Christian Peace
and
Nonviolence

ALSO BY MICHAEL G. LONG

Marshalling Justice:
The Early Civil Rights Letters of Thurgood Marshall

Resist! Christian Dissent for the Twenty-first Century

First Class Citizenship:
The Civil Rights Letters of Jackie Robinson

The Legacy of Billy Graham:
Critical Reflections on America's Greatest Evangelist

God and Country: Diverse Perspectives on Christianity and Patriotism
(with Tracy Wenger Sadd)

Billy Graham and the Beloved Community:
America's Evangelist and the Dream of Martin Luther King, Jr.

Martin Luther King, Jr. on Creative Living

Against Us, but for Us:
Martin Luther King, Jr. and the State

Christian Peace and Nonviolence

A Documentary History

Edited by
Michael G. Long

Foreword by
Stanley Hauerwas

ORBIS BOOKS

Maryknoll, New York 10545

Founded in 1970, Orbis Books endeavors to publish works that enlighten the mind, nourish the spirit, and challenge the conscience. The publishing arm of the Maryknoll Fathers and Brothers, Orbis seeks to explore the global dimensions of the Christian faith and mission, to invite dialogue with diverse cultures and religious traditions, and to serve the cause of reconciliation and peace. The books published reflect the views of their authors and do not represent the official position of the Maryknoll Society. To learn more about Maryknoll and Orbis Books, please visit our website at www.maryknollsociety.org.

Copyright © 2011 by Michael G. Long

Published by Orbis Books, Maryknoll, NY 10545-0302.

Sources and permissions for the writings collected in this volume can be found on pages 333-339.

The publishers wish to thank Mr. and Mrs. Harold M. Isbell for their generous support of the publication of this volume.

Manufactured in the United States of America.

Library of Congress Cataloging-in-Publication Data

Christian peace and nonviolence : a documentary history / edited by Michael G. Long.
    p. cm.
    Includes index.
    ISBN 978-1-57075-922-2 (pbk.)
    1. Peace—Religious aspects—Christianity—History. 2. Nonviolence—Religious aspects—Christianity—History. I. Long, Michael G.
    BT736.4.C443 2011
    261.8'73—dc22
                          2010036751

For Jack and Nate,
my favorite resisters

Love your enemies …
JESUS

CONTENTS

Contents

PART III
Medieval Voices

CONTENTS

PART IV
Late Scholastic Period and the Reformation

CONTENTS

Contents

PART VI
Early Twentieth Century (1900-1949)

CONTENTS

Contents

PART VII
Mid-Twentieth Century (1950-1974)

CONTENTS

PART VIII
Late Twentieth Century (1975-2000)

Contents

PART IX
Twenty-first Century

FOREWORD

Stanley Hauerwas

Our commitment to Christian nonviolence can invite us to imagine we are a bit isolated. After all, we are often told we represent a minority voice in the larger Christian tradition. And when those who do not share our commitment to nonviolence describe us as "prophetic" (while at the same time curiously suggesting we are irresponsible), we may even be tempted to enjoy our separated status. But that is a game, a trade-off, which this extremely important book should forever bring to an end.

These extraordinary documents, which bear witness to the Christian commitment to peace across time, clarify that nonviolence is not a mere "exception"—it is at the very heart of what it means to be a follower of Christ. Indeed, from what we can gather, particularly from the witness of the early church, Christians did not even find it necessary to declare they were nonviolent—exactly because the way of nonviolence could not be distinguished from what it meant for them to be Christian. To worship Jesus, to follow Jesus, was to assume a way of life that altogether precluded the question of whether one might need to kill; it simply did not come up.

They did not assume they could not kill because, as has often been claimed, they had not yet gained social and political standing. Rather, they were excluded from certain forms of life because they worshiped Jesus, making it impossible for them even to ask questions about the permissibility of the use of violence. As the selections in *Christian Peace and Nonviolence* make clear, nonviolence was not some further implication that might be drawn from fundamental Christian convictions—nonviolence was constitutive of the Christian conviction that Jesus is Lord.

That conviction, moreover, did not lead to Christian withdrawal from the world. The refusal to kill did not mean, as the essays in this book make clear, that Christians thought they should withdraw from social and political engagement. Christians committed to nonviolence were, and are, anything but passive. Indeed, it was Christians committed to nonviolence who took the lead, for example, in challenging the presumption that Christians could own slaves.

Pacifists have often been, and still are, people determined to make a difference. But they understand that the difference they desire must be schooled by the patience of the cross. That patience, the patience of the cross, turns out to be the way of peace that quite literally turns the world "upside down." It does so because death has been defeated through the cross and resurrection of Jesus. Christians are, therefore, able to live nonviolently because, in the words of Justin Martyr, while we know that our enemies can kill us, "they cannot do us any real harm."

In *Nonviolence: A Brief History*, John Howard Yoder observes that every renewal of the future demands a vision of the past. He further notes that accounts of our history too often seek to retell a story from the perspective of the winning party. Subsequently, such revisionist histories, with their efforts to convince us that the way things turned out were simply inevitable, are part of the old game of letting history be the history of conflicts and battles—a history that serves to legitimate and glorify the present regime. Yoder, therefore, argues that a more fundamental historical revision is necessary—one that chronicles not how dynasties clashed over borders, but how parents raised their children, or how a blacksmith's discovery for sharpening implements changed farming practices so that the quality of ordinary human existence was made better, or how a community found ways of cooperation that avoided violence. The documents gathered in *Christian Peace and Nonviolence* are the start of the kind of historiography that Yoder suggested we desperately need if we are to provide an alternative to the presumption that violence is inevitable.

The many voices heard throughout this text are ones often left out of standard anthologies of Christian theological and ethical reflection. I take this to be an indication that these writings can help us imaginatively recapture what it means to be a people who live in a world that has been turned on its head. For example, the inclusion of Benedict's Rule, with its exhortation to let the virtue of humility make us refrain from unnecessary speech, is wonderfully suggestive for helping us remember that a life of nonviolence involves how we negotiate the everyday. The inclusion of texts from the Lollards, as well as those from non-Christians such as Clarence Darrow, is a reminder that those who are often described as unorthodox, even non-Christian, are part of the story we have to tell.

I cannot imagine that *Christian Peace and Nonviolence,* with its strong collection of Christian theologians and thinkers, will not become an essential teaching resource not only for thinking through nonviolence but also for understanding the very character of Christianity. The resources represented in this book cut across the sterile debates associated with ecclesial identities and suggest that a story—a truly coherent story—can be told about the Christian commitment to nonviolence that hopefully points to an increasing awareness that the church is "catholic."

Truth, moreover, is the heart of the matter. John Haynes Holmes bluntly but truthfully puts the matter thus: "If war is right then Christianity is false, a lie." But we believe that Christ has defeated death, making Christians to be witnesses to the truth. Truth is simply another way of naming Christ's peace. In her wonderful work entitled "Training," Muriel Lester observes that for "nonviolence to be effective [it] must be allied with the vow of truth," a vow that may well mean that at times we will have to refuse to cooperate with what many assume is a "good cause."

That said, however, I am extremely appreciative that Long has included selections in the book from those identified with liberation theology, the civil rights struggle, and feminism. By doing so, he is able to help us see more clearly that there is no intrinsic conflict between nonviolence and a challenge to the current politics. Indeed, as many of the selections in this book suggest, commitment to nonviolence is a necessary condition for creating imaginative responses to injustice without having to use violence.

Augustine, Aquinas, Luther, Calvin, and Reinhold Niebuhr do not appear in *Christian Peace and Nonviolence.* They, of course, were not pacifist, but I urge those committed to Christian nonviolence to read them, for I think you will discover they often sound very much like many of the figures whose work is collected here. They should be read, moreover, because our commitment to nonviolence requires listening to those who do not share our convictions. And one can only hope that many of our Christian brothers and sisters who think war cannot be avoided will also read this book.

I think if they do so they cannot help but be moved by the witness of their sisters and brothers in Christ who have argued that Christians cannot kill. Those committed to nonviolence, as well as those who are not, will find that the material gathered in this book is not only intellectually compelling but also inspirational. We are in Michael Long's debt for this extraordinary collection that bears witness to Christ's peace.

Notes on the Text

In editing this volume, I have sought to be far from heavy-handed in changing—or correcting—the grammar used by individual authors or translators. I have deleted outmoded grammar (for example, the use of a comma immediately before a dash) at some points, and in those places where I did retain the use of archaic grammar, it was to preserve the historic feel of the written word. It is one thing to edit nineteenth- or twentieth-century translations of writings from the early church, after all, and quite another to edit the writings of pacifists in colonial Pennsylvania. In all cases, however, my changes are silent; they are not marked by the use of brackets or [*sic*].

I have also tried to exercise great care when excerpting the selected pieces. Almost all of the writings here are shortened in some way, some of them quite liberally, and I have used ellipses to indicate where I have made deletions. Although ellipses sometimes break the flow of reading, I find them important for preserving the integrity of the piece as it was written or translated.

Careful readers will note that this volume lacks notes that appeared in original documents. Simply stated, given my own self-imposed constraints of space, I deleted notes, all of them, so that I could include more selections. Had I included notes, this book would have ended up excluding pieces I consider essential for a peace reader like this one. On a similar note, I did not write my own notes to explicate material in the text. Nor have I relied on brackets to add information; if the reader comes across such use of brackets, it is because I have retained their use by a prior editor of a particular selection.

The most difficult choices I faced centered on the selection of texts—which to include and exclude. The good news is that there were so many choices—far more than I originally thought—and that these choices came in many languages and from many cultures. The bad news, of course, is that I could not include them all.

Even a cursory look at the table of contents will show that I have largely (but not solely) focused on the historic roots and expressions of Christian nonviolence in North America, especially as it took form in the twentieth century. This decision is in accord with—and reflects—not only my own base of knowledge but also the intended market and readership for the book.

Readers will also quickly see that this volume includes pieces from authors who seem to accept violence at certain points or who may not even identify themselves as Christian. I will not take the fun away from those who want to struggle with discovering my particular reasons for selecting certain authors, but I will state this much: there is no author in this volume whose thought does not strongly emphasize—and extol—the virtues and practices of Christian peace and nonviolence. I should add here that I did not rely on a tight definition of "Christian peace" or "Christian nonviolence" in the selection process, although I believe that it is possible (and often desirable) to provide tight definitions for both of those phrases.

Finally, I chose to work on the overall project not only because I wanted to give my students easy access to some of the most important primary sources in the field of Christian peace and conflict studies, but especially because I wanted to contribute, however modestly, to the legacy of Jesus of Nazareth in this awful Age of Terror.

If the words of this volume, some simple and others difficult, can help some of us confront the raging politics of fear with the breathtaking courage of Jesus—the courage to love our enemies—perhaps we can hope against hope and begin to breathe life anew into a church that began to die the very second it took up the sword and honored it as the work of God and the will of Christ. Wielding the sword was the first heresy of the Christian church, and it remains with us to this day as the worst heresy of the church.

May we resist the sword—and at last be faithful to Jesus.

Michael G. Long

PART I
Scriptures of Peace

1. HEBREW SCRIPTURES

Isaiah 11:6-9

The wolf shall live with the lamb, the leopard shall lie down with the kid, the calf and the lion and the fatling together, and a little child shall lead them.

The cow and the bear shall graze, their young shall lie down together; and the lion shall eat straw like the ox.

The nursing child shall play over the hole of the asp, and the weaned child shall put its hand on the adder's den.

They will not hurt or destroy on all my holy mountain; for the earth will be full of the knowledge of the Lord as the waters cover the sea.

Jeremiah 6:13-14

For from the least to the greatest of them, everyone is greedy for unjust gain; and from prophet to priest, everyone deals falsely.

They have treated the wound of my people carelessly, saying, "Peace, peace," when there is no peace.

Micah 4:1-4

In days to come the mountain of the Lord's house shall be established as the highest of the mountains, and shall be raised up above the hills. Peoples shall stream to it,

and many nations shall come and say: "Come, let us go up to the mountain of the Lord, to the house of the God of Jacob; that he may teach us his ways and that we may walk in his paths." For out of Zion shall go forth instruction, and the word of the Lord from Jerusalem.

He shall judge between many peoples, and shall arbitrate between strong nations far away; they shall beat their swords into plowshares, and their spears into pruning hooks; nation shall not lift up sword against nation, neither shall they learn war any more;

but they shall all sit under their own vines and under their own fig trees, and no one shall make them afraid; for the mouth of the Lord of hosts has spoken.

2. Walter Brueggemann

Living toward a Vision

Walter Brueggemann (b. 1933), the William Marcellus McPheeters Professor of Old Testament Emeritus at Columbia Theological Seminary in Georgia, is the world's leading interpreter of the Hebrew Scriptures. His writings on social ethics and the Bible, including his book Peace, *excerpted below, are so important because they demonstrate that the biblical vision of peace is inextricably linked with economic justice, social inclusiveness, personal righteousness, and community life.*

I will give you your rains in their season, and the land shall yield its produce, and the trees of the field shall yield their fruit. Your threshing shall overtake the vintage, and the vintage shall overtake the sowing; you shall eat your bread to the full, and live securely in your land. And I will grant peace in the land, and you shall lie down, and no one shall make you afraid; I will remove dangerous animals from the land, and no sword shall go through your land.

Leviticus 26:4-6

For he is our peace; in his flesh he has made both groups into one and has broken down the dividing wall, that is, the hostility between us.

Ephesians 2:14

The central vision of world history in the Bible is that all of creation is one, every creature in community with every other, living in harmony and security toward the joy and well-being of every other creature. *In the community of faith in Israel,* this vision is expressed in the affirmation that Abraham is father of all Israel and every person is his child (see Genesis 15:5; Isaiah 41:8; 51:2). Israel has a vision of all people drawn into community around the will of its God (Isaiah 2:2-4). *In the New Testament, the church* has a parallel vision of all persons being drawn under the lordship and fellowship of Jesus (Matthew 28:16-20; John 12:32) and therefore into a single community (Acts 2:1-11). As if those visions were not sweeping enough, the most stag-gering expression of the vision is that *all persons* are *children of a single family,* members of a single tribe, heirs of a single hope, and bearers of a single destiny, namely, the care and management of all God's creation.

That persistent vision of joy, well-being, harmony, and prosperity is not captured in any single word or idea in the Bible; a cluster of words is required to express its many dimensions and subtle nuances: love, loyalty, truth, grace, salvation, justice, blessing, righteousness. But the term that in recent discussions has been used to summarize that controlling vision is *shalom.* Both in such discussion and in the Bible itself, it bears tremendous freight—the freight of a dream of God that resists all our tendencies to division, hostility, fear, drivenness, and misery.

Shalom is the substance of the biblical vision of one community embracing all creation. It refers to all those resources and factors that make communal harmony joyous and effective. Ezekiel in a visionary passage expresses its meaning:

I will make with them a covenant of *shalom* and banish wild beasts from the land, so that they may dwell securely in the wilderness and sleep in the woods. And I will make them and the places round about my hill a blessing; and I will send down the showers in their season; they shall be showers of blessing. And the trees of the field shall yield their fruit, and the earth shall yield its increase, and they shall be secure in their land. They shall no more be a prey to the nations, nor shall the beasts of the land devour them; they shall dwell securely, and none shall make them afraid. And I will provide for them plantations of *shalom*. (Ezekiel 34:25-29a, author's translation)

The origin and the destiny of God's people are to be on the road of *shalom,* which is to live out of joyous memories and toward greater anticipations.

This passage from Ezekiel and the one from Leviticus quoted at the beginning of the chapter show *shalom* in all its power. It is well-being that exists in the very midst of threats—from sword and drought and wild animals. It is well-being of a material, physical, historical kind, not idyllic "pie in the sky," but "salvation" in the midst of trees and crops and enemies—in the very places where people always have to cope with anxiety, to struggle for survival, and to deal with temptation. It is well-being of a very personal kind—the address in Leviticus 26 is to a single person, but it is also deliberately corporate. If there is to be well-being, it will not be just for isolated, insulated individuals; it is, rather, security and prosperity granted to a whole community—young and old, rich and poor, powerful and dependent. Always we are all in it together. Together we stand before God's blessings and together we receive the gift of life, if we receive it at all. *Shalom* comes only to the inclusive, embracing community that excludes none.

The vision of wholeness, which is the supreme will of the biblical God, is the outgrowth of a covenant of *shalom* (see Ezekiel 34:25), in which persons are bound not only to God but to one another in a caring, sharing, rejoicing community with none to make them afraid.

Dimensions of Shalom

The scope of this communal vision is an important element in understanding its power. In its most inclusive dimension it is *a vision encompassing all reality,* expressed in the mystery and majesty of creation image:

[without *shalom*]
The earth was a formless void and darkness covered the face of the deep. (Genesis 1:2a)

[with *shalom*]
The wolf shall live with the lamb,
   the leopard shall lie down with the kid,
the calf and the lion and the fatling together,
   and a little child shall lead them.
The cow and the bear shall graze,
   their young shall lie down together;
   and the lion shall eat straw like the ox …
They will not hurt or destroy
   on all my holy mountain.
                                    (Isaiah 11:6-7, 9a)

[from chaos to *shalom*]
A great windstorm arose, and the waves beat into the boat, so that the boat was already being swamped … and they woke him up and said to him, "Teacher, do you not care that we are perishing?" He woke up and rebuked the wind, and said to the sea, "Peace! Be still!" Then the wind ceased, and there was a dead calm. (Mark 4:37-39)

The Greek word translated *peace* here means *quiet* rather than *shalom,* but the passage still applies. The storm at sea represents all the same ominous, chaotic forces presented in Genesis 1:2. And the word of Jesus in Mark serves the same purpose as the hovering spirit of God in Genesis 1:2, namely, to bring fundamental disorder under God's rule—into harmony—so that light, life, and joy become possible. Creation in Genesis and by Jesus (see Colossians 1:17) is the establishment of *shalom* in a universe that apart from God's rule is disordered, unproductive, and unfulfilling.

In the same symbolic word, the messianic vision of Isaiah (11:6-9) is of a world in which creation is reconciled and harmony appears between children and snakes, among all kinds of natural enemies. *Shalom* is creation time, when all God's creation eases up on hostility and destruction and finds another way of relating. No wonder creation culminates in the peace and joy of the Sabbath (Genesis 2:1-4a) when all lie down and none make them afraid. No wonder our most familiar Sabbath blessing ends: "The Lord lift up his countenance upon you, and give you peace *(shalom)*" (Numbers 6:26), for the benediction is the affirmation of Sabbath, the conclusion of creation, when harmony has been brought to all the warring elements in our existence.

A second dimension of *shalom* is the *historic political community.* Absence of *shalom* and lack of harmony are expressed in social disorder as evidenced in economic inequality, judicial perversion, and political oppression and exclusivism. Of course, the prophets speak boldly against such disruption of community, which is the absence of *shalom:*

> Alas for those who devise wickedness
> and evil deeds on their beds! …
> They covet fields, and seize them;
> houses, and take them away;
> they oppress householder and house.
> (Micah 2:1-2)

> Hear this word, you cows of Bashan,
> who are on Mount Samaria,
> who oppress the poor, who crush the needy,
> who say to their husbands,
> "Bring something to drink!"
> (Amos 4:1)

These offenses are viewed by the prophets not simply as ethical violations but as the disruption of God's intention for *shalom,* the perversion of the community God wills for people in history. Their call is continually a call for righteousness and justice:

> Seek good and not evil, that you may live …
> Hate evil and love good,
> and establish justice in the gate.
> (Amos 5:14-15a)

> Wash yourselves; make yourselves clean;
> remove the evil of your doings
> from before my eyes;
> cease to do evil,
> learn to do good;
> seek justice,
> rescue the oppressed,
> defend the orphan,
> plead for the widow.
> (Isaiah 1:16-17)

The doing of righteousness and justice results in the building of viable community, that is, *shalom,* in which the oppressed and disenfranchised have dignity and power.

> Depart from evil, and do good;
> Seek peace (*shalom*), and pursue it.
> (Psalm 34:14)

> Then justice will dwell in the wilderness,
> and righteousness abide in the fruitful
> field.
> The effect of righteousness will be peace
> (*shalom*),
> and the result of righteousness, quietness
> and trust forever.
> (Isaiah 32:16-17)

The consequence of justice and righteousness is *shalom,* an enduring Sabbath of joy and well-being. But the alternative is injustice and oppression, which lead inevitably to turmoil and anxiety, with no chance of well-being (Isaiah 48:22; 57:21).

Jesus' ministry to the excluded (see Luke 4:16-21) was the same, the establishment of community between those who were excluded and those who had excluded them. His acts of healing the sick, forgiving the guilty, raising the dead, and feeding the hungry are all actions of reestablishing God's will for *shalom* in a world gone chaotic by callous self-seeking.

The cosmic and historical-political aspects of *shalom* point to a third dimension, which the Bible usually assumes but does not discuss. It is the *shalom* sense of well-being experienced by *the person* who lives a caring, sharing, joyous life in community. By way of contrast, covetousness is presented as one aspect of the self-seeking life that is never satiated but always pursues selfish security only to discover that it leads to destruction:

> Because of the iniquity of his covetousness
> I was angry, I smote him,
> I hid my face and was angry …
> *Shalom, shalom,* to the far and to the near,
> says the Lord;
> and I will heal him.

But the wicked are like the tossing sea;
for it cannot rest,
and its waters toss up mire and dirt.
There is no *shalom,* says my God, for the
wicked.
>(Isaiah 57:17, 19-21, author's transla-
tion; compare Joshua 7)

And in Jesus' teaching, covetousness leads to a
tormenting anxiety:

>"Teacher, tell my brother to divide the family
inheritance with me." ... And he said to them,
"Take care! Be on your guard against all kinds
of greed; for one's life does not consist in the
abundance of possessions." ... He said to his
disciples, "Therefore, I tell you, do not worry
about your life, what you will eat, or about
your body, what you will wear." (Luke 12:13,
15, 22; compare Acts 5:1-14)

Thus, in creation, the forces of chaos are
opposed by God's powerful will *for orderly fruitfulness.* In historic community, the forces of injustices and exploitation are opposed by God's will for
responsible, equitable justice, which yields security.
In personal existence, driven, anxious self-seeking
is opposed by God's will for *generous caring.* The
biblical vision of *shalom* functions always as a firm
rejection of values and lifestyles that seek security and well-being in manipulative ways at the
expense of another part of creation, another part
of the community, or a brother or sister. The vision
of the biblical way affirms that communal well-
being comes by living God's dream, not by idolatrous self-aggrandizement. The alternative is to so
distort creation as never to know what it means to
celebrate the Sabbath. Either we strive to secure our
own existence or we celebrate the joy and rest of
Sabbath, knowing that God has already secured it
for us. *Shalom* is received by grateful creation.

Maintaining the Vision

The Bible is not romantic about its vision. It never
assumes *shalom* will come naturally or automatically. Indeed, there are many ways of compromising God's will for *shalom.*

One way the community can say no to the vision
and live without *shalom* is to deceive itself into
thinking that its *private arrangements* of injustice
and exploitation are suitable ways of living:

>For from the least to the greatest of them,
every one is greedy for unjust gain;
and from prophet to priest,
every one deals falsely.
They have healed the wound of my people
lightly,
saying, "*Shalom, shalom,*" when there is no
shalom.
>>(Jeremiah 6:13-14, author's translation;
compare Ezekiel 13:10, 16 and Amos
6:1-6)

Shalom in a special way is the task and burden
of the well-off and powerful. They are the ones held
accountable for *shalom.* The prophets persistently
criticized and polemicized against those well-off
and powerful ones who legitimized their selfish
prosperity and deceived themselves into thinking
it was permanent. The prophetic vision of *shalom*
stands against all private arrangements, all "separate pieces," all ghettos that pretend the others are
not there (compare Luke 16:19-31). Religious legitimacy in the service of self-deceiving well-being is
a form of chaos. *Shalom* is never the private property of the few.

A second way of perverting the vision is to take
a *short-term view.* Isaiah preserves a story of King
Hezekiah, who bargained the future of his people
for present accommodation. He is condemned for
thinking: "There will be peace *(shalom)* and security in my days" (Isaiah 39:8). A moment of well-
being can be had today with enormous charges
made against tomorrow. Parents pile up debts of
hatred and abuse for their children to pay off. But
the prophet is clear. *Shalom* is never short-range;
eventually, someone must pay dearly. Caring for
creation is never a one-generation deal (see Jeremiah 31:29-30; Ezekiel 18:2).

A third way of abusing God's will for *shalom*
is to *credit certain props* as sources of life—for
example, to idolize political or religious furniture
and pretend it is the power of God. Jeremiah saw
that his people regarded the temple as a way of

shalom, apparently thinking it was available and cheap without regard to demands that came with the package (Jeremiah 7:1-10). Similarly, Jesus exposed a self-deceiving mentality that valued particular moral rules at the expense of persons (Matthew 15:1-20). The vision of *shalom* is so great that it would be nice to manage and control it—to know the formula that puts it at our disposal—either by a religion of piety or morality or by a technology that puts it on call (see Deuteronomy 18:9-14). But *shalom* is not subject to our best knowledge or our cleverest gimmicks. It comes only through the costly way of caring.

A Vital Hope

Shalom is an enduring vision. It is promised persistently and hoped for always. But there are occasions when it is an especially vital hope. One such time was during Israel's exile. Among the eloquent spokesmen for the vision in that period was Jeremiah. And among the most extraordinary texts is this letter he wrote to the exiles urging the validity of the vision even among displaced persons:

> I will fulfill to you my promise and bring you back to this place. For surely I know the plans I have for you, says the Lord, plans for your welfare *(shalom)* and not for harm, to give you a future with hope … When you search for me, you will find me; if you seek me with all your heart, I will let you find me, says the Lord, and I will restore your fortunes.(Jeremiah 29:10-11, 13-14a)

On the face of it, the text is simply a promise that the exile will eventually end. But the structure moves from promise (verse 10) to land (place, verse 14). So again Israel is set on that joyous, tortuous path from promise to land, from wandering to security, from chaos to *shalom.* Thus, the experience of exile—like every experience—gets read as a part of the pilgrimage of this incredible vision of God with the people of Israel.

In a letter to the exiles in Babylon, Jeremiah uses our term twice. Jeremiah 29:11 has the affirmation that God wills *shalom* even for the exiles. God does not will evil, even though exile feels like evil. God

wills a future and a hope—a promise thrusting to reality. We take the affirmation routinely. But its boldness can surprise when it is spoken in a time of despair and cynicism, when "the center cannot hold," when everything has collapsed and everyone is weary, with hope exhausted. At the root of history is the One who wills *shalom.* At its end is the One who calls us to *shalom,* secure community, a golden calf that frequently seems to be against all the stubborn facts. A lesser resource will scarcely refute despair or enable alienated ones to care. Only being grasped by the Holy One will do this— the One who dares to promise and dream when the rest of us have given up.

And what does Jeremiah mean? Simply that God is there. We are not abandoned. (Note the affirmation in exilic texts, Isaiah 41:10, 14; 43:1-2, 5; 49:14-15; 54:7-10 and, in a quite different context, Matthew 28:20.) We are heard by God, who also answers (Exodus 3:7ff.; Isaiah 65:24). Ours is not an empty world of machinery where we get what we have coming to us. No! Caring, healing communication is still possible. There is this *Thou* who calls every historical *I* to community. Life is not a driven or an anxious monologue. The Lord is findable, which is a gospel theme of great importance when God seems dead or hidden (see Deuteronomy 4:29-31; Isaiah 55:6, both texts from the exile). The vision of *shalom* is most eloquently expressed in times very much like our own, when resources for faith to endure are hardly available. Thus, for example, in Isaiah 65:21, *shalom* motifs come together; in 65:25, reconciled creation; in 65:24, assured dialogue. It is natural that the question of *shalom* should vex the church precisely when life seems so much a monologue.

The other use of *shalom* in Jeremiah's letter to the exiles is in 29:7:

> But seek the *shalom* of the city where I have sent you into exile, and pray to the Lord on its behalf, for in its *shalom* you will find your *shalom.* (author's translation)

Imagine that! A letter written to displaced persons in hated Babylon, where they have gone against their will and watched their life and culture collapse. And they are still there, yearning to go home, despising their captors and resenting their God—if, indeed, God is still their God. And the speaker for the vision dares to say, "Your *shalom* will be found in Babylon's *shalom*." The well-being of the chosen ones is tied to the well-being of the hated metropolis, which the chosen people fear and resent. It is profound and disturbing to discover that this remarkable religious vision will have to be actualized in the civil community. The stuff of well-being is the sordid collection of rulers, soldiers, wardens, and carpetbaggers in Judah and in every place of displaced, exhausted hope. It is an incredible vision even now for people of faith who feel pressed and angry about the urban shape of our existence, to say nothing about the urban shape of our vision. But again it is affirmed that God's *shalom* is known only by those in inclusive, caring community.

The letter of Jeremiah to the displaced persons surely did not meet expectations. No doubt they hoped for a purer gospel, a neater promise, a distinctive future. But God's exiles are always learning the hard way that the thrust toward viable unity must find a way to include the very ones we prefer to exclude. Depending on how deep the hatred and how great the fear, this promise of *shalom* with hated Babylon is a glorious promise or a sobering thought; but it is our best vision, a vision always rooted in and addressed to historical realities.

The Embodiment of Shalom

The only *shalom* promised is one in the midst of historical reality, which comes close to saying "incarnation." The only God we know entered history, appeared as a person. *Shalom* of a biblical kind is always somewhat scandalous—never simply a liturgical experience or a mythical statement, but one facing our deepest divisions and countering with a vision.

The Pauline letters speak of this. There seem to be so many categories and divisions and discriminating marks that separate and pigeonhole, but there is also this:

There is no longer Jew or Greek, there is no longer slave or free, there is no longer male and female; for all of you are one in Christ Jesus. And if you belong to Christ, then you are Abraham's offspring, heirs according to the promise. (Galatians 3:28-29)

Called to the Lord's single community, bearers of God's single promise, children of the one Abraham. Paul runs blatantly over our favorite divisions—black-white, rich-poor, male-female, East-West, old-young, or whatever—finding them unreal and uninteresting. Those factors count not at all—our anxiety, drivenness, covetousness, injustice, chaos—none of these ever secures our existence. Yet we are secure, called to *shalom* from all our desperate efforts at security and our foolish manipulations to ensure dominance. Then Paul comes right out and says it ever more flatly: "He [Jesus] is our peace *(shalom)*" (Ephesians 2:14).

He got the lepers and the Pharisees all together again, the sons of Isaac and the heirs of Hagar, or so the vision lets us hope. He is known in the breaking of bread; he is crucified and risen; he is coming again—he who draws all people to himself, who rose from the dead and defied the governor, but who could not save himself. We say he embodies our vision and empowers us to live it.

We are sometimes children of the eighth day. And we risk an embracing of the vision. It is remarkable that lions and lambs share fodder, that widows and people of means have a common heritage, that our future is not in compulsive drivenness but in free caring. That vision surrounds us and addresses us, but we see only in a glass darkly.

3. SERMON ON THE MOUNT

Matthew 5:1-12

When Jesus saw the crowds, he went up the mountain; and after he sat down, his disciples came to him. Then he began to speak, and taught them, saying:

"Blessed are the poor in spirit, for theirs is the kingdom of heaven.

"Blessed are those who mourn, for they will be comforted.

"Blessed are the meek, for they will inherit the earth.

"Blessed are those who hunger and thirst for righteousness, for they will be filled.

"Blessed are the merciful, for they will receive mercy.

"Blessed are the pure in heart, for they will see God.

"Blessed are the peacemakers, for they will be called children of God.

"Blessed are those who are persecuted for righteousness' sake, for theirs is the kingdom of heaven.

"Blessed are you when people revile you and persecute you and utter all kinds of evil against you falsely on my account. Rejoice and be glad, for your reward is great in heaven, for in the same way they persecuted the prophets who were before you."

Matthew 5:38-42

"You have heard that it was said, 'An eye for an eye and a tooth for a tooth.' But I say to you, Do not resist an evildoer. But if anyone strikes you on the right cheek, turn the other also; and if anyone wants to sue you and take your coat, give your cloak as well; and if anyone forces you to go one mile, go also the second mile. Give to everyone who begs from you, and do not refuse anyone who wants to borrow from you."

4. WALTER WINK

Jesus and Nonviolence: A Third Way

Walter Wink (b. 1935) is professor emeritus of biblical interpretation at Auburn Theological Seminary in New York City, the author of an acclaimed trilogy on powers and principalities, and the editor of Peace Is the Way: Writings on Nonviolence from the Fellowship of Reconciliation. *His creative work on the third way of Jesus is one of the most important contemporary contributions to the field of Christian pacifism and biblical interpretation.*

Many of those who have committed their lives to ending injustice simply dismiss Jesus' teachings about nonviolence out of hand as impractical idealism. And with good reason. "Turn the other cheek" suggests the passive, Christian doormat quality that has made so many Christians cowardly and complicit in the face of injustice. "Resist not evil" seems to break the back of all opposition to evil and to counsel submission. "Going the second mile" has become a platitude meaning nothing more than "extend yourself," and rather than fostering structural change, encourages collaboration with the oppressor.

Jesus obviously never behaved in any of these

ways. Whatever the source of the misunderstanding, it is clearly neither in Jesus nor in his teaching, which, when given a fair hearing in its original social context, is arguably one of the most revolutionary political statements ever uttered:

> You have heard that it was said, "An eye for an eye and a tooth for a tooth." But I say to you, Do not resist an evildoer. But if anyone strikes you on the right cheek, turn the other also; and if anyone wants to sue you and take your coat, give your cloak as well; and if anyone forces you to go one mile, go also the second mile. (Matt. 5:38-41 NRSV)

When the court translators working in the hire of King James chose to translate *antistenai* as "*Resist not evil*," they were doing something more than rendering Greek into English. They were translating nonviolent resistance into docility. Jesus did *not* tell his oppressed hearers not to resist evil. That would have been absurd. His entire ministry is utterly at odds with such a preposterous idea. The Greek word is made up of two parts: *anti*, a word still used in English for "against," and *histemi*, a verb that in its noun form (*stasis*) means violent rebellion, armed revolt, sharp dissention....

A proper translation of Jesus' teaching would then be, "Don't strike back at evil (or, one who has done you evil) in kind." "Do not retaliate against violence with violence." The Scholars Version is brilliant: "Don't react violently against the one who is evil." Jesus was no less committed to opposing evil than the anti-Roman resistance fighters. The only difference was over the means to be used: *how* one should fight evil.

There are three general responses to evil: (1) passivity, (2) violent opposition, and (3) the third way of militant nonviolence articulated by Jesus. Human evolution has conditioned us for only the first two of these responses: flight or fight....

Neither of these alternatives has anything to do with what Jesus is proposing. It is important that we be utterly clear about this point before going on: *Jesus abhors both passivity and violence as responses to evil.* His is a third alternative not even touched by these options. *Antistenai* cannot be construed to mean submission.

Jesus clarifies his meaning by three examples. "If anyone strikes you on the right cheek, turn to him the other also." Why the *right* cheek? How does one strike another on the right cheek anyway? Try it. A blow by the right fist in that right-handed world would land on the *left* cheek of the opponent. To strike the right cheek with the fist would require using the left hand, but in that society the left hand was used only for unclean tasks. Even to gesture with the left hand at Qumran carried the penalty of exclusion and ten days' penance (The Dead Sea Scrolls, 1QS 7). The only way one could strike the right cheek with the right hand would be with the *back of the right hand.* What we are dealing with here is unmistakably an insult, not a fistfight. The intention is not to injure but to humiliate, to put someone in his or her "place." One normally did not strike a peer thus, and if one did, the fine was exorbitant.... A backhand slap was the normal way of admonishing inferiors. Masters backhanded slaves; husbands, wives; parents, children; men, women; Romans, Jews. *We have here a set of unequal relations, in each of which retaliation would be suicidal.* The only normal response would be cowering submission.

It is important to ask who Jesus' audience is. In every case, Jesus' listeners are not those who strike, initiate lawsuits, or impose forced labor, but their victims....

Why then does he counsel these already humiliated people to turn the other cheek? Because this action robs the oppressor of the power to humiliate. The person who turns the other cheek is saying, in effect, "Try again. Your first blow failed to achieve its intended effect. I deny you the power to humiliate me. I am a human being just like you. Your status does not alter that fact. You cannot demean me." ...

The second example Jesus gives is set in a court of law. Someone is being sued for his outer garment. Who would do that and under what circumstances? The Old Testament provides the clues.

> When you make your neighbor a loan of any sort, you shall not go into his house to fetch his pledge. You shall stand outside, and the man to whom you make the loan shall bring the pledge out to you. *And if he is a poor*

man, you shall not sleep in his pledge; when the sun goes down, you shall restore to him the pledge that he may sleep in his cloak and bless you.... You shall not take a widow's garment in pledge. (Deut. 24:10-13, 17)

Only the poorest of the poor would have nothing but an outer garment to give as collateral for a loan. Jewish law strictly required its return every evening at sunset, for that was all the poor had in which to sleep. The situation to which Jesus alludes is one with which all his hearers would have been all too familiar: the poor debtor has sunk even deeper into poverty, the debt cannot be repaid, and his creditor has hauled him into court to try to seize his property by legal means.

Indebtedness was the most serious social problem in first-century Palestine. Jesus' parables are full of debtors struggling to salvage their lives. The situation was not, however, a natural calamity that had overtaken the incompetent. It was the direct consequence of Roman imperial policy. Emperors taxed the wealthy ruthlessly to fund their wars. Naturally, the rich sought non-liquid investments to secure their wealth. Land was best, but there was a problem: it was not bought and sold on the open market as today but was ancestrally owned and passed down over generations. Little land was ever for sale, in Palestine at least. Exorbitant interest, however, could be used to drive landowners into even deeper debt until they were forced to sell their land. By the time of Jesus we see this process already far advanced: large estates (*latifundia*) owned by absentee landlords, managed by stewards, and worked by servants, sharecroppers, and day laborers. It is no accident that the first act of the Jewish revolutionaries in 66 C.E. was to burn the Temple treasury, where the record of debts was kept.

It is in this context that Jesus speaks. His hearers are the poor ("if any one would sue *you*"). They share a rankling hatred for a system that subjects them to humiliation by stripping them of their lands, their goods, and finally even their outer garments.

Why then does Jesus counsel them to give over their inner garment as well? This would mean stripping off all their clothing and marching out of court stark naked! Put yourself in the debtor's place, and imagine the chuckles this saying must have evoked. There stands the creditor, beet-red with embarrassment, your outer garment in one hand, your underwear in the other. You have suddenly turned the tables on him. You had no hope of winning the trial; the law was entirely in his favor. But you have refused to be humiliated, and at the same time you have registered a stunning protest against a system that spawns such debt. You have said in effect, "You want my robe? Here, take everything! Now you've got all I have except my body. Is that what you'll take next?"

Nakedness was taboo in Judaism, and shame fell not on the naked party, but on the person viewing or causing one's nakedness (Gen. 9: 20-27). By stripping you have brought the creditor under the same prohibition that led to the curse of Canaan. As you parade into the street, your friends and neighbors, startled, aghast, inquire what happened. You explain. They join your growing procession, which now resembles a victory parade. The entire system by which debtors are oppressed has been publicly unmasked. The creditor is revealed to be not a "respectable" moneylender but a party in the reduction of an entire social class to landlessness and destitution. This unmasking is not simply punitive, however; it offers the creditor a chance to see, perhaps for the first time in his life, what his practices cause, and to repent. Far from collaborating in injustice, the poor man has used the law, aikido-like, to make an exploitative law a laughing stock....

Jesus' third example, the one about going the second mile, is drawn from the very enlightened practice of limiting the amount of forced labor that Roman soldiers could levy on subject peoples. Jews would have seldom encountered legionnaires except in time of war or insurrection. It would have been auxiliaries who were headquartered in Judea, paid at half the rate of legionnaires and rather a scruffy bunch. In Galilee, Herod Antipas maintained an army patterned after Rome's; presumably it also had the right to impose labor. Mile markers were placed regularly beside the highways. A soldier could impress a civilian to carry his pack one mile only; to force the civilian to go farther carried with it severe penalties under military law. In this way Rome attempted to limit the anger of the occupied people and still keep its armies on the move. Nevertheless, this levy was a bitter reminder to the Jews that they were a subject people even in the Promised Land.

To this proud but subjugated people Jesus does not counsel revolt. One does not "befriend" the soldier, draw him aside, and drive a knife into his ribs. Jesus was keenly aware of the futility of armed revolt against Roman imperial might and minced no words about it, though it must have cost him support from the revolutionary factions.

But why walk the second mile? Is this not to rebound to the opposite extreme: aiding and abetting the enemy? Not at all. The question here, as in the two previous instances, is how the oppressed can recover the initiative, how they can assert their human dignity in a situation that cannot for the time being be changed. The rules are Caesar's, but not how one responds to the rules—that is God's, and Caesar has no power over that.

Imagine then the soldier's surprise when, at the next mile marker, he reluctantly reaches to assume his pack (sixty-five to eighty-five pounds in full gear), and you say, "Oh, no, let me carry it another mile." Why would you do that? What are you up to? Normally he has to coerce your kinsmen to carry his pack, and now you do it cheerfully and *will not stop!* Is this a provocation? Are you insulting his strength? Being kind? Trying to get him disciplined for seeming to make you go farther than you should? Are you planning to file a complaint? Create trouble?

From a situation of servile impressments, you have once more seized the initiative. You have taken back the power of choice....

These three examples amplify what Jesus means in his thesis statement: "Don't react violently against the one who is evil." Instead of the two options ingrained in us by millions of years of unreflective, brute response to biological threats from the environment—flight or fight—Jesus offers a third way. This new way marks a historic mutation in human development: the revolt against the principle of natural selection. With Jesus a way emerges by which evil can be opposed without being mirrored:

Jesus' Third Way
- Seize the moral initiative
- Find a creative alternative to violence
- Assert your own humanity and dignity as a person
- Meet force with ridicule or humor
- Break the cycle of humiliation
- Refuse to submit or to accept the inferior position
- Expose the injustice of the system
- Take control of the power dynamic
- Shame the oppressor into repentance
- Stand your ground
- Force the Powers to make decisions for which they are not prepared
- Recognize your own power
- Be willing to suffer rather than to retaliate
- Cause the oppressor to see you in a new light
- Deprive the oppressor of a situation where a show of force is effective
- Be willing to undergo the penalty for breaking unjust laws
- Die to fear of the old order and its rules ...

5. NEW TESTAMENT TEXTS

Romans 5:8-10; 12:14, 16a, 17-21

But God proves his love for us in that while we still were sinners Christ died for us. Much more surely then, now that we have been justified by his blood, will we be saved through him from the wrath of God. For if while we were enemies, we were reconciled to God through the death of his Son, much more surely, having been reconciled, will we be saved by his life.

Bless those who persecute you; bless and do not curse them.

Live in harmony with one another.

Do not repay anyone evil for evil, but take thought for what is noble in the sight of all. If it is possible, so far as it depends on you, live peaceably with all. Beloved, never avenge yourselves, but leave room for the wrath of God; for it is written, "Vengeance is mine, I will repay, says the Lord." No, "if your enemies are hungry, feed them; if they are thirsty, give them something to drink; for by doing this you will heap burning coals on their heads." Do not be overcome by evil, but overcome evil with good.

Hebrews 10:32-34

[Y]ou endured a hard struggle with sufferings, sometimes being publicly exposed to abuse and persecution, and sometimes being partners with those so treated. For you had compassion for those who were in prison, and you cheerfully accepted the plundering of your possessions, knowing that you yourselves possessed something better and more lasting.

1 Peter 2:21, 23

For to this you have been called, because Christ also suffered for you, leaving you an example, so that you should follow in his steps.

When he was abused, he did not return abuse; when he suffered, he did not threaten; but he entrusted himself to the one who judges justly.

6. RICHARD B. HAYS

Violence in Defense of Justice

Like Brueggemann and Wink, Richard B. Hays (b. 1948) is a contemporary biblical scholar whose writings are well known for their attention to issues of war and peace. Hays is profes- sor of New Testament at Duke University, and the following excerpt, taken from The Moral Vision of the New Testament: A Contemporary Introduction to New Testament Ethics, *is a landmark study in biblical pacifism.*

Our exegetical investigation of Matthew 5:38-48 has led to the conclusion that the passage teaches a norm of nonviolent love of enemies. Within the context of Matthew's Gospel, the directive to "turn the other cheek" functions as more than a bare rule; instead, as a "focal instance" of discipleship, it functions metonymically, illuminating the life of a covenant community that is called to live in radical faithfulness to the vision of the kingdom of God disclosed in Jesus' teaching and example. Taken alone, this text would certainly preclude any justifi- cation for Jesus' disciples to resort to violence. The question that we must now consider is how Mat- thew's vision of the peaceful community fits into the larger witness of the canonical New Testament. Do the other texts in the canon reinforce the Ser- mon on the Mount's teaching on nonviolence, or do they provide other options that might allow or require Christians to take up the sword?

When the question is posed this way, the imme- diate result—as Barth observed—is to under- score how impressively univocal is the testimony of the New Testament writers on this point. The evangelists are unanimous in portraying Jesus as a Messiah who subverts all prior expectations by assuming the vocation of suffering rather than conquering Israel's enemies. Despite his sting- ing criticism of those in positions of authority, he never attempts to exert force as a way of gaining social or political power.... He imposes an order of silence to keep his disciples from proclaiming him as Messiah until he has redefined the title in terms of the cross, and he instructs the disciples that their vocation must be the same as his (Mark

8:27-9:1). He withdraws from the crowd that wants to "take him by force to make him king" (John 6:15). At every turn he renounces violence as a strategy for promoting God's kingdom (e.g., Luke 9:51-56, where he rebukes James and John for wanting to call down fire from heaven to consume unreceptive Samaritans), and he teaches his followers to assume the posture of servanthood (Mark 10:42-45; John 13:1-7) and to expect to suffer at the hands of the world's authorities (Mark 13:9-13; John 15:18-16:4a). The hope of vindication and justice lies not with worldly force—that is the satanic temptation rejected at the beginning of his ministry—but in God's eschatological power. Jesus' death is fully consistent with his teaching; he refuses to lift a finger in his own defense, scolds those who do try to defend him with the sword, and rejects calling down "legions of angels" to fight a holy war against his enemies (Matt. 26:53). In Luke's account, he intercedes for the enemies responsible for his execution (Luke 23:34a, if this belongs to the text).

In the Acts of the Apostles, Luke tells a story of an emergent movement whose activity consists of preaching, healing, worship, and sharing. Those who carry the word to the various outposts of the Roman world do not claim territory through military operations; rather, they proclaim the gospel and often find themselves the targets of violence. The Christian response to this violence is modeled by the martyr Stephen, who in turn mirrors Jesus in his death by praying for the forgiveness of his enemies (Acts 7:60).

In the letters of Paul, the death of Christ is interpreted as God's peace initiative.... How does God treat enemies? Rather than killing them, Paul declares, he gives his Son to die for them. This has profound implications for the subsequent behavior of those who are reconciled to God through Jesus' death: to be "saved by his life" means to enter into a life that recapitulates the pattern of Christ's self-giving. As we have argued above, the imitation of Christ in his self-emptying service for the sake of others is a central ethical motif in Paul (e.g., Phil. 2:1-13). It is evident, then, that those whose lives are reshaped in Christ must deal with enemies in the same way that God in Christ dealt with enemies.

The most important Pauline hortatory passage that deals directly with the issue of violence (Rom. 12:14-21) bears so many material similarities to the Sermon on the Mount that some critics have sought to demonstrate Paul's dependence here on Jesus-tradition, despite the sparsity of verbatim agreement.... Though the governing authorities bear the sword to execute God's wrath (13:4), that is not the role of believers. Those who are members of the one body in Christ (12:5) are never to take vengeance (12:19); they are to bless their persecutors and minister to their enemies, returning good for evil. There is not a syllable in the Pauline letters that can be cited in support of Christians employing violence. Paul's occasional uses of military imagery (e.g., 2 Cor. 10:3-6; Phil. 1:27-30) actually have the opposite effect: the warfare imagery is drafted into the service of the gospel, rather than the reverse. He appropriates battle imagery as a way of describing the apocalyptic context in which the community lives, but the actual "fighting" is done through the proclamation of the gospel and through obedient yielding of one's members to God as *hopla* ("weapons") of righteousness (Rom. 6:13). The implications of this metaphorical logic are nicely summarized in 2 Corinthians 10:3-4: "For though we live in the flesh, we do not wage war according to the flesh, for the weapons of our warfare are not fleshly" (RH). This revisionary imagery is subsequently further elaborated by Ephesians 6:10-20: the community's struggle is not against human adversaries but against "spiritual forces of darkness," and its armor and weapons are truth, righteousness, peace, faith, salvation, and the word of God. Rightly understood, these metaphors witness powerfully *against* violence as an expression of obedience to God in Christ.

Likewise, in Hebrews and the catholic Epistles we encounter a consistent portrayal of the community as called to suffer without anger or retaliation. The author of Hebrews asks the readers to recall their earlier experience [of persecution].... Having been through such experiences in the past, the readers are exhorted to maintain their confidence and to remain faithful in the present. The plundering of possessions is to be accepted "with joy" (*meta charas*) rather than resisted by force. Here, without the slightest verbal echo, we find a substantive parallel to Matthew 5:40. Similarly, 1 Peter is pervasively concerned with the community's response to trials and suffering (1 Pet. 1:6-7, 3:13-18, 4:12-19, 5:8-10). Such afflictions are interpreted, in a manner reminiscent of Paul, as "sharing Christ's sufferings" (4:13). Even more explicitly than Paul, however, the author of 1 Peter holds up the suffering of Christ as a paradigm for Christian faithfulness [2:21, 23].... The appeal is to Jesus' conduct in his passion, not to any specific teaching of Jesus, but the familiar picture that emerges here is thoroughly consonant with the texts that we have been considering in the Sermon on the Mount. A final passage that should be noted is James 4:1-3, which attributes "wars and fightings" to the "cravings" that are at war within the individual: "You want something and do not have it; so you commit murder." James never entertains the notion that there might be circumstances in which fighting and killing are necessary for some good purpose.

The Apocalypse ... has often been misconstrued as a warrant for warlike attitudes among Christians. In fact ... such a reading of the text is far wide of the mark. In fact, the book seeks to inculcate in its readers precisely the same character qualities that we have seen extolled through the rest of the New Testament canon: faithful endurance in suffering, trust in God's eschatological vindication of his people, and a response to adversity modeled on the paradigm of "the Lamb who was slaughtered." The saints conquer the power of evil through "the blood of the Lamb and by the word of their testimony" (Rev. 12:11), not through recourse to violence.

Thus, from Matthew to Revelation we find a consistent witness against violence and a calling to the community to follow the example of Jesus in *accepting* suffering rather than *inflicting* it....

PART II
Early Christian Voices

7. Justin Martyr

Justin (c. 100-c. 165), a Christian apologist from Syrian Palestine, was martyred during the violent reign of Marcus Aurelius, but not before leaving behind landmark contributions to early Christian literature, including the First Apology *and* Dialogue with Trypho. *Immediately below is an excerpt from the* First Apology, *in which Justin implores the imperial rulers and people of Rome to stop persecuting Christians as threats to state and society. Part of his eloquent defense, which follows his opening words to his addressees, is an argument about the revolutionary peacefulness of Christian teaching and practices.*

First Apology

1. To the Emperor Titus Aelius Hadranius Antoninus Pius Augustus Caesar, and to Verissimus his son, the Philosopher, son of Caesar by nature and of Augustus by adoption, a lover of culture, and to the Sacred Senate and the whole Roman people—on behalf of men of every nation who are unjustly hated and reviled, I, Justin, son of Priscus and grandson of Bacchius, of Flavia Neapolis in Syria Palestina, being myself one of them, have drawn up this plea and petition.

2. ... in these pages we do not come before you with flattery, or as if making a speech to win your favor, but asking you to give judgment according to strict and exact inquiry—not, moved by prejudice or respect for superstitious men, or by irrational impulse and long-established evil rumor, giving a vote which would really be against yourselves. For we are firmly convinced that we can suffer no evil unless we are proved to be evildoers or shown to be criminals. You can kill us, but cannot do us any real harm.

3. But so no one may think that this is an unreasonable and presumptuous utterance, we ask that the charges against us be investigated. If they are true, [let us] be punished as is proper. But if nobody has proofs against us, true reason does not allow [you] to wrong innocent men because of an evil rumor—or rather [to wrong] yourselves when you decide to pass sentence on the basis of passion rather than judgment....

14. ... Those who once rejoiced in fornication now delight in continence alone; those who made use of magic arts have dedicated themselves to the good and unbegotten God; we who once took most pleasure in the means of increasing our wealth and property now bring what we have into a common

fund and share with everyone in need; we who hated and killed one another and would not associate with men of different tribes because of [their different] customs, now after the manifestation of Christ live together and pray for our enemies and try to persuade those who unjustly hate us, so that they, living according to the fair commands of Christ, may share with us the good hope of receiving the same things [that we will] from God, the master of all. So that this may not seem to be sophistry, I think fit before giving our demonstration to recall a few of the teachings which have come from Christ himself. It is for you then, as mighty emperors, to examine whether we have been taught and do teach these things truly. His sayings were short and concise, for he was no sophist, but his word was the power of God.

15. ... This is what he taught on affection for all men: "If you love those who love you, what new thing do you do? for even the harlots do this. But I say to you, Pray for your enemies and love those who hate you and bless those who curse you and pray for those who treat you despitefully" ...

16. About being long-suffering and servants to all and free from anger, this is what he said: "To him that smites you on one cheek turn the other also, and to him that takes away your cloak do not deny your tunic either. Whoever is angry is worthy of the fire. And whoever compels you to go one mile, follow him for two. Let your good works shine before men, that they as they see may wonder at your Father who is in heaven."

For we ought not to quarrel; he has not wished us to imitate the wicked, but rather by our patience and meekness to draw all men from shame and evil desires. This we can show in the case of many who were once on your side but have turned from the ways of violence and tyranny, overcome by observing the consistent lives of their neighbors, or noting the strange patience of their injured acquaintances, or experiencing the way they did business with them....

39. When the prophetic Spirit speaks as prophesying things to come, he says: "For the law will go forth from Zion and the Word of the Lord from Jerusalem, and he shall judge in the midst of the nations and rebuke much people; and they shall beat their swords into plowshares and their spears into pruning hooks, and nation will not lift up sword against nation, neither shall they learn to war anymore." We can show you that this has really happened. For a band of twelve men went forth from Jerusalem, and they were common men, not trained in speaking, but by the power of God they testified to every race of mankind that they were sent by Christ to teach to all the Word of God; and [now] we who once killed each other not only do not make war on each other, but in order not to lie or deceive our inquisitors we gladly die for the confession of Christ....

Dialogue with Trypho

In his dialogue with Trypho, a Jew, Justin once again refers to the passage from Micah which prophesies that nations will beat their swords into plowshares and refuse to undertake war against one another. Justin was convinced that the Christians of his age had been transformed from warriors to peacemakers and thus had already fulfilled part of the prophecy of Micah.

60. ... and we who were filled with war, and mutual slaughter, and every wickedness, have each through the whole earth changed our warlike weapons—our swords into ploughshares, and our spears into implements of tillage—and we cultivate piety, righteousness, philanthropy, faith, and hope, which we have from the Father Himself through Him who was crucified ... Now it is evident that no one can terrify or subdue us who have believed in Jesus all over the world. For it is plain that, though beheaded, and crucified, and thrown to wild beasts, and chains, and fire, and all other kinds of torture, we do not give up our confession; but the more such things happen, the more do others and in larger numbers become faithful, and worshippers of God through the name of Jesus. For just as if one should cut away the fruit-bearing parts of a vine, it grows up again, and yields other branches flourishing and fruitful; even so the same thing happens with us. For the vine planted by God and Christ the Savior is His people.

8. ATHENAGORUS

A Plea Regarding Christians

Athenagorus (?-c. 160) was a Christian apologist based in Athens whose major extant work,
A Plea Regarding Christians, *defended Christians against charges of cannibalism, incest,
and insurrection. Like Justin, Athenagorus was deeply concerned about persecution, and he
addressed his plea to the Roman emperors, Marcus Aurelius and Lucius Aurelius Commodus, to assure them that Christians were not threats to the civil order but rather unlettered
women and men devoted to Roman laws and the peaceful teachings of Christianity.*

1. ... while everyone admires your mildness and gentleness and your peaceful and kindly attitude toward all, they enjoy equal rights under the law. The cities, according to their rank, share in equal honor; and the whole Empire through your wisdom enjoys profound peace.

But you have not cared for us who are called Christians in this way. Although we do no wrong, but, as we shall show, are of all men most religiously and rightly disposed toward God and your Empire, you allow us to be harassed, plundered, and persecuted, the mob making war on us only because of our name. We venture, therefore, to state our case before you. From what we have to say you will gather that we suffer unjustly and contrary to all law and reason. Hence we ask you to devise some measures to prevent our being the victims of false accusers.

The injury we suffer from our persecutors does not concern our property or our civil rights or anything of less importance. For we hold these things in contempt, although they appear weighty to the crowd. We have learned not only not to return blow for blow, nor to sue those who plunder and rob us, but to those who smite us on one cheek to offer the other also, and to those who take away our coat to give our overcoat as well. But when we have given up our property, they plot against our bodies and souls, pouring upon us a multitude of accusations which have not the slightest foundation, but which are the stock in trade of gossips and the like.

2. If, indeed, anyone can convict us of wrongdoing, be it trifling or more serious, we do not beg off punishment, but are prepared to pay the penalty however cruel and unpitying....

11. ... Although what I have said has raised a loud clamor, permit me here to proceed freely, since I am making my defense to emperors who are philosophers. Who of those who analyze syllogisms, resolve ambiguities, explain etymologies, or [teach] homonyms, synonyms, predicates, axioms, and what the subject is and what the predicate—who of them do not promise to make their disciples happy through these and similar disciplines? And yet who of them have so purified their own hearts as to love their enemies instead of hating them; instead of upbraiding those who first insult them (which is certainly more usual), to bless them; and to pray for those who plot against them? On the contrary, they ever persist in delving into the evil mysteries of their sophistry, ever desirous of working some harm, making skill in oratory rather than proof by deeds their business. With us, on the contrary, you will find unlettered people, tradesmen and old women, who, though unable to express in words the advantages of our teaching, demonstrate by acts the value of their principles. For they do not rehearse speeches, but evidence good deeds. When struck, they do not strike back; when robbed, they do not sue; to those who ask, they give, and they love their neighbors as themselves.

12. If we do not think that a God ruled over the human race, would we live in such purity? The idea is impossible. But since we are persuaded that we must give an account of all our life here to God who made us and the world, we adopt a temperate, generous, and despised way of life. For we think that, even if we lose our lives, we shall suffer here no evil to be compared with the reward we shall receive

from the great Judge for a gentle, generous, and modest life.…

35. Since this is our character, what man of sound judgment would say that we are murderers? For you cannot eat human flesh until we have killed someone. If their first charge against us is a fiction, so is the second. For if anyone were to ask them if they had seen what they affirm, none of them would be so shameless as to say he had.

Moreover, we have slaves: some of us more, some fewer. We cannot hide anything from them; yet not one of them has made up such tall stories against us. Since they know that we cannot endure to see a man being put to death even justly, who of them would charge us with murder or cannibalism? Who among our accusers is not eager to witness contests of gladiators and wild beasts, especially those organized by you? But we see little difference between watching a man being put to death and killing him. So we have given up such spectacles. How can we commit murder when we will not look at it, lest we should contract the stain of guilt? What reason would we have to commit murder when we say that women who induce abortions are murderers, and will have to give account of it to God? For the same person would not regard the fetus in the womb as a living thing and therefore an object of God's care, and at the same time slay it, once it had come to life. Nor would he refuse to expose infants, on the ground that those who expose them are murderers of children, and at the same time do away with the child he has reared. But we are altogether consistent in our conduct. We obey reason and do not override it.

9. Letter to Diognetus

The Letter to Diognetus *has both an anonymous author and an indeterminate date, although it seems to have been written between the late second and the late third century* C.E. *Not much is known about the addressee, either, except for his status as a cultural elite. But the point of the writing is clearly apologetic: the author explains Christian beliefs in response to critics and encourages the addressee to convert to Christianity. Perhaps most striking is the text's rich depiction of Christians as peaceful and the wider world as violent. According to the author, peaceful Christians even represent a "new race or way of life."*

To His Excellency, Diognetus:

I understand, sir, that you are really interested in learning about the religion of the Christians, and that you are making an accurate and careful investigation of the subject. You want to know, for instance, what God they believe in and how they worship him, while at the same time they disregard the world and look down on death, and how it is that they do not treat the divinities of the Greeks as gods at all, although on the other hand they do not follow the superstition of the Jews. You would also like to know the source of the loving affection that they have for each other. You wonder, too, why this new race or way of life has appeared on earth now and not earlier. I certainly welcome this keen interest on your part, and I ask God, who gives us the power to speak and the power to listen, to let me speak in such a way that you may derive the greatest possible benefit from listening, and to enable you to listen to such great effect that I may never have a reason for regretting what I have said.…

[C]hristians cannot be distinguished from the rest of the human race by country or language or customs.… Yet, although they live in Greek and barbarian cities alike, as each man's lot has been cast, and follow the customs of the country in clothing and food and other matters of daily living, at the same time they give proof of the remarkable and admittedly extraordinary constitution of their own commonwealth. They live in their own countries, but only as aliens.… They busy themselves on earth, but their citizenship is in heaven. They obey the established laws, but in their own lives they go far beyond what the laws require. They love all men, and by all men are persecuted. They are unknown, and still they are condemned; they are put to death, and yet they are brought to life. They are poor, and yet they make many rich; they are completely destitute, and yet they enjoy complete abundance. They are dishonored, and in their very dishonor are glorified; they are defamed, and are vindicated. They are reviled, and yet they bless; when they are affronted, they still pay due respect. When they do good, they are punished as evildoers; undergoing punishment, they rejoice because they are brought to life. They are treated by the Jews as foreigners and enemies, and are hunted down by the Greeks; and all the time those who hate them find it impossible to justify their enmity.

To put it simply: What the soul is in the body, that Christians are in the world…. The flesh hates the soul and treats it as an enemy, even though it has suffered no wrong, because it is prevented from enjoying its pleasures; so too the world hates Christians, even though it suffers no wrong at their hands, because they range themselves against its pleasures. The soul loves the flesh that hates it, and its members; in the same way, Christians love those who hate them…. The soul, when faring badly as to food and drink, grows better; so too Christians, when punished, day by day increase more and more. It is to no less a post than this that God has ordered them, and they must not try to evade it.

10. TERTULLIAN

Tertullian (c. 155-c. 225) was a well-heeled and highly educated lay theologian from Carthage. Most of his thirty-one extant writings are polemical treatises directed against pagans, Marcionites, and Gnostics—writings whose trinitarian and christological language continues to find expression even in contemporary Christian theology. Although he was not a strict pacifist—his Apology, *for instance, accepted the emperor's wars and noted that Christians pray for "brave armies"—it would be inaccurate to suggest that Tertullian was not favorably inclined to nonviolence as a way of life for Christians. Written for Emperor Septimus Severus in 197 C.E., the* Apology, *excerpted below, depicts Christians as those who could be a threat to the emperor but whose teachings forbid retaliation and extol nonviolent love.*

Apology

37. If we are enjoined, then, to love our enemies, as I have remarked above, whom have we to hate? If injured, we are forbidden to retaliate, lest we become as bad ourselves: who can suffer injury at our hands? In regard to this, recall your own experiences. How often you inflict gross cruelties on Christians, partly because it is your own inclination, and partly in obedience to the laws! How often, too, the hostile mob, paying no regard to you, takes the law into its own hand, and assails us with stones and flames! With the very frenzy of the Bacchanals, they do not even spare the Christian dead, but tear them, now sadly changed, no longer entire, from the rest of the tomb, from the asylum we might say of death, cutting them in pieces, rending them asunder. Yet, banded together as we are, ever so ready to sacrifice our lives, what single case of revenge for injury are you able to point to, though, if it were held right among us to repay evil by evil, a single night with a torch or two could achieve an ample vengeance? But away with the idea of a sect divine avenging itself by human fires, or shrinking from the sufferings in which it is tried. If we desired, indeed, to act the part of open enemies, not merely of secret avengers, would there be any lacking in strength, whether of numbers or resources? … We are but of yesterday, and we have filled every place among you—cities, islands, for-

tresses, towns, marketplaces, the very camp, tribes, companies, palace, senate, forum—we have left nothing to you but the temples of your gods. For what wars should we not be fit, not eager, even with unequal forces, we who so willingly yield ourselves to the sword, if in our religion it were not counted better to be slain than to slay? Without arms even, and raising no insurrectionary banner, but simply in enmity to you, we could carry on the contest with you by an ill-willed severance alone. For if such multitudes of men were to break away from you, and betake themselves to some remote corner of the world, why, the very loss of so many citizens, whatever sort they were, would cover the empire with shame; nay, in the very forsaking, vengeance would be inflicted. Why, you would be horror-struck at the solitude in which you would find yourselves, at such an all-prevailing silence, and that stupor as of a dead world. You would have to seek subjects to govern. You would have more enemies than citizens remaining. For now it is the immense number of Christians which makes your enemies so few—almost all the inhabitants of your various cities being followers of Christ. Yet you choose to call us enemies of the human race, rather than of human error. Nay, who would deliver you from those secret foes, ever busy both destroying your souls and ruining your health? Who would save you, I mean, from the attacks of those spirits of evil, which without reward or hire we exorcise? This alone would be revenge enough for us, that you were henceforth left free to the possession of unclean spirits. But instead of taking into account what is due to us for the important protection we afford you, and though we are not merely no trouble to you, but in fact necessary to your well-being, you prefer to hold us enemies, as indeed we are, yet not of man, but rather of his error.

On Idolatry

Tertullian wrote another famous treatise, On Idolatry, *after he had authored* Apology, *and it appears to offer an elucidation of his earlier position on Christians and the military. It is not true that Christians were a nonviolent lot until Emperor Constantine corrupted them in the fourth century, and Tertullian earlier conceded, without protesting,* *that Christians served in the military. But now, in* On Idolatry, *he unqualifiedly argues that because Jesus disarmed Peter, Christians may not wear the military uniform. Although he believed that Jesus' teachings disarmed Christians, Tertullian was also no doubt concerned about religious demands on Roman soldiers—after all, he uses a treatise on idolatry to clarify his opposition to Christians serving in the military. Indeed, Roman military camps at this point practiced what Tertullian identified as "worship of the standards" (Apology 16.8): soldiers pledged their ultimate allegiance to the emperor, abided by a calendar of religious festivals honoring the emperor's deities, and offered sacrifice to these same gods.*

19.1-3. But the question now is whether a member of the faithful can become a soldier and whether a soldier can be admitted to the Faith even if he is a member of the rank and file who are not required to offer sacrifice or decide capital cases. There can be no compatibility between an oath made to God and one made to man, between the standard of Christ and that of the devil, between the camp of light and the camp of darkness. The soul cannot be beholden to two masters, God and Caesar. Moses, to be sure, carried a rod; Aaron wore a military belt and John had a breastplate. If one wants to play around with the topic, Jesus, son of Nun [i.e., Joshua], led an army and the Jewish nation went to war. But how will a Christian do so? Indeed how will he serve in the army even during peacetime without the sword that Jesus Christ has taken away? Even if soldiers came to John and got advice on how they ought to act, even if the centurion became a believer, the Lord, by taking away Peter's sword, disarmed every soldier thereafter. We are not allowed to wear any uniform that symbolizes a sinful act.

The Shows

Tertullian's condemnation of the killing of humans is especially visible in his treatise on the gladiatorial shows that were so popular among his contemporary Carthaginians. Although the residents of the city were becoming Christian, they continued to practice the habit of going to "the shows." Tertullian expresses his disgust for this bloody practice and draws a sharp distinction between the shows and the will of God for Christians.

2. … There is a vast difference between the corrupted state and that of primal purity, just because there is a vast difference between the Creator and the corruptor. Why, all sorts of evils, which as indubitably evils even the heathens prohibit, and against which they guard themselves, come from the works of God. Take, for instance, murder, whether committed by iron, by poison, or by magical enchantments. Irons and herbs and enchantments are all equally creatures of God. Has the Creator, withal, provided these things for man's destruction? Nay, He puts His interdict on every sort of man-killing by that one summary precept: "Thou shalt not kill." … Man himself, guilty as he is of every iniquity, is not only a work of God—he is His image, and yet both in soul and body he has severed himself from his Maker. For we did not get eyes to minister to lust, and the tongue for speaking evil with, and ears to be the receptacle of evil speech, and the throat to serve the vice of gluttony, and the belly to be gluttony's ally, and the genitals for unchaste excesses, and hands for deeds of violence, and the feet for an erring life….

On the Crown

The issue of idolatry and the military reappears in his treatise On the Crown. *Tertullian wrote the treatise in response to a Christian soldier who seems to have been put to death for refusing to abide by the dress code for a military parade honoring Emperor Caracalla. The code called for the wearing of a military crown (one that evoked Roman military religion), and the Christian solider had refused to wear the idolatrous symbol. Nevertheless, it is not only idolatry that Tertullian finds so troubling about military life; he is also disturbed by the military's opposition to Christian teachings about revenge.*

11.1-7. Before treating the matter of a military crown I think we must first ask whether military service is appropriate for Christians at all. What is the point in talking about incidental matters when the assumptions which they rest on are wrong from the start. Do we think that one can rightfully super-

impose a human oath on one made to God? and that a man can answer to a second lord once he has acknowledged Christ? and that he can abjure father, mother, and all his neighbors when the Law prescribes that they be honored and loved next to God and the Gospel holds them in the same high esteem, valuing only Christ himself above them? Is it right to make a profession of the sword when the Lord has proclaimed that the man who uses it will perish by it?

Will a son of peace who should not even go to court take part in battle? Will a man who does not avenge wrongs done to himself have any part in chains, prisons, tortures and punishments? Will he perform guard duty for anyone other than Christ, or will he do so on the Lord's day when he is not doing it for Christ Himself? Will he stand guard at the temples which he has foresworn? Will he go to a banquet at places where the apostle disapproves of it? At night will he protect those [demons] that he has exorcised during the day, leaning and resting all the while on the spear that pierced the side of Christ? Will he carry the standards that rival Christ's? Will he ask his commander for a password when he has already received one from God? At the moment of death will he be disturbed by the trumpeter's horn if he looks forward to being awakened by the horn of the angel? Will he be cremated according to the usual practice when this has been forbidden him and when he has been freed by Christ from the punishment of fire? By looking around one can see how many other forms of wrongdoing are involved in fulfilling the duties of military camps, things which must be considered violations of God's law. Carrying the title "Christian" from the camp of life to the camp of darkness is itself a violation.

The situation is different if the faith comes to a man after he is in the army, as with the soldiers whom John admitted to baptism and the converted centurion whom Christ praised and the one whom Peter instructed in the faith. Nonetheless, once a man has accepted the faith and has been marked with its seal, he must immediately leave the service, as many have done, or he has to engage in all kinds of quibbling to avoid offending God in ways that are forbidden to men even outside the service. Or, finally, he will have to endure for God what civilian members of the faith have been no less willing to accept. Military service offers neither impunity for wrongdoing nor immunity from martyrdom. The Gospel is one and the same for Christians everywhere. Jesus will deny everyone who denies Him and will acknowledge everyone who acknowledges Him. He will save the life that has been given up for his Name's sake but will destroy the one that was saved at the expense of his Name for money's sake. In his eyes the faithful civilian is as much a soldier as the faithful soldier is a civilian. There is no allowance for a plea of necessity. No necessity for wrongdoing is incumbent on those for whom the only necessity is to avoid wrongdoing. Someone, you say, is pressed into sacrificing or officially denying Christ by the inevitability of torture or punishment. All the same, church discipline does not wink even at that kind of necessity because the necessity to fear denial and to suffer martyrdom is greater than the necessity to avoid martyrdom and to make the required offering. What is more, a pretext like this undercuts the whole meaning of the baptismal oath, thereby opening the door to even voluntary sins. For desire itself could be considered necessity inasmuch as it is a matter of compulsion. On the matter of official crowns, I would give the same answer to other arguments that are used to bolster the familiar cry of necessity because we must either refuse offices in order to avoid falling into sin or we must undergo martyrdom in order to be freed from these obligations.

On Marcion

Tertullian's writings on Christ and peace are also present in his treatise against Marcion (d. c. 160). Tertullian considered Marcion a heretic for identifying the Christian gospel as one merely of love (not law, too) and for rejecting the Hebrew Scriptures on the grounds that the creator depicted therein was directly at odds with the revelation of love in the New Testament. Below is a brief excerpt in which Tertullian claims to see the nonviolent Christ of the New Testament prefigured in the Psalms—a claim he connects to his interpretation of "sword."

3.14. This interpretation of ours will derive confirmation, when, on your supposing that Christ is in any passage called a warrior, from the mention of certain arms and expressions of that sort, you weigh well the analogy of their other meanings, and draw your conclusions accordingly. "Gird on Thy sword," says David, "upon Thy thigh." But what do you read about Christ just before? "Thou art fairer than the children of men; grace is poured forth upon Thy lips." It amuses me to imagine that blandishments of fair beauty and graceful lips are ascribed to one who had to gird on His sword for war! So likewise, when it is added, "Ride on prosperously in Thy majesty," the reason is subjoined: "Because of truth, and meekness, and righteousness." But who shall produce *these* results with the sword, and not their opposites rather—deceit, and harshness, and injury—which, it must be confessed, are the proper business of battles? Let us see, therefore, whether that is not some other sword, which has so different an action. Now the Apostle John, in the Apocalypse, describes a sword which proceeded from the mouth of God as "a doubly sharp, two-edged one." This may be understood to be the Divine Word, who is doubly edged with the two testaments of the law and the gospel—sharpened with wisdom, hostile to the devil, arming us against the spiritual enemies of all wickedness and concupiscence, and cutting us off from the dearest objects for the sake of God's holy name. If, however, you will not acknowledge John, you have our common master Paul, who "girds our loins about with truth, and puts on us the breastplate of righteousness, and shoes us with the preparation of the gospel of peace, not of war; who bids us take the shield of faith, wherewith we may be able to quench all the fiery darts of the devil, and the helmet of salvation, and the sword of the Spirit, which (he says) is the word of God." This sword the Lord Himself came to send on earth, and not peace. If he is your Christ, then even he is a warrior. If he is not a warrior, and the sword he brandishes is an allegorical one, then the Creator's Christ in the psalm too may have been girded with the figurative sword of the Word, without any martial gear. The above-mentioned "fairness" of His beauty and "grace of His lips" would quite suit such a sword, girt as it even then was upon His thigh in the passage of David, and sent as it would one day be by Him on earth. For this is what He says: "Ride on prosperously in Thy majesty"—*advancing* His word into every land, so as to call all nations: destined to *prosper* in the success of that faith which received Him, and *reigning*, from the fact that He conquered death by His resurrection. "Thy right hand," says He, "shall wonderfully lead Thee forth," even the might of Thy spiritual grace, whereby the knowledge of Christ is spread. "Thine arrows are sharp"; everywhere Thy precepts fly about, Thy threatenings also, and convictions of heart, pricking and piercing each conscience. "The people shall fall under Thee," that is, in adoration. Thus is the Creator's Christ mighty in war, and a bearer of arms; thus also does He now take the spoils, not of Samaria alone, but of all nations. Acknowledge, then, that His spoils are figurative, since you have learned that His arms are allegorical. Since, therefore, both the Lord speaks and His apostle writes such things in a figurative style, we are not rash in using His interpretations, the records of which even our adversaries admit; and thus in *so* far will it be Isaiah's Christ who has come, in as far as He was not a warrior, because it is not of such a character that He is described by Isaiah.

On Patience

Finally, as his treatise On Patience *suggests, the starting point of Tertullian's Christian teachings on nonviolence is his understanding of the nature of God as revealed in the life of Jesus.*

3. And *this* species of the divine patience indeed being, as it were, at a distance, may perhaps be esteemed as among "things too high for us"; but what is that which, in a certain way, has been grasped by hand among men openly on the earth? God suffers Himself to be conceived in a mother's womb, and awaits *the time for birth*; and, when born, bears *the delay* of growing up; and, when grown up, is not eager to be recognized, but is furthermore contumelious to Himself, and is baptized by His own servant; and repels with words alone the assaults of the tempter; while from being "Lord" He becomes "Master," teaching

man to escape death, having been trained to the exercise of the absolute forbearance of offended patience. He did not strive; He did not cry aloud; nor did any hear His voice in the streets. He did not break the bruised reed; the smoking flax He did not quench: for the prophet—nay, the attestation of God Himself, placing His own Spirit, together with patience in its entirety, in His Son—had not falsely spoken. There was none desirous of cleaving to Him whom He did not receive. No one's table or roof did He despise: indeed, Himself ministered to the washing of the disciples' feet; not sinners, not publicans, did He repel; not with that city even which had refused to receive Him was He wroth, when even the disciples had wished that the celestial fires should be forthwith hurled on so contumelious a town. He cared for the ungrateful; He yielded to His ensnarers. This were a small matter, if He had not had in His company even His own betrayer, and steadfastly abstained from pointing him out. Moreover, while He is being betrayed, while He is being led up "as a sheep for a victim" (for "so He no more opens His mouth than a lamb under the power of the shearer"), He to whom, had He willed it, legions of angels would at one word have presented themselves from the heavens, approved not the avenging sword of even one disciple. The patience of the Lord was wounded in (the wound of) Malchus. And so, too, He cursed for the time to come the works of the sword; and, by the restoration of health, made satisfaction to him whom Himself had not hurt, through Patience, the mother of Mercy. I pass by in silence (the fact) that He is crucified, for this was the end for which He had come; yet had the death which must be undergone need of contumelies likewise? *Nay*, but, when about to depart, He wished to be sated with the pleasure of patience. He is spitted on, scourged, derided, clad foully, more foully crowned. Wondrous is the faith of equanimity! He who had set before *Him* the concealing of Himself in man's shape, imitated nought of man's impatience! Hence, even more than from any other trait, ought ye, Pharisees, to have recognized the Lord. Patience of this kind none of *men* would achieve. Such and so mighty evidences—the *very* magnitude of which proves to be among the nations indeed a cause for rejection of the faith, but among us its reason and rearing—proves manifestly enough (not by the sermons only, in enjoining, but likewise by the sufferings of the Lord in enduring) to them to whom it is given to believe, that as the effect and excellence of some inherent propriety, patience is God's nature.

11. ORIGEN

Origen (c. 185-c. 253) was reared in a Christian family in Alexandria and educated in the city's major schools of philosophy. As a prolific theologian, biblical scholar, teacher, and preacher, Origen was no stranger to controversy: his rational approach to the Bible resulted in conflicts with Christian leaders of his day, and his unorthodox ordination met with the disapproval of Alexandria's bishop, Demetrius. After Demetrius had removed him from his teaching post and the priesthood, Origen left Alexandria for Caesaria, where he continued to write, teach, and preach. Two decades after his departure from Alexandria, Origen died of complications from torture during the reign of Emperor Decius.

Historians have differed over the proper interpretation of Origen's views on the use of force: some have described him as a pacifist, pure and simple, while others have characterized his thought as foundational for the just war tradition. If we consider the major emphases in Origen's thoughts on the issue, especially as he sketched them in Against Celsus *(c. 248), his apologetic reply to charges that Christians were uncivil in their refusal to participate in political and military life, it is remarkably clear that he encouraged a life of nonviolence for Christians. Although he conceded that "a righteous cause" may be the driving force of a war, he nowhere suggested that the execution of wars was itself morally permissible. To classify his thought as foundational for just war theory is thus to claim too much; it is one thing to grant that soldiers fight for a just cause and quite another to concede the moral permissibility of using force for a just cause.*

Below are a few excerpts from Against Celsus, *in which Origin criticizes Celsus—a pagan philosopher who had denounced Christianity in* True Discourse, *the oldest extant literary attack on Christian beliefs and practices—for mischaracterizing the origins of Christianity and misunderstanding the ways in which Christians support the emperor.*

Against Celsus

3.7. The assertion that "certain Jews at the time of Christ revolted against the Jewish community and followed Jesus" is not less false than the claim "that the Jews had their origin in a revolt of certain Egyptians." Celsus and those who agree with him will not be able to cite a single act of rebellion on the part of the Christians. If a revolt had indeed given rise to the Christian community, if Christians took their origin from the Jews, who were allowed to take up arms in defense of their possessions and to kill their enemies, the Christian Lawgiver would not have made homicide absolutely forbidden. He would not have taught that his disciples were never justified in taking such action against a man even if he were the greatest wrongdoer. [Jesus] considered it contrary to his divinely inspired legislation to approve any kind of homicide whatsoever. If Christians had started with a revolt, they would never have submitted to the kind of peaceful laws which permitted them to be slaughtered "like sheep" (Ps. 44.11) and which made them always incapable of taking vengeance on their persecutors because they followed the law of gentleness and love....

5.33. To those who ask about our origin and our founder we reply that we have come in response to Jesus' commands to beat into plowshares the rational swords of conflict and arrogance and to change into pruning hooks those spears that we used to fight with. For we no longer take up the sword against any nation, nor do we learn the art of war anymore. Instead of following the traditions that made us "strangers to the covenants" (Ephesians 2:12), we have become sons of peace through Jesus our founder....

8.73. Celsus goes on to encourage us "to assist the emperor with all our strength, to work with him on just undertakings, to fight for him and to serve in his army, if he requires it, either as a soldier or a general." To this we should reply that when the occasion arises, we provide the emperors with divine assistance, as it were, by putting on the "armor of God" (Ephesians 6:11). We do so in obedience to the voice of the Apostle, who says, "My advice is that first and foremost you offer prayers, supplications, petitions and thanksgiving for all men, especially for the emperors and all those in authority" (I Timothy 2:1-2). To be sure, the more pious a man is, the more effectively does he assist the emperors—more so than the troops that go out and kill as many of the enemy as possible on the battle line. This would be our answer to those who are strangers to our faith and who ask us to take up arms and to kill men for the common good. Even in your religion priests attached to certain images and guardians of temples which are dedicated to what you believe are gods should keep their right hand undefiled for sacrifice so as to make their usual offerings to beings that you consider deities with hands that are free of blood and murder. And, of course, in wartime you do not enlist your priests. If this is a reasonable procedure, how much more so is it for Christians to fight as priests and worshipers of God while others fight as soldiers. Though they keep their right hands clean, the Christians fight through their prayers to God on behalf of those doing battle in a just cause and on behalf of an emperor who is ruling justly in order that all opposition and hostility toward those who are acting rightly may be eliminated. What is more, by overcoming with our prayers all the demons who incite wars, who violate oaths and who disturb the peace we help emperors more than those who are supposedly doing the fighting ... We do not go out on the campaign with him [i.e., the emperor] even if

he insists, but we do battle on his behalf by raising a special army of piety through our petitions to God.

The violence of the Hebrew Scriptures posed difficulties for Christians advocating nonviolence, and Origen offered his own solution to the problem in both Against Celsus *(the first section below) and* Homilies on Joshua *(the second section).*

7.25. Celsus then extracts from the Gospels the precept, "To him who strikes thee once, thou shalt offer thyself to be struck again," although without giving any passage from the Old Testament, which he considers opposed to it. On the one hand, we know that "it was said to them in old time, An eye for an eye, and a tooth for a tooth"; and on the other, we have read, "I say unto you, Whoever shall smite thee on the one cheek, turn to him the other also." But as there is reason to believe that Celsus produces the objections which he has heard from those who wish to make a difference between the God of the Gospel and the God of the law, we must say in reply that this precept ... is not unknown in the older Scriptures. For thus, in the Lamentations of Jeremiah, it is said, "It is good for a man that he bear the yoke in his youth: he sitteth alone, and keepeth silence, because he hath borne it upon him. He giveth his cheek to him that smiteth him; he is filled full with reproach." There is no discrepancy, then, between the God of the Gospel and the God of the law, even when we take literally the precept regarding the blow on the face. So, then, we infer that neither "Jesus nor Moses has taught falsely." The Father in sending Jesus did not "forget the commands which he had given to Moses"; He did not "change his mind; condemn His own laws, and send His messenger counter instructions."

7.26. However, if we must refer briefly to the difference between the constitution which was given to the Jews of old by Moses and that which the Christians, under the direction of Christ's teaching, wish now to establish, we would observe that it must be impossible for the legislation of Moses, taken literally, to harmonize with the calling of the Gentiles, and with their subjection to the Roman government; and on the other hand, it would be impossible for the Jews to preserve their civil economy unchanged, supposing that they should embrace the Gospel. For

Christians could not slay their enemies, or condemn to be burned or stoned, as Moses commands, those who had broken the law, and were therefore condemned as deserving of these punishments; since the Jews themselves, however desirous of carrying out their law, are not able to inflict these punishments. But in the case of the ancient Jews, who had a land and a form of government of their own, to take from them the right of making war upon their enemies, of fighting for their country, of putting to death or otherwise punishing adulterers, murderers, or others who were guilty of similar crimes, would be to subject them to sudden and utter destruction whenever the enemy fell upon them; for their very laws would in that case restrain them, and prevent them from resisting the enemy. And that same providence which of old gave the law, and has now given the Gospel of Jesus Christ, not wishing the Jewish state to continue longer, has destroyed their city and their temple ... And as it has destroyed these things, not wishing that they should longer continue, in like manner it has extended day by day the Christian religion, so that it is now preached everywhere with boldness, and that in spite of the numerous obstacles which oppose the spread of Christ's teaching in the world. But since it was the purpose of God that the nations should receive the benefits of Christ's teaching, all the devices of men against Christians have been brought to nought; for the more that kings, and rulers, and peoples have persecuted them everywhere, the more they have increased in number and grown in strength.

Homilies on Joshua

15.1. Unless those carnal wars [i.e., of the Old Testament] were a symbol of spiritual wars, I do not think that the Jewish historical books would ever have been passed down by the Apostles to be read by Christ's followers in their churches ... Thus, the Apostle, being aware that physical wars are no longer to be waged by us but that our struggles are to be only battles of the soul against spiritual adversaries, gives orders to the soldiers of Christ like a military commander when he says, "Put on the armor of God so as to be able to hold your ground against the wiles of the devil" (Ephesians 6:11).

12. CYPRIAN

In 248, only two years after he had converted to Christianity, Cyprian (c. 200-258), formerly a secular rhetorician, was elected bishop of Carthage. He left Carthage a few months later, when the Decian persecution threatened his life, but then returned to the city in 251. Known especially for insisting that because there is no salvation outside the church, schismatics had to be rebaptized within the church, Cyprian was martyred during the reign of Emperor Valerian in 258.

Although he was not a strict pacifist, it is certainly true that Cyprian's denunciation of murder, wars, and military life served to encourage Christian nonviolence. One of his most famous extant letters, To Donatus, *excerpted below, draws the sharpest of contrasts between worldly violence and the patience of Jesus, and even offers a liturgical case for Christian nonviolence.*

To Donatus

6. But in order that the characteristics of the divine may shine more brightly by the development of the truth, I will give you light to apprehend it, the obscurity caused by sin being wiped away. I will draw away the veil from the darkness of this hidden world. For a brief space conceive yourself to be transported to one of the loftiest peaks of some inaccessible mountain, thence gaze on the appearances of things lying below you, and with eyes turned in various directions look upon the eddies of the billowy world, while you yourself are removed from earthly contacts—you will at once

begin to feel compassion for the world, and with self-recollection and increasing gratitude to God, you will rejoice with all the greater joy that you have escaped it. Consider the roads blocked up by robbers, the seas beset with pirates, wars scattered all over the earth with the bloody horror of camps. The whole world is wet with mutual blood; and murder, which in the case of an individual is admitted to be a crime, is called a virtue when it is committed wholesale. Impunity is claimed for the wicked deeds, not on the plea that they are guiltless, but because the cruelty is perpetrated on a grand scale.

7. And now, if you turn your eyes and your regards to the cities themselves, you will behold a concourse more fraught with sadness than any solitude. The gladiatorial games are prepared, that blood may gladden the lust of cruel eyes. The body is fed up with stronger food, and the vigorous mass of limbs is enriched with brawn and muscle, that the wretch fattened for punishment may die a harder death. Man is slaughtered that man may be gratified, and the skill that is best able to kill is an exercise and an art. Crime is not only committed, but it is taught. What can be said more inhuman—what more repulsive? Training is undergone to acquire the power to murder, and the achievement of murder is its glory....

11. But that we may not perchance appear as if we were picking out extreme cases, and with the view of disparagement were seeking to attract your attention to those things whereof the sad and revolting view may offend the gaze of a better conscience, I will now direct you to such things as the world in its ignorance accounts good. Among these also you will behold things that will shock you. In respect of what you regard as honors, of what you consider the fasces, what you count affluence in riches, what you think power in the camp, the glory of the purple in the magisterial office, the power of license in the chief command—there is hidden the virus of ensnaring mischief, and an appearance of smiling wickedness, joyous indeed, but the treacherous deception of hidden calamity. Just as some poison, in which the flavor having been medicated with sweetness, craftily mingled in its deadly juices, seems, when taken, to be an ordinary draught, but when it is drunk up, the destruction that you have swallowed assails you. You see, forsooth, that man distinguished by his brilliant dress, glittering, as he

thinks, in his purple. Yet with what baseness has he purchased this glitter! …

14. Hence, then, the one peaceful and trustworthy tranquility, the one solid and firm and constant security, is this, for a man to withdraw from these eddies of a distracting world, and, anchored on the ground of the harbor of salvation, to lift his eyes from earth to heaven; and having been admitted to the gift of God, and being already very near to his God in mind, he may boast, that whatever in human affairs others esteem lofty and grand, lies altogether beneath his consciousness. He who is actually greater than the world can crave nothing, can desire nothing, from the world. How stable, how free from all shocks is that safeguard; how heavenly the protection in its perennial blessings—to be loosed from the snares of this entangling world, and to be purged from earthly dregs, and fitted for the light of eternal immortality! He will see what crafty mischief of the foe that previously attacked us has been in progress against us. We are constrained to have more love for what we shall be, by being allowed to know and to condemn what we were. Neither for this purpose is it necessary to pay a price either in the way of bribery or of labor; so that man's elevation or dignity or power should be begotten in him with elaborate effort; but it is a gratuitous gift from God, and it is accessible to all. As the sun shines spontaneously, as the day gives light, as the fountain flows, as the shower yields moisture, so does the heavenly Spirit infuse itself into us. When the soul, in its gaze into heaven, has recognized its Author, it rises higher than the sun, and far transcends all this earthly power, and begins to be that which it believes itself to be.

On the Advantage of Patience

Cyprian did not just denounce violence (and political life) as outside the gift of life granted by the Spirit of God. More positively, he also depicted the Christian life as properly imitative of the patience of Jesus. Below are excerpts from his treatise titled On the Advantage of Patience.

5. And that we may more fully understand, beloved brethren, that patience is a thing of God, and that whoever is gentle, and patient, and meek, is an imitator of God the Father; when the Lord in

His Gospel was giving precepts for salvation, and, bringing forth divine warnings, was instructing His disciples to perfection, He laid it down, and said, "Ye have heard that it is said, Thou shalt love thy neighbor, and have thine enemy in hatred. But I say unto you, Love your enemies, and pray for them which persecute you; that ye may be the children of your Father which is in heaven, who maketh His sun to rise on the good and on the evil, and raineth upon the just and on the unjust. For if ye love them which love you, what reward shall ye have? do not even the publicans the same? And if ye shall salute your brethren only, what do ye more (than others)? do not even the heathens the same thing? Be ye therefore perfect, even as your Father in heaven is perfect." He said that the children of God would thus become perfect. He showed that they were thus completed, and taught that they were restored by a heavenly birth, if the patience of God our Father dwell in us—if the divine likeness, which Adam had lost by sin, be manifested and shine in our actions. What a glory is it to become like to God! What and how great a felicity, to possess among our virtues, that which may be placed on the level of divine praises!

6. Nor, beloved brethren, did Jesus Christ, our God and Lord, teach this in words only; but He fulfilled it also in deeds.... He wrestles with the devil tempting Him; and, content only to have overcome the enemy, He strives no farther than by words. He ruled over His disciples not as servants in the power of a master; but, kind and gentle, He loved them with a brotherly love. He deigned even to wash the apostles' feet, that since the Lord is such among His servants, He might teach, by His example, what a fellow-servant ought to be among his peers and equals. Nor is it to be wondered at, that among the obedient He showed Himself such, since He could bear Judas even to the last with a long patience—could take meat with His enemy—could know the household foe, and not openly point him out, nor refuse the kiss of the traitor....

7. And moreover, in His very passion and cross, before they had reached the cruelty of death and the effusion of blood, what infamies of reproach were patiently heard, what mockings of contumely were suffered, so that *He* received the spittings of insulters, who with His spittle had a little

before made eyes for a blind man; and He in whose name the devil and his angels is now scourged by His servants, Himself suffered scourgings! He was crowned with thorns, who crowns martyrs with eternal flowers. He was smitten on the face with palms, who gives the true palms to those who overcome. He was despoiled of His earthly garment, who clothes others in the vesture of immortality. He was fed with gall, who gave heavenly food. He was given to drink of vinegar, who appointed the cup of salvation....

8. And after all these things, He still receives His murderers, if they will be converted and come to Him; and with a saving patience, He who is benignant to preserve, closes His Church to none. Those adversaries, those blasphemers, those who were always enemies to His name, if they repent of their sin, if they acknowledge the crime committed, He receives, not only to the pardon of their sin, but to the reward of the heavenly kingdom. What can be said more patient, what more merciful? Even he is made alive by Christ's blood who has shed Christ's blood. Such and so great is the patience of Christ; and had it not been such and so great, the Church would never have possessed Paul as an apostle.

9. But if we also, beloved brethren, are in Christ; if we put Him on, if He is the way of our salvation, who follow Christ in the footsteps of salvation, let us walk by the example of Christ, as the Apostle John instructs us, saying, "He who saith he abideth in Christ, ought himself also to walk even as He walked." Peter also, upon whom by the Lord's condescension the Church was founded, lays it down in his epistle, and says, "Christ suffered for us, leaving you an example, that ye should follow His steps, who did no sin, neither was deceit found in His mouth; who, when He was reviled, reviled not again; when He suffered, threatened not, but gave Himself up to him that judged Him unjustly."

10. Finally, we find that both patriarchs and prophets, and all the righteous men who in their preceding likeness wore the figure of Christ, in the praise of their virtues were watchful over nothing more than that they should preserve patience with a strong and steadfast equanimity. Thus Abel, who first initiated and consecrated the origin of martyrdom, and the passion of the righteous man, makes no resistance nor struggles against his frat-

ricidal brother, but with lowliness and meekness he is patiently slain. Thus Abraham, believing God, and first of all instituting the root and foundation of faith, when tried in respect of his son, does not hesitate nor delay, but obeys the commands of God with all the patience of devotion. And Isaac, prefigured as the likeness of the Lord's victim, when he is presented by his father for immolation, is found patient. And Jacob, driven forth by his brother from his country, departs with patience; and afterwards with greater patience, he suppliantly brings him back to concord with peaceful gifts, when he is even more impious and persecuting. Joseph, sold by his brethren and sent away, not only with patience pardons them, but even bountifully and mercifully bestows gratuitous supplies of corn on them when they come to him. Moses is frequently condemned by an ungrateful and faithless people, and almost stoned; and yet with gentleness and patience he entreats the Lord for those people. But in David, from whom, according to the flesh, the nativity of Christ springs, how great and marvelous and Christian is the patience, that he often had it in his power to be able to kill king Saul, who was persecuting him and desiring to slay him; and yet, chose rather to save him when placed in his hand, and delivered up to him, not repaying his enemy in turn, but rather, on the contrary, even avenging him when slain! In fine, so many prophets were slain, so many martyrs were honored with glorious deaths, who all have attained to the heavenly crowns by the praise of patience. For the crown of sorrows and sufferings cannot be received unless patience in sorrow and suffering precede it.

11. But that it may be more manifestly and fully known how useful and necessary patience is, beloved brethren; let the judgment of God be pondered, which even in the beginning of the world and of the human race, Adam, forgetful of the commandment, and a transgressor of the given law, received. Then we shall know how patient in this life we ought to be who are born in such a state, that we labor here with afflictions and contests. "Because," says He, "thou hast hearkened to the voice of thy wife, and hast eaten of the tree of which alone I had charged thee that thou shouldest not eat, cursed shall be the ground in all thy works: in sorrow and in groaning shalt thou eat of it all the days of thy life. Thorns and thistles shall it give forth to thee, and thou shalt eat the food of the field. In the sweat of thy face shalt thou eat thy bread, till thou return into the ground from which thou wast taken: for dust thou art, and to dust shalt thou go." We are all tied and bound with the chain of this sentence, until, death being expunged, we depart from this life. In sorrow and groaning we must of necessity be all the days of our life: it is necessary that we eat our bread with sweat and labor.

12. Whence every one of us, when he is born and received in the inn of this world, takes his beginning from tears; and, although still unconscious and ignorant of all things, he knows nothing else in that very earliest birth except to weep.... for us who, besides the various and continual battles of temptations, must also in the contest of persecutions forsake our patrimonies, undergo imprisonment, bear chains, spend our lives, endure the sword, the wild beasts, fires, crucifixions—in fine, all kinds of torments and penalties, to be endured in the faith and courage of patience; as the Lord Himself instructs us, and says, "These things have I spoken unto you, that in me ye might have peace. But in the world ye shall have tribulation; yet be confident, for I have overcome the world." And if we who have renounced the devil and the world, suffer the tribulations and mischiefs of the devil and the world with more frequency and violence, how much more ought we to keep patience, wherewith as our helper and ally, we may bear all mischievous things! ...

14. But patience, beloved brethren, not only keeps watch over what is good, but it also repels what is evil.... Let patience be strong and steadfast in the heart.... nor, after the Eucharist carried in it, is the hand [to be] spotted with the sword and blood.

15. Charity is the bond of brotherhood, the foundation of peace, the holdfast and security of unity, which is greater than both hope and faith, which excels both good works and martyrdoms, which will abide with us always, eternal with God in the kingdom of heaven. Take from it patience; and deprived of it, it does not endure....

13. APOSTOLIC TRADITION

Apostolic Tradition (c. 235) details rules and regulations for the early Christian church. Its authorship is in dispute—some scholars claim it was written by the Roman theologian Hippolytus—but whoever the author may be, Apostolic Tradition, *with written instructions on such things as communion, baptism, prayer, ecclesial order, fasting, caring for the sick, and more, is one of the most significant documents of early church-order literature. The section on trades and professions, excerpted below, gives some idea of the importance of peacemaking in the early church movement. It seems likely that the author was gravely concerned about Christians undertaking two practices common in the military life—killing and idolatry.*

1. Those things, then, concerning spiritual gifts, which are worthy of note, we have set forth. God gave these gifts to people in the beginning in accordance with his will, presenting them with his own image, which had been lost. And now, out of love for all the saints, we have reached the summit of the tradition which is proper for the churches, so that those who are well-taught should guard the tradition which has come down to us now, and which we are now going to consider, and so be confirmed in their knowledge. Because of the error or falling-away that has now come about through ignorance, and through those who are ignorant, the Holy Spirit gives perfect grace to those who rightly believe, so that they should know in what manner those who are preeminent in the church should defend and pass on all these things....

16. On trades and profession

Enquiry should be made concerning the crafts and occupations of those who are brought to be instructed.

If any is a pimp or procurer of prostitutes he should desist or he should be rejected. If any is a sculptor or a painter he should be instructed not to make idols; he should desist or he should be rejected. If any is an actor, or makes presentations in the theater, he should desist, or he should be rejected. If somebody teaches children it is better that he desist; if he have no other trade let him be allowed. Likewise a charioteer who competes, or anyone who goes to the races, should desist or be rejected. If any is a gladiator, or trains gladiators in fighting, or one who fights with beasts in the games, or a public official engaged in gladiatorial business should desist, or he should be rejected. If any is a priest of idols, or a guardian of idols, he should desist, or he should be rejected. A soldier in command must be told not to kill people; if he is ordered so to do, he shall not carry it out. Nor should he take the oath. If he will not agree, he should be rejected. Anyone who has the power of the sword, or who is a civil magistrate wearing the purple, should desist, or he should be rejected. If a catechumen or a believer wishes to become a soldier they should be rejected, for they have despised God.

14. EARLY CHRISTIAN MARTYRS

Early Christian literature includes several accounts, some of them very graphic, of Christian martyrs—their faith, witness, and nonviolent resistance against violent rulers. It may be mistaken to identify early Christian saints like Perpetua and Felicity, or Montanus and

Sebastian, as Christian pacifists, but there is no reason to doubt that they assumed a non-violent approach when facing some of the most horrific methods of their rulers, or that their stories have served to inspire countless Christian pacifists through the centuries. One of the inspiring accounts is the story of Maximilian, a young man whose father had taken him to Numidia in 295 to enlist in the military under the proconsul Dion. In the following dialogue, Dion makes it clear that Christians were no strangers to military life. Less clear, however, are the exact reasons for Maximilian's faith-fueled resistance to the military, although it is quite possible that he was concerned about both idolatry and the shedding of blood.

The Acts of Maximilian

Dion the proconsul said, "What is your name?" Maximilian answered, "What do you want to know my name for? It is not right for me to serve in the army since I am a Christian."

Dion said, "Get him ready." While this was being done, Maximilian responded, "I cannot serve in the army; I cannot engage in wrongdoing; I am a Christian."

Dion remarked, "Measure him." When this had been done, the staff member called out, "He is five feet, ten."

Dion said to the staff member, "Give him the seal." But Maximilian continued to resist, saying, "I'm not going to do it; I cannot serve in the army."

Dion said, "Join up if you don't want to die." "I will not," Maximilian replied. "Cut off my head. I will serve in the army of my God, not in any that belongs to this world."

Dion the proconsul said, "Who has led you to this position?" "Only my own soul," replied Maximilian, "and he who called me."

Dion said to the young man's father, Victor, "Talk to your son." Victor replied, "He knows what's at stake and can counsel himself about the best course of action."

To Maximilian, Dion the proconsul said, "Join up and accept the military seal."

"I will not take it," he answered. "I already have a seal, the seal of Christ, my God." Dion said, "I'll soon send you to your Christ." "If only you would!" he answered. "That would be glory for me."

Dion said to the staff member, "Give him the seal." Maximilian would have none of it, and he remarked, "I am not going to receive a seal that belongs to this world. If you put it on me, I will smash it because it has no power. I am a Christian; I may not carry a piece of lead around my neck now that I have accepted the saving seal of my Lord Jesus Christ, son of the living God. You know nothing about him, but he suffered for our salvation, and he was delivered up by God for our sins. It is he whom all of us Christians serve; it is he whom we follow as life's sovereign and as the author of salvation."

Dion said, "Join up and receive the seal or you will die a miserable death."

"I won't die," Maximilian replied. "My name is already in the presence of my Lord. I cannot serve in the army."

Dion said, "Consider your age and join up. It is fitting for a young man to do so."

Maximilian answered, "I am committed to serve my Lord; I cannot serve in an army of this world. As I have already said, I am a Christian."

Dion the proconsul said, "The sacred bodyguard of our sovereigns Diocletian and Maximian, Constantius and Maximus, includes Christians who serve."

"They know what is in their own best interest," Maximilian answered, "but I am a Christian, and I cannot do what is wrong."

Dion said, "What are you doing that is wrong?" "You know what they do," Maximilian answered. Dion the proconsul said, "Join up. Do not bring a miserable death upon yourself by disdaining the service."

Maximilian answered, "I am not going to die. And if I leave this world, my soul goes on living with Christ my Lord" (1-2).

The Acts of Marcellus

Idolatry seems to be the major issue in this account of a Christian soldier who sheds his military belt during a feast for the emperors Diocletian and Maximilian in Tingis, North Africa, in 298. Historian Louis Swift has rightly noted that in the following account "there is no mention of bloodshed or other immoral acts associated with military life."

In the city of Tingis, while Fortunatus was governor, it was the celebration of the emperor's birthday. At length, when everyone was dining at the banquet table, a centurion named Marcellus rejected these pagan festivities, and after throwing down his soldier's belt in front of the legionary standards which were there at the time, he bore witness in a loud voice: "I am a soldier of Jesus Christ, the eternal king. From now I cease to serve your emperors and I despise the worship of your gods of wood and stone, for they are deaf and dumb images."

Now the soldiers that heard this were amazed, and arresting him, they threw him into prison and went to report the affair to the governor Fortunatus. When he had heard the story he ordered Marcellus to be kept in prison. After the banquet was over, he ordered Marcellus to be brought into his council chamber. When the centurion Marcellus was brought in, the prefect Anastasius Fortunatus spoke to him as follows: "What was your intention in violating military discipline by taking off your belt and throwing it down with your staff?"

"On July 21," Marcellus replied, "while you were celebrating the emperor's feast day, I declared clearly and publicly before the standards of this legion that I was a Christian, and said that I could not serve under this military oath, but only for Christ Jesus, the son of God the Father almighty."

The prefect Fortunatus said, "I cannot conceal your rash act. And so I must report this to the emperors and to Caesar; and you will be handed over to my lord Aurelius Agricolanus, deputy for

the praetorian prefects, with Caecilius Arva, staff-officer, in charge."

On 30 October, at Tingis, when Marcellus of the rank of centurion was brought into court, one of the court secretaries announced: "The prefect Fortunatus has referred the case of the centurion Marcellus to your jurisdiction. There is a letter from him here, which I shall read with your permission."

Agricolanus said: "Have it read."

The secretary read: "To you, my lord, from Fortunatus ..." (and so forth).

After the letter was read, Agricolanus said: "Did you say the things that are recorded in the prefect's reports?"

"Yes, I did," answered Marcellus.

"You held the military rank of centurion, first class?" asked Agricolanus.

"Yes," said Marcellus.

"What madness possessed you," asked Agricolanus, "to throw down the symbols of your military oath and to say the things you did?"

Marcellus replied: "No madness possesses those who fear the Lord."

"Then you did say all of those things," asked Agricolanus, "that are set down in the prefect's report?"

"Yes, I said them," answered Marcellus.

"Agricolanus said: "You threw down your weapons?"

Marcellus replied: "Yes, I did. For it is not fitting that a Christian, who fights for Christ his Lord, should fight for the armies of this world."

Agricolanus said: "What Marcellus has done merits punishment according to military rules. And so, whereas Marcellus, who held the rank of centurion, first class, has confessed that he had disgraced himself by publicly renouncing his military oath, I hereby sentence him to death by the sword."

As Marcellus was being led out to execution he said, "Agricolanus, may God reward you." Thus it was fitting that Marcellus should depart a glorious martyr from this world.

15. Arnobius

Against the Heathen

Arnobius (d. c. 330) was a Christian apologist in Sicca, Africa, during the reign of Diocletian. The treatise Against the Heathen, *which defends Christianity against the charge that it was responsible for the many social problems of Roman life, is his only extant work. Interestingly, part of his defense states that since the inception of Christianity, "there were countless victories over conquered armies, the empire's boundaries were expanded, and nations which had never been heard of were brought under our control" (1.14). This defense is especially curious when we consider his critical assessment of Roman wars and his sense that the peacefulness of Christianity has led to peace in the Roman world. Although his writing on war and peace is puzzling at times, Arnobius seemed to believe, as suggested in the excerpts below, that the life and teachings of Jesus are directly contrary to Roman wars.*

1.6. Although you allege that those wars which you speak of were excited through hatred of our religion, it would not be difficult to prove, that after the name of Christ was heard in the world, not only were they not increased, but they were even in great measure diminished by the restraining of furious passions. For since we, a numerous band of men as we are, have learned from His teaching and His laws that evil ought not to be requited with evil, that it is better to suffer wrong than to inflict it, that we should rather shed our own blood than stain our hands and our conscience with that of another, an ungrateful world is now for a long period enjoying a benefit from Christ, inasmuch as by His means the rage of savage ferocity has been softened, and has begun to withhold hostile hands from the blood of a fellow-creature. But if all without exception, who feel that they are men not in form of body but in power of reason, would lend an ear for a little to His salutary and peaceful rules, and would not, in the pride and arrogance of enlightenment, trust to their own senses rather than to His admonitions, the whole world, having turned the use of steel into more peaceful occupations, would now be living in the most placid tranquility, and would unite in blessed harmony, maintaining inviolate the sanctity of treaties....

2.1. ... If you think it no dishonor to answer when asked a question, explain to us and say what is the cause, what the reason, that you pursue Christ with so bitter hostility? or what offences you remember which He did, that at the mention of His name you are roused to bursts of mad and savage fury? Did He ever, in claiming for Himself power as king, fill the whole world with bands of the fiercest soldiers; and of nations at peace from the beginning, did He destroy and put an end to some, *and* compel others to submit to His yoke and serve Him? Did He ever, excited by grasping avarice, claim as His own by right all that wealth to have abundance of which men strive eagerly? Did He ever, transported with lustful passions, break down by force the barriers of purity, or stealthily lie in wait for other men's wives? Did He ever, puffed up with haughty arrogance, inflict at random injuries and insults, without any distinction of persons? (B) And if He was not worthy that you should listen to and believe *Him, yet* He should not have been despised by you even on this account, that He showed to you things concerning your salvation, that He prepared for you a path to heaven, and the immortality for which you long; although He neither extended the light of life to all, nor delivered *all* from the danger which threatens them through their ignorance.

16. LACTANTIUS

The Divine Institutes

Like his teacher Arnobius, Lactantius (c. 250-c. 325) was a Christian apologist. He lost his job as a teacher of rhetoric at Nicomedia when the Diocletian persecution erupted in 303, but his career was far from finished; he eventually landed the position of tutor to Emperor Constantine's son, Crispus. Lactantius's main extant work, Divine Institutes, *excerpted below, offers a systematic defense of Christianity for those who were highly educated. It also decries Roman wars and gladiatorial contests, and even presents the theological case that killing people is always and everywhere wrong. In later works—ones he authored after Constantine rose to power—Lactantius would leave behind the absolute proscription against violence and celebrate Constantine's military victories as God's own.*

1.18. [The Romans] think the only path to immortality is that of leading armies, devastating foreign territories, leveling cities, destroying towns and killing free men or subjecting them to slavery. The more men they beat up, rob or kill, the more distinguished and famous they think they are. Captivated by the vision of empty glory they call their criminal acts virtue. It would be better, I think, for them to fashion their concept of deity from the slaughter of wild animals than to accept such a bloody kind of immortality. If a man throttles a single individual, he is considered a vile criminal and people think it wrong to allow him to enter the earthly dwellings of the gods. But a man who has killed countless thousands, has made the fields run with blood and has polluted rivers is admitted not only into the temples but into heaven itself....

5.8. But if God only were worshipped, there would not be dissensions and wars, since men would know that they are the sons of one God; and, therefore, among those who were connected by the sacred and inviolable bond of divine relationship, there would be no plottings, inasmuch as they would know what kind of punishments God prepared for the destroyer of souls, who sees through secret crimes, and even the very thoughts themselves. There would be no frauds or plunderings if they had learned, through the instruction of God, to be content with all which was their own, though little, so that they might prefer solid and eternal

things to those which are frail and perishable.... There would not, therefore, as I have said, be these evils on the earth, if there were by common consent a general observance of the law of God, if those things were done by all which our people alone perform. How happy and how golden would be the condition of human affairs, if throughout the world gentleness, and piety, and peace, and innocence, and equity, and temperance, and faith, took up their abode! In short, there would be no need of so many and varied laws to rule men, since the law of God alone would be sufficient for perfect innocence; nor would there be any need of prisons, or the swords of rulers, or the terror of punishments, since the wholesomeness of the divine precepts infused into the breasts of men would of itself instruct them to works of justice. But now men are wicked through ignorance of what is right and good.... Therefore the unjust and impious worship of the gods has introduced all the evils by which mankind in turn destroy one another....

5.10. ... What then, or where, or of what character is piety? Truly it is among those who are ignorant of wars, who maintain concord with all, who are friendly even to their enemies, who love all men as brethren, who know how to restrain their anger, and to soothe every passion of the mind with calm government....

5.20. There is no occasion for violence and injury, for religion cannot be imposed by force; the matter must be carried on by words rather than by blows, that the will may be affected. Let them unsheath the weapon of their intellect; if their system is true, let it be asserted....

Oh, with what an honorable inclination the wretched men go astray! For they are aware that there is nothing among men more excellent than religion, and that this ought to be defended with the whole of our power; but as they are deceived in the matter of religion itself, so also are they in the manner of its defense. For religion is to be defended, not by putting to death, but by dying; not by cruelty, but by patient endurance; not by guilt, but by good faith: for the former belong to evils, but the latter to goods; and it is necessary for that which is good to have place in religion, and not that which is evil. For if you wish to defend religion by bloodshed, and by tortures, and by guilt, it will no longer be defended, but will be polluted and profaned. For nothing is so much a matter of freewill as religion; in which, if the mind of the worshipper is disinclined to it, religion is at once taken away, and ceases to exist. The right method therefore is, that you defend religion by patient endurance or by death; in which the preservation of the faith is both pleasing to God Himself, and adds authority to religion....

5.21. ... But we, on the contrary, do not require that anyone should be compelled, whether he is willing or unwilling, to worship our God, who is the God of all men; nor are we angry if anyone does not worship Him. For we trust in the majesty of Him who has power to avenge contempt shown towards Himself, as also He has power to avenge calamities and injuries inflicted on His servants. And therefore, when we suffer such impious things, we do not resist even in word; but we remit vengeance to God, not as they act who would have it appear that they are defenders of their gods, and rage without restraint against those who do not worship them. From which it may be understood how it is good not to worship their gods, since men ought to have been led to that which is good by good, and not by evil....

6.10. I have said what is due to God, I will now say what is to be given to man; although this very thing which you shall give to man is given to God, for man is the image of God. But, however, the first office of justice is to be united with God, the second with man. But the former is called religion; the second is named mercy or kindness; which virtue is peculiar to the just, and to the worshippers of God, because this alone comprises the principle of common life. For God, who has not given wisdom to the other animals, has made them more safe from attack in danger by natural defenses. But because He made him naked and defenseless, that He might rather furnish him with wisdom, He gave him, besides other things, this feeling of kindness; so that man should protect, love, and cherish man, and both receive and afford assistance against all dangers. Therefore kindness is the greatest bond of human society; and he who has broken this is to be deemed impious, and a parricide. For if we all derive our origin from one man, whom God created, we are plainly of one blood; and therefore it must be considered the greatest wickedness to hate a man, even though guilty. On which account God has enjoined that enmities are never to be contracted by us, but that they are always to be removed, so that we soothe those who are our enemies, by reminding them of their relationship. Likewise, if we are all inspired and animated by one God, what else are we than brothers? And, indeed, the more closely united, because we are united in soul rather than in body. Accordingly Lucretius does not err when he says: "In short, we are all sprung from a heavenly seed; all have that same father." Therefore they are to be accounted as savage beasts who injure man; who, in opposition to every law and right of human nature, plunder, torture, slay, and banish. On account of this relationship of brotherhood, God teaches us never to do evil, but always good. And He also prescribes in what this doing good consists: in affording aid to those who are oppressed and in difficulty, and in bestowing food on those who are destitute. For God, since He is kind, wished us to be a social animal....

6.11. Therefore humanity is to be preserved, if we wish rightly to be called men. But what else is this preservation of humanity than the loving a man because he is a man, and the same as ourselves? Therefore discord and dissension are not in accordance with the nature of man; and that expression of Cicero is true, which says that man, while he is obedient to nature, cannot injure man. Therefore, if it is contrary to nature to injure a man, it must be in accordance with nature to benefit a man; and he who does not do this deprives himself of the title of a man, because it is the duty of humanity to succor the necessity and peril of a man....

6.19. But the just man will omit no opportunity of doing anything mercifully.... If anyone reviles, he must answer him with a blessing; he himself must never revile, that no evil word may proceed out of the mouth of a man who reveres the good Word. Moreover, he must also diligently take care, lest by any fault of his he should at any time make an enemy; and if anyone should be so shameless as to inflict injury on a good and just man, he must bear it with calmness and moderation, and not take upon himself his revenge, but reserve it for the judgment of God. He must at all times and in all places guard innocence. And this precept is not limited to this, that he should not himself inflict injury, but that he should not avenge it when inflicted on himself. For there sits on the judgment seat a very great and impartial Judge, the observer and witness to all.... Cicero says [that a just person should] "at once teach himself that he is a good man who ... injures no one unless provoked by injury."

Oh how he marred a simple and true sentiment by the addition of two words! For what need was there of adding these words, "unless provoked by injury"? that he might append vice as a most disgraceful tail to a good man, and might represent him as without patience, which is the greatest of all the virtues. He said that a good man would inflict injuries if he were provoked: now he must necessarily lose the name of a good man from this very circumstance, if he shall inflict injury. For it is not less the part of a bad man to return an injury than to inflict it. For from what source do contests, from what source do fightings and contentions, arise among men, except that impatience opposed to injustice often excites great tempests? But if you meet an injustice with patience ... it will immediately be extinguished, as though you should pour water upon a fire. But if that injustice which provokes opposition has met with impatience equal to itself, as though overspread with oil, it will excite so great a conflagration, that no stream can extinguish it, but only the shedding of blood. Great,

therefore, is the advantage of patience.... For this alone causes that no evil happens; and if it should be given to all, there will be no wickedness and no fraud in the affairs of men....

6.20. [S]ince they are the greatest incitement to vices, and have a most powerful tendency to corrupt our minds, they ought to be taken away from us; for they not only contribute in no respect to a happy life, but even inflict the greatest injury. For he who reckons it a pleasure, that a man, though justly condemned, should be slain in his sight, pollutes his conscience as much as if he should become a spectator and a sharer of a homicide which is secretly committed. And yet they call these sports in which human blood is shed. So far has the feeling of humanity departed from the men, that when they destroy the lives of men, they think that they are amusing themselves with sport, being more guilty than all those whose blood-shedding they esteem a pleasure.

I ask now whether they can be just and pious men, who, when they see men placed under the stroke of death, and entreating mercy, not only suffer them to be put to death, but also demand it, and give cruel and inhuman votes for their death, not being satiated with wounds nor contented with bloodshed. Moreover, they order them, even though wounded and prostrate, to be attacked again, and their caresses to be wasted with blows, that no one may delude them by a pretended death. They are even angry with the combatants, unless one of the two is quickly slain; and as though they thirsted for human blood, they hate delays. They demand that other and fresh combatants should be given to them, that they may satisfy their eyes as soon as possible. Being imbued with this practice, they have lost their humanity. Therefore they do not spare even the innocent, but practice upon all that which they have learned in the slaughter of the wicked. It is not therefore befitting that those who strive to keep to the path of justice should be companions and sharers in this public homicide. For when God forbids us to kill, He not only prohibits us from open violence, which is not even allowed by the public laws, but He warns us against the commission of those things which are esteemed lawful among men. Thus it will be neither lawful for a just man to engage in warfare, since his warfare is justice itself, nor to accuse any one of a capital charge, because it makes no difference whether you put a man to death by word, or rather by the sword, since it is the act of putting to death itself which is prohibited. Therefore, with regard to this precept of God, there ought to be no exception at all; but that it is always unlawful to put to death a man, whom God willed to be a sacred animal.

Therefore let no one imagine that even this is allowed, to strangle newly born children, which is the greatest impiety; for God breathes into their souls for life, and not for death. But men, that there may be no crime with which they may not pollute their hands, deprive souls as yet innocent and simple of the light which they themselves have not given. Can anyone, indeed, expect that they would abstain from the blood of others who do not abstain even from their own? But these are without any controversy wicked and unjust. What are they whom a false piety compels to expose their children? Can they be considered innocent who expose their own offspring as a prey to dogs, and as far as it depends upon themselves, kill them in a more cruel manner than if they had strangled them? Who can doubt that he is impious who gives occasion for the pity of others? For, although that which he has wished should befall the child—namely, that it should be brought up—he has certainly consigned his own offspring either to servitude or to the brothel? But who does not understand, who is ignorant what things may happen, or are accustomed to happen, in the case of each sex, even through error? For this is shown by the example of Oedipus alone, confused with twofold guilt. It is therefore as wicked to expose as it is to kill. But truly parricides complain of the scantiness of their means, and allege that they have not enough for bringing up more children; as though, in truth, their means were in the power of those who possess them, or God did not daily make the rich poor, and the poor rich. Wherefore, if any one on account of poverty shall be unable to bring up children, it is better to abstain from marriage.

If, then, it is in no way permitted to commit homicide, it is not allowed us to be present at all, lest any bloodshed should overspread the conscience, since that blood is offered for the gratification of the people.

PART III
Medieval Voices

17. BASIL OF CAESARIA

Canon 13

Basil (c. 330-379) was educated in Caesaria, Constantinople, and Athens, converted to Christianity in 357, and joined a monastic community at Amnesia. In 370, after Eusebius of Caesarea died, Basil was elected bishop and wrote treatises that helped develop trinitarianism, Eastern asceticism, and canon law. Although he did not write a systematic treatise on war and peace, Basil's canonical epistles deal with this issue, as well as many other social problems, and helped to form the substance of the ethics of early Eastern monasticism. Some Christian pacifists will no doubt be disappointed that Basil has been included here, but it would be negligent to fail to recognize Basil's writings as a clear alternative to the emerging just war theory proposed by Augustine and others. Immediately below is a short excerpt from one of Basil's numerous epistles.

Our fathers did not consider killings committed in the course of wars to be classifiable as murders at all, on the score, it seems to me, of allowing a pardon to men fighting in defense of sobriety and piety. Perhaps, though, it might be advisable to refuse them communion for three years, on the ground that their hands are not clean.

JOHN ANTHONY MCGUCKIN
Nonviolence and Peace in Early and Eastern Christianity

No one has explained this fairly obtuse passage better than John Anthony McGuckin, professor of early church history at Union Theological Seminary and Columbia University, and below is an excerpt of McGuckin's article on nonviolence and peace traditions in early and Eastern Christianity.

Basil of Caesarea was a younger contemporary of Eusebius, and in the following generation of the Church of the late fourth century, he emerged as one of the leading theorists of the Christian movement. His letters and instructions on the ascetic life, and his "Canons" (ethical judgments as from a ruling bishop to his flock) on morality and practical issues became highly influential in the wider church because of his role as one of the major monastic theorists of early Christianity. His canonical epistles were transmitted wherever monasticism went: and in the Eastern Church of antiquity (because monasticism was the substructure of the spread of the Christian movement), that more or less meant his canonical views became the standard paradigm of Eastern Christianity's theoretical approach to the morality of war and violence, even though the writings were local and occasional in origin....

Basil has several things to say about violence and war in his diocese. It was a border territory of the empire, and his administration had known several incursions by "barbarian" forces. Canon 13 of the 92 considers war: "Our fathers did not consider killings committed in the course of wars to be classifiable as murders at all, on the score, it seems to me, of allowing a pardon to men fighting in defense of sobriety and piety. Perhaps, though, it might be advisable to refuse them communion for three years, on the ground that their hands are not clean."

The balance and sense of discretion is remarkable in this little comment, one that bears much weight in terms of Eastern Orthodox understandings of the morality of war. The "fathers" in question refers to Athanasius of Alexandria, the great Nicene Orthodox authority of the fourth-century church. Athanasius's defense of the Nicene creed, and the divine status of Christ, had won him immense prestige by the end of the fourth century, and as his works were being collated and disseminated (in his own lifetime his reputation had been highly conflicted, his person exiled numerous times, and his writings proscribed by imperial censors), Basil seems to wish to add a cautionary note: that not everything a "father" has to say is equally momentous, or universally authoritative. In his Letter to Amun, Athanasius had apparently come out quite straightforwardly about the legitimacy of killing in time of war, saying: Although one is not supposed to kill, the killing of the enemy in time of war is both a lawful and praiseworthy thing. This is why we consider individuals who have distinguished themselves in war as being worthy of great honors, and indeed public monuments are set up to celebrate their achievements. It is evident, therefore, that at one particular time, and under one set of circumstances, an act is not permissible, but when time and circumstances are right, it is both allowed and condoned.

This saying was being circulated, and given authority as a "patristic witness" simply because it had come from Athanasius. In fact the original letter had nothing whatsoever to do with war. The very example of the "war-hero" is a sardonic reference ad hominem since the letter was addressed to an aged leader of the Egyptian monks who described themselves as Asketes, that is, those who labored and "fought" for the virtuous life. The military image is entirely incidental, and Athanasius in context merely uses it to illustrate his chief point in the letter—which is to discuss the query Amun had sent on to him as Archbishop: "did nocturnal emissions count as sins for desert celibates?" Athanasius replies to the effect that with human sexuality, as with all sorts of other things, the context of the activity determines what is moral, not some absolute standard which is superimposed on moral discussion from the outset. Many ancients, Christian and pagan, regarded sexual activity as inherently defiling, and here Athanasius decidedly takes leave of them. His argument, therefore, is falsely attributed when (as is often the case) read out of context as an apparent justification of killing in time of war. He is not actually condoning the practice at all, merely using the rhetorical example of current opinion to show Amun that contextual variability is very important in making moral judgments.

In his turn, Basil wishes to make it abundantly clear for his Christian audience that such a reading, if applied to the Church's tradition on war, is simplistic, and that it is just plain wrongheadedness to conclude that the issue ceases to be problematic if one is able to dig up a justificatory "proof text" from scripture or patristic tradition (as some seem to have been doing with these words of Athanasius). And so, Basil sets out a nuanced corrective exegesis of what the Church's canon law should really be in terms of fighting in time of hostilities. One of the ways he does this is to attribute this aphorism of Athanasius to indeterminate "fathers," who can then be legitimately corrected by taking a stricter view than they appeared to allow. He also carefully sets his own context: what he speaks about is the canonical regulation of war in which a Christian can engage and be "amerced"; all other armed conflicts are implicitly excluded as not being appropriate to Christian morality. Basil's text on war needs, therefore, to be understood in terms of an "economic" reflection on the ancient canons that forbade the shedding of blood in blanket terms. This tension between the ideal standard (no bloodshed) and the complexities of the context in which a local church finds itself thrown in times of conflict and war is witnessed in several other ancient laws, such as Canon 14 of Hippolytus (also from the fourth century). The reasons Basil gives for suggesting that killing in time of hostilities could be distinguished from voluntary murder pure and simple (for which the canonical penalty was a lifelong ban from admission to the churches and from the sacraments) is set out as the "defense of sobriety and piety." This is code language for the defense of Christian borders from the ravages of pagan marauders. The difficulty Basil had to deal with was not war on the large-scale, but local tribal insurgents who were mounting attacks on Roman border towns, with extensive rapinage. In such circumstances Basil has little patience for those who do not feel they can fight because of religious scruples. His sentiment is more that a passive non-involvement betrays the Christian family (especially its weaker members who cannot defend themselves but need others to help them) to the ravages of men without heart or conscience to restrain them. The implication of his argument, then, is that the provocation to fighting, which Christians ought at some stage to accept (to defend the honor and safety of the weak), will be inherently a limited and adequate response, mainly because the honor and tradition of the Christian faith (piety and sobriety) in the hearts and minds of the warriors will restrict the bloodshed to a necessary minimum. His "economic" solution nevertheless makes it abundantly clear that the absolute standard of Christian morality turns away from war as an unmitigated evil. This is why we can note that the primary reason Basil

gives that previous "fathers" had distinguished killing in time of war, from the case of simple murder, was "on the score of allowing a pardon." There was no distinction made here in terms of the qualitative horror of the deed itself, but rather in terms of the way in which the deed could be "cleansed" by the Church's system of penance.

Is it logical to expect a Christian of his diocese to engage in the defense of the homeland, while simultaneously penalizing him if he spills blood in the process? Well, one needs to contextualize the debarment from the sacrament in the generic fourth-century practice of the reception of the Eucharist, which did not expect regular communication to begin with (ritual preparation was extensive and involved fasting and almsgiving and prayer), and where a sizeable majority of adult Christians in a given church would not have yet been initiated by means of baptism, and were thus not bound to keep all the canons of the Church. By his regulation and by the ritual exclusion of the illumined warrior from the sacrament (the returning "victor" presumably would have received many other public honors and the gratitude of the local folk), Basil is making sure at least one public sign is given to the entire community that the Gospel standard has no place for war, violence and organized death. He is trying to sustain an eschatological balance: that war is not part of the Kingdom of God (signified in the Eucharistic ritual as arriving in the present) but is part of the bloody and greed-driven reality of world affairs which is the "Kingdom-Not-Arrived." By moving in and out of Eucharistic reception, Basil's faithful Christian (returning from his duty with blood on his hands) is now in the modality of expressing his dedication to the values of peace and innocence, by means of the lamentation and repentance for life that has been taken, albeit the blood of the violent. Basil's arrangement that the returning noble warrior should stand in the Church (not in the narthex where the other public sinners were allocated spaces) but refrain from communion makes the statement that a truly honorable termination of war, for a Christian, has to be an honorable repentance.

Several commentators (not least many of the later western Church fathers) have regarded this as "fudge," but it seems to me to express, in a finely tuned "economic" way, the tension in the basic Christian message that there is an irresolvable shortfall between the ideal and the real in an apocalyptically charged religion. What this Basilian canon does most effectively is to set a "No Entry" sign to any potential theory of just war within Christian theology, and should set up a decided refusal of post-war, church-sponsored, self-congratulations for victory. All violence, local, individual, or nationally sanctioned, is here stated to be an expression of hubris that is inconsistent with the values of the Kingdom of God, and while in many circumstances that violence may be "necessary" or "unavoidable" (Basil states the only legitimate reasons as the defense of the weak and innocent), it is never "justifiable." Even for the best motives in the world, the shedding of blood remains a defilement, such that the true Christian, afterwards, would wish to undergo the cathartic experience of temporary return to the lifestyle of penance, that is, "be penitent." Basil's restriction of the time of penance to three years (seemingly harsh to us moderns) was actually a commonly recognized sign of merciful leniency in the ancient rule book of the early Church.

We might today regard such early attempts by Christians as quaintly naive. They are wired through the early penitential system, clearly, and have a fundamental "economic" character about them. By "economy" the early church meant the art of doing what was possible when a higher ideal standard was not sustained. In the case of war Basil and the canonical tradition are tacitly saying that when the Kingdom ideals of peace and reconciliation collapse, especially in times of war when decisive and unusual action is required, and the ideals of reconciliation and forgiveness fall into chaos in the very heart of the Church itself, as members go off to fight, then the ideal must be reasserted as soon as possible—with limitations to the hostilities a primary concern, and a profound desire to mark the occasion retrospectively with a public "cleansing." While the honor of the combatants is celebrated by Basil (even demanded as an act of protection for the weak), one essential aspect of that honor is also listed as being the public acceptance of the status of penitent shedder of blood. The clergy (as with other economic concessions of morality operative in the church's canons) are the only ones not allowed benefit of necessity. In no case is violent action permitted to one who stands at the altar of God. Even if a cleric spills blood accidentally (such as in an involuntary manslaughter) such a person would be deposed from active presbyteral office. The sight of "warrior-bishops" in full military regalia, passing through the streets of Constantinople in the Fourth Crusade, left its mark on contemporary Greek sources as one of the greatest "shocks" to the system, and one of the incidentals that were taken by the Greeks as proof positive that Latin Christianity in the thirteenth century had a serious illness at its center.

More than naive, perhaps, might we regard such a morality of war as seriously "underdeveloped"? Can such an important issue really be dealt with by so few canons of the ancient Eastern church, and even then, by regulations that are so evidently local and occasional in character? Well, the charges of inconsistency (praising a noble warrior and then subjecting him to penance) and muddle-headedness, were raised in early times, especially by Latin theologians who wanted to press the envelope and arrive at a more coherent and all-embracing theory of war: one that balanced the apparent biblical justifications of hostility on the part of the chosen people, with the need to limit the obvious bloodlust of our species. The Latin theory of just war was one result. Considered primarily (as it was meant to be) as a theory of the limitation of hostilities in the ancient context (hand to hand fighting of massed armies whose very size limited the time of possible engagement to a matter of months at most), it too was an "economic" theory that had much merit. Its usefulness became moot in the medieval period when armament manufacture took ancient warfare into a new age, and it has become utterly useless in the modern age of mechanized warfare, where it could not stop the fatal transition ... to the centrally important role of the murder of noncombatants. Be that as it may, it is not the purpose of the present essay to offer a sustained critique on just war theory—merely to raise up a mainline Christian tradition of the ancient East which has never believed in just war—and to offer, instead of an elegant theory, a poor threadbare suggestion of old saints: that war is never justified or justifiable, but is de facto a sign and witness of evil and sin....

18. PELAGIUS

On Riches

Pelagius (c. 350-c. 425) was a theologian and reformer who believed that humanity enjoyed the capacity to undertake the simple lifestyle exemplified in the life of Jesus. As a committed ascetic, Pelagius was sometimes mistaken for a monk because of his own simple living. He is known in contemporary Christianity primarily because of Augustine's uncharitable refutation of his theological anthropology, but Pelagius also wrote widely on issues of Christian ethics, especially those related to economics. Below is an excerpt from a treatise on the subject of riches, and although it is unclear whether Pelagius or one of his disciples authored the text, there is no doubt that he and his followers were among the earliest Christians to see inextricable links between wealth and violence.

6, 1. … Note carefully, I beg you, what a great sign of arrogance and pride it is to want to be rich when we know that Christ was poor, and to take upon ourselves any of the power that comes with lordship, when he took on the outward form of a servant, as it is written: Have this in mind among yourselves, which is yours in Christ Jesus, who, though he was in the form of God, did not count equality with God a thing to be grasped, but emptied himself, taking the form of a servant (Phil. 2:5-8). Surely everyone who is called a Christian professes that he is Christ's disciple, and Christ's disciple should follow his teacher's example in all things, so that in the deportment and conduct of the pupil his manner and doctrine may be in accord with that of his master.

2. What pattern of Christ is revealed in such a rich man? What likeness to him is shown in such a possessor of wealth? How can poverty be compared with affluence? What has humility in common with pride? What similarity is there between the man who has nothing and the man who has superfluous possessions? I shall say no more about material fortune; but let us see if the rich man's way of life has any similarity with that of Christ. There is none that I can see: the one is haughty, the other downcast; the one is proud, the other humble; the one is full of fury, the other of gentleness; the one is angry, the other long-suffering; the one is boastful, the other self-effacing; the one abhors the poor, the other embraces them; the one abuses them, the other extols them. The rich, with that vainglorious

and proud spirit in which they covet for themselves the glory of this world, are sometimes accustomed to solicit earthly power and to take their seat upon that tribunal before which Christ stood and was heard. How intolerable is the presumption of human pride! You may see the servant sitting where the master stood, and judging where he was judged. What is this, Christian? What is this, disciple of Christ? This is not the pattern given by your teacher. *He* stood humbly before the tribunal; *you* sit on the tribunal, above those who stand before you, propped up by your pride, perhaps about to judge a poor man. *You* ask the questions, *he* was heard; *you* judge, *he* was subjected to the judge's decision; in your presumption *you* utter your judgment, in his innocence *he* received it, as if guilty; *he* said that his kingdom was not of this world, but to *you* the glory of a worldly kingdom is so desirable that you procure it at vast expense or acquire it with unworthy and wearisome servitude and flattery.

3. And all the time you convince yourself that it is from God that you receive what, in fact, you either procure with your ill-gotten gains or acquire at the price of shameful sycophancy and oft-repeated acts of obeisance.…

5. What is the reason, I beg you, for so great a discrepancy between persons who are called Christians by the same name and are bound by solemn obligation to the same religion that some of them engage in such unholy acts of cruelty that they are not afraid to oppress, rob, torture and, finally, kill, while others are so frightened by their feelings of

compassion and sense of duty that they fear to be lacking in mercy to those whom the others have destroyed without any fear at all. It is worth giving careful consideration to what causes such diversity in men of the same faith. Has the same law of Christian conduct not been given to all who are called Christians? Or are they perhaps bound by two kinds of commandments different from each other, one by which some are by necessity bound to fulfill the obligations of compassion and sense of duty, the other by which others are given leave to perform acts of irresponsible cruelty? Or is a cooler fire made ready in hell for those whom it pleases to commit cruel acts and a hotter one for those who must practice godliness? We know that we are "one body," in the words of the apostle (I Cor. 12:13); if we are truly one, then we should act as one. There is no room for such variety in the same people. Let us search the scriptures and weigh up with serious and careful thought which law we should adhere to and then choose one of these two alternatives, either to be compassionate or, shocking though it may be to hear, to live a life of professed cruelty, if that is what is expedient in our opinion....

17, 1. I wish to add something that no wise man will be able to dispute, namely, that it is difficult to acquire riches without committing every kind of evil. They are procured by calculated lies or clever theft or fraudulent deceit or robbery with violence or barefaced falsification. They are frequently accumulated by plunder of widows or oppression of orphans or bribery or, much more cruel still, by the shedding of innocent blood. If that is so, how can we imagine that something which is acquired by such a variety of crimes has the sanction of God? Far, far from our thoughts be a notion so ungodly! For God either forbids all the crimes mentioned above if they have not yet been committed, or con-

demns them when they have been perpetrated. So we have no grounds whatsoever for regarding as conferred by God wealth which has been acquired by means which he forbids....

3. Hence the Lord deservedly censures and condemns excessive wealth, since he saw greed for it to be the cause of sin. For what wise or sensible man would doubt that greed is the occasion of all evils, the root of crimes, the fuel of wrongdoing, the source of transgressions? Because of it no one can live in safety or travel without fear on land, sea or anywhere else for that matter. It is through greed that we have pirates on the ocean waves, highwaymen on the roads, burglars in towns and villages, and plunderers everywhere; it is greed that motivates fraudulent practices, pillage, falsehood, perjury, false witness, cheating, ungodly and cruel acts and every conceivable kind of misdeed. For its sake the earth is daily stained with innocent blood, the poor man is stripped of his property, the wretched man is trodden underfoot and not even widows or orphans are spared. Greed drives men to spurn God's law almost every moment of the day and to outrage heaven's decree by committing transgressions of all kinds one after the other; on account of it modesty is often assaulted, chastity over-powered, and shameless lust given free rein to revel in its forbidden pleasures; in order to satisfy it, parricide is often committed in thought or by deed, since a man will wish for his parents' death or even bring it about, when he is in haste to acquire riches and is driven to extremes by the force of his impatience and greed.

4. ... What man is there, however gentle, humble, patient, kindly and moderate in his poverty, who does not become puffed up with haughtiness, swollen with pride, inflamed with anger and goaded into madness as his riches increase? ...

19. Paulinus of Nola

Poem 17
Letters 18 and 25

Paulinus of Nola (c. 352-431) was a Roman aristocrat who served as a senator and governor of Campania before converting to Christianity around 390. After his conversion, he and his wife, Therasia, then moved to northern Spain, where he became a priest in 393 or 394, distributed part of his vast wealth, and even took monastic vows. He lived the monastic life near the tomb of St. Felix at Nola and was elected bishop in Campania between 403 and 413. Known especially for his celebrated poetry, Paulinus was also friend to Martin of Tours, Ambrose, Jerome, and Augustine. His extant poems and correspondence reveal his Christian commitment to peace in the age of the barbarian invasions of the Roman Empire, and immediately following here is an excerpt of a poetic profile of his friend Nicetas of Remesiana (d. c. 414), who devoted part of his life to converting barbarians and Bessian rebels. Paulinus contrasts the peaceful ways of Nicetas with the violent ways of the barbarians and rebels, and praises Nicetas's conversion practices as a form of peacemaking.

189. ... You will journey through the territory of Philippi in Macedonia and through the city of Tomi; you will be a visitor from Troy to the Scupi who border on your land. With what cries of joy will that land now ring, when you teach those arctic peoples to bend their fierce necks to the gentle Christ! Where the north wind binds the rivers with thick frost in Rhiphaean lands, you thaw minds stiff with ice by your heavenly fire. For the Bessians, whose minds are harder than their lands, who indeed are harder than their own snow, have now become sheep, and you lead them as they flock to the hall of peace. Those necks which they always refused to bow to slavery, since they were always unsubdued in war, they now rejoice to bend in submission to the yoke of the true Lord. Now the Bessians are richer, and delight in the reward of toil. The gold which they previously sought from the earth with their hands they now gather with their minds from heaven....

217. What a change and happy transformation in the world! Those mountains once trackless and bloodstained now protect brigands turned monks, pupils of peace. The land once drenched in blood is now the land of life; the violence of brigands is turned devotedly towards heaven, and Christ smiles on the plundering which lays hold of heaven's kingdom. Where once existed the rule of beasts, there is now the vigorous life of angels. The just man now lives his hidden life in the caves where the brigand dwelt. The plunderer of old is become the plunder of holy men, and the murderer groans because the losses he inflicted are reversed, for Christ despoils him, and he is rightly stripped of the weapons of sinning. With the fall of Satan the envious Cain perishes in turn, and Abel reborn feeds the lambs redeemed at the cost of flowing blood....

237. Well done, Nicetas, goodly servant of Christ, who permits you to transform stones into stars and to build consecrated temples on rocks that live. You tread trackless glades and deserted ranges in your search for the way. You prevail over the barren woodland of unkempt minds, and you transform it into fertile fields. The whole region of the north calls you farther. The Scythians become gentle at your words; at war with each other, they abandon their aggressive spirit under your schooling....

253. Your work is the creation of calves from wolves, and the feeding with hay of lion and ox yoked together, and the opening of dens of vipers to children without harm. For you persuade wild beasts to join with domesticated animals and to abandon their fierce ways when you flood men's

wild minds with your civilizing discourse. In this mute region of the world, the barbarians through your schooling learn to make Christ's name resound from Roman hearts, and to live in purity and tranquil peace. So the wolf lies tamed in your sheepfold, the calf eats in harmony with the lion, the child plays in those grim caves from which the snake has been driven.

We can also detect Paulinus's commitment to peace in his numerous extant letters, and in the following letter (18) to his friend Victricius (c. 330-c. 407), who served as bishop of Rouen, Paulinus contrasts the soldier's "arms of blood" with the Christian's "arms of peace."

7. But by what paths did He lead you to the way of his truth? He schooled you first in duties of the flesh to lead you to the spiritual tasks of His virtue. He first appointed as soldier one whom He later chose as bishop. He allowed you to fight for Caesar so that you could learn to fight for God, in order that whilst exercising your bodily vigor in the work of the army, you could strengthen yourself for spiritual battles, reinforcing your spirit to confess the faith and hardening your body for suffering.

Your subsequent abandonment of military service and your entry into the faith showed that divine providence had attached to you an important design. As soon as you were fired with love for Christ, the Lord Himself arranged a display of His activity. You marched on to the parade ground on the day designated for military assembly. You were clad in all the adornment of the armor of war which by then you had mentally rejected. All were admiring your most punctilious appearance and your awe-inspiring equipment, when suddenly the army gaped with surprise. You changed direction, altered your military oath of allegiance, and before the feet of your impious commanding officer you threw down the arms of blood to take up the arms of peace. Now that you were armed with Christ, you despised weapons of steel.

Straightaway the commander was roused to fury by the venom of the serpent of old. You were stretched out for scourging and beaten with huge sticks; but you were not conquered because you leaned on the wood of the Cross. Next your physi-

cal pain was redoubled. Your limbs, lacerated by great blows, were stretched out over sharp fragments of earthenware. But Christ gave you softer support, for His bosom was your bed and His right hand your pillow. So before your wounds were healed, you advanced eagerly and more bravely on a greater enemy, for you were restored by courage which was fired rather than broken by the pain of your wounds.

You were handed over to the commanding general, but your triumph over this more powerful enemy was more glorious still. The clients of the devil did not dare to pile on further the torture which you had overcome, but they mooted the death penalty so that their defeats might end at any rate with the termination of your bodily life. But our *Lord who is strong and mighty and unconquered in battle* shattered their hearts, however obstinate, with notable miracles. For on that journey on which you followed your assassin as a sacred victim, the executioner with menacing taunts laid a rash hand on your neck, stroking with a hand which sought to foreshadow the sword the spot where his blow would strike. But there and then his eyes were torn from him, and he was struck with blindness. What love Christ's indescribable goodness proffers to His own! …

In this striking letter (25), Paulinus even counsels an anonymous soldier in no uncertain terms to leave the military and its blood-shedding ways.

Do not go on loving this world and the military service that is part of it because Scripture bears witness that anyone who is "a friend of the world is an enemy of God" (Letter of James 4:4). The man who fights with the sword is an agent of death, and whoever sheds his own blood or someone else's will have death as his wages. He will be responsible for his own death or for the crime of bringing it on another because, of necessity, the soldier in war, even though he fights for someone else rather than himself, either meets death in defeat or attains victory through killing. One cannot be victorious except through shedding blood. For this reason the Lord says, "You cannot serve two masters" (Matt. 6:24), that is, both the one God and mammon, both Christ and Caesar, although Caesar himself now wants to be the servant of Christ in order that he might deserve to be ruler over certain nations. For no earthly king is king of the whole world. That belongs to Christ who is God because "all things were made through him, and without him nothing was made" (John 1:3). He is both the King of kings and the Lord of lords (Rev. 17:14). "He does whatever he wishes on the earth, in the sea and in the depths" (Psalm 135:6).

20. SULPICIUS SEVERUS

Life of St. Martin

Sulpicius Severus (c. 360-420) was a Roman aristocrat from Aquitaine who converted to Christian asceticism around 394, some time after receiving encouragement from his friends Paulinus of Nola and Martin of Tours. His most influential work was the Life of St. Martin *(c. 397), a colorful hagiography of the monk whose life centered on ascetic practices and missionary work and who was elected bishop of Tours. Below is Severus's famous account of Martin's transformation from a military soldier to a nonviolent "soldier of Christ." The scene of the conversion is somewhere near Worms, in Gaul, in c. 356, and one of the main protagonists is Julian, the future Roman emperor, who had gathered his troops on the eve of yet another battle so that he could bestow gifts upon them. Although the account is no doubt embellished, Sulpicius's depiction of Martin's nonviolent commitment as exemplary for those who wish to follow Jesus is striking, especially given the violence of the age.*

Military Service of St. Martin

Martin, then, was born at Sabaria in Pannonia, but was brought up at Ticinum, which is situated in Italy. His parents were, according to the judgment of the world, of no mean rank, but were heathens. His father was at first simply a soldier, but afterwards a military tribune. He himself in his youth following military pursuits was enrolled in the imperial guard, first under king Constantine, and then under Julian Caesar. This, however, was not done of his own free will, for, almost from his earliest years, the holy infancy of the illustrious boy aspired rather to the service of God. For, when he was of the age of ten years, he betook himself, against the wish of his parents, to the Church, and begged that he might become a catechumen. Soon afterwards, becoming in a wonderful manner completely devoted to the service of God, when he was twelve years old, he desired to enter on the life of a hermit; and he would have followed up that desire with the necessary vows, had not his as yet too youthful age prevented. His mind, however, being always engaged on matters pertaining to the monasteries or the Church, already meditated in his boyish years what he afterwards, as a professed servant of Christ, fulfilled. But when an edict was issued by the ruling powers in the state, that the sons of veterans should be enrolled for military service, and he, on the information furnished by his father (who looked with an evil eye on his blessed actions), having been seized and put in chains, when he was fifteen years old, was compelled to take the military oath, then showed himself content with only one servant as his attendant. And even to him, changing places as it were, he often acted as though, while really master, he had been inferior; to such a degree that, for the most part, he drew off his [servant's] boots and cleaned them with his own hand; while they took their meals together, the real master, however, generally acting the part of servant. During nearly three years before his baptism, he was engaged in the profession of arms, but he kept completely free from those vices in which that class of men become too frequently involved. He showed exceeding kindness towards his fellow-soldiers, and held them in wonderful affection; while his patience and humility surpassed what seemed possible to human nature. There is no need to praise the self-denial which he displayed: it was so great that, even at that date, he was regarded not so much as being a soldier as a monk. By all these qualities he had so endeared himself to the whole body of his comrades, that they esteemed him while they marvelously loved him. Although not yet made a new creature in Christ, he, by his good works, acted the part of a candidate for baptism. This he did, for instance, by aiding those who were in trouble, by furnishing assistance to the wretched, by supporting the needy, by clothing the naked, while he reserved nothing for himself from his military pay except what was necessary for his daily sustenance. Even then, far from being a senseless hearer of the Gospel, he so far complied with its precepts as to take no thought about the morrow.

Christ Appears to St. Martin

Accordingly, at a certain period, when he had nothing except his arms and his simple military dress, in the middle of winter, a winter which had shown itself more severe than ordinary, so that the extreme cold was proving fatal to many, he happened to meet at the gate of the city of Amiens a poor man destitute of clothing. He was entreating those that passed by to have compassion upon him, but all passed the wretched man without notice, when Martin, that man full of God, recognized that a being to whom others showed no pity, was, in that respect, left to him. Yet, what should he do? He had nothing except the cloak in which he was clad, for he had already parted with the rest of his garments for similar purposes. Taking, therefore, his sword with which he was girt, he divided his cloak into two equal parts, and gave one part to the poor man, while he again clothed himself with the remainder. Upon this, some of the by-standers laughed, because he was now an unsightly object, and stood out as but partly dressed. Many, however, who were of sounder understanding, groaned deeply because they themselves had done nothing similar. They especially felt this, because, being

possessed of more than Martin, they could have clothed the poor man without reducing themselves to nakedness. In the following night, when Martin had resigned himself to sleep, he had a vision of Christ arrayed in that part of his cloak with which he had clothed the poor man. He contemplated the Lord with the greatest attention, and was told to own as his the robe which he had given. Ere long, he heard Jesus saying with a clear voice to the multitude of angels standing round—"Martin, who is still but a catechumen, clothed me with this robe." The Lord, truly mindful of his own words (who had said when on earth—"Inasmuch as ye have done these things to one of the least of these, ye have done them unto me"), declared that he himself had been clothed in that poor man; and to confirm the testimony he bore to so good a deed, he condescended to show him himself in that very dress which the poor man had received. After this vision the sainted man was not puffed up with human glory, but, acknowledging the goodness of God in what had been done, and being now of the age of twenty years, he hastened to receive baptism. He did not, however, all at once, retire from military service, yielding to the entreaties of his tribune, whom he admitted to be his familiar tent-companion. For the tribune promised that, after the period of his office had expired, he too would retire from the world. Martin, kept back by the expectation of this event, continued, although but in name, to act the part of a soldier, for nearly two years after he had received baptism.

Martin Retires from Military Service

In the meantime, as the barbarians were rushing within the two divisions of Gaul, Julian Cæsar, bringing an army together at the city of the Vaugiones, began to distribute a donative to the soldiers. As was the custom in such a case, they were called forward, one by one, until it came to the turn of Martin. Then, indeed, judging it a suitable opportunity for seeking his discharge—for he did not think it would be proper for him, if he were not to continue in the service, to receive a donative—he said to Caesar, "Hitherto I have served *you* as a soldier: allow me now to become a soldier to God: let the man who is to serve thee receive thy donative:

I am the soldier of Christ: it is not lawful for me to fight." Then truly the tyrant stormed on hearing such words, declaring that, from fear of the battle, which was to take place on the morrow, and not from any religious feeling, Martin withdrew from the service. But Martin, full of courage, yea all the more resolute from the danger that had been set before him, exclaims, "If this conduct of mine is ascribed to cowardice, and not to faith, I will take my stand unarmed before the line of battle tomorrow, and in the name of the Lord Jesus, protected by the sign of the cross, and not by shield or helmet, I will safely penetrate the ranks of the enemy." He is ordered, therefore, to be thrust back into prison, determined on proving his words true by exposing himself unarmed to the barbarians. But, on the following day, the enemy sent ambassadors to treat about peace and surrendered both themselves and all their possessions. In these circumstances who can doubt that this victory was due to the saintly man? It was granted him that he should not be sent unarmed to the fight. And although the good Lord could have preserved his own soldier, even amid the swords and darts of the enemy, yet that his blessed eyes might not be pained by witnessing the death of others, he removed all necessity for fighting. For Christ did not require to secure any other victory in behalf of his own soldier, than that, the enemy being subdued without bloodshed, no one should suffer death.

21. BENEDICT OF NURSIA

The Rule of St. Benedict

Benedict (c. 480-c. 547) was one of the most important founders of Western monasticism. The details of his life are sketchy, but it seems that he was born in Nursia, received his education at Rome, and became so repulsed by Roman society that he eventually withdrew to a cave, perhaps around 500, near Subiaco. After living as a hermit and then as an (unsuccessful) abbot of a monastery in the area, Benedict joined several monks in establishing a new monastery in Monte Cassino, where he drafted his famous "rule" for the monastic life. Now known as the Rule of St. Benedict, the document details the character and practices of the good monk and his abbot. The rule's section on humility has been especially formative for Christian monks seeking to live a nonviolent life and, consequently, for countless Christians who have since committed themselves to Benedictine spirituality. It is important to note, however, that even as he called for nonviolent humility Benedict also permitted the physical striking of monks under certain circumstances and encouraged the use of the rod against unruly children.

1. The Word of God in scripture teaches us in clear and resounding terms that anyone who lays claim to a high position will be brought low and anyone who is modest in self-appraisal will be lifted up. This is Christ's teaching about the guest who took the first place at the king's banquet: All who exalt themselves, he said, will be humbled and all who humble themselves will be exalted. He taught us by these words that whenever one of us is raised to a position of prominence, there is always an ele-ment of pride involved. The psalmist shows his concern to avoid this when he says: There is no pride in my heart, O Lord, nor arrogance in the look of my eyes; I have not aspired to a role too great for me nor to the glamour of pretensions that are beyond me. We should be wary of such pride. And why does he say this? It is because lack of humility calls for correction and so the psalm goes on: If I failed to keep a modest spirit and raised my ambitions too high, then your correction would

come down on me as though I were nothing but a newly weaned child on its mother's lap.

3. This ladder, then, will symbolize for each of us our life in this world during which we aspire to be lifted up to heaven by the Lord if only we can learn humility in our hearts. We can imagine that he has placed the steps of the ladder, held in place by the sides which signify our living body and soul, to invite us to climb on them. Paradoxically, to climb upward will take us down to earth but stepping down will lift us toward heaven. The steps themselves, then, mark the decision we are invited by God to make in the exercise of humility and self-discipline.

4. The first step of humility is to cherish at all times the sense of awe with which we should ever turn to God. It should drive all forgetfulness away; it should keep our minds alive to all God's guidance and commandments; it should make us reflect in our hearts again and again that those who despise God and reject his love prepare for themselves that irreversible spiritual death which is meant by hell, just as eternal life is prepared for those who fear God.

5. One who follows that way finds protection at all times from sin and vice of thought, of tongue, of hand, of foot, of self-will, and of disordered sensual desire, so as to lead a life that is completely open before the scrutiny of God and of his angels who watch over us from hour to hour. This is made clear by the psalmist who shows that God is always present to our very thoughts when he says: God searches the hearts and thoughts of men and women. And again: The Lord knows the thoughts of all. And: From afar you know my thoughts. And again: The thoughts of men and women shall give you praise. Thus it may help one concerned about thoughts that are perverse to repeat the psalmist's heartfelt saying: I shall be blameless in his sight only if I guard myself from my own wickedness.

6. As to pursuing our own will, we are warned against that when scripture says to us: Turn away from your own desires; and in the Lord's Prayer itself we pray that his will may be brought to fulfillment in us. It is therefore right that we should learn not to seek our own will and to learn from that warning in holy scripture which says: There are ways which seem right to human eyes, but their end plunges down into the depths of hell. Another good sign is to be afraid of what scripture says of those who reject such advice: They are corrupt and have become depraved in their pleasure seeking.

7. As to sensual desires we should believe that they are not hidden from God, for the psalmist says to the Lord: All my desires are known to you. We must indeed be on our guard against evil desires because spiritual death is not far from the gateway to wrongful pleasure, so that scripture gives us this clear direction: Do not pursue your lusts. And so, if the eyes of the Lord are watching the good and the wicked, and if at all times the Lord looks down from heaven on the sons and daughters of men to see if any show understanding in seeking God, and if the angels assigned to care for us report our deeds to the Lord day and night, then we must be on our guard every hour or else, as the psalmist says, the time may come when God will observe us falling into evil and so made worthless. He may spare us for a while during this life, because he is a loving Father who waits and longs for us to do better, but in the end his rebuke may come upon us with the words: You were guilty of these crimes and I was silent.

8. The second step of humility is not to love having our own way nor to delight in our own desires. Instead we should take as our model for imitation the Lord himself when he says: I have come not to indulge my own desires but to do the will of him who sent me. Again remember that scripture says: Punishment awaits us for following our own will, but there is a crown of victory for doing what is required of us.

9. The third step of humility is to submit oneself out of love of God to whatever obedience under a superior may require of us; it is the example of the Lord himself that we follow in this way, as we know from Saint Paul's words: He was made obedient even unto death.

10. The fourth step of humility is to go even further than this by readily accepting in patient and silent endurance, without thought of giving up or avoiding the issue, any hard and demanding things that may come our way in the course of that obedience, even if they include harsh impositions which are unjust. We are encouraged to such patience by the words of scripture: Whoever perseveres to the

very end will be saved. And again there is the saying of the psalm: Be steadfast in your heart and trust in the Lord. Then again there is that verse from another psalm: It is for you we face death all the day long and are counted as sheep for the slaughter.

11. Those who follow in that way have a sure hope of reward from God and they are joyful with Saint Paul's words on their lips: In all these things we are more than conquerors through him who loved us. They remember also the psalm: You, O God, have tested us and have tried us as silver is tried; you led us, God, in to the snare; you laid a heavy burden on our backs. Then this is added in the psalm: You placed leaders over us to show how we should be under a superior. In this way they fulfill the Lord's command through patience in spite of adversity and in spite of any wrongs they may suffer; struck on one cheek, they offer the other; when robbed of their coat, they let their cloak go also; pressed to go one mile, they willingly go two; with the Apostle Paul they put up with false brethren and shower blessings on those who curse them.

12. The fifth step of humility is that we should not cover up but humbly confess to our superior or spiritual guide whatever evil thoughts come into our minds and the evil deeds we have done in secret. That is what scripture urges on us when it says: Make known to the Lord the way you have taken and trust in him. Then again it says: Confess to the Lord, for he is good, for his mercy endures for ever. And again: I have made known to you my sin and have not covered over my wrongdoing. I have said: Against myself I shall proclaim my own faults to the Lord, and you have forgiven the wickedness of my heart.

13. The sixth step of humility for monks or nuns is to accept without complaint really wretched and inadequate conditions, and then whatever the task they may be ordered to perform, they should think of themselves as poor workers not worthy of consideration, saying quietly to themselves with the psalmist: I am of no account and lack understanding, no better than a beast in your sight. Yet I am always in your presence.

14. The seventh step of humility is that we should be ready to speak of ourselves as of less important and less worthy than others, not as a mere phrase on our lips, but as something we believe in the secret conviction of our hearts. Thus in a spirit of humility we make the psalmist's words our own: I am despised by all and cast out by my own people. I was raised up high in honor, but then I was humbled and overwhelmed with confusion. In the end we may learn to say: It was good for me, Lord, that you humbled me so that I might learn your precepts.

15. The eighth step of humility teaches us to do nothing as monks and nuns which goes beyond what is approved and encouraged by the common rule of the monastery and the example of our seniors.

16. The ninth step of humility leads us to refrain from unnecessary speech and to guard our silence by not speaking until we are addressed. That is what scripture recommends with these sayings: Anyone who is forever chattering will not escape sin, and there is another saying from a psalm: One who never stops talking loses the right way in life.

17. The tenth step of humility teaches us not to be given to empty laughter on every least occasion because: A fool's voice is forever raised in laughter.

18. The eleventh degree of humility is concerned with the manner of speech appropriate in a monastery. We should speak gently and seriously with words that are unassuming but serious. We should be brief and reasonable in whatever we have to say and not raise our voices to insist on our own opinions. We should remember the saying that the wise are to be recognized by the fewness of their words.

19. The twelfth step of humility is concerned with the external impression conveyed by those dedicated to monastic life. The humility of their hearts should ever be apparent to all who see them, even in their bodily movements. Whether they are at the work of God, at prayer in the oratory, walking about the monastery, in the garden, on a journey, or in the fields, wherever they may be, whether sitting, walking, or standing, they should be free of any hint of arrogance or pride in their manner or the way they look about them. They should guard their eyes and look down. They should remember that they are at all times answerable for their sins just as though they already stood before the awesome judgment of God, repeating always in their hearts the words of the publican in the gospel as he stood with his eyes cast down, saying: Lord, I am not wor-

thy, sinner that I am, to lift my eyes to the heavens. Or the words of the psalmist might fit just as well: I am bowed down and utterly humbled.

20. Any monk or nun who has climbed all these steps of humility will come quickly to that love of God which in its fullness casts out all fear. Carried forward by that love, they will begin to observe without effort as though naturally from good habit all those precepts which in earlier days were kept at least partly through fear. A new motive will have taken over, not fear of hell but the love of Christ. Good habit and delight in virtue will carry them along. This happy state the Lord will bring about through the Holy Spirit in his servant, whom he has cleansed of vice and sin and taught to be a true and faithful worker in the kingdom.

22. PENITENTIALS

Penitential books originated in the Celtic church in the sixth century and were initially intended as manuals for confessors, giving specific directives about penances in relation to a long list of particular sins. This individualistic, and mechanistic, approach to sin offended those committed to public penance, but it eventually found favor at the Council of Chalon-sur-Saone between 647 and 653. Although the penitentials rose in popularity following the council's stamp of approval, their popularity began to drop off as confessors became frustrated with their inconsistencies and abuses.

It should come as no surprise that penitentials detailed penalties for such acts as murder, but it is quite striking, even shocking, for the contemporary reader to see that the manuals prescribed penalties for killing in a public war and in response to the command of military authorities. Historian Ronald Musto has suggested that the penitentials "reveal a growing awareness of Gospel ideals in a barbarized society."

Penitential of Finnian (525-550)

6. If anyone has started a quarrel and plotted in his heart to strike or kill his neighbor, if [the offender] is a cleric, he shall do penance for half a year with an allowance of bread and water and for a whole year abstain from wine and meats, and thus he will be reconciled to the altar.

7. But if he is a layman, he shall do penance for a week, since he is a man of this world and his guilt is lighter in this world and his reward less in the world to come.

8. But if he is a cleric and strikes his brother or his neighbor or sheds blood, it is the same as if he had killed him, but the penance is not the same. He shall do penance with bread and water and be deprived of his clerical office for an entire year, and he must pray for himself with weeping and tears, that he may obtain mercy from God, since the Scripture says: "Whosoever hateth his brother is a murderer," how much more he who strikes him.

9. But if he is a layman, he shall do penance forty days and give some money to him whom he struck, according as some priest or judge determines. A cleric, however, ought not to give money, either to the one or the other.

Penitential of Theodore (668-690)

IV. Of Manslaughter

1. If one slays a man in revenge for a relative, he shall do penance as a murderer for seven or ten years. However, if he will render to the relatives the legal price, the penance shall be lighter, that is, [it shall be shortened] by half the time.

2. If one slays a man in revenge for a brother, he shall do penance for three years. In another place it is said that he should do penance for ten years.

3. But a murderer, ten or seven years.

4. If a layman slays another with malice aforethought, if he will not lay aside his arms, he shall do penance for seven years; without flesh and wine, three years.

5. If one slays a monk or a cleric, he shall lay aside his arms and serve God, or he shall do penance for seven years. He is in the judgment of his bishop. But as for one who slays a bishop or a presbyter, it is for the king to give judgment in his case.

6. One who slays a man by command of his lord shall keep away from the church for forty days; and one who slays a man in public war shall do penance for forty days.

7. If through anger, he shall do penance for three years; if by accident, for one year; if by a potion or any trick, seven years or more; if as a result of a quarrel, ten years.

2. He who slays a layman with malice aforethought or for the possession of his inheritance, four years.

3. He who slays to avenge a brother, one year and in the two following years the three forty-day periods and the appointed days.

4. He who slays through sudden anger and a quarrel, three years.

5. He who slays by accident, one year.

6. He who slays in public warfare, forty days.

7. He who slays at the command of his master, if he is a slave, forty days; he who, being a freeman, at the command of his superior slays an innocent person, one year and for the two [years] following, the three forty-day periods and the appointed days.

Penitential Ascribed to Bede (c. 750)

II. Of Slaughter

1. He who slays a monk or a cleric shall lay aside his weapons and serve God or do penance for seven years.

23. SMARAGDUS

Commentary on the Rule of Saint Benedict

Smaragdus (d. c. 825), the abbot of St. Mihiel during the demise of the Carolingian Empire, wrote the following exposition on the Rule of Benedict sometime after 817. It provides yet another sharp contrast to the violence of medieval Europe.

Introduction

Large numbers of monks are practicing shrewdness as they look for interpretations of the words in the Rule of blessed Benedict, and an understanding of its various statements. When I perceived this, and saw that they were also looking for a way of distinguishing between the many judgments to be found in the Rule concerning faults, and their vari-

ous types and degrees, of my own accord and also under pressure from other brothers, I undertook to expound the Rule. Although the learned do not need to have it expounded, still a simple exposition of it is pleasing to simple monks. Those who yearn to reach the heavenly kingdom by observing it are anxious to hear frequently even a few words about it. And those who hold to the uprightness of life it teaches, and hope thereby to enjoy eternal happiness, listen gladly and often to a discourse on the Rule. With the Lord's grace to assist me, I shall now begin to expound its words in an orderly fashion.

Book One of the Commentary

Prologue to the Rule

… **Intending to do military service to the Lord Christ the true king.** He is called Lord because he has lordship over the whole of his creation, or at all events because the whole of creation is subject to his lordship. He is called Christ from the word "chrism." What in Greek is called "chrism" is in Latin called "anointing." This name also suits our Lord Jesus Christ, whom God the Father anointed not with a visible but with an invisible and spiritual oil. Hence in the Acts of the Apostles the Father is told: "They are gathered together in this city against your Son whom you anointed." And the writer of the psalm says to the Son: *God, your God, has anointed you with the oil of gladness,* and so forth.

He is called the true king because he rightly sustains, governs, protects and rules everything he created. Although holy men may loosely be called kings … yet Christ the Lord is the true king because he is the Son of the true King.… For Christ the Lord is in truth shown to be the true King of kings and Lord of lords, because just as every creature is known to have been made through him, it is also shown to be ruled and governed through him. For the world has its soldiers and Christ has his. Now the world's soldiers take up weak and slippery weapons, whereas Christ's soldiers take up strong and bright ones. The former fight against their enemies, and the result is they bring themselves and those they kill to eternal punishment; the latter fight against the vices, so that after death they may be able to gain eternal life and its rewards; the former fight, and the result is they go down into hell, the latter fight that they may ascend to glory; the former fight and so after death are enslaved with the demons in hell, the latter fight so that they may always rejoice with the angels; the former fight and so will always mourn with the devil, the latter fight so that they may always exult with Christ. The apostle Paul sums up both kinds of soldiers in one sentence: *No one serving as God's soldiers involves himself in worldly matters,* thus showing that there are soldiers belonging to God just as there are soldiers belonging to the world.

Therefore the two kinds of military service mark out the two kinds of soldiers. A spiritual military service leads some to the heavenly camp through the gratuitous grace of the heavenly commander; a corporal military service binds others to labor with the world according to the will of an earthly king. The world's soldiers are held bound by passions and desires, while God's soldiers *crucify their flesh with its vices and concupiscences.* The former are nourished with banquets, the latter with virtues; the former endeavor to seize the possessions of others, the latter desire either patiently to endure the loss of what belongs to them or in the exercise of mercy to give these away. The former perform deeds for which they may be extolled with false praises; the latter seek ways of being honored with everlasting rewards. Vanity bestows on the former an appearance of happiness, while truth confers true joys on the latter. The former consult their own advantage; the latter seek the common good. The former, who are destined to perish, hasten to preserve what is destined to perish; the latter desire to possess what will never perish so that they may not eternally perish. For the former, to live is hard labor and to die is torment; for the latter, *to live is Christ and to die is gain.* The former battle against visible, the latter against invisible enemies. Avarice makes the former cruel; mercy makes the latter kind. Envy makes the former quarrelsome, while meekness makes peacemakers of the latter. The former, out of pride, engage in disputes for the sake of their own honor; as for the latter, humility makes one person think another superior to himself. Babylon is ruled by the former, while through and in the latter the heavenly Jerusalem is administered by the Lord. Prosperity lifts up and adversity casts down the world's soldiers, whereas God's soldiers are immovable in their perseverance, whether in prosperity or in adversity.

You take up the strong bright weapons of obedience. Blessed Benedict called them the strong weapons of obedience because the labor of obedience surpasses all human labors that are done voluntarily. For what can be stronger than that a man should make himself in all respects servant to a man and, although free and held in honor, should present himself to all as a lowly purchased slave, despised and abject, so that he can say: *But I am a worm and no man, the reproach of men and despised by the people?* What can be stronger than that when struck on one cheek he should offer the other, should surrender his cloak to one who is taking away his tunic, that for one who is forcing him to go one mile he should go two? And that in all these things he should rejoice, because he has been considered worthy to suffer insults for the Lord's name? What can be stronger or more resistant than that a man should voluntarily subject himself to a man in all obedience, and in the very obedience should patiently bear the hard and contrary injustices inflicted on him, than that he should be content with great poverty and hardship, and be ready for everything enjoined on him; than that not only with his tongue he declare himself, but also in his heart consider himself inferior to and of less value than everyone else, and wherever he is, whether sitting or walking, with his head always bowed and his eyes fixed on the ground, he consider himself guilty of his sins, saying: Lord, I am not worthy to look up and see the height of heaven on account of my injustices?

Let us see why blessed Benedict said that the weapons of obedience are *very strong and bright.* They are very strong because, as we have said above, the labor of obedience surpasses all the voluntarily performed labors of the human race. The strong weapons of obedience are that a man should deny himself in regard to himself, the bright weapons, that he should follow Christ; the very strong, that he should turn from evil, the bright, that he should do good; the very strong, that he should not render evil for evil, the bright, that he should render good for evil; the very strong, that he should not curse one who curses him, the bright, that he should even bless him; the very strong, that he should not hold hatred in his heart, the bright, that he should love both enemy and neighbor as himself; very strong, inasmuch as the monk is despised, bright, when it comes to performing some work; very strong in endurance, bright in obedience; very strong in continued fasting, bright in refreshing the poor; strong, *Let your loins be girt,* bright, *and your lamps be burning.* They are very strong when they endure their own weakness, bright when they visit others who are weakly; very strong when they are not undone by the deceitfulness of vanity, bright when they speak the truth with heart and mouth; very strong when they bear injustices patiently, bright when they do not inflict injuries for others to bear; very strong when they rein in the appetite of gluttony, bright when they love frugality and sparingness; very strong when they chastise the body, bright when they love chastity....

Seek peace and follow it.... Peace is mind's serenity, spirit's tranquility, heart's simplicity, love's bond, charity's fellowship. This it is that takes away secret hatreds, puts an end to wars, suppresses angry outbursts, treads down the proud, loves the humble, quiets those involved in discord, brings enemies to concord; it is pleasing to all, does not seek what belongs to others, regards nothing as its own, teaches how to love since it does not know how to hate; it does not know what it is to be lifted up or puffed up. Let him who has received this hold on to it; let him who has lost it search for it again; let him who has let go of it seek it out carefully; because he who is not found in peace is disowned by the Father, disinherited by the Son, and no less made a stranger by the Holy Spirit.

24. PEACE OF GOD

In 975, Bishop Guy of Anjou, France, responded to the pervasive, and ongoing, violence of his home diocese in Le Puy by calling together a group of knights and peasants to discuss the most effective methods for limiting violence. The bishop used the meeting to call upon the warring parties to refrain from destroying the property of churches and the poor in his diocese. The violence of medieval Europe troubled other bishops, too, and following the example set by Guy, a group of bishops gathered together at Charroux several years later and set forth the "Peace of God," a proclamation that called upon the warring parties to cease attacking churches, clerics, and the poor. Other proclamations followed the one promulgated at Charroux in 989, excerpted below, and Peace of God rallies, with large groups of men and women calling for peace, began to take place across some sections of medieval Europe by the end of the tenth century.

I, Gumbald, Archbishop of Aquitania secunda, and all my coprovincial bishops, together with religious clerics and others of both sexes, met at the hall, which is called Karrof.... Thus solemnly assembled in God's name we decreed thus:

1. Anathema for violators of churches: if anyone breaks into a sacred church, or violently removes anything thence, unless he makes satisfaction, let him be anathema.

2. Anathema for spoilers of the poor: if anyone robs peasants or other poor of a sheep, ox, ass, cow, goat, or pigs, unless by the other's fault, and if he neglect to make full reparation, let him be anathema.

3. Anathema for those who assault the clergy: if anyone attacks, captures or assaults a priest or deacon or any clergyman, who is not carrying arms (that is, shield, sword, coat of mail and helmet), but quietly going on his way or remaining at home, that sacrilegious man shall be held to be cast forth from the holy church of God, unless he makes satisfaction, after the clergyman has been examined by his bishop to see if he was at fault.

25. THE MARTYRDOM OF BORIS AND GLEB

The Martyrdom of Boris and Gleb *has long inspired Christian peacemakers in the Eastern tradition, and contemporary Orthodox Christians continue to embrace the story as an example of Christian nonviolence worthy of devotion and emulation. The story depicts in vivid detail the murders of Boris and Gleb in 1015, following the death of their father, Vladimir, the grand prince of Kiev. The murders were plotted and ordered by Sviatopolk, the eldest of the three brothers, who appears in this account as an eleventh-century Cain. The Orthodox faith refers to the two slain brothers, Boris and Gelb, as "passion-bearers," since they followed the example of Jesus in refusing to resist their executioners.*

Sviatopolk settled in Kiev after his father's death, and after calling together all the inhabitants of Kiev, he began to distribute largess among them. They accepted it, but their hearts were not with him, because their brethren were with Boris. When Boris returned with the army, not having met with the Pechenegs, he received the news that his father was dead. He mourned deeply for him, for he was beloved of his father before all the rest.

When he came to the Alta, he halted. His father's retainers then urged him to take his place in Kiev on his father's throne, since he had at his disposal the latter's retainers and troops. But Boris protested: "Be it not for me to raise my hand against my elder brother. Now that my father has passed away, let him take the place of my father in my heart." When the soldiery heard these words, they departed from him, and Boris remained with his servants.

But Sviatopolk was filled with lawlessness. Adopting the device of Cain, he sent messages to Boris that he desired to live at peace with him, and would increase the patrimony he had received from his father. But he plotted against him how he might kill him. So Sviatopolk came by night to Vyshegorod. After secretly summoning to his presence Putsha and the boyars of the town, he inquired of them whether they were wholeheartedly devoted to him. Putsha and the men of Vyshegorod replied: "We are ready to lay down our lives for you." He then commanded them to say nothing to any man, but to go and kill his brother Boris. They straightway promised to execute his order. Of such men Solomon has well said: "They make haste to shed blood unjustly. For they promise blood, and gather evil. Their path runneth to evil, for they possess their souls in dishonor" (Proverbs 1:16-19).

These emissaries came to the Alta, and when they approached, they heard the sainted Boris singing vespers. For it was already known to him that they intended to take his life. Then he arose and began to chant, saying: "O Lord, how are they increased who come against me! Many are they that rise up against me" (Psalms 3:1). And also: "Thy arrows have pierced me, for I am ready for wounds and my pain is before me continually" (Psalms 38:2, 17). And he also uttered this prayer: "Lord, hear my prayer, and enter not into judgment with thy servant, for no living man shall be just before thee. For the enemy hath crushed my soul!" (Psalms 140:1-3). After ending the six psalms, when he saw how men were sent out to kill him, he began to chant the Psalter, saying: "Strong bulls encompassed me, and the assemblage of the evil beset me. O Lord my God, I have hoped in thee; save me and deliver me from my pursuers" (Psalms 22:12, 16; 7:1). Then he began to sing the canon. After finishing vespers, he prayed, gazing upon the icon, the image of the Lord, with these words: "Lord Jesus Christ, who in this image hast appeared on earth for our salvation, and who, having voluntarily suffered thy hands to be nailed to the cross, didst endure thy passion for our sins, so help me now to endure my passion. For I accept it not from those who are my enemies, but from the hand of my own brother. Hold it not against him as a sin, O Lord!"

After offering this prayer, he lay down upon his couch. Then they fell upon him like wild beasts about the tent, and overcame him by piercing him with lances. They also overpowered his servant, who cast himself upon his body. For he was beloved of Boris. He was a servant of Hungarian race, George by name, to whom Boris was greatly attached. The prince had given him a large gold necklace which he wore while serving him. They also killed many other servants of Boris. But since they could not quickly take the necklace from George's neck, they cut off his head, and thus obtained it. For this reason his body was not recognized later among the corpses.

The murderers, after attacking Boris, wrapped him in a canvas, loaded him upon a wagon, and dragged him off, though he was still alive. When the impious Sviatopolk saw that he was still breathing, he sent two Varangians to finish him. When they came and saw that he was still alive, one of them drew his sword and plunged it into his heart. Thus died the blessed Boris, receiving from the hand of Christ our God the crown among the righteous. He shall be numbered with the prophets and the Apostles, as he joins with the choirs of martyrs, rests in the lap of Abraham, beholds joy ineffable, chants with the angels, and rejoices in company with the choirs of saints. After his body had been carried in secret to Vyshegorod, it was buried in the church of St. Basil.

The impious Sviatopolk then reflected: "Behold, I have killed Boris; now how can I kill Gleb?" Adopting once more Cain's device, he craftily sent messages to Gleb to the effect that he should come quickly, because his father was very ill and desired his presence. Gleb quickly mounted his horse, and set out with a small company, for he was obedient to his father. When he came to the Volga, his horse stumbled in a ditch on the plain, and broke his leg. He arrived at Smolensk, and setting out thence at dawn, he embarked in a boat on the Smiadyn. At this time, Yaroslav received from Predslava the tidings of their father's death, and he sent word to Gleb that he should not set out, because his father was dead and his brother had been murdered by Sviatopolk. Upon receiving these tidings, Gleb burst into tears, and mourned for his father, but still more deeply for his brother. He wept and prayed with the lament: "Woe is me, O Lord! It were better for me to die with my brother than to live on in this world. O my brother, had I but seen thy angelic countenance, I should have died with thee. Why am I now left alone? Where are thy words that thou didst say to me, my brother? No longer do I hear thy sweet counsel. If thou hast received affliction from God, pray for me that I may endure the same passion. For it were better for me to dwell with thee than in this deceitful world."

While he was thus praying amid his tears, there suddenly arrived those sent by Sviatopolk for Gleb's destruction. These emissaries seized Gleb's boat, and drew their weapons. The servants of Gleb were terrified, and the impious messenger, Goriaser, gave orders that they should slay Gleb with dispatch. Then Gleb's cook, Torchin by name, seized a knife, and stabbed Gleb. He was offered up as a sacrifice to God like an innocent lamb, a glorious offering amid the perfume of incense, and he received the crown of glory. Entering the heavenly mansions, he beheld his long-desired brother, and rejoiced with him in the joy ineffable which they had attained through their brotherly love.

"How good and fair it is for brethren to live together!" (Psalms 133:1). But the impious ones returned again, even as David said, "Let the sinners return to hell" (Psalms 9:17). When they returned to Sviatopolk, they reported that his command had been executed. On hearing these tidings, he was puffed up with pride, since he knew not the words of David: "Why art thou proud of thy evildoing, O mighty one? Thy tongue hath considered lawlessness all the day long" (Psalms 52:1).

After Gleb had been slain, his body was thrown upon the shore between two tree trunks, but after-ward they took him and carried him away, to bury him beside his brother Boris in the Church of St. Basil. United thus in body and still more in soul, ye dwell with the Lord and King of all, in eternal joy, ineffable light, bestowing salutary gifts upon the land of Russia. Ye give healing to other strangers who draw near with faith, making the lame to walk, giving sight to the blind, to the sick health, to captives freedom, to prisoners liberty, to the sorrowful consolation, and to the oppressed relief. Ye are the protectors of the land of Russia, shining forever like beacons and praying to the Lord in behalf of your countrymen. Therefore must we worthily magnify these martyrs in Christ, praying fervently to them and saying: "Rejoice, martyrs in Christ from the land of Russia, who gave healing to them who draw near to you in faith and love. Rejoice, dwellers in heaven. In the body ye were angels, servants in the same thought, comrades in the same image, of one heart with the saints. To all that suffer ye give relief. Rejoice, Boris and Gleb, wise in God. Like streams ye spring from the founts of life-giving water which flow for the redemption of the righteous. Rejoice, ye who have trampled the serpent of evil beneath your feet. Ye have appeared amid bright rays, enlightening like beacons the whole land of Russia. Appearing in faith immutable, ye have ever driven away the darkness. Rejoice, ye who have won an unslumbering eye, ye blessed ones who have received in your hearts the zeal to fulfill God's only commandments. Rejoice, brethren united in the realms of golden light, in the heavenly abodes, in glory unfading, which ye through your merits have attained. Rejoice, ye who are brightly irradiate with the luminance of God, and travel throughout the world expelling devils and healing diseases. Like beacons supernal and zealous guardians, ye dwell with God, illumined forever with light divine, and in your courageous martyrdom ye enlighten the souls of the faithful. The light-bringing heavenly love has exalted you, wherefore ye have inherited all fair things in the heavenly life: glory, celestial sustenance, the light of wisdom, and beauteous joys. Rejoice, ye who refresh our hearts, driving out pain and sickness and curing evil passions. Ye glorious ones, with the sacred drops of your blood ye have dyed a robe of purple which ye wear in beauty, and reign forevermore with Christ, interceding with him for his new Christian nation and for your fellows, for our land is hallowed by your blood. By virtue of your relics deposited in the church, ye illumine it with the Holy Spirit, for there in heavenly bliss, as martyr among the army of martyrs, ye intercede for our nation. Rejoice, bright daysprings, our Christ-

loving martyrs and intercessors! Subject the pagans to our princes, beseeching our Lord God that they may live in concord and in health, freed from intestine war and the crafts of the devil. Help us therefore who sing and recite your sacred praise forever unto our life's end."

26. TRUCE OF GOD

After the Peace of God movement declined in the middle of the eleventh century, clergy, bishops, and nobility sought yet again to limit violence in medieval Europe, and the result was the "Truce of God," proclamations that ordered warring parties to cease their fighting on certain days of the week, identified individuals who should never be attacked (as well as property that should be safeguarded), and even proscribed the use of certain weapons. Below are examples of proclamations from the Truce of God movement.

There is little doubt that the Peace and Truce of God proclamations gave substance to future just war theorists, Gratian among them, contemplating such things as noncombatant immunity, but the documents are included here because they sought to limit violence and create sanctuaries of peace in an extremely violent world. They were not designed to give religious legitimacy to the execution of war and other violent acts, but rather to create times, places, and personalities that would be free of violence. That, in and of itself, was a peaceful act, even as it unfairly favored Christians in general and clergy and the poor in particular.

The Earliest Truce of God, Proclaimed in the Diocese of Elne, 1027

And so the said bishops, with all the clergy and the faithful people, provided that [1] throughout the whole of the said country and bishopric no one should attack his enemy from the ninth hour on Saturday until the first hour on Monday, so that everyone may perform his religious duties on Sunday. [2] And none shall attack a monk or a clergyman who is unarmed, nor any man going to or coming from a church or a council, nor a man accompanied by a woman. [3] And none shall dare to violate a church or the houses within thirty paces of a church.

Truce of God, Proclaimed at the Council of Narbonne, August 25, 1054

1. First, we order that no Christian shall slay his fellow Christian. For he who kills a Christian, without doubt sheds the blood of Christ. If anyone unjustly kills a man, he shall pay the penalty according to the law.

2. We confirm the truce of God, which was long ago established by us and now is broken by evil men. Henceforth it shall be faithfully observed by all. Accordingly we adjure in God's name every Christian not to do hurt to any other Christian from sunset on Wednesday till sunrise on Monday.

3. From the first Sunday in Advent till the octave

of Epiphany; from the Sunday before Lent till the octave of Easter; from the Sunday before Ascension Day till the octave of Whitsunday; and on the following feasts and their vigils—those of St. Mary, John the Baptist, apostles, St. Peter in Chains, Justus and Pastor, St. Laurence, St. Michael, All Saints, St. Martin; and in the four periods of Ember Days: we forbid any Christian to attack another Christian during any of the said fasts, feasts and vigils or to insult him or to seize his property. ...

9. Olive trees, which, we read, were used as a sign that peace had returned to the earth at the time of the flood, and from whose oil the holy chrism is made, shall be so strictly protected that no Christian shall dare to cut them down or injure them or seize their fruit.

10. Sheep and their pastors, while tending them, shall also be under the truce of God on all days in all places.

Canons of the Second Lateran Council, 1123

Canon 11: We command also that priests, clerics, monks, travelers, merchants, country people going and returning, and those engaged in agriculture, as well as the animals with which they till the soil and that carry the seeds to the field, and also their sheep, shall at all times be secure.

Canon 12: We decree that the truce of God be strictly observed by all from the setting of the sun on Wednesday to its rising on Monday, and from Advent to the octave of Epiphany and from Quinquagesima to the octave of Easter. If anyone shall violate it and does not make satisfaction after the third admonition, the bishop shall direct against him the sentence of excommunication and in writing shall announce his action to the neighboring bishops. No bishops shall restore to communion the one excommunicated; indeed every bishop should confirm the sentence made known to him in writing....

Canon 15: If anyone at instigation of the devil incurs the guilt of this sacrilege, namely, that he has laid violent hands on a cleric or monk, he shall be anathematized and no bishop shall dare absolve him, except *mortis urgente periculo,* till he be presented to the Apostolic See and receive its mandate. We command also that no one shall dare lay hands on those who have taken refuge in a church or cemetery. Anyone doing this, let him be excommunicated....

Canon 18: By the authority of God and the blessed Apostles Peter and Paul we absolutely condemn and prohibit that most wicked, devastating, horrible, and malicious work of incendiaries; for this pest, this hostile waste, surpasses all other depredations. No one is ignorant of how detrimental this is to the people of God and what injury it inflicts on souls and bodies. Every means must be employed, therefore, and no effort must be spared that for the welfare of the people such ruin and such destruction may be eradicated and extirpated. If anyone, therefore, after the promulgation of this prohibition, shall through malice, hatred, or revenge set fire, or cause it to be set, or knowingly by advice or other connivance have part in it, let him be excommunicated. Moreover, when incendiaries die, let them be deprived of Christian burial. Nor shall they be absolved until, as far as they are able, they have made reparation to those injured and have promised under oath to set no more fires. For penance they are to spend one year in the service of God either in Jerusalem or in Spain....

Canon 29: We forbid under penalty of anathema that that deadly and God-detested art of stingers and archers be in the future exercised against Christians and Catholics.

27. PETER DAMIAN

Letter to Bishop Olderic

Peter Damian (c. 1007-1072) was born in Ravenna and became a monk in Fonte Avella in 1035. Known for his devotion to extreme austerity, Damian became prior in 1043, led the monastic reform movement of his day, and was appointed cardinal bishop of Ostia in 1057. His numerous extant works focus on sacraments as God's free gifts, on personal and social holiness, and on monastic practices, especially the vow of poverty. Although Damian was not a strict pacifist, some of his letters to secular and religious rulers demand the cessation of violence, especially against the poor. For instance, in his letter to Bishop Olderic of Fermo, excerpted below, Damian draws an inextricable connection between Christianity and non-violence and calls upon church leaders to show the way of nonviolence.

Damian's calls for church leaders to help end violence went largely unheeded, of course, and a few decades later Pope Urban II delivered his famous speech at the Council of Clermont (1095)—a speech that inspired countless Christians to carry out bloody crusades against Muslims.

…Wars wage so bitterly every day, battle formations rush forward, hostile attacks bristle so that the sword seems to remove more people as soldiers than bodily illness finishes them lying quietly on their sick beds.…

But when among the other evils that have emerged in our time, violent men also oppress churches insolently and invade the estates and whatever other goods [protected by] the sacred law, it moves some [to consider] whether the rectors of the churches ought to seek revenge, as they return evil for evil, according to the custom of the world. For there are soon very many who, as the force of injury strikes them, leap up immediately to declare wars. They draw up their armed wedges of soldiers, and so they slash their enemies with far more bitterness than they were wounded.

This to me plainly enough appears to be absurd, that the very priests of the Lord seek after what is prohibited to the laity, and what their words struggle against, their deeds assert. For what appears to be more contrary to the Christian law than avenging injuries? Where, I ask, are the many proclamations of the Scriptures? Where is what the Lord said, "and do not ask for your property back from someone who takes it" [Lk. 6:30]. For if it is not allowed us to ask back for those things that are taken from us, how are these people allowed to inflict a wound in further retribution? Where is, "if anyone hits you on the right cheek, offer him the other as well; if someone wishes to go to law with you to get your tunic, let him have your cloak as well. And if anyone requires you to go one mile, go two miles with him" [Mt. 5:39-42]?

But perhaps someone will object that the mass of laity has been ordered to do this, but not the priests, undoubtedly, of course, because the hierarchy of the Church ought to preach, but not obey, this. But what fool feels this way, when the Lord says, "anyone who infringes even one of the least of these commandments and teaches others to do the same will be considered the least in the kingdom of heaven; but the person who keeps them and teaches them will be considered great in the kingdom of heaven" [Mt. 5:19]? Therefore the priest, who wishes to be great in the kingdom of heaven, may be first among the people if what he dictates to his followers in words, he himself first fulfills with his living actions.

Therefore, in order to avoid every chance that his understanding will be perverted, the one who is first among the priests of the Church does not say, "Lord, how many times must a brother sin against a brother and he forgive him?" but rather establishing the case of all priests in his one person, "Lord," he [Peter] says, "how often must I forgive my brother if he wrongs me? As often as seven times?" [Mt. 18:21]. And when Jesus tells him to forgive "seventy times seven" [Mt. 18:22] there appears no ambiguity left that it is a universal command to be obeyed by priests....

Indeed, among all the gems of virtue that our Savior brought from heaven, he demonstrated that two shine out more famously and clearly, which he expressed first in himself and taught so that they might be imprinted in us: namely, love and patience. Of love the Apostle [Paul] says, "but God, on account of the great love with which he loved the world, sent his Son" [cf. Eph. 2:4]. But of patience, he says, "and all these things which were written so long ago were written so that we, learning patience [perseverance] and the encouragement which the scriptures give, should have hope" [Rom. 15:4]. Through love the Son of God came down from Heaven; but through patience he overcame the devil.

Fortified with these virtues, the apostles founded and established the holy Church; and his champions, the holy martyrs, triumphantly carried through the various entreaties of those who were killed. If, therefore, on behalf of the faith by which the universal Church lives, one is never allowed to take up weapons of iron, how is it that for the earthly and transitory possessions of the Church armored battle lines rush madly upon swords? Indeed, when the saints prevailed they never destroyed heretics and idolaters; but far more likely did not flee from being destroyed by them for the sake of the Catholic faith. Why, therefore, because of an injury over worthless things, does a believer attack a believer with swords, whom he well knows is redeemed just like him, by the blood of Christ?

In the far reaches of Gaul I heard of the events I now relate. Between an abbot and a certain nobleman there arose a not minor dispute over some possession. After the vassals of both sides had long disputed and quarreled, at last on both sides it was agreed that it would be settled by arms.

After the nobleman had outfitted his soldiers, he entered the field ready for battle, he set up his battle formations, he inflamed everyone's mind to acting bravely. A forest of swords sprang up all around, shields glistened red, a shouting clamor rose, the swaggering threats of soldiers began to swell, the webs began to draw tighter. The only thing that awaited was the onslaught of the opposing parties rushing against one another with outstretched arms.

The abbot, on the other hand, set his hopes not on earthly weapons, but on the author of human salvation. He forbade everyone who had come to his levy to brandish weapons on his behalf. He put only his own monks on horses. He ordered their heads helmeted with their monks' hoods. Thus along with them, as if they were helmeted, and protected by the breastplate of faith, he arrived at the battleground with the cross for a standard.

And when that nobleman did not see iron weapons, as he had hoped, but rather celestial ones; and when, face to face, he perceived a battle formation of angels, such a huge horror—the fear of God—filled him and all his vassals, that they threw down their arms and jumped from their horses immediately; and they stretched themselves humbly out on the ground, and they earnestly begged forgiveness. Yes, yes, of course he obtained the titles of triumphant victory. He did not place his hope in numerous horses, nor in glittering swords, but he trusted so much in the strength of divine power.

If someone objects that Pope Leo [IX, 1049-54] frequently involved himself in violent means, but that, nevertheless, he is blessed, I say what I feel: Peter did not obtain the apostolic supremacy because of the fact that he denied [Jesus] [see Mk. 14:66-72]; nor did David merit the prophet's tongue because he had invaded the marriage bed of another man [see 2 Sam. 11]. Good and bad deeds are not judged according to the general merits of their doers, but ought to be judged on their own intrinsic value.

Did anyone ever read that Gregory [I, the Great, 590-604] either did or taught his [behavior] in letters, who had suffered so much rapine and violence through the savagery of the Lombards? Did Ambrose ever wage war on the Arians who cruelly infested him and his church? Was it ever related that the holy popes rose up in arms? ...

28. FRANCIS OF ASSISI

Francis of Assisi (c. 1182-1226), the founder of the Franciscan Order, was reared in a wealthy family and joined his father's commercially successful cloth business before going off to war against Perugia. After serving as a prisoner of war for more than a year, he returned to his old life at Assisi but was called to war again in 1204. Diverted by a vision, he went back to Assisi and began to redirect his life away from his family and towards a simple lifestyle. Around this time, two events were catalytic in affecting his conversion to a new way of living. First, he encountered a leper who both repulsed him and forced him to rethink the way he treated those with leprosy. Second, after he had left his father's business and begun to repair churches, he heard a sermon extolling Jesus' counsel to his disciples to leave behind all they possessed. Francis was so moved by Matthew 10:7-19 that he left behind all of his worldly goods, draped himself in the clothes of a peasant, and began to live the life of an itinerant Christian preacher. His itinerancy, coupled with his simple lifestyle and teachings of poverty and humility, attracted a small core of followers, which later grew in number and influence, leading Pope Innocent III to offer his official approval for a rule that Francis had drafted for his followers. The monastic rules, excerpted here, reveal that Francis sought to form the character and actions of his followers in accord with the peaceful ways of Jesus. The rules thus stand in marked contrast to the bloodthirsty practices of the medieval crusades.

The Earlier Rule
1209/10-1221

Chapter XI: The Brothers Should Not Revile or Detract, But Should Love One Another

Let all the brothers be careful not to slander or engage in disputes; let them strive, instead, to keep silence whenever God gives them the grace. Let them not quarrel among themselves or with others but strive to respond humbly, saying: *I am a useless servant.* Let them not become angry because *whoever is angry with his brother is liable to judgment; whoever says to his brother "fool" shall be answerable to the Council; whoever says "fool" will be liable to fiery Gehenna.*

Let them love one another, as the Lord says: *This is my commandment: love one another as I have loved you.* Let them express the love they have for one another by their deeds, as the Apostle says: *Let us not love in word or speech, but in deed and truth.*

Let them revile no one. Let them not grumble or detract from others, for it is written: *Gossips and detractors are detestable to God.* Let them be *modest by showing graciousness toward everyone.* Let them not judge or condemn. As the Lord says, let them not consider the least sins of others; instead, let them reflect more upon their own sins *in the bitterness of their soul.* Let them struggle *to enter through the narrow gate,* for the Lord says: *The gate is narrow and the road that leads to life constricted; those who find it are few....*

Chapter XIV: How the Brothers Should Go through the World

When the brothers go through the world, let them take *nothing for the journey, neither knapsack, nor purse, nor bread, nor money, nor walking stick. Whatever house they enter,* let them first say: Peace to this house. They may eat and drink *what is placed before them* for as long as they stay *in that house. Let them not resist anyone evil, but whoever strikes them on one cheek, let them offer him the other as well. Whoever takes their cloak, let them not withhold their tunic. Let them give to all who ask of them and whoever takes what is theirs, let them not seek to take it back....*

Chapter XVI: Those Going among the Saracens and Other Nonbelievers

… Wherever they may be, let all my brothers remember that they have given themselves and abandoned their bodies to the Lord Jesus Christ. For love of Him, they must make themselves vulnerable to their enemies, both visible and invisible, because the Lord says: *Whoever loses his life because of me will save it* in eternal life. *Blessed are they who suffer persecution for the sake of justice, for theirs is the kingdom of heaven. If they have persecuted me, they will also persecute you. If they persecute you in one town, flee to another. Blessed are you when people hate you, speak evil of you, persecute, expel, and abuse you, denounce your name as evil and utter every kind of slander against you because of me. Rejoice and be glad on that day because your reward is great in heaven.*

I tell you, my friends, do not be afraid of them and do not fear those who kill the body and afterwards have nothing more to do. See that you are not alarmed. For by your patience, you will possess your souls; whoever perseveres to the end will be saved....

Chapter XXII: An Admonition to the Brothers

All my brothers: let us pay attention to what the Lord says: *Love your enemies* and *do good to those who hate you* for our Lord Jesus Christ, Whose footprints we must follow, called His betrayer a friend and willingly offered Himself to His executioners.

Our friends, therefore, are all those who unjustly inflict upon us distress and anguish, shame and injury, sorrow and punishment, martyrdom and death. We must love them greatly for we shall possess eternal life because of what they bring us....

Francis's famous canticle, below, is one of the first Christian texts that draws a close connection between peacemaking and a reverential—even mystic— appreciation for the God of nature and creation itself.

The Canticle of the Creatures (1225)

Most High, all-powerful, good Lord,
 Yours are *the praises, the glory,* and *the honor,*
  and all *blessing.*
To You alone, Most High, do they belong,
 and no human is worthy to mention Your
  name.
Praised be You, my *Lord,* with all *Your creatures,*
 especially Sir Brother Sun,
 Who is the day and through whom You give us
  light.
And he is beautiful and radiant with great
  splendor;
 and bears a likeness of You, Most High One.
Praised be You, my Lord, through Sister *Moon* and
  the stars,
 in heaven. You formed them clear and precious
  and beautiful.
Praised be You, my Lord, through Brother
  Wind,
 and through the air, cloudy and serene, and
  every kind of weather,
 through whom You give sustenance to Your
  creatures.
Praised be you, my Lord, through Sister *Water,*
 who is very useful and humble and precious
  and chaste.
Praised be You, my Lord, through Brother *Fire,*
 through whom *You light the night,*
 and he is beautiful and playful and robust and
  strong.
Praised be You, my Lord, through our Sister
  Mother *Earth,*
 who sustains and governs us,
 and who produces various *fruit* with colored
  flowers and *herbs.*

Praised be You, my Lord, through those who give
  pardon for Your love,
 and bear infirmity and tribulation.
Blessed are those who endure in peace
 for by You, Most High, shall they be crowned.

Praised be You, my Lord, through our Sister
  Bodily Death,
 from whom no one living can escape.
Woe to those who die in mortal sin.

Blessed are those whom death will find in Your
most holy will,
    for *the second death* shall do them no harm.

Praise and *bless* my *Lord* and give Him thanks
    and serve Him with great humility.

29. HUMBERT OF ROMANS

Short Work in Three Parts

In approximately 1272, Pope Gregory X asked Humbert of Romans (d. 1277), the fifth Master of the Dominican Order, to write a report in preparation for the Second Council of Lyons. Humbert's document, Short Work in Three Parts, *addressed the division between Catholics and Greek Orthodox, the reform of the Latin church, and the revival of the crusades. The first part of Humbert's work, excerpted below, includes his enthusiastic case for supporting the pope's plan to wage war against the Saracens (that is, the Muslims). Because his case reviews positions that dissented from the pope's, Humbert's historic work provides written evidence of peaceful movements that were sharply critical of the crusades. The peace movements of this era, although largely forgotten in contemporary histories of war and peace, also stood in contrast to the just war theory that Aquinas sketched in his* Summa Theologiae *(1268-1271).*

10. It should be noted that there are certain people given to hate, fleeing all labors for Christ, who are used to protesting the campaign that the church has taken up against the Saracens. They are like those ... who are used to passing judgment on everyone else, while they themselves know how to do nothing....

So with their dissent certain of these dissuade many from the path that leads to heaven, namely that of the crusade, and cause them to remain with them in their inertia. What is worse, they are like heretics who are used to making many jokes about those taking such a pilgrimage, and about those returning, and those who have sustained misfortunes.

11. There are certain of these protestors who say that it is not proper for the Christian religion to thus shed blood, even that of evil infidels. For Christ did not do so; to the contrary, when he was arrested [in the garden], he did not threaten (or resist), and he surrendered to him who judged him unjustly, as Peter says.

Nor did Christ teach this; on the contrary, he said to Peter, who wished to defend him, "Put your sword in its sheath" [Mt. 26:52]. Nor did the Apostles do this; on the contrary, they went rejoicing from their court appearances, since they were ready to suffer physical outrage for the name of Christ.

And not only did the Apostles teach this. For this reason Paul said to the Romans: "Do not defend yourselves, beloved. How much greater are they who do not resist?" [Cf. Romans 12]. And Peter: "Do not repay evil for evil, nor curse for curse, but bless those who curse you" [I Pet. 3:9].

Not even the holy martyrs [used violence]. On the contrary, Mauricius with his entire [Theban] legion of [Christian] soldiers did not resist their killers. And the same can be said for innumerable other martyrs, who indeed hurried to martyrdom and for God's sake were murdered and were considered like lambs for sacrifice.

The ancient Fathers did not even teach this [violence]. And there are innumerable authorities of holy authors, of popes and councils that appear to condemn wars. From these, then, it is concluded that the Christian religion, which ought to follow the example and doctrine of Christ and the saints, ought not to any degree enter into war, through which so much blood is spilled.

12. ... There are those who say that even if Saracen blood is not to be spared, nevertheless, the blood-spilling and death of Christians should be prevented. But in this type of pilgrimage against the Saracens innumerable [Christians] die, as much on the high seas as through disease, as in war, as from scarcity or excess of food, and not only common folk, but also kings and princes, and people very precious to Christendom [as in the case of King (Saint) Louis]. What wisdom is there in exposing such people to death and of emptying Christendom of so many and such good people?

13. Others say that when our people go across the sea against the Saracens, the conditions of war are much worse for us. For there we are very few in comparison to their multitude. Again, we are in a strange land, they in their own. Again, we are in an unaccustomed climate, they in an accustomed one. Again we have to use many kinds of strange food, but they are used to them. They know the terrain [the dangerous and winding passes] but we don't. We frequently lack supplies there; they, however, have an abundance. And so it appears to be tempting to God or to be a great lack of faith to enter such a conflict. Therefore, since wisdom is the highest necessity in war, it appears that wars of this type should never be attempted by Christians.

14. There are those who say that even if we ought to *defend* ourselves against the Saracens when they invade us, nevertheless, when they leave us in peace, it does not seem that we ought to invade them.

15. There are some who say: if we're supposed to wipe the Saracens off the earth, why not do the same to the Jews, and why don't we do the same to the Saracens whom we have under our power? Why don't we persecute with the same zeal other pagans who still inhabit the world? Why don't we also do the same to the Tartars and to the barbarian nations of this type who are all infidels?

16. Some say: "What use is there in this campaign against the Saracens? For they will not be led to conversion in this way, but more strongly provoked against the Christian faith. Again, when we conquer and kill them, we send them to hell, which appears to be against charity. Again, when we take their lands, we do not hold those who populate and cultivate them, since our own people do not want to remain in those parts. And thus it does not appear that there is any fruit, either spiritually, materially, or temporally, from this expedition."

17. Some say that it does not appear to be the will of God that Christians should proceed thus against the Saracens, because of the misfortunes that God has permitted and permits to happen to the Christians in pursuit of this campaign. For how could God permit that Saladin [in 1187] could so quickly take from us again almost the entire land taken with so much Christian blood and sweat? And that Emperor Frederick [Barbarossa], heading to the rescue, should perish in a puddle of water? And that King Louis of happy memory be captured in Egypt with his brother and almost all of the nobility of France [in 1250]? And again starting off on the Tunisian campaign was killed with his son? And that so many of the ships returning from there with the survivors were sunk in a storm off Sicily? And that such a huge army accomplished nothing, and the same for innumerable similar armies, if God favored such proceedings? ... It should be said that those who talk like this don't yet really understand God's ways.

30. The Twelve Conclusions of the Lollards

As followers of John Wyclif in the late 1300s, Lollards emphasized personal piety, divine election, and the authority of the Bible over all other sources for Christian living. The Twelve Conclusions, excerpted below, provide an early sketch of the main tenets of their beliefs, including opposition to such things as church hierarchy, transubstantiation, required confession, celibacy, indulgences, and the veneration of icons. Most important for our purposes is their conclusion that killing in secular war is wrong. The Lollards posted their conclusions on Westminster Hall and St. Paul's Church in London in 1395, and because neither parliament nor the church looked kindly upon the Lollards and their conclusions, in the early 1400s a royal statute called for their persecution by burning at the stake.

We poor men, treasurers of Christ and the apostles, declare to the [House of] Lords and Commons of the Parliament certain conclusions and truths for the reformation of the holy Church of England, the which has been blind and leprous for many years because of the doing of arrogant prelates borne up by the curried favors of the religious, who have become a great and onerous burden to the people here in England....

[10.] The tenth conclusion is that manslaughter in battle or by pretended law of justice for a temporal cause, without spiritual revelation, is expressly contrary to the New Testament, which is a law of grace and full of mercy. This conclusion is openly proved by the examples of Christ's preaching here on earth, for he specially taught man to love and have mercy on his enemies and not to slay them. The reason is this, that for the most part, when men fight, after the first blow, charity is broken; and whoever dies without charity goes on the high road to hell. And beyond this we know well that no cleric can by Scripture or by lawful reason remit the punishment of death for one mortal sin and not for another; but the law of mercy that is the New Testament forbids all manslaughter; in the Gospel, "it was said unto them, thou shalt not kill." The corollary is: it is indeed robbery of the poor people when lords purchase indulgences from punishment and guilt for those who aid their army to kill a Christian people in distant lands for temporal gain, just as we have seen knights who run into heathendom to get them a name for the slaughter of men; much more do they deserve ill thanks from the king of peace. For by meekness and patience was our faith multiplied, and Jesus Christ hates and threatens fighters and manslayers [when he says]: "He who lives by the sword, shall perish by the sword." ...

This is our embassy, which Christ commands us to pursue, very necessary at this time for several reasons. And although these matters have been briefly noted here, they are declared in another book at greater length, and many others as well, in our language, which we wish were accessible to all true Christian people. We pray God in his endless goodness to reform our church, which is all out of joint, to the perfection of the first beginning. Amen.

31. PETER CHELCICKY

On the Triple Division of Society

Peter Chelcicky (c. 1385-c. 1460) was a radical Christian separatist from Hussite Bohemia and an intellectual leader of the Czech Reformation. Chelcicky decried the violence of the Taborites, as well as the hierarchy of the Roman Catholic Church, and influenced Christian communalists and pacifists for years to come. The Unity of the Brethren and Leo Tolstoy are among those who were deeply influenced by Chelcicky's pointed treatises. Below is a short excerpt from his work titled "On the Triple Division of Society." It is included here because of its pioneering contrast between worldly power and the power of Jesus and his followers.

... either the secular powers are to be assured of salvation under the Law of Christ, and their path is to be shown them through the Law, or they have to be confirmed through something else, apart from the Law, as they are now falsely secured in Christ's faith by many of the clergy, in their writings. But these writings never have in them the fundamental sense of the scriptural passages on this subject that the Holy Spirit has inspired, although the clergy interpret them thus, to the deception of the princes and lords. For if power were supposed to be administered through Christ's faith by means of battles and punishments, and try to benefit Christ's faith with those battles and punishments, then why would Christ have abolished the Jewish Law and established a different, spiritual one? If he had wanted people to cut each other up, to hang, drown, and burn each other, and otherwise pour out human blood for his Law, then that Old Law could also have stood unchanged, with the same bloody deeds as before.

Therefore take from this what seems right to you, and reflect seriously on what basis you wish to give power, with its battles, punishments, and even cruelties, a path in Christ's faith. For there can be no power without cruelty. If power forgives, it prepares its own destruction, because none will fear it when they see that it uses love and not the force before which one trembles. Therefore the sweet fig, the fat olive, the grapevine, which gladden men, are none of them fit to wield power as is the cruel thorn, which has no qualms about grieving a man, striking him, flaying him as though stripping bark from a linden tree, throwing him into prison, and

killing him. Power will better prosper and endure by these means than by feeding the hungry, clothing the naked, healing the sick, without ever being able to wound and grieve, as would be the case if power stood according to love. There is thus a great difference between power and love.

… all lands need some sort of justice and peace, and without them people could not survive on earth. Because there are many nations in the world who do not have in themselves any virtue or knowledge of God, and who preserve no justice toward others, God, desiring that these many peoples continue to exist in the world, establishes kings and princes over them, so that they may be kept in peace by the latter's power, and so that every sort of injustice may find remedy, every complaint have recourse, through power. And that thanks to this power no one may wrong another nor deprive him by violence of his possessions, nor steal from him, nor disturb the boundaries.…

Power is thus the foundation of a country and preserves its stability against disruption. But the things of power are used only by the worst people, who are without faith or any virtue; through cruel punishments, power forcibly imposes such justice on evil people in external matters that those inclined to harm others do not undertake such action or, having begun, stop. Power does all this for its own benefit, so that over no man will its dominion be negated through injuries done by some to others.… But the justice and peace enforced by power are far removed from Christ's faith; people are safeguarded through the success of secular power only in their temporal good.…

But we must now speak more attentively about the order which Christ introduced as his own true one, according to the virtue and love of the Holy Spirit. For God, through a prophet, said of Christ that "He will rule my people of Israel." And Christ established his people under the Law of love and gave them a Law under which there are no complaints, in order that real spiritual order, similar to that of the angels in heaven, might exist in the people, as well as the peace of undivided union, like that of many limbs in one body, and also perfect justice, superior by far to that which stands on earth through the power of princes and to that which was brought about by the Old Law. For Christ rejected the justice of the Old Law, saying: "If your justice be not more abundant than that of the Jews, you will not enter the Kingdom of Heaven." When therefore we are established under mercy and without complaints, we have in ourselves and in our hearts the foundation of the higher justice that has love for all. Where that love prevails, it wishes good to all from its heart, and it not only wishes but does good to all, as it is able according to its strength, goods, and understanding. Nor does it wish, ask, or do evil to anybody; nor does it deprive, hinder, or torture anyone, but rather consoles and helps everyone according to its power and the other's need. Even more, that love suffers the injustice done by others, and in return loves, prays for, and benefits those who scorn or harm it.

Thus those who belong under that Law do not lodge complaints because, observing the kind of conduct described above, they abolish complaint on both sides: they do not harm anybody, so that no one can justly complain of them, and when they are wronged they suffer it. Turbulent complaints and quarrels do not therefore find any place among them, and with them secular courts are a shame and a sin, according to the words of the Apostle, who said: "And if there are courts among you, then already there is certainly sin among you" [I Cor. 6:7; q.v.]. The justice of such people is perfect, because they truly love God and their fellows, and seek peace with all in what is good. This sort of order, which prevails and should prevail among God's people, cannot be taught by any wisdom of this world, nor can it be enforced by any secular power, but it is born from the heart of good will,

a heart not in servitude as a slave but under love as a son. These people are taught by the Law of Truth written down in the Scriptures, and are led into this order by the Holy Spirit, according to the words of the Apostle, that those who are sons of God are governed by the Holy Spirit [Rom. 8:14]. The power of the world, on the other hand, can dispose of cases only on the basis of what can be established in them through witnesses, and it uses power to settle matters, all of which is far removed from the heart of good will. For he [who is outside of the order of love] has to be just toward others in spite of his own will, and he will not tell the truth against himself in a dispute until he is confronted with witnesses. Such a person is not just in his heart, but in the end he must be summoned by power against his will concerning the external injustice between him and his neighbor. It is for such unjust people that the secular power is established because they have neither the knowledge nor the fear of God in them, and because only the terrible power of the sword can become a law to their unjust and unfair wills.

This division in two parts, the secular order through power and Christ's order through love, sets them far apart, and it must be understood that these two orders cannot stand together so that both would be included under the name of one Christian faith. The order of Christ and the secular order cannot exist together, nor can Christ's order become the secular order. That which is done through power and under compulsion is one thing, while that which is done through love and good will is another, which stands on the words of Truth. It is thus clear that as far as secular power is from Christ's Truth written in his Law, so far is Christ's faith from the requirements of secular power. Power is not regulated by faith, and faith does not need power—as though faith were to have its fulfillment and preservation through power. As much as many goods, large bodies of soldiers, strong castles and towns, constitute the fullness of power, so God's wisdom and the strength of the Holy Spirit constitute the fullness and welfare of faith. Therefore faith, having spiritual power, prospers without the power that induces fear and drives people to do its bidding through terror and against their will; for the Apostle says, "You have not received the Spirit once more in fear, but you have received the Spirit of election as sons of God, in which Spirit we call out, 'Father, Father'" [Rom. 8:15; *q.v.*]. Therefore I consider those who belong under this order to be the spiritual Body of Christ. . . .

It will thus be seen that there is a grave confusion in the faith when the fullness of Christ's faith is ascribed to power—so that what power does, in ordinary nations that are outside the faith and the Law of God—so that this originally pagan affair becomes Christ's affair. So that power, now existing under the faith, should shed much blood in battles, inflict many punishments, according to the doctrine drawn by the priests from the Jewish Law, and, according to pagan laws, inflict many deaths, by hanging, drowning, burning, beheading, breaking on the wheel, letting people die in prisons, strangling them, plundering and otherwise tormenting them, and grinding the people down with violence. And because this power has been admitted under the faith, the things it does are things of Christ's faith. And so Christ, who shed his blood for the sinning people, has had his faith enriched with the secular power by the priest Sylvester, so that this power might, in the name of Christ, drain much blood from the people in battles and other acts of killing, and so that everything thus done by power should count as the richness of the Christian faith. But since we believe that Christ won us from the Devil's power through the weakness and humbleness of his Cross, we cannot agree that he causes our perfection in the faith through the secular power, as though power were more beneficial to us than faith. Nor can we believe that everything done by power in the ways we have described belongs to Christ's faith or is its fullness, unless all these acts be founded in Christ's Law; for only his Law is man's life, and only if all the works of power are commensurate with his Law can power be our life.

PART IV
Late Scholastic Period and the Reformation

32. Desiderius Erasmus

The Education of a Christian Prince

Desiderius Erasmus (c. 1469-1536) joined forces with Thomas More in blending humanistic principles of the Renaissance with classical Christian theology. As a Christian humanist, Erasmus satirized scholastic theology and favored an inner spirituality focused on Christ over external displays of public piety. He was the most famous scholar of his age and was known especially for his own edition of the Greek New Testament and his translation of the text into classical Latin. Although an early advocate of Luther, Erasmus eventually separated from Luther's movement and extolled humanistic reform within the Catholic Church.

His humanistic theology opposed the just war tradition as well as Christians who used force in the religious wars throughout Europe. Below is his anti-war writing in The Education of a Christian Prince *(1516), which appeared just three years after Niccolo Machiavelli had completed his famous writing on political realism,* The Prince. *As Machiavelli dedicated his work to a prince, Lorenzo Medici, Erasmus dedicated his writing to Prince Charles, soon to become Emperor Charles V.*

On Starting War

Although the prince will never make any decision hastily, he will never be more hesitant or more circumspect than in starting a war; other actions have their different disadvantages, but war always brings about the wreck of everything that is good, and the tide of war overflows with everything that is worst; what is more, there is no evil that persists so stubbornly. War breeds war; from a small war a greater is born, from one, two; a war that begins as a game becomes bloody and serious; the plague of war, breaking out in one place, infects neighbors too and, indeed, even those far from the scene.

The good prince will never start a war at all unless, after everything else has been tried, it cannot by any means be avoided. If we were all agreed on this, there would hardly ever be a war among men. In the end, if so pernicious a thing cannot be avoided, the prince's first concern should be to fight with the least possible harm to his subjects, at the lowest cost in Christian blood, and to end it as quickly as possible.

The truly Christian prince will first ponder how much difference there is between man, a creature born to peace and good will, and wild animals and beasts, born to pillage and war, and in addition how much difference there is between a man and a Christian. He should then consider how desirable, how honorable, how wholesome a thing is peace; on the other hand, how calamitous as well as wicked a thing is war, and how even the most just of wars brings with it a train of evils—if indeed any war can really be called just. Finally, putting aside all emotion, let him apply just a little reason to the problem by counting up the true cost of the war and deciding whether the object he seeks to achieve by it is worth that much, even if he were certain of victory, which does not always favor even the best of causes. Weigh up the anxieties, expense, dangers, the long and difficult preparations. You must call in a barbarian rabble, made up of all the worst scoundrels, and, if you want to be thought more of a man than the rival prince, you have to flatter and defer to these mercenaries, even after paying them, although there is no class of men more abject and indeed more damnable. Nothing is more precious to the good prince than that his people should be as virtuous as possible. But could there be a greater and more immediate threat to morality than war? The prince should pray for nothing more fervently than to see his subjects secure and prosperous in every way. But while he is learning to wage war, he is compelled to expose young men to all kinds of peril and to make countless orphans, widows, and childless old people, and to reduce countless others to beggary and misery, often in a single hour.

The world will have paid too high a price to make princes wise, if they insist on learning by experience how dreadful war is, so that as old men they can say: "I never thought war could be so pernicious." But, immortal God! what incalculable suffering has it cost the whole world to teach you that truism! One day the prince will realize that it was pointless to extend the frontiers of his kingdom and that what seemed at the outset to be a profitable enterprise has resulted in terrible loss to him; but before then many thousands of men have been either killed or maimed. These things would be better learned from books, from the reminiscences of old men, or from the tribulations of neighbors. For years now this prince or that has been fighting for this or that realm: how much greater are their losses than their gains!

The good prince will arrange these matters so that they will be settled once and for all. A policy adopted on impulse will seem satisfactory for as long as the impulse has hold of you; a policy adopted after due consideration, and which satisfies you as a young man, will satisfy you as an old man too. This is never more relevant than when starting a war.

Plato calls it sedition, not war, when Greek fights Greek, and advises that, if this does occur, the war must be fought with the utmost restraint. What word, then, do we think should be used when Christian draws the sword against Christian, since they are bound to one another by so many ties? What shall we say when the cruelest wars, prolonged for year after year, are fought on some slender pretext, some private quarrel, a foolish or immature ambition?

Some princes deceive themselves as follows: "Some wars are entirely just, and I have just cause for starting one." First, I will suspend judgment on whether any war is entirely just; but who is there who does not think his cause just? Amid so many shifts and changes in human affairs, amid the making and breaking of so many agreements and treaties, how could anyone not find a pretext, if any sort of pretext is enough to start a war?

It can be argued that papal laws do not condemn all war. Augustine too approves it somewhere. Again, St. Bernard praises some soldiers. True enough, but Christ himself, and Peter, and Paul, always teach the opposite. Why does their authority carry less weight than that of Augustine or Bernard? Augustine does not disapprove of war in one or two passages, but the whole philosophy of Christ argues against war. Nowhere do the Apostles approve it, and as for those holy doctors who are alleged to have approved of war in one or two passages, how many passages are there where they condemn and curse it? Why do we gloss over all these and seize on the bits which support our wickedness? In fact, anyone who examines the matter more closely will find that none of them approves of the kind of war which is usually fought today.

Certain arts, such as astrology and what is called alchemy, were banned by law because they were too close to fraud and were generally managed by trickery, even if it were possible for a man to practice them honestly. This would be far more justifiable in the case of wars, even if some of them might be just—although with the world in its present state, I am not sure that any of that kind could be found, that is, wars not caused by ambition, anger, arrogance, lust or greed. It often happens that the leaders of men, more extravagant than their private resources will allow, will take a chance to stir up war in order to boost their own finances, even by pillaging their own people. This is sometimes done by princes in collusion with one another, on some trumped-up pretext, in order to weaken the people and to strengthen their own position at the expense of the state. For these reasons the good Christian prince must be suspicious of all war, however just.

Some, of course, will protest that they cannot give up their rights. First of all, these "rights," if acquired by marriage, are largely the prince's private concern; how unjust it would be, while pursuing these rights, to inflict enormous damage on the people, and to pillage the whole kingdom bringing it to the brink of disaster, while pursuing some small addition to his own possessions. Why should it affect the population as a whole when one prince offends another in some trifling matter, and a personal one at that, connected with a marriage or something similar?

The good prince uses the public interest as a yardstick in every field, otherwise he is no prince. He has not the same rights over men as over cattle. Government depends to a large extent on the consent of the people, which was what created kings in the first place. If some dispute arises between princes, why do they not take it to arbitration instead? There are plenty of bishops, abbots, scholars, plenty of grave magistrates whose verdict would settle the matter more satisfactorily than all this carnage, pillaging, and universal calamity.

First of all, the Christian prince must be suspicious about his "rights," and then, if they are established beyond doubt, he must ask himself whether they have to be vindicated to the great detriment of the whole world. Wise men prefer sometimes to lose a case rather than pursue it, because they see that it will cost less to do so. I believe that the emperor would prefer to give up rather than pursue the rights to the ancient monarchy which jurists have conferred on him in their writings.

But, people will say, if no one pursues his rights will anything be safe? Let the prince pursue his rights by all means, if it is to the state's advantage, so long as his rights do not cost his subjects too dear. After all, is anything ever safe nowadays when everyone pursues his right to the letter? We see wars causing wars, wars following wars, and no limit or end to these upheavals. It is clear enough that nothing is achieved by these methods, and so other remedies should be tried. Even between the best of friends the relationship will not last long without some give and take. A husband often overlooks some fault in his wife to avoid disturbing their harmony. What can war produce except war? But consideration breeds consideration, and fairness, fairness.

The godly and merciful prince will also be influenced by seeing that the greatest part of all the great evils which every war entails falls on people unconnected with the war, who least deserve to suffer these calamities.

When the prince has made his calculations and reckoned up the total of all these woes (if indeed they could ever by reckoned up), then let him say to himself: "Shall I alone be the cause of so much woe? Shall so much human blood, so many widows, so many grief-stricken households, so many childless old people, so many made undeservedly poor, the total ruin of morality, law and religion: shall all this be laid at my door? Must I atone for all this before Christ?"

A prince cannot revenge himself on his enemy without first opening hostilities against his own subjects. The people will have to be pillaged, the soldier (not for nothing called "godless" by Virgil) will have to be called in. Citizens must be expelled from places where they have been accustomed to enjoy their property; citizens must be shut in in order to shut in the enemy. It happens all too often that we commit worse atrocities against our own citizens than against the enemy.

It is more difficult, and so more admirable, to build a fine city than to demolish one. We observe, however, that the most prosperous cities are built by private citizens, simple men, but are demolished by the wrath of princes. All too often we go to more trouble and expense to demolish a town than would be needed to build a new one, and we fight wars with such extravagance, at such expense, and with such enthusiasm and diligence, that peace could have been preserved for a tenth of all that.

The good prince should always seek the kind of glory that is bloodless and involves no harm to anyone. However well a war may turn out, there can be success only on one side, and on the other is ruin. Very often the victor too laments a victory bought too dearly.

If religion does not move us, or the misfortunes of the world, at least the honor of the Christian name should move us. What do we imagine the Turks and Saracens say about us, when they see that for hundreds of years the Christian princes have been utterly unable to agree among themselves? That peace never lasts, despite all the treaties? That there is no limit to the shedding of blood? And that there are fewer upheavals among the pagans than among those who preach perfect concord according to the doctrine of Christ?

How fleeting, how brief, how fragile is the life of a man, and how subject to misfortune, assailed already by a multitude of diseases and accidents, buildings which collapse, shipwrecks, earthquakes, lightning! We do not need to add war to our woes, and yet it causes more woe than all the others.

It used to be the task of preachers to root out all hostile feelings from the hearts of the common people. Nowadays the Englishman generally hates the Frenchman, for no better reason than that he is French. The Scot, simply because he is a Scot, hates the Englishman, the Italian hates the German, the Swabian the Swiss, and so on; province hates province, city hates city. Why do these ridiculous labels do more to separate us than the name of Christ, common to us all, can do to reconcile us?

Even if we allow that some wars are just, yet since we see that all mankind is plagued by this madness, it should be the role of wise priests to turn the minds of people and princes to other things. Nowadays we often see them as very firebrands of war. Bishops are not ashamed to frequent the camp; the cross is there, the body of Christ is there, the heavenly sacraments become mixed up in this worse than hellish business, and the symbols of perfect charity are brought into these bloody conflicts. Still more absurd, Christ is present in both camps, as if fighting against himself. It is not enough for war to be permitted between Christians; it must also be accorded the supreme honor.

If the teaching of Christ does not always and everywhere attack warfare, if my opponents can find one passage approving war, then let us fight as Christians. The Hebrews were allowed to engage in war, but with God's permission. On the other hand, our oracle, which reechoes again and again in the pages of the Gospel, argues against war—and yet we make war with more wild enthusiasm than the Hebrews. David was beloved of God for his other virtues, and yet he was forbidden to build his temple for the simple reason that he was a man of blood, that is, a warrior—God chose the peaceful Solomon for this task. If such things happened among the Jews, what will become of us Christians? They had only the shadow of Solomon, we have the true Solomon, Christ, the lover of peace, who reconciles all things in heaven and on earth.

However, I do not think, either, that war against the Turks should be hastily undertaken, remembering first of all that the kingdom of Christ was created, spread, and secured by very different means. Perhaps it should not be defended by other means than those which created and spread it. In addition we can see that wars of this kind have too frequently been made an excuse to fleece the Christian people—and then nothing else has been done. If it is done for the faith, this has been increased and enhanced by the suffering of martyrs, not by military force; if the battle is for power, wealth, and possessions, we must constantly consider whether such a course does not savor too little of Christianity. Indeed, judging by the people who fight this kind of war nowadays, it is more likely that we shall turn into Turks than that our efforts will make them into Christians. Let us first make sure that we are truly Christians ourselves and then, if it seems appropriate, let us attack the Turks.

But I have written a great deal elsewhere on the evils of war, and this is not the place to repeat it. I would merely exhort the princes who bear the name of Christian to set aside all trumped-up claims and spurious pretexts and apply themselves seriously and wholeheartedly to making an end of this long-standing and terrible mania among Christians for war, and to establishing peace and harmony among those who are united by so many common interests. To achieve this, they should exercise their talents, employ their resources, draw up common plans, and stretch every sinew. It is in this way that those whose ambition it is to be considered great will prove their greatness. Anyone who can achieve this will have performed a far more dazzling deed than if he had subdued all Africa by arms. Nor should it prove too difficult to achieve, if each of us will cease to urge his own case, if we will set aside our personal feelings and work for the common cause, if our guide is Christ, not the world. At present, while each man looks out for himself, while popes and bishops are preoccupied with power and wealth, while princes are made reckless by ambition or anger, and while everyone else finds it to his advantage to defer to them, we are running headlong into the storm with folly as our guide. But if we acted with common purpose in our common affairs, even our private business would prosper. At the moment, even the things we are fighting for are destroyed.

I have no doubt, most illustrious Prince, that you are of one mind with me, by your birth and by your upbringing at the hands of the best and most upright of men. For the rest, I pray that Christ, perfect and supreme, will continue to favor your noble enterprises. He left a kingdom unstained by blood and he would have it remain unstained. He rejoices to be called the Prince of Peace; may he do the same for you, that your goodness and wisdom may at last give us relief from these insane wars. Even the memory of past troubles will commend peace to us, and the misfortunes of days gone by will make your good deed doubly welcome.

33. CONRAD GREBEL

Letter to Thomas Müntzer

The Reformation era led by Martin Luther and John Calvin was one of the causal factors in the wars of sixteenth- and seventeenth-century Europe, including the Peasants' War in Germany (1524 to 1525), the Thirty Years War (1618 to 1648), and the English Civil War (1642 to 1660).

Like Augustine, both Luther and Calvin believed that under certain circumstances war could be just and should be executed by secular authorities. Both reformers, of course, also opposed the pope's use of the sword for religious reasons.

More particularly, Luther justified and called for the use of force against the peasants in their war against the secular authorities in southern Germany, especially when he believed that they were becoming too bloodthirsty and ferocious in their killings. Opposing Luther was Thomas Müntzer, the radical Protestant reformer who advocated the peasants' use of force.

Conrad Grebel (c. 1498-1526), one of the first Anabaptists and a founding member of the Swiss Brethren, took a stance against both Luther and Müntzer. Some of the clearest expressions of this radical Reformer, especially his principled opposition to violence, appear in his extant letters, including the one below to Thomas Müntzer.

Zurich, September 5, 1524

Peace, grace, and mercy from God our Father and Jesus Christ our Lord be with us all, Amen.

Dear Brother Thomas.

For the sake of God, please do not let it surprise you that we address you without title and ask you as a brother henceforth to exchange ideas with us by correspondence, and that we, unsolicited and unknown to you, have dared to initiate such future dialogue. God's Son, Jesus Christ, who offers himself as the only Master and Head to all who are to be saved and commands us to be brethren to all brethren and believers through the one common Word, has moved and impelled us to establish friendship and brotherhood and to bring the following theses to your attention. Also the fact that you have written two booklets on phony faith has led us to write to you. Therefore, if you will accept it graciously for the sake of Christ our Savior, it may, if God wills, serve and work for the good. Amen.

Just as our forefathers had fallen away from the true God and knowledge of Jesus Christ and true faith in him, from the one true common divine Word and from the godly practices of the Christian love and way, and lived without God's law and gospel in human, useless, unchristian practices and ceremonies and supposed they would find salvation in them but fell far short of it, as the evangelical preachers have shown and are still in part showing, so even today everyone wants to be saved by hypocritical faith, without fruits of faith, without the baptism of trial and testing, without hope and love, without true Christian practices, and wants to remain in all the old ways of personal vices and common antichristian ceremonial rites of baptism and the Lord's Supper, dishonoring the divine Word, but honoring the papal word and the antipapal preachers, which is not like or in accord with the divine Word. In respect of persons and all manner of seduction they are in more serious and harmful error than has ever been the case since the foundation of the world. We were also in the same aberration because we were only hearers and readers of the evangelical preachers who are responsible for all this error as our sins deserved. But after we took the Scripture in hand and con-sulted it on all kinds of issues, we gained some insight and became aware of the great and harmful shortcomings of the shepherds as well as our own in that we do not daily cry earnestly to God with constant sighs to be led out of the destruction of all godly living and out of human abominations and enter into true faith and practices of God. In all this, a false forbearance is what leads to the suppression of God's Word and its mixture with the human. Indeed, we say it brings harm to all and does disservice to all the things of God—no need for further analysis and detail.

While we were noting and lamenting these things, your writing against false faith and baptism was brought out here to us and we are even better informed and strengthened and were wonderfully happy to have found someone who is of a common Christian mind with us and ventures to show the evangelical preachers their shortcomings—how in all the major issues they practice false forbearance and set their own opinions and even those of antichrist above God and against God, not as befits messengers of God to act and to preach. Therefore we ask and admonish you as a brother in the name, power, Word, Spirit, and salvation which comes to all Christians through Jesus Christ our Master and Savior, to seek earnestly to preach only God's Word unflinchingly, to establish and defend only divine practices, to esteem as good and right only what can be found in definite clear Scripture, and to reject, hate, and curse all the schemes, words, practices, and opinions of all men, even your own....

March forward with the Word and create a Christian church with the help of Christ and his rule such as we find instituted in Matthew 18 and practiced in the epistles. Press on in earnest with common prayer and fasting, in accord with faith and love without being commanded and compelled. Then God will help you and your lambs to all purity, and the chanting and the tablets will fall away. There is more than enough wisdom and counsel in the Scripture on how to teach, govern, direct and make devout all classes and all men. Anyone who will not reform or believe and strives against the Word and acts of God persists therein, after Christ and his Word and rule have been preached to him, and he has been admonished with the three witnesses before the church, such a man we say on the basis of God's Word shall not be put to death but regarded as a heathen and publican and left alone.

Moreover, the gospel and its adherents are not to be protected by the sword, nor [should] they [protect] themselves, which as we have heard through our brother is what you believe and maintain. True believing Christians are sheep among wolves, sheep for the slaughter. They must be baptized in anguish and tribulation, persecution, suffering, and death, tried in fire, and must reach the fatherland of eternal rest not by slaying the physical but the spiritual. They use neither worldly sword nor war, since killing has ceased with them entirely, unless indeed we are still under the old law, and even there (as far as we can know) war was only a plague after they had once conquered the Promised Land. No more of this....

Zurich, Sent with
Letter of September 5, 1524

Dearly beloved brother Thomas.

... Hujuff's brother writes that you have preached against the princes, that they should be combated with the fist. If that is true, or if you intend to defend war, the tablets, chanting or other things for which you do not find a clear word (as you do not find for any of these aforementioned points), I admonish you by the salvation common to all of us that if you will desist from them and all opinions of your own now and henceforth, you will become completely pure, for you satisfy us on all other points better than anyone else in this German and other lands.... God grant you and us grace, for our shepherds are also fierce and enraged against us, reviling us from the public pulpit as rascals and *Satanas in angelos lucis conversos* [Satans turned into angels of light]. In time we too will see persecution come upon us through them. Therefore pray to God for us. Once more we admonish you, because we love and respect you so sincerely for the clarity of your words, and we confidently venture to write to you: Do not act, teach, or establish anything according to human opinion, your own or borrowed, repeal what has been established, and teach only the clear Word and rites of God, including the rule of Christ, the unadulterated baptism and unadulterated Supper, which we touched upon in our first letter and upon which you are better informed than a hundred of us.

34. JUAN LUIS VIVES

Introduction to Wisdom

Juan Luis Vives (1492-1540) was a Spanish humanist who was fired from his teaching post at Oxford after he sided with Catherine of Aragon, one of his former pupils, in the famous controversy surrounding Henry VIII's decision to divorce her. Vives was known not only for his efforts in educational reform—his writings called for increasing education for women— but also for his ethical writings against poverty and for peace with justice. Like Erasmus, Vives taught Christian nonviolence, and below is an excerpt from his Introduction to Wisdom, *which includes a series of pithy arguments for peace. In the same year that Vives published this book—1524—the radical Protestant reformer Andreas Karlstadt published a work calling upon the German peasants to arm themselves against their "godless" rulers.*

349. A great likeness among men can be observed in body and mind, for we have all been brought into this world under the same jurisdiction, made for a common society of life. For the lat-

ter's preservation, Nature has proclaimed this law, "Let no man do to another what he does not want done to himself."

350. He who restored our fallen nature has professed this one doctrine to be His, both explicating and illustrating it Himself.

351. In order that He might elevate human nature to the likeness of God up to the highest point possible, He commanded us not only to love one another, but also to love those who hate us.

352. Thus, we will be like the Father of heaven Who sincerely loves His enemies, as He declares by His many benefits pursuing them. He hates no one whatever.

353. Such is the condition of men that they want others to bear good will to them, even those whom they resent.

354. That most wise Master and Author of our life has given us this one instruction for living: that is, to love one another. By this rule, we might skillfully lead a most blessed life, without need of any other law.

355. Nothing is more blessed than to love: therefore God and His angels, who love all things, are most blessed.

356. Nothing is more wretched than to hate: for which reason the devils are most miserable.

357. True love balances everything equally. Where it thrives, no man seeks preferment. No man robs someone he loves, by accounting things to be his which are his friend's. Love contends not

with his dear brother, nor does he think himself afflicted with any injury by him....

388. God introduced us to peace, concord, and love.

389. The devil (that most expert schemer) invented parties, factions, private profits, and other damning action such as dissensions, brawls, contentions, and wars.

390. God, willing our salvation, sows among us benevolence; the devil, willing our destruction, sows enmities.

391. Fellowship unites in small issues; discord dissipates in great concerns.

392. They who study to bring peace among men, and to preserve tranquility safe and sound, shall be called the children of God, as Christ testifies [Mt. 5:9]. These are the true peacemakers of whom he spoke. Contrarily, those who sow discord and destroy charity among men are sons of the devil.

393. The greatest enmity, in which man surpasses the ferocity of wild animals, is war, a matter of inhumanity which is best described by the term "beastly."

394. How Nature herself abhors war! For she brought forth man into this world unarmed, and shaped him to meekness and to sociability. God also abhors the same, for He willed and commanded mutual love between man and man.

395. Man cannot war against man, nor harm another, without serious offense....

35. BROTHERLY UNION OF A NUMBER OF CHILDREN OF GOD CONCERNING SEVEN ARTICLES (THE SCHLEITHEIM CONFESSION)

In 1527 Anabaptist leaders gathered together at Schleitheim, Switzerland, and adopted a doctrinal confession of faith, most likely written by the reformer Michael Sattler, as a way of seeking to identify their movement against the rest of Protestantism. This confession stressed the significance of adult baptism, the use of the ban as a form of excommunication, the separation of Christians from an evil world, and communion as a memorial to Jesus Christ. In addition, the Swiss Brethren made sure to emphasize that Christian discipleship demanded the practice of nonviolence.

May joy, peace, mercy from our Father, through the atonement of the blood of Christ Jesus, together with the gifts of the Spirit—who is sent by the Father to all believers to [give] strength and consolation and constance in all tribulation until the end, Amen, be with all who love God and all children of light, who are scattered everywhere, wherever they might have been placed by God our Father, wherever they might be gathered in unity of spirit in one God and Father of us all; grace and peace of heart be with you all. Amen.

Beloved brothers and sisters in the Lord: first and primordially we are always concerned for your consolation and the assurance of your conscience (which was sometimes confused), so that you might not always be separated from us as aliens and by right almost completely excluded, but that you might turn to the true implanted members of Christ, who have been armed through patience and the knowledge of self, and thus be again united with us in the power of a godly Christian spirit and zeal for God.

It is manifest with what manifold cunning the devil has turned us aside, so that he might destroy and cast down the work of God, which in us mercifully and graciously has been partially begun. But the true Shepherd of our souls, Christ, who has begun such in us, will direct and teach the same unto the end, to His glory and our salvation, Amen.

Dear brothers and sisters, we who have been assembled in the Lord at Schleitheim on the Randen make known, in points and articles, unto all that love God, that as far as we are concerned, we have been united to stand fast in the Lord as obedient children of God, sons and daughters, who have been and shall be separated from the world in all that we do and leave undone, and (the praise and glory be to God alone) uncontradicted by all the brothers, completely at peace. Herein we have sensed the unity of the Father and of our common Christ as present with us in their Spirit. For the Lord is a Lord of peace and not of quarrelling, as Paul indicates. So that you understand at what points this occurred, you should observe and understand [what follows]: …

The articles which we have dealt with, and in which we have been united, are these: baptism, ban, the breaking of bread, separation from abomination, shepherds in the congregation, the sword, the oath.…

II. We have been united as follows concerning the ban. The ban shall be employed with all those who have given themselves over to the Lord, to walk after [Him] in His commandments; those who have been baptized into the one body of Christ, and let themselves be called brothers or sisters, and still somehow slip and fall into error and sin, being inadvertently overtaken. The same [shall] be warned twice privately and the third time be publicly admonished before the entire congregation according to the command of Christ (Mt. 18). But this shall be done according to the ordering of the Spirit of God before the breaking of bread, so that we may all in one spirit and in one love break and eat from one bread and drink from one cup.…

IV. We have been united concerning the separation that shall take place from the evil and the wickedness which the devil has planted in the world, … that we have no fellowship with them, and do not run with them in the confusion of their abominations. So it is; since all who have not entered into the obedience of faith and have not united themselves with God so that they will to do His will, are a great abomination before God, therefore nothing else can or really will grow or spring forth from them than abominable things. Now there is nothing else in the world and all creation than good or evil, believing and unbelieving, darkness and light, the world and those who are [come] out of the world, God's temple and idols, Christ and Belial, and none will have part with the other.

To us, then, the commandment of the Lord is also obvious, whereby He orders us to be and to become separated from the evil one, and thus He will be our God and we shall be His sons and daughters.

Further, He admonishes us therefore to go out from Babylon and from the earthly Egypt, that we may not be partakers in their torment and suffering, which the Lord will bring upon them.

From all this we should learn that everything which has not been united with our God in Christ is nothing but an abomination which we should shun. By this are meant all popish and repopish works and idolatry, gatherings, church attendance, winehouses, guarantees and commitments of unbelief, and other things of the kind, which the world regards highly, and yet which are carnal or flatly counter to the command of God, after the pattern of all the iniquity which is in the world. From all this we shall be separated and have no part with such, for they are nothing but abominations, which cause us to be hated before our Christ Jesus, who has freed us from the servitude of the flesh and fitted us for the service of God and the Spirit whom He has given us.

Thereby shall also fall away from us the diabolical weapons of violence—such as sword, armor, and the like, and all of their use to protect friends or against enemies—by virtue of the word of Christ: "you shall not resist evil." ...

VI. We have been united as follows concerning the sword. The sword is an ordering of God outside the perfection of Christ. It punishes and kills the wicked, and guards and protects the good. In the law the sword is established over the wicked for punishment and for death, and the secular rulers are established to wield the same.

But within the perfection of Christ only the ban is used for the admonition and exclusion of the one who has sinned, without the death of the flesh, simply the warning and the command to sin no more.

Now many, who do not understand Christ's will for us, will ask: whether a Christian may or should use the sword against the wicked for the protection and defense of the good, or for the sake of love.

The answer is unanimously revealed: Christ teaches and commands us to learn from Him, for He is meek and lowly of heart and thus we shall find rest for our souls. Now Christ says to the woman who was taken in adultery, not that she should be stoned according to the law of His Father (and yet He says, "what the Father commanded me, that I do") but with mercy and forgiveness and the warning to sin no more, says: "Go, sin no more." Exactly thus should we also proceed, according to the rule of the ban.

Second, is asked concerning the sword: whether a Christian shall pass sentence in disputes and strife about worldly matters, such as the unbelievers have with one another. The answer: Christ did not wish

to decide or pass judgment between brother and brother concerning inheritance, but refused to do so. So should we also do.

Third, is asked concerning the sword: whether the Christian should be a magistrate if he is chosen thereto. This is answered thus: Christ was to be made king, but He fled and did not discern the ordinance of His Father. Thus we should also do as He did and follow after Him, and we shall not walk in darkness. For He Himself says: "Whoever would come after me, let him deny himself and take up his cross and follow me." He Himself further forbids the violence of the sword when He says: "The princes of this world lord it over them, etc., but among you it shall not be so." Further Paul says, "Whom God has foreknown, the same he has also predestined to be conformed to the image of His Son," etc. Peter also says, "Christ has suffered (not ruled) and has left us an example, that you should follow after in his steps."

Lastly one can see in the following points that it does not befit a Christian to be a magistrate: the rule of the government is according to the flesh, that of the Christians according to the spirit. Their houses and dwelling remain in this world, that of the Christians is in heaven. Their citizenship is in this world, that of the Christians is in heaven. The weapons of their battle and warfare are carnal and only against the flesh, but the weapons of Christians are spiritual, against the fortification of the devil. The worldly are armed with steel and iron, but Christians are armed with the armor of God, with truth, righteousness, peace, faith, salvation, and with the Word of God. In sum: as Christ our Head is minded, so also must be minded the members of the body of Christ through Him, so that there be no division in the body, through which it would be destroyed....

Dear Brothers and Sisters in the Lord: these are the articles which some brothers previously had understood wrongly and in a way not conformed to the true meaning. Thereby many weak consciences were confused, whereby the name of God has been grossly slandered, for which reason it was needful that we should be brought to agreement in the Lord, which has come to pass. To God be praise and glory! ...

36. JAKOB HUTTER

Letter to Johann Kuna von Kunstadt

Jacob Hutter (c. 1500-1536) was a leader of an Anabaptist movement based mostly in Moravia and marked by its devotion to communal living. In 1535 the Hutterites were expelled from Moravia, even though they were peaceful disciples of Jesus, and became refugees on the move. Below is the letter that Hutter penned to the governor of Moravia, Johann Kuna von Kunstadt, protesting the expulsion and warning him of his disobedience to God. Most striking about this letter is its description of both the nonviolent behavior of the Hutterites and their belief that an avenging God will extract blood from the secular rulers who sent them into exile. The letter was not warmly received, and Hutter was eventually imprisoned, tortured, and burned at the stake for refusing to recant his beliefs.

We are brothers who love God and His truth, we are witnesses of our Lord Jesus Christ, and we have been driven out of many countries for the sake of God's Name. We arrived here in Moravia where we have been living together under the Lord Marshal through God's protection. To God alone we give praise forever.

This letter is to let you know, dear Governor of Moravia, that we received the order delivered by your servants. We already answered you by word of mouth and now want to do it also in writing. This is our answer: We have left the world and all its wrong and godless ways. We believe in God the Almighty and in His Son, Jesus Christ, who will protect us from evil forevermore. We have given ourselves to God the Lord in order to live according to His divine will and keep His commandments in the way Jesus Christ showed us.

Because we serve Him, do His will, keep His commandments, and leave behind all sin and evil, we are persecuted and despised by the whole world and robbed of all our goods. The same was done to all the men of God, to the prophets, and to Christ Himself. King Ferdinand in particular has put many of our innocent brothers and sisters to death. He has robbed us of our homes and all our goods and persecuted us terribly. But through God's grace we were able to move to this country and have lived here for a time, recently under the Lord Marshal. We have not troubled or harmed anyone and have lived faithfully in the fear of God; everybody will confirm this. But now even the Marshal has given us notice and forced us to leave our houses and property.

So we now find ourselves out in the wilderness, under the open sky on a desolate heath. This we accept patiently, praising God that He has made us worthy to suffer for His Name. Yet we feel great pain of heart for you, that you treat God's faithful children so cruelly. We cry to Him about your wretchedness. The enormous injustice increases daily. Day and night we plead with God the Lord to protect us from evil; we trust Him to lead us through, according to His will and mercy. And God will surely do so; He is our Captain and Protector and will fight for us. The Prophets Isaiah and Esdras foretold that all who turn away from evil, all who love God from their hearts, who fear and serve Him and keep His commandments, are bound to be robbed and driven from their homes. This shows that we are fellow heirs of His glory, that He loves us and is pleased with us, and that we belong to the believers. Therefore we quietly suffer all this, and our hearts are comforted by His Holy Spirit.

But woe to all who persecute, expel, and hate us without cause, simply because we stand for God's truth! Their condemnation and punishment is approaching and will overtake them terrifyingly, here and in Eternity. According to His holy prophets, God will call the persecutors most terribly to account for the suffering and innocent blood of His children.

Now since you have commanded us to leave without delay, we give you this answer: We know of no place to go. We are surrounded by the King's lands. In every direction we would walk straight into the jaws of robbers and tyrants, like sheep cast among ravenous wolves. Besides, we have among us many widows and orphans, many sick people and helpless little children who are unable to walk or travel. Their fathers and mothers were murdered by that tyrant Ferdinand, an enemy of divine justice. He also robbed them of their goods. These poor and weak ones are entrusted to us by God the Almighty, who commands us to feed, clothe, and house them, and in every way to serve them in love. So we cannot leave them behind or send them away—truly, may God protect us from ever doing that! We dare not disobey God for the sake of man's command, though it cost our life. We must obey God rather than men.

We have not had time to sell our homes and possessions. They were earned by honest, hard labor, by the sweat of our brows, and rightly belong to us before God and men. We also need time because of the sick, the widows and orphans, and the small children. Praise God, there are not just few but many of these helpless ones among us, about as many as able-bodied people. Now, by God's will, we are out on the open heath, harming no one. We do not want to hurt or wrong anyone, not even our worst enemy, be it Ferdinand or anyone else. All our doing, our words and way of life, are there for all men to see. Rather than knowingly wrong a man to the value of a penny, we would let ourselves be robbed of a hundred florins; rather than strike our worst enemy with the hand—to say nothing of spears, swords, and halberds as the world does—we would let our own lives be taken.

As anyone can see, we have no physical weapons, neither spears nor muskets. No, we want to show by our word and deed that men should live as true followers of Christ, in peace and unity and in God's truth and justice. We are not ashamed to give an account of ourselves to anyone. It does not trouble us that many evil things are said about us, for Christ foretold all this. It has been the lot of all believers, of Christ himself, and of all His apostles, from the beginning.

It is rumored that we took possession of the field with so many thousands, as if we were going to war, but only a callow, lying scoundrel could talk like that. We lament that there are so few believers (such as we truly are). We wish all the world lived like us; we would like to convince and turn all men to this faith, for that would mean the end of warfare and injustice.

In our present situation we just do not know how we can leave the country unless God the Lord in Heaven shows us where to go. You cannot simply deny us a place on the earth or in this country. For the earth is the Lord's, and all that is in it belongs to our God in Heaven. Besides, even if we did agree to go, and planned to do so, we might not be able to keep our word, for we are in God's hands and He does with us whatever His will is. Perhaps God wants us to remain in this country to test our faith. This we do not know, but we trust in the eternal and true God.

On the other hand, it is a fact that we are being persecuted and driven out, so we tell you that if the almighty God showed us enough cause to leave the country and move somewhere else, if He gave us good proof that this were His will, we would do it gladly, without waiting for any command from men. Once God's will about where we should go is clear to us, we will not hesitate. We will not and cannot disobey His divine will; neither can you, even though you may think you can. God the Almighty may suddenly reveal to us, even overnight, that we should leave you. Then we will not delay but be prepared to do His will—either to leave or to die. Perhaps you are not worthy to have us among you any longer.

Therefore woe to you Moravian lords forever, that you have given in to Ferdinand, the awful tyrant and enemy of divine truth, that you have agreed to drive those who love and fear God out of your lands. You fear a weak, mortal man more than the living, eternal, and almighty God. You are willing to expel and ruthlessly persecute the children of God, old and young, even the Lord's widows and orphans in their need and sorrow, and to deliver them up to plunder, fear, great suffering, and extreme poverty. It is as if you strangled them with your own hands. We would rather be murdered for the Lord's sake than witness such misery inflicted on innocent, God-fearing hearts. You will have to pay dearly for it and will have no more excuse than Pilate, who also did not want to crucify and kill the Lord Jesus. Yet when the Jews threatened him (by God's plan), fear of the Emperor made him condemn an innocent man. You do the same, using the King as your excuse.

God has made it known through the mouth of His prophets that He will avenge innocent blood with terrible might on all who stain their hands with it. Therefore you will earn great misfortune and distress, deep sorrow—indeed, eternal torment. They are ordained for you by God in Heaven, in this life and forever. In the name of our Lord Jesus Christ, we declare that this will certainly happen, and you will soon see that we have spoken the truth. This we declare to you and to all who sin against God.

We wish you could escape this judgment and that you and all men might be saved with us and inherit eternal life. For the sake of God we plead with you to accept His word and our warning and to take them to heart, for we testify to what we know and to the truth of God. And we do this from a pure fear of God and because we love God and all men.

And now we entrust ourselves to the protection of the eternal Lord. May He be gracious to us and forever dwell with us, through Jesus Christ. Amen. As for you, may God the Lord allow you to understand His fatherly warning and discipline, and may He be merciful to you through our Lord Jesus Christ. His will be done. Amen.

37. PETER RIEDEMANN

Account of Our Religion, Doctrine and Faith

Peter Riedemann (1506-1556) was the most important intellectual leader of the early Hutterites. During various imprisonments resulting from his Anabaptism, Riedemann penned several versions of Account of Our Religion, Doctrine and Faith, *excerpted below. Riedemann's explication of Hutterite theology, including its opposition to warfare, remains the Hutterites' confession of faith even today.*

Concerning Governmental Authority

Governmental authority is appointed and ordained by God as a rule of his anger for the discipline and punishment of the evil and profligate nation. Therefore doth Paul name it a servant of God's vengeance, by means of which God will avenge himself on their sins and bring the evil they have done upon their own head, that their wickedness might not continue to spread and that the whole earth might not on their account become blemished and unclean. Therefore one should be obedient and subject to rulers as ordained by God for the purpose of protection, in so far as they do not attack the conscience or command what is against God. As Peter exhorteth us saying, "Submit yourselves to every ordinance of man for the Lord's sake: whether it be to the king, as supreme; or unto the governors, as unto them that are sent by him." And Paul saith, "Remind them to be subject to the principalities and powers, to obey magistrates, to be ready to every good work."

Therefore is one rightly obedient and subject to them, and the more diligent one is therein, the better is it and the more pleasing to God. For whosoever resisteth this, resisteth the ordinance of God. Where, however, the rulers command and act against God, there one must leave their command undone, and obey God rather than man. For the conscience hath been set free and is reserved for God alone, that he and no human being may be Lord of the same and rule over, teach and direct it whithersoever it pleaseth him. Therefore wherever the government presumeth to lay hands upon the conscience and to control the faith of man, there it is robbing God of what is his. Therefore it is wrong to obey it in this. Now, since the office of government is an ordinance and establishment of God and because it hath been appointed and ordained by God, within its own limits it is right and good, but where it is abused, this same misuse is wrong. The office, nevertheless, remaineth as it was ordained. Therefore is the office to be honored. For, even though godless men fill it, the office is not thereby annulled. And God permitteth this to the godless for the greater punishment of the people. But just as a godless government is given to the nation by God as a punishment, even so is a disobedient nation given to the godless government, that they might tear and devour one another and at last be consumed together.

Why Governmental Authority Hath Been Ordained

Governmental authority hath been ordained by God because of the turning aside of the people, in that they turned away from him and walked according to the flesh. For God saith, "My Spirit shall not always strive with men, for they are flesh." For this reason, after the flood, he ordained governmental authority for them to be a rod of the anger and vengeance of God, to shed the blood of those who have shed blood....

Therefore the government is a picture, sign and reminder of man's departure from God, and ought well to be to all men an urge to retire within themselves and to consider to what they have come and to what they have fallen, that they might with all the more haste turn back to God to receive again the grace they had lost. There are few, however, who consider thus, therefore do they remain in their sins.

Over and above all this, because governmental authority is a servant of God's anger and vengeance, as long as it hath being it indicateth that God's anger and wrath is still over sinners and is not at an end.

Whether Rulers Can Also Be Christians

Here beginneth a quite other kingdom and reign, therefore that which is old must stop and come to an end, as also the symbol of the Jewish royal house signifieth, which was there until Christ came, as the scriptures declare, "The scepter shall not depart from Judah until the hero, Christ, shall come." Therefore it is ended, stopped and broken in Christ. He now sitteth upon the throne of his father, David, and hath become a king of all true Israelites. He also hath now begun a new regime that is not like the old one and is not supported by the temporal sword.

Now, since the regime of the Jews, who until then were God's people, came to an end in Christ, ceased and was taken from them, it is clear that it should be no more in Christ, but it is his desire to rule over Christians with his spiritual sword alone. That the power of the temporal sword was taken from the Jews and hath passed to the heathen signifieth that from henceforth the people of God ought no longer to use the temporal sword and rule therewith; but ought to be ruled and led by the one Spirit of Christ alone. And that it hath gone to the heathen signifieth that those who do not submit themselves to the Spirit of Christ—that is, all heathen and unbelievers—should be disciplined and punished therewith. Therefore hath governmental authority its place outside Christ, but not in Christ.

Thus God in Christ, alone, is king and commander of his people, as it is written, "God hath set a ruler over every people, but over Israel he alone is Lord." Even as he is a spiritual king hath he also spiritual servants and wieldeth a spiritual sword—both he and all his servants—that pierceth soul and spirit.

Now because the Son was appointed by the Father, as it is written, "I have set my king upon my holy hill of Zion," and given not in anger like the other but in blessing, and hath become a source of blessing to us all (as, indeed, it had been promised that in him all peoples should be blessed), therefore, even as the other was ordained to shed the blood of him who sheddeth a man's blood, this king hath been ordained to preserve the souls of men; as the other to take vengeance on evil, this to recompense it with good; as the other to hate the enemy, this is ordained to love. Thus is Christ King of all kings, and at the same time the opposite of all the rulers of this world; therefore doth he say, "My kingdom is not of this world: if my kingdom were of this world then would my servants fight for me."

Thus, he setteth up quite a different kingdom and rule and desireth that his servants submit themselves to it and become like him; therefore doth he say to them, "The princes of the world are called gracious lords, and the powerful exercise dominion over the people, but it shall not be so among you: but let him who is the greatest among you be your minister." Thus the glory of Christ and of his servants consisteth in the putting off of all worldly glory. And the more one putteth this aside, the more glorious doth he become in Christ's kingdom, as the word showeth, "Whosoever exalteth himself shall be abased, and whosoever humbleth himself shall be exalted."

Now because in Christ our King is the full blessing of God—yea, he is himself the blessing—all that was given in wrath must come to an end and cease in him, and hath no part in him. But governmental authority was given in wrath, and so it can neither fit itself into nor belong to Christ. Thus no Christian is a ruler and no ruler is a Christian, for the child of blessing cannot be the servant of wrath. Thus, in Christ not the temporal, but the spiritual sword doth rule over men, and so ruleth that they deserve not the temporal sword, therefore also have no need of it....

Concerning Warfare

Now since Christ, the Prince of Peace, hath prepared and won for himself a kingdom, that is a Church, through his own blood; in this same kingdom all worldly warfare hath an end, as was promised aforetime, "Out of Zion shall go forth the law, and the word of the Lord from Jerusalem, and shall judge among the heathen and shall draw many peoples, so that they shall beat their swords into ploughshares and their lances or spears into pruning hooks, sickles and scythes, for from thenceforth nation shall not lift up sword against nation, nor shall they learn war anymore."

Therefore a Christian neither wages war nor wields the worldly sword to practice vengeance, as Paul also exhorteth us saying, "Dear brothers, avenge not yourselves, but rather give place unto the wrath of God, for the Lord saith, Vengeance is mine; I will repay it." Now if vengeance is God's and not ours, it ought to be left to him and not practiced or exercised by ourselves. For, since we are Christ's disciples, we must show forth the nature of him who, though he could, indeed, have done so, repaid not evil with evil. For he could, indeed, have protected himself against his enemies, the Jews, by striking down with a single word all who wanted to take him captive.

But though he might well have done this, he did not himself and would not permit others to do so. Therefore he said to Peter, "Put up again thy sword into its place." Here one can see how our King setteth out with a powerful host against his enemy; how he defeateth the enemy and how he taketh vengeance: in that he taketh Malchus' ear, that had been struck off, and putteth it on again. And he who did this saith, "Whosoever will be my disciple, let him take his cross upon him and follow me."

Now, therefore, Christ desireth that we should act even as he did, so he commandeth us, saying, "It hath been said to the men of old, 'An eye for an eye, and a tooth for a tooth,' but I say unto you, that ye resist not evil: but whosoever shall smite them on thy right cheek, turn and offer to him the other also." Here it is clearly to be seen that one ought neither to avenge oneself nor to go to war, but rather offer his back to the strikers and his cheeks to them that pluck off the hair—that is, suffer with patience and wait upon God, who is righteous, and who will repay it.

If one should say that David, who was loved by God, and other saints, went to war, and therefore one should still do so when one hath right and justification thereto, we say, "No." That David and other saints did this, but that we ought not so to do, can be seen by all from the words quoted above, "To them of old is said, 'An eye for an eye and a tooth for a tooth,' but I say unto you, that ye resist not evil!" Here Christ maketh the distinction himself. There is therefore no need for many words, for it is clear that Christians can neither go to war nor practice vengeance. Whosoever doeth this hath forsaken and denied Christ and Christ's nature....

Concerning the Making of Swords

Since, as hath been said above, Christians should beat their swords into ploughshares and take up arms no more—still less can they make the same, for they serve for naught else than to slay, harm and destroy men—and Christ hath not come to destroy men …

Now, since Christians must not use and practice such vengeance, neither can they make the weapons by which such vengeance and destruction may be practiced by others, that they be not partakers of other men's sins. Therefore we make neither swords, spears, muskets nor any such weapons.

What, however, is made for the benefit and daily use of man, such as bread knives, axes, hoes and the like, we both can and do make. Even if one were to say, "But one could therewith harm and slay others," still they are not made for the purpose of slaying and harming, so there is naught to prevent our making them. If they should ever be used to harm another, we do not share the harmer's guilt, so let him bear the judgment himself.

38. MENNO SIMONS

Reply to False Accusations

Menno Simons (1496-1561) was a parish priest in Dutch Friesland, but after many conversations with Melchiorites, the nonviolent followers of Melchior Hoffman, who preached adult baptism throughout the Netherlands, Simons left the priesthood, received adult baptism, and spent the remainder of his life leading the Dutch Anabaptists (or, as they would be later called, the Mennonites). Simons's theology, like the Swiss Brethren's, stressed adult baptism, communion as a symbolic memorial, use of the ban, a connectional church structure, and nonviolence. In "Reply to False Accusations" (1552), excerpted below, Simons defends his followers from charges leveled by their critics, including the accusation that the Mennonites, like the followers of Thomas Müntzer, embraced violence as a means of social transformation.

I. In the first place, they complain and accuse us of being Münsterites; and warn all people to beware of us and take an example from those of Münster.

Answer. We do not like to reprove and judge those who are already reproved and judged of God and man; yet since we are assailed so fiercely with this matter and without basis in truth, therefore we would say this much in defense of all of us—that we consider the doctrine and practice of those of Münster in regard to king, sword, rebellion, retaliation, vengeance, polygamy, and the visible kingdom of Christ on earth a new Judaism and a seductive error, doctrine, and abomination, far removed from the Spirit, Word and example of Christ. Behold, in Christ Jesus, we lie not.…

In short, we herewith testify and confess before God, before you, and before the whole world that we from our inmost hearts detest the errors of the Münsterites, as well as every other sect which is at variance with the Spirit, Word, and ordinance for the Lord. Before God in Christ Jesus, we neither seek nor desire anything more than that we may turn the whole world which lies in sin from its wickedness to the right way, and that we may by the Word, grace, and power of the Lord deliver many souls from the kingdom of the devil and gain them to the kingdom of Christ; that we may lead a pious, humble, and godly life in Christ Jesus, and that we may glorify His great and glorious name forever. We firmly believe and confess that all false doctrine, idolatry, ungodliness, and sin are of the devil and that the reward of sin is everlasting death. Therefore we labor diligently and earnestly, and desire, the Lord knows, to be pious and to fear God. And we poor people are so lamentably reviled and frequently and in many places even slain because of this.

II. In the second place, they say that we will not obey the magistracy.

Answer. The writings which we have published during the several years past prove clearly that this accusation against us is untrue and false. We publicly and unequivocally confess that the office of the magistrate is ordained of God, even as we have always confessed, since according to our small talent we have served the Word of the Lord. And moreover, in the meantime, we have obeyed them when not contrary to the Word of God. We intend to do so all our lives. For we are not so stupid as not to know what the Lord's Word commands in this respect. Taxes and tolls we pay as Christ has taught and Himself practiced. We pray for the imperial majesty, kings, lords, princes and all in authority. We honor and obey them. I Tim. 2:2; Rom. 13:1. And yet they cry that we will not obey the magistrates, in order that they may disturb the hearts of those that have authority and excite them to all unmercifulness, wrath, and bitterness against us, and that by their continual agitation the bloody sword may be used against us without mercy and never be sheathed, as may be seen.

They ceaselessly excite the magistracy by such gross falsehood, and moreover say Yea and Amen to everything the magistracy commands or does, whether it is agreeable to the Scriptures or not. Thus they by their pleasant doctrine lead these souls into destruction and loss. They seek not their salvation but their own enjoyment and gain. Therefore before God, it is the truth; love compels us respectfully and humbly to show all high officials (some of whom would do right if they knew it and had some Hanani to point it out to them, since it is concealed by the preachers) what the Word of the Lord commands them, how they should be minded, and how they should rightfully execute their office to the praise and glory of the Lord....

Behold, beloved rulers and judges, if you take to heart these Scriptures and diligently ponder them, then you will observe, first, that your office is not your own but God's, so that you may bend your knees before His majesty; fear His great and adorable name, and rightly and reasonably execute your ordained office. Then you will not so freely with your perishable earthly power invade and transgress against Christ, the Lord of lords in His kingdom, power, and jurisdiction, and with your iron sword adjudicate in that which belongs exclusively to the eternal judgment of the Most High God, such as in faith and matters pertaining to faith. In the same vein Luther and others wrote in the beginning, but after they came to greater and higher estate they forgot it all. Dear sirs, observe how very much Moses, Joshua, David, Ezekiel, Josiah, Zerubbabel, and others are praised in the Scriptures because they feared the Lord, and faithfully and diligently kept His commandments, counsel, and word....

Secondly, you may understand from these Scriptures that you are all called of God and ordained to your offices to punish the transgressors and protect the good; to judge rightly between a man and his fellows; to do justice to the widows and orphans, to the poor, despised stranger and pilgrim; to protect them against violence and tyranny; to rule cities and countries justly by a good policy and administration not contrary to God's Word, in peace and quiet, unto the benefit and profit of the common people, to rule well. You should eagerly seek and love the holy Word (by which the soul must live), the name and the glory of God, and in Scriptural fairness promote and maintain the same as much as possible.

You see, dear sirs and rulers, this is really the office to which you are called. Whether you fulfill these requirements piously and faithfully, I will leave to your own consideration....

III. In the third place, they say that we are seditionists and that we could take cities and countries if we had the power.

Answer. This prophecy is false and will ever remain so; and by the grace of God, as time and experience will prove that those who thus prophesy according to the Word of Moses are not of God. Faithful reader, understand what I write.

The Scriptures teach that there are two opposing princes and two opposing kingdoms: the one is the Prince of peace; the other the prince of strife. Each of these princes had his particular kingdom and as the prince is so is also the kingdom. The Prince of peace is Christ Jesus; His kingdom is the kingdom of peace, which is His church; His messengers are the messengers of peace; His word is the word of peace; His body is the body of peace; His children are the seed of peace; and His inheritance and reward are the inheritance and reward of peace. In short, with this King, and in His kingdom and reign, it is nothing but peace. Everything that is seen, heard, and done is peace.

We have heard the word of peace, namely, the consoling Gospel of peace from the mouth of His messengers of peace. We, by His grace, have believed and accepted it in peace and have committed ourselves to the only, eternal, and true Prince of peace, Christ Jesus, in His kingdom of peace and under His reign, and are thus by the gift of His Holy Spirit, by means of faith, incorporated into His body. And henceforth we look with all the children of His peace for the promised inheritance and reward of peace.

Such exceeding grace of God has appeared unto us poor, miserable sinners that we who were formerly no people at all and who knew of no peace are now called to be such a glorious people of God, a church, kingdom, inheritance, body, and possession of peace. Therefore we desire not to break this peace, but by His great power by which He has called us to this peace and portion, to walk in this grace and peace, unchangeably and unwaveringly unto death.

Peter was commanded to sheathe his sword. All Christians are commanded to love their enemies; to do good unto those who abuse and persecute them; to give the mantle when the cloak is taken, the other cheek when one is struck. Tell me, how can a Christian defend Scripturally retaliation, rebellion, war, striking, slaying, torturing, stealing, robbing and plundering and burning cities, and conquering countries?

The great Lord who has created you and us, who has placed our hearts within us knows, and He only knows that our hearts and hands are clear of all sedition and murderous mutiny. By His grace we will ever remain clear. For we truly confess that all rebellion is of the flesh and of the devil.

O beloved reader, our weapons are not swords and spears, but patience, silence, and hope, and the Word of God. With these we must maintain our heavy warfare and fight our battle. Paul says, The weapons of our warfare are not carnal; but

mighty through God. With these we intend and desire to storm the kingdom of the devil; and not with sword, spears, cannon, and coats of mail. For He esteemeth iron as straw, and brass as rotten wood. Thus may we with our Prince, Teacher, and Example Christ Jesus, raise the father against the son, and the son against the father, and may we cast down imagination and every high thing that exalteth itself against the knowledge of God, and bring into captivity every thought in obedience to Christ.

True Christians do not know vengeance, no matter how they are mistreated. In patience they posses their souls. Luke 21:18. And they do not break their peace, even if they should be tempted by bondage, torture, poverty and besides, by the sword and fire. They do not cry, Vengeance, vengeance, as does the world; but with Christ they supplicate and pray: Father, forgive them; for they know not what they do. Luke 23:34; Acts 7:60.

According to the declaration of the prophets they have beaten their swords into plowshares and their spears into pruning hooks. They shall sit every man under his vine and under his fig tree, Christ; neither shall they learn war anymore. Isa. 2:4; Mic. 4:3.

They do not seek your money, goods, injury, nor blood, but they seek the honor and praise of God and the salvation of your souls. They are the children of peace; their hearts overflow with peace; their mouths speak peace, and they walk in the way of peace; they are full of peace. They seek, desire, and know nothing but peace; and are prepared to forsake country, goods, life, and all for the sake of peace. For they are the kingdom, people, congregation, city, property, and body of peace, as has been heard....

The other prince is the prince of darkness, Antichrist, and Satan. This prince is a prince of all tumult and blood. Raging and murder is his proper nature and policy. His commandments and teaching and his kingdom, body, and church are of the same nature. I John 3. Here we need not much Scripture, for seeing, hearing, and daily experience prove the truth.

Our opponents invent that we are intent upon rebellion; something of which we have never thought. But we say, and that truthfully, that they and their ancestors for more than a thousand years have been that which they make us out to be. Read history and you will be convinced of this. All those who place themselves in opposition to their shamefulness, dishonor, and evildoing have had to suffer for it. Even so it is today.

For what they have done these last few years by their writings, teachings, and cries, cities and countries prove. How neatly they have placed one ruler against the others saying, Since the sword is placed in your hands you may maintain the Word of the Lord thereby, until they prevailed on them and have shed human blood like water, torn the hearts from each other's bodies, and have made countless harlots, rogues, widows, and orphans. The innocent citizen they have devoured and plundered; cities and lands they have destroyed. In short, they have done as if neither prophet nor Christ nor apostle nor the Word of God had ever been upon the earth. Notwithstanding, they wish to be called holy,

Christian church and body. O dear Lord, how lamentably is Thy holy, worthy Word mocked, and Thy glorious work derided, as if Thy divine and powerful activity in Thy church were nothing but reading, shouting, water, bread, wine, and name; and as if rebellion, warring, robbing, murder, and devilish works were permissible. Dear reader, behold and observe, and learn to know this kingdom and body. For if they with such actions and doing were the kingdom and body of Christ, as the learned ones assure them, then Christ's holy, glorious kingdom, church, and body would be an inhuman, cruel, rebellious, bloody, rapacious, noisy, unmerciful, and unrighteous people. This is incontrovertible. Oh, damnable error, dark blindness! …

Kind reader, earnestly reflect upon this our brief delineation of the two princes and their kingdoms, and by the grace of God, it will give you no mean insight into the Scriptures.

39. BARTOLOMÉ DE LAS CASAS

The Only Way

Bartolomé de Las Casas (1484-1566) was a Spanish Dominican friar who devoted his life to criticizing Spanish colonialism in the New World and defending the rights of aboriginal Americans. His record is not without blemish, however; in his zeal to defend the Indians, he tolerated the importation of African slaves.

Some of his writings, for example, The Only Way *(1550s), excerpted below, are important because they offer a progressive (and pioneering) take on sharing the Gospel peacefully. Unlike so many others of his age, Las Casas opposed evangelism by force and found religious wars to be anything but reflective of the nonviolent Christ. Nevertheless, even as he preached against conversion by force, he accepted the legitimacy of a state's right to defend itself.*

The Only Way
Winning the Mind and Will

One way, one way only, of teaching a living faith, to everyone, everywhere, always, was set by Divine Providence: the way that wins the mind with reasons, that wins the will with gentleness, with invitation. It has to fit all people on earth, no distinction made for sect, for error, even for evil.…

By the Way of Christ

Divine Wisdom, Divine Providence are behind the way, the form Christ fashioned and prescribed in preaching and teaching His gospel, His belief, to all and sundry, everywhere, every time, from His ascension into heaven until the day of judgment. But that way, that form, wins the mind with reasons, wins the will with gentleness, with invitation.

So Divine Wisdom, Divine Providence are behind this way of teaching people a living faith, winning their minds, winning their wills, etc....

Christ commanded a special greeting, used the words, "Peace to this house!" [Mt. 10:22]. It was a strong custom among Hebrews and Syrians to use this greeting, as Jerome implies, commenting on Matthew. The apostles worked among Hebrews and Syrians. Or it was that no other greeting seemed to embrace more blessings than wishing someone peace. All greetings are prayers for blessings, but more are enveloped in this particular one because peace is the tranquility of order, as Augustine says in *The City of God,* bk. 19, chap. 13. Where the tranquility of order prevails, blessings abound. Peace is a state of calm and quiet and of multiple friendships according to Isidore in his *Etymologies*. Everyone is made for happiness. Where the tranquility of order prevails, everyone is happy since nothing upsets the order. If tranquility exists, people want the quiet life; they work for it. Should something block it, they must pursue it. They will have it and not a counterfeit. Peace is a supreme good, there is nothing more beautiful than it in society. ...

By the Example of the Apostles

The apostles preached peace first—a value so wanted, so palatable, so loved and lovable by those people who lived in city, town and household that it's clear they could only attract such people! And render them gracious and kind enough to welcome the apostles and shelter them generously and warmly and listen to their teaching willingly.

It is very winning to see the apostles poor, humble, kind—not after gold, not after silver, not after coin, not after stuff of any kind, not the least thing earthly or passing, not even asking for the meal they needed unless from people willing to provide it....

After the Lord taught his apostles and disciples the form and fashion of their behavior toward the city, the town, the household that took them in, willingly, even graciously, He then gave them a norm they should act on toward those who are resistant. "Whoever is unreceptive, who does not listen to your words, leave the house, the town, shake its dust off your feet. I tell you solemnly it will go easier for Sodom and Gomorrah [biblical symbols of inhospitality] on judgment day than for that town" [Mt. 10:14].

What is clear is that Christ gave His apostles permission and power to teach the gospel to those willing to hear it, and that only! Not power to punish the unwilling by force, pressure or harshness. He granted no power to apostle or preacher of the faith to force the unwilling to listen, no power to punish even those who drove the apostles out of town. He decreed punishment in eternity, not in time. "Whoever is unreceptive and does not listen to your words, leave the place." He did not say, "Confront them! Preach to them willy nilly! If they persist tenaciously in trying to drive you out, do not hesitate to use human punishment!" ...

Every evangelist shows that Christ taught, that Christ set the peaceful way not just by His words but also by His deeds. He was humble and meek. He would teach others meekness and humility. From the outset of His preaching therefore, He dealt humbly and meekly with people so he could draw people to Himself with peaceful behavior, could get them to trust being able to approach God. In the words of Romans 5:2, "We have an approach to God through Him." ...

No one should conclude from this that warfare is forbidden to Christian leaders when it is necessary for the defense of the nation. It is one thing to speak of the way to preach the law of Christ and thereby gather, settle, and secure a Christianity in which He rules spiritually. It is another to speak of saving the nation, of using sound judgment which sometimes dictates waging a defensive war, or offensive war, against tyranny. Grace does not contradict nature but perfects it.

You see what power the weapons of Christ have for conquering the world, you see what destruction, what captivity is worked on enemies! Different from the spirit of tyrants and slaughterers who cannot win the souls or affections of those they conquer, though they conquer body and property and locale and kingdom with their physical weapons. Physical weapons can bring ruin on people, irreparable harm, but cannot reach beyond body, property, or place, as I said earlier.

That rule is tyrannical, violent, and never long lasting which is acquired by force of arms, or gotten without some consent of the conquered [Aristotle, *Ethics,* Bk. 3]. Tyranny is the worst of all political systems of rule [Aristotle, *Ethics,* Bk. 8]. The rule which people grant to someone as a gift, grant it freely, with no force or fear or coercion involved, so someone rules willing subjects—that rule is a noble rule, natural, just, virtuous, and judge the best....

The Opposite Way: Violating the Mind and Will

The opposite way would clearly be this ...

War brings with it cannon fire, surprise attacks, shore raids that are lawless and blind, violence, riots, scandals, corpses, carnage, butchery, robbery, looting, parent split from child, child from parent, slavery, the ruin of states and kingdoms, of lords and local rulers, the devastation of cities and towns and people without number. War fills here and there and everywhere with tears, with sobs, with keening over every pitiful spectacle possible.

People the world over know too well the evil effects war causes or brings to birth. Let me name a few of the many listed by jurists: War, like a tornado, like a tidal wave of evils, runs amok destroying everything, whole cities, whole regions. War paves the way for atrocities, it causes bitter hatreds, it makes people boldly vicious. It beggars a people, it torments them, etc. In war cattle are raided, crops ruined, peasants slaughtered, ancestral villas torched, and prosperous cities leveled by the one blast of all those deplorable hostilities. War is a curse not a blessing. Families live in fear, they feud, they carp; everything is depressed; the crafts go dead; the poor are forced into starvation or into a lawless life; the rich resent their loss of wealth, they fear further loss, they are doubly trapped. Raped women marry, though seldom and sadly; and widow women live in barren homes; law is gagged, decency ridiculed, justice pitched out, religion mocked, nothing is sacred, everything is up for grabs. Each nook and cranny of war is stuffed with crooks, with thieves, with rapists, with arsonists, with killers. War is a license to kill and steal; what else can it be? The wider the war, the wickeder, the more thousands of innocent victims are dragged into the lethal conflict and they [the victims] gave no cause for the harm. People lose their souls in war, they lose their lives and their livelihood.

The next step is to see how opposed to the peaceful way of preaching the faith, how utterly opposed the violent way is. It is the dead opposite, the reverse of preaching the faith and drawing people gently into the flock of Christ, of reaching the goal God wants from the preaching, honor for the divine name, change of heart and eternal life for the human soul....

Wars Contradict the Way of Christ

I must further the argument and prove how the war/conversion approach is a flat and absolute contradiction of what Christ wanted and willed.

The first proof is easy enough. Christ willed it, through the way He did His own preaching, that the preachers of His law, before they said or did anything else, should offer peace to the pagan people of whatever place they entered, fort or farm or city, even before peace was offered them. And Christ forbade His preachers to carry even a staff, so that they could be seen as peaceful men right from the start. But the method we contradict says we should conquer pagan peoples, should call down on their heads a welter of suffering and death. This way pagans are not only shamed and cursed by the words we bring; but also they are beaten, bruised, wounded and killed, by our deadly deeds. Conclusion: the way of war contradicts the way Christ willed, the one He taught when He preached His gospel.

Second. Through His own way of preaching the gospel, Christ commanded His apostles and those who later carried on their missionary role, to heal the sick, to raise the dead, to cleanse the lepers, to expel the demons. War says and does the opposite in fact. It makes pagans who have done Christians no harm—to my knowledge—undergo a living death first, then die. It makes sound and healthy people sick unto death through the horrors they are forced to accept. It makes those who were leprosy-free suffer worse leprosies, those caused by the plagues the warrior brings. There is no doubt of it.

The way of war provides a shortcut for demons to pour into people's souls, whose bodily health prevented it before then. The victims will surely hate, with an implacable hatred, those who wage war against them, hate them as enemies. The next thing is that the victims who are killed are damned eternally since they die in unbelief. And the killers, no doubt of it either, they are possessed by demons in the waging of war. They will burn in the same eternal flames along with their victims, if they do not repent. And so this new bizarre way of conversion contradicts the way Christ wanted and willed it to be when He Himself preached the gospel.

Third. Again, by the way He preached the gospel, Christ willed that His missionaries should be meek as lambs, simple as doves. His words were: "I send you like sheep among wolves" [Luke 10:3]. And: "Be simple, like doves" [Mt. 10:16]. He further willed that they should learn from Him to be meek and humble of heart, both in word and deed. But the way of first conquering pagans in war does not smack of the meekness of lambs nor the simplicity of doves. It is all a roar of lions, bears, tigers, all a howling of wolves, howling of horrible monsters, it is crafty as a fox at maliciousness. It almost outdoes the devil himself in pride and ferocity of thought and word and deed. Warrior preachers are—or are sent as—ravening wolves among flocks of sheep, not flocks of sheep among ravening wolves. And that is an utter contradiction of the true way....

At His birth the angels sang peace, not war songs, not songs of victory in war! [Luke 2:14]. When alive, He offered peace and He ordered it offered [Luke 10:5-6]. When dying, He bequeathed peace [John 14:27]. When risen, He repeated His offer! [John 20:26]. Scrutinize His whole teaching once again. You will find nothing that is not redolent of peace, that does not ring with friendship, that is not rinsed with charity. For this one reason He gave His command to love—filled with love Himself—for it to produce peace, for it to nourish the peace produced, for it to preserve the same! [John 14:27; 15:13].

The kingly dignity of Christ, His kingly generosity would not stoop to using war as a way to gain a people, nor war to expand, enrich, ensure a kingdom. Only through peace. So it is not the way of Christ or Christian or apostle, the way of war, with its fearful clash of weaponry, to gain a kingdom. It is the way of robbers, of pirates, of tyrants, of heretics, of faithless people, of ravenous, murderous wolves who come only to rip, to madden, kill, wipe out the flock of Christ, the flock that exists, and the sheep on the threshold of the flock who would enter it with little trouble if not blocked, if not slaughtered by such hoodlums! …

Wars Contradict the Way of the Missionary

… For this kind of man brings cruel war to bear on those who never harmed him, never insulted him, people he never knew before, of that we are sure, people who never plotted evil against him. He kills, he slaughters human beings—never mind their sex or age—with a sword, with a spear, off with their heads! One stroke, head from neck, and plunges the souls of his wretched victims into instant hellfire. Disgusting!

Conquerors steal others' wives, force them into adultery. They don't have to steal! They own everything! And incest, the lewdness, and concubinage, up to the minute they die! I tell you they steal servant and maid and ox and ass and anything else on the landscape! I say not a word about stripping legitimate kings and princes of the honor and respect due to them, not a word about those who survived the sword to lead a life more bitter than death. And not a word about the wounded, their arms cut off, their hands or feet or other parts, then plunged into perpetual slavery, slavery they can never hope to escape except through death.

As if this is not enough, missionaries fanatic for the spread of faith in Christianity, so that they themselves can apply the full weight of divine sanction, malign the natives a million ways, even to the point of perjury, calling them dogs, idolaters, accomplices in rotten crimes, stupid morons, unfit, incapable of Christian faith and moral life. The things they then do to these people under the pretext of a lie—a false, a wicked, a heretical lie, a deadly detestable lie—might then seem just, or at least pardonable. "But I am who I am, I am not blind, says the Lord!" …

Do you keep the command—"You are not to shed your neighbor's blood"—by mass slaughter in which everything reeks of human blood? Or do you keep it by not slaughtering innocent life, by not betraying your kindred, by suppressing your bad behavior, by getting justice done, by helping victims, aiding orphans, protecting widows, keep it by not harassing others—no violence, no robbery—by feeding the hungry? Or do you rather keep the bread, and so create famine and death for thousands and thousands of people, men and women of every type and rank and age? And what about the command not to put faith in a lie since it leads us nowhere? Do you obey it by stealing, robbery, murder, adultery, lewdness, by fouling everything with incest all around, by lying under oath, by the cult of Baal, i.e., the special idol of marauders, who has a hold over them as over subjects, who possesses them? A Baal is a lust for power, a huge hunger to get rich; limitless lust, hopeless hunger, and "that is an idolatry" [Col. 3:5]. "A Baal is something I so idolize that it dominates me, it possesses me," Jerome says. Baals are kith and kin to lustful, hungry, greedy men, to preachers of war, to rotten and damnable tyrants....

All those who wage wars of conversion, all those who unleash them, have no love of God; they have a hatred of God, they live without charity....

PART V
Modern Period (1600-1900)

40. Gerrard Winstanley

The True Levellers Standard

In April 1649, Gerrard Winstanley (1609-1676) helped to establish a colony of "Diggers" (also known as the "True Levellers") on St. George's Hill in Surrey, England, with the purpose of creating a commune that would enact their belief that God originally desired for the Earth to be a "common treasury" shared by all. Winstanley wrote more than twenty tracts explaining the teachings of the Digger movement—which the propertied class of England eventually crushed—and was the intellectual leader of the movement. Below is an excerpt from The True Levellers Standard, *which Winstanley wrote ten days after he and other Diggers occupied St. George's Hill. Like Pelagius centuries before him, Winstanley believed there was a close link between private property and violence.*

A DECLARATION TO THE POWERS OF ENGLAND, AND TO ALL THE POWERS OF THE WORLD, shewing the cause why the common people of England have begun, and gives consent to digge up, manure, and sowe corn upon George-Hill in Surrey; by those that have subscribed, and thousands more that gives consent.

In the beginning of Time, the great Creator Reason, made the Earth to be a Common Treasury, to preserve Beasts, Birds, Fishes, and Man, the lord that was to govern this Creation; for Man had Domination given to him, over the Beasts, Birds, and Fishes; but not one word was spoken in the beginning, That one branch of mankind should rule over another.

And the Reason is this, Every single man, Male and Female, is a perfect Creature of himself; and the same Spirit that made the Globe, dwells in man to govern the Globe; so that the flesh of man being subject to Reason, his Maker, hath him to be his Teacher and Ruler within himself, therefore needs not run abroad after any Teacher and Ruler without him, for he needs not that any man should teach him, for the same Anoynting that ruled in the Son of man, teacheth him all things.

But since humane flesh (that king of Beasts) began to delight himself in the objects of the Creation, more then in the Spirit Reason and Righteousness, who manifests himself to be the indweller in the Five Sences, of Hearing, Seeing, Tasting, Smelling, Feeling; then he fell into blindness of mind and weakness of heart, and runs abroad for a Teacher and Ruler: And so selfish imaginations taking possession of the Five Sences, and ruling as King in the room of Reason therein, and working with Covetousnesse, did set up one man to teach and rule over another; and thereby the Spirit was killed, and man was brought into bondage, and became a greater Slave to such of his own kind, then the Beasts of the field were to him.

And hereupon, The Earth (which was made to be a Common Treasury of relief for all, both Beasts and Men) was hedged in to In-closures by the teachers and rulers, and the others were made Servants and Slaves: And that Earth that is within this Creation made a Common Store-house for all, is bought and sold, and kept in the hands of a few, whereby the great Creator is mightily dishonoured, as if he were a respecter of persons, delighting in the comfortable Livelihood of some, and rejoycing in the miserable povertie and straits of others. From the beginning it was not so....

. . . But for the present state of the old World that is running up like parchment in the fire, and wearing away, we see proud Imaginary flesh, which is the wise Serpent, rises up in flesh and gets dominion in some to rule over others, and so forces one part of the Creation man, to be a slave to another; and thereby the Spirit is killed in both. The one looks upon himself as a teacher and ruler, and so is lifted up in pride over his fellow Creature: The other looks upon himself as imperfect, and so is dejected in his spirit, and looks upon his fellow Creature of his own Image, as a Lord above him.

And thus *Esau*, the man of flesh, which is Covetousness and Pride, hath killed *Jacob*, the Spirit of meeknesse, and righteous government in the light of Reason, and rules over him: And so the Earth that was made a common Treasury for all to live comfortably upon, is become through mans unrighteous actions one over another, to be a place, wherein one torments another. . . .

Now the great Creator, who is the Spirit Reason, suffered himself thus to be rejected, and troden underfoot by the covetous proud flesh, for a certain time limited; therefore saith he, The Seed out of whom the Creation did proceed, which is my Self, shall bruise this Serpents head, and restore my Creation again from this curse and bondage; and when I the King of Righteousnesse reigns in every man, I will be the blessing of the Earth and the joy of all Nations.

And since the coming in of the stoppage, or the Adam, the Earth hath been inclosed and given to the Elder brother Esau, or man of flesh, and hath been bought and sold from one to another; and Jacob, or the younger brother, that is to succeed or come forth next, who is the universal spreading power of righteousnesse that gives liberty to the whole Creation, is made a servant.

And this Elder Son, or man of bondage, hath held the Earth in bondage to himself, not by a meek Law of Righteousnesse, but by subtle selfish Councels, and by open and violent force; for wherefore is it that there is such Wars and rumours of Wars in the Nations of the Earth? and wherefore are men so mad to destroy one another? But only to uphold Civil propriety of Honor, Dominion and Riches one over another, which is the curse the Creation groans under, waiting for deliverance.

But when once the Earth becomes a Common Treasury again, as it must, for all the Prophesies of Scriptures and Reason are Circled here in this Community, and mankind must have the Law of Righteousness once more writ in his heart, and all must be made of one heart, and one mind.

Then this Enmity in all Lands will cease, for none shall dare to seek a Dominion over others, neither shall any dare to kill another, nor desire more of the Earth then another; for he that will rule over, imprison, oppresse, and kill his fellow Creatures, under what pretence soever, is a destroyer of the Creation, and an actor of the Curse, and walks contrary to the rule of righteousnesse: *(Do, as you would have others do to you; and love your Enemies, not in words, but in actions)....*

The Work we are going about is this, To dig up *Georges-Hill* and the waste Ground thereabouts, and to Sow Corn, and to eat our bread together by the sweat of our brows.

And the First Reason is this, That we may work in righteousness, and lay the Foundation of making the Earth a Common Treasury for All, both Rich and Poor, That every one that is born in the Land, may be fed by the Earth his Mother that brought him forth, according to the Reason that rules in the Creation. Not Inclosing any part into any particular hand, but all as one man, working together, and feeding together as Sons of one Father, members of one Family; not one Lording over another, but all looking upon each other, as equals in the Creation; so that our Maker may be glorified in the work of his own hands, and that every one may see, he is no respecter of Persons, but equally loves his whole Creation, and hates nothing but the Serpent, which is Covetousness, branching forth into selfish Imagination, Pride, Envie, Hypocrisie, Uncleanness; all seeking the ease and honor of flesh, and fighting against the Spirit Reason that made the Creation; for that is the Corruption, the Curse, the Devil, the Father of Lies; Death and Bondage that Serpent and Dragon that the Creation is to be delivered from....

41. George Fox

Paper to Friends to Keep Out of Wars and Fights

George Fox (1624-1691) founded a movement in England that was initially referred to as Friends of the Truth and later became known as the Religious Society of Friends (the Quakers). After leaving family and friends in search of religious enlightenment in 1643, Fox began preaching his own unique message in 1647—that truth can be found in the voice of God that speaks to one's soul. Although he was imprisoned at times for preaching his doctrine of "inner light," Fox was able to take his message to the West Indies, America, Germany, and the Netherlands. A key part of his teaching focused on Christian peace, and in 1660 he and eleven other Quakers submitted a declaration of peace to King Charles II. One of the purposes of the declaration was to let the king know that the Quakers were distinct from the Fifth Monarchy, a violent group of radical Christians who opposed the restoration of the monarchy following the execution of Charles I in 1649 (and the resulting reign of parliament, Oliver Cromwell, and his son Richard). Because they believed that Jesus would soon return, the Fifth Monarchy sought to overthrow the government, thereby making way for King Jesus, in 1661. Several years before he and other Friends submitted this declaration, Fox also authored a paper imploring his friends to keep out of wars and fights. This lesser-known document, below, has no exact date and most likely was not widely circulated.

All friends everywhere, keep out of plots and bustling and the arm of flesh: for all that is among Adam's sons in the fall, where they are destroying men's lives like dogs and beasts and swine, goring, rending and biting one another, and destroying one another, and wrestling with flesh and blood. From whence rises wars but from the lust and killing? And all this is in Adam in the fall out of Adam that never fell, in whom there is peace and life. And ye are called to peace, therefore follow it. And Christ is that Peace, and Adam is in the fall. For all that pretends to fight for Christ, they are deceived, for his kingdom is not of this world; therefore his servant doth not fight. Therefore fighters are not of Christ's kingdom, and are without Christ's kingdom, for his kingdom stands in peace and righteousness. And so fighters are in the lust, and all that would destroy men's lives are not of Christ's mind, who comes to save men's lives. Christ's kingdom is not of this world, it is peaceable; and all that be in strifes are not of his kingdom, and all such as pretends to fight for the Gospel (the Gospel is the power of God, before the devil or fall of man was), which are ignorant of the Gospel, and all that talk of fighting for Sion, are in darkness; for Sion needs no such helpers. And all such as profess themselves to be ministers of Christ and Christians, and go beat down the whore with outward carnal weapons, the flesh and the whore are got up in themselves in a blind zeal. That which beats down the whore, which got up by the inward ravening from the spirit of God, the beating down of the whore must be by the inward rising of the sword of the spirit within. All such as pretend Christ Jesus and confesseth him and runs into carnal weapons, wrestling with flesh and blood, throws away the spiritual; (they) that would be wrestlers with flesh and blood, they throw away Christ's doctrine, and flesh is got up in them, and they are weary of their sufferings; and such as would revenge themselves be out of

Christ's doctrine; and such as would be stricken on the one cheek, and would not turn the other be out of Christ's doctrine, and such as do not love one another and love enemies be out of Christ's doctrine. And therefore you that be heirs of the blessings of God, which was before the curse and the fall was, come to inherit your portions. And you that be heirs with the Gospel of peace before the devil was, live in the Gospel of peace.

Let your conversation preach to all men and your innocent lives, that they which speak evil of you and beholding your Godly conversation may glorify your father which is in heaven. And all friends everywhere this I charge you, which is the word of the Lord God unto you all, live in peace, in Christ the way of peace, and in which seek the peace of all men and no man's hurt. And therefore live in the peaceable life, doing good to all men, and seeking the good and welfare of all men.

G.F.

Let this go among friends everywhere.

42. Robert Barclay

Epistle of Love and Friendly Advice

Robert Barclay (1648-1690) was the preeminent theologian among the early Quakers. Unlike Fox, whose writings were largely occasional, Barclay systematized Quaker principles, perhaps most ably in his Apology, *which, because of its articulate defense of the doctrine of "inner light," became one of the most important foundational documents of Quakerism. Although he was imprisoned for his beliefs at various times, Barclay eventually found favor among some royals, especially the Duke of York, and even helped William Penn as he sought to transfer Quaker principles to what would become Pennsylvania. Barclay was an eloquent defender of Christian peace, and in the writing below,* An Epistle of Love and Friendly Advice *(1678), which he sent to ambassadors negotiating the end of the third Dutch War of 1672-1678, he encourages the warring parties to see the peacefulness of the light of Christ.*

... The chief ground, cause and root then of all this misery among all those called Christians, is, because they are only such in name, and not in nature, having only a form and profession of Christianity in show and words, but are still strangers, yea, and enemies to the Life and Virtue of it; own-

ing God and Christ in words, but denying them in works; and therefore the Lord Jesus Christ will not own them as his Children, nor Disciples. For while they say, they are his followers; while they preach and exalt his precepts; while they extol his life, patience, and meekness, his self-denying, perfect resignation and obedience to the will of his Father; yet themselves are out of it: and so bring shame and reproach to that honorable Name, which they assume to themselves in the face of the nations, and give an occasion for Infidels (Turks, Jews and Atheists) to profane and blaspheme the Holy Name of Jesus. Is it not so? While so much ambition, pride, vanity, wantonness and malice, murder, cruelty, and oppression, yea, and all manner of abominations abounds and is openly practiced; yea, while those, that should be patterns and examples of justice, virtue and sobriety to others, do for the most part exceed most in those things. So that the Courts of Christian Princes (who while in words seem more to glory in being professors and protectors of Christianity, than in their outward crowns) which should be colleges of virtue and piety, are mostly scenes of greatest wickedness, and nests and receptacles of all the buffoons, stage-players, and other vilest vermin not fit to be mentioned. I say, is it not so? While upon every slender pretext, such as their own small discontents, or that they judge, the present Peace they have with their neighbour, cannot suit with their grandeur and worldly glory, they sheath their swords in one another's bowels; ruin waste and destroy whole Countries; expose to the greatest misery many thousand families; make thousands of widows and ten thousands of orphans; cause the banks to overflow with the blood of those, for whom the Lord Jesus Christ shed his precious Blood; and spend and destroy many of the good creatures of God. And all this while they pretend to be followers of the lamb-like Jesus; who came not to destroy men's lives, but to save them; the song of whose appearance to the world was, "Glory to God in the highest, and good will and peace to all men" (Luke 2:4): not to kill, murder and destroy men; not to hire and force poor men to run upon and murder one another, merely to satisfy the lust and ambition of great men; they being oftentimes ignorant of the ground of the quarrel, and not having the least occasion of evil will or prejudice against those their fellow Christians, whom they thus kill; amongst whom not one of a thousand perhaps ever saw another before. Yea, is it not so, that there is only a name, and nothing of the true nature of Christians especially manifest in the Clergy, who pretend not only to be professors, but preachers,

promoters and exhorters of others to Christianity, who for the most part are the greatest promoters and advancers of those wars; and by whom upon all such occasions the Name of God and Jesus Christ is most horribly abused, profaned and blasphemed, while they dare pray to God, and thank him for the destruction of their brethren Christians, and that for and against, according to the changeable wills of their several Princes: yea so, that some will join in their prayers with and for the prosperity of such as their Profession obliges them to believe to be heretical and anti-Christian; and for the destruction of those whom the same profession acknowledges to be good and orthodox Christians. Thus the French, both Papists and Protestants join in their prayers, and rejoice for the destruction of the Spanish Papists and Dutch Protestants: the like may be said of the Danish, Swedish and German Protestants, as respectively concerned in this matter. Yea, which is yet more strange, if either constraint or interest do engage any Prince or State to change his party, while the same war and cause remains; then will the Clergy presently accommodate their prayers to the case, in praying for prosperity to those, to whom they instantly before wished ruin; and so on the contrary: as in this present war, in the case of the Bishop of Münster is manifest. Was there ever, or can there be any more horrible profanations of the Holy and Pure Name of God, especially to be done by those, who pretend to be worshippers of the true God, and Disciples of Jesus Christ? This not only equals, but far exceeds the wickedness of the Heathens: for they only prayed such gods to their assistance, as they fancied allow their ambition, and accounted their warring a virtue; whom they judged changeable like themselves, and subject to such quarrels among themselves, as they that are their worshippers: but for those to be found in these things, who believe, there is but one only God, and have, or at least profess to have such notions of his justice, equity and mercy, and of the certainty of his punishing the transgressors of his Law, is so horrible and abominable, as cannot sufficiently be neither said, or written.

The ground then of all this is the want of true Christianity, because the nature of it is not begotten, nor brought forth in those called Christians; and therefore they bear not the image, nor bring not forth the fruits of it. For albeit they have the Name; yet the nature they are strangers to: the Lamb's nature is not in them, but the doggish nature, the wolfish nature, that will still be quarrelling and destroying; the cunning, serpentine, subtle nature, and the proud ambitious, Luciferian nature, that sets Princes and States a work to contrive and foment wars, and engages people to fight together, some for ambition and vain glory; and some for covetousness and hope of gain: and the same cause doth move the Clergy to concur with their share in making their prayers turn and twine; and so all are here out from the state of true Christianity. And as they keep the Name of being Christians; so also upon the same pretext each will pretend to be for peace, while their fruits manifestly declare the contrary. And how hath and doth experience daily discover this deceit! For how is peace brought about? Is it not, when the weaker is forced to give way to the stronger, without respect to the equity of the cause? Is it not just so, as among the wild and devouring beasts? who when they fight together, the weaker is forced to give way to the stronger, and so desist, until another occasion offer? So who are found weakest, who are least capable to hold out, they must bear the inconveniency; and he gets the most advantage, however frivolous, yea, unjust his pretence be, who is most able to vindicate his claim, and preserve it not by equity, but force of arms: so that the peace-contrivers' rule is not the equity of the cause, but the power of the parties. Is not his known and manifest in many, if not most of the pacifications, that have been made in Christendom.

It is therefore in my heart, in the Name and behalf of the Lord Jesus Christ, to warn you to consider of those things: and therefore be not unwilling to hear one, that appears among you for the interest of Christ his King and Master. Not as if thereby he denied the just authority of Sovereign Princes; or refused to acknowledge the subjection himself owes to his lawful Prince and Superior; or were any ways inclined to favour the dreams of such, as under the pretence of crying up King Jesus, and the Kingdom of Christ, either deny, or seek to overturn all Civil Government; nay, not at all: but I am one, who do reverence and honour Magistracy, and acknowledge subjection due unto them by

their respective people in all things just and lawful; knowing, "that Magistracy is an ordinance of God, and the Magistrates are his ministers, who bear not the sword in vain" (Rom. 13:1-4). Yet nevertheless I judge it no prejudice to the Magistracy, nor injury to any, for one that is called of the Lord Jesus, to appear for him in this affair; for he is not a little concerned, as by all their confession, so by right are his subjects (unless they willfully render themselves to another, even to the Adversary) for he is heir of all, and therefore it is fit, that they, who speak in his name, be heard; for his Honour and Glory is concerned; his Authority has been condemned; his Laws broken; his Life oppressed; his Standard of Peace pulled down and rent; his Government encroached upon: what shall I say! his precious Blood shed, and himself afresh crucified, and put to open shame by the murders and cruelties, that have attended those wars. If then ye come not under a deep and weighty sense of those things, so as to apply yourselves to seek after some effectual way to remedy these evils; however you may seek to please Princes and States by patching up a reconciliation, and troubling yourselves to satisfy their covetous and ambitious wills, who make such a notice and stir in the world about their glory, and do not mind the Glory and Honour of the Lord Jesus Christ, so as to give him the right, that is due unto him in the first place (not in a bare sound of words; he will not accept of such a compliment, while the evil works remain); I testify in his Name, and Power and Authority, your work be imperfect, and not prosperous.

For although those Kings and Princes, that are now at variance, may be by your means brought to lay down arms and appear to be good friends, and dear allies; yet unless the Lord Jesus Christ can be restored to his Kingdom in their hearts, and that evil ground of ambition, for pride, and lust, and vain glory be removed that so they may rule in the Wisdom and Power of God, and not according to their lusts; that evil ground and devouring nature being still alive and predominant in them, will quickly stir some of them up again, so soon as opportunity offers fit for their advantage: they will kindle the flame again, and all your Articles will not bind them; but they will break them like straws: and their counselors, who flatter them, and seek to please them, will quickly find out a pretext for a breach, such as have taught them these hellish maxims, *Qui nescit dissimulare, nescit regnare*, i.e., that such, as make conscience to lie (or serve the Devil) but to obey Christ, are not fit to rule; and that Kings must not be slaves to their words. And perhaps, if they find it difficult to hit upon any probable ground or pretence; if they judge themselves strong enough, they will neither trouble themselves, nor the world to give a reason, but tell, that to be at Peace is no longer consistent with their glory: and when they have brought about, what they have determined, they will let the world know the reason of it. Hath not manifold experience proved those things to be true? And seeing it is so, there is, nor can no settled, firm, established Peace be brought to Christendom, until the Devil's Kingdom be rooted out of men's hearts, from which wars come, as the Apostle James testifies (James 4:1-7); and the Kingdom of Jesus come to be established in the hearts of Kings, and Princes, and People, whose Kingdom is a Kingdom of Righteousness and Peace, and joy in the Holy Spirit: until he come to rule in and among them, and his enemies, viz. every evil lust be thrown out from him so that his heavenly Wisdom may take place, "which is pure, and peaceable, and easy to be entreated" (James 3:17). And therefore to bring this about, is the one and great thing needful to be minded and considered of, and effectually to be pressed after, as that, by the accomplishing whereof the present evils can alone be cured and removed.

Therefore be not mistaken, neither deceive yourselves to think, ye can accomplish this work by your worldly and human wisdom; the wisdom of the flesh will not do it, neither that of the first birth, which must die and be crucified, ere the Heavenly Wisdom, the beginning whereof is the fear of the Lord (Prov. 1:7), be revealed, by which alone this work can both be truly begun and finished. For the worldly and carnal wisdom is the cause of the war: it is by it, that men have been, and are stirred up to it, even the wisdom of the first fleshy birth, which leaves men not to be content with their own, but to covet their neighbour's, and to quarrel and fight in the hopes of advantage: therefore that wisdom, which is the cause of the mischief, will, nor can never cure it. Try and examine yourselves there-fore seriously in the sight of God, whether you be led, acted and influenced in your present negotiation by the wisdom of this world, the wisdom of the first birth, which is sensual, devilish and from below; or by the Heavenly and Pure Wisdom of God, which is from above, and is the fruit of the second birth (James 3:17), the new birth by Christ Jesus formed and brought forth in the soul, and the Light of Jesus Christ in you, which shows you all your thoughts, and has reproved every one of you for your unrighteousness, even from your childhood up: that will manifest unto you (if you mind it, and heed it) which wisdom you are acted by; and discover to you, whether it be your thoughts and purposes to glorify God over all, and to remove, so far as in you lies, what is contrary to his Holy and Pure Will; and whether you be more concerned for the particular interest and interests of your several Princes, to satisfy or obviate their designs, or to bring about that, by which God's holy witness in every conscience may be answered, and the pure life of Jesus: that by these doings the oppressed may be eased, and suffered to arise. For if this be little in your minds, as a thing not much regarded, but neglected by you, I must intimate to you in the Name of the Lord, that your work will not be blessed by him; neither will it prosper: for although you may make peace for a time; yet (as I have aforesaid) it will not be firm, nor of any long continuance; but the old root still remaining, will send forth its evil fruit again, and all your labour will quickly be undone.

Let me exhort you then seriously to examine yourselves by the Light of Jesus Christ in you, that can alone discover unto you your own hearts, and will not flatter you (as men may) whether you be fit for this work you are set about? Which you cannot be, until you have seriously applied yourselves to the killing and crucifying of that nature in yourselves, from which all this evil flows: if the warring part be removed out of you, and the corrupted wisdom done away, and the peaceable wisdom brought up, then are you fit to consult, and bring about the peace of Christendom. But this cannot be accomplished in you, until you have first believed in the Light of Jesus Christ, wherewithal you, as well as all men are enlightened; and which is given you as a sufficient Guide and Leader, to lead out of darkness, to lead out of strife, to lead out of the lusts, from which wars come (Jam. 4:1), unto the ways of righteousness and peace; which leads not to destroy, but to love, and forgive enemies: it is the minding of this, and being led and guided by it, that only can fit you for so great and good a work; for this is the Fruit of the Father's love to mankind, and the gift of God, even Christ Jesus, who was given for a Light to enlighten the Gentiles, and for his salvation unto the ends of the earth (Isa. 49:6, Luke 2:32). So it is by turning to this, and following it, and obeying it (in which is sufficiency, and which gives power to the receivers of it to become the sons of God) that the true nature of Christianity can be brought forth and restored; and by which Kings and Princes, Rulers and People may be brought out of lust, envy, warring and strife, to true peace with God, and one with another.

And therefore the cause of all the mischief, that is in Christendom, is, because this Light has not been minded, nor regarded in the heart; but has been hated and overlooked, as a low and insufficient thing: and therefore the Seed of the Kingdom, this gift of the Father's love, this little Leaven, this Pearl of great Price, this Talent being hid in the ground, condemned and despised, and the world and worldly mind being set over it, notwithstanding all the preaching and praying, and professing of Christ in words (that has been only one outward show and appearance, by which men might the more easily be deceived, and live more securely in their wickedness) the innocent life of Christ hath not been known, and all Christendom has brought forth bitter and sour grapes under all their talk and form of worship; and not the sweet and peaceable Fruits of Righteousness: which can never be brought, until all come to him, to the Light of Christ in their consciences, to follow and obey it, and acknowledge it, as that which is given them of God, and sufficient to lead them to Life and Salvation. For as this is thus received and entertained, the true nature of Christ will be begotten and brought forth in people; and then the contrary nature, in which the enmity and strife is, will die and pass away: and so Truth and Peace will come and be settled and firmly established. And for this end the Lord God Almighty

is arisen, and arising in his own Power and glory, who out of his infinite compassion, having regard to the present distracted and desolate condition of Christendom (as seeing them strangers to his Life and Power, and led and guided at will to the utter ruin and destruction both of body and soul by the Adversary of mankind's true happiness) that he might reveal the Light of his Truth even of true Christianity to those, who have the name only, hath turned many, who are strangers and enemies thereunto in their minds by wicked works, to this precious Light, by which Judgment has been laid to the line, and righteousness to the plummet in them (Isa. 28:7, Matt. 12:20), and the evil works and nature in them have been judged and condemned; and they have willingly abode under it, until it hath been brought forth to victory in them. And many of them, who have been wise according to the wisdom of the world, have learned to lay it down at the feet of Jesus, that they might receive from him of his Pure and Heavenly Wisdom; being contented in the enjoyment of that by the world to be accounted fools: and also many of them who were fighters, and even renowned for their skill and valour in warring, have come by the influence of this Pure Light to "beat their swords into plowshares, and their spears into pruning hooks and not learn carnal war any more" (Isa. 2:4), being redeemed from the lusts, from which fighting comes. And there are thousands, whom God hath brought here already; who see to the end of all contention and strife, and that for which the world contends: and albeit the Devil be angry at them, and rage against them in the mere nominal and literal Christians, because he knows, they strike at the very root and foundation of his Kingdom in men's hearts; and therefore he prevails in his followers, to wit, in these literal, nominal Christians, to persecute, kill, beat, banish and imprison, and many ways vex them: yet because the Lord has chosen them to be a First Fruit of that Glorious Work, which he is bringing about in the Nations; therefore they hitherto have, notwithstanding of all that opposition, and yet shall prosper: by a patient enduring in the Spirit of Jesus, they do and shall OVERCOME.

And therefore there is nothing can so much tend to the good and universal peace of Christendom, than for all and every one to mind this gift of God in themselves; and not only to suffer, but to rejoice at the preaching and promulgating of the universality of this glorious Light, whereunto God is now calling many: for as the resisting and slaying of this in themselves, as well as in those, who come in the Name of God to declare it, is the cause of all the mischief, that Christendom labours under; so also its being received and taking place would remove and do it away.

43. WILLIAM PENN

An Essay towards the Present and Future Peace of Europe

William Penn (1644-1718), a Quaker and the founder of Pennsylvania, was a prolific writer and philosopher who published numerous works on politics and religion, including the one excerpted here, An Essay towards the Present and Future Peace of Europe *(1693). Following the internationalism of his day, and especially the great Catholic internationalists Emeric Cruce and Charles François Irenee Castel de Saint-Pierre, Penn calls for establishing a European parliament that would avert the "evils of war."*

To the Reader:

I have undertaken a Subject that I am very sensible requires one of more Sufficiency than I am Master of to treat it, as in Truth, it deserves, and the growing State of Europe calls for; but since Bunglers may Stumble upon the Game, as well as Masters, though it belongs to the Skillful to hunt and catch it, I hope this Essay will not be charged upon me for a Fault, if it appear to be neither Chimerical nor Injurious, and may provoke abler Pens to improve and perform the Design with better Judgment and Success. I will say no more in Excuse of myself, for this Undertaking, but that it is the Fruit of my solicitous Thoughts, for the Peace of Europe, and they must want Charity as much as the World needs Quiet, to be offended with me for so Pacifick a Proposal. Let them censure my Management, so they prosecute the Advantage of the Design; for, till the Millenary doctrine be accomplished, there is nothing appears to me so beneficial and Expedient to the Peace and Happiness of this Quarter of the World.

I. The Evils of War, and the Benefits of Peace

The terrible mortality and the heavy economic burdens of the present war illustrate the inevitable evils of war. Peace, on the contrary, insures the possession of property, foreign commerce, domestic industry, philanthropy, and public and private tranquility. War, like the frost of 1683, seizes all these comforts at once, and stops the civil channel of society. What the peace gave, the war devours.

II. The Causes of War, and Justice as the Means of Its Prevention

Most wars are due to wrongs received or to rights refused. Hence *Justice* is the best means of preventing wars, both at home and abroad.

Wars of aggression are due to ambition and the pride of conquest; but such wars are relatively few in history. As *Leviathans* appear rarely in the world; considering how few there are of those *Sons of Prey,* and how early [seldom?] they show themselves—it may be not once in an Age or two; the League of Nations, when established, will prove an impassable limit to their ambition.

Wars of defense and offense are for the purpose of keeping or recovering national rights. These rights can best be defined, and defended or bestowed, by the League of Nations. For each nation to be judge and executioner in its own cause means injustice and war.

III. The Origin of Government, and Justice as Its Function

Governments arose when men, desirous of peace and justice, formed a political society and imposed obligations upon themselves, thereby surrendering their right of acting as judge in their own cause and as avenger of their own wrong.

The most natural and human government is that which governs by *consent;* for that binds freely, as when men hold their liberty by true obedience to rules of their own making.

The end of government is the prevention or cure of disorder; hence it is the means of justice, as justice is of peace.

IV. The League of Nations

1. A Society of Nations and International Government

The sovereign princes of Europe, if they truly love peace and justice, should follow the precedent of peace-loving men and form a Society of Nations. This society should impose obligations upon itself and its members by means of an international government.

2. The International Parliament

The rules of justice to be observed by the sovereign princes one to another are to be established by deputies in a *General Dyet, Estates,* or *Parliament,* to be called *The Sovereign* or *Imperial Dyet, Parliament,* or *State, of Europe....*

3. The International Court and Councils of Conciliation

All differences pending between one sovereignty and another, which cannot be made up by "private embassies," should be brought before the international parliament, before a session begins. All complaints should be delivered in writing, in the form of memorials.

4. The International Sanction

If any of the sovereignties that constitute the Imperial Diet shall refuse to submit their claim or pretensions to it, or to abide and perform the judgment thereof, and seek their remedy by arms, or delay their compliance beyond the time prescribed in the decision, all the other sovereignties, united as one strength, shall compel the submission and performance of the sentence, with damages to the suffering party, and charges to the sovereignties that obliged their submission.

No sovereignty in Europe would have the power, and therefore could not show the will to dispute the conclusion. The strongest and richest sovereignty is not stronger and richer than all the rest.

5. The Reduction and Limitation of Armaments

With judicial settlement established, no sovereignty would have more occasion for war than any other. Nor is it to be thought that any one will keep up such an army, after the league is on foot, as would hazard the safety of the others. However, if it be found needful, the question may be asked, by order of the Sovereign States, why such an one either raises or keeps up a formidable body of troops, and he be obliged forthwith to reduce them: lest any one, by keeping up a great body of troops, should surprise a neighbor. But only a small force in every other sovereignty, such as it is capable or accustomed to maintain, will certainly prevent that danger and vanquish any such fear....

VI. Benefits of the League of Nations

First: Let it not be considered the least benefit that the league would prevent the spilling of so much human blood; for a thing so offensive to God, and terrible and afflicting to men, must recommend our expedient beyond all objections. Although the chief men in government positions are seldom personally exposed in war, yet it is a duty incumbent upon them to be tender of the lives of their people; since, without all doubt, they are accountable to God for the blood that is spilt in their service. Besides the loss of so many lives, of importance to any nation both for labor and propagation, the cries of so many widows, parents and fatherless, would be prevented.

Second, by means of this peaceable expedient the reputation of Christianity would in some degree be recovered. Christians have warred with non-Christians, and with other Christians; the same kinds of Christians have fought with one another: at the same time, invoking and interesting, all they could, the good and merciful God to prosper their arms to their brethren's destruction. Yet their Savior has told them that he came to save and not to destroy the lives of men, to give and plant peace among men; and if any sense he may be said to send war, it is the Holy War indeed, for it is against the Devil, and not against the persons of men. Here is a wide field for service on the part of the reverend clergy of Europe, who have so much the possession of princes and people too. May they recommend and labor this pacific means I offer, which will end bloodshed, if not strife; and then reason, founded upon free debate, and not the sword, will be judge, and both justice and peace will result.

Third: Money would be saved both to governments and people, and popular discontent which follows the devouring expenses of war would be prevented. Both governments and people would be enabled to expend larger sums upon learning, charity, industry, and other things which are the virtue of governments and the ornaments of nations.

Fourth: Towns, cities and countries laid waste by war would be preserved. What this would mean, let Flanders, Hungary, and the borders of England and Scotland answer!

Fifth: It would make easy and secure both travel and trade, which has never been fully realized since the Roman Empire was broken into so many sovereignties. A passport issued by any member of the league would be honored by all the other states, and it could be used in peace as it cannot be in war. This would lead to the benefit of a world-monarchy, without the disadvantages that attend it: to the peace and security which alone could render a universal monarchy desirable.

Sixth: It would secure Christian Europe against the inroads of the Turks. For it would have been impossible for the Porte to have prevailed so often and so far upon Christendom, except for the indifference or willful connivance, if not aid, of some Christian princes. For the same reason that no Christian monarch would venture to oppose or break such a league, the Sultan will find himself obliged to concur—if he desires to secure that which he holds in Europe; for, with all his strength, he would feel the league an overmatch for him.

Seventh: The league would beget and increase personal friendship between governments and peoples, which would itself tend to prevent war and to plant peace in a deep and fruitful soil. The tranquility of the world would be greatly promoted if rulers could freely converse face to face and personally and reciprocally give and receive marks of civility and kindness. International emulation would then consist in such things as goodness, laws, customs, learning, arts, buildings and particularly those that relate to charity.…

44. JOHN WOOLMAN

Journal of John Woolman

John Woolman (1720-1772) was an itinerant Quaker preacher in America who became known for his abolitionism—his stance against slavery—and his advocacy for a just land policy for the Indians. Woolman was especially concerned about the payment of a tax that would fund the war against the Indians, and in the following 1757 writing from his journal, which was first published in 1774, he recounts his struggle of conscience in relation to the tax. In the second journal excerpt, written in 1758, Woolman reports on his principled opposition to the keeping of slaves.

A FEW years past, money being made current in our province for carrying on wars, and to be called in again by taxes laid on the inhabitants, my mind was often affected with the thoughts of paying such taxes; and I believe it right for me to preserve a memorandum concerning it. I was told that Friends in England frequently paid taxes, when the money was applied to such purposes. I had conversation with several noted Friends on the subject, who all favored the payment of such taxes; some of them I preferred before myself, and this made me easier for a time; yet there was in the depth of my mind a scruple which I never could get over; and at certain times I was greatly distressed on that account.

I believed that there were some upright-hearted men who paid such taxes, yet could not see that their example was a sufficient reason for me to do so, while I believe that the spirit of truth required of me, as an individual, to suffer patiently the distress of goods, rather than pay actively.

To refuse the active payment of a tax which our Society generally paid was exceedingly disagreeable; but to do a thing contrary to my conscience appeared yet more dreadful. When this exercise came upon me, I knew of none under the like difficulty; and in my distress I besought the Lord to enable me to give up all that so I might follow him wheresoever he was pleased to lead me. Under this exercise I went to our Yearly Meeting at Philadelphia in the year 1755; at which a committee was appointed of some from each Quarterly Meeting, to correspond with the meeting for sufferers in London; and another to visit our Monthly and Quarterly Meetings. After their appointment, before the last adjournment of the meeting, it was agreed that these two committees should meet together in Friends' schoolhouse in the city, to consider some things in which the cause of truth was concerned. They accordingly had a weighty conference in the fear of the Lord; at which time I perceived there were many Friends under a scruple like that before mentioned.

As scrupling to pay a tax on account of the application hath seldom been heard of heretofore, even amongst men of integrity, who have steadily borne their testimony against outward wars in their time, I may therefore note some things which have occurred to my mind, as I have been inwardly exercised on that account. From the steady opposition which faithful Friends in early times made to wrong things then approved, they were hated and persecuted by men living in the spirit of this world, and suffering with firmness, they were made a blessing to the Church, and the work prospered. It equally concerns men in every age to take heed to their own spirits; and in comparing their situation with ours, to me it appears that there was less danger of their being infected with the spirit of this world, in paying such taxes, than is the case with us now. They had little or no share in civil government, and many of them declared that they were, through the power of God, separated from the spirit in which wars were, and being afflicted by the rulers on account of their testimony, there was less likelihood of their uniting in spirit with them in things inconsistent with the purity of truth. We, from the first settlement of this land, have known little or no troubles of that sort. The profession of our predecessors was for a time accounted reproachful, but at length their uprightness being understood by the rulers, and their innocent sufferings moving them, our way of worship was tolerated, and many of our members in these colonies became active in civil government. Being thus tried with favor and prosperity, this world appeared inviting; our minds have been turned to the improvement of our country, to merchandise and the sciences, amongst which are many things useful, if followed in pure wisdom; but in our present condition I believe it will not be denied that a carnal mind is gaining upon us. Some of our members, who are officers in civil government, are in one case or other, called upon in their respective stations to assist in things relative to the wars; but being in doubt whether to act or to crave to be excused from their office, if they see their brethren united in the payment of a tax to carry on the said wars, may think their case not much different, and so might quench the tender movings of the Holy Spirit in their minds. Thus, by small degrees, we might approach so near to fighting that the distinction would be little else than the name of a peaceable people.

It requires great self-denial and resignation of ourselves to God, to attain that state wherein we can freely cease from fighting when wrongfully invaded, if, by our fighting, there were a probability of overcoming the invaders. Whoever rightly attains to it does in some degree feel that spirit in which our Redeemer gave his life for us; and through divine goodness many of our predecessors, and many now living, have learned this blessed lesson; but many others, having their religion chiefly by education, and not being enough acquainted with that cross which crucifies to the world, do manifest a temper distinguishable from that of an entire trust in God. In calmly considering these things, it hath not appeared strange to me that an exercise hath now fallen upon some, which, with respect to the outward means, is different from what was known to many of those who went before us.

Some time after the Yearly Meeting, the said committees met at Philadelphia, and, by adjournments, continued sitting several days. The calamities of war were now increasing; the frontier inhabitants of Pennsylvania were frequently surprised; some were slain, and many taken captive by the Indians; and while these committees sat, the corpse of one so slain was brought in a wagon, and taken through the streets of the city in his bloody garments, to alarm the people and rouse them to war.

Friends thus met were not all of one mind in relation to the tax, which, to those who scrupled it, made the way more difficult. To refuse an active payment at such a time might be construed into an act of disloyalty, and appeared likely to displease the rulers not only here but in England; still there was a scruple so fixed on the minds of many Friends that nothing moved it. It was a conference the most weighty that ever I was at, and the hearts of many were bowed in reverence before the Most High. Some Friends of the said committees who appeared easy to pay the tax, after several adjournments, withdrew; others of them continued till the last. At length an epistle of tender love and caution to Friends in Pennsylvania was drawn up, and being read several times and corrected, was signed by such as were free to sign it, and afterward sent to the Monthly and Quarterly Meetings....

The Monthly Meeting of Philadelphia having been under a concern on account of some Friends who this summer (1758) had bought negro slaves, proposed to their Quarterly Meeting to have the minute reconsidered in the Yearly Meeting, which was made last on that subject, and the said Quarterly Meeting appointed a committee to consider it, and to report to their next. This committee having met once and adjourned, and I, going to Philadelphia to meet a committee of the Yearly Meeting, was in town the evening on which the Quarterly Meeting's committee met the second time, and finding an inclination to sit with them, I, with some others, was admitted, and Friends had a weighty conference on the subject. Soon after their next Quarterly Meeting I heard that the case was coming to our Yearly Meeting. This brought a weighty exercise upon me, and under a sense of my own infirmities, and the great danger I felt of turning aside from perfect purity, my mind was often drawn to retire alone, and put up my prayers to the Lord that he would be graciously pleased to strengthen me; that setting aside all views of self-interest and the friendship of this world, I might stand fully resigned to his holy will.

In this Yearly Meeting several weighty matters were considered, and toward the last that in relation to dealing with persons who purchase slaves. During the several sittings of the said meeting, my mind was frequently covered with inward prayer, and I could say with David, "that tears were my meat day and night." The case of slave-keeping lay heavy upon me, nor did I find any engagement to speak directly to any other matter before the meeting. Now when this case was opened several faithful Friends spake weightily thereto, with which I was comforted; and feeling a concern to cast in my mite, I said in substance as follows:

In the difficulties attending us in this life nothing is more precious than the mind of truth inwardly manifested; and it is my earnest desire that in this weighty matter we may be so truly humbled as to be favored with a clear understanding of the mind of truth, and follow it; this would be of more advantage to the Society than any medium not in the clearness of divine wisdom. The case is difficult to some who have slaves, but if such set aside all self-interest, and come to be weaned from the desire of getting estates, or even from holding them together, when truth requires the contrary, I believe the way will so open that they will know how to steer through those difficulties.

Many Friends appeared to be deeply bowed under the weight of the work, and manifested much firmness in their love to the cause of truth and universal righteousness on the earth. And though none did openly justify the practice of slave-keeping in general, yet some appeared concerned lest the meeting should go into such measures as might give uneasiness to many brethren, alleging that if Friends patiently continued under the exercise, the Lord in his time might open a way for the deliverance of these people. Finding an engagement to speak, I said,

My mind is often led to consider the purity of the Divine Being, and the justice of his judgments; and herein my soul is covered with awfulness. I cannot omit to hint of some cases where people have not been treated with the purity of justice, and the event hath been lamentable. Many slaves on this continent are oppressed, and their cries have reached the ears of the Most High. Such are the purity and certainty of his judgments, that he cannot be partial in our favor. In infinite love and goodness, he hath opened our understanding from one time to another concerning our

duty towards this people, and it is not a time for delay. Should we now be sensible of what he requires of us, and through a respect to the private interest of some persons, or through a regard to some friendships which do not stand on an immutable foundation, neglect to do our duty in firmness and constancy, still waiting for some extraordinary means to bring about their deliverance, God may by terrible things in righteousness answer us in this matter.

Many faithful brethren labored with great firmness, and the love of truth in a good degree prevailed. Several who had negroes expressed their desire that a rule might be made to deal with such Friends as offenders who bought slaves in future. To this it was answered that the root of this evil would never be effectually struck at until a thorough search was made in the circumstances of such Friends as kept negroes, with respect to the righteousness of their motives in keeping them, that impartial justice might be administered throughout. Several Friends expressed their desire that a visit might be made to such Friends as kept slaves, and many others said that they believed liberty was the negro's right; to which, at length, no opposition was publicly made. A minute was made more full on that subject than any heretofore; and the names of several Friends entered who were free to join in a visit to such as kept slaves.

45. Pennsylvania Mennonites and German Baptists

A Short and Sincere Declaration

In colonial America, and especially at the time of the time of the Revolutionary War, Mennonites and German Baptists in Pennsylvania sought exemption from military service because of their religious beliefs. The Pennsylvania Assembly granted them the exemption, and in reply they offered the following statement of their thanks, as well as a commitment to serve the commonwealth in ways other than through the bearing of arms. The following short note appears at the end of the document: "The above Declaration, signed by a Number of Elders and Teachers of the Society of Mennonites, and some of the German Baptists, presented to the Honorable House of Assembly on the 7th Day of November, 1775, was most graciously received."

To our *Honorable Assembly,* and all others in high or low Station of *Administration,* and to all Friends and Inhabitants of this Country, to whose Sight this may come, be they ENGLISH or GERMANS.

In the first place we acknowledge us indebted to the most high God, who created Heaven and Earth, the only good Being, to thank him for all his great Goodness and manifold Mercies and Love through our Savior Jesus Christ, who is come to save the Souls of Men, having all Power in Heaven and Earth.

Further we find ourselves indebted to be thankful to our late worthy Assembly, for their giving so good an Advice in these troublesome Times to all Ranks of People in *Pennsylvania,* particularly in allowing those, who, by the Doctrine of our Savior Jesus Christ, are persuaded in their Consciences to love their Enemies, and not to resist Evil, to enjoy the Liberty of their Conscience, for which, as also for all the good Things we enjoyed under their Care, we heartily thank that worthy Body of Assembly, and all high and low in Office, who have advised to such a peaceful Measure, hoping and confiding that they, and all others entrusted with Power in this hitherto blessed Province, may be moved by the same Spirit of Grace, which animated the first Founder of this Province, our late worthy Proprietor *William Penn,* to grant Liberty of Conscience to all its inhabitants, that they may in the great and memorable Day of Judgment be put on the right Hand of the just Judge, who judgeth without Respect of Person, and hear of him these blessed Words. *Come, ye blessed of my Father, inherit the Kingdom prepared for you, &c. What ye have done unto one of the least of these my Brethren, ye have done unto me,* among which Number *(i.e., the least of Christ's Brethren)* we by his grace hope to be ranked; and every Lenity and Favor shewn to such tender conscienced, although weak Followers of this our blessed Savior, will not be forgotten by him in that great Day.

The Advice to those who do not feel Freedom of Conscience to take up Arms, that they ought to be helpful to those who are in Need and distressed Circumstances, we receive with Cheerfulness towards all Men of what Station they may be—it being our Principle to feed the Hungry and give the Thirsty Drink; we have dedicated ourselves to serve all Men in every Thing that can be helpful to the Preservation of Men's Lives, but we find no Freedom in giving, or doing, or assisting any Thing by which Men's Lives are destroyed or hurt—We beg the patience of all those who believe we err on this point.

We are always ready, according to Christ's Command to *Peter,* to pay the Tribute, that we may offend no Man, and so we are willing to pay taxes, *and to render unto Caesar those things that are Caesar's, and to God those Things that are God's,* although we think ourselves very weak to give God his due Honor, he being a Spirit and Life, and we only Dust and Ashes.

We are also willing to be subject to the higher Powers, and to give in the manner *Paul* directs us— *for he beareth the Sword not in vain, for he is the Minister of God, a Revenger to execute Wrath upon him that doeth Evil.*

This Testimony we lay down before our worthy Assembly, and all other Persons in Government, letting them know, that we are thankful as above-mentioned, and that we are not at Liberty in Conscience to take up Arms to conquer our Enemies, but rather to pray to God, who has Power in Heaven and on Earth, for *US* and *THEM.*

We also crave the Patience of all the Inhabitants of this Country—what they think to see clearer in the Doctrine of the blessed Jesus Christ, we will leave to them and God, finding ourselves very poor; for Faith is to proceed out of the Word of God, which is Life and Spirit, and a Power of God, and our Conscience is to be instructed by the same, therefore we beg for Patience.

Our small Gift, which we have given, we gave to those who have Power over us, that we may not offend them, as Christ taught us by the Tribute Penny.

We heartily pray that God would govern all Hearts of our Rulers, be they high or low, to mediate those good Things which will pertain to *OUR* and *THEIR* Happiness.

46. DAVID DODGE

War Inconsistent with the Religion of Jesus Christ

In 1815, David Dodge (1774-1852), a wealthy Presbyterian merchant, founded the first formal peace organization in the United States—the New York Peace Society. This society would merge with others in 1828 to become the American Peace Society, and Dodge played a leading role in the APS until the following decade. Dodge was also a famous tract writer, and three years before he founded the New York Peace Society, he authored the pamphlet excerpted below, War Inconsistent with the Religion of Jesus Christ, *which arrived on the heels of the War of 1812. Especially noteworthy in the text is his attention to the effects of war on "God's animal creation," and, more generally, his graphic descriptions of the ravages of war. These descriptions stand in sharp contrast to the largely septic analyses of war by many contemporary Christian writers on war and peace.*

Humanity, wisdom, and goodness at once combine all that can be great and lovely in man. Inhumanity, folly, and wickedness reverse the picture, and at once represent all that can be odious and hateful. The former is the spirit of Heaven, and the latter the offspring of hell. The spirit of the gospel not only "breathes glory to God in the highest, but on earth peace, and good will to men." The wisdom from above is first pure, then peaceable, gentle, easy to be entreated; but the wisdom from beneath is earthly, sensual, and devilish.

It is exceedingly strange that anyone under the light of the gospel, professing to be guided by its blessed precepts, with the Bible in his hand, while the whole creation around him is so often groaning under the weight and terrors of war, should have doubts whether any kinds of wars under the gospel dispensation, except spiritual warfare, can be the dictate of any kind of wisdom except that from beneath; and much more so, to believe that they are the fruit of the Divine Spirit, which is love, joy, and peace.

An inspired apostle has informed us from whence come wars and fightings. They come from the lusts of men that war in their numbers. Ever since the fall, mankind have had naturally within them a spirit of pride, avarice, and revenge. The gospel is directly opposed to this spirit. It teaches humility, it inculcates love, it breathes pity and forgiveness even to enemies, and forbids rendering evil for evil to any man.

Believing as I do, after much reflection and, as I trust, prayerful investigation of the subject, that all kinds of carnal warfare are unlawful upon gospel principles, I shall now endeavor to prove that WAR is INHUMAN, UNWISE, and CRIMINAL, and then make some general remarks, and state and answer several objections....

I. War Is Inhuman, Because It Hardens the Heart and Blunts the Tender Feelings of Mankind

That it is the duty of mankind to be tenderhearted, feeling for the distress of others, and to do all in their power to prevent and alleviate their misery, is evident not only from the example of the Son of God but the precepts of the gospel.

When the Savior of sinners visited this dark and cruel world he became a man of sorrow and was acquainted with grief, so that he was touched with the feeling of our infirmities. He went about continually healing the sick, opening the eyes of the blind, unstopping the ears of the deaf, raising the dead, as well as preaching the gospel of peace to the poor.... Love to God and man flowed from his soul pure as the river of life, refreshing the thirsty desert around him. He was affectionate not only to his friends but kind to his enemies. He returned love for their hatred, and blessing for their curse....

The apostle exhorts Christians, saying, "Be ye kind and tenderhearted, forgiving one another, even as God for Christ's sake hath forgiven you."

Authority in abundance might be quoted to show that the spirit of the gospel absolutely requires the exercise of love, pity, and forgiveness, even to enemies.

But who will undertake to prove that soldiers are usually kind and tenderhearted, and that their employment has a natural tendency to promote active benevolence, while it requires all their study of mind and strength of body to injure their enemies to the greatest extent? ...

Is it not a fact that those who are engaged in the spirit of war, either in the council or in the field, are not usually so meek, lowly, kind, and tenderhearted as other men? Does the soldier usually become kind and tenderhearted while trained to the art of killing his fellowman, or more so when engaged in the heat of the battle, stepping forward over the wounded and hearing the groans of the expiring? Does he actually put on bowels of tenderness, mercy, and forgiveness, while he bathes his sword in the blood of his brother? Do these scenes generally change the lion into the lamb? ...

It is a fact, however, so notorious that the spirit and practice of war do actually harden the heart and chill the kind and tender feelings of mankind, that I think few will be found to deny it, and none who have ever known or felt the spirit of Christ....

II. War Is Inhuman,
As in Its Nature and Tendency
It Abuses God's Animal Creation

... Though God has decorated the earth with beauty and richly clothed it with food for man and beast, yet where an all-devouring army passes, notwithstanding the earth before them is like the garden of Eden, it is behind them a desolate wilderness; the lowing ox and bleating sheep may cry for food, but, alas! the destroyer hath destroyed it.

The noble horse, which God has made for the use and pleasure of man, shares largely in this desolating evil....

... the horse rushes into the combat not knowing that torture and death are before him. His sides are often perforated with the spur of his rider, notwithstanding he exerts all his strength to rush into the heat of the battle, while the strokes of the sabers and the wounds of the bullets lacerate his body, and instead of having God's pure air to breathe to alleviate his pains, he can only snuff up the dust of his feet and the sulphurous smoke of the cannon, emblem of the infernal abode....

But if such is the cruelty to beasts in persecuting war, what is the cruelty to man, born for immortality?

No wonder that those who feel so little for their fellowman should feel less for beasts....

III. War Is Inhuman,
As It Oppresses the Poor

To oppress the poor is everywhere in the Scriptures considered as a great sin ...

That war actually does oppress the poor may be heard from ten thousand wretched tongues who have felt its woe. Very few, comparatively, who are instigators of war actually take the field of battle, and are seldom seen in the front of the fire. It is usually those who are rioting on the labors of the poor that fan up the flames of war. The great mass of soldiers are generally from the poor of a country. They must gird on the harness and for a few cents per day endure all the hardships of a camp and be led forward like sheep to the slaughter....

War cannot be prosecuted without enormous expenses. The money that has been expended the last twenty years in war would doubtless have been sufficient not only to have rendered every poor person on earth comfortable—so far as money could do it—during the same period, but, if the residue had been applied to cultivate the earth, it would have literally turned the desert into a fruitful field....

The vast expenses of war must be met by corresponding taxes, whether by duties on merchandise or direct taxes on real estate; yet they fall most heavily on the poor.... In times of war the prices of the necessaries of life are generally very much increased, but the prices of the labor of the poor do not usually rise in the same proportion, therefore it falls very heavily on them. When the honest laborers are suddenly called from the plow to take the sword and leave the tilling of the ground, either its seed is but sparingly sown or its fruit but partially gathered, scarcity ensues, high prices are the consequence …

These are some of the evils of war at a distance, but when it comes to their doors … they fly from their habitations, leaving their little all to the fire and pillage, glad to escape with their lives, though destitute and dependent … Thus does war not only oppress the poor but also adds multitudes to their number who before were comfortable.…

IV. War Is Inhuman, As It Spreads Terror and Distress among Mankind

In the benign reign of Messiah on earth the earth will be filled with the abundance of peace; there will be nothing to hurt or destroy; every one will sit quietly under his own vine and fig tree, having nothing to molest or make him afraid. But in times of war, mankind are usually full of anxiety, looking for those things which are coming upon our wicked world.

One of the most delightful scenes on earth is a happy family where all the members dwell together in love, being influenced by the blessed precepts of the gospel of peace. But how soon does the sound of war disturb and distress the happy circle! …

Who can describe the distress of a happy village suddenly encompassed by two contending armies … hundreds of cannon are vomiting destruction in every quarter; the hoofs of horses trampling down everything in their way; bullets, stones, bricks, and splinters flying in every direction; houses pierced with cannon shot and shells which carry desolation in their course; without, multitudes of men rushing with deadly weapons upon each other with all the rage of tigers, plunging each other into eternity, until the streets are literally drenched with the blood of men.…

V. War Is Inhuman, As It Involves Men in Fatigue, Famine, and All the Pains of the Mutilated

… There [on the field of battle] thousands of mangled bodies lie on the cold ground hours, and sometimes days, without a friendly hand to bind up a wound; not a voice is heard except the dying groans of their fellow soldiers around them. No one can describe the horrors of the scene: here lies one with a fractured skull, there another with a severed limb, and a third with a lacerated body; some fainting with the loss of blood, others distracted, and others again crying for help.

If such are some of the faint outlines of the fatigues and sufferings of soldiers, then their occupation must be an inhuman employment, for they are instrumental in bringing the same calamities on others which they suffer themselves; and of course it is unfriendly to the spirit of the gospel and wrong for Christians to engage in it.…

VI. War Is Inhuman, As It Destroys the Youth and Cuts Off the Hope of Gray Hairs

Mankind are speedily hastening into eternity, and it might be supposed sufficiently fast without the aid of all the ingenuity and strength of man to hurry them forward; yet it is a melancholy truth that a great proportion of the wealth, talents, and labors of men are actually employed in inventing and using means for the premature destruction of their fellow-beings.…

No pen, much less this writer's, can describe the inhumanity and horrors of a battle.… Hundreds are parrying the blows; hundreds more are thrusting their bayonets into the bowels of their fellow mortals, and many, while extricating them, have their own heads cleft asunder by swords and sabers; and all are hurried together before the tribunal Judge, with hearts full of rage and hands dyed in the blood of their brethren.…

VII. War Is Inhuman, As It Multiplies Widows and Orphans, and Clothes the Land in Mourning

The widow and fatherless are special objects of divine compassion, and Christianity binds men under the strongest obligation to be kind and merciful towards them, as their situation is peculiarly tender and afflicting. "A father of the fatherless, and a judge of the widow, is God in his holy habitation." ...

To be active in any measure which has a natural tendency to wantonly multiply widows and orphans in a land is the height of inhumanity as well as daring impiety.

I will venture to say that no one circumstance in our world has so greatly multiplied widows and fatherless children as that of war....

In times of war thousands of virtuous women are deprived of their husbands and ten thousands of helpless children of their fathers. The little tender children may now gather round their disconsolate mothers, anxiously inquiring about their fathers, remembering their kind visages, recollecting how they used fondly to dandle them on their knees and affectionately instruct them; but now they are torn from their embraces by the cruelty

of war, and they have no fathers left them but their Father in heaven....

Surely Christians cannot be active in such measures without incurring the displeasure of God, who styles himself the father of the fatherless and the judge and avenger of the widow....

Dodge goes on the describe war as "unwise," primarily because it encourages soldiers to lead an immoral lifestyle, and as "criminal" when judged against the moral standards of the Gospel. More particularly, war is criminal because it intoxicates soldiers with temptation, encourages pride, infringes on individual conscience, opposes "patient suffering," disobeys the Golden Rule, undermines mercy, requires justice rather than forgiveness, and returns evil for evil.

47. PRISCILLA CADWALLADER

Sermon against War

Priscilla Cadwallader (1786-1859) was a prominent Quaker minister who, while based at the Blue River Monthly Meeting in Washington County, Indiana, traveled and spoke across the United States in the early- to mid-1800s. In the sermon below, which she delivered in Darby, Pennsylvania, in 1831, she predicts a coming war occasioned by the evils of slavery. The sermon was published and distributed as part of her memoirs in the very midst of the Civil War, and following the text of her sermon is a brief account of her own interpretation of the sermon: "I cannot tell when it will be accomplished; but whoever lives 50 years longer, will see America very different from what it now is, in regard to African Slavery."

"What shall I do unto thee? O Ephraim; O Judah, what shall I do unto thee, for your goodness is as the morning cloud and as the early dew that passes away. Therefore get thee into thy tent, and dwell in it lest that which has been so abundantly handed forth shall be entirely withdrawn." This language was sounded in my ears soon after I took my seat among you.... I was willing to take it to myself, conceal it in my own breast, and improve upon it. But finding it is not for me alone, I feel a woe if I warn not this people, and take not warning myself. Therefore, my beloved friends, let us gather

home; let us dwell in our tent, and that is God. And there is no other tent, in which the mind of man can safely dwell. And I believe there never was a day nor a time when there was more need for this people to dwell in their tents—for here our safety assuredly lies. For I believe, from awful impressions as I pass through the land, there are more storms arising, greater than have yet been witnessed by this people. And those who are not founded in God, whose souls are not anchored in perfect love, will be wiped away, and carried wholly into the vortex of confusion. For behold there cometh *storms* and *tempests* and a *deluge of blood*. And I do not find that I have much more to say unto you, than to warn you to gather home to your God—for nothing else will screen you from danger, and no other arm can protect you.

Do I not hear, in my spiritual ear—I have long heard it—the alarm of war, the loud roar of cannon, the clashing of swords, and horsemen rushing to battle. And I believe that this day is nigher at hand than many are aware of; a day of treading down, and a day of bloodshed; and it will be "seen that every battle of the warrior is with confused noise and garments rolled in blood." But this shall be a day, like the day of the Lord, "that cometh with burning and fuel of fire." And I entreat you to be willing to *come* to *this* that is "*with burning and fuel of fire*," that it may consume all the sin and transgression of the heart, purify the soul, and bring it unto God. I can tell you, beloveds, and I do tell you in awful fear, that I have long seen, *sons* wrestling in bonds, and their bands will burst, and they will leap as tigers, from their dens, and then, wo, wo, to the inhabitants of North America. Thus I feel engaged to warn all that are now present, and to invite you to come home and centre in Him who is perfect love. And there is no other weapon that will defend you but perfect love, and you will find this to be a rock of safety; and although the deluge of blood may come, yet this will bear your souls above all. For God will preserve his children who depend upon him, and who have no other arm nor place of refuge: these he will marvellously protect and hold in the hollow of his holy hand. And all who do experience this day of the Lord, do find the truth of this, that it comes with "burning and fuel of fire," and will consume all that is comparable to wood, hay or stubble: it will burn up all vain notions. And thus it is that righteousness will come unto us, and the Sun of righteousness arise with healing in his wings, as was declared by the mouth of one of the prophets: "Behold the day cometh, saith the Lord, that shall burn as an oven, and all that are proud, and all that do wickedly, shall be as stubble, and the fire of the Lord shall utterly consume them; but unto you that fear my name, shall the Sun of righteousness arise, with healing in his wings." Now this is the reward of the righteous, and these have nothing to fear. But

the sinner and transgressor must perish, fearfulness shall surprise the hypocrite, and sinners will be made afraid. This language was used formerly, and it may be used in the present day—and the time is near at hand when it will be applicable; for "the sinners in Zion will be made afraid, fearfulness [shall] surprise the hypocrite." Now, "who among us shall dwell with everlasting burnings; who among us shall dwell with the devouring fire? he that worketh righteousness, and speaketh uprightly; he that despises the gain of oppression; that shutteth his hands from the holding of bribes; that stoppeth his ears from the hearing of blood; and shutteth his eyes from seeing evil—his place of defence shall be the munition of rocks—his bread shall be given him, his water shall be sure."

Here the righteous can dwell in safety, and be at peace with God. And blessed are they who receive him in the way of his coming, and who endure this day that consumes all that his holy will hath a controversy with; blessed are those who can, in sincerity of heart, adopt the language of Jesus Christ: "Not my will, but thine, O God, be done." For in this blessed state, where the mind comes to dwell in perfect love, all fear is cast out, and where there is no fear there is no torment, said one of the Apostles—and if our souls dwell in this perfect love, we have nothing to fear; for it is this that triumphs over death, hell, and the grave. It is this that makes us perfect, even as our Father who is in heaven is perfect; and though many may think this is an impossibility—and say it is impossible for man to become as perfect as God—yet there is nothing required of us but what we have ability given us to perform, and this is a divine commandment, an injunction of Jesus Christ: "Be ye therefore *perfect* even as your Father who is in heaven is perfect." And how are we to come to this? The only way that we can come to it, is to live in perfect obedience to the Divine will. And as we come to dwell in God, and God in us, we shall dwell in perfection, for God is perfect, and we shall dwell in perfection, just so far, as we live in obedience to the Father's will; and every rational soul may come and dwell in the love of God; all have power to receive his kind offers. He is a God nigh at hand—He is Omnipresent, and all who come unto Him, are enlightened to walk in the paths of peace and perfection. But if we remain in darkness and ignorance, the fault is our own—for man was not designed to dwell in darkness; he was made to inherit the bright regions of eternal day, to come forth in light, and to be alive in the eternal Word. Therefore if man remains in darkness it is his own fault, and the reason is, because he transgresses the Divine law: he will not hearken to the call of God, nor open to the beloved of souls; while he stands inviting all, wooing all, calling all—saying unto them, "Open unto me." Now here is the express invitation of his eternal love: "Behold I stand at the door and knock, if any man will hear my voice and open unto me, I will come in to him, and sup with him, and he with me."

48. WILLIAM LLOYD GARRISON

Nonresistance Society: Declaration of Principles

On January 1, 1831, William Lloyd Garrison (1805-1879) published the first edition of the Liberator, *an anti-slavery newspaper that he would keep in business until the end of the Civil War. In addition to calling for an immediate end to slavery, Garrison also lobbied for the abolition of capital punishment and war, and he and others founded the New England Non-Resistance Society in 1838. Below is the statement of beliefs that Garrison drafted for the new society.*

Assembled in Convention, from various sections of the American Union, for the promotion of peace on earth and good will among men, we, the undersigned, regard it as due to ourselves, to the cause which we love, to the country in which we live, and to the world, to publish a Declaration, expressive of the principles we cherish, the purposes we aim to accomplish, and the measures we shall adopt to carry forward the work of the peaceful and universal reformation.

We cannot acknowledge allegiance to any human government; neither can we oppose any such government, by a resort of physical force. We recognize but one King and Lawgiver, one Judge and Ruler of Mankind. We are bound by the laws of a kingdom which is not of this world; the subjects of which are forbidden to fight; in which Mercy and Truth are met together, and Righteousness and Peace have kissed each other; which has no state lines, no national partitions, no geographical boundaries; in which there is no distinction of rank, or division of caste, or inequality of sex; the officers of which are Peace, its exactors Righteousness, its walls Salvation, and its gates Praise; and which is destined to break in pieces and consume all other kingdoms.

Our country is the world, our countrymen are all mankind. We love the land of our nativity, only as we love all other lands. The interests, rights, and liberties of American citizens are no more dear to us, than are those of the whole human race. Hence, we can allow no appeal to patriotism, to revenge any national insult or injury. The Prince of Peace, under whose stainless banner we rally, came not to destroy, but to save, even the worst of enemies. He has left us an example, that we should follow his steps. "God commandeth his love towards us, in that while we were yet sinners, Christ died for us."

We conceive, that if a nation has no right to defend itself against foreign enemies, or to punish its invaders, no individual possesses that right in his own case. The unit cannot be of greater importance than the aggregate. If one man may take life, to obtain or defend his rights, the same license must necessarily be granted to communities, states, and nations. If he may use a dagger or a pistol, they may employ cannon, bombshells, land and naval forces. The means of self-preservation must be in proportion to the magnitude of interests at stake, and the manner of lives exposed to destruction. But if a rapacious and bloodthirsty soldiery, thronging these shores from abroad, with intent to commit rapine and destroy life, may not be resisted by the people or magistracy, then ought no resistance to be offered to domestic troublers of the public peace, or of private security. No obligation can rest upon Americans to regard foreigners as more sacred in their persons than themselves, or to give them a monopoly of wrongdoing with impunity.

The dogma, that all the governments of the world are approvingly ordained of God, and that the powers that be in the United States, in Russia, in Turkey, are in accordance with His will, is not less absurd than impious. It makes the impartial Author of human freedom and equality, unequal and tyrannical. It cannot be affirmed, that the powers that be, in any nation, are actuated by the spirit, or guided by the example of Christ, in the treatment of enemies: therefore, they cannot be agreeable to the will of God: and, therefore, their overthrow, by a spiritual regeneration of their subjects, is inevitable.

We register our testimony, not only against all wars, whether offensive or defensive, but all preparations for war; against every naval ship, every arsenal, every fortification; against the militia system and a standing army; against all military chieftains and soldiers; against all monuments commemorative of victory over a foreign foe, all trophies won in battle, all celebrations in honor of military or naval exploits; against all appropriations for the defense of a nation by force and arms on the part of any legislative body; against every edict of government, requiring of its subjects military service. Hence, we deem it unlawful to bear arms, or to hold a military office.

As every human government is upheld by physical strength, and its laws are enforced virtually at the point of the bayonet, we cannot hold any office which imposes upon its incumbent the obligation to do right, on pain of imprisonment or death. We therefore voluntarily exclude ourselves from every legislative and judicial body, and repudiate all human politics, worldly honors, and stations of authority. If *we* cannot occupy a seat in

the legislature, or on the bench, neither can we elect *others* to act as our substitutes in any such capacity.

It follows, that we cannot sue any man at law, to compel him by force to restore any thing which he may have wrongfully taken from us or others; but, if he has seized our coat, we shall surrender up our cloak, rather than subject him to punishment.

We believe that the penal code of the old covenant, An eye for an eye, and a tooth for a tooth, has been abrogated by Jesus Christ; and that, under the new covenant, the forgiveness, instead of the punishment of enemies, has been enjoined upon all his disciples, in all cases whatsoever. To extort money from enemies, or set them upon a pillory, or cast them into prison, or hang them upon a gallows, is obviously not to forgive, but to take retribution. "Vengeance is mine—I will repay, saith the Lord."

The history of mankind is crowded with evidences, proving that physical coercion is not adapted to moral regeneration; that the sinful disposition of man can be subdued only by love; that evil can be exterminated from the earth only by goodness; that it is not safe to rely upon an arm of flesh, upon man, whose breath is in his nostrils, to preserve us from harm; that there is great security in being gentle, harmless, long-suffering, and abundant in mercy; that it is only the meek who shall inherit the earth, for the violent, who resort to the sword, shall perish with the sword. Hence, as a measure of sound policy, of safety to property, life, and liberty, of public quietude and private enjoyment, as well as on the ground of allegiance to Him who is King of kings, and Lord of lords, we cordially adopt the nonresistance principle; being confident that it provides for all possible consequences, will ensure all things needful to us, is armed with omnipotent power, and must ultimately triumph over every assailing force.

We advocate no jacobinical doctrines. The spirit of jacobinism is the spirit of retaliation, violence and murder. It neither fears God, nor regards man. We would be filled with the spirit of Christ. If we abide by our principles, it is impossible for us to be disorderly, or plot treason, or participate in any evil work: we shall submit to every ordinance of man, for the Lord's sake; obey all the requirements of government, except such as we deem contrary to the commands of the gospel; and in no wise resist the operation of law, except by meekly submitting to the penalty of disobedience.

But, while we shall adhere to the doctrines of nonresistance and passive submission to enemies, we purpose, in a moral and spiritual sense, to speak and act boldly in the cause of God; to assail iniquity in high places and in low places; to apply our principles to all existing civil, political, legal, and ecclesiastical institutions; and to hasten the time, when the kingdoms of this world shall become the kingdoms of our Lord and of his Christ, and he shall reign for ever.

It appears to us a self-evident truth, that, whatever the gospel is designed to destroy at any period of the world, being contrary to it, ought now to be abandoned. If, then, the time is predicted, when swords shall be beaten into ploughshares, and spears into pruning hooks, and men shall not learn the art of war any more, it follows that all who manufacture, sell, or wield those deadly weapons, do thus array themselves against the peaceful dominion of the Son of God on earth.

Having thus briefly, but frankly, stated our principles and purposes, we proceed to specify the measures we propose to adopt, in carrying our object into effect.

We expect to prevail through the foolishness of preaching—striving to commend ourselves unto every man's conscience, in the sight of God. From the press, we shall promulgate our sentiments as widely as practicable. We shall endeavor to secure the cooperation of all persons, of whatever name or sect. The triumphant progress of the cause of Temperance and of Abolition in our land, through the instrumentality of benevolent and voluntary associations, encourages us to combine our own means and efforts for the promotion of a still greater cause. Hence we shall employ lecturers, circulate tracts and publications, form societies, and petition our state and national governments in relation to the subject of Universal Peace. It will be our leading object to devise ways and means for effecting a radical change in the views, feelings and practices of society respecting the sinfulness of war, and the treatment of enemies.

In entering upon the great work before us, we are not unmindful that, in its prosecution, we may be called to test our sincerity, even as in a fiery ordeal. It may subject us to insult, outrage, suffering, yea, even death itself. We anticipate no small amount of misconceptions, misrepresentation, calumny. Tumults may arise against us. The ungodly and violent, the proud and pharisaical, the ambitious and tyrannical, principalities and powers, and spiritual wickedness in high places, may combine to crush us. So they treated the Messiah, whose example we are humbly striving to imitate. If we suffer with him, we know that we shall reign with him. We shall not be afraid of their terror, neither be troubled. Our confidence is in the Lord Almighty, not in man. Having withdrawn from human protection, what can sustain us but the faith which overcomes the world? We shall not think it strange concerning the fiery trial which is to try us, as though some strange thing had happened unto us; but rejoice, inasmuch as we are partakers of Christ's sufferings. Wherefore, we commit the keeping of our souls to God, in well-doing, as unto a faithful Creator. "For everyone that forsakes houses, or brethren, or sisters, or father, or mother, or wife, or children, or lands, for Christ's sake, shall receive an hundred fold, and shall inherit everlasting life."

Firmly relying upon the certain and universal triumph of the sentiments contained in this Declaration, however formidable may be the opposition arrayed against them, in solemn testimony of our faith in their divine origin, we hereby affix our signatures to it; commending it to the reason and conscience of mankind, giving ourselves no anxiety as to what may befall us, and resolving, in the strength of the Lord God, calmly and meekly to abide the issue.

49. Frederick Douglass

My Opposition to War

Whipped and beaten as a slave, Frederick Douglass (1818-1895) freed himself on September 3, 1838, while working at a shipyard in Baltimore. After traveling by train and steamboat to New York City, Douglass eventually settled in Massachusetts, where he became an active abolitionist and spoke regularly for the Massachusetts Anti-Slavery Society. In 1845, he published his famous autobiography, Narrative of the Life of Frederick Douglass, an American Slave, Written by Himself, *and for the next few years toured England, Ireland, and Scotland. Below is the text of* My Opposition to War, *an address he delivered in London, England, on May 19, 1846. It is perhaps the clearest statement of his nonviolence at this point in his life. (During the Civil War, Douglass would recruit northern blacks for the Union Army.)*

1. I experience great pleasure in rising to support the resolution which has been so ably advocated by the gentleman preceding me. You may think it somewhat singular, that I, a slave, an American slave, should stand forth at this time as an advocate of peace between two countries situated as this and the United States are, when it is universally believed that a war between them would eventuate in the emancipation of three millions of my brethren who are now held in most cruel bonds in that country. I believe this would be the result; but such is my regard for the principle of peace—such is my deep, firm conviction that nothing can be attained for liberty universally by war, that were I to be asked the question as to whether I would have my emancipation by the shedding of one single drop of blood, my answer would be in the negative. (Loud cheers.)

2. I am opposed to war, because I am a believer in Christianity. I am opposed to war, because I am a lover of my race. The first gleam of Christian truth that beamed upon my dark mind, after having escaped the clutches of those who held me in slavery, was accompanied by the spirit of love. I felt at that moment as if I were embracing the whole world in the arms of love and affection. I could not have injured one hair of the head of my worst enemy, although that enemy might have been at that very time imbruing his hands in the blood of a brother or a sister. I believe all who have experienced this love, who are living in the enjoyment of this love, feel this same spirit, this same abhorrence of injuring a single individual, no matter what his conduct happens to be.

3. One of my reasons for hating war, and by which my attention was first attracted to its many evils, was a circumstance which occurred a few years since in the city of New York. During the revolutionary war, an attempt was made to bombard many of our cities on the coast. Some of the bombshells had been recently found that were thrown during that war. One was taken from the shores of New Jersey, and sent to an ironmonger in the city of New York. When in the shop, one of the workmen took it out of doors, and finding it had not been discharged, he commenced with a hammer and chisel to take out its contents; and in so doing, by one stroke with the hammer, a spark was emitted, and at once the shell exploded, blowing the poor man to atoms—his legs one way, his arms another, his skull, his whole person was shattered by this single bomb. Pieces passed into several dwellings and three or four women and one or two children were killed in consequence of that single bombshell. The thought struck me, what must be the state of things when hundreds of these are thrown into innocent families, not among the hostile parties, not among those on the field of battle,

armed and equipped, infuriated with the spirit of war, but into the domestic circle, among children some of whom may have been intended by the Creator to fill a prominent place in the reformation and purification of the world—these all destroyed by the demon, war. On reading an account of this, I thought if I had power within me, it should be used, whenever it could, in opposition to the demoniacal spirit of war. (Cheers.)

4. Some people contend that they can fight in love. I have heard individuals say they could go to war in love. Yes, this foul reproach has been brought upon Christianity, and ministers have been heard to say that they could go to war in love. This was answered very well by an advocate of peace in the United States, and I am happy to inform the good people here that advocates of peace are multiplying in the United States. (Cheers.) An advocate of peace was arguing this question with a brother who was a minister of the gospel. The minister was against it; in fact, they were both ministers. He was asked, "If he believed Christianity was a religion of love? If the spirit of Christ breathed love?" He admitted it—he said, "God is love." "Then," said the other, "all that dwell in him should dwell in love." This he admitted at once. "Then we should do nothing but what can be done in entire consistency with love?" Of course this must be granted. "Well," said he, "can you go to war in love?" "Oh! yes. (Laughter and cheers.) "Can you kill an enemy in love?" "Oh! yes. I can conceive of circumstances when I should be bound by love to kill him." "What, throw bombshells, shoot cannon, use the sword in love?" "Yes."

"Well," said my good friend, "if you can do all these things in love, what can you do in hate?" (Laughter and cheers.)

5. I believe, if there is one thing more than another that has brought a reproach upon the Christian religion, it is the spirit of war. Why, a little while ago, in the Congress of the United States, a member arose and proposed the appropriation of a large sum to the support of the chaplaincy in the navy. Our Congress is made up of various materials; among the number there is an infidel, the son of Robert Owen. That infidel, Mr. Owen, rose in his place at once, and opposed the proposition to support the chaplaincy; and on what ground, do you suppose? He did it, he said, on patriotic grounds. He was opposed to the introduction of the Scriptures in the navy, for, he said, "If the principles of Christianity, if the doctrines inculcated in the New Testament are carried out in the lives of our soldiers, they would do the very opposite to that for which we enlist them in the service. (Cheers.) Instead of shooting their enemies, they would love them; instead of butchering them, they would bind up their wounds; instead of blowing them into atoms, they would seek to preserve their lives." He added, "I am utterly and unequivocally opposed to any support being given to the chaplaincy—they would preach the doctrines of the New Testament." What a stain, what a blot: an infidel rising up and rebuking ministers claiming to be ministers of the God of love; rebuking them for their delinquency, and preaching a higher Christianity than those to whom he has been accustomed to look! (Cheers.)

50. Adin Ballou

Christian Nonresistance

Adin Ballou (1803-1890) was the founder of the Hopedale Community in 1842, a utopian group whose "practical Christianity" stood opposed to intemperance, slavery, the degradation of women, and war. A Universalist minister, Ballou joined forces with the abolitionist William Lloyd Garrison in founding the New England Non-Resistance Society in 1838. The society chose Ballou as its president in 1843, and three years later he authored a book titled Christian Nonresistance. *Excerpted below, the book represents one of the first systematic articulations of the definition of "nonresistance."*

The Term Christian Nonresistance

Whence originated the term *Christian nonresistance*? Nonresistance comes from the injunction, "*resist not evil,*" Matt. 5:39. The words "*resist not,*" being changed from the form of a *verb* to that of a substantive, give us *nonresistance*. This term is considered more strikingly significant than any other, of the *principle* involved, and the *duty* enjoined in our Savior's precept. Hence its adoption and established use. It is denominated *Christian* nonresistance, to distinguish it, as the genuine primitive doctrine, from mere *philosophical, sentimental* and *necessitous* nonresistance. Literally, then, *Christian nonresistance* is the original nonresistance taught and exemplified by Jesus Christ; the bearings, limitations and applications which are to be learned from the Scriptures of the New Testament....

The Key Text of Nonresistance

Now let us examine Matt. 5: 39. "I say unto you, resist not evil," &c. This single text, from which, as has been stated, the term nonresistance took its rise, if justly construed, furnishes a complete key to the true bearings, limitations and applications of the doctrine under discussion.... What did the divine teacher mean by the word "*evil,*" and what by the word "*resist*"? There are several kinds of *evil*. 1. Pain, loss, damage, suffered from causes involving no moral agency, or *natural evil*. 2. Sin in general, or *moral evil*. 3. Temptations to sin, or *spiritual evil*. 4. Personal wrong, insult, outrage, injury—or *personal evil*. Which of these kinds of evil does the context show to have been in our Savior's mind when he said "*resist not evil*"? Was he speaking of fires, floods, famine, disease, serpents, wild beasts, or any other mere *natural evil agents*? No. Then of course he does not prohibit our resisting *such evil*. Was he speaking of sin in general? No. Then of course he does not prohibit our resisting *such evil* by suitable means. Was he speaking of temptations addressed to our propensities and passions, enticing us to commit sin? No. Then of course he does not prohibit our resisting the *devil*, withstanding the *evil* suggestions of our own carnal mind, and suppressing our *evil* lusts. Was he speaking of *personal evil,* injury personally inflicted by man on man? Yes....

But what did Jesus mean by the words "*resist not evil.*" There are various kinds of *resistance,* which may be offered to personal injury, when threatened or actually inflicted. There is *passive* resistance—a dead silence, a sullen inertia, a complete muscular helplessness—an utter refusal to speak or move. Does the context show that Jesus contemplated, pro or con, any such resistance in his prohibition? No. There is an active righteous moral resistance—a meek firm remonstrance, rebuke, reproof, protestation. Does the context show that Jesus prohibits this kind of resistance? No. There is an active, firm, compound, moral and physical resistance, *uninjurious* to the evil doer, and only calculated to restrain him from deadly violence or extreme outrage. Was Jesus contemplating such modes of resisting personal injury? Does the context show that he intended to prohibit all resistance of evil by such means? No. There is a determined resistance of *personal injury* by means of *injury inflicted;* as when man deliberately takes life to save life, destroys an assailant's eye to save an eye, inflicts a violent blow to prevent a blow; or, as when, in retaliation, he takes life for life, eye for eye, tooth for tooth, hand for hand, &c.; or, as when, by means of governmental agencies, he causes an injurious person to be punished by the infliction of some injury equivalent to the one he has inflicted or attempted. It was of such resistance as this, that our Savior was speaking. It is such resistance as this, that he prohibits. His obvious doctrine is: *Resist not personal injury with personal injury....* It bears on all mankind, in every social relation of life.... But they are not prohibited from resisting, opposing, preventing, or counteracting the injuries inflicted, attempted or threatened by man on man, in the use of any *absolutely uninjurious* forces, whether moral or physical. On the contrary, it is their bounden duty, by all such benevolent resistance, to promote the safety and welfare, the holiness and happiness of all human beings, as opportunity may offer....

What a Christian Nonresistant Cannot Consistently Do

It will appear from the foregoing exposition, that a true Christian nonresistant *cannot,* with deliberate intent, knowledge or conscious voluntariness, compromise his principles by either of the following acts.

1. He cannot kill, maim, or otherwise *absolutely injure* any human being, in personal self-defense, or for the sake of his family, or anything he holds dear.

2. He cannot participate in any lawless conspiracy, mob, riotous assembly, or disorderly combination of individuals, to cause or countenance the commission of any such absolute personal injury.

3. He cannot be a member of any voluntary association, however orderly, respectable or allowable by law and general consent, *which declaratively* holds as *fundamental truth,* or claims as an essential right, or distinctly inculcates as sound doctrine, or approves as commendable in practice, *war, capital punishment,* or any other absolute personal injury.

4. He cannot be an *officer* or *private,* chaplain or retainer, in the army, navy or militia of any nation, state, or chieftain.

5. He cannot be an officer, elector, agent, legal prosecutor, passive constituent or approver of any government, as a sworn or an otherwise pledged supporter thereof, whose civil constitution and fundamental laws, require, authorize or tolerate war, slavery, capital punishment, or the infliction of any absolute injury.

6. He cannot be a member of any chartered corporation, or body politic, whose articles of compact oblige or authorize its official functionaries to resort for compulsory aid, in the conducting of its affairs, to a government of constitutional violence.

7. Finally, he cannot do any act, either in person or by proxy; nor abet or encourage any act in others; nor demand, petition for, request, advise or approve the doing of any act, by an individual, association or government, *which* act would inflict, *threaten* to inflict, or *necessarily* cause to *be* inflicted *any absolute personal injury,* as herein before defined.

Such are the necessary bearings, limitations and applications of the doctrine of Christian nonresistance. Let the reader be careful not to misunderstand the positions laid down. The platform of principle and action has been carefully founded, and its essential peculiarities plainly delineated. Let it not be said that the government goes against all religion, government, social organization, constitutions, laws, order, rules and regulations. It goes against none of these things, *per se.* It goes for them, in the highest and best sense. It goes only against *such* religion, government, social organization, constitutions, laws, order, rules, regulations and restraints, as are unequivocally contrary to the law of Christ; as sanction taking "life for life, eye for eye, tooth for tooth"; as are based on the assumption, that it is *right* to resist *injury with injury, evil with evil.*

The Principle and Sub-principle of Nonresistance

… What is the principle from which it proceeds? It is a principle from the inmost bosom of God. It proceeds from all perfect love, that absolute, independent, unerringly wise, holy *love,* which distinguishes the *Divine* from all inferior natures … This love is not mere natural affection, nor sentimental passion, but a pure, enlightened, conscientious *principle.* It is a *divine spring of action,* which intuitively and spontaneously dictates the doing of good to others, whether *they* do good or evil. It operates independently of external influences, and being in its nature absolutely *un*selfish, is not affected by the merit or demerit of its objects. It does not inquire "am I loved? have I been benefitted? have my merits been appreciated? shall I be blessed in return? Or am I hated, injured, cursed and condemned?" …

… What is the sub-principle which constitutes its immediate moral basis? The essential efficacy of *good,* as the counteracting force with which to resist evil.…

The Conclusion

But the Son of the Highest, the great self-sacrificing Nonresistant, is our prophet, priest, and king. Though the maddened inhabitants of the earth have so long turned a deaf ear to his voice, he shall yet be heard. He declares that *good* is the only antagonist of *evil,* which can conquer the deadly foe.… This is the sub-principle of Christian nonresistance. "Evil can be overcome only with good." Faith, then, in the inherent superiority of *good* over *evil,* truth over error, right over wrong, love over hatred, is the immediate moral basis of our doctrine.…

51. ALEXANDER CAMPBELL

An Address on War

Alexander Campbell (1788-1866) was a cofounder of the Disciples of Christ. He and Barton Stone, the other cofounder, were the namesakes of the "Stone-Campbell Restoration Movement," which intended to "restore" New Testament practices and thereby create church unity before the millennial reign of Christ. Campbell was also the editor of The Christian Baptist *(1823-1830) and* Millennial Harbinger *(1830-1870), and both publications included numerous reflections on the question of Christian participation in war. Below is the conclusion of Campbell's "An Address on War," which he delivered in Wheeling, West Virginia, in 1848, two years after the beginning of the Mexican-American War.*

To sum up the whole we argue:

1. The right to take away the life of the murderer does not of itself warrant war, inasmuch as in that case none but the guilty suffer, whereas in war the innocent suffer not only with, but often without, the guilty. The guilty generally make war and the innocent suffer from its consequences.

2. The right given to the Jews to wage war is not vouchsafed to any other nation, for they were under a theocracy, and were God's sheriff to punish nations; consequently no Christian can argue from the wars of the Jews in justification or in extenuation of the wars of Christendom. The Jews had a Divine precept and authority; no existing nation can produce such a warrant.

3. The prophecies clearly indicate that the Messiah himself would be "the Prince of Peace," and that under his reign "wars should cease" and "nations study it no more."

4. The gospel, as first announced by the angels, is a message which results in producing "peace on earth and good will among men."

5. The precepts of Christianity positively inhibit war—by showing that "wars and fightings come from men's lusts" and evil passions, and by commanding Christians to "follow peace with all men."

6. The beatitudes of Christ are not pronounced on patriots, heroes, and conquerors but on peacemakers, on whom is conferred the highest rank and title in the universe: "Blessed are the peacemakers, for they shall be called the sons of God."

7. The folly of war is manifest in the following particulars: First. It can never be the criterion of justice of a proof of right. Second. It can never be a satisfactory end of the controversy. Third. Peace is always the result of negotiation, and treaties are its guaranty and pledge.

8. The wickedness of war is demonstrated in the following particulars:

First. Those who are engaged in killing their brethren, for the most part, have no personal cause of provocation whatever.

Second. They seldom, or never, comprehend the right or the wrong of the war. They, therefore, act without the approbation of conscience.

Third. In all wars the innocent are punished with the guilty.

Fourth. They constrain the soldier to do for the state that which, were he to do it for himself, would, by the law of the state, involve forfeiture of his life.

Fifth. They are the pioneers of all other evils to society, both moral and physical. In the language of Lord Brougham, "Peace, peace, peace! I abominate war as un-Christian. I hold it the greatest of human curses. I deem it to include all others—violence, blood, rapine, fraud, everything that can deform the character, alter the nature, and debase the name of man." Or with Joseph Bonaparte, "War is but organized barbarism—an inheritance of the savage state." With Franklin I, therefore, conclude, "There never was a good war, or a bad peace."

No wonder, then, that for two or three centuries after Christ all Christians refused to bear arms. So depose Justin Martyr, Tatian, Clement of Alexandria, Tertullian, Origen, and so forth.

In addition to all these considerations, I further say, were I not a Christian, as a political economist even, I would plead this cause. Apart from the mere claims of humanity, I would urge it on the ground of sound national policy.

Give me the money that's been spent in wars and I will clear up every acre of land in the world that ought to be cleared, drain every marsh, subdue every desert, fertilize every mountain and hill, and convert the whole earth into a continuous series of fruitful fields, verdant meadows, beautiful villas, hamlets, towns, cities, standing along smooth and comfortable highways and canals, or in the midst of luxuriant and fruitful orchards, vineyards, and gardens, full of fruits and flowers, redolent with all that pleases the eye and regales the senses of man. I would found, furnish, and endow as many schools, academies, and colleges as would educate the whole human race, would build meeting houses, public halls, lyceums, and furnish them with libraries adequate to the wants of a thousand millions of human beings.

Beat your swords into plowshares, your spears into pruning hooks, convert your warships into missionary packets, your arsenals and munitions of war into Bibles, school books, and all the appliances of literature, science, and art, and then ask, "What would be wanting on the part of man to 'make the wilderness and solitary peace glad,' to cause 'the desert to rejoice and blossom as the rose,' to make our hills 'like Carmel and Sharon,' and our valleys as 'the garden of God'?" All this being done, I would doubtless have a surplus for some new enterprise.

On reviewing the subject in the few points only that I have made and with the comparatively few facts I have collected, I must confess that I both wonder at myself and am ashamed to think that I have never before spoken out my views, nor even written an essay on this subject. True, I had, indeed, no apprehension of ever again seeing or even hearing of a war in the United States. It came upon me so suddenly, and it so soon became a party question, that, preserving, as I do, a strict neutrality between party politics, both in my oral and written addresses on all subjects, I could not for a time decide whether to speak out or be silent. I finally determined not to touch the subject till the war was over. Presuming that time to have arrived, and having resolved that my first essay from my regular course, at any foreign point should be on this subject, I feel that I need offer no excuse, ladies and gentlemen, for having called your attention to the matter in hand. I am sorry to think—very sorry indeed to be only of the opinion—that probably even this much published by me some three years or even two years ago, might have saved some lives that since have been thrown away in the desert—some hot-brained youths—"Whose limbs, unburied on the shore, Devouring dogs or hungry vultures tore."

We have all a deep interest in the question; we can all do something to solve it; and it is everyone's duty to do all the good he can. We must create a public opinion on this subject. We should inspire a pacific spirit and urge on all proper occasions the chief objections to war. In the language of the eloquent Grimke, we must show that "the great objection to war is not so much the number of lives and the amount of property it destroys, as its moral influence on nations and individuals. It creates and perpetuates national jealousy, fear, hatred, and envy. It arrogates to itself the prerogative of the Creator alone—to involve the innocent multitude in the punishment of the guilty few. It corrupts the moral taste and hardens the heart; cherishes and strengthens the base and violent passions; destroys the distinguishing features of Christian charity—its universality and its love of enemies; turns into mockery and contempt the best virtue of Christians—humility; weakens the sense of moral obligation; banishes the spirit of improvement, usefulness, and benevolence; and inculcates the horrible maxim that murder and robbery are matters of state expediency."

Let everyone, then, who fears God and loves man put his hand to the work; and the time will not be far distant when—

"No longer hosts encountering hosts
Shall crowds of slain deplore:
They'll hang the trumpet in the hall,
And study war no more."

52. SOJOURNER TRUTH

Narrative of Sojourner Truth

*Sojourner Truth (c. 1797-1883) was a former slave who became a leader in the aboli-
tionist and women's movement of the nineteenth century. Like Douglass, Truth eventually
recruited troops for the Union Army, but in the middle of the nineteenth century, when an
autobiographical narrative of her life appeared in print, she was a Christian pacifist. The
extract below, taken from the* Narrative of Sojourner Truth, *shows her early embrace of
pacifist principles.*

Meeting in New Lisbon

Sojourner Truth interested an audience in New
Lisbon, Ohio, at the Methodist Episcopal Church,
for nearly an hour, talking of slavery in this country, and the suffering and injustice inseparable
from it. If earnestness is eloquence, she has a just
claim to that appellation; for she makes some powerful appeals, which cannot but strike a chord of
sympathy in every human heart.

She sang the following original song at the close
of the meeting:

I am pleading for my people—
A poor, down-trodden race,
Who dwell in freedom's boasted land,
With no abiding place.

I am pleading that my people
May have their rights astored [restored];
For they have long been toiling,
And yet had no reward.

They are forced the crops to culture,
But not for them they yield,
Although both late and early
They labor in the field.

Whilst I bear upon my body
The scars of many a gash,
I am pleading for my people
Who groan beneath the lash.

I am pleading for the mothers
Who gaze in wild despair

Upon the hated auction-block,
And see their children there.

I feel for those in bondage—
Well may I feel for them;
I know how fiendish hearts can be
That sell their fellow-men.

Yet those oppressors steeped in guilt—
I still would have them live;
For I have learned of Jesus
To suffer and forgive.

I want no carnal weapons,
No enginery of death;
For I love not to hear the sound
Of war's tempestuous breath.

I do not ask you to engage
In death and bloody strife,
I do not dare insult my God
By asking for their life.

But while your kindest sympathies
To foreign lands do roam,
I would ask you to remember
Your own oppressed at home.

I plead with you to sympathize
With sighs and groans and scars,
And note how base the tyranny
Beneath the stripes and stars.

53. William C. Thurman

Nonresistance, or the Spirit of Christianity Restored

In 1862, the same year he was elected as a Brethren minister, William C. Thurman (c. 1830-1906) wrote a pamphlet on Christian nonresistance that was widely circulated among Christian pacifists in the North and the South. In his preface to the second edition of the pamphlet, Thurman wrote: "This tract was first published in the South, soon after the commencement of the present war. In 1862 it was sent to the Southern Congress, at Richmond, as a means of procuring the exemption of those who, thinking that 'we ought to obey God rather than man,' could not by the powers of earth be prevailed upon to draw that sword which Christ had commanded his people to put up." The Confederate Congress did, indeed, pass an exemption act in the same year, and whether or not Thurman's tract played a significant role, his writing is one of the clearest Christian statements against war during the Civil War. The tract is seventy pages in length and full of numerous scriptural references; excerpted here is the tract's conclusion—a brief section titled "The Christian's Pledge."

Having vowed eternal allegiance to "The Prince of Peace," even the Son of the Living God, who does not only forbid our resisting "the powers that be," but lays us under obligation to be as harmless as doves, we, whose names are hereto affixed, do hereby promise and solemnly pledge ourselves that, yielding a lamblike, passive submission to the powers that be, we will neither, by proxy nor the use of the sword ourselves, nor by casting a vote for those who are thus placed in authority, nor in any other way, save that of paying a legal tribute, give any support whatever to any of the hostile powers under the canopy of heaven. For he that aids the enraged nations of the earth, or bids them "God speed," is partaker of their evil deeds; and it being "impossible for God to lie," "all they that take the sword shall perish with the sword."

54. Joshua Blanchard

Hostile Brotherhood

Joshua Blanchard (c. 1782-1868) was a wealthy Boston merchant who was active in several peace organizations at various points in his adult years, including the Massachusetts Peace League, the New England Non-Resistance Society, the American Peace Society, the Universal Peace Union, and the League of United Brotherhood. He was a cofounder of the latter group, and for many years he served as a leading officer of APS. A close friend of Elihu Burritt, Blanchard was an absolute pacifist who, unlike many other leading players in U.S. pacifism, refused to suspend his principles during the Civil War. Blanchard penned sharply critical letters and articles against those who, like William Lloyd Garrison, gave up their nonviolent stance during the war, and in an 1862 letter to Garrison, he wrote that "putting aside the idea of the criminality of war in itself, as extensive murder, and regarding only expediency, it is still a question whether the abolition of slavery, enormous as that evil is, does not cost too much, in the slaughters, losses and sorrows of war. It may be indeed said, that slavery is a crime as well as war. True; but it is a crime which States exempt from it are not called upon to remove or punish." Blanchard favored "advocating the independence of the seceded states" as a way to avert war. Below is an 1865 essay in which he laments the demise of the League of Universal Brotherhood—and the Christian principles on which it stood.

A generation has not passed away since thousands of persons in England and America, of both sexes, united themselves in a League, by a solemn pledge, not only to endeavor to abolish all war, and all its preparations and manifestations, but even to abolish all human institutions and customs which did not recognize a brother in every man, which literally was not intended. All is silence on these Resolutions now: the *Bond of Brotherhood* is the only relic of this sublime, all-embracing movement: the voices of peace, justice and benevolence are indeed yet faintly audible and affecting, but the claim of brotherhood from a common nature is hushed.

Why is this abandonment of an enterprise, once so boldly, so enthusiastically urged, by the learned as well as by the ignorant, by the eminent as by the obscure? Has the increased wisdom of the age exposed its fallacy; or has its short experience shown it to be unsuited to the character of man? But it was itself a revolution from preceding maxims, found erroneous in reflection, and pernicious in experience. Nor is the principle in theory yet repudiated; its former advocates still cherish it in belief and admiration, while they depart from it almost to the opposite extreme in action.

Has the terrible voice of war overpowered the pleadings of love uttered on the mount of Galilee? Has the natal voice of angels chanting "peace on earth," been unheard in the distance of ages? Has the martyr spirit of Christianity been quenched in fear, and timid humanity yielded to imperious power? Yet in the service of martial malignity, no deficiency of courage is seen; but life, limbs, comforts and the dearest affections are resolutely sacrificed to it; and the compassionate kindness which relieves distress was never more apparent.

Perhaps while the principle of peaceful brotherhood was seen to be divine and righteous, it was deemed that the ultra maintenance of it was too extravagant. The people of the nations were not prepared for so vastly wide an aberration from the long cherished sentiment of chivalric honor; that the teachings of Christian forbearance could not be suddenly forced upon that sentiment, but should be worked into it as a leaven, by which gradually and in process of time, all the unfriendly dispositions of men shall be changed, and universal, affectionate brotherhood be everywhere established. Alas! it is not perceived by the world, that the principles of Christian love and martial hostility are irreconcilable—the charm of forbearing benevolence is lost in the excitement of miscalled patriotism.

No grafting of moral principle is available in moral truth; the axe must be laid to the root of evil: the radical principle of fraternal love must still be taught, and the world prepared for it, by martyrs' testimony and reforming boldness; especially the masses of the ignorant and servile must be taught that they are the brothers of those called their enemies, whom they are enjoined to love; that they should refuse to be led, like subjected brutes at command, to inflict or suffer the crime of martial murder; to be offered as a sacrifice to the demon of war for the luxury of the few who rule them. When the truth of the divine fraternity of men shall burst upon all the ignorant, the impoverished, and the enslaved; when obedience to military authority shall no longer be a merit, but a disgraceful tyranny, war shall then sink into its bloody grave; the voices of angels, which predicted "peace on earth, and good will to men," shall again sound in trumpet tones of rejoicing over its blessed accomplishment."

55. Lucretia Mott

The Subject of Peace Is Taking Hold

Lucretia Mott (1793-1880) was a Quaker minister and one of the leading activists for women's rights in the early nineteenth century. Influenced by William Lloyd Garrison, Mott became very involved in the abolitionist movement and attended the World Anti-Slavery Conference in 1840, where, much to her dismay, women were prohibited from speaking. This experience, along with many others, led her to join forces with Elizabeth Cady Stanton in organizing the famous Seneca Falls Convention in 1848—a progressive convention dedicated to the advancement of women's rights. A few years later, Mott published Discourse on Woman *and was elected president of the American Equal Rights Association. Although known primarily for her advocacy of women's rights, Mott was also dedicated to the issues of higher education, becoming a founder of Swarthmore College in 1864, and to peace and nonviolence. Below is a speech she delivered at the Abington Peace Meeting in Abington, Pennsylvania, on September 19, 1869—"The Subject of Peace Is Taking a Deep Hold."*

I feel greatly comforted in seeing such a large gathering here. There has been evidence ever since our late war, that the subject of peace is taking a deep hold on the minds of many persons, especially those who were engaged in that contest, many of these came home more opposed to war than ever before, and those in our society who enlisted in the war because they felt that it was necessary to overthrow the great evil of slavery which threatened the destruction of the government. These friends have been willing to go as far as they could in acknowledging the evils of war, and the great regret that the country was thus involved. I rejoice that there is this evidence of interest in the cause of Peace.

The treatment of the Indians may seem, by some, not to be strictly relevant to the subject of peace, and one for the Peace Society to take up, but we know as in the great crime of human slavery, that it never could have gone to the extent it has, but for war, so with the Indians they never could have arrived at the state of revenge and cruelty towards the white inhabitants of this land, if they had not set the example by taking the sword.

Our friend mentioned that one great object of this society, was the education of the people of this country. I knew not what branch of this subject would be considered at this meeting.

Greatly interested as I am in this question of Peace, it occurred to me as I was coming to this meeting, that what ought to be considered was the condition of our country and our State. I know there is an effort to have a portion of the education in the Public Schools of the country of a military character.

I do not know how far military tactics, training, and preparations have been introduced among the little children in our public schools. It seems to me that it is a duty that we owe to ourselves and to our children, to our State and to the world, as a Peace Society, if this practice is still continued, to bear our testimony against it—to center some protest against it, and urge that States shall not introduce anything of this kind. I met a few days ago a Roman Catholic father, and in speaking of the education of that society, he said the Catholics never have given attention to the education of their people, said he, how could that be carried on in our country, when the popular education was not in accordance with their most conscientious belief—they could not send their children to public schools.

I believe there never was more willingness and openness in the minds of the people, to hear appeals made for peace in a way that can be carried out, than at present. I know that we cannot availingly advocate peace principles, until we are prepared to carry out the spirit of peace—that spirit which delights not in anything like revenge, and indulging in any feeling towards the wrongdoer, but a spirit of forgiveness. That this is attainable the testimonies on record go to show, and very desirable is it that there should be a sufficient number of the advocates of peace, so grounded and settled in the principles of peace, that they may know of what they speak, and thus be enabled to labor to prepare the minds of the people, for a better way of settling their disputes.

It may not be necessary to hold up the idea that all must attain to this state before Peace can be established. I believe as it was in the past, ten righteous on the subject of slavery redeemed the country.

It was by the means of the moral warfare that was carried on that slavery was brought to an end, long before the slave holding spirit was put an end to.

It was the great moral warfare that made our Congress anti-slavery, that made our Country ready to plead for, and hold up the great duty of abolishing slavery. So I fully believe with regard to war, and those who are grounded in the principles of peace, and have the subject near and dear to their hearts.

First I believe that those who are interested in this Peace Society, will be blessed in their labors, and be able to induce many, even though they may not have attained to the full spirit of Peace within themselves, to see how barbarous the spirit of war is, and how comparatively easy it would be for nations to settle their difficulties by the same means that individuals do, and that would do away with the barbarism of the sword and of war.

Some of the best writers of the age have pronounced war to be a barbarism, second only to the great evil of religious persecution. It seems to me that the continual holding up to the people of the evil consequences which result to all who are engaged in warfare, the great expense to the country, the evils which result from exciting the passions of men, will tend to the instruction of the people, and that war may be presented to the intelligent minds of the country in such a manner as to induce the Government to abandon it. If the council of the political men (and women I trust too) will ere long be induced to look at this subject in all its

aspects, we will be able to show how greatly to be desired is peace, and other means of settling all difficulties, and bringing to an end the evils which result from war.

Our friend has spoken of the barbarities which have been practiced toward the Indians, and of their present condition of degradation in contrast with their condition when William Penn landed on this continent. It occurred to me to ask if Friends were truly alive to their situation, and to the fact of the treatment they have received from the agents that have been employed by the Government, and who have wronged them so shamefully, whether there would not have been more frequent and more earnest protest and appeals to the Government on their behalf. I know there have been individuals who have been willing to sacrifice their time and leave their families, to devote themselves to the amelioration of the condition of the Indians. I remember Adin T. Corey, Griffith M. Cooper, Halliday Jackson and more recently our friend Joseph Walton and many others who were disposed to do what they could in their limited way.

We have never considered the wrongs of the Indian as our own. We have aided in driving them further and further west, until as the poor Indian has said, "You will drive us away, until we go beyond the setting sun." I would ask if, with the profession that we as Friends have made, of care for the Indians, we have been active enough in our labors. I believe they were saved by the Indian Committees appointed among Friends, from being driven entirely away from the Cattaraugus and other reservations in New York. So far as we have labored by means of Committees, we have in various ways done great good to the Indians.

So also on the subject of Peace, it is a question that has often been with me whether as a religious body we have borne our testimony faithfully enough; whether it would not have prevented so many of our "young men and strong" from being induced to enter the army. I know it is a very delicate subject, and many most conscientiously entered into the strife with the hope of doing what they might to bring peace in the right way, without slavery in the land, for they knew that the war which had been waged was against the colored people, was far greater than any war we could have where there was an equal conflict. Considerations of this kind were apologies, as they deemed, for entering upon this. But all that has passed, and there certainly has been a leniency on the part of the meetings where they have brought these members under dealings, and there has been a disposition to pass all by; but I trust not with anything like a compromise of the principle. I do hope we are all as a body, more desirous to promote "peace on earth and goodwill among men" than ever before, for now that slavery is done away, we may see how in many ways the spirit of war may be opposed, and appeals made for peace that would not have been while we were engaged in such a barbarous warfare as slavery. I want we should all be willing to look at this subject of war in its true light, and not feel because it is sanctioned as yet by all the nations of the earth, and there is so much glory given to those who are the leaders in warfare, that therefore we should not seek to expose its barbarities. It seems to me that it should be the especial duty of those who love and honor the name of Jesus to be opposed to war. I marvel when I see so much in his life and character in favor of Peace, that in his testimonies he so clearly pointed out these things, when he declared: "Ye have heard it said an eye for an eye and a tooth for a tooth, but I say unto you resist not evil—love thine enemy." How he taught that they should do good for evil, that they should put up the sword, for he that taketh the sword shall perish by the sword—which means if they indulge in this spirit it will return to them, and one of the apostles asks: From whence come wars and fightings; come they not from the lusts that war in the members?

I want to hold up the highest principles for our consideration and see how far we can act them out. Even in the Old Testament we find many prophecies in regard to the coming of a better era, when there should be no more war and bloodshed upon the earth. I know there are those who have quoted these Scriptures as authority for war. It was so in regard to slavery. It is so now in reference to the Temperance movement. It has been retarded doubtless by the appeals that have been made to the Scriptures placing them as authority for the wrong, rather than to present the many beautiful examples that are in favor of the right. Although it is true that we have done wrong, that nations have not obeyed the Lord, and they have been given over to their own destruction, as was said formerly, I proclaim that I leave you to your wars, to famine, to pestilence, but this was never uttered by the Highest Powers, the principles of Divine Love have never led any to war. We must go so far as to be afraid to speak of war or any other evil that has ever existed in the world.

With God there is neither variableness nor shadow of turning. Let us have faith in this, and we shall find it is much easier to carry out every principle of right.

I was glad to hear how this peace principle was progressing. If we can once do away with the practice of taking life, it will be a great advance in the world. I have been glad that in the Peace Society a strong protest has been made against capital punishment. That we have petitioned to remove the death penalty on the ground of right. Let us never be afraid to take hold of the right, however error and wrong may be sanctioned by usage, and by some quotations from Scripture. We know that the general run of these is for the right, else they would not be so valuable, if it were not that we found the testimonies of eternal truth in them. We must not take the examples of semi-barbarous nations as authority for our action.

56. CHARLES SPURGEON

Periodical War Madness

Charles Spurgeon (1834-1892) was the most famous Baptist preacher in nineteenth-century England, and his popularity extended across the Atlantic when U.S. newspapers began to publish the sermons he preached weekly at the Metropolitan Tabernacle in Newington Causeway. Spurgeon was not a theological liberal, nor would anyone ever have mistaken him for a progressive biblical exegete. His biblical ethics, however, led him to denounce war, imperialism, and racial discrimination in no uncertain terms. Below is an anti-war essay, "Periodical War Madness," that Spurgeon published in 1878.

A friend who was some long time ago prostrated by African fever assures us that he still feels it once a year. The enemy was repulsed in its first assault, but it annually resumes the attack, and will probably do so as long as our friend survives. This curious phenomenon has its parallel in the moral world, for certain evils may be subdued and apparently driven out of a man, and yet they return with great fury and resume their former sway. The like is true of races and nations. At intervals the world goes mad, and mad in the very same direction in which it had confessed its former insanity, and resolved never to rave again. England, at set seasons, runs wild with the war lunacy, foams at the mouth, bellows out "Rule Britannia," shows her teeth, and in general behaves herself like a mad creature: then her doctors bleed her, and put her through a course of depletion until she comes to her senses, settles down to her cotton-spinning and shop-keeping, and wonders what could have ailed her. A very few months ago it would have been difficult to discover an apologist for the Crimean war, and yet in this year of grace 1878 we find ourselves surrounded by a furious crowd whose intemperate language renders it almost a miracle that peace yet continues. If they do not desire war, they are mere bullies; but if they do desire it, they certainly go the right way to bring it about.

One stands amazed at the singular change which has come over the populace, who, if they are faithfully represented by their journals, have learned nothing by experience, but long to thrust their burned hand again into the fire. The mistakes of former days should minister to the wisdom of the present generation, for history is a nation's education; it is, therefore, to the last degree, unfortunate when the people relapse into their acknowledged errors, and repeat the blunders of their sires. If our country has been fairly depicted by the advocates for war, its condition is disappointing to the believer in progress, and alarming to the patriot who gazes into the future. We are still pugnacious, still believers in brute force, still ready to shed blood, still able to contemplate ravaged lands and murdered thousands without horror, still eager to test our ability to kill our fellow men. We are persuaded that a large portion of our fellow citizens are clear of this charge, but the noisier, if not the more numerous party, clamor for a warlike policy as loudly as if it involved no slaughter, and were rather a boon to mankind than an unmitigated curse. A mysterious argument, founded upon the protection of certain mythical "British interests" is set up as an excuse, but the fact is that the national bulldog wants to fix his teeth into somebody's leg, and growls because he does not quite see how to do it. The fighting instinct is asking to be gratified, and waxes violent because it is denied indulgence.

It is cause for gratitude that the cool heads among us are now sufficiently numerous to act as a check upon the more passionate. We are not now all mad at the same time, nor are quite so many bitten by the ban-dog. When last our people barked at the Russian bear, Messrs. Cobden and Bright and a small band of sensible men entered a protest which only enraged the fighting party; but now, thank God, the advocates of peace are heard, and even though abused, their power is felt. They may be unpopular, but they are certainly influential; their opponents have to stand upon the defensive, and exhibit some show of apologetic argument, whereas aforetime they laughed the peace-man to scorn as un-English, fanatical, and idiotic. Though our people have not advanced as we could desire, yet there has been progress, and that of a solid kind. Statesmen are now found who forgo considerations of party to obey the higher dictates of humanity; ministers of the gospel now more frequently denounce the crime of carnage and pray for peace and among the masses there are juster ideas of the lamentable results of war. We are bound to be thankful even for small mercies, and on that ground we rejoice in the faintest sign of advance towards truthful estimates of bloodshed; but we are sorry to temper our rejoicing with a large measure of regret that our fellow countrymen, aye, and fellow Christians are still so far from being educated upon this most important subject. Many who did run well apparently, and were theoretical lovers of peace, lost their heads in the general excitement and went over to the enemy; some of them, fearful lest English prestige, alias British swagger, should suffer; others afraid that Russia, by capturing Constantinople, would block our road to India; and a third class, carried away by unreasoning sympathy with the dominant feeling around them. Times of feverish excitement test our attachment to great principles, and are probably intended by providence to act as a gauge as to their real growth; viewing the past few months in that light, there has been cause for congratulation, but greater reason for regret.

What is the cause of these periodical outbreaks of passion? Why does a peaceful nation bluster and threaten for a few months, and even commence fighting, when in a short time it sighs for peace, and illuminates its streets as soon as peace is proclaimed? The immediate causes differ, but the abiding reason is the same—man is fallen, and belongs to a race of which infallible revelation declares "their feet are swift to shed blood; destruction and misery are in their ways, and the way of peace they have not known." Wars and fightings arise from the inward lusts of the corrupt heart, and so long as human nature is unrenewed, battles and sieges, wars and rumors of wars will make up the history of nations. Civilized man is the same creature as the savage; he is washed and clothed, but intrinsically he is the same being. As beneath the Russian's skin you find the Tartar, so the Englishman is the savage Briton, or plundering Saxon, wearing broadcloth made from the wool of the sheep, but with a wild fierce heart within his breast. A prizefight a few years ago excited universal interest, and would do so again if it exhibited gameness and pluck, endurance and mettle. As a race we have these qualities and admire them, and it is idle to deny that if we were unrestrained by education and unrenewed by grace, there is not a man among us but would delight to see, or at least to read of, a fair stand-up fight, whether between fighting men or fighting cocks. We are not cruel, and therefore the brutal contests of Roman gladiators, or the disgusting scenes of Spanish bullfights, would never be tolerated among us; but we are a fighting nation, and are never better pleased than when we see an exhibition of spirit and courage. Doubtless some good runs side by side with this characteristic of our countrymen, and we are far from wishing to depreciate bravery and valor, but at the same time this is one of the difficulties which the peace advocate must not fail to recognize. A tamer people might more readily adopt our tenets, not from conviction, but from force of circumstances; we find a warrior race slow to learn the doctrine of "peace on earth, good will toward men"; nor may this discourage us, for such a race is worth instructing, and when thoroughly indoctrinated will be mighty to spread abroad the glorious truth. Rome covets England because she knows it to be the centre and pivot of the world, and we covet it also for the self-same reason: let Great Britain once declare from her heart that her empire is peace, and the whole earth shall be in a fair way to sit still and be at rest. We are far from this consummation at present, nor need we wonder when we remember the hearts of men and the passions which rage therein, and especially when we note the peculiarly warlike constituents of which our nation is composed. Observe the bold dash of the Irish, the stern valor of the Scotch, the fierce fire of the Welsh, and the dogged resolution of the English, and you see before you stormy elements ready at any time to brew a tempest.

What, then, is to be done? Shall we unite with

the clamorous patriots of the hour and sacrifice peace to political selfishness? Or shall we in silence maintain our own views, and despair of their ever being received by our own countrymen?

There is no need to take either course: let us believe in our principles, and wait till the present mania comes to an end. We would persuade all lovers of peace to labor perseveringly to spread the spirit of love and gentleness, which is indeed the spirit of Christ, and to give a practical bearing to what else may become mere theory. The fight-spirit must be battled with in all its forms, and the genius of gentleness must be cultivated. Cruelty to animals, the lust for destroying living things, the desire for revenge, the indulgence of anger—all these we must war against by manifesting and inculcating pity, compassion, forgiveness, kindness, and goodness in the fear of the Lord. Children must be trained with meekness and not with passion, and our dealings with our fellowmen must manifest our readiness to suffer wrong rather than to inflict it upon others. Nor is this all: the truth as to war must be more and more insisted on: the loss of time, labor, treasure, and life must be shown, and the satanic crimes to which it leads must be laid bare. It is the sum of all villainies, and ought to be stripped of its flaunting colors, and to have its bloody horrors revealed; its music should be hushed, that men may hear the moans and groans, the cries and shrieks of dying men and ravished women. War brings out the devil in man, wakes up the hellish legion within his fallen nature, and binds his better faculties hand and foot. Its natural tendency is to hurl nations back into barbarism, and retard the growth of everything good and holy. When undertaken from a dire necessity, as the last resource of an oppressed people, it may become heroic, and its after results may compensate for its immediate evils; but war wantonly undertaken, for self-interest, ambition, or wounded pride is evil, only evil, and that continually. It ought not to be smiled upon as a brilliant spectacle, nor talked of with a light heart; it is a fitter theme for tears and intercessions. To see a soldier a Christian is a joy; to see a Christian a soldier is another matter. We may not judge another man, but we may discourage thoughtless inclinations in the young and ignorant. A sweeping condemnation would arouse antago-

nism, and possibly provoke the very spirit we would allay; while quiet and holy influence may sober and ultimately overcome misdirected tendencies. Many of our bravest soldiers are on the side of peace, and in the present crisis have spoken out more boldly on the right side than we might reasonably have expected of them. This must be duly acknowledged and taken into account, and we must speak accordingly. Rash advocates mar the cause they love, and this also is not to be wondered at, since a portion of the same fighting nature is in them also, and leads them to be furious for peace, and warlike on behalf of love. The temptation to fight Christ's battles with the devil's weapons comes upon us all at times, and it is not marvelous that men speak of "fighting Quakers," and "bigots for liberality." We must guard our own spirits, and not lend ourselves to the service of strife by bitter contentions for peace; this, we fear, has not always been remembered, and the consequences have been more lamentable than would at first sight appear: opponents have been needlessly created, and prejudices have been foolishly confirmed. Let us profit by all the mistakes of zealots, and at the same time let us not become so extremely prudent as to lose all earnestness. The cause is a good one, let us urge it onward with blended vigor and discretion.

Seeing that the war-spirit is not slain, and only at the best wounded, we must in quiet times industriously inculcate the doctrines of peace. The work begun must be deepened and made more real, and where nothing has been taught we must begin in real earnest. It is wise to keep the evil spirit down when it is down. We had better shear its locks while it sleeps, for if once the giant awakes it snaps all arguments as Samson broke the new ropes. As a drunkard should be reasoned with in his sober intervals, and not when he is in liquor, so must our nation be instructed in peace when its fit of passion is over, and not when it is enraged. Have we well and wisely used the period since the last great war? Perhaps not; and it may be that the late ebullition has come to warn us, lest we beguile ourselves into the false notion that a millennium has commenced, and dream that men are about to beat their spears into pruning-hooks. Peace teaching, which is but another name for practical gospel teaching, must be incessant, line upon line, precept upon precept, here a little and there a little. "Thou shalt love thy neighbor as thyself" must resound from our pulpits, and be practiced in our homes. "Let us love one another, for love is of God," must be more in our hearts and lives. Above all we must evangelize the masses, carry the truth of the loving God to their homes, preach Jesus and his dying love in their streets, and gather men to his fold. All soul-saving work is a blow at the war-spirit. Make a man a Christian, and he becomes a lover of his race; instruct him, and he becomes ashamed of blows and battles; sanctify him, and he sweetens into an embodiment of love. May the Holy Ghost do such work on all sides among our countrymen, and we shall see their outbursts of rage become less frequent and less violent, for there will be a strong counteracting influence to keep down the evil, and to restrain it when in a measure it breaks loose.

57. DWIGHT L. MOODY

Good News

Dwight L. Moody (1837-1899), the most famous Protestant evangelist of nineteenth-century America, preached his evangelistic sermons, with their focus on individual conversion, throughout the United States, England, Scotland, and Ireland. He was also deeply committed to Christian education, leading the Sunday School movement and founding such schools as the Northfield Seminary for Young Women, the Mount Hermon School for Young Men, and the Bible Institute Colportage Association (which enabled him to disseminate countless religious tracts). Far less known than Moody's evangelical fervor is his commitment to Christian pacifism. During the Civil War, he ministered to both Union and Confederate soldiers rather than following the advice of friends who counseled him to join the Union Army. "There has never been a time in my life," Moody said, "when I felt that I could take a gun and shoot down a fellow being. In this respect, I am a Quaker." Unfortunately, Moody did not outline his pacifist principles in careful fashion, but we can see part of his thoughts in the following excerpt of "Good News," one of his many published sermons.

And then it is *a free* gospel; any one may have it. You need not ask, "For whom is this good news." It is for yourself. If you would like Christ's own word for it, come with me to that scene in Jerusalem where the disciples are bidding Him farewell. Calvary with all its horrors is behind Him; Gethsemane is over, and Pilate's judgment hall. He has passed the grave, and is about to take his place at the right hand of the Father. Around Him stands his little band of disciples, the little church He was to leave behind Him to be his witnesses. The hour of parting has come, and He has some "last words" for them. Is He thinking about Himself in these closing moments? Is He thinking about the throne that is waiting Him, and the Father's smile that will welcome Him to heaven? Is He going over in memory the scenes of the past; or is He thinking of the friends who have followed Him so far, who will miss Him so much when He is gone? No, He is thinking about *you*. You imagined He would think of those who loved Him? No, sinner, He thought of you then. He thought of his enemies, those who shunned Him, those who despised Him, those who killed Him—He thought what more He could do for them. He thought of those who would hate Him, of those who would have none of his gospel, of those who would say it was too good to be true, of those who would make excuse that He never died for *them*. And then turning to his disciples, his heart just bursting with compassion, He gives them his farewell charge, "Go ye into ALL the world and preach the gospel To EVERY CREATURE." They are almost his last words, "to every creature."

I can imagine Peter saying, "Lord, do you really mean that we shall preach the gospel to *every* creature?" "Yes, Peter." "Shall we go back to Jerusalem and preach the gospel to those Jerusalem sinners who murdered you?" "Yes, Peter, go back and tarry there until you are endued with power from on high. Offer the gospel to them first. Go search out that man who spat in my face; tell him I forgive him; there is nothing in my heart but love for him. Go, search out the man who put that cruel crown of thorns on my brow; tell him I will have a crown ready for him in my kingdom, if he will accept salvation; there shall not be a thorn in it, and he shall wear it for ever and ever in the kingdom of his Redeemer. Find out that man who took the reed from my hand, and smote my head, driving the thorns deeper into my brow. If he will accept salvation as a gift, I will give him a sceptre, and he shall sway it over the nations of the earth. Yes, I will give him to sit with Me upon my throne. Go, seek that man who struck Me with the palm of his hand; find him, and preach the gospel to him; tell him that the blood of Jesus Christ cleanseth from all sin, and my blood was shed for him freely." Yes, I can imagine Him saying, "Go, seek out that poor soldier who drove the spear into my side; tell him that there is a nearer way to my heart than that. Tell him that I forgive him freely; and tell him I will make him a soldier of the cross, and my banner over him shall be love."

58. Jane Addams

The Subjective Necessity for Social Settlements

In 1889, Jane Addams (1860-1935) and Ellen Starr purchased a large home built by Charles Hull in Chicago and transformed it into one of the most important centers of civic responsibility in the United States. Dedicated to Christian humanitarianism, including a lifestyle of nonviolence, Hull House focused on helping local neighbors to combat poverty, poor education, and discrimination. Addams was also an influential advocate for both women's rights and world peace. In 1907 she published Newer Ideals of Peace, *and several years later she opposed the entry of the United States into World War I. In 1915 she became chair of the Women's Peace Party in the U.S., serving later as president of the Women's International League for Peace and Freedom. Addams was reared a Quaker, maintained a membership in the Presbyterian church, and attended Unitarian services, but she was known less for her religious views than her activist efforts to bring peace and justice to the world. Below is an excerpt of an essay she wrote to explain the motivations behind Hull House and the wider settlement house movement.*

... The third division of motives which I believe make toward the Settlement is the result of a certain *renaissance* going forward in Christianity. The impulse to share the lives of the poor, the desire to make social service, irrespective of propaganda, express the spirit of Christ, is as old as Christianity itself. We have no proof from the records themselves that the early Roman Christians, who strained their simple art to the point of grotesqueness in their eagerness to record a "good news" on the walls of the catacombs, considered this "good news" a religion. Jesus had no set of truths labeled "Religious." On the contrary, his doctrine was that all truth is one, that the appropriation of it is freedom. His teaching had no dogma to mark it off from truth and action in general. He himself called it a revelation—a life. These early Roman Christians received the Gospel message, a command to love all men, with a certain joyous simplicity. The image of the Good Shepherd is blithe and gay beyond the gentlest shepherd of Greek mythology; the hart no longer pants, but rushes to the water brooks. The Christians looked for the continuous revelation, but believed what Jesus said, that this revelation to be held and made manifest must be put into terms of action; that action is the only medium man has for receiving and appropriating truth. "If any man do His will, he shall know of the doctrine."

That Christianity has to be revealed and embodied in the line of social progress is a corollary to the simple proposition that man's action is found in his social relationships in the way in which he connects with his fellows, that his motives for action are the zeal and affection with which he regards his fellows. By this simple process was created a deep enthusiasm for humanity, which regarded man as at once the organ and object of revelation; and by this process came about that wonderful fellowship, that true democracy of the early Church, that so captivates the imagination. The early Christians were preeminently nonresistant. They believed in love as a cosmic force. There was no iconoclasm during the minor peace of the Church. They did not yet denounce, nor tear down temples, nor preach the end of the world. They grew to a mighty number, but it never occurred to them, either in their weakness or their strength, to regard other men for an instant as their foes or as aliens. The spectacle of the Christians loving all men was the most astounding Rome had ever seen. They were eager to sacrifice themselves for the weak, for children and the aged. They identified themselves with slaves and did not avoid the plague. They longed to share the common lot that they might receive the constant revelation. It was a new treasure which the early Christians added to the sum of all treasures, a joy hitherto unknown in the world—the joy of finding the Christ which lieth in each man, but which no man can unfold save in fellowship. A happiness ranging from the heroic to the pastoral enveloped them. They were to possess a revelation as long as life had new meaning to unfold, new action to propose.

I believe that there is a distinct turning among young men and women toward this simple accep-

tance of Christ's message. They resent the assumption that Christianity is a set of ideas which belong to the religious consciousness, whatever that may be, that it is a thing to be proclaimed and instituted apart from the social life of the community. They insist that it shall seek a simple and natural expression in the social organism itself. The Settlement movement is only one manifestation of that wider humanitarian movement which throughout Christendom, but preeminently in England, is endeavoring to embody itself, not in a sect, but in society itself. Tolstoi has reminded us all very forcibly of Christ's principle of nonresistance. His formulation has been startling and his expression has deviated from the general movement, but there is little doubt that he has many adherents, men and women who are philosophically convinced of the futility of opposition, who believe that evil can be overcome only with good and cannot be opposed. If love is the creative force of the universe, the principle which binds men together, and by their interdependence on each other makes them human, just so surely is anger and the spirit of opposition the destructive principle of the universe, that which tears down, thrusts men apart, and makes them isolated and brutal.

I cannot, of course, speak for other Settlements, but it would, I think, be unfair to Hull House not to emphasize the conviction with which the first residents went there, that it would simply be a foolish and an unwarrantable expenditure of force to oppose or to antagonize any individual or set of people in the neighborhood; that whatever of good the House had to offer should be put into positive terms; that its residents should live with opposition to no man, with recognition of the good in every man, even the meanest. I believe that this turning, this *renaissance* of the early Christian humanitarianism, is going on in America, in Chicago, if you please, without leaders who write or philosophize, without much speaking, but with a bent to express in social service, in terms of action, the spirit of Christ. Certain it is that spiritual force is found in the Settlement movement, and it is also true that this force must be evoked and must be called into play before the success of any Settlement is assured....

59. Leo Tolstoy

Letter to Ernest Howard Crosby

Leo Tolstoy (1828-1910), the famed Russian writer of such works as War and Peace *and* Anna Karenina, *denounced the formalism of the Orthodox Church, the ownership of private property, abstruse theological doctrines disconnected from social reform, and violence in all of its forms, especially capital punishment, imprisonment, and war. His Christian writings extolled the Sermon on the Mount as the essence of the Gospel, and he called upon Christians to follow one law—the law of love—and to spread the love of God through one's soul and the wider world so that the kingdom of God would finally come. As an anarchist, Tolstoy opposed the kingdom of God to the workings of the state and its violent order. Below is his 1896 letter to Ernest Howard Crosby, a New York-based reformer who was the leading exponent of Tolstoy's works in the United States.*

Tradition—the collective wisdom of my greatest forerunners—tells me that I should do unto others as I would that they should do unto me. My reason shows me that only by all men acting thus is the highest happiness for all men attainable. Only when I yield myself to that intuition of love which demands obedience to this law is my own heart happy and at rest. And not only can I then know how to act, but I can and do discern that work, to coöperate in which my activity was designed and is required. I cannot fathom God's whole design, for the sake of which the universe exists and lives; but the divine work which is being accomplished in this world, and in which I participate by living, is comprehensible to me.

This work is the annihilation of discord and strife among men, and among all creatures; and the establishment of the highest unity, concord, and love. It is the fulfillment of the promises of the Hebrew prophets, who foretold a time when all men should be taught by truth, when spears should be turned into reaping-hooks, swords be beaten to plowshares, and the lion lie down with the lamb. So that a man of Christian intelligence not only knows what he has to do, but he also understands the work he is doing. He has to act so as to coöperate toward the establishment of the kingdom of God on earth. For this, a man must obey his intuition of God's will, *i.e.,* he must act lovingly toward others, as he would that others should act toward him. Thus the intuitive demands of man's soul coincide with the external aim of life which he sees before him.

Man in this world, according to Christian teaching, is God's laborer. A laborer does not know his master's whole design, but he does know the immediate object which he is set to work at. He receives definite instructions what to do, and especially what not to do, lest he hinder the attainment of the very ends toward which his labor must tend. For the rest he has full liberty given him. And therefore, for a man who has grasped the Christian conception of life, the meaning of his life is perfectly plain and reasonable; nor can he have a moment's hesitation as to how he should act, or what he should do to fulfill the object for which he lives.

And yet, in spite of such a twofold indication, clear and indubitable to a man of Christian understanding of what is the real aim and meaning of human life, and of what men should do and should not do, we find people (and people calling themselves Christians) who decide that in such and such circumstances men ought to abandon God's law and reason's guidance, and act in opposition to them; because, according to their conception, the effects of actions performed in submission to God's law may be detrimental or inconvenient.

According to the law, contained alike in tradition, in our reason, and in our hearts, man should always do unto others as he would that they should do unto him; he should always cooperate in the development of love and union among created beings. But on the contrary, in the judgment of these people who look ahead, as long as it is premature, in their opinion, to obey this law, man should do violence, imprison or kill people, and thereby evoke anger and venom instead of loving union in the hearts of men. It is as if a bricklayer, set to do a particular task, and knowing that he was coöperating with others to build a house, after receiving clear and precise instructions from the master himself how to build a certain wall, should receive from some fellow bricklayers (who like himself knew neither the plan of the house nor what would fit in with it) orders to cease building his wall, and instead rather to pull down a wall which other workmen had erected.

Astonishing delusion! A being who breathes one day and vanishes the next receives one definite, indubitable law to guide him through the brief term of his life; but instead of obeying that law he prefers to fancy that he knows what is necessary, advantageous, and well-timed for men, for all the world—this world which continually shifts and evolves; and for the sake of some advantage (which each man pictures after his own fancy) he decides that he and other people should temporarily abandon the indubitable law given to one and to all, and should act, not as they would that others should act toward them, bringing love into the world, but instead do violence, imprison, kill, and bring into the world enmity whenever it seems profitable to do so. And he decides to act thus, though he knows that the most horrible cruelties, martyrdoms, and murders—from the inquisitions, and the murders, and horrors of all the revolutions, down to the violences of contemporary anarchists, and their slaughter by the established authorities—have only occurred because people will imagine that they know what is necessary for mankind and for the world. But are there not always, at any given moment, two opposite parties, each of which declares that it is necessary to use force against the other—the "law and order" party against the "anarchist"; the "anarchist" against the "law and order" men; English against Americans, and Americans against English, and English against Germans; and so forth in all possible combinations and rearrangements?

A man enlightened by Christianity sees that he has no reason to abandon the law of God, given to enable him to walk with sure foot through life, in order to follow the chance, inconstant, and often contradictory demands of men. But besides this, if he has lived a Christian life for some time, and has developed in himself a Christian moral sensibility, he literally cannot act as people demand of him. Not this reason only, but his feeling also, makes it impossible. To many people of our society it would be impossible to torture or kill a baby, even if they were told that by so doing they could save hundreds of people. And in the same way a man, when he has developed a Christian sensibility of heart, finds a whole series of actions are become impossible for him. For instance, a Christian who is obliged to take part in judicial proceedings in which a man may be sentenced to death, or who is obliged to take part in evictions, or in debating a proposal leading to war, or to participate in preparations for war (not to mention war itself), is in a position parallel to that of a kindly man called on to torture or to kill a baby. It is not reason alone that forbids him to do what is demanded of him; he feels instinctively that he cannot do it. For certain actions are morally impossible, just as others are physically impossible. As a man cannot lift a mountain, and as a kindly man cannot kill an infant, so a man living the Christian life cannot take part in deeds of violence. Of what value then to him are arguments about the imaginary advantages of doing what is morally impossible for him to do?

But how is a man to act when he sees clearly an evil in following the law of love and its corollary law of non-resistance? How (to use the stock example) is a man to act when he sees a criminal killing or outraging a child, and he can only save the child by killing the criminal? When such a case is put, it is generally assumed that the only possible reply is that one should kill the assailant to save the child. But the answer is given so quickly and decidedly only because we are all so accustomed to the use of violence, not only to save a child, but even to prevent a neighboring government altering its frontier at the expense of ours, or to prevent some one from smuggling lace across that frontier, or even to defend our garden fruit from a passerby. It is assumed that to save the child the assailant should be killed.

But it is only necessary to consider the question, "On what grounds ought a man, whether he be or be not a Christian, to act so?" in order to come to the conclusion that such action has no reasonable foundation, and only seems to us necessary because up to two thousand years ago such conduct was considered right, and a habit of acting so had been formed. Why should a non-Christian, not acknowledging God, and not regarding the fulfillment of His will as the aim of life, decide to kill the criminal in order to defend the child? By killing the former he kills for certain; whereas he cannot know positively whether the criminal would have killed the child or not. But letting that pass, who shall say whether the child's life was more needed, was better, than the other's life? Surely, if the non-Christian knows not God, and does not see life's meaning to be in the performance of His will, the only rule for his actions must be a reckoning, a conception, of which is more profitable for him and for all men, a continuation of the criminal's life or of the child's. To decide that, he needs to know what would become of the child whom he saves, and what, had he not killed him, would have been the future of the assailant. And as he cannot know this, the non-Christian has no sufficient rational ground for killing a robber to save a child.

If a man be a Christian, and consequently acknowledges God, and sees the meaning of life in fulfilling His will, then, however ferocious the assailant, however innocent and lovely the child, he has even less ground to abandon the God-given law, and to do to the criminal as the criminal wishes to do to the child. He may plead with the assailant, may interpose his own body between the assailant and the victim; but there is one thing he cannot do—he cannot deliberately abandon the law he has received from God, the fulfillment of which alone gives meaning to his life. Very probably bad education, or his animal nature, may cause a man, Christian or non-Christian, to kill an assailant, not to save a child, but even to save himself or to save his purse. But it does not follow that he is right in acting thus, or that he should accustom himself or others to think such conduct right. What it does show is that, notwithstanding a coating of education and of Christianity, the habits of the stone age are yet so strong in man that he still commits actions long since condemned by his reasonable conscience.

I see a criminal killing a child, and I can save the child by killing the assailant—therefore, in certain cases, violence must be used to resist evil. A man's life is in danger, and can be saved only by my telling a lie—therefore, in certain cases, one must lie. A man is starving, and I can only save him by stealing—therefore, in certain cases, one must steal. I lately read a story by Coppée, in which an orderly kills his officer, whose life was insured, and thereby saves the honor and the family of the officer, the moral being that, in certain cases, one must kill. Such devices, and the deductions from them, only prove that there are men who know that it is not well to steal, to lie, or to kill, but who are still so unwilling that people should cease to do these things that they use all their mental powers to invent excuses for such conduct. There is no moral law concerning which one might not devise a case in which it is difficult to decide which is more moral, to disobey the law or to obey it? But all such devices fail to prove that the laws, "Thou shalt not lie, steal, or kill," are invalid.

It is thus with the law of non-resistance. People know it is wrong to use violence, but they are so anxious to continue to live a life secured by "the strong arm of the law," that, instead of devoting their intellects to the elucidation of the evils which have flowed, and are still flowing, from admitting that man has a right to use violence to his fellow-men, they prefer to exert their mental powers in defense of that error. *"Fais ce que dois, advienne que pourra"*—"Do what's right, come what may"—is an expression of profound wisdom. We each can know indubitably what we ought to do, but what results will follow from our actions we none of us either do or can know. Therefore it follows that, besides feeling the call of duty, we are further driven to act as duty bids us by the consideration that we have no other guidance, but are totally ignorant of what will result from our action.

Christian teaching indicates what a man should do to perform the will of Him who sent him into life; and discussion as to what results we anticipate from such or such human actions have nothing to do with Christianity, but are just an example of the error which Christianity eliminates. None of us has ever yet met the imaginary criminal with the imaginary child, but all the horrors which fill the annals of history and of our own times came, and come, from this one thing, namely, that people will believe they really foresee speculative future results of actions.

The case is this. People once lived an animal life, and violated or killed whom they thought well to violate or to kill. They even ate one another, and public opinion approved of it. Thousands of years ago, as far back as the times of Moses, a day came when people had realized that to violate or kill one another is bad. But there were people for whom the reign of force was advantageous, and these did not approve of the change, but assured themselves and others that to do deeds of violence and to kill people is not always bad, but that there are circumstances when it is necessary and even moral. And violence and slaughter, though not so frequent or so cruel as before, continued, only with this difference, that those who committed or commended such acts excused themselves by pleading that they did it for the benefit of humanity.

It was just this sophistical justification of violence that Christ denounced. When two enemies fight, each may think his own conduct justified by the circumstances. Excuses can be made for every use of violence, and no infallible standard has ever been discovered by which to measure the worth of these excuses. Therefore Christ taught us to disbelieve in any excuse for violence, and (contrary to what had been taught by them of old times) never to use violence. One would have thought that those who have professed Christianity would be indefatigable in exposing deception in this matter; for in such exposure lay one of the chief manifestations of Christianity. What really happened was just the reverse. People who profited by violence, and who did not wish to give up their advantages, took on themselves a monopoly of Christian preaching, and declared that, as cases can be found in which non-resistance causes more harm than the use of violence (the imaginary criminal killing the imaginary child), therefore Christ's doctrine of non-resistance need not always be followed; and that one may deviate from His teaching to defend one's life or the life of others; or to defend one's country,

to save society from lunatics or criminals, and in many other cases.

The decision of the question in what cases Christ's teaching should be set aside was left to the very people who employed violence. So that it ended by Christ's teaching on the subject of not resisting evil by violence being completely annulled. And what was worst of all was that the very people Christ denounced came to consider themselves the sole preachers and expositors of His doctrines. But the light shines through the darkness, and Christ's teaching is again exposing the pseudoteachers of Christianity. We may think about rearranging the world to suit our own taste— no one can prevent that; and we may try to do what seems to us pleasant or profitable, and with that object treat our fellow creatures with violence on the pretext that we are doing good. But so acting we cannot pretend that we follow Christ's teaching, for Christ denounced just this deception. Truth sooner or later reappears, and the false teachers are shown up, which is just what is happening today.

Only let the question of man's life be rightly put, as Christ put it, and not as it has been perversely put by the Church, and the whole structure of falsehood which the Church has built over Christ's teaching will collapse of itself. The real question is not whether it will be good or bad for a certain human society that people should follow the law of love and the consequent law of non-resistance. But it is this: Do you, who today live and tomorrow will die, you who are indeed tending deathward every moment, do you wish now, immediately and entirely, to obey the law of Him who sent you into life, and who clearly showed you His will, alike in tradition and in your mind and heart; or do you prefer to resist His will? And as soon as the question is put thus, only one reply is possible: I wish now, this moment, without delay or hesitation, to the very utmost of my strength, neither waiting for one or counting the cost, to do that which alone is clearly demanded by Him who sent me into the world; and on no account, and under no conditions, do I wish to, or can I, act otherwise—for herein lies my only possibility of a rational and unharassed life.

PART VI
Early Twentieth Century
(1900-1949)

60. Clarence Darrow

Resist Not Evil

Clarence Darrow (1857-1938), perhaps the most famous attorney of the radical left in U.S. political history, defended the right of John Scopes to teach evolution in the famous case Scopes v. State. *Although he is known especially for squaring off against William Jennings Bryan at that trial, Darrow also devoted himself to the cause of agnosticism. But, as evident in* Resist Not Evil *(1902), a book long ignored in the literature of peace studies, Darrow was the type of agnostic who drew upon Christian principles when criticizing traditional Christianity, especially its embrace of state-sanctioned violence.*

The Nature of the State

In this heroic age, given to war and conquest and violence, the precepts of peace and good will seem to have been almost submerged. The pulpit, the press, and the school unite in teaching patriotism and in proclaiming the glory and beneficence of war; and one may search literature almost in vain for one note of that "Peace on earth, and good will toward men" in which the world still professes to believe; and yet these benign precepts are supposed to be the basis of all the civilization of the western world.

The doctrine of nonresistance if ever referred to is treated with derision and scorn. At its best

the doctrine can only be held by dreamers and theorists, and can have no place in daily life. Every government on earth furnishes proof that there is nothing practical or vital in its teachings. Every government on earth is the personification of violence and force, and yet the doctrine of nonresistance is as old as human thought—even more than this, the instinct is as old as life upon earth....

Armies and Navies

How is the authority of the state maintained? In whatever guise, or however far removed from the rudest savage tribe to the most democratic state, this autocratic power rests on violence and force

141

alone. The first great instrument which supports every government on earth is the soldier with his gun and sword. True, the army may be but rarely used. The civil power, the courts of justice, the policemen and jails generally suffice in civilized lands to maintain existing things; but back of these, to enforce each decree, is the power of armed men with all the modern implements of death.

Thousands of church organizations throughout the Christian world profess the doctrine of nonresistance to evil, of peace on earth and good will to men, and yet each of these Christian lands trains great bodies of armed men to kill their fellows for the preservation of existing things. Europe is made up of great military camps where millions of men are kept apart from their fellows and taught the trade of war alone. And democratic America, feeling the flush of victory and the glow of conquest, is turning her energies and strength to gathering armies and navies that shall equal those across the sea. Not only are these trained soldiers a living denial of the doctrines that are professed, but in obedience to an external law, deeper and more beneficent than any ever made by man, these mighty forces are working their own ruin and death. These great armies and navies which give the lie to our professions of faith exist for two purposes: first, to keep in subjection the people of their own land; second, to make war upon and defend against the other nations of the earth. The history of the world is little else than the story of the carnage and destruction wrought on battlefields; carnage and destruction springing not from any difference between the common people of the earth, but due alone to the desires and passions of the rulers of the earth. This ruling class, ever eager to extend its power and strength, and ever looking for new people to govern and new lands to tax, has always been ready to turn its face against other powers to satisfy the ruler's will, and without pity or regret, these rulers have depopulated their kingdoms, and carried ruin and destruction to every portion of the earth for gold and power.

Not only do these European rulers keep many millions of men whose only trade is war, but these must be supported in worse than useless idleness by the labor of the poor. Still other millions are trained to war and are ever ready to answer to their master's call, to desert their homes and trades and offer up their lives to satisfy the vain ambitions of the ruler of the state. Millions more must give their strength and lives to build forts and ships, make guns and canon and all the modern implements of war. Apart from any moral question of the right of man to slay his fellow man, all this great burden rests upon the poor. The vast expense of war comes from the production of the land and must serve to weaken and impair its industrial strength. This very force must destroy itself. The best talent of every nation is called upon to invent new implements of destruction—faster sailing boats, stronger forts, more powerful explosives and more deadly guns. As one nation adds to its military stores, so every other nation is also bound to increase its army and navy too. Thus the added force does not augment the military power, but only makes larger the burden of the state; until today, these great armies, aside from producing the moral degradation of the world, are sapping and undermining and consuming the vitality and strength of all the nations of the earth. Cost of labor and strength means cost of life. Thus in their practical results these armies are destroying millions of lives that a policy of peace and nonresistance would conserve and save.

But when the armies are in action how stands the case? Over and over again the world has been submerged by war. The strongest nations of the earth have been almost destroyed. Devastating wars have left consequences that centuries could not repair. Countless millions of men have been used as food for guns. The miseries and sufferings and brutality following in the wake of war have never been described or imagined, and yet the world persists in teaching the glory and honor and greatness of war. To excuse the wholesale butcheries of men by the governing powers, learned apologists have taught that without the havoc and cruel devastation of war the human race would overrun the earth; and yet every government in the world has used its power and influence to promote and encourage marriage and the rearing of children, to punish infanticide and abortion, and make criminal every device to prevent population; have used their power to heal the sick, to alleviate misery and to prolong life. Every movement to overcome disease, to make cities sanitary, to produce and maintain men and women and children has received the sanction and encouragement of all governments; and still these glorious rulers have ruthlessly slaughtered in the most barbarous and cruel way tens of millions of their fellow men, to add to their glory and perpetuate their names. And philosophers have told us that this was necessary to prevent the overpopulation of the earth!

No single ruler, however cruel or ambitious, has ever yet been able to bring the whole world beneath his sway, and the ambitions and lusts of these separate chiefs have divided the world into hostile camps and hostile states. Endless wars have been waged to increase or protect the territory governed by these various rulers. In these bloody conflicts the poor serfs have dumbly and patiently met death in a thousand sickening ways to uphold the authority and prowess of the ruler whose sole function has ever been to pillage and rob the poor victims that fate has placed within his power. To these brutal, senseless, fighting millions the boundaries of the state or the color of the flag that they were taught to love could not in the least affect their lives. Whoever their rulers, their mission has been to toil and fight and die for the honor of the state and the glory of the chief.

But, today, even national preservation demands that the rule of peace shall give place to the rule of war. In the older countries of the earth the great drains made upon industry and life to support vast armies and equip them for slaughter is depopulating states and impoverishing the lands. And besides all this, so far as external power is concerned, no nation adds to its effectiveness to battle with the others by increasing its army and navy. This simply serves to increase the strength of the enemy's guns and to make new combinations between hostile lands, until the very strength of a nation becomes its weakness and must in turn lead to its decay and overthrow. The nation that would today disarm its soldiers and turn its people to the paths of peace would accomplish more to its building up than by all the war taxes wrung from its hostile and unwilling serfs. A nation like this would exhibit to the world such an example of moral grandeur and true vitality and worth that no nation, however powerful, would dare to invite the odium and hostility of the world by sending arms and men to conquer a peaceful, productive, nonresistant land. If the integrity and independence of a nation depended upon its forts and guns the smaller countries of Europe would at once be wiped from the map of the world. Switzerland, Holland, Greece, Italy, and Spain are absolutely powerless to defend themselves by force. If these nations should at once disarm every soldier and melt every gun and turn the worse than wasted labor into productive, life-saving work, they could but greatly strengthen themselves amongst the other nations of the earth. Not only this, their example would serve to help turn the tide of the world from the barbarous and soul-destroying path of war toward the higher, nobler life of peace and good will toward men.

But not alone are these small nations made still weaker by war, but every battleship that is built by England, Russia, France, Germany, or the United States really weakens those nations too. It weakens them not alone by the loss of productive power but by the worse than wasted energy which is required to support these implements of death, from the time their first beam is mined in the original ore, until scarred and worthless and racked by scenes of blood and violence and shame, they are thrown out upon the sands to rot. But every battleship weakens a nation by inviting the hostility of the other peoples of the earth, by compelling other rulers to weaken their kingdoms, to build mighty ships and powerful guns. Every preparation for war and violence is really a violation of the neutrality under which great nations profess to live. They are a reflection upon the integrity and humanity of their own people and an insult to every other land on earth. The building of a man of war, the rearing of a fort, or the planting of a gun can be likened only to a man who professes to live in peace and quiet with his neighbors and his friends and who goes about armed with pistol and with dirk.

But these patent evils and outrages are after all the smallest that flow from violence and strife. The whole pursuit of war weakens the aspirations and ideals of the race. Rulers have ever taught and encouraged the spirit of patriotism, that they might call upon their slaves to give their labor to the privileged class and to freely offer up their lives when the king commands. Every people in the world is taught that their country and their government is the best on earth, and that they should be ever ready to desert their homes, abandon their hopes, aspirations, and ambitions when their ruler calls, and this regardless of the right or wrong for which they fight. The teaching of patriotism and war permeates all society; it reaches to the youngest child and even shapes the character of the unborn babe. It fills the soul with false ambitions, with ignoble desires, and with sordid hopes.

Every sentiment for the improvement of men, for human injustice, for the uplifting of the poor, is at once stifled by the wild, hoarse shout for blood. The lowest standard of ethics of which a right-thinking man can possibly conceive is taught to the common soldier whose trade is to shoot his fellow man. In youth he may have learned the command, "Thou shalt not kill," but the ruler takes the boy just as he enters manhood and teaches him that his highest duty is to shoot a bullet through his neighbor's heart—and this unmoved by passion or feeling or hatred, and without the least regard to right or wrong, but simply because his ruler gives the word. It is not the privilege of the common soldier to ask questions, to consider right and wrong, to think of the misery and suffering his act entails upon others innocent of crime. He may be told to point his gun at his neighbor and his friend, even

at his brother or father; if so he must obey commands.

> Theirs not to reason why
> Theirs but to do and die,

represents the code of ethics that governs a soldier's life.

And yet from men who believe in these ideals, men who sacrifice their right of private judgment in the holiest matter that can weigh upon the conscience and the intellect, the taking of human life—men who place their lives, their consciences, their destinies, without question or hesitation, into another's keeping, men whose trade is slaughter and whose cunning consists in their ability to kill their fellows—from such men it is expected to build great states and rear a noble humanity!

These teachings lead to destruction and death; the destruction of the body and the destruction of the soul. Even on the plea of physical evolution in the long sweep of time, these men must give way to the patient, peaceful, nonresistants, who love their brothers and believe in the sacredness of life. Long ago it was written down that "He who takes the sword shall perish by the sword."

61. A. J. TOMLINSON

The Awful War Seems Near

A. J. Tomlinson (1865-1943) was one of the founders of the Church of God (Cleveland, Tennessee) and became general overseer of the Pentecostal denomination in 1914. Although he was elected for life, an accounting controversy led to his removal, and Tomlinson then founded the Church of God Prophecy. Reared in a Quaker family, Tomlinson was committed to Christian peace, and at the beginning of World War I, he used his denominational paper, The Church of God Evangel, *to publicize his concerns about the emerging war. The following 1917 piece is titled "The Awful War Seems Near."*

It may be that war will have been declared between the United States of America and Germany before this message reaches its readers. But I am sure many prayers are being offered up just now for our rulers and those in authority that we may

be kept at peace and have the privilege of living a peaceable and quiet life. I Tim. 2:1, 2.

But in spite of all the prayers and good desires for peace and good will to men, the inevitable seems about to burst in upon our nation with all its horrors and slaughter. Excitement and the spirit of patriotism is rising and running at a pretty high tide. Nobody knows what the final outcome will be.

War is butchery and contrary to the spirit of Christianity. We, as a nation, make a boast of being a Christian nation, but how little the spirit of Christianity prevails. We are a boastful, proud nation, running to many excesses, and spending much of our time in mere play. In order for God to answer the many prayers that are constantly ascending the hill of the Lord, He will have to bring about a state of humility that does not now exist, and how do we know but what this is to be accomplished, by passing us over into the power of Satan for the destruction of our pride and haughtiness. I Cor. 5:5.

While the awful war seems near, the saints of God should still remember that they are not of this world even as their Lord was not of the world. John 17:16. Our citizenship is not here, but in heaven. Phil. 3:20. Jesus said if His kingdom was of this world His servants would fight, but as it was not, there would be no fighting for the mastery. John 18:36. Therefore He was delivered over to His enemies and slain by them because He would not fight.

Here is an example for us. If our Lord could submit to His enemies and be imposed upon by them rather than fight, where is the authority for us to flee to arms and engage in the wholesale slaughter of our enemies because they are trampling upon our rights?

Indeed we love our country, and hope for peace and prosperity, but to level our guns and mow down our enemies like grass and hasten their souls to hell is not the spirit of our Master. And we are to follow Him. He is our example and we must follow in His steps. I Peter 1:21. We are not cowards, but we want to follow the example and teaching of our Lord. If He joined the army and fought for His country then we should do likewise. But as He did not do this, we cannot.

Yes, the awful war seems near, but we cannot fight in carnal warfare when Jesus taught differently, both by precept and example. We might go on the battlefield and care for the wounded and dying, and lend our assistance in the hospitals, and preach to the soldiers, but we cannot take a gun and kill and mangle our enemies, when Jesus commands us to love them and do them good instead of evil. Matt. 5:44.

No doubt many of the saints of God are perplexed about the war problem. They are wondering what is right for them to do in case war is declared. Then they look still farther on and wonder what they should do in case the war becomes so fierce and far-reaching that they will be forced into the service against their will. We have but one way to determine our course. What would Jesus do? Ask ourselves this question and study the life and character of our blessed Jesus and apply it to ourselves and the problem is solved. I cannot dictate to any one in detail. Matters of great moment will have to be decided by the individual on the spur of the moment. The instructions of Jesus that were given to follow in case of being brought before magistrates and officers will be safe to follow in such cases: "And when they shall bring you * * * unto magistrates, and powers, take no thought how or what thing ye shall answer, or what ye shall say: For the Holy Ghost shall teach you in the same hour what ye ought to say." Luke 12:11, 12. Every child of God needs to get so close to God and live so in His presence that he can have the assistance of the Holy Ghost in these perilous times.

There is one thing sure, we cannot fight, but just how or what to do when the crisis comes to the individual will have to be determined at the moment. But as it is the duty of the Holy Ghost to help us at such extreme moments, I fully believe He will stand by us and lend us the necessary help. I am sure He will not forsake us at such a time if we live to please him until that particular moment.

There never has been a time when it was more necessary for God's people to live close to Him than now. There have been times of greater persecution than now, but now is the time for us to live in constant expectancy of our Lord's return to redeem us from the awful tribulations that it seems are almost ready to burst forth with all the hellish fury of his satanic majesty. The coming of the Lord is drawing nigh; and this is an epoch the world has never known.

While the awful war is raging, and the nations are vying with each other and engaging in the wholesale slaughter of men, the church must shine and bless humanity regardless of the world war.

As members of His church, this is our duty and glorious privilege. And we must bless people of other nations as well as our own. There can be no respecter of persons with us. Help one as well as another when opportunity affords was the spirit of Him who wore the seamless coat. "As we have therefore opportunity, let us do good unto all men," says Paul. Gal. 6:10.

I love for people to become enthused when their enthusiasm and energy can be spent in the right manner. But the saints of God have no surplus enthusiasm and energy to spend in fighting Germany. We need to use all of such that we have, to spread the glorious gospel into all the world to tell them of good things that can be obtained through our Christ.

I warn our people against enthusiasm and excitement over the war. This is a time for us to keep cool and continue in our efforts to evangelize the world. If there are any advantages to be gained in this respect by the awful world war, then we must utilize them and make progress while others may be giving their attention more to the war. If others who profess religion want to give their time and attention to the war, let them go, but we should bend all our energies to the one thing undivided.

The secular newspapers are full of the spirit of the world and calculated to inflame the minds of the American people with patriotic zeal. If war is declared public speakers will soon be infesting our country to enthuse the war spirit into our young men to induce them to volunteer to fight for their country, but we must guard against such things as much as possible on account of our religion. We have already enlisted to fight in a spiritual warfare for our Great General and Chief Executive and we must not betray our trust.

We cannot afford to forsake the work of the Lord to display our patriotic zeal and bravery in a war against people for whom Christ died the same as He did for us. While others may do this, we cannot. Our young men need to spend their energy and strength in planting the gospel among the Germans rather than killing them and thus send-ing their souls to hell. We may not be able to take the gospel to Germany just now, but we can go elsewhere and we trust the time will come before long when we can plant the Church of God on German soil. I admit that there will be awful wars and bloodshed, and so much that blood will flow down the valleys like rivers, but nowhere does the Scripture show that the saints of God shall engage in this awful carnage. The Lord is to fight our battles for us while we spread the glorious gospel of love and cheer to the benighted and darkened souls of men and women of earth.

The CHURCH MUST SHINE AND BLESS HUMANITY regardless of the world war. Now is the time for the "black woman" of Solomon's Song to keep and prune the vineyards of others in almost absolute forgetfulness of self interests. Solomon's Song 1:5, 6. Now is the time for the daughter to forget her own people and abandon herself to the service of the king. Psalm 45:10. Now is the time for the preparation for the great day of the Lord. The signs are so plain that we need not be in darkness nor in doubt about the time in which we are living.

When we know of this and how the time is so short, we cannot afford to idle away our moments by taking an active hand in the world war, nor spend our strength and energies in that kind of service when we should spend and be spent for God and His beautiful Church. This is the time for the church to come forth by leaps and bounds and make herself felt in this dark world. She has been hidden for ages, but now she must come forth, assert and show her power, and shine. "Arise, shine for thy light is come, and the glory of the Lord is risen upon thee" (Isa 6:1) means the Church of God. It means the Church of God now. Then as we are members and loyal to His service we can have a part in this wonderful blessedness.

Come on beloved, let us go into the battle in which we are engaged with a little more zeal, enthusiasm, and courage than ever, and continue the work God has given us to do, even if our country is enthralled with war.

62. John Haynes Holmes

A Statement to My People on the Eve of War

As a young socialist, John Haynes Holmes (1879-1964) helped to found the Unitarian Fellowship for Social Justice in 1908. A year later he was a founding member of the National Association for the Advancement of Colored People, and he later played a leading role in forming the American Civil Liberties Union and the U.S. branch of the Fellowship of Reconciliation. No stranger to controversy, he frequently preached on issues of peace and justice from his pulpit in New York City, and in 1917, with World War I on the horizon, he set forth his "A Statement to My People on the Eve of War," excerpted below. It is perhaps his most famous work on issues of peace and justice.

Tomorrow morning (April 2), there will assemble in the capital city of the nation the Congress of these United States, called together in a special session by proclamation of the President, to consider matters of grave moment in the life of the Republic. This assemblage of the chosen representatives of our people promises to be the most fateful in our history. Unless events now unforeseen, unexpected and in the highest degree improbable intervene, the Congress will either affirm that this country is in a state of war, or will do the more formal and decisive thing of issuing a declaration of war against the Imperial German Government....

On the morning of Sunday, March 7, 1915, I declared in this church my absolute and unalterable opposition to war. "War," I said, "is never justifiable at any time or under any circumstances. No man is wise enough, no nation is important enough, no human interest is precious enough, to justify the wholesale destruction and murder which constitute the essence of war.... War is hate, and hate has no place within the human heart. War is death, and death has no place within the realm of life. War is hell, and hell has no more place in the human order than in the divine." I then asked what "this means in practical terms of today?" And I answered, "It means not only that war is unjustifiable in general, but that this English war is unjustifiable for Englishmen, and this German war is unjustifiable for Germans. It means that this war which may in the folly of men, come to American tomorrow, is unjustifiable for Americans."

These words spoken in this place more than two years ago, I must reaffirm this day. Nothing has happened in this period of time to change my opinion of war. On the contrary, much has happened to strengthen and confirm it. I do not deny that war, like polygamy, slavery and cannibalism, was inseparable from early and low stages of social life. I do not deny that war, like pestilence, famine and conflagration, has often helped forward the civilization of mankind, for thus does God make the wrath, as well as the agony of men, to praise him. I do not even deny that there have been times in the past when war, like the storms of the sea, has seemed to be unavoidable. What I do deny is that these facts of history touch in any remotest way the judgment of ethics and religion that war is wrong, or should swerve by so much as a hair's breadth the decision of any one of us to have nothing to do with it. War is an open and utter violation of Christianity. If war is right, then Christianity is wrong, false, a lie. If Christianity is right, then war is wrong, false, a lie. The God revealed by Jesus, and by every great spiritual leader of the race, is no God of battles. He lifts no sword—he asks no sacrifice of blood. He is the Father of all men, Jew and Gentile, bond and free. His spirit is love, his rule is peace, his method of persuasion is forgiveness. His law, as interpreted and promulgated by the Nazarene, is "love one another," "resist not evil with evil," "forgive seventy times seven," "overcome evil with good," "love your enemies, bless them that curse you, do good to them that hate you, pray for them which despitefully use you and persecute you." Such a God and such a law, others may reconcile with war, if they can. I cannot—and what I cannot do, I will not profess to do.

But I must go farther—I must speak not only of war in general, but of this war in particular....

If you tell me that this war is fought for the integrity of international law, I must ask you why it is directed only against Germany and not also against England, which is an equal although far less terrible violator of covenants between nations? If you say that it is fought on behalf of the rights of neutrals, I must ask you where, when and by which belligerent the rights of neutrals have been conserved in this war, and what guarantee you can offer that, after all our expenditure of blood and money for defense, these rights will not be similarly violated all over again in the next war by any nation which is battling for its life? If you say that it is fought for the security of American property and lives, I must ask you how and to what extent it will be safer for our citizens to cross the seas after the declaration of war than it was before? If you say that it is fought in vindication of our national honor, I must ask you why no harm has come to the honor of other nations, such as Holland and Scandinavia, for example, which have suffered even more than we, but, for prudential reasons, refuse to take up arms? If you say that this is a war of defense against wanton and intolerable aggression, I must reply that every blow which we have endured has been primarily a blow directed not against ourselves but against England, and that it has yet to be proved that Germany has any intention or desire of attacking us. If you say that this war is a life-and-death struggle for the preservation of civilization against barbarism, I must ask you why we remained neutral when Belgium was raped, and were at last aroused to action not by the cries of the stricken abroad, but by our own losses in men and money? If you say that this war is a last resort in a situation which every other method, patiently tried, has failed to meet, I must answer that this is not true—that other ways and means of action, tried by experience and justified by success, have been laid before the administration and willfully rejected.

In its ultimate causes, this war is the natural product and expression of our unchristian civilization. Its armed men are grown from the dragon's teeth of secret diplomacy, imperialistic ambitions, dynastic pride, greedy commercialism, economic exploitation at home and abroad. In the sowing of these teeth, America has had her part; and it is therefore only proper, perhaps, that she should have her part also in the reaping of the dreadful harvest. In its more immediate causes, this war is the direct result of unwarrantable, cruel, but nonetheless inevitable interferences with our commercial relations with one group of the belligerents. Our participation in the war, therefore, like the war itself, is political and economic, not ethical, in its character....

When hostilities begin, it is universally assumed that there is but a single service which a loyal citizen can render to the state—that of bearing arms and killing the enemy. Will you understand me if I say, humbly and regretfully, that this I cannot, and will not, do. If any man or boy in this church answers the call to arms, I shall bless him as he marches to the front. When he lies in the trenches, or watches on the lonely sentinel posts, or fights in the charge, I shall follow him with my prayers. If he is brought back dead from hospital or battlefield, I shall bury him with all the honors not of war but of religion. He will have obeyed his conscience and thus performed his whole duty as a man. But I also have a conscience, and that conscience I also must obey. When, therefore, there comes a call for volunteers, I shall have to refuse to heed. When, or if, the system of conscription is adopted, I shall have to decline to serve. If this means a fine, I will pay my fine. If this means imprisonment, I will serve my term. If this means persecution, I will carry my cross. No order of president or governor, no law of nation or state, no loss of reputation, freedom or life, will persuade me or force me to this business of killing. On this issue, for me at least, there is "no compromise." Mistaken, foolish, fanatical, I may be; I will not deny the charge. But false to my own soul I will not be. Therefore here I stand. God help me! I cannot do other! ...

63. GENERAL COUNCIL OF THE ASSEMBLIES OF GOD

Resolution Concerning the Attitude of the General Council of the Assemblies of God toward Any Military Service Which Involves the Actual Participation in the Destruction of Human Life

The following statement by the General Council of the Assemblies of God appeared in a 1917 Weekly Evangel *article titled "The Pentecostal Movement and the Conscription Law."*

While recognizing Human Government as of Divine ordination and affirming our unswerving loyalty to the Government of the United States, nevertheless we are constrained to define our position with reference to the taking of human life.

WHEREAS, in the Constitutional Resolution adopted at the Hot Springs General Council, April 1-10, 1914, we plainly declare the Holy Inspired Scriptures to be the all-sufficient rule of faith and practice, and

WHEREAS, the Scriptures deal plainly with the obligations and relations of humanity, setting forth the principles of "Peace on earth, good will toward men" (Luke 2:14); and

WHEREAS we, as followers of the Lord Jesus Christ, the Prince of Peace, believe in implicit obedience to the Divine commands and precepts which instruct us to "Follow peace with all men" (Heb. 12:14); "Thou shalt not kill" (Exod. 20:13); "Resist not evil" (Matt. 5:39); "Love your enemies" (Matt. 5:44); etc., and

WHEREAS these and other Scriptures have always been accepted and interpreted by our churches as prohibiting Christians from shedding blood or taking human life;

THEREFORE we, as a body of Christians, while purposing to fulfill all the obligation of loyal citizenship, are nevertheless constrained to declare we cannot conscientiously participate in war and armed resistance which involves the actual destruction of human life, since this is contrary to our view of the clear teachings of the inspired Word of God, which is the sole basis of our faith.

64. AMMON HENNACY

Love Your Enemies?

Ammon Hennacy (1893-1970) was imprisoned during World War I for his conscientious objection. The federal prison near Atlanta, Georgia, allowed Hennacy to read the Bible, and he soon found himself embracing Christian anarchism and pacifism. As an advocate for peace, he spent many years writing for the Catholic Worker *and agitating against capital punishment and the payment of taxes to support wars. With his holistic, activist approach to peace, Hennacy was also a vegetarian. He was known later in his life for establishing the Joe Hill House in Salt Lake City, Utah, dedicated to serving the city's homeless. Below is an excerpt from a journal he penned during his World War I imprisonment.*

Love Your Enemies?

That night I was nervous and tore off the buttons from my clothing in order to have something to do to sew them on again. I paced my eight and a half steps back and forth for hours and finally flung myself on the bunk. It must have been the middle of the night when I awoke. I had not had a note from anyone for a month. Were my friends forgetting me? I felt weak, lonesome, and alone in the world. Here I had been singing defiance at the whole capitalistic world but a few hours before and had boasted to the warden how I would bravely do my time; now I wondered if anyone really cared. Perhaps by this time Selma might be married to someone else with a real future ahead of him instead of being lost in a jail. The last letter I had received from her was rather formal. Would she understand why I did not write; and could I be sure that some of the letters I had sent her had been received, with the officials opening the mail I had sent to my sister Lola? How could one end it all? The sharp spoon with which I had carved poems and my calendar on the wall could cut my wrist and I could bleed to death before a guard arrived. But then that would be such a messy death. Then the warden would be sorry for the lies he had told me and the tricks he had tried to play. The last thing I could remember before falling asleep was the long wailing whistle of the freight train as it echoed in the woods nearby.

The next day the deputy came to my cell and said that I was looking very pale, that number 7440, a man just two numbers from me who had come in the same day with me, had died of the flu, and that thirty others were buried that week. If I did not get out and breathe the fresh air it was likely that I would die sooner than the others, he said. Why should I not tell what I knew and get out? In reply I asked the deputy to talk about the weather, as I was not interested in achieving the reputation of a rat. He asked me if it was a prisoner or a guard who had sent out my letters. I walked up to him closely and in a confidential tone said, "It was a prisoner or a guard."

I did not know the nature of the flu but thought that this might be a good way to die if I could only get it. Fate seemed to seal me up in a place where I could not get any germs. (Now that I think of it

my "Celestial Bulldozer," guardian angel, or whatever the name may be must have been in charge of events. In those days I believed in germs and doctors, and out in the prison I might have absorbed their fears and succumbed. I was saved until I could emancipate my mind from medical as well as other kinds of slavery.) Late that afternoon I was called across the hall to take a bath. The guard accidentally left my wooden door open when he was called to answer a telephone. I could not see anywhere except across the hall to the solid door of another cell, but I could hear Popoff in the next cell groaning and calling for water. He was still hanging from his hands for eight hours a day as he had been for months. As the guard came down the hall he opened Popoff's door, dipping his tin cup in the toilet and threw the dirty water in Popoff's face. Then he came and slammed my door shut and locked it. How soon would I be strung to the bars? How long could a fellow stand such treatment?

As soon as it was dark, I sharpened my spoon again and tried it gently on my wrist. The skin seemed to be quite tough, but then I could press harder. If I cut my wrist at midnight, I could be dead by morning. I thought I ought to write a note to Selma and to my mother and I couldn't see to do it until morning. Well, I had waited that long, I could wait a day longer. That night my dreams were a mixture of Victor Hugo's stories of men hiding in the sewers of Paris, I.W.W. songs, blood flowing from the pigs that had been butchered on the farm when I was a boy, and the groans of Popoff.

The sun shone brightly in my cell the next morning for the first time in weeks. I crouched again by the door and saw Berkman's [Alexander Berkman, a famous anarchist] bald head. Tears came into my eyes, and I felt ashamed of myself for my cowardly idea of suicide just because I had had a few reverses. Here was Berkman who had passed through much more than I would ever have to endure if I stayed two more years in solitary. How was the world to know more about the continued torture of Popoff and others if I gave up? The last two verses of the I.W.W. Prison Song now had a real meaning to me as I sang them again. I was through with despair. I wanted to live to make the world better. Just because most prisoners and, for all that, most people on the outside did not understand and know what solitary meant was all the more reason why I should be strong. I sang cheerfully:

By all the graves of Labor's dead,
By Labor's deathless flag of red,
We make a solemn vow to you,
We'll keep the faith, we will be true.
For freedom laughs at prison bars,
Her voice reechoes from the stars;
Proclaiming with the tempest's breath
A Cause beyond the reach of death.

Two months later I heard the whistles blow and shouts resound throughout the prison. The war was over. The Armistice had been signed. It was not until then that I was informed in a note from Berkman that November 11 was also an anarchist anniversary: The date of the hanging of the Chicago anarchists of the Haymarket in 1887. I had ceased by this time my nervous running back and forth like a squirrel in my cell and was now taking steady walks in my cell each day and also hours of physical exercise. I was going to build myself up and not get sick and die. I would show my persecutors that I would be a credit to my ideals.

I had painted the ceiling of the Catholic chapel in flat work before I got in solitary and had left no brush marks. The priest appreciated my good work. He knew I was an Irishman who was not a Catholic, but he never tried to convert me. Now, as I studied the Bible, I was not thinking of any church but just wanted to see what might be worthwhile in it. I had now read it through four times and had read the New Testament many times and the Sermon on the Mount scores of times. I had made up games with pages and chapters and names of characters in the Bible to pass away the time. I had memorized certain chapters that I like. As I read of Isaiah, Ezekiel, Micah and other prophets and of Jesus, I could see that they had opposed tyranny. I had also spent many days reviewing all of the historical knowledge that I could remember and in trying to think through a philosophy of life. I had passed through the idea of killing myself. This was an escape, not any solution to life. The remainder of my two years in solitary must result in a clear-cut plan whereby I could go forth and be a force in the world. I could not take any halfway measures.

If assassination, violence, and revolution were the better way, then military tactics must be studied and a group of fearless rebels organized. I remembered again what Slim, the Robin Hood Wobblie who was in on some larceny charge, had told me once to the effect that one could not be a good rebel unless he became angry and vengeful. Then I heard Popoff curse the guards, and I heard them beat him. I remembered the Negro who had sworn at the guard in the tailor shop and was killed. I had read of riots in prison over food, and I remembered the peaceful victory that we had in our strike against the spoiled fish. I also remembered what Berkman had said about being firm, but quiet. He had tried violence but did not believe in it as a wholesale method. I read of the wars and hatred in the Old Testament. I also read of the courage of Daniel and the Hebrew children who would not worship the golden image, of Peter who chose to obey God rather than the properly constituted authorities who placed him in jail, and of the victory of these men by courage and peaceful methods. I read of Jesus, who was confronted with a whole world empire of tyranny and chose not to overturn the tyrant and make Himself king but to change the hatred in the hearts of men to love and understanding—to overcome evil with goodwill.

I had called loudly for the sword and mentally listed those whom I desired to kill when I was free. Was this really the universal method that should be used? I would read the Sermon on the Mount again. When a child I had been frightened by hell fire into proclaiming a change of life. Now I spent months making a decision; there was no sudden change. I had all the time in the world and no one could talk to me or influence me. I was deciding this idea for myself. Gradually, I came to gain a glimpse of what Jesus meant when He said, "The Kingdom of God is within you." In my heart now after six months I could love everybody in the world but the warden, but if I did not love him then the Sermon on the Mount meant nothing at all. I really saw this and felt it in my heart, but I was too stubborn to admit it in my mind. One day I was walking back and forth in my cell when, in turning, my head hit the wall. Then the thought came to me: "Here I am locked up in a cell. The warden was never locked up in any cell, and he never had a chance to know what Jesus meant. Neither did I until yesterday. So I must not blame him. I must love him." Now the whole thing was clear. This Kingdom of God must be in everyone: in the deputy, the warden, the rat, and the pervert—and now I came to know it—in myself. I read and reread the Sermon on the Mount: the fifth, sixth, and seventh chapters of Matthew thus became a living thing to me. I tried to take every sentence and apply it to my present problems. The warden had said that he did not understand political prisoners. He and the deputy, in plain words, didn't know any better; they had put on the false face of sternness and tyranny because this was the only method they knew. It was my job to teach them another method: that of goodwill overcoming their evil intentions or, rather, habits. The opposite of the Sermon on the Mount was what the whole world had been practicing, in prison and out of prison; and hate piled on hate had brought hate and revenge. It was plain that this system did not work. I would never have a better opportunity than to try out the Sermon on the Mount right now in my cell. Here was deceit, hatred, lust, murder, and every kind of evil in this prison. I reread slowly and pondered each verse: "Ye have heard that it hath been said, An eye for an eye, and a tooth for a tooth … Whoever shall smite thee on thy right

cheek turn to him the other also … take therefore no thought for the morrow … therefore all things whatsoever ye would that men should do to you, do ye even so to them."

I fancied what my radical friends in and out of prison would say when I spoke of the above teachings of Jesus. I knew that I would have to bear their displeasure, just as I had borne the hysteria of the patriots and the silence of my friends when I was sent to prison. This did not mean that I was going to "squeal" and give in to the officials, but in my heart I would try to see the good in them and not hate them. Jesus did not give in to His persecutors. He used strong words against the evildoers of His time, but He had mercy for the sinner. I was not alone fighting the world for I had him as my helper. I saw that if I held this philosophy for myself I could not engage in violence for a revolution—a good war, as some might call it—but would have to renounce violence even in my thought. Would I be ready to go the whole way? At that time I had not heard of Tolstoy and his application of Christ's teachings to society.… The most difficult animosity for me to overcome was a dislike of hypocrites and church people who had so long withheld the real teachings of Jesus. I could see no connection between Jesus and the church.…

65. HOWARD THURMAN

Peace Tactics and a Racial Minority

Howard Thurman (1899-1981), an ordained Baptist minister, was a professor of religion and director of religious life at Morehouse College and Spelman College throughout the middle of the twentieth century. A student of Rufus Jones, Thurman was profoundly influenced by Quaker thought, and his corpus of work is remarkable for its integration of Christian mysticism and nonviolence. Not long after Thurman completed his seminal Jesus and the Disinherited *(1949), his name appeared on a national magazine list of the greatest preachers and teachers in America. Indeed, his influence was wide and deep, especially in African American communities, and Martin Luther King, Jr., Jesse Jackson, and Vernon Jordan, among others, considered Thurman among their mentors. The 1928 article below— "Peace Tactics and a Racial Minority"—is progressive for its connection between race and peace.*

I

It is a very simple matter for people who form the dominant group in a society to develop what they call a philosophy of pacifism that makes few if any demands upon their ethical obligation to minority groups with which they may be having contacts. Such a philosophy becomes a mere quietus to be put into the hands of the minority to keep them peaceful and controllable.

The difficulty a minority group faces is twofold. First, there is always present the danger which comes from the imitation of the dominant majority. In its position as a minority it may live vicariously the total life of the group which is contributing so largely to its discomfort. A careful study of the life of minorities usually reveals this imitation of the majority. Often when the dominant group is heartily hated, the imitation takes the form of compensation. That is, those who ride on top in a minority group may treat those below them, so to speak, as they themselves are treated by the dominant majority. This grave danger is certainly one which is, for example, facing the Negro in American life. It is entirely possible to love people so much that one becomes like them. It is also equally possible and perhaps more thoroughly feasible to hate people so bitterly that one becomes like them. This imitation may range all the way from the cut of clothes to small-town economic "imperialism."

The second danger is even more imminent and deadly: a dread despair due to the overwhelming expression of domination and control which emanate everywhere from a powerful majority. All the current symbols of "civilization" which reach their clammy hands into the most intimate social processes of Negro life bespeak the will of the majority. A sense of helplessness and despair is apt to work its way into the very soul of such a stigmatized minority group. This helplessness expresses itself in many ways. I was going through a section in Atlanta called Beaver's Slide when my attention was attracted by a deep baritone voice singing this refrain:

Been down so long—
Down don't worry me.

A Negro man whose soul had given up the ghost! Or this helplessness may express itself as the motive which drives a brilliant Negro holding two degrees from one of the dominant group's best symbols of "education" to become a dining car waiter—the light was faded from his eyes!

II

I have gone to great length before attempting to state the thesis of this little discussion. The editors have asked me to discuss the philosophy of pacifism as it may be applied to the relationship between Negroes and white people in America. Fundamentally this means as it may be applied to the relationship between a stigmatized minority and a dominant more or less hostile majority.

A philosophy of pacifism implies the will to share joyfully the common life and the will to love all healingly and redemptively. It springs out of a sense of the unity, the basic interrelation, and the sacredness of all life. This means at least two things for Negroes and white people who must live together in America. First, it means that white people who make up the dominant majority in American life must relax their will to dominate and control the Negro minority. Second, Negroes must develop a minority technique which I choose to call a technique of relaxation sufficiently operative in group life to make for vast creativity, with no corresponding loss of self-respect. I shall discuss each in turn.

III

At the present time in America the will of the dominant group is tense; it is increasingly concentrated upon the domination and control of the minority group, utilizing all the machinery at its disposal to that end. Nothing is spared: the press, including the comic sheet and the high-brow journal; the church, including the pulpit and much "religious" activity; and for the most part the technique and philosophy of education.

The relaxation of this will to dominate and control would be far-reaching because it would demand an evolutionary, if not revolutionary, shifting of a group mindset, and the discovery of a new basis for group security. This is most difficult because of the historical relationship between these two groups in America.

Slavery would have been impossible without a stern relentless will to dominate and control the life of the slave group. For many generations the springs of such a will were fed by education, by religion, and by observation. The security of the group rested in the unchanging quality of this relationship. This type of education, et cetera, included the slave group as well. My grandmother has often told me how she was taught as a little child just who she was and where she fitted into the scheme of the plantation. And as a nurse in the master's household she saw how careful the training was with reference to the status of the master and his family.

So thorough-going was the whole procedure that, far from questioning the ethics of the position, a master-slave ethic evolved which has not entirely lost its power even today. The sanction for this ethic was not far to seek. I quote here in outline the position as used by Mode in his *Sourcebook for American Church History* (p. 573ff.):

Slave holding does not appear in any catalogue of sins or disciplinable offences given us in the New Testament.

This fact, which none will call in question, is presumptive proof that neither Christ nor his Apostles regarded slave-holding as a sin or an offence. That we may give to this presumption its proper weight, we must take account of such facts as the following:

First. The Catalogues of Sins and Disciplinable Offences, given us in the New Testament are numerous, and in some instances, extended and minute.

Second. All the books of the New Testament were written in slave-holding states, and were originally addressed to persons and churches in slave-holding states: One of them—the epistle to Philemon—is an address to a slave-holder....

Third. The condition of slaves in Judea, in our Lord's day, was no better than it now is in our Southern states, whilst in all other countries it was greatly worse....

Fourth. Slavery, and the relations which it establishes are frequently spoken of, and yet more frequently referred to by Christ and his Apostles.

The Apostles Received Slave-Holders into the Christian Church, and Continued them therein, without giving any intimation either at the time of their Reception, or Afterwards that Slave-Holding was a sin before God, or to be accounted an offence by the Church. Proof. Eph. 6:9; Col. 4:1; I Tim. 6:2; Philem. 2....

Paul sent back a Fugitive Slave, after the Slave's hopeful Conversion, to his Christian Master again, and assigns his reason for so doing that Master's right to the services of his Slave. Proof: Philem. 10-19.

The Apostles repeatedly enjoin the relative Duties of Masters and Slaves, and enforce their Injunctions upon both alike, as Christian Men, by Christian Motives; uniformly treating the Evils which they sought to correct as incidental Evils, and not part and parcel of slavery itself. Proof. Eph 6:5-9; Col. 3:22-25; 4:1; I Tim. 6:1, 2; Titus 2:9, 10; I Pet. 2:18, 19.

Now let us put alongside this outline a very impressive statement written by Professor Coe in his Social Theory of Religious Education:

When we who pray to God as father, and call humanity a family and exalt the idea of service, nevertheless take unprotesting comfort in the anti-domestic, unbrotherly, caste-like inequalities of opportunity that prevail in the world, then, however conscious we may be of compromising our religion, we actually become teachers of an anti-Christian ethic.

Nothing can take the place of or atone for the profound shifting of this old point of view. Anything less than this, however sincere may be the motive, the devotion, the words uttered by Jesus (a member of a stigmatized minority with regard to the dominant more or less hostile majority) are true: "And Jesus said unto them, the kings of the Gentiles exercise lordship over them, and they that exercise authority upon them are called benefactors."

It is outside the scope of this paper to suggest ways for bringing about a new group mindset. I am profoundly convinced, however, that if this will to dominate and control is to be relaxed the answer must come in terms of a new philosophy of education and a more adequate philosophy of religion. In other words, it must be placed at the springs which feed the school, the church, the home.

IV

In the second place, Negroes must develop a minority technique which I choose to call a technique of relaxation sufficiently operative to make for creative living. And this without a corresponding loss in self-respect—perhaps an impossible situation!

The supposedly ignorant Negro who does much of the heavy work of the South has mastered such a technique in some of its aspects. In the midst of a hostile dominating, controlling white majority he relaxes and oftentimes becomes remarkably creative. When he swears or laughs or sings, the gods tremble. He transcends his environment and in that degree he is free.

But what happens to those who are in the schools? Ideally stated, it seems to me that the goal of education is to make people at home in the world so that they may live fully and creatively. It aims to put at their disposal a technique of mastery over themselves and over their environment as far as possible. This may mean different things for two different groups who live together as a basis of caste. To the dominant group it may mean that it must be at home in the world so that it may live fully and creatively—"fully and creatively" being interpreted in terms of the life within the group but not at all with reference to the minority. When it thinks of the mastery of its environment, it may think of the minority group as being a part of its environment! It is conceivable that people so educated would eventually harness social forces to the extent that their position in society would be secure. As a matter of fact it is just this thing that has happened in American life. The great emphasis is upon the technique of mastery. This is a most useful tool.

Now I raise my previous question. What happens to those of the minority group who are the products of these schools? The same thing happens to them that happens to the members of the dominant group. With what result? Very soon it is discovered that the technique is one which is to be used by those who stand in society in a position of advantage. (I do not refer here to the subject matter as such—majority and minority group mathematics is the same.) But the Negro stands in a position of disadvantage. Meanwhile the gulf between him and the great majority of his own group widens. They look on each other with eyes that do not understand. Perhaps this is inevitable. But an education which tends to throw a member of a minority group out of sympathy with the life and struggles of the greater number of his group to whose fate his fate is also tied is suicidal.

A minority technique which I am calling a technique of relaxation would put the group into the frame of mind that would make it possible to detach itself from the clash of minority and majority sufficiently to interpret the relationship between them in the light of a will to share and a will to love. The same thing would obtain with the dominant group. For the moment that it relaxes its will to dominate and control, the way is open for summarizing the relationship on a new basis. To this end all social forces operating separately and jointly among both groups must be harnessed.

In my opinion, all our attempts to bring about brotherhood, sympathetic understanding, good will are dashed to pieces against an adamant wall. On the one side it is labeled: The Will to Control and Dominate. On the other it is labeled: The Will to Hate the Man who tries to Dominate and Crush me. When these wills are relaxed, then the way is clear for the operation of the will to share joyfully in the common life—the will to love healingly and redemptively.

66. HARRY EMERSON FOSDICK

The Unknown Solider

Harry Emerson Fosdick (1878-1969), like Howard Thurman, was one of the most famous preachers in the United States in the first half of the twentieth century. He served at First Presbyterian Church and later at Riverside Church in New York City, and his books on Christian living sold millions of copies. His untiring advocacy for liberal Christianity won him countless critics, William Jennings Bryan among them; and although Fosdick's reputation is firmly rooted in his public agitation against fundamentalism, his pacifism was no less important. Below is a sermon titled "The Unknown Soldier," which he saw important enough to include in a 1934 book of sermons.

It was an interesting idea to deposit the body of an unrecognized soldier in the national memorial of the Greatest War, and yet, when one stops to think of it, how strange it is! Yesterday, in Rome, Paris, London, Washington, and how many capitals beside, the most stirring military pageantry, decked with flags and exultant with music, centered about the bodies of unknown soldiers. That is strange. So this is the outcome of Western civilization, which for nearly two thousand years has worshiped Christ, and in which democracy and science have had their widest opportunity, that the whole nation pauses, its acclamations rise, its colorful pageantry centers, its patriotic oratory flourishes around the unrecognizable body of the soldier blown to bits on the battlefield. That is strange.

It was the war lords themselves who picked him out as the symbol of war. So be it! As a symbol of war we accept him from their hands.

You may not say that I, being a Christian minister, did not know him. I knew him well. From the north of Scotland, where they planted the sea with mines, to the trenches of France, I lived with him and his fellows—British, Australian, New Zealander, French, American. The places where he fought, from Ypres through the Somme battlefield to the southern trenches, I saw while he still was there. I lived with him in his dugouts in the trenches, and on destroyers searching for submarines off the shores of France. Short of actual battle, from training camp to hospital, from the fleet to No Man's Land, I, a Christian minister, saw the

war. Moreover, I, a Christian minister, participated in it. I too was persuaded that it was a war to end war. I too was a gullible fool and thought that modern war could somehow make the world safe for democracy. They sent men like me to explain to the army the high meanings of war and, by every argument we could command, to strengthen their morale. I wonder if I ever spoke to the Unknown Soldier.

One night, in a ruined barn behind the lines, I spoke at sunset to a company of hand-grenaders who were going out that night to raid the German trenches. They told me that on the average no more than half a company came back from a raid, and I, a minister of Christ, tried to nerve them for their suicidal and murderous endeavor. I wonder if the Unknown Soldier was in the barn that night.

Once in a dugout which in other days had been a French wine cellar I bade Godspeed at two in the morning to a detail of men going out on patrol in No Man's Land. They were a fine company of American boys fresh from home. I recall that, huddled in the dark, underground chamber, they sang,

Lead, kindly Light, amid th'encircling gloom,
　Lead thou me on.
The night is dark, and I am far from home—
　Lead thou me on.

Then, with my admonitions in their ears, they went down from the second- to the first-line trenches and so out to No Man's Land. I wonder if the Unknown Soldier was in that dugout.

You here this morning may listen to the rest of this sermon or not, as you please. It makes much less difference to me than usual what you do or think. I have an account to settle in this pulpit today between my soul and the Unknown Soldier.

He is not so utterly unknown as we sometimes think. Of one thing we can be certain: he was sound of mind and body. We made sure of that. All primitive gods who demanded bloody sacrifices on their altars insisted that the animals should be of the best, without mar or hurt. Turn to the Old Testament and you find it written there: "Whether male or female, he shall offer it without blemish before Jehovah." The god of war still maintains the old demand. These men to be sacrificed upon his altars were sound and strong. Once there might have been guessing about that. Not now. Now we have medical science, which tests the prospective soldier's body. Now we have psychiatry, which tests his mind. We used them both to make sure that these sacrifices for the god of war were without blemish. Of all insane and suicidal procedures, can you imagine anything madder than this, that all the nations should pick out their best, use their scientific skill to make certain that they are the best, and then in one mighty holocaust offer ten million of them on the battlefields of one war?

I have an account to settle between my soul and the Unknown Soldier. I deceived him. I deceived myself first, unwittingly, and then I deceived him, assuring him that good consequence could come out of that. As a matter of hardheaded, biological fact, what good can come out of that? Mad civilization, you cannot sacrifice on bloody altars the best of your breed and expect anything to compensate for the loss.

Of another thing we may be fairly sure concerning the Unknown Soldier—that he was a conscript. He may have been a volunteer but on an actuarial average he probably was a conscript. The long arm of the nation reached into his home, touched him on the shoulder, saying, You must go to France and fight. If someone asks why in this "land of the free" conscription was used, the answer is, of course, that it was necessary if we were to win the war. Cer-

tainly it was. And that reveals something terrific about modern war. We cannot get soldiers—not enough of them, not the right kind of them—without forcing them. When a nation goes to war now, the entire nation must go. That means that the youth of the nation must be compelled, coerced, conscripted to fight.

When you stand in Arlington before the tomb of the Unknown Soldier on some occasion, let us say, when the panoply of military glory decks it with music and color, are you thrilled? I am not—not any more. I see there the memorial of one of the saddest things in American history, from the continued repetition of which may God deliver us!— the conscripted boy.

He was a son, the hope of the family, and the nation coerced him. He was, perchance, a lover and the deepest emotion of his life was not desire for military glory or hatred of another country or any other idiotic thing like that, but love of a girl and hope of a home. He was, maybe, a husband and a father, and already, by that slow and beautiful gradation which all fathers know, he had felt the deep ambitions of his heart being transferred from himself to his children. And the nation coerced him. I am not blaming him; he was conscripted. I am not blaming the nation; it never could have won the war without conscription. I am simply saying that *that* is modern war, not by accident but by necessity, and with every repetition that will be more and more the attribute of war.

Last time they coerced our sons. Next time, of course, they will coerce our daughters, and in any future war they will absolutely conscript all property. Old-fashioned Americans, born out of the long tradition of liberty, some of us have trouble with these new coercions used as short cuts to get things done, but nothing else compares with this inevitable, universal, national conscription in time of war. Repeated once or twice more, it will end everything in this nation that remotely approaches liberty.

If I blame anybody about this matter, it is men like myself who ought to have known better. We went out to the army and explained to these valiant men what a resplendent future they were preparing for their children by their heroic sacrifice. O Unknown Soldier, however can I make that right with you? For sometimes I think I hear you asking me about it:

Where is this great, new era that the war was to create? Where is it? They blew out my eyes in the Argonne. Is it because of that that now from Arlington I strain them vainly to see the great gains of the war? If I could see the prosperity, plenty and peace of my children for which this mangled body was laid down!

My friends, sometimes I do not want to believe in immortality. Sometimes I hope that the Unknown Soldier will never know.

Many of you here knew these men better, you may think, than I knew them, and already you may be relieving my presentation of the case by another picture. Probably, you say, the Unknown Soldier enjoyed soldiering and had a thrilling time in France. The Great War, you say, was the most exciting episode of our time. Some of us found in it emotional release unknown before or since. We escaped from ourselves. We were carried out of ourselves. Multitudes were picked up from a dull routine, lifted out of the drudgery of common days with which they were infinitely bored, and plunged into an exciting adventure which they remember yet as the most thrilling episode of their careers.

Indeed, you say, how could martial music be so stirring and martial poetry so exultant if there were not at the heart of the war a lyric glory? Even in the churches you sing,

Onward, Christian soldiers,
Marching as to war.

You, too, when you wish to express or arouse ardor and courage, use war's symbolism. The Unknown Soldier, sound in mind and body—yes! The Unknown Soldier a conscript—probably! But be fair and add that the Unknown Soldier had a thrilling time in France.

To be sure, he may have had. Listen to this from a wounded American after a battle. "We went over the parapet at five o'clock and I was not hit till nine. They were the greatest four hours of my life." Quite so! Only let me talk to you a moment about that. *That* was the first time he went over the parapet.

Anything risky, dangerous, tried for the first time, well handled, and now escaped from, is thrilling to an excitable and courageous soul. What about the second time and the third time and the fourth? What about the dreadful times between, the long-drawn-out, monotonous, dreary, muddy barrenness of war, concerning which one who knows said, "Nine-tenths of war is waiting"? The trouble with much familiar talk about the lyric glory of war is that it comes from people who never saw any soldiers except the American troops, fresh, resilient, who had time to go over the parapet about once. You ought to have seen the hardening-up camps of the armies which had been at the business since 1914. Did you ever see them? Did you look, as I have looked, into the faces of young men who had been over the top, wounded, hospitalized, hardened up—over the top, wounded, hospitalized, hardened up—four times, five times, six times? Never talk to a man who has seen that about the lyric glory of war.

Where does all this talk about the glory of war come from, anyway?

"Charge, Chester, charge! On Stanley, on!"

Were the last words of Marmion. That is Sir Walter Scott. Did he ever see war? Never.

And how can man die better
    Than facing fearful odds,
For the ashes of his fathers,
    And the temples of his Gods?

That is Macaulay. Did he ever see war? He was never near one.

Storm'd at with shot and shell,
Boldly they rode and well,
Into the jaws of Death,
Into the mouth of Hell,
    Rode the six hundred.

That is Tennyson. Did he ever see war? I should say not.

There is where the glory of war comes from. We have heard very little about it from the real soldiers of this last war. We have had from them the appalling opposite. They say what George Washington said: it is "a plague to mankind." The glory of war comes from poets, preachers, orators, the writers of martial music, statesmen preparing flowery proclamations for the people, who dress up war for other men to fight. They do not go to the trenches. They do not go over the top again and again and again.

Do you think that the Unknown Soldier would really believe in the lyric glory of war? I dare you; go down to Arlington and tell him that *now*.

Nevertheless, some may say that while war is a grim and murderous business with no glory in it in the end, and while the Unknown Soldier doubtless knew that well, we have the right in our imagination to make him the symbol of whatever was most idealistic and courageous in the men who went out to fight. Of course we have. Now, let us do that! On the body of a French sergeant killed in battle was found a letter to his parents in which he said, "You know how I made the sacrifice of my life before leaving." So we think of our Unknown Soldier as an idealist, rising up in answer to a human call and making the sacrifice of his life before leaving. His country seemed to him like Christ himself, saying, "If any man would come after me, let him deny himself, and take up his cross daily, and follow me." Far from appealing to his worst, the war brought out his best—his loyalty, his courage, his venturesomeness, his care for the downtrodden, his capacity for self-sacrifice. The noblest qualities of his young manhood were aroused. He went out of France a flaming patriot and in secret quoted Rupert Brook to his own soul:

If I should die, think only this of me:
That there's some corner of a foreign field
That is forever England.

There, you say, is the Unknown Soldier.

Yes, indeed, did you suppose I never had met him? I talked with him many a time. When the words that I would speak about war are blistering fury on my lips and the encouragement I gave to war is a deep self-condemnation in my heart, it is of him that I think. For I watched war lay its hands on these strongest, loveliest things in men and use the noblest attributes of the human spirit for what ungodly deeds! Is there anything more infernal

than this, to take the best that is in man and use it to do what war does? This is the ultimate description of war—it is the prostitution of the noblest powers of the human soul to the most dastardly deeds, the most abysmal cruelties of which our human nature is capable. That *is* war.

Granted, then, that the Unknown Soldier should be to us a symbol of everything most idealistic in a valiant warrior, I beg of you, be realistic and follow through what war made the Unknown Soldier do with his idealism. Here is one eyewitness speaking:

"Last night, at an officer's mess there was great laughter at the story of one of our men who had spent his last cartridge in defending an attack. 'Hand me down your spade, Mike,' he said; and as six Germans came one by one round the end of a traverse, he split each man's skull open with a deadly blow." The war made the Unknown Soldier do *that* with his idealism.

"I can remember," says one infantry officer, "a pair of hands (nationality unknown) which protruded from the soaked ashen soil like the roots of a tree turned upside down; one hand seemed to be pointing at the sky with an accusing gesture.... Floating on the surface of the flooded trench was the mask of a human face which had detached itself from the skull." War harnessed the idealism of the Unknown Soldier to *that*!

Do I not have an account to settle between my soul and him? They sent men like me into the camps to awaken his idealism, to touch those secret, holy springs within him so that with devotion, fidelity, loyalty, and self-sacrifice he might go out to war. O war, I hate you most of all for this, that you do lay your hands on the noblest elements in human character, with which we might make a heaven on earth, and you use them to make a hell on earth instead. You take even our science, the fruit of our dedicated intelligence, by means of which we might build here the City of God, and, using it, you fill the earth instead with new ways of slaughtering men. You take our loyalty, our unselfishness, with which we might make the earth beautiful, and, using these our finest qualities, you make death fall from the sky and burst up from the sea and hurtle from unseen ambuscades sixty miles away; you blast fathers in the trenches with gas while you are starving their children at home by blockades;

and you so bedevil the world that fifteen years after the Armistice we cannot be sure who won the war, so sunk in the same disaster are victors and vanquished alike. If war were fought simply with evil things, like hate, it would be bad enough but, when one sees the deeds of war done with the loveliest faculties of the human spirit, he looks into the very pit of hell.

Suppose one thing more—that the Unknown Soldier was a Christian. Maybe he was not, but suppose he was, a Christian like Sergeant York, who at the beginning intended to take Jesus so seriously as to refuse to fight but afterward, otherwise persuaded, made a real soldier. For these Christians do make soldiers. Religion is a force. When religious faith supports war, when as in the Crusades, the priests of Christ cry, "Deus Vult"—God wills it— and, confirming ordinary motives, the dynamic of Christian devotion is added, then an incalculable resource of confidence and power is released. No wonder the war departments wanted the churches behind them!

Suppose, then, that the Unknown Soldier was a Christian, I wonder what he thinks about war now. Practically all modern books about war emphasize the newness of it—new weapons, new horrors, new extensiveness. At times, however, it seems to me that still the worst things about war are the ancient elements. In the Bible we read terrible passages where the Hebrews thought they had command from Jehovah to slaughter the Amalekites, "both man and women, infant and suckling, ox and sheep, camel and ass." Dreadful! we say, an ancient and appalling idea! Ancient? Appalling? Upon the contrary, that is war, and always will be. A military order issued in our generation by an American general in the Philippines and publicly acknowledged by his counsel afterwards in military court, commanded his soldiers to burn and kill, to exterminate all capable of bearing arms, and to make the island of Samar a howling wilderness. Moreover, his counsel acknowledged that he had specifically named the age of ten with instructions to kill every one over that. Far from launching into a denunciation of that American general, I am much more tempted to state his case for him. Why not? Cannot boys and girls of eleven fire a gun? Why not kill

everything over ten? That is war, past, present, and future. All that our modern fashions have done is to make the necessity of slaughtering children not the comparatively simple and harmless matter of shooting some of them in Samar, one by one, but the wholesale destruction of children, starving them by millions, impoverishing them, spoiling the chances of unborn generations of them, as in the Great War.

My friends, I am not trying to make you sentimental about his. I want you to be hardheaded. We can have this monstrous thing or we have Christ, but we cannot have both. O my country, stay out of war! Coöperate with the nations in every movement that has any hope for peace; enter the World Court, support the League of Nations, contend undiscourageably for disarmament, but set your face steadfastly and forever against being drawn into another war. O church of Christ, stay out of war! Withdraw from every alliance that maintains or encourages it. It was not a pacifist, it was Field Marshal Earl Haig who said, "It is the business of the churches to make my business impossible." And O my soul, stay out of war!

At any rate, I will myself do the best I can to settle my account with the Unknown Soldier. I renounce war. I renounce war because of what it does to our own men. I have watched them coming gassed from the frontline trenches. I have seen the long, long hospital trains filled with their mutilated bodies. I have heard the cries of the crazed and the prayers of those who wanted to die and could not, and I remember the maimed and ruined men for whom the war is not yet over. I renounce war because of what it compels us to do to our enemies, bombing their mothers in villages, starving their children by blockades, laughing over our coffee cups about every damnable thing we have been able to do to them. I renounce war for its consequences, for the lies it lives on and propagates, for the undying hatreds it arouses, for the dictatorships it puts in the place of democracy, for the starvation that stalks after it. I renounce war and never again, directly or indirectly, will I sanction or support another! O Unknown Soldier, in penitent reparation I make you that pledge.

67. Evelyn Underhill

The Church and War

Evelyn Underhill (1875-1941) was an acclaimed novelist, editor, and spiritual writer in England during the first half of the twentieth century, with her most popular book, Mysticism, *appearing in print in 1911. Underhill worked for naval intelligence in World War I, but by 1936 she had begun to embrace Christian pacifism. Four years later she wrote the selection below—an influential pamphlet titled* The Church and War—*for the Anglican Peace Fellowship based in London.*

We are moving—perhaps more rapidly than we realize—towards a moment in which the Church, if she is to preserve her integrity and her spiritual influence, will be compelled to define her attitude towards war; to clear her own mind as to the true reason why her members, by the mere fact of their membership, are bound to repudiate war, not only in principle but also in fact. The reason, for there is only one, is simple and conclusive. The Christian Church is the Body of Christ. Her mission on earth is to spread the Spirit of Christ, which is the creative spirit of wisdom and love; and in so doing bring in the Kingdom of God. Therefore, she can never support or approve any human action, individual or collective, which is hostile to wisdom and love.

This is the first and last reason why, if she remains true to her supernatural call, the Church cannot acquiesce in war. For war, however camouflaged or excused, must always mean the effort of one group of men to achieve their purpose—get something which they want, or prevent something happening which they do not want—by inflicting destruction and death on another group of men. When we trace war to its origin, that origin is always either mortal sin—Pride, Anger, Envy, Greed—or else that spirit of self-regarding Fear, which is a worse infidelity to God than any mortal sin. The Christian cannot serve these masters, even though they are wearing national dress. His attitude to the use of violence "justifiable" or "unjustifiable," was settled once and for all in Gethsemane. Our Lord's rebuke to St. Peter condemns all "righteous" wars, all resort to arms, even in the defense of the just and holy. No cause indeed could have been more just and holy than that of his disciples who sought to defend the Redeemer from His enemies; from their point of view, they would have been fighting for the Kingdom of God, and the highest claims of patriotism must fade before this. Yet it was not by any resort to arms that the world was to be saved; but by the suffering, patience and sacrificial love of the Cross.

To defeat the power of evil by the health-giving power of love and thus open a channel for the inflow of the creative grace of God is therefore the only struggle in which the realistic Christian can take part. No retaliation. No revenge, national or personal. No "defensive wars"—i.e., destroying our brother to prevent him from destroying us. "Fear not him that can kill the body," says the Church—or so at least the Church ought to say. Yet armament factories working full time announce to the world that we do fear him very much indeed; and are determined, if it comes to the point, to kill his body before he can kill ours. This attitude is one with which the Christian Church must never come to terms; for questions of expediency, practicality, national prestige and national safety do not as such concern her. All these derive from human egotism and human fear. Her single business is to apply everywhere and at all times the law of charity; and so bring the will of man, whether national or individual, into harmony with the Will of God. Charity means a loving and selfless co-operation of man with God; and because of this, loving and selfless co-operation between men. In this the Church has a constructive program far more complete, definite, and truly practical—and also far more exacting—than that of any political reformer; for she looks towards a transfigured world, in which the energies now wasted on conflict shall be turned to the purposes of life, and calls upon every one of her members to work for this transfigured world. But she will not make her message effective until she shows the courage of her convictions, and makes her own life, individual and corporate, entirely consistent with the mandate she has received. She cannot minister with one hand the Chalice of Salvation, while with the other she blesses the instruments of death.

Certainly she can, and perhaps must, under present conditions, approve the use of such discipline as is needed to check the turbulent, protect the helpless, and keep order between man and man and between group and group. But such a use of force is never by intention destructive, and works for the ultimate good of those to whom it is applied. It is often difficult to define the boundary which divides this legitimate police action from military action: nevertheless, Christians must try to find that boundary, and having found it must observe it. Christianity is not anarchy; and the right ordering of society for the good of all is a part of her creative task. But on the question of war between man and man she cannot compromise; for this is in direct conflict with her law of brotherly love. Nor can the Church put this question aside as "none of her business," and create for herself a devotional bomb-proof shelter in which to take refuge and meditate upon God, while those to whom she is sent violate His laws.

The Church is in the world to save the world. The whole of human life is her province, because Christianity is not a religion of escape but a religion of incarnation, not standing alongside human life, but working in and through it. So, she is bound to make a choice and declare herself on the great issues of that life, and carry through her choice into action however great the cost. War means men pressing their own claims and demands, or resisting another's claims and demands, to the point of destruction. At best this is atavism, at worst it is devilry. The individual sacrifices for which it calls are sacrifices indeed, but they are not made at the only altar which Christians can acknowledge—the altar of the Divine Love. Therefore the Church cannot acquiesce in war, nor can any communicant who is true to the costly realities of faith take part in it. Christianity stands for absolute values, and the Church falls from grace every time she compromises about them, for she is a supernatural society, consisting of persons who have crossed over from the world's side to God's side and have accepted service under the august standard of the Cross, with all that service of the Cross implies. Necessarily then, though in the world the Church can never be of it. For the world detests absolute values; they are so inconvenient. "Marvel not, my brethren, if the world hate you."

It is true that in this realistic sense the Church is a small body and Christians are a small party, but the Holy Spirit "works through minorities," and it may be that He is in this present hour giving the Church one of the greatest opportunities she has been offered in the course of her career. That stirring of men's minds to a desire for peace which is the most striking fact of our present situation is a manifest working of the Spirit of God. The first business of the Church is surely to give unlimited support to this movement wherever it appears, invest it with the fire, the passion, the beauty proper to humanity's greatest aspirations, invite all whom it has touched to a share in her sources of power, and offer them constructive work that they can do. Here each communicant has a direct obligation, for the decisive factor in the establishment of a peace-loving community is such a disciplining of the individual heart and mind as shall enable every circumstance of daily life to be received in a spirit of peaceful love, and made an occasion for the deepening of charity. The Church is, or should be, the rallying point for all those who believe in the creative and redeeming power of this tranquil and generous love, for those who trust God, and are sure that those hidden, spiritual forces which condition and support our life can and will intervene—not to save us from suffering or material loss, not in the interest of personal or national selfishness, but to secure in the teeth of opposition the ultimate triumph of God's Will.

Now, as never before, men's consciences are moved and their fear is roused by the awful spectacle of war allied with science and allowed to work out unchecked the consequences of this dread partnership—the mind of man, and the will of man, wreaking destruction on God's world. Only Christianity can say why these things are evil, and offer a method whereby this evil can be dealt with at the source, namely, in the hearts of men. Christianity alone holds the solution of humanity's most terrible and most pressing problem. She alone has something really practical to say, for to her has been confided the Word of God for men. It is the Church's hour; and she will not face it, because like the hour of birth it means risk, travail, inevitable pain. We are forced to the bitter conclusion that the members of the Visible Church as a body are not good enough, not brave enough to risk everything for that which they know to be the Will of God and the teaching of Christ. For it does mean risking everything, freedom, reputation, friend-

ship, security—life itself. It is the folly of the Cross, in the particular form in which our generation is asked to accept it; that absolute choice which the Rich Young Man could not make. "If I were still pleasing men, I should not be the slave of Christ," said St. Paul to the Galatians. The Church is still very busy pleasing men. She has yet to accept with all its penalties the fact of being in the world and not of it, of having renounced the world's methods and standards and put all her confidence in God's method and standards. Because of this, her supernatural life is weak and ineffective, and her influence on the nations is slight. Only when she does make that crucial act of acceptance will she become in the full sense that which she is meant to be: the organ on earth of the Divine transforming power.

68. MURIEL LESTER

Training

Muriel Lester (1883-1968) was known affectionately as "the Jane Addams of London." She and her sister Doris bought and converted a chapel in Bow, an impoverished area of London, into a community center, Kingsley Hall, where neighborhood residents could find the resources they needed, including education, for a better life. Lester was a pacifist by 1914, and a year later she joined the Fellowship of Reconciliation. She was present for the first meetings of the International Fellowship of Reconciliation in 1919 and traveled on behalf of the organization for the rest of her life. As a pacifist known worldwide, Lester formed a friendship with Gandhi in the mid-1920s and hosted him on his visit to Great Britain in 1931. Below is her 1942 writing titled "Training."

In Germany and Russia they specialize in the disciplined life. Our lives have to be even more disciplined. We must out-train the totalitarians, out-match their "intrepidity, contempt for comfort, surrender of private interest, obedience to command" with a superior courage, frugality, loyalty and selflessness.

Our job is bigger than theirs. It is to spread the Kingdom of Heaven, the Rule of God. Our business is to stop war, to purify the world, to get it saved from poverty *and* riches, to make people like each other, to heal the sick, and comfort the sad, to wake

up those who have not yet found God, to create joy and beauty wherever we go, to find God in everything and in everyone.

Without confidence the body politic tends to disintegrate. Without confidence business is impossible. Without confidence we can do nothing. There is power, unseen, indefinable, inherent in the stuff of life which always responds to confidence. How can we link all of ourselves to this power? What must we do to acquire the strength of spirit, the carefree joy without which life is a lame and rather smirched affair? Are there any rules?

During the past few years groups of people, young mostly—in America, in Berlin, in Vienna, in Fano and in England—have met together at odd and awkward hours to work out a set of techniques for living the disciplined life. Here are some:

To disarm—not only our bodies by refusing to kill, or to make killing instruments in munitions factories—but to disarm our minds of anger, pride, envy, hate and malice. We should stop praying the Lord's Prayer until we can see that "Our Father" means we are "tied to the same living tether" not only with fellow countrymen but with everybody on this planet. In this perspective, righteous indignation is soon found to be a noxious growth, fostered by the pleasure we feel unconsciously in comparing our imagined rectitude with the obvious evil of other nations. Owning up to our own share of blame in any awkward situation that arises in international as well as home or church or social life, is a precondition of getting a new start made. Usually it is the most sensible and perhaps least blameworthy person who makes the first move. He may not be conscious of any particular guilt of his own, but he takes it for granted that, being in general a sinner, he had some hand in it, and he sets the healing process going by not excusing himself, and by shouldering his share of the general blame. No matter how morally superior we feel, this fact remains: no one can suddenly become our enemy because he happens to have been born on the other side of the river, or a strip of sea, and two governments have signed a bit of paper called an ultimatum. Violence creates violence. This applies to our mental moods. Our anger, pride, envy, hate, malice and "righteous indignation" are murderous. However deep they have twined into our personality, we must pluck them out, though such drastic uprooting may entail agony. Self-pity also has to go. Self-pity is a perfect preparation for dictatorship.

What we call nonviolence is not enough. It may still be camouflaged cowardice. Nonviolence to be effective must be allied with the vow of truth. To pretend that the aggressor is not aggressing, as was done by certain great powers during the rape of Manchuria and the destruction of Spain, is to stultify personality; it is to destroy morale and imperil the future by destroying the ability to think straight.

Gandhi's followers train themselves to speak the truth without fear and without exaggeration; to tell it to people who do not want to hear it, or in the quarters where the telling of it may lose them their jobs or land them in jail. Gandhi was obeying the vow of truth when he declared that the British *government* was "Satanic" but that the British *people* must be loved and on occasion copied, for they have certain virtues which the Indian lacks, just as the Indian has virtues which the British lack.

But even nonviolence plus truth is not enough. There is a third necessity—noncooperation. This takes sublime courage; the courage not to raise one's hand and say "Heil Hitler"; the courage of Japanese soldiers who have refused to kill Chinese. War resistance implies noncooperation.

If our country were suddenly Hitlerized, or Stalinized, we should have to refuse to keep the imposed laws at whatever cost. This implies that we must make ourselves spiritually and physically fit to endure torture.

We must keep at the top of our form, ready for anything. It is rather an insult to God to make it appear that He is such a bad engineer as to be continually turning out machines that don't work. Poise, endurance, strength, the serenity that comes from the open-air life—all these things characterized Jesus. To walk three or four miles a day is one step in this direction. (Mr. Ford will somehow survive.) The body is the temple of something far more holy than we may suspect. Holiness means health, wholeness and completeness. To let the spirit of God thus rule our lives eventually brings real fulfillment. On that basis problems such as sex solve themselves. And voluntary simplicity becomes exhilarating just as going without pie sharpens the alertness and staying power of a long distance runner.

We must face the fact that the present economic order is not God's. Why do we wait for revolutions or elections? Why not begin now to readjust our personal economic life? "If you possess superfluities, while your brethren lack necessities, you are possessing the goods of others and are therefore stealing." A growing number of people realize that they have the right to satisfaction of their needs, physical and cultural, but beyond that their property is not really theirs at all. According to the law of the land it belongs to them. According to the law of God it belongs to the people who need it—God's other children. It's rather a lark working out all these commonsense ideas, even in the midst of the distraught and distressing world. We might meet with likeminded people, a group of three is enough to begin with, and state how much money each of us received during the previous month by earnings, income or gift, and exactly how we spent it; confessing thus the measure of our greed and our need with equal frankness. The persistence of the worship of the golden calf is due in part to a secrecy and pride and false sanctity with which we treat money matters.

We discuss with our friends our thoughts, our religious ideas, our love affairs, but we rarely let them know our income.

We might leave out one meal a week, not only to provide a little fund for the propagation of our ideas, but to recall our errant thoughts to the hunger of many friends, and raise other people's standard of living by lowering our own. Ours, even in peacetime, not to promulgate vegetarianism, to despise the delight of chocolates, to fear the effects of nicotine, but it seems a bit vulgar to consume in a few seconds the price of a week's food for a Chinese family. The more we like candy, smokes and cakes, the more potent reminders they become, when we refuse to take them, of our unemployed friends and of the undernourished millions in the Orient. To do without dessert so that a Chinese child may be kept alive for a whole day (it only costs three cents to do that!) does not rob one of the energy. It enhances one's sense of solidarity. It makes one more alive.

There is a plentitude in the world of all good things; enough raw materials for food, fuel and clothing to satisfy the needs of every inhabitant of the globe. But we cannot enjoy too much cake while others have no bread.

If you and I love God with all our hearts and all our wills and all our wits, we will not leave the job of breaking down barriers of class, nation or race to isolated efforts here and there. We will work together with other people in organized social pressures to distribute goods according to a sound economic plan so that the "haves" and "have-nots" shall gain equitable access to the abundance of this

earth. Ought not all the Lord's people to be ready to speak out the truth to face officials, magistrates, editors, archbishops and dictators, and give them a message of commonsense in the name of God and the common people? "I claim no privileges that others cannot have the counterpart of on the same terms," said Eugene V. Debs (a labor organizer and cofounder of the Socialist Party). Can't we who are relatively over-privileged go a little way toward his position?

The idea of being stripped of superfluities is so that others may enjoy what otherwise we should be stealing from them. It is also so that we ourselves may be more athletic, more alert to expect "that of God" in every man we meet. Let us remember that it is far easier to love enemies whom we have never seen, who live hundreds of miles away, than our next-door neighbor whose dog or radio irritates us. The vertical barriers that separate country from country are easier to break through than the horizontal barriers that separate man from man in the same city; barriers between those of different races, class and character. When one has learned to recognize a spark of God's spirit in the least reputable of one's neighbors, one has more power to drop all labels and to work for that justice which must underlie the making of peace.

The only way to get strong enough to keep at it is to practice the presence of God. We have to force ourselves to return many times in the morning from worry and self-pity, from fear and defeatism, from conceit and callousness, to the Unseen Reality of the Eternal.

When we are overtaken in a fault, in sin, in a new realization of our own pitiful weakness, and hypocrisy we do not grieve overmuch. We lift up our hearts to God immediately as Brother Lawrence advises, not delaying a second, and we say: "Lord, I shall always go on doing such and such, unless I keep closer to Thee." Those who are not rooted deeply enough in God, who are not disciplined by prayer to face facts and repent of sins and gain power to make a fresh start, tend to project their self-disgust onto others. They lose confidence in the future, in life itself.

We keep silent, solitary, if possible, for half an hour a day. During this period we enjoy completely relaxed muscles and nerves. We walk or sit or lie and we let our breathing become slow, and deep and regular. The surprising restfulness that ensues at the end of fifteen minutes or so makes one understand that the rhythm of the Universe of God's is keeping our own bodies and minds sane and sound. God's spirit breathed into man's nostrils the breath of life and he became a living soul. His Creative Spirit is also the Recreative Spirit. Our nights and our awakening are no longer haunted by apprehensions of things undone, by self-disgust, by dread of some coming ordeal, for each of these fears and shames is faced in the presence of God. How is it possible to dread an interview with anyone, when we know God will be the third Person present at the conversation? The world is God's, though one has to rally all one's forces to keep aware of the fact. The world is God's, though our breakfast coffee is spoiled by its proximity to a newspaper full of horrors.

We can no longer make the affirmation lightheartedly. Yet to confess that the world is not God's, to say He has failed, abdicated, that another method, not God's, must be adopted, is to court disintegration, to commit the ultimate blasphemy. It would blacken the skies with bombing airplanes and with despair. And by no stretch of the imagination could it be called a noble despair. For if we forcibly detach ourselves from our particular fears and hates, recrimination and regrets, if we submit ourselves to the cleansing power of events, we see that our narrow vision, our callous self-indulgence, our lazy, purposeless living, our profit-seeking, our tenacious hold on national, racial and personal privileges, *have materially helped to create the present agony.*

In quietness and confidence is our strength. From now on, we're committed to the exciting, dangerous but never dull task of using all our available powers. It is because we have used only a fraction of our available powers that our bodies have been poisoned with silly, bitter, angry thoughts, or the sense that we have no place in the world.

We accept the fact that most of God's work is done slowly, remembering how long it takes Him to make a tree. Lots of His work is done in the dark, in secret, underground. Isn't it an honor for us to be given work like that, quiet and low and regular, rather than the showy kind? We may face the firing squad. Again, nothing externally dramatic like that may ever happen to us. What difference?

Ours is to keep sensitive enough to be in contact with God daily, to practice life as an art. Many times a day we are to sharpen our hunger for that perfection which is the goal of all art by putting ourselves through certain necessary scales and exercises just as a good pianist does.

***

Under such discipline the pride of the whole world, regimented, mechanized, apparently almighty, may be arrayed against us. Even so, we will not "bow our heads to insolent might." We cannot say why God has revealed it to us, but having once seen we cannot un-see it. It is the will of the Eternal that we should refuse any longer to hate and lie and kill. And we can discover our individual lives merging themselves ever more completely into the life of the world....

69. Georgia Harkness

The Christian's Dilemma

Born at a time when there were few options open to women seeking to serve the church in an official capacity, Georgia Harkness (1891-1974) managed to become the first female professor of theology in a U.S. seminary. A theologian and a pacifist, Harkness published over thirty books and held numerous professorships at seminaries and liberal arts institutions alike. She wrote the following essay, "The Christian's Dilemma," just four months before the attack on Pearl Harbor. Her main conversation partner here is the most influ-

ential theologian of this era, Reinhold Niebuhr (1892-1971), who, though once a Christian pacifist, had become the nation's leading exponent of Christian realism.

A paradoxical situation prevails in our churches. On the one hand, there is ground for rejoicing that within the church, in spite of differences of opinion, there continues to be a potent moral and spiritual leadership. There is now in the church more fellowship among those of divergent political opinions, more spiritual steadiness in the face of nationalistic hysteria, more determination to work creatively for a just and enduring peace, than in any other of our social institutions. There is hope in the fact that there is apparently far greater resoluteness at these points now than was characteristic of the churches of twenty-five years ago.

On the other hand, many persons are confused because the leaders of the church do not agree as to America's duty, or the individual Christian's duty, in the present crisis. Christian leaders, equally sincere and greatly trusted, are passionately urging opposite courses. It is not surprising that the man on the street, whether churchgoer or onlooker, often fails to find in the church any clear guide to action.

Basic theological presuppositions have more to do with the problem than is commonly realized. Among Christian leaders who understand their faith and who take it seriously there are some important agreements. Non-theological factors being given due allowance, it is these agreements in faith that are binding us together and giving the church its moral effectiveness. There are also certain fundamental differences in theological emphasis which go far toward explaining differences of alignment in international policy. To understand these foundations should help us to work together more effectively and to maintain tolerance at those points where our decisions must differ. It is the purpose of this article to outline some of these differences and agreements. After surveying the Christian pacifist and non-pacifist presuppositions I shall suggest some bases of united action.

I

Christian pacifism grows best in the soil of social-gospel liberalism, where the central ethical emphasis is drawn, not from the Old Testament or from Paul, but from Jesus. This helps to explain why there is more pacifism among the great preachers of America than among the theologians. In Union and Princeton seminaries, where the prevailing political climate is that of interventionism, the dominant theological mood is the new orthodoxy with a strongly Hebraic-Pauline-Augustinian note. On the other hand, most of our outstanding preachers were reared in liberalism and, though their liberalism has been chastened and deepened in recent years, they are still liberals. Whether this is stigma or compliment depends on the point of view! To mention Fosdick, Buttrick, Tittle, Palmer ... Halford Luccock, E. Stanley Jones—and others whose names will as readily occur to the reader—is both to call the roll of America's leading pacifist preachers and to name some of our most forthright crusaders for a liberal social gospel. It is, of course, impossible to equate liberalism with pacifism, since such stalwart liberals as Henry Sloane Coffin and Henry P. Van Dusen are in the ranks of the interventionists.

If pacifists are for the most part liberals, even though not all the liberals are pacifists, what are the basic postulates which give pacifism a growing point?

The familiar charges brought against Christian pacifism by its critics are that it is "perfectionist," "utopian" and "idealistic"; that it is based on a false and sentimental optimism about human nature; that it misunderstands or at least misapplies the ethics of Jesus; that it has a wrong conception of the Kingdom of God and of man's relation to it; that in exalting the love of God it gives too little place to the God of judgment. In a recent statement, Reinhold Niebuhr brings together most of these charges when he writes:

It is the fruit of a "religious idealism" which never gauged the tragic factors of human sin in human history adequately. It was an idealism ostensibly devoted to the "truth," but yet unwilling to face the truth about men.... This is the final fruit of a theological movement which thinks that the Kingdom of God is a simple extension of human history and that men may progress from the one to the other at any time if they have become sufficiently courageous, pure and selfless. All such illusions finally end in disaster. Communist utopianism ends in the sorry realities of Stalinism and this liberal-Christian utopianism ends by giving the dubious politics of "America First" the sanctity of the Sermon on the Mount.

Since my purpose is not polemic I shall not attempt to answer these charges. Dr. Niebuhr will doubtless tell us whether his brand of interventionism can find a better bedfellow in "the sorry realities of Stalinism" than in the "liberal-Christian utopianism" which he so vigorously renounces. While these charges as they are commonly set forth are a caricature of the Christian pacifist position, they stem from certain vital emphases.

Christian pacifism roots primarily in four theological convictions: a doctrine of God, a doctrine of man, a moral attitude toward Jesus, and a conception of man's responsibility with reference to the Kingdom of God. Each of these is a great subject, the outlines of which can only be suggested here.

1. God is the Father of all men. His character is Christ-like. His primary method of dealing with men is redemptive love. He dwells both within and beyond history. His cause may be temporarily thwarted but it cannot be defeated. Each of these convictions for the Christian pacifist has important consequences for action.

If God is the Father of all men, he is the Father of the enemies of our state as well as our compatriots. Their wrongs ought to be rectified and the sufferings relieved instead of their being slain. If God's character is Christ-like, then one will not participate in war as the will of God unless one believes that Christ could have done so. If God deals with men by the method of redemptive love, not only our ends but our means for the restraint of evil must be prompted by love. If God is both within and beyond the human scene, he cannot be indifferent to the human struggle and, however deferred the victory, good must in the long run triumph. Knowing that God is on the side, not of the heaviest battalions but of justice and love, we can labor for peace by such ways of peace as are available, and leave with God the outcome.

2. The Christian pacifist's doctrine of man is by no means as naïve about human sin as it is sometimes represented to be. It is precisely because the pacifist knows men to be sinful and life to be full of conflict that he sees no good to be gained by the colossal sin and conflict of war. On the other hand, he sees in every man the image of God, however much defaced by sin, and he cannot therefore adopt a devil theory of history. He sees in every war a conflict, not between an all-good and an all-bad state, but between states composed of men who are sons of God and who, like ourselves, are mixtures of good and evil. With this perspective he may—and must—judge some men and movements to be more evil than others and in need of restraint for the common good. But since he sees in every man the divine image he cannot judge any man to merit death for the sin of his national affiliation.

3. All Christian pacifism worthy of the name stems from the revelation of God in Jesus Christ. Pacifism's affiliation with liberalism and the social gospel is evident in the high estimate it places on the words and deeds of the Jesus of history. The Synoptic Gospels are its major authority and source. Yet regarding the nonresistance enjoined by Jesus there is no single point of view. Some pacifists literalize the injunctions of the Sermon on the Mount while others do not. Some are disturbed by the incident of the moneychangers, while others see no close analogy between this relatively mild and harmless use of force and the total destructiveness of modern war. Those are on safest ground who do not deny that Jesus in at least one instance used physical coercion and that he said nothing specific about war.

If one believes that Jesus regarded persons—all persons—as of supreme worth, this is bedrock for the pacifist position. Add to it the fact that Jesus himself chose the way of the cross instead of military force in a situation tense with nationalism, and one finds more potent testimony in this fact than in any specific word about nonresistance. The charter of the Christian pacifist's obligation to a positive ministry of reconciliation was stated in classic terms by Paul: "God was in Christ, reconciling the world unto himself, not imputing their trespasses unto them; and hath committed unto us the word of reconciliation."

4. With reference to the Kingdom, there is both wide variation among pacifists and close agreement between pacifists and non-pacifists. That it is not impossible for pacifism and apocalypticism to form a working partnership is demonstrated by Jehovah's Witnesses, to say nothing of the early Christians. On the other hand, there are probably as many non-pacifists as pacifists who talk about "building the Kingdom."

The central focus of the matter lies in man's responsibility for the Kingdom and the means to be used in the exercise of this responsibility. As the Madras report declared, the Kingdom is "both present and future; both a growth and a final consummation by God. It is our task and our hope.... We work for it and we wait for it." To most Christian pacifists, this means active responsibility for helping to create those conditions of economic justice, international cooperation and personal understanding through which God can progressively establish his Kingdom. This does not mean perfectionism or utopianism or a doctrine of automatic progress. It does not make the Kingdom "a simple extension of history" or assume that we shall ever have a sinless political or social order. It does mean a hope and an effort born of the conviction that God will use man's labor to bring the Kingdom nearer to fulfillment on earth if man will seek to use God's methods. But not otherwise. Specifically, this means the faith that war is not ineradicable, but that it can be eradicated only by means consonant with God's governance of his Kingdom in justice and love.

II

At many points the non-pacifist understanding of the Christian faith converges with the pacifist. However, important differences in emphasis cause different conclusions to be drawn. I shall mention some of these matters with reference again to God, man, Jesus, the Kingdom.

1. God is Creator, Judge, Redeemer, and the Lord of history. He is a God of mercy as well as of justice; he saves and redeems unworthy men by his grace when in our sin we forsake his paths. Thus far the pacifist and non-pacifist can walk together. The non-pacifist believes that the pacifist inadequately reckons with the sovereign righteousness of God. God is the righteous Ruler before whom evil men and movements are weighed in the balance, and he does not draw back from using even dire catastrophe to enact his will. Some non-pacifists argue that because God uses force to bring to pass his judgments, men may and must do likewise. All hold that men must be his instruments, even at the cost of the sternest measures, to check tyranny and defeat evil enterprises.

2. Man is a sinner and must ever, even at his highest moments, stand under judgment. Since men are evil, all political systems are infested with evil. So far, pacifist and non-pacifist agree. Divergence arises when the non-pacifist affirms that war, if fought for a good end, may be the lesser of two evil courses. To refuse to take this course is to lapse into political irresponsibility and do incalculable harm to persons whose freedom ought to be defended.

3. Positions vary widely as to the moral absolutes of Jesus. Explanations in terms of an "interim ethic" are less commonly advanced than the view that Jesus was concerned only with the individual, in whose relations nonresistance, though never perfectly attained, is at least a feasible possibility. The pacifist is charged with illicitly transforming "nonresistance," which Jesus enjoins upon individuals but not upon states, into "nonviolent resistance," which he enjoins upon nobody. Frederick C. Grant, in *The Gospel of the Kingdom*, makes Jesus' pacifism depend not on a universal spiritual principle but on his intellectual discernment of the futility of resistance under the circumstances of his time. The familiar argument that Jesus was himself not a pacifist because he said, "I came not to bring peace but a sword," and used a whip on the moneychangers, is seldom adduced by the more competent non-pacifist scholars.

4. With reference to the Kingdom, the non-pacifist position strikes in at two different angles. On the one hand, there are those who hold that Jesus' primary concern was with an otherworldly Kingdom. His Kingdom has its foregleams upon earth, not in a transformed society but in the souls of redeemed individuals who in repentance and faith receive forgiveness by God's grace. This position, which dominates Continental theology, provides little soil for

pacifism to grow in, for it tends to turn over to the state the management of the social order. It correlates closely with the doctrine of "the orders," long familiar in Lutheran thought and now being widely adduced by non-Lutherans. According to this position the state is an order ordained of God, and therefore it is a God-given duty, not as a Christian but as a citizen, to go to war when the state so ordains.

On the other hand, interventionism, like pacifism, springs from the soil of American social-gospel liberalism. Man must act with God to help bring in the Kingdom and establish justice upon earth. And he must act by any means available. The non-pacifist, differing radically from the pacifist at this point, holds that there are no specifically Christian means. It is always better to act in peace than in war if one can, but in some circumstances, so this argument runs, war is the only instrument by which men may move toward a more just society. To participate in a just war and to give oneself sacrificially to its high ends then becomes the first duty of the Christian.

III

In a welter of such diverse opinion, is there any common ground? It is my conviction that there is, and that we must increasingly discover and act upon it.

First, we can agree upon the evil and unchristian character of war. This does not mean that we shall all agree to be pacifists. It does mean that all Christians can endorse the Oxford Conference statement, unanimously adopted, that "war is a peculiar manifestation of the power of sin in the world; and is a defiance of the righteousness of God as revealed in Jesus Christ and him crucified." This paragraph is the only one italicized in full in the Oxford report. It may seem on the face of it not to be worth much, since Christians keep on fighting each other in good conscience. Yet it means a great deal for the most inclusive body in Christendom to declare officially that war is sin. This judgment has been passed many times by individuals and by individual churches; it was never before spoken with the united voice of the church.

Whether as the result of Oxford or of the cumulative peace effort of the past twenty years, this judg-ment has been bearing fruit. Even among those Christians who believe most ardently that American intervention is necessary to save democracy, there is an almost unanimous judgment that war, though it may check evil, cannot create good. The disposition to look beyond the battle to lay now the foundations of a just and durable peace is altogether Christian and almost wholly new. Only as Christians unitedly keep this perspective can anything constructive come out of the present holocaust.

Second, we can agree to avoid the extremes of a utopian optimism and of a defeatist pessimism. The world will not be free of sin as long as there are men in it, and as we judge evil to be present we must always ourselves in humility and penitence stand under judgment. But there need not be so much evil as there is. To adopt one of Reinhold Niebuhr's most constructive phrases, love is always an "impossible possibility"; and if we emphasize its possibilities as grounded in the nature of God, there is no upper limit set to its achievements. All that is most vital in the Christian's faith in the eternal and living God—a God of Christ-like love whose purposes are long and whose victories are sure—corroborates this hope.

Third, we can avoid both acquiescence in evil and ruthlessness in the attempt to overcome it. No space need be taken to demonstrate that Christian pacifism is not an irresponsible tolerance of colossal wrongs. It is not a "sit-down strike" in the presence of tyranny. Those non-pacifists who know us best do not make this charge. On the other hand, it needs to be pointed out that among those non-pacifists who see with clearest vision, there is an endeavor to prevent war from becoming mere retaliation and barbarism. Those who read the *British Christian Newsletter* cannot fail to be moved by the greatness of spirit of Dr. J. H. Oldham and his collaborators, who, though not pacifists, have argued repeatedly against reprisals, the bombing of civilian populations, and the loss of Christian understanding and fellowship through war. Should our country become a belligerent, it is devoutly to be hoped that our churches will have leaders equally empowered by Christian insights to see "above the battle."

Fourth, Christians can agree on the duty of absolute loyalty to God alone. Whatever our difference as to moral decision arising from this loyalty, the obligation to obey God rather than men remains unequivocal. The Christian's primary devotion is to the God who is above all gods.

Finally, we must—and can—maintain our faith in God and our faith in one another. In the Christian gospel the two are indissolubly connected. We sever them at our peril. If we love not our brother whom we have—or have not—seen, how shall we love God? And how shall we find in God our refuge and strength? The Christian church exists to bring to men in a living fellowship the power of the living God. The Christian gospel is the gospel of Jesus Christ our common Lord. Before him we can stand in differences of opinion but not in dissensions of spirit. In him our dilemmas of thought are resolved in love.

70. ERNEST FREMONT TITTLE

If America Is Drawn into the War, Can You, as a Christian, Participate in It, or Support It?

Ernest Fremont Tittle (1885-1949), minister of the First Methodist Church in Evanston, Illinois, was yet another famous Protestant preacher in the first half of the twentieth century. During World War I, Tittle took a position with the YMCA and served the humanitarian needs of troops in Europe. But after witnessing the carnage of the war, he became devoted to Christian pacifism and remained a pacifist throughout the rest of his life, even as he faced sharp criticism during World War II. Below is a piece that Tittle wrote for the Christian Century *in 1941. The liberal Protestant periodical had asked ten individuals to offer their written reflections on the question, "If America is drawn into the war, can you, as a Christian participate in it, or support it?"*

In 1917, I believed that war was the only means of preserving a humane and civilized culture. In that conviction, I left a wife and three children and went to France. I undertook to promote a fighting morale. I did what little I could, at a first aid dressing station, to relieve the suffering of wounded men. On the way to the front, I came upon a poem that deeply moved me. It was found on the body of a dead and unidentifiable Australian, who had written:

Rejoice, whatever anguish rend the heart,
  That God has given you a priceless dower
To live in these great times and have your part
  In freedom's crowning hour,
That ye may tell your sons, who see the light
  High in the heavens, their heritage to take,
I saw the powers of darkness put to flight,
  I saw the morning break.

But the powers of darkness were not put to flight. Men were killed, millions of them, including promising young writers and artists and musicians and scientists and philosophers. Women were left desolate, multitudes of them. Wealth was destroyed. Hunger stalked and pestilence raged over vast areas of the earth. Thirty million civilians were liquidated. The world was set on the road to an economic debacle. But justice was not achieved. Liberty was not secured. The rights and liberties of small nations were not guaranteed. Brute force was not banished from international affairs. The world was not made safe for democracy or for morality or for Christianity or for anything else that decent men care for and would be glad to die for. A heritage there was for the sons of men who died in the First World War, but it was not light "high in the heavens" or anywhere else. It was the descending darkness of the present war.

I am now convinced that war, being, as the Oxford Conference said, "a defiance of the righteousness of God as revealed in Jesus Christ and him crucified," cannot serve the ends of freedom and justice but is certain to defeat them. So, if the United States becomes a belligerent in Europe or in Asia, I shall undertake to contribute in some way to the good of my country, but I shall not "support" the war.

I

The present war in Europe is not only a clash of imperialisms; it is also a conflict of ideologies and ways of life. There is now far more at stake than there was in 1917. Prussianism threatened the world with whips; Hitlerism threatens it with scorpions. It is now all-essential to the welfare and progress of humanity that Hitlerism be overcome. On this point American Christians are agreed. The point on which they are not agreed is the means by which Hitlerism *can be* overcome. Christian pacifists do not proclaim that tyranny is better than war; they proclaim that tyranny cannot be overcome by war. They believe with the late Lord Lothian that "the triumph of Hitler grew out of the despair that settled on central Europe in the years of war, defeat, inflation and revolutionary propaganda." And they believe that this war is now producing political, economic and psychological conditions that make for the survival and spread of Hitlerism.

1. I believe that war as we know it cannot pave the way for doing good. When the fighting ends, who makes the peace? Not the men who actually fought the war, nor the parsons who blessed it, nor the professors who glorified it. When the fighting ends, the people who make the peace are the same people whose ambitions and practices created the situation which bred the war....

It has been said of the pacifist that he has "a confidence in human nature that human nature cannot support." As a matter of fact, it is the non-pacifist, not the pacifist, who believes that after a long-drawn-out orgy of indiscriminate killing and wholesale destruction people may be expected to think rationally and act justly. The pacifist has no such confidence in human nature.

2. I believe that war as we now know it cannot even hold evil in check. Total war is itself a most active and destructive evil: It knows no distinction of guilty and innocent or even of combatant and non-combatant. It has no "reverence for personality." It treats human beings as if they were things. It demands the distortion of truth. It knows no distinction of right and wrong but only military necessity. It requires men to believe that the end for which they are fighting is so important that it justifies the use of any means. It is now persuading men that a food blockade, although it may bring starvation, disease and death to innocent aged persons and women and children, is justified on the ground that it is essential to the preservation of civilization!

Can war, nevertheless, be made to hold evil in check? I have no confidence in attempts to preserve civilization by means that are themselves a denial and betrayal of everything that is essential to a humane and civilized culture. When men do evil that good may come, what they get is not the good they seek but the evil they do. History joins the New Testament in saying, "Be not deceived; God is not mocked; for whatsoever a man soweth, that shall he also reap."

II

It is the Christian faith that the cross of Christ is the supreme revelation of God's method of dealing with evil. The Son of God goes about doing good. He encounters opposition, but when he is reviled He reviles not again. He does not try to overcome evil with more evil. He undertakes to overcome evil with good. He resists evil but never with its own weapons. Condemning it unsparingly, he resists it with truth and love even unto death—his own death on a cross. That, Christianity maintains, is God's way of dealing with evil. That, St. Paul declares, is the power of God and the wisdom of God. That, pacifists believe, is the only way out of the world's misery.

I am convinced that the doing of good is the only way to put an end to aggression. Under present conditions, aggression may not be wholly unprovoked.... To say this is by no means to condone aggression, which in any case is an infamous thing; it is only to face the fact that, rooted in historical

172

events and psychological situations, aggression is seldom unprovoked. Nations that benefit from a world situation which denies equality of opportunity may view with abhorrence any attempt to change it by force. But if they themselves refuse to consent to peaceful change through discussion and negotiation, their refusal may be as immoral as the aggression it provokes.

In a world that is suffering from injustice piled upon injustice, the immediate overcoming of evil may be impossible. There may be no escape from the wages of sin. The question then is, What course, if faithfully followed, would eventually lead to a better state of affairs? War, I am convinced, is not the answer.... On the contrary, it can only provide new soil for the growth of dictatorship and aggression. The answer, I believe, is the persistent doing of good. Injustice breeds injustice. Hatred breeds hatred. Cruelty breeds cruelty. War breeds war. And no less surely does good beget good.

If the United States were invaded I should feel called upon to resist the invader by refusing to become his accomplice in the doing of evil. Both in South Africa and India this kind of resistance has produced notable results.... It produces a situation which the aggressor is unprepared to handle. Air raid for air raid, blockade for blockade, evil for evil—this he has been taught to expect, and when it occurs he knows what to do. But what is he to do when the pastors of all the Protestant churches of the Netherlands read from their pulpits a vigorous protest, in the name of Christ, against any attempt to force upon their country an anti-Jewish program? Nonviolent resistance forces the aggressor to think, which he can hardly do without a disastrous loss of military morale. It forces him to think because, although it refuses to become his accomplice, it does not seek to hurt him.

Pacifists do not suppose that nonviolent resistance can be offered without risk of arrest, imprisonment, and death. There would doubtless be many casualties, just as in war. Yet the end result, pacifists believe, would be far different; for war produces in victor and vanquished alike a state of mind that forbids the making of a just and durable peace, whereas nonviolent resistance, which appeals to the best in the aggressor and calls forth the best in his victim, may hope to be redemptive. Of course, nonviolent resistance to evil is not enough. It must be accompanied by a positive program of good which seeks long-range objectives.

III

I believe that Christian pacifism has relevance to the relations between nations as well as to the relations of the individual to his fellows. The doing of good is not only the way of life for the individual; it is also the way of life for society....

What would pacifism as our national policy require? ... As a national policy, pacifism would require the United States to set its own house in order. It would seek a real solution (which peacetime conscription is not) for the problem of unemployment and equality of opportunity for all Americans, including Negroes.... It would lead the United States to become indeed a good neighbor, concerned that all nations should have equal access to raw materials and needed markets for their industrial goods.

In the present crisis, pacifism as a national policy would constrain the United States to announce to the world (1) its readiness to associate itself with other nations in the building of a new world order; (2) its determination in any case to order its own life with a sensitive regard for the well-being of other peoples; (3) its desire to contribute to the relief of human suffering in war-stricken regions, through gifts of food, clothing and medical supplies; and (4) its readiness at the war's end to make loans for economic rehabilitation, if convinced of the desirability of the projects for which the money was sought. This foundation of justice being laid, pacifism would constrain the United States to appeal for an armistice and for an earnest attempt through discussion and negotiation to find a fundamental solution of world problems in a just peace....

Pacifism as a national strategy would pursue a policy not of appeasement but of reconciliation. Between these policies there is a vast range of difference. Appeasement is concerned only to safeguard individual and national self-interest at whatever cost to others; reconciliation seeks to promote fellowship through justice and good will. Pacifism finds the surest grounds of security not in concession or in conquest but in confidence.

"Good will" is a recognized asset in business; it is equally crucial in the affairs of nations. To seek good will is not impractical idealism; it is the most hard-headed realism.

But would it not be an act of insanity to trust Hitler? Yes, under present conditions. It is a fact, however, that Hitler has power only so long as the German army chooses to support him. And it is *not* a fact that the German people are wholly devoid of human decency or that they have no appreciation of the things which make for peace. To say that the Germans have ceased to be a civilized people is to reveal oneself a victim of war-born bitterness and confusion. It would not, in my judgment, be an act of insanity to seek an official statement of peace aims, a reasonable basis for the cessation of hostilities, and opportunity through discussion and negotiation to find a fundamental solution of world problems in a just peace. On the contrary, it would be an act of high statesmanship which would indicate that the responsible leadership of the United States has decided to trust in God and in the power of justice and good will, not merely in human cunning and brute force.

War is an attempted shortcut to the solution of terrific social problems, which it does not solve but only makes more difficult of solution. It is thought to be, but never is, a relatively quick way out of an intolerable situation. I can see ruin ahead if the United States becomes a belligerent in Europe or in Asia—ruin for us and for all mankind. The only way out of the world's misery is, I believe, the doing of good. That way I feel bound to take and advocate for my country.

71. DOROTHY DAY

Our Country Passes from Undeclared War to Declared War; We Continue Our Christian Pacifist Stand

Dorothy Day (1897-1980) partnered with Peter Maurin in founding The Catholic Worker *in 1933. Day was a socialist committed to the immediate advancement of worker's rights, women's rights, and civil rights, and the force of her writings and personality resulted in a social movement that, among other things, constructed hospitality houses to assist impoverished neighborhoods across the country. Perhaps more than any other Catholic in mid-century America, Day blended spirituality with the demands of social justice and Christian pacifism. The 1942 article below—"Our Country Passes from Undeclared War to Declared War; We Continue Our Christian Pacifist Stand"—reveals her faith-based opposition to U.S. participation in World War II.*

Dear Fellow Workers in Christ:

Lord God, merciful God, our Father, shall we keep silent, or shall we speak? And if we speak, what shall we say?

I am sitting here in the church on Mott Street writing this in your presence. Out on the streets it is quiet, but you are there too, in the Chinese, in the Italians, these neighbors we love. We love them because they are our brothers, as Christ is our Brother and God our Father.

But we have forgotten so much. We have all forgotten. And how can we know unless you tell us. "For whoever calls upon the name of the Lord shall be saved." How then are they to call upon Him in whom they have not believed? But how are they to believe Him whom they have not heard? And how are they to hear, if no one preaches? And how are men to preach unless they be sent? As it is written, "How beautiful are the feet of those who preach the gospel of peace." (Romans X)

Seventy-five thousand *Catholic Workers* go out every month. What shall we print? We can print still what the Holy Father is saying, when he speaks of total war, of mitigating the horrors of war, when he speaks of cities of refuge, of feeding Europe....

We will print the words of Christ who is with us always, even to the end of the world. "Love your enemies, do good to those who hate you, and pray for those who persecute and calumniate you, so that you may be children of your Father in heaven, who makes His sun to rise on the good and the evil, and sends rain on the just and unjust."

We are at war, a declared war, with Japan, Germany and Italy. But still we can repeat Christ's words, each day, holding them close in our hearts, each month printing them in the paper. In times past, Europe has been a battlefield. But let us remember St. Francis, who spoke of peace, and we will remind our readers of him, too, so they will not forget.

In *The Catholic Worker* we will quote our Pope, our saints, our priests. We will go on printing the articles which remind us today that we are "called to be saints," that we are other Christs, reminding us of the priesthood of the laity.

We are still pacifists. Our manifesto is the Sermon on the Mount, which means that we will try to be peacemakers. Speaking for many of our conscientious objectors, we will not participate in armed warfare or in making munitions, or by buying government bonds to prosecute the war, or in urging others to these efforts.

But neither will we be carping in our criticism. We love our country and we love our President. We have been the only country in the world where men of all nations have taken refuge from oppression. We recognize that while in the order of intention we have tried to stand for peace, for love of our brother, in the order of execution we have failed as Americans in living up to our principles.

We will try daily, hourly, to pray for an end to the war, such an end, to quote Father Orchard, "as would manifest to all the world, that it was brought about by divine action, rather than by military might or diplomatic negotiation, which men and nations would then only attribute to their power or sagacity."

"Despite all calls to prayer," Father Orchard concludes, "there is at present all too little indication anywhere that the tragedy of humanity and the desperate need of the world have moved the faithful, still less stirred the thoughtless masses, to turn to prayer as the only hope for mankind in this dreadful hour.

"We shall never pray until we feel more deeply, and we shall never feel deeply enough until we envisage what is actually happening in the world, and understand what is possible in the will of God; and that means until sufficient numbers realize that we have brought things to a pass which is beyond human power to help or save.

"Those who do feel and see, however inadequately, should not hesitate to begin to pray, or fail to persevere, however dark the prospects remain. Let them urge others to do likewise; and then, first small groups, and then the Church as a whole, and at last the world, may turn and cry for forgiveness, mercy and deliverance for all.

"Then we may be sure God will answer, and effectually; for the Lord's hand is not shortened that it cannot save, nor His ear heavy that it cannot hear." Let us add, that unless we combine this prayer with almsgiving, in giving to the least of God's children, and fasting in order that we may help feed the hungry, and penance in recognition of our share in the guilt, our prayer may become empty words.

Our works of mercy may take us into the midst of war. As editor of *The Catholic Worker,* I would urge our friends and associates to care for the sick and the wounded, to the growing of food for the hungry, to the continuation of all our works of mercy in our houses and on our farms. We understand, of course, that there is and that there will be great differences of opinion even among our own groups as to how much collaboration we can have with the government in times like these. There are differences more profound and there will be many continuing to work with us from necessity, or from choice, who do not agree with us as to our position on war, conscientious objection, etc. But we beg that there will be mutual charity and forbearance among us all.

This letter, sent to all our Houses of Hospitality and to all our farms, and being printed in the January issue of the paper, is to state our position in this most difficult time.

Because of our refusal to assist in the prosecution

of war and our insistence that our collaboration be one for peace, we may find ourselves in difficulties. But we trust in the generosity and understanding of our government and our friends, to permit us to continue, to use our paper to "preach Christ crucified."

May the Blessed Mary, Mother of love, of faith, of knowledge and of hope, pray for us.

72. Bayard Rustin

Letter to Local Draft Board No. 63

Bayard Rustin (1912-1987) was not only the leading tactician of the civil rights movement but also an openly gay man who schooled Martin Luther King, Jr., and other civil rights leaders in the demands of Christian nonviolence. Reared in a Quaker household, Rustin refused to serve as a soldier in World War II, and the following is his 1943 letter to Local Draft Board No. 63 in New York City.

Gentlemen:

For eight years I have believed war to be impractical and a denial of our Hebrew-Christian tradition. The social teachings of Jesus are: (1) Respect for personality; (2) Service to the "summum bonum"; (3) Overcoming evil with good; and (4) The brotherhood of man. These principles as I see it are violated by participation in war.

Believing this, and having before me Jesus' continued resistance to that which he considered evil, I was compelled to resist war by registering as a Conscientious Objector in October 1940.

However, a year later, September 1941, I became convinced that conscription as well as war equally is inconsistent with the teachings of Jesus. I must resist conscription also.

On Saturday, November 13, 1943, I received from you an order to report for a physical examination to be taken Tuesday, November 16, at eight o'clock in the evening. I wish to inform you that I cannot voluntarily submit to an order springing from the Selective Service and Training Act for War.

There are several reasons for this decision, all stemming from the basic spiritual truth that men are brothers in the sight of God:

1. War is wrong. Conscription is a concomitant of modern war. Thus conscription for so vast an evil as war is wrong.

2. Conscription for war is inconsistent with freedom of conscience, which is not merely the right to believe, but to act on the degree of truth that one receives, to follow a vocation which is God-inspired and God-directed.

   Today I feel that God motivates me to use my whole being to combat by nonviolent means the ever-growing racial tension in the United States; at the same time the State directs that I shall do its will; which of these dictates can I follow—that of God or that of the State? Surely, I must at all times attempt to obey the law of the State. But when the will of God and the will of the State conflict, I am compelled to follow the will of God. If I cannot continue in my present vocation, I must resist.

3. The Conscription Act denies brotherhood—the most basic New Testament teaching. Its design and purpose is to set men apart—German against American, American against Japanese. Its aim springs from a moral impossibility—that ends justify means, that from unfriendly acts a new and friendly world can emerge.

   In practice further, it separates black from white—those supposedly struggling for a common freedom. Such a separation also is based on the moral error that racism can overcome racism, that evil can produce good, that men virtually in slavery can struggle for a freedom they are denied. This means that I must protest racial discrimination in the armed forces, which is not only morally indefensible but also in clear violation of the Act. This does not, however, imply that I could have a part in conforming to the Act if discrimination were eliminated.

Segregation, separation, according to Jesus, is the basis of continuous violence. It was such an observation which encouraged him to teach, "It has been said to you in olden times that thou shalt not kill, but I say unto you, do not call a man a fool"—and he might have added: "for if you call him such, you automatically separate yourself from him and violence begins." That which separates man from his brother is evil and must be resisted.

uation. It is always timely and virtuous to change—to take in all humility a new path.

Though joyfully following the will of God, I regret that I must break the law of the State. I am prepared for whatever may follow.

I herewith return the material you have sent me, for conscientiously I cannot hold a card in connection with an Act I no longer feel able to accept and abide by.

Today I am notifying the Federal District Attorney of my decision and am forwarding him a copy of this letter.

I appreciate now as in the past your advice and consideration, and trust that I shall cause you no anxiety in the future. I want you to know I deeply respect you for executing your duty to God and country in these difficult times in the way you feel you must. I remain

Sincerely yours,
Bayard Rustin

I admit my share of guilt for having participated in the institutions and ways of life which helped bring fascism and war. Nevertheless, guilty as I am, I now see as did the Prodigal Son that it is never too late to refuse longer to remain in a non-creative sit-

P.S. I am enclosing samples of the material which from time to time I have sent out to hundreds of persons, Negro and white, throughout our nation. This indicates one type of the creative work to which God has called me.

73. ANDRÉ TROCMÉ

Message to the Church of Le Chambon-sur-Lignon

André Trocmé (1901-1971) was a Protestant minister serving the French village of Le Chambon-sur-Lignon, with its population of five thousand, when France fell to Germany in 1940. Trocmé preached Christian nonviolent resistance before, during, and after the defeat, and when it became clear that Jews were in need of a safe haven, Trocmé, his wife, Magda, and their fellow Huguenot villagers opened their homes and farms to as many as five thousand Jews fleeing deportation and death at the hands of Nazi collaborators and occupiers. Below is a sermon of encouragement that Trocmé preached to his congregation in 1944.

Dear Brothers and Sisters,

… Major trials are still ahead for our country, and perhaps ahead of our Church. We learn bit

by bit to know the war in all its forms, and we are now plunged into the furnace with the rest of the country. However, our few difficulties are nothing compared to those of bombed out, starving towns and localities where there is fighting. Major tests always result in a sorting among men: Some entrench themselves in an egoist life, or even seek to profit from their brothers' suffering. Others get carried away in a spirit of enthusiasm, sacrifice and devotion.

Between the two attitudes, a disciple of Jesus Christ would not hesitate: He must offer his life and his resources.

But always remember that the disciples' devotion to Jesus has a specific character:

1. The Christian does not seek the Kingdom of this world, but the Kingdom of God.

2. He does not use, to fight against all forms of evil, the earthly weapons of violence, lies, and vengeance. I was very happy, when I arrived, to ascertain that you were calm and stable. A spirit of moderation and gentleness must thrive among us.

3. The gift of our lives. Calm and confidence does not suffice, however. It is also necessary to use God's positive weapons, much more effective than the others, although less visible.

If evil responds to evil, how will we extinguish it?

But if the power of the Crucified Christ responds to evil, it will extinguish the characteristics of evil. We must therefore have the Holy Spirit in us, because God gives it to those who ask for it.

4. Finally, remember that the Christian is a persevering man. He knows that nothing serious is accomplished in noise, excitement, tempers, followed by panics and depressions in an hour of danger.

If he undertakes to construct a tower, he calculates ahead of time if he will be able to complete it....

God is the Christian's source of this patience and perseverance, and He makes the fruits of this earth grow slowly but surely.

Through prayer, we enter into communication with God, who fills us with all the persistence which we need to manage our enterprises well.

Because it is a question of something completely different, brothers and sisters, than just a short crisis … It is a question of a huge battle of love against hate, light against shadows, truth against lies, and Christ's cross against the power of sin.

After the present crisis, other forms of struggle will follow this form: It will be a matter of the evangelization of France, of Europe and of the entire world, which must be submissive to Jesus Christ.

Therefore, Christians, who are awakened because of the massive suffering and injustice in the world and who are now ready to give their lives, know that their involvement is the involvement of *their whole existence* towards God.

Only in this condition, in perseverance and love, will their sacrifice have any use.

Finally, brothers and sisters, let us recall that men pass and human enterprises rise up and crumble down. Only God endures, only God can act. It is only He who can really move mountains. We must not substitute ourselves for God and push Him aside in our undertakings. Faith consists of having confidence in Him alone, and in obeying Him without reserve, in order to obtain serious results. Let us therefore direct all our lively energies to his service in unconditional obedience.

Without faith, we are likely to stir up a lot of dust but then discover that all our work was in vain. But through faith we will see miracles accomplished. I'm sure of it, and I ask you to share in this conviction.

74. TAKASHI NAGAI

The Bells of Nagasaki

Takashi Nagai (1908-1951) was a radiation researcher and medical doctor working in Nagasaki when the atomic bomb dropped there on August 9, 1945. His wife was burned to ashes, but Nagai survived and helped to lead his hospital staff in rescue efforts and medical treatment for those scorched by the horrific blast. As a devoted Catholic, Nagai interpreted his relief work through the lenses of his faith, and below are his reflections on the time immediately following the explosion—an excerpt drawn from The Bells of Nagasaki *(1946).*

Chimoto-san was cutting grass on Mount Kawabira. From where he worked he could see Urakami three kilometers down to the southwest. The hot summer sun was shining lazily over the beautiful town and its hills. Suddenly Chimoto-san heard the familiar, still faint sound of a plane. Sickle in hand, he straightened his body and looked up at the sky. It was more or less clear, but just above his head there floated a big cloud the shape of a human hand. Yes, the sound of the plane came from above that cloud. And as he watched, out it came. "It's a B-29." From the tip of the middle finger of the hand-shaped cloud, a small flashing silver plane appeared. It must have been eight thousand meters up in the sky. "Oh, it's dropped something. A long, narrow, black object. A bomb! A bomb!" Chimato-san threw himself to the ground. Five seconds. Ten seconds. Twenty seconds. One minute. As he held his breath, an eternity seemed to pass.

Suddenly there was a blinding flash of light; an awful brightness but no noise. Nervously Chimato-san raised his head. "A bomb! It's at Urakami." And in the area above the church he saw an enormous cloud of white smoke float upward, swelling rapidly as it rose. But what struck terror into his heart was the huge blast of air like a hurricane that rushed toward him. It came from under the white smoke and rolled over the hills and fields with terrifying speed and power. Houses and trees and everything else collapsed before it. They fell to the ground; they were smashed to pieces; the debris was blown this way and that. Clumps of trees disappeared before his very eyes as this violent force rushed up the slopes of Mount Kawabira. What was it? He could only think of an enormous, invisible bulldozer moving forward and leveling everything in its path. I'm going to be crushed to powder, he thought. Joining his hands in supplication, he cried out: "My God! My God!" and again he pressed his face to the ground.

Then a deafening noise struck his ears and he was thrown into the air and hurled five meters against a brick wall. Finally he opened his eyes and looked around. The trees were torn from their roots. There were no branches, no leaves, no grass. Everything had vanished. All that remained was the smell of resin....

Behind the Department of Pharmacy, Professor Seiki and his students were hard at work digging a shelter. The professor was digging inside, while the students were carrying the earth away. Who could have guessed that at that moment they were drawing lots? Those outside were choosing death, while those inside were choosing life. Wearing short pants, they looked like miners as they vigorously dug into the ground. They were some four hundred meters from the center of the explosion.

A blinding flash lit up the dugout to its very depth. Then came the terrible roar. Tomita, who, basket in hand, was working at the entrance, was blown inside, hitting the back of Professor Seiki who was crouching down and working with his spade.

"What's going on?" shouted the professor angrily, as he straightened his back. But after Tomita, pieces of wood and shreds of clothing and bits of tile came hurtling through the air. A big piece of wood hit the professor full in the back and he fell unconscious in the mud.

Only a few minutes seemed to pass. Professor Seiki regained consciousness and found himself lying in a maelstrom of smoke and fumes filling the shelter. The hot air kept pouring in, but the professor, tottering to his feet, made his way to the entrance. At first he felt relieved that he had survived. But the feeling of relief did not last for long. Unconsciously he dropped his spade and stood aghast with mouth and eyes wide open, dazed by what he saw.

The large buildings of the Department of Pharmacy were no longer there. The biochemistry classroom was not there. The pharmacology classroom was not there. The fence was not there. The houses outside the fence were not there. Everything had disappeared and all that remained was a sea of fire.

Atomic specialist and doctor of physics though he was, Seiki did not realize that this was an atomic bomb. He never dreamed that American scientists had made such progress.

But what about the students? He looked at the ground around him and a cold shiver went through his whole body. "Is it possible that these lifeless beings are my students? No, it can't be! In the shelter I was struck in the back and I'm still unconscious. It's a nightmare. No matter how awful war is, it can't be this cruel." He pinched his thigh. He felt his pulse. Yes, his body was awake and alive. "If this isn't a nightmare, what is it? It's worse than any dream."

The professor went quickly to the first charred body that lay nearby. "Hey! Hey!" he shouted. But there was no answer. He grabbed the shoulders with both hands and tried to lift the body, but the flesh peeled off like the skin of a peach. Okamato was dead.

The boy beside him groaned and turned over. "Murayama! Murayama! Hold on!" cried the professor as he cradled in his arms the student whose skin was peeling off. "Professor! Professor! … Ah!" And with these words Murayama rolled over on his side. He was dead. With a deep sigh, Dr. Seiki laid the cold, naked body on the earth, joined his hands in silent prayer, and crouched down beside the next charred body.

Araki was swollen like a pumpkin and the skin was peeling off his face. But the narrow white eyes were open as he said quietly, "Professor, I'm finished. There's no hope for me. Thanks for everything."

Blood flowed from the ears and noses of the dead and dying students. Some had had their skulls smashed and had died instantly. Evidently they had been thrown violently to the ground. There were others from whose mouths bubbles of blood were flowing like froth….

Professor Seiki shouted out: "Help! Help! Someone come!" He faced north and shouted. He faced east and shouted. Then he faced west and shouted again. He strained his ears and listened. But the atmosphere had not yet returned to normal. Restless gusts of wind were swirling fiercely on all sides. And mingled with the sound of that wind, from beneath the broken and crushed roof,

he could hear endless cries, voices screaming for help.

"Help! Help! I'm in agony!"

"Come, somebody!"

"I'm burning! Throw water on me! Water!"

"Mommy! Mommy!"

The professor felt dizzy. Again he lost consciousness and fell to the ground. After some time he opened his eyes to find that a thick, black, solid cloud filled the whole sky. The sun had lost its light and looked like a reddish brown disc. It was dark like evening. It was cold.

Seiki strained his ears and listened. The number of voices crying for help had somewhat diminished. The child screaming for its mother must have been burned to death….

Dr. Yamada threw herself on the floor and thus was saved. She alone survived to tell the tale. Beside her, Tsujita-san fell dying. "Oh! the pain! The pain!" she gasped. And with these words she died. It was like a dream. The bacteriology classroom became a ball of fire. Professor Naito and all the others were killed instantly.

When Dr. Yamada dragged herself out of the building, everything was dark and the wind was moaning. And what a scene met her eyes! The huge pines and camphor trees were torn up by the roots and all the school buildings had collapsed. As for the cathedral, about one-third of the building was blown down, including the fifty-meter-tall bell tower, and the remnant looked like a ruin of ancient Rome. On the stone fences, people were hanging upside down with arms and legs torn off. The road was dotted with fallen men, women, and children. In the field, innumerable corpses lay as far as the eye could see….

I myself was buried beneath a heap of debris. But finally I managed to extricate myself by my own efforts and make my way to the photography room where I found Professor Fuse with Nurse Hashimoto, the chief nurse, and the others. They all ran to me. "Oh, good! Good!" they kept shouting as they threw their arms around me joyfully….

"Doctor, help me!"

"Give me medicine!"

"Look at this wound!"

"Doctor, I'm cold. Give me clothes!"

A strange group of naked human beings

crowded around us, all shouting. These were the people who somehow survived when everybody and everything was swept into the air and hurled in all directions by the explosion.

Since the bomb had fallen just when the outpatients were coming in great numbers for consultation, this part of the corridor and the waiting room were littered with an enormous number of fallen people. Their clothes had been torn off; their skin was cut and peeling away. Covered with dirt and smoke, they were gray like phantoms, and it was difficult to believe they were human or that they belonged to this world....

The force of the bomb is so terrible that it cannot be expressed in words. People who were fully exposed to it—namely, people who were outside or on the roof of a building or standing at a window—were beaten down or blown away. Those who were within a kilometer of the explosion died instantly or in a few minutes.

Five hundred meters from the explosion lay a mother with her stomach split open while her future baby attached by the umbilical cord dangled between her legs. There were corpses with the belly gaping and the entrails exposed. Seven hundred meters away were heads that had been torn from the trunks of bodies. There were broken skulls with blood dripping from the ears....

I hear my five-year-old daughter Kayano talking to herself. Going outside, I find her playing the housewife with her toys. The head of a doll, some bottles, plates, the frame of a mirror are gathered together on a scorched rock. All her friends are dead.

She is chattering to herself. "Kaya-chan's house was big, wasn't it? It had an upstairs. My mom was there. She gave me bean-jam cakes to eat. I slept with a quilt. We had electricity."

I stood there silently. Kayano kept talking about memories, one after another. As she chattered on, I closed my eyes and within me rose a vision of a life that had passed. It was like the legend of a magnificent palace at the bottom of the ocean. I opened my eyes and, like Urashima who dwelt in that place for one hundred years, I saw my beautiful dream collapse and disappear. Before me lay nothing but an arid, atomic wasteland.

The autumn wind wailed. The tiles on the roof seemed to weep.

Suddenly Ichitaro appeared. He was wearing his military uniform with the bottom of his trousers tied around his ankles. As soon as he had been demobilized he had returned in haste, to find his city in ruins and his house a heap of ashes, while the charred, black bones of his beloved wife and five children were scattered here and there.

"I have no joy in life," he lamented.

"Who has joy when we've been defeated in war?" I replied....

"Look, the day after tomorrow there will be a funeral service at Urakami Cathedral for the victims of the bomb. As the representative of the Christians, I've written a speech which I intend to read there. Would you like to read it now?"

Ichitaro took the paper and began to read. At first his voice was vigorous and strong, but as he proceeded he would pause for a moment to reflect. Tears flowed down his cheeks.

Here is the text of my speech:

Funeral Address for the Victims of the Atom Bomb

On August 9, 1945, at 10:30 A.M. a meeting of the Supreme Council of War was held at the Imperial Headquarters to decide whether Japan should capitulate or continue to wage war. At that moment the world was at a crossroads. A decision was being made that would either bring about a new and lasting peace or throw the human family into further cruel bloodshed and carnage.

And just at that same time, at two minutes past eleven in the morning, an atomic bomb exploded over our district of Urakami in Nagasaki. In an instant, eight thousand Christians were called into the hands of God, while in a few hours the fierce flames reduced to ashes this sacred territory of the East. At midnight of that same night the cathedral suddenly burst into flames and was burned to the ground. And exactly at that time in the Imperial Palace, His Majesty the Emperor made known his sacred decision to bring the war to an end.

On August 15, the Imperial Rescript which

put an end to the fighting was formally promulgated, and the whole world welcomed a day of peace. This day was also the great feast of the Assumption of the Virgin Mary. It is significant to reflect that Urakami Cathedral was dedicated to her. And we must ask if this convergence of events—the ending of the war and the celebration of her feast—was merely coincidental or if there was here some mysterious providence of God.

I have heard that the second atomic bomb, calculated to deal a deadly blow to the war potential of Japan, was originally destined for another city. But since the sky over that city was covered with clouds, the American pilots found it impossible to aim at their target. Consequently, they suddenly changed their plans and decided to drop the bomb on Nagasaki, the secondary target. However, yet another hitch occurred. As the bomb fell, cloud and wind carried it slightly north of the munitions factory over which it was supposed to explode and it exploded above the cathedral.

This is what I have heard. If it is true, the American pilots did not aim at Urakami. It was the providence of God that carried the bomb to that destination.

Is there not a profound relationship between the destruction of Nagasaki and the end of the war? Nagasaki, the only holy place in all Japan—was it not chosen as a victim, a pure lamb, to be slaughtered and burned on the altar of sacrifice to expiate the sins committed by humanity in the Second World War?

The human family has inherited the sin of Adam who ate the fruit of the forbidden tree; we have inherited the sin of Cain who killed his younger brother; we have forgotten that we are children of God; we have believed in idols; we have disobeyed the law of love. Joyfully we have hated one another; joyfully we have killed one another. And now at last we have brought this great and evil war to an end. But in order to restore peace to the world it was not sufficient to repent. We had to obtain God's pardon through the offering of a great sacrifice.

Before this moment there were many opportunities to end the war. Not a few cities were totally destroyed. But these were not suitable sacrifices; nor did God accept them. Only when Nagasaki was destroyed did God accept the sacrifice. Hearing the cry of the human family, He inspired the emperor to issue the sacred decree by which the war was brought to an end.

Our church of Nagasaki kept the faith during four hundred years of persecution when religion was proscribed and the blood of martyrs flowed freely. During the war this same church never ceased to pray day and night for a lasting peace. Was it not, then, the one unblemished lamb that had to be offered on the altar of God? Thanks to the sacrifice of this lamb many millions who would otherwise have fallen victim to the ravages of war have been saved.

How noble, how splendid was that holocaust of August 9, when flames soared up from the cathedral, dispelling the darkness of war and bringing the light of peace! In the very depth of our grief we reverently saw here something beautiful, something pure, something sublime. Eight thousand people, together with their priests, burning with pure smoke, entered into eternal life. All without exception were good people whom we deeply mourn.

How happy are those people who left this world without knowing the defeat of their country! How happy are the pure lambs who rest in the bosom of God! Compared with them how miserable is the fate of us who have survived! Japan is conquered. Urakami is totally destroyed. A waste of ash and rubble lies before our eyes. We have no houses, no food, no clothes. Our fields are devastated. Only a remnant has survived. In the midst of the ruins we stand in groups of two or three looking blankly at the sky.

Why did we not die with them on that day, at that time, in this house of God? Why must we alone continue this miserable existence?

It is because we are sinners. Ah! Now

indeed we are forced to see the enormity of our sins! It is because I have not made expiation for my sins that I am left behind. Those are left who are so deeply rooted in sin that they were not worthy to be offered to God.

We Japanese, a vanquished people, must now walk along a path that is full of pain and suffering. The reparations imposed by the Potsdam Declaration are a heavy burden. But this painful path along which we walk carrying our burden—is it not also the path of hope which gives to us sinners an opportunity to expiate our sins?

"Blessed are those that mourn for they shall be comforted." We must walk this way of expiation faithfully and sincerely. And as we walk in hunger and thirst, ridiculed, penalized, scourged, pouring with sweat and covered with blood, let us remember how Jesus Christ carried His cross to the hill of Calvary. He will give us courage.

"The Lord has given: the Lord has taken away. Blessed be the name of the Lord!"

Let us give thanks that Nagasaki was chosen for the sacrifice. Let us give thanks that through this sacrifice peace was given to the world and freedom of religion to Japan.

May the souls of the faithful departed, through the mercy of God, rest in peace. Amen.

Ichitaro finished reading and closed his eyes.

After a while he spoke quietly: "Then my wife and children didn't go to hell. That's for sure! … But, Doctor," he went on, "what about us who're left behind?"

"You and I, both of us, have failed the entrance exam to heaven!"

"We failed the exam! Ha! Ha!"

Together we raised our voices and laughed heartily. It was as though a heavy burden had fallen from our shoulders.…

The insects are chirping and singing. I am in bed with Kayano in my arms. She keeps groping for her mother's breasts, only to find she is with her father. She begins to sob gently. Then her breathing tells me that she has fallen into a deep sleep.

I am not alone in this suffering. Tonight in this atomic waste, how many orphans are weeping! How many widows are weeping!

The night is long but my sleep is short. My dreams fly away as the white light of the morning filters through the cracks in the shutters.

"Bong! … Bong! … Bong!"

The bells are ringing. These are the bells of the Angelus ringing from the ruined cathedral, echoing across the atomic wilderness and telling us that dawn has come. Under the direction of Ichitaro, Iwanaga and the young men of Honno dug up those bells from beneath the atomic rubble and debris. The bells had fallen fifty meters from the cathedral tower but were not broken.

On Christmas night, Iwanaga and his companions hoisted them up and rang them morning, noon, and night until they clanged with the nostalgic sound we had often heard before.

"The angel of the Lord declared unto Mary.…" Makoto and Kayano have jumped out of bed and, sitting on the blanket, are reciting their morning prayers.

"Bong! … Bong! … Bong!"

The clear sound of those bells!—ringing out the message of peace and its blessings. These are the bells that did not ring for weeks and months after the disaster. May there never again be a time when they do not ring! May they ring out this message of peace until the morning of the day on which the world ends!

Men and women of the world, never again plan war! With this atomic bomb, we can only mean suicide for the human race. From this atomic waste the people of Nagasaki confront the world and cry out: No more war! Let us follow the commandment of love and work together. The people of Nagasaki prostrate themselves before God and pray: Grant that Nagasaki may be the last atomic wilderness in the history of the world.

The bells continue to ring.

"O Mary, conceived without sin, pray for us who have recourse to thee."

Makato and Kayana make the sign of the cross as they finish their prayers.

75. TOYOHIKO KAGAWA

We Have Abandoned War

Toyohiko Kagawa's (1888-1960) first formal introduction to Christianity came when he enrolled in an English-language Bible class as a means to learn the language. His later conversion to Christianity as a teenager and subsequent enrollment in Presbyterian College in Tokyo cost him the only remaining family he had. As an adult, he devoted his life to helping the poor, living with them in the Kobe slums. In 1941 Kagawa left Japan to visit the United States in a futile attempt to prevent war between the two countries.

A typical modern state, cumbered with its heavy armament but well-nigh bereft of other values, reminds one of nothing so much as a naked savage, lugging around his javelin and poisoned arrows. States today seem nearer to the stage of barbarism than do many individuals.

By the abandonment of war, we in Japan have merged from an era of barbarism. Thus we have been accorded a chance to make ourselves the most progressive and civilized of all the nations.

If only we had done this willingly ten years ago, history would have taken another course. But it not too late for us.

Our new constitution will become a milestone in the realization of world peace. For the first time in human history, by our abandonment of war, the warning of Christ has been accepted by a national government: "All they that take the sword shall perish by the sword."

We are going to alter the definition of a "great" state. A truly great state is not necessarily big, nor rich, nor quarrelsome with its neighbors. The great state is the one which is wise, moral and God-fearing. The ideal we pursue is that of making Japan a state with which God can be pleased. Thus may we arrive at the summit of civilization and set an example of a peace-loving state. Though not large, nor rich, nor strong, we may thus become truly great.

76. A. J. MUSTE

Theology of Despair: An Open Letter to Reinhold Niebuhr

A. J. Muste (1885-1967) was the leading pacifist in the United States at this point, and Reinhold Niebuhr (1892-1971) was the nation's leading exponent of Christian political realism. A minister of the Dutch Reformed Church, Muste became involved in revolutionary politics, especially with the labor movement, in the 1920s. But by 1937 he devoted himself anew to pacifism, and he became executive secretary of the Fellowship of Reconciliation in 1940, a position he held until 1953. Muste's thought and actions served to influence many Christian pacifists in the latter half of the twentieth century, including Bayard Rustin and Martin Luther King, Jr. In the essay below—"Theology of Despair: An Open Letter to Reinhold Niebuhr"—Muste makes reference to Jan Masaryk, who served as foreign minister in pre-communist Czechoslovakia and then regretted his decision to retain this post after the communist takeover, led by Klement Gottwald, in 1948.

Dear Dr. Niebuhr:

I have just finished reading your editorial, "Amid Encircling Gloom," in *Christianity and Crisis* and the "Editorial Notes" immediately following. The experience has saddened and dismayed me, not alone because of the defeatism and despair that pervade both, but because of the *justification* for despair and even suicide I found there.

In the editorial you point out that "our possession of a monopoly in atomic weapons and our fear that the monopoly will run out" in a few years make it possible that Americans may plunge into a "preventative" war against Russia, and certainly make it likely that they will not exercise "the forbearance without which it will be impossible to prevent present tensions from breaking out into conflict."

You warn that we shall have to walk the tight rope of avoidance of such a course even while we "defend" ourselves by both military and political weapons—atomic not excluded—against communism, a counsel which is no whit different from that which we may hear from enlightened secular sources! Aside from this, what do you, widely regarded as America's foremost theologian, have to say that might avert the tragedy and lead men out of the "encircling gloom"?

What you offer is a variation on the only text about which you ever preach or write any more, though there are so many other texts and—I venture to say—more Christian ones, in the Scriptures. If the world is plunged into war, you say, "it would be indeed the final ironic and tragic culmination of the pretensions of modern man." Men drawn into war, though not wishing to be, "would merely"—what does that assumption-laden, emotion-ridden word "merely" signify in this context?—"illustrate the human predicament confessed by St. Paul in the words: 'For the good that I would I do not....'"

As befits a Christian prophet, you warn that in these circumstances "we face not merely a Russian or communist peril but the threat of divine judgment." But you do not conclude, as did the prophets that were before you, by calling upon your hearers to repent, act and so flee from the judgment. Instead, you finish with a solemn statement which, I am bound to say, makes little sense if taken at face value: "We are drifting toward a possible calamity in which even the most self-righteous assurance of the justice of our cause will give us no easy conscience."

Here is an illustration, it seems to me, of your tendency to blur all distinctions, in disregard of your own insistently proclaimed doctrine that there are relative differences that matter. What the sentence just quoted does in the political realm—on the *existential* level, shall we say?—is to convey to people the subtle suggestion that they are paralyzed, under a judgment which they cannot escape, that in the now-so-familiar phrase, "there isn't anything they can do about it." They will feel when they go to war that it is right, necessary, or even holy—and yet they will not have easy consciences! They will not have easy consciences, and yet they will feel self-righteous! That is the human condition.

So there is no true tension, but only *anxiety*, or a pervading sense of futility, for tension in the biblical sense is surely characteristic of a situation where man stands before his God and makes a *decision*. Here, no decision is possible any more. The important decisions have all been made, or are being made, but always by something or somebody else. (I do not mean to say that you deliberately try to convey this subtle suggestion of paralysis and helplessness, but I believe it is the effect of your writing. And a confession on your part that this might be another illustration of how men do the evil which they would not—a confession I well know you are humble enough to make—would not do a thing to mend matters.)

The habit of utterance which seems to me to have grown upon you, and which dismays and disturbs me so, is illustrated again in the editorial note about the Palestine partition question in the same issue. After pointing out that in spite of what the Jews endured at Hitler's hands, they have been grievously wounded again "and not even the Stratton bill has been passed as a balm for those wounds," you conclude: "The whole situation is almost too tragic that the perplexities of this particular problem only engage a fraction of our conscience." There it is again. The tragic plight of the Jews. What to do? It can "only engage a fraction of our conscience."

Sandwiched between these two items is your comment on Jan Masaryk's suicide. It seems to me very revealing. You recall that many people felt that Masaryk's willingness to become foreign secretary of a communist government, in spite of his well-known aversion to communism, demonstrated a lack of inner integrity. But, you assert, "he proved himself in possession of a final resource of such integrity by taking his life." You recognize, of course, that "suicide is not an ideal way of coming to terms with the issues of life," but, not being a "perfectionist," you are certain that men cannot attain the ideal anyway. And, having reached the point where the battle against "perfectionists" has become practically your sole occupation, now for the third time with rather obvious avidity you seize the opportunity to emphasize the complete hopelessness of man's estate and to pour sarcasm upon "the pretensions of modern man." Young Masaryk "proved his loyalty to his father's political ideas by violating his father's scruples against suicide," and from this you conclude, "that men may be forced into a position in which they can maintain the integrity of their soul *only* (italics mine) by taking their life, points to a dimension of human selfhood which makes nonsense of most modern theories of 'self-realization'!"

I am not suggesting that Jan Masaryk may not indeed have been truer to his father's ideals and to his own attachment to democratic principles by committing suicide—if that is what occurred—than he would have been by continuing to serve in the communist government of Czechoslovakia after the coup. But the assertion that suicide was the "only" way of proving the integrity of his soul is, I think, a very revealing one. So is the fact that every tragedy as it passes in review before you is the occasion for just one comment: that it proves the validity of a theory of human depravity or, more accurately, futility.

The upshot of the business is that Jan Masaryk commits suicide—and it is really the only thing he can do. On the larger scale of world politics the conclusion likewise is that mankind—or at least western civilization—commits suicide in atomic war. When it comes to a showdown that is the only thing it can do! Surely it is not altogether inappropriate to raise the question whether something like a "death-wish" is not operating here. The one positive element in the situation is that the thesis of

man's utter futility has been vindicated!

This philosophy of fatalism and "inevitability" has its parallel in the Marxist-Leninist-Stalinist dogma of the "inevitability" of war between "the workers' fatherland" and the capitalist-imperialist world. That dogma also is linked to a low view of human nature and an essentially fatalistic one. It declares that man and his history are chiefly, if not entirely, the product of economic forces. According to this view of things, also, the living human beings in Russia, the United States, and elsewhere are essentially spectators at a tragedy of which they are also, alas, the victims, but which, nevertheless, they have no alternative but to play through to the bloody end.

The parallel does not end there. All is happily resolved—in theory—after the "inevitable" catastrophe has taken place. In the Marxist case, the solution is "within history," in the free society which grows out of "the dictatorship of the proletariat." In the other case, the resolution is "beyond history." Actual human beings, living and suffering, killing and being killed, today are offered "pie in the sky" under both systems!

One other observation remains to be made about how your thesis works out in contemporary affairs. In essential matters—support of the Marshall Plan, the need of fighting communism and Russia by both military and "peaceful" means, and so on—your political position today cannot be distinguished from that of John Foster Dulles, who is Thomas E. Dewey's choice for Secretary of State. For you, a Socialist who knows how to make use of certain parts of the Marxian analysis, who has been the nemesis not only of conservatives but of liberals for these many years, this conjunction certainly should give pause.

Considered as a political phenomenon it is not an accident that Reinhold Niebuhr, the radical, and John Foster Dulles, the Wall Street attorney and one of the chief architects of the bipartisan foreign policy of the United States, should now be virtually a team. For, if war is "inevitable," whether on the basis of the Marxist class war and materialistic interpretation of history, or on the basis of the theory of human depravity and the necessity of exposing "the pretensions of modern man," in actuality the war will be between Stalinist Russia and imperialist United States, for "communism" on the one hand and "free enterprise" on the other. Let me emphasize that I am not saying that war is "inevitable," only that *if* there is war, it will be this kind and no other. These are the elements that have an "interest" in making war and that possess the resources with which to make war.

However, in lining up the masses of people for war, these elements must have at least the acquiescence of the Church and of Christian leaders, if not their unequaled blessing. They must have, in both the conservative and the progressive camps, men who are regarded as idealists but who, being practical, know that you have to meet Soviet military might with American military might, including atomic bombs, even while they also use other means; "practical" idealists who will not seriously interfere with war preparations; who are, whether conscious of it or not, and despite disclaimers, pretty well convinced in their hearts that war *is* inevitable—hence the constellation of Niebuhr and Dulles.

To Jan Masaryk, there was open another way than suicide to prove his integrity: open refusal to serve in the post-coup cabinet, and a public statement, either in Czechoslovakia or in exile, of the reasons therefore. This probably would have had little immediate or obvious political effect. Many would have regarded it as a foolish gesture, or even as an exhibition of addiction to "perfectionism." He might have lost his life in that case, too. But, as it is, his suicide served only to dramatize what the discerning already knew and the American government had already accepted as the basis of its policy, namely, that in the final analysis Soviet totalitarianism will not compromise on essentials. Had he been killed for public repudiation of the Stalinist course, democracy and truth would have had a martyr, Bohemia perhaps another Jan Hus.

The world does not have to go to war and commit suicide, either. But it can escape that calamity only if there are those who do not believe that catastrophe is inevitable; who do not believe that you have to line up with one side or the other in the "cold" war; who are willing to pursue a course that will seem politically ineffective and foolish in the estimation of "the wise of this world"; who will not, indeed, ask for victims for executioners, in the name of any cause or theory, but who will be prepared to lay down their own lives if the call comes, since they have learned, from the most authoritative of all teachers, that most infallible and inexorable of all laws: unless the seed falls into the ground and dies, it bears no fruit; but if it die, it brings forth much fruit.

The Scriptures are not simply an extended commentary on the single text, "vanity of vanities, all is vanity." We read in them the commandment, "Be ye prefect as your heavenly Father is perfect," and the promise, "Behold, I make all things new." Even Paul declared, "I can do all things in him that strengtheneth me." Pacifists verily need to be on guard both against the error of over-simplification and the sin of self-righteousness, but it does not follow that nonviolence as political strategy and pacifism as a way of life are invalidated. For Christian leaders to reject them may be in truth to condemn the Church and our age to futility and doom.

PART VII
Mid-Twentieth Century
(1950-1974)

77. KIRBY PAGE

The Faith of a Christian Pacifist

Kirby Page (1890-1957) was a famous Protestant evangelist and prolific author in the early to middle part of the twentieth century. As a writer and editor for publications such as The World Tomorrow *and* Christian Century, *Page was one of the most important Christian commentators on social and economic problems of his day. He lived out his pacifist principles not only by writing—his most famous book was* War, Its Causes, Consequences and Cure *(1923)—but also by serving as a leader of the Fellowship of Reconciliation. Page authored the following 1950 essay—"The Faith of a Christian Pacifist"—partly in response to the brewing crisis in Korea.*

We Christian pacifists must confess that we have often underestimated the power of entrenched evil. Sometimes we have presented pacifism as a sure way to achieve justice and security. Frequently we have substituted generalities for specific programs of action. Much too often we have been self-righteous and arrogant, not sufficiently appreciative and considerate of those from whom we have differed. We must confess our full share of responsibility for the divided ranks and tragic ineffectiveness of Christian forces in this ominous hour of world crisis. Nevertheless, in spite of all this (and much more), I am more than ever convinced of the validity of Christian pacifism.

I hold the conviction that the method of war is contrary to the will of the God and Father of our Lord Jesus Christ. My mind goes along with the pronouncement of the Oxford Conference in 1937 that "war is a particular demonstration of the power of sin in this world and a defiance of the righteousness of God as revealed in Jesus Christ and him crucified."

My conviction that the method of war is in defiance of God's will has been strengthened by recent changes in the nature of warfare. I agree with the Theologian's Report when it included "the massacre of the civilian populations" as a practice which "cannot be regarded by the church as justifiable." I further agree with its denial that "modern war may properly, even in cases of extreme peril to nation, church, or culture, become total war."

The evidence convinces me that the massacre

189

of civilian populations has become part of modern war. General Arnold reported that obliteration bombing destroyed an average of 42 percent of 68 cities in Japan with a total population of 21 million people. He further reported that "on the morning of 22 February 1945, more than ten thousand Allied planes were airborne from their bases in England, France, Holland, Belgium and Italy. The 200 individual targets covered an area of nearly a quarter of a million square miles." The official figure is that 50 million firebombs were used by the Allies against the Axis powers.

I am convinced also that a third world war would include the massacre of civilians through widespread obliteration bombing, and probably through the use of atomic bombs, atomic dust, and possibly bacterial and hydrogen weapons. I agree with the Theologian's Report that "the march toward total war, which this commission and other theologians have judged irreconcilable with Christian principles, has been advanced a giant step further," and that "the logical end would be total war in grim truth." I share the feeling of Admiral Leahy, when he writes in *The Atlantic Monthly* concerning the atomic bomb: "Future commentators may trace the new Dark Age back to America's adoption of the ethics of total war and the official endorsement of ways to increase the slaughter of civilians—almost to the point of annihilation."

Believing that total war is contrary to the will of God, I have no faith in it as an instrument of righteousness. I cannot believe that God wants us to follow a course of action which we acknowledge to be contrary to his will.

In an imperfect and sinful society, situations arise frequently where there is no way to stop exploitation and injustice immediately and completely. Our Lord did not succeed in delivering his countrymen from bondage and exploitation, but he was nevertheless loyal to the will of God. It is better to do God's will and fail to deliver the exploited than attempt to serve God's children by acts of rebellion against his will.

As citizens we must advocate a polity which seems to us to be right and work for its adoption. For three decades I have worked for the League of Nations and the United Nations and world government, for economic cooperation in a worldwide effort to help peoples everywhere to achieve a good life, for the creation of the international mind and the international heart, and for universal disarmament.

In the present crisis, precipitated by communist flagrant aggression in the invasion of South Korea, my conviction that the method of war is contrary to the will of God remains unchanged. This is war and already it reveals signs of becoming obliteration war. The action taken by the United Nations has not changed the weapons of modern warfare. The massacre of civilians appears to me to be still defiance of God's will even if ordered by the United Nations. Military victory over the Communists in Korea is not likely to bring peace. On the contrary, Soviet Russia will probably increase its revolutionary activities in many parts of the earth, and speed up preparedness for atomic, bacterial and hydrogen warfare. The Koreans themselves are more likely to be destroyed by military action than they are to be safeguarded. And we must face the appalling possibility that the third world war has already begun in Korea, and that it may not end until another civilization has been added to the fourteen which Professor Toynbee reminds us have already been destroyed by war. Let us, therefore, urge the United Nations to call an immediate conference for the purpose of attempting to negotiate a treaty of worldwide economic cooperation and of universal disarmament. If civilization survives, such a conference must someday be held. If it were convened now, it might help to preserve divination from destruction.

Our hope of deliverance is not to be found in man's wisdom, not in his military or political action, and not in his pacifism. Nothing less than a miracle of God can save us, a mighty work of the Eternal wrought in the minds and lives of peoples and leaders of governments. Our part is to provide God with opportunity to enlighten us and empower us. This we can do by dominant desire to know his holy will and to do it. Fidelity is required of every soul. Therefore, in contrition and with determination, let every individual, to the utmost of his ability, do the will of God with the power which comes from God. Let him take up his cross and follow wherever it leads, leaving the results in God's hands, and proceeding with faith in the ultimate triumph of his kingdom.

78. HISTORIC PEACE CHURCHES AND THE INTERNATIONAL FELLOWSHIP OF RECONCILIATION COMMITTEE

Peace Is the Will of God

In 1951, the Continuation Committee of Historic Peace Churches and the International Fellowship of Reconciliation, in response to an invitation from W. A. Visser't Hoof, the general secretary of the World Council of Churches, drafted a document titled "War Is Contrary to the Will of God." Because the final document offered four different statements on war, one from each of the representatives of the invited bodies (the Mennonites, Quakers, Brethren, and the IFOR), the WCC staff, always concerned about unity, encouraged the Continuation Committee to draft a new document, this one a statement with which all the members of the Committee could agree. The result of this collaborative effort was the 1953 document titled "Peace Is the Will of God," and below are excerpts from sections two and three.

II. G. The Compatibility of War with Christian Love

Some hold that a Christian spirit of love toward the enemy may be maintained even in the act of killing. But such a benevolent sentiment, even if it could be preserved by the killer, is not love, for "love worketh no ill" (Rom. 13:10, KJV). Furthermore a "love" that expresses itself in violence is for the victim indistinguishable from hatred, and can only call forth hatred and violence in return. Indeed, the higher the values in the name of which violence is done, the deeper will be the resentment of the victims against the "love" that kills them or their loved ones. The unhappy effect of colonial exploitation on Christian missions is sufficient demonstration that according Christian sanction to violence compromises the communication of the Gospel of love.

III. The Christian Nonresistant Pacifist Position

A. Love and the Way of the Cross

Christians all agree that the essence of the gospel is the love of God reaching down to redeem and transform the imperfections and sin which mar the life of men, and further, that this love must call forth in man a like expression of redemptive love for his fellowman. "This is my commandment, that you love one another as I have loved you" (John 15:12, RSV).

Those who read the New Testament in this perspective will find themselves in agreement with the numerous competent Christian scholars who have examined the passages commonly quoted in discussion of the peace and war issue, studying them objectively and with no attempt to read meanings into them. They will recognize that the words and spirit of the gospels fully warrant the Amsterdam statement that "war is incompatible with the teachings and example of Christ"; furthermore, that the cross of Christ, the heart of our faith, the means by which God's love operates redemptively in a world of sin, speaks against war, for it stands for the acceptance of unlimited suffering, the utter denial of self, and the complete dedication of life to the ministry of redemption.

But that cross is not merely exemplary, nor is the love to which it gives expression only redemptive, for beyond the cross lies the resurrection, and the moral renewal of the believer, "so that as Christ was raised from the dead by the Father's glorious power, we too should begin living a new life" (Rom. 6:4, NJB). Thus through the Scriptures and the light of Christ shining into the human heart man is made aware of the vital distinction in the sight of God between good and evil, right and wrong: aware that the problem of good and evil is bound up with the problem of his relationship with his brother; and aware increasingly that the overcoming of evil with good and the establishment of relationships of love and cooperation with this fellowman are possible to him only by the power of God working within him. The clear teachings of Christ: "Love your enemies"; "Do good to them that hate you"; "Resist not evil"; etc., bear the unmistakable authority both of his spoken Word as recorded in Scripture and of the inner witness of his Spirit. The Sermon on the Mount is in spirit declarative as well as imperative—such is the natural conduct of the children of God.

These assertions do not mean that we can achieve an easy perfection nor do they assume that human endeavor alone can bring about a warless world within history. Sin and violence will remain with us as long as man continues to abuse his moral freedom. The Christian himself is still subject to sin and to human limitation and still beset by the violence of the world. It is only the miracle of divine love that lifts him up, enabling him to realize the divine purpose of his existence. But he cannot claim that love without accepting the discipleship it entails with all its consequences. It is the heart of our position that once having been laid hold of by God through Christ the Christian owes him unqualified obedience. He may not calculate in advance what this may mean for himself or for society and obey only so far as seems practicable. The Christian is thus placed in a position of inevitable and endless tension. Though he lives in the world and participates in the activities that belong to human life, he must recurrently face situations where loyalty to Christ, to the new *aeon* in which he already stands, means refusal to the world, *in which* he is, but *of which* he is not. Perhaps nowhere does this conflict of loyalties become more articulate or more acute than in the question of war. But here as elsewhere in life the Christian has but one weapon, to "overcome evil with good." His whole life must be one of unflinching fidelity to the way of redemptive love, even though it be the way of the cross.

B. The Church

In his discipleship, however, the Christian is not an isolated individual whose faith is a matter merely of private interest. He is a member of the church, the universal community established by Christ in which his Spirit must reign and his will must be done, and from which must go out into all society the saving and healing ministry of the gospel.... In her transcendent life the church already lives in the new aeon which she is called to manifest. As [the body of Christ] she lives according to the new "law of liberty," and we who are her members are called to "stand fast . . . in the liberty wherewith Christ hath made us free" (Gal. 5:1, KJV), a freedom which no exercise of earthly authority can ever impair or usurp. Her source of life is the final and absolute reality of God in Christ, who in her existence manifests that power which will ultimately triumph over all the forces of darkness. To her has been entrusted the ministry of reconciliation, and henceforth neither she nor her members can engage in activities contrary to that mission. She is the herald of the new order, the kingdom of God, and her members must live within that order. Where in the supposed interest of the new order they revert to the method of violence characteristic of the old they thwart the very process of redemption to which as Christians they are dedicated, for righteousness cannot spring up from unrighteousness, nor love from strife.

For Christians to allow themselves to be drawn into taking sides in war is a denial of the unity of the body of Christ. The Christian church is not provincial or national, it is universal. Therefore every war in which churches on each side condone or support the national effort becomes a civil war within the church. Is not this state of affairs where Christian kills Christian an even greater breach of ecumenical fellowship than the deplorable confessional differences that have rent our unity? Indeed, can we Christians expect the Lord to restore our unity in worship as long as we put one another to death on the field of battle? Therefore we humbly submit: The refusal to participate in and to support war in any form is the only course compatible with the high calling of the church of Jesus Christ.

C. Church and State

The church has to fulfill her mission not in a perfect society but in a world of men and nations who are free to spurn the will of God, in an aeon which Scripture itself recognizes will be marked by the continuing presence of evil. In the face of social disharmony both the Old and the New Testament recognize the authority of the state, as instituted to maintain order by force. This seeming contradiction of the ethic of love is clearly the heart of the problem of the Christian attitude toward war.

The classic New Testament passage dealing with this question, Romans 13, says unequivocally that the state is "ordained by God" as an institution of order, whose responsibility is the promotion of the good in society and the suppression of evil. Paul even concedes to the magistrate who bears the sword the lofty title, "minister of God." Acceptance of and obedience to the state is hence a matter of conscience. It is true that the state, particularly as we know it today, performs a host of other functions not connected with the execution of justice but salutary and necessary to society. But whatever may be the desirability of these functions in terms of political philosophy, the primary task of the state is still to be guarantor of order, the role in which it is a "minister of God to thee for good."

In the same breath, however, this passage asserts that "there is no power but of God." The state has therefore only a delegated and limited authority. It possesses nothing of a mystical or metaphysical quality, no autonomous norms or existence, no ultimate source of justice. Indeed this passage appears in a context where Paul had quoted God's words from the Song of Moses, "Vengeance is mine, I will repay" (Deut. 32:35, Rom. 12:19). Thus it is clear that whatever authority the state exercises, whatever justice it may be called upon to achieve, is purely of a delegated, relative, and provisional nature. At no point may its functions presume a suspension of the divine will.

Furthermore, the New Testament, and particularly the Apocalypse, sees in the state also a demonic quality. In this respect it is implicated in the usurped temporal power of the "prince of this world." This element, like a dominant trait in a biological organism, constantly seeks to assert itself, and leads a state, particularly one whose power is growing, to overstep its boundaries, to forget its derivative character, and to abuse its authority, as for example in the prosecution of modern warfare. In the eschatological vision of Scripture the kingdoms of this world are therefore visited with the righteous wrath of God. The authority which they are given becomes the very occasion of their downfall, and ultimately every functionary of the state stands before God as any other individual. For him therefore to kill men on the field of battle at the state's behest does not divest the deed of its sinful character, even though it appears to be a sin less heinous than private murder.

In the Old Testament, the first clear reference to the institution of justice in human hands follows the Noachian flood, where God declares: "If anyone shed the blood of man, by man shall his blood be shed" (Gen. 9:6, NAB), stating thus a maxim later formulated as "Eye for eye, tooth for tooth" (Exod. 21:24). In the course of Jewish history, God appears to legitimatize military action, in contrast to his own prohibition of murder: "You shall not kill" (Exod. 20:13, NJB). But these behests stood in the context of human disobedience, where the people of Israel had to bear the consequences of their own wrongdoing. The resulting bloodshed was thus not God's original will for man but rather his judgment on human disobedience, whereby "sin was chastened by sin." We see this clearly in the great drama of Old Testament nations (e.g., Isa. 10), where God uses the spontaneous evil designs of one nation to punish another only for the first to fall under divine judgment itself, often for that very act, even though he had made it subserve his purposes. The principle is still operative today in the achieving of justice and order on the level of divine preservation, on which level war occurs. Here we stand before that humanly impenetrable mystery whereby the wrath of men, while judged by God, is nevertheless so diverted as to serve his glory, a mystery which we encounter even more strikingly in the crucifixion itself.

The role which war plays in the Old Testament has been a source of difficulty for many people, particularly for those who are most deeply convinced of the unity of the holy Scriptures. On the other hand the Old Testament especially has been a source book for many who have sought or felt called to give religious sanction to military enterprise. Obviously the various parts of the Bible cannot be examined here in regard to this question. The basic problem, however, constituted by the seeming contradiction between the Old and New Testaments, finds its answer in the progression of redemptive revelation which culminated in Christ and in the corresponding progressive preparation of man for his advent. The pre-Christian covenants provided for man's provisional pardon, but they did not alter his fallen state. When Christ said, "Ye had heard that it had been said," he referred to the old dispensation, where provisional justice and order were achieved through the natural laws of "eye for eye" and "tooth for tooth," although this was contrary to God's real intent then as now. But for those who have been renewed and placed into the new dispensation he goes on to prescribe a wholly different sort of conduct. "I tell you: do not take revenge on someone who wrongs you.... Love your enemies" (Matt. 5:39, 44, TEV). In the new economy of grace this vicious cycle of human sin is broken; henceforth the Christian is restored from his sinful state and is lifted into the new aeon, "into the glorious liberty of the children of God" (Rom. 8:21, KJV).

A distinction hereby becomes apparent between the dispensation of providence on the one hand, where violence, including that exercised by the state, remains embedded in the structure of unredeemed society, and the dispensation of redemption on the other, where man is restored to unity with God and made "a new creation": where "the old order is gone and a new being is there to see" (2 Cor. 5:17, NJB), where he cannot "continue in sin" because he is "dead" to it (Rom. 6:1-2, KJV). There is no provision for the Christian to revert, under force of circumstance, to the sub-Christian code of conduct. Hence it is clear that man's primary responsibility to God may never be annulled by the claims of the state. Under no circumstances, according to our understanding, may the Christian take the life of his fellow man, who also was created in the image of God and for whom Christ died.

War therefore presents itself to the Christian as a two-dimensional problem, not only because he himself stands in two "worlds," but also because in another sense the state too is of a dual character.

In keeping with his conscientious affirmation of the state, he seeks through every legitimate secular or political means to help build the kind of society which can avoid war. Moreover, with war and its origin so intricately interwoven in the texture of social and particularly of economic life, the Christian conscience cannot renounce war while tolerating other abuses equally incompatible with the Christian ethic. In the highest sense, however, the Christian must regard his direct economic and political efforts as secondary, inasmuch as they are at best ameliorative and can never deal with the ultimate root of war, which is in the perverted human personality. Consequently, paradoxical as it may seem, he entertains no utopian illusions that the ethic of the gospel will be applied in its real meaning in international affairs as long as men reject the basic claims of Christ, for their acceptance alone can produce that ethic as fruit.

It follows that the Christian endeavor to eliminate war by political and other secular means does not constitute the heart of the church's peace effort. The task of the church does not consist in the statements she makes on international affairs or in the influence she exerts on national policies. Whether or not the church and Christians engage in war is not dependent on whether or not war can be avoided. The church's most effective witness and action against war comes on a different level and consists simply in the stand she takes in and through her members in the face of war. Unless the church, trusting the power of God in whose hand the destinies of nations lie, is willing to "fall into the ground and die," to renounce war absolutely, whatever sacrifice of freedoms, advantages, or possessions this might entail, even to the point of counseling a nation not to resist foreign conquest and occupation, she can give no prophetic message for the world of nations. As the Oxford report stated so aptly in another connection, "The first duty of the church, and its greatest service to the world, is that it be in very deed the church" (57-Ox, already quoted).

Such a position will admittedly often be misunderstood by the world as negativism, evasion of responsibility, and even betrayal. Indeed this is precisely the point that even Christians find difficult to comprehend. We cannot hope to convince alone by appeal to reason, for the issue here is one of faith and obedience which the "natural man" cannot comprehend (1 Cor. 2:4, 14). We can, however, point out that it is not a question here of evading responsibility but one of correct diagnosis and remedy. Certainly the church is the first to oppose evil wherever it is found, but she cannot fight this spiritual battle with physical weapons. Even though the problem of society is not in all respects the same as the problem of the individual, it remains true that moral evil has no existence in a community except as the effect of the evil will of members of the community, and consequently that social evil cannot be resolved by violence. Whatever our theory of evil we know that in practice it lies in the heart of man. It is not something external to him which can be struck and smashed or carted away, or which can be destroyed by an atom bomb. The waging of war only aggravates and spreads the trouble, and the Christian must turn from this to the far more difficult and unpopular task of attacking evil at its root. The only way to end war is to cease to fight, for the devil cannot be driven out by Beelzebub.

79. MARTIN LUTHER KING, JR.

Nonviolence and Racial Justice

Martin Luther King, Jr. (1929-1968) was the most important civil rights leader in the latter half of the twentieth century. He led the famous Montgomery bus boycott from 1955-1956, founded the Southern Christian Leadership Conference in 1957, and directed major campaigns for civil rights in the Deep South and even Chicago throughout the late 1950s and 1960s. In 1964 he was awarded the Nobel Peace Prize for his nonviolent methods in securing constitutional rights for African Americans, and a few years later he assumed a leading role in the peace movement against the Vietnam War. Below is one of the many articles he wrote on the relationship between peace and race—"Nonviolence and Racial Justice" (1957).

It is commonly observed that the crisis in race relations dominates the arena of American life. This crisis has been precipitated by two factors: the determined resistance of reactionary elements in the South to the Supreme Court's momentous decision outlawing segregation in the public schools, and the radical change in the Negro's evaluation of himself. While southern legislative halls ring with open defiance through "interposition" and "nullification," while a modern version of the Ku Klux Klan has arisen in the form of "respectable" white citizens' councils, a revolutionary change has taken place in the Negro's conception of his own nature and destiny. Once he thought of himself as an inferior and patiently accepted injustice and exploitation. Those days are gone.

The first Negroes landed on the shores of this nation in 1619, one year ahead of the Pilgrim Fathers. They were brought here from Africa and, unlike the Pilgrims, they were brought against their will, as slaves. Throughout the era of slavery the Negro was treated in inhuman fashion. He was considered a thing to be used, not a person to be respected. He was merely a depersonalized cog in a vast plantation machine. The famous Dred Scott decision of 1857 well illustrates his status during slavery. In this decision the Supreme Court of the United States said, in substance, that the Negro is not a citizen of the United States; he is merely property subject to the dictates of his owner.

After his emancipation in 1863, the Negro still confronted oppression and inequality. It is true that for a time, while the army of occupation remained in the South and Reconstruction ruled, he had a brief period of eminence and political power. But he was quickly overwhelmed by the white majority. Then in 1896, through the *Plessy v. Ferguson* decision, a new kind of slavery came into being. In this decision the Supreme Court of the nation established the doctrine of "separate but equal" as the law of the land. Very soon it was discovered that the concrete result of this doctrine was strict enforcement of the "separate," without the slightest intention to abide by the "equal." So the Plessy doctrine ended up plunging the Negro into the abyss of exploitation where he experienced the bleakness of nagging injustice.

A Peace That Was No Peace

Living under these conditions, many Negroes lost faith in themselves. They came to feel that perhaps they were less than human. So long as the Negro maintained this subservient attitude and accepted the "place" assigned him, a sort of racial peace existed. But it was an uneasy peace in which the Negro was forced patiently to submit to insult, injustice and exploitation. It was a negative peace. True peace is not merely the absence of some negative force—tension, confusion or war; it is the presence of some positive force—justice, good will and brotherhood.

Then circumstances made it necessary for the Negro to travel more. From the rural plantation he migrated to the urban industrial community. His economic life began gradually to rise, his crippling illiteracy gradually to decline. A myriad of factors came together to cause the Negro to take a new look at himself. Individually and as a group, he began to reevaluate himself. And so he came to feel that he was somebody. His religion revealed to him that God loves all his children and that the important thing about a man is "not his specificity but his fundamentum," not the texture of his hair or the color of his skin but the quality of his soul.

This new self-respect and sense of dignity on the part of the Negro undermined the South's negative peace, since the white man refused to accept the change. The tension we are witnessing in race relations today can be explained in part by this revolutionary change in the Negro's evaluation of himself and his determination to struggle and sacrifice until the walls of segregation have been finally crushed by the battering rams of justice.

Quest for Freedom Everywhere

The determination of Negro Americans to win freedom from every form of oppression springs from the same profound longing for freedom that motivates oppressed peoples all over the world. The rhythmic beat of deep discontent in Africa and Asia is at bottom a quest for freedom and human dignity on the part of people who have long been victims of colonialism. The struggle for freedom on the part of oppressed people in general and of the American Negro in particular has developed slowly and is not going to end suddenly. Privileged groups rarely give up their privileges without strong resistance. But when oppressed people rise up against oppression there is no stopping point short of full freedom. Realism compels us to admit that the struggle will continue until freedom is a reality for all the oppressed peoples of the world.

Hence the basic question which confronts the world's oppressed is: How is the struggle against the forces of injustice to be waged? There are two possible answers. One is resort to the all too prevalent method of physical violence and corroding hatred. The danger of this method is its futility. Violence solves no social problems; it merely creates new and more complicated ones. Through the vistas of time a voice still cries to every potential Peter, "Put up your sword!" The shores of history are white with the bleached bones of nations and communities that failed to follow this command. If the American Negro and other victims of oppression succumb to the temptation of using violence in the struggle for justice, unborn generations will live in a desolate night of bitterness, and their chief legacy will be an endless reign of chaos.

Alternative to Violence

The alternative to violence is nonviolent resistance. This method was made famous in our generation by Mohandas K. Gandhi, who used it to free India from the domination of the British empire. Five points can be made concerning nonviolence as a method in bringing about better racial conditions.

First, this is not a method for cowards; it does resist. The nonviolent resister is just as strongly opposed to the evil against which he protests as is the person who uses violence. His method is passive or nonaggressive in the sense that he is not physically aggressive toward his opponent. But his mind and emotions are always active, constantly seeking to persuade the opponent that he is mistaken. This method is passive physically but strongly active spiritually; it is nonaggressive physically but dynamically aggressive spiritually.

A second point is that nonviolent resistance does not seek to defeat or humiliate the opponent, but to win his friendship and understanding. The nonviolent resister must often express his protest through noncooperation or boycotts, but he realizes that noncooperation and boycotts are not ends themselves; they are merely means to awaken a sense of moral shame in the opponent. The end is redemption and reconciliation. The aftermath of nonviolence is the creation of the beloved community, while the aftermath of violence is tragic bitterness.

A third characteristic of this method is that the attack is directed against forces of evil rather than against persons who are caught in those forces. It is evil we are seeking to defeat, not the persons victimized by evil. Those of us who struggle against racial injustice must come to see that the basic tension is not between races. As I like to say to the people in Montgomery, Alabama: "The tension in this city is not between white people and Negro people. The tension is at bottom between justice and injustice, between the forces of light and the forces of darkness. And if there is a victory it will be a victory not merely for 50,000 Negroes, but a victory for justice and the forces of light. We are out to defeat injustice and not white persons who may happen to be unjust."

A fourth point that must be brought out concerning nonviolent resistance is that it avoids not only external physical violence but also internal violence of spirit. At the center of nonviolence stands the principle of love. In struggling for human dignity the oppressed people of the world must not allow themselves to become bitter or indulge in hate campaigns. To retaliate with hate and bitterness would do nothing but intensify the hate in the world. Along the way of life, someone must have sense enough and morality enough to cut off the chain of hate. This can be done only by projecting the ethics of love to the center of our lives.

The Meaning of "Love"

In speaking of love at this point, we are not referring to some sentimental emotion. It would be nonsense to urge men to love their oppressors in an affectionate sense. "Love" in this connection means understanding good will. There are three words for love in the Greek New Testament. First, there is *eros*. In Platonic philosophy *eros* meant the yearning of the soul for the realm of the divine. It has come now to mean a sort of aesthetic or romantic love. Second, there is *philia*. It meant intimate affectionateness between friends. *Philia* denotes a sort of reciprocal love: the person loves because he is loved. When we speak of loving those who oppose us we refer to neither *eros* nor *philia*; we speak of a love which is expressed in the Greek word *agape*. *Agape* means nothing sentimental or basically affectionate; it means understanding, redeeming good will for all men, an overflowing love which seeks nothing in return. It is the love of God working in the lives of men. When we love on the *agape* level we love men not because we like them, not because their attitudes and ways appeal to us, but because God loves them. Here we rise to the position of loving the person who does the evil deed while hating the deed he does.

Finally, the method of nonviolence is based on the conviction that the universe is on the side of justice. It is this deep faith in the future that causes the nonviolent resister to accept suffering without retaliation. He knows that in his struggle for justice he has cosmic companionship. This belief that God is on the side of truth and justice comes down to us from the long tradition of our Christian faith. There is something at the very center of our faith which reminds us that Good Friday may reign for a day, but ultimately it must give way to the triumphant beat of the Easter drums. Evil may so shape events that Caesar will occupy a palace and Christ a cross, but one day that same Christ will rise up and split history into A.D. and B.C., so that even the life of Caesar must be dated by his name. So in Montgomery we can walk and never get weary, because we know that there will be a great camp meeting in the promised land of freedom and justice.

This, in brief, is the method of nonviolent resistance. It is a method that challenges all people struggling for justice and freedom. God grant that we wage the struggle with dignity and discipline. May all who suffer oppression in this world reject the self-defeating method of retaliatory violence and choose the method that seeks to redeem. Through using this method wisely and courageously we will emerge from the bleak and desolate midnight of man's inhumanity to man into the bright daybreak of freedom and justice.

80. Marjorie Swann

Statement by Marjorie Swann, Participant in Omaha Action

Marjorie Swann (b. 1922) was one of the founding members of the Committee for Nonviolent Action, a group of radical pacifists who protested the testing of nuclear weapons and led direct action campaigns against the nuclear arms race. In 1959 Swann was arrested for her participation in a protest against nuclear weapons at an intercontinental ballistic missiles base near Omaha, Nebraska. She was convicted in federal court and served six months in jail for trespassing at the military base. In the trial and sentencing period, some of her opponents characterized her as an unfit mother willing to desert her children, and below is Swann's eloquent statement about this and other criticisms.

To my fellow Americans—

As a child, I went with my mother—who was Rehabilitation Chairman of the Legion Auxiliary of which I was also a member—to the Hines Veteran Hospital near Chicago. There I saw the horrible physical and psychological results of war—results minor compared to those which will come from a nuclear war with missiles and H-bombs—but still so terrible that even then I could see no way to justify the cause of this damage to the human body and soul.

My father was shell-shocked and gassed in World War I, and even though these injuries were not as serious as those I saw at the hospital, my brother and sisters and I experienced in our own lives the direct effects of war. My brother was in the army in World War II, driving supply trucks from India across the Himalayas into China, and I know the awful tension of waiting and wondering if that final telegram is going to come from the War Department.

As I grew up, I was taught in Sunday School that God is Love, that *all* men are brothers, that we should love our enemies as ourselves. In school I was taught the futility of World War I, and my high school principal organized an international relations club for high school students which emphasized understanding and good will among the people of all nations, and the necessity of settling international conflict without war. I heard my father and his fellow Legionnaires say many times, "Never will *my* son go to war!" I believed all these things and took them seriously.

About the age of 17, I came to understand that the anti-war attitudes of the twenties and thirties were not sufficient; that these laudable sentiments had to be translated into political and economic reality; and that the welfare of each human being *is* the responsibility of every other human being— that we are in truth our brother's keeper ... our Russian, German, Chinese, African brother as well as those in our own country. So I became a pacifist—not a self-righteous pacifist, I hope, but one who does have sincere disagreement with most of you about how to achieve and maintain peace in this one world of which we are all citizens.

"But," many of you say, including Judge Robinson of the Federal District Court, "What are we to do; let the Russians walk over us? How can we give up our arms and our missiles if they don't give up theirs? We certainly can't trust them."

There is no simple answer to that question; none of us in Omaha Action would want you to believe we have a blueprint. Many proposals have been made; if you seriously wish to do so, you will have no difficulty in discovering and studying these proposals. A nonviolent alternative to war is admittedly risky, but let me ask you just one question: what kind of risk are we taking now? One hundred percent is the only answer, if we continue in our present direction.

Possibly not 100 percent risk of war, if there is any validity in the deterrent theory, although history and commonsense tell us that an arms race inevitably ends in war. But can you try to imagine what kind of "democracy" we will have if we continue on our present course of military buildup and control? It is not only physical survival with which we must be concerned, but also survival of the human spirit—of the divine right of human beings to think and feel for themselves, to make their own choices and live their own lives, and the divine duty to share, voluntarily, not because we are forced to by a despotic government.

It is part of the law of the universe that ends and means must be consistent. True peace cannot come by means of war. We will have peace when we are ready to pay as much for it as we pay for war, with sacrifice as soldiers, wives and parents sacrifice in war with all the energy and creative talent which is now perverted to plans for mass destruction, with humility and the replacing of our national pride with pride in the human race.

I know many of you ask why I take this action of deliberately violating an order of the United States government. Particularly, why a mother who has the responsibility of raising four children? Do I not feel guilty in disgracing them by going to prison, and in leaving them without my care for a number of months?

I can only say that the guilt I may feel now, and the pain at leaving my husband and children, is nothing compared to the guilt and pain I will feel—if I am still alive—at seeing my children blasted to death by an H-bomb; die slowly of radiation sickness; wander starving and in rags down a cratered road as did the children of Korea; or become robots in a militarized and totalitarian state which must obliterate freedom in order to survive.

Look at your children and grandchildren. Think what is in store for them. Accept your responsibility for their future. That is what my friends and I ask as we go to prison. If you will try to save the children of all the world, prison is a small price for us to pay.

81. POPE JOHN XXIII

Pacem in Terris

John XXIII (1881-1963) was the 261st pope of the Roman Catholic Church. His most famous action was to convene the Second Vatican Council, which eventually led to dramatic changes in, among other things, Catholic liturgy and ecumenical ministries. His papal reign was set against the darkest hours of the Cold War, and he played a crucial role in helping to facilitate communication between East and West. Among his important contributions to the case of peace was his encyclical Pacem in Terris *(1963), excerpted below, in which he calls upon world leaders to halt the nuclear arms race. Just two years earlier, Paul Ramsey, a Protestant ethicist and the prime exponent of just war theory in the generation following Reinhold Niebuhr, had argued against nuclear pacifism in a book titled* War and the Christian Conscience.

Peace on earth—which man throughout the ages has so longed for and sought after—can never be established, never guaranteed, except by the diligent observance of the divinely established order.

III

State-to-State Relations

80. With respect to states themselves, our predecessors have constantly taught, and we wish to lend the weight of our own authority to their teaching, that nations are the subjects of reciprocal rights and duties. Their relationships, therefore, must likewise be harmonized in accordance with the dictates of truth, justice, willing cooperation, and freedom. The same law of nature that governs the life and conduct of individuals must also regulate the relations of political communities with one another.

81. This will be readily understood when one reflects that it is quite impossible for political leaders to lay aside their natural dignity while acting in their country's name and in its interests. They are still bound by the natural law, which is the rule that governs all moral conduct, and they have no authority to depart from its slightest precepts.

82. The idea that men, by the fact of their appointment to public office, are compelled to lay aside their own humanity, is quite inconceivable. Their very attainment to this high-ranking office was due to their exceptional gifts and intellectual qualities, which earned for them their reputation as outstanding representatives of the body politic.

83. Moreover, a ruling authority is indispensable to civil society. That is a fact which follows from the moral order itself. Such authority, therefore, cannot be misdirected against the moral order. It would immediately cease to exist, being deprived of its whole raison d'être. God himself warns us of this: "Hear, therefore, ye kings, and understand: learn, ye that are judges of the ends of the earth. Give ear, you that rule the people, and that please yourselves in multitudes of nations. For power is given you by the Lord, and strength by the Most High, who will examine your works, and search out your thoughts."

84. And lastly one must bear in mind that, even when it regulates the relations between states, authority must be exercised for the promotion of the common good. That is the primary reason for its existence.

85. But one of the principal imperatives of the common good is the recognition of the moral order and the unfailing observance of its precepts. "A firmly established order between political communities must be founded on the unshakable and unmoving rock of the moral law, that law which is revealed in the order of nature by the creator himself, and engraved indelibly on men's hearts . . . Its principles are beacon lights to guide the policies of men and nations. They are also warning lights—providential signs—which men must heed if their laborious efforts to establish a new order are not to encounter perilous storms and shipwreck."

86. The first point to be settled is that mutual ties between states must be governed by truth. Truth calls for the elimination of every trace of racial discrimination, and the consequent recognition of the inviolable principle that all states are by nature equal in dignity. Each of them accordingly has the right to exist, to develop, and to possess the necessary means and accept a primary responsibility for its own development. Each is also legitimately entitled to its good name and to the respect which is its due.

87. As we know from experience, men frequently differ widely in knowledge, virtue, intelligence and wealth, but that is no valid argument in favor of a system whereby those who are in a position of superiority impose their will arbitrarily on others. On the contrary, such men have a greater share in the common responsibility to help others to reach perfection by their mutual efforts.

88. So, too, on the international level: some nations may have attained to a superior degree of scientific, cultural and economic development. But that does not entitle them to exert unjust political domination over other nations. It means that they have to make a greater contribution to the common cause of social progress.

89. The fact is that no one can be by nature superior to his fellows, since all men are equally noble in natural dignity. And consequently there are no differences at all between political communities from the point of view of natural dignity. Each state is like a body, the members of which are human beings. And, as we know from experience, nations can be highly sensitive in matters in any way touching their dignity and honor; and with good reason....

91. Relations between states must furthermore be regulated by justice. This necessitates both the recognition of their mutual rights, and, at the same time, the fulfillment of their respective duties.

92. States have the right to existence, to self-development, and to the means necessary to achieve this. They have the right to play the leading part in the process of their own development, and the right to their good name and due honors. Consequently, states are likewise in duty bound to safeguard all such rights effectively, and to avoid any action that could violate them. And just as individual men may not pursue their own private interests in a way that is unfair and detrimental to others, so too it would be criminal in a state to aim at improving itself by the use of methods which involve other nations in injury and unjust oppression. There is a saying of St. Augustine which has particular relevance in this context: "Take away justice, and what are kingdoms but mighty bands of robbers."

93. There may be, and sometimes is, a clash of interests among states, each striving for its own development. When differences of this sort arise, they must be settled in a truly human way, not by armed force nor by deceit or trickery. There must be a mutual assessment of the arguments and feelings on both sides, a mature and objective investigation of the situation, and an equitable reconciliation of opposing views.

94. A special instance of this clash of interests is furnished by that political trend (which since the nineteenth century has become widespread throughout the world and has gained in strength) as a result of which men of similar ethnic background are anxious for political autonomy and unification into a single nation. For many reasons this cannot always be effected, and consequently minority peoples are often obliged to live within the territories of a nation of a different ethnic origin. This situation gives rise to serious problems.

95. It is quite clear that any attempt to check the vitality and growth of these ethnic minorities is a flagrant violation of justice; the more so if such perverse efforts are aimed at their very extinction.

96. Indeed, the best interests of justice are served by those public authorities who do all they can to improve the human conditions of the members of these minority groups, especially in what concerns their language, culture, ancient traditions, and their economic activity and enterprise.

97. It is worth noting, however, that these minority groups, in reaction, perhaps, to the enforced hardships of their present situation, or to historical circumstances, frequently tend to magnify unduly characteristics proper to their own people. They even rate them above those human values which are common to all mankind, as though the good of the entire human family should subserve the interests of their own particular groups. A more reasonable attitude for such people to adopt would be to recognize the advantages, too, which accrue to them from their own special situation. They should realize that their constant association with a people steeped in a different civilization from their own has no small part to play in the development of their own particular genius and spirit. Little by little they can absorb into their very being those virtues which characterize the other nation. But for this to happen these minority groups must enter into some kind of association with the people in whose midst they are living, and learn to share their customs and way of life. It will never happen if they sow seeds of disaffection which can only produce a harvest of evils, stifling the political development of nations.

98. Since relationships between states must be regulated in accordance with the principles of truth and justice, states must further these relation-

ships by taking positive steps to pool their material and spiritual resources. In many cases this can be achieved by all kinds of mutual collaboration; and this is already happening in our own day in the economic, social, political, educational, health and athletic spheres—and with beneficial results. We must bear in mind that of its very nature civil authority exists, not to confine men within the frontiers of their own nations, but primarily to protect the common good of the state, which certainly cannot be divorced from the common good of the entire human family.

99. Thus, in pursuing their own interests, civil societies, far from causing injury to others, must join plans and forces whenever the efforts of particular states cannot achieve the desired goal. But in doing so great care must be taken. What is beneficial to some states may prove detrimental rather than advantageous to others.

100. Furthermore, the universal common good requires the encouragement in all nations of every kind of reciprocation between citizens and their intermediate societies. There are many parts of the world where we find groupings of people of more or less different ethnic origin. Nothing must be allowed to prevent reciprocal relations between them. Indeed such a prohibition would flout the very spirit of an age which has done so much to nullify the distances separating peoples. Nor must one overlook the fact that whatever their ethnic background, men possess, besides the special characteristics which distinguish them from other men, other very important elements in common with the rest of mankind. And these can form the basis of their progressive development and self-realization especially in regard to spiritual values. They have, therefore, the right and duty to carry on their lives with others in society.

101. As everyone is well aware, there are some countries where there is an imbalance between the amount of arable land and the number of inhabitants; others where there is an imbalance between the richness of the resources and the instruments of agriculture available. It is imperative, therefore, that nations enter into collaboration with each

other, and facilitate the circulation of goods, capital and manpower.

102. We advocate in such cases the policy of bringing the work to the workers, wherever possible, rather than bringing workers to the scene of the work. In this way many people will be afforded an opportunity of increasing their resources without being exposed to the painful necessity of uprooting themselves from their own homes, settling in a strange environment, and forming new social contacts. ...

107. We therefore take this opportunity of giving our public approval and commendation to every undertaking, founded on the principles of human solidarity or of Christian charity, which aims at relieving the distress of those who are compelled to emigrate from their own country to another.

108. And we must indeed single out for the praise of all right-minded men those international agencies which devote all their energies to this most important work.

The Arms Race

109. On the other hand, we are deeply distressed to see the enormous stocks of armaments that have been, and continue to be, manufactured in the economically more developed countries. This policy is involving a vast outlay of intellectual and material resources, with the result that the people of these countries are saddled with a great burden, while other countries lack the help they need for their economic and social development.

110. There is a common belief that under modern conditions peace cannot be assured except on the basis of an equal balance of armaments and that this factor is the probable cause of this stockpiling of armaments. Thus, if one country increases its military strength, others are immediately roused by a competitive spirit to augment their own supply of armaments. And if one country is equipped with atomic weapons, others consider themselves justified in producing such weapons themselves, equal in destructive force.

111. Consequently people are living in the grip of constant fear. They are afraid that at any moment the impending storm may break upon them with horrific violence. And they have good reasons for their fear, for there is certainly no lack of such weapons. While it is difficult to believe that anyone would dare to assume responsibility for initiating the appalling slaughter and destruction that war would bring in its wake, there is no denying that the conflagration could be started by some chance and unforeseen circumstance. Moreover, even though the monstrous power of modern weapons does indeed act as a deterrent, there is reason to fear that the very testing of nuclear devices for war purposes can, if continued, lead to serious danger for various forms of life on earth.

112. Hence justice, right reason, and the recognition of man's dignity cry out insistently for a cessation to the arms race. The stockpiles of armaments which have been built up in various countries must be reduced all round and simultaneously by the parties concerned. Nuclear weapons must be banned. A general agreement must be reached on a suitable disarmament program, with an effective system of mutual control. In the words of Pope Pius XII: "The calamity of a world war, with the economic and social ruin and the moral excesses and dissolution that accompany it, must not on any account be permitted to engulf the human race for a third time."

113. Everyone, however, must realize that, unless this process of disarmament be thoroughgoing and complete, and reach men's very souls, it is impossible to stop the arms race, or to reduce armaments, or—and this is the main thing—ultimately to abolish them entirely. Everyone must sincerely cooperate in the effort to banish fear and the anxious expectation of war from men's minds. But this requires that the fundamental principles upon which peace is based in today's world be replaced by an altogether different one, namely, the realization that true and lasting peace among nations cannot consist in the possession of an equal supply of armaments but only in mutual trust. And we are confident that this can be achieved, for it is a thing which not only is dictated by common sense, but is in itself most desirable and most fruitful of good.

114. Here, then, we have an objective dictated first of all by reason. There is general agreement—or at least there should be—that relations between states, as between individuals, must be regulated not by armed force, but in accordance with the principles of right reason: the principles, that is, of truth, justice and vigorous and sincere cooperation.

115. Secondly, it is an objective which we maintain is more earnestly to be desired. For who is there who does not feel the craving to be rid of the threat of war, and to see peace preserved and made daily more secure?

116. And finally it is an objective which is rich with possibilities for good. Its advantages will be felt everywhere, by individuals, by families, by nations, by the whole human race. The warning of Pope Pius XII still rings in our ears: "Nothing is lost by peace; everything may be lost by war."

117. We therefore consider it our duty as the vicar on earth of Jesus Christ—the saviour of the world, the author of peace—and as interpreter of the most ardent wishes of the whole human family, in the fatherly love we bear all mankind, to beg and beseech mankind, and above all the rulers of states, to be unsparing of their labor and efforts to ensure that human affairs follow a rational and dignified course.

118. In their deliberations together, let men of outstanding wisdom and influence give serious thought to the problem of achieving a more human adjustment of relations between states throughout the world. It must be an adjustment that is based on mutual trust, sincerity in negotiation, and the faithful fulfillment of obligations assumed. Every aspect of the problem must be examined, so that eventually there may emerge some point of agreement from which to initiate treaties which are sincere, lasting, and beneficial in their effects.

119. We, for our part, will pray unceasingly that God may bless these labors by his divine assistance, and make them fruitful.

Preserving Freedom

120. Furthermore, relations between states must be regulated by the principle of freedom. This means that no country has the right to take any action that would constitute an unjust oppression of other countries, or an unwarranted interference in their affairs. On the contrary, all should help to develop in others an increasing awareness of their duties, an adventurous and enterprising spirit, and the resolution to take the initiative for their own advancement in every field of endeavor.

121. All men are united by their common origin and fellowship, their redemption by Christ, and their supernatural destiny. They are called to form one Christian family. In our encyclical *Mater et Magistra*, therefore, we appealed to the more wealthy nations to render every kind of assistance to those states which are still in the process of economic development.

122. It is no small consolation to us to be able to testify here to the wide acceptance of our appeal, and we are confident that in the years that lie ahead it will be accepted even more widely. The result we look for is that the poorer states shall in as short a time as possible attain to a degree of economic development that enables their citizens to live in conditions more in keeping with their human dignity.

123. Again and again we must insist on the need for helping these peoples in a way which guarantees to them the preservation of their own freedom. They must be conscious that they are themselves playing the major role in their economic and social development; that they are themselves to shoulder the main burden of it.

124. Hence the wisdom of Pope Pius XII's teaching: "A new order founded on moral principles is the surest bulwark against the violation of the freedom, integrity and security of other nations, no matter what may be their territorial extension or their capacity for defense. For although it is almost inevitable that the larger states, in view of their greater power and vaster resources, will themselves decide on the norms governing their economic associations with small states, nevertheless these smaller states cannot be denied their right, in keeping with the common good, to political freedom, and to the adoption of a position of neutrality in the conflicts between nations. No state can be denied this right, for it is a postulate of the natural law itself, as also of international law. These smaller states have also the right of assuring their own economic development. It is only with the effective guaranteeing of these rights that smaller nations can fittingly promote the common good of all mankind, as well as the material welfare and the cultural and spiritual progress of their own people."

125. The wealthier states, therefore, while providing various forms of assistance to the poorer, must have the highest possible respect for the latter's national characteristics and time-honored civil institutions. They must also repudiate any policy of domination. If this can be achieved, then "a precious contribution will have been made to the formation of a world community, in which each individual nation, conscious of its rights and duties, can work on terms of equality with the rest for the attainment of universal prosperity."

126. Men nowadays are becoming more and more convinced that any disputes which may arise between nations must be resolved by negotiation and agreement, and not by recourse to arms.

127. We acknowledge that this conviction owes its origin chiefly to the terrifying destructive force of modern weapons. It arises from fear of the ghastly and catastrophic consequences of their use. Thus, in this age which boasts of its atomic power, it no longer makes sense to maintain that war is a fit instrument with which to repair the violation of justice.

128. And yet, unhappily, we often find the law of fear reigning supreme among nations and causing them to spend enormous sums on armaments. Their object is not aggression, so they say—and there is no reason for disbelieving them—but to deter others from aggression.

129. Nevertheless, we are hopeful that, by establishing contact with one another and by a policy of negotiation, nations will come to a better recognition of the natural ties that bind them together as men. We are hopeful, too, that they will come to a fairer realization of one of the cardinal duties deriving from our common nature: namely, that love, not fear, must dominate the relationships between individuals and between nations. It is principally characteristic of love that it draws men together in all sorts of ways, sincerely united in the bonds of mind and matter; and this is a union from which countless blessings can flow.

IV

Collaboration towards the Universal Common Good

130. Recent progress in science and technology has had a profound influence on man's way of life. This progress is a spur to men all over the world to extend their collaboration and association with one another in these days when material resources, travel from one country to another, and technical information have so vastly increased. This has led to a phenomenal growth in relationships between individuals, families and intermediate associations belonging to the various nations, and between the public authorities of the various political communities. There is also a growing economic interdependence between states. National economies are gradually becoming so interdependent that a kind of world economy is being born from the simultaneous integration of the economies of individual states. And finally, each country's social progress, order, security and peace are necessarily linked with the social progress, order, security and peace of every other country.

131. From this it is clear that no state can fittingly pursue its own interests in isolation from the rest, nor, under such circumstances, can it develop itself as it should. The prosperity and progress of any state is in part consequence, and in part cause, of the prosperity and progress of all other states.

132. No era will ever succeed in destroying the unity of the human family, for it consists of men who are all equal by virtue of their natural dignity. Hence there will always be an imperative need—born of man's very nature—to promote in sufficient measure the universal common good; the good, that is, of the whole human family.

133. In the past rulers of states seem to have been able to make sufficient provision for the universal common good through the normal diplomatic channels, or by top-level meetings and discussions, treaties and agreements; by using, that is, the ways and means suggested by the natural law, the law of nations, or international law.

134. In our own day, however, mutual relationships between states have undergone a far-reaching change. On the one hand, the universal common good gives rise to problems of the utmost gravity, complexity and urgency—especially as regards the preservation of the security and peace of the whole world. On the other hand, the rulers of individual nations, being all on an equal footing, largely fail in their efforts to achieve this, however much they multiply their meetings and their endeavors to discover more fitting instruments of justice. And this is no reflection on their sincerity and enterprise. It is merely that their authority is not sufficiently influential.

135. We are thus driven to the conclusion that the shape and structure of political life in the modern world, and the influence exercised by public authority in all the nations of the world, are unequal to the task of promoting the common good of all peoples.

136. Now, if one considers carefully the inner significance of the common good on the one hand, and the nature and function of public authority on the other, one cannot fail to see that there is an intrinsic connection between them. Public authority, as the means of promoting the common good in civil society, is a postulate of the moral order. But the moral order likewise requires that this authority be effective in attaining its end. Hence the civil institutions in which such authority resides, becomes operative and promotes its ends, are endowed with a certain kind of structure and

efficacy: a structure and efficacy which make such institutions capable of realizing the common good by ways and means adequate to the changing historical conditions.

137. Today the universal common good presents us with problems which are worldwide in their dimensions; problems, therefore, which cannot be solved except by a public authority with power, organization and means coextensive with these problems, and with a worldwide sphere of activity. Consequently the moral order itself demands the establishment of some such general form of public authority.

138. But this general authority equipped with worldwide power and adequate means for achieving the universal common good cannot be imposed by force. It must be set up with the consent of all nations. If its work is to be effective, it must operate with fairness, absolute impartiality, and with dedication to the common good of all peoples. The forcible imposition by the more powerful nations of a universal authority of this kind would inevitably arouse fears of its being used as an instrument to serve the interests of the few or to take the side of a single nation, and thus the influence and effectiveness of its activity would be undermined. For even though nations may differ widely in material progress and military strength, they are very sensitive as regards their juridical equality and the excellence of their own way of life. They are right, therefore, in their reluctance to submit to an authority imposed by force, established without their cooperation, or not accepted of their own accord.

139. The common good of individual states is something that cannot be determined without reference to the human person, and the same is true of the common good of all states taken together. Hence the public authority of the world community must likewise have as its special aim the recognition, respect, safeguarding and promotion of the rights of the human person. This can be done by direct action, if need be, or by the creation throughout the world of the sort of conditions in which rulers of individual states can more easily carry out their specific functions.

140. The same principle of subsidiarity which governs the relations between public authorities and individuals, families and intermediate societies in a single state, must also apply to the relations between the public authority of the world community and the public authorities of each political community. The special function of this universal authority must be to evaluate and find a solution to economic, social, political and cultural problems which affect the universal common good. These are problems which, because of their extreme gravity, vastness and urgency, must be considered too difficult for the rulers of individual states to solve with any degree of success.

141. But it is no part of the duty of universal authority to limit the sphere of action of the public authority of individual states, or to arrogate any of their functions to itself. On the contrary, its essential purpose is to create world conditions in which the public authorities of each nation, its citizens and intermediate groups, can carry out their tasks, fulfill their duties and claim their rights with greater security.

The United Nations

142. The United Nations Organization (U.N.) was established, as is well known, on 26 June 1945. To it were subsequently added lesser organizations consisting of members nominated by the public authority of the various nations and entrusted with highly important international functions in the economics, social, cultural, educational and health fields. The United Nations Organization has the special aim of maintaining and strengthening peace between nations, and of encouraging and assisting friendly relations between them, based on the principles of equality, mutual respect, and extensive cooperation in every field of human endeavor.

143. A clear proof of the farsightedness of this organization is provided by the Universal Declaration of Human Rights passed by the United Nations General Assembly on 10 December 1948. The preamble of this declaration affirms that the genuine recognition and complete observance of all the rights and freedoms outlined in the decla-

206

ration is a goal to be sought by all peoples and all nations.

144. We are, of course, aware that some of the points in the declaration did not meet with unqualified approval in some quarters; and there was justification for this. Nevertheless, we think the document should be considered a step in the right direction, an approach toward the establishment of a juridical and political ordering of the world community. It is a solemn recognition of the personal dignity of every human being; an assertion of everyone's right to be free to seek out the truth, to follow moral principles, discharge the duties imposed by justice, and lead a fully human life. It also recognized other rights connected with these.

145. It is therefore our earnest wish that the United Nations Organization may be able progressively to adapt its structure and methods of operation to the magnitude and nobility of its tasks. May the day be not long delayed when every human being can find in this organization an effective safeguard of his personal rights; those rights, that is, which derive directly from his dignity as a human person, and which are therefore universal, inviolable and inalienable. This is all the more desirable in that men today are taking an ever more active part in the public life of their own nations, and in doing so they are showing an increased interest in the affairs of all peoples. They are becoming more and more conscious of being living members of the universal family of mankind.

82. THOMAS MERTON

Blessed Are the Meek: The Roots of Christian Nonviolence

Thomas Merton (1915-1968) was a Trappist monk whose many writings, especially his famous autobiography, The Seven Storey Mountain *(1948), described his conversion and his path to the monastery. In the early 1960s he began to branch out beyond his writings on prayer and spirituality to address social issues—particularly the threat of nuclear war, racism, and violence. While not an activist, Merton was no less an advocate of Christian nonviolence. His writings on the subject, like the 1967 essay below, "Blessed Are the Meek: The Roots of Christian Nonviolence," had a broad influence on Christian peacemakers and activists.*

It would be a serious mistake to regard Christian nonviolence simply as a novel tactic which is at once efficacious and even edifying, and which enables the sensitive man to participate in the struggles of the world without being dirtied with blood. Nonviolence is not simply a way of proving one's point and getting what one wants without being involved in behavior that one considers ugly and evil. Nor is it, for that matter, a means which anyone legitimately can make use of according to his fancy for any purpose whatever. To practice nonviolence for a purely selfish or arbitrary end would in fact discredit and distort the truth of nonviolent resistance.

Nonviolence is perhaps the most exacting of all forms of struggle, not only because it demands first of all that one be ready to suffer evil and even face the threat of death without violent retaliation, but because it excludes mere transient self-interest from its considerations. In a very real sense, he who practices nonviolent resistance must commit himself not to the defense of his own interests or even those of a particular group: he must commit himself to the defense of objective truth and right and above all of *man*. His aim is then not simply to "prevail" or to prove that he is right and the adversary wrong, or to make the adversary give in and yield what is demanded of him.

Nor should the nonviolent resister be content to prove *to himself* that *he* is virtuous and right, that *his* hands and heart are pure even though the adversary's may be evil and defiled. Still less should he seek for himself the psychological gratification of upsetting the adversary's conscience and perhaps driving him to an act of bad faith and refusal of the truth. We know that our unconscious motives may, at times, make our nonviolence a form of moral aggression and even a subtle provocation designed (without our awareness) to bring out the evil we hope to find in the adversary, and thus to justify ourselves in our own eyes and in the eyes of "decent people." Wherever there is a high moral ideal there is an attendant risk of pharisaism and nonviolence is no exception. The basis of pharisaism is division: on one hand this morally and socially privileged self and the elite to which it belongs. On the other hand, the "others," the wicked, the unenlightened, whoever they may be, communists, capitalists, colonialists, traitors, international Jewry, racists, etc.

Christian nonviolence is not built on a presupposed division, but on the basic unity of man. It is not out for the conversion of the wicked to the ideas of the good, but for the healing and reconciliation of man with himself, man the person and man the human family.

The nonviolent resister is not fighting simply for "his" truth or for "his" pure conscience, or for the right that is on "his side." On the contrary, both his strength and his weakness come from the fact that he is fighting for *the* truth, common to him and to the adversary, *the* right which is objective and universal. He is fighting for *everybody*.

For this very reason, as Gandhi saw, the fully consistent practice of nonviolence demands a solid metaphysical and religious basis both in being and in God. This comes *before* subjective good intentions and sincerity. For the Hindu this metaphysical basis was provided by the Vedantist doctrine of the Atman, the true transcendent Self which alone is absolutely real, and before which the empirical self of the individual must be effaced in the faithful practice of *dharma*. For the Christian the basis of nonviolence is the Gospel message of salvation for all and the Kingdom of God to which *all* are summoned. The disciple of Christ, who has heard the good news, the announcement of the Lord's coming and of victory, and is aware of the definitive establishment of the Kingdom, proves his faith by the gift of his whole self to the Lord in order that *all* may enter the Kingdom.

The great historical event, the coming of the Kingdom, is made clear and is "realized" in proportion as Christians themselves live the life of the Kingdom in the circumstances of their own place and time. The saving grace of God in the Lord Jesus is proclaimed to man existentially in the love, the openness, the simplicity, the humility and the self-sacrifice of Christians. By their example of a truly Christian understanding of the world, expressed in a living and active application of the Christian faith to the human problems of their own time, Christians manifest the love of Christ for men (John 13:35, 17:21), and by that fact make him visibly present in the world. The religious basis of Christian nonviolence is then faith in Christ the Redeemer and obedience to his demand to love and manifest himself in us by a certain manner of acting in the world and in relation to other men. This obedience enables us to live as true citizens of the Kingdom, in which the divine mercy, the grace, favor and redeeming love of God are active in our lives. Then the Holy Spirit will indeed "rest upon us" and act in us, not for our own good alone but for God and his Kingdom. And if the Spirit dwells in us and works in us, our lives will be a continuous and progressive conversion and transformation in which we also, in some measure, help to transform others and allow ourselves to be transformed by and with others, in Christ.

The chief place in which this new mode of life is set forth in detail is the Sermon on the Mount. At the very beginning of this great inaugural discourse, the Lord numbers the beatitudes, which are the theological foundation of Christian nonviolence: Blessed are the poor in spirit . . . blessed are the meek (Matthew 5:3-4).

This does not mean "blessed are they who are endowed with a tranquil natural temperament, who are not easily moved to anger, who are always quiet and obedient, who do not naturally resist." Still less does it mean "blessed are they who passively submit to unjust oppression." On the contrary, we know that the "poor in spirit" are those of whom the prophets spoke, those who in the last days will be the "humble of the earth," that is to say the oppressed who have no human weapons to rely on and who nevertheless are true to the commandments of Yahweh, and who hear the voice that tells them: "Seek justice, seek humility, perhaps you will find shelter on the day of the Lord's wrath." (Sophia 2:3). In other words they seek justice in the power of the truth and of God, not by the power of man. Note that Christian meekness, which is essential to true nonviolence, has this eschatological quality about it. It refrains from self-assertion and from violent aggression because it sees all things in the light of the great judgment. Hence it does not struggle and fight merely for this or that ephemeral gain. It struggles for the truth and the right which alone will stand in that day when all is to be tried by fire (I Corinthians 3:10-15).

Furthermore, Christian nonviolence and meekness imply a particular understanding of the power of human poverty and powerlessness when they are united with the invisible strength of Christ. The beatitudes indeed convey a profound existential understanding of the dynamic of the Kingdom of God—a dynamic made clear in the parables of the mustard seed and of yeast. This is a dynamism of patient and secret growth, in belief that out of the smallest, weakest, and most insignificant seed the greatest tree will come. This is not merely a matter of blind and arbitrary faith. The early history of the Church, the record of the apostles and martyrs remains to testify to this inherent and mysterious dynamism of the ecclesial "event" in the world of history and time. Christian nonviolence is rooted in this consciousness and this faith.

This aspect of Christian nonviolence is extremely important and it gives us the key to a proper understanding of the meekness which accepts being "without strength" (*gewaltlos*) not out of masochism, quietism, defeatism or false passivity, but trusting in the strength of the Lord of truth. Indeed, we repeat, Christian nonviolence is nothing if not first of all a formal profession of faith in the Gospel message that the *Kingdom has been established* and that the Lord of truth is indeed risen and reigning over his Kingdom.

Faith of course tells us that we live in a time of eschatological struggle, facing a fierce combat which marshals all the forces of evil and darkness against the still invisible truth, yet this combat is already decided by the victory of Christ over death and over sin. The Christian can renounce the protection of violence and risk being humble, therefore *vulnerable*, not because he trusts in the supposed efficacy of a gentle and persuasive tactic that will disarm hatred and tame cruelty, but because he believes that the hidden power of the Gospel is demanding to be manifested in and through his own poor person. Hence in perfect obedience to the Gospel, he effaces himself and his own interests and even risks his life in order to testify not simply to "the truth" in a sweeping, idealistic and purely platonic sense, but to the truth that is incarnate in a concrete human situation, involving living persons whose rights are denied or whose lives are threatened.

Here it must be remarked that a holy zeal for the cause of humanity in the abstract may sometimes be mere lovelessness and indifference for concrete and living human beings. When we appeal to the highest and most noble ideals, we are more easily tempted to hate and condemn those who, so we believe, are standing in the way of their realization.

Christian nonviolence does not encourage or excuse hatred of a special class, nation or social group. It is not merely *anti-* this or that. In other words, the evangelical realism which is demanded of the Christian should make it impossible for him to generalize about "the wicked" against whom he takes up moral arms in a struggle for righteousness. He will not let himself be persuaded that the adversary is totally wicked and can therefore never be reasonable or well-intentioned, and hence need never be listened to. This attitude, which defeats the very purpose of nonviolence—openness, communication, dialogue—often accounts for the fact that some acts of civil disobedience merely antagonize the adversary without making him willing to communicate in any way whatever, except with bullets or missiles. Thomas à Becket, in Eliot's play *Murder in the Cathedral*, debated with himself, fearing that he might be seeking martyrdom merely in order to demonstrate his own righteousness and the King's injustice: "This is the greatest treason, to do the right thing for the wrong reason."

Now all these principles are fine and they accord

with our Christian faith. But once we view the principles in the light of current facts, a practical difficulty confronts us. If the Gospel is preached to the poor, if the Christian message is essentially a message of hope and redemption for the poor, the oppressed, the underprivileged and those who have no power humanly speaking, how are we to reconcile ourselves to the fact that Christians belong for the most part to the rich and powerful nations of the earth? Seventeen percent of the world's population control eighty percent of the world's wealth, and most of these seventeen percent are supposedly Christian. Admittedly those Christians who are interested in nonviolence are not ordinarily wealthy ones. Nevertheless, like it or not, they share in the power and privilege of the most wealthy and mighty society the world has ever known. Even with the best subjective intentions in the world, how can they avoid a certain ambiguity in preaching nonviolence? Is this not a mystification?

We must remember Marx's accusation that, "The social principles of Christianity encourage dullness, lack of self-respect, submissiveness, self-abasement, in short all the characteristics of the proletariat." We must frankly face the possibility that the nonviolence of the European or American preaching Christian meekness may conceivably be adulterated by bourgeois feelings and by an unconscious desire to preserve the status quo against violent upheaval.

Let us however seriously consider at least the *conditions* for relative honesty in the practice of Christian nonviolence.

1. Nonviolence must be aimed above all at the transformation of the present state of the world, and it must therefore be free from all occult, unconscious connivance with an unjust use of power. This poses enormous problems—for if nonviolence is too political it becomes drawn into the power struggle and identified with one side or another in that struggle, while if it is totally apolitical it runs the risk of being ineffective or at best merely symbolic.

2. The nonviolent resistance of the Christian who belongs to one of the powerful nations and who is himself in some sense a privileged member of world society will have to be clearly not *for himself* but *for others*, that is for the poor and under-

privileged. (Obviously in the case of the Negroes in the United States, though they may be citizens of a privileged nation, their case is different. They are clearly entitled to wage a nonviolent struggle for their rights, but even for them this struggle should be primarily for *truth itself*—this being the source of their power.)

3. In the case of nonviolent struggle for peace—the threat of nuclear war abolishes all privileges. Under the bomb there is not much distinction between rich and poor. In fact the richest nations are usually the most threatened. Nonviolence must simply avoid the ambiguity of an unclear and *confusing protest* that hardens the warmakers in their self-righteous blindness. This means in fact that *in this case above all nonviolence must avoid a facile and fanatical self-righteousness*, and refrain from being satisfied with dramatic self-justifying gestures.

4. Perhaps the most insidious temptation to be avoided is one which is characteristic of the power structure itself: this fetishism of immediate visible results. Modern society understands "possibilities" and "results" in terms of a superficial and quantitative idea of efficacy. One of the missions of Christian nonviolence is to restore a different standard of practical judgment in social conflicts. This means that the Christian humility of nonviolent action must establish itself in the minds and memories of modern man not only as *conceivable* and possible, but as a *desirable alternative* to what he now considers the only realistic possibility: namely political technique backed by force. Here the human dignity of nonviolence must manifest itself clearly in terms of a freedom and a nobility which are able to resist political manipulation and brute force and show them up as arbitrary, barbarous and irrational. This will not be easy. The temptation to get publicity and quick results by spectacular tricks or by forms of protest that are merely odd and provocative but whose human meaning is not clear, may defeat this purpose. The realism of nonviolence must be made evident by humility and self-restraint which clearly show frankness and open-mindedness and invite the adversary to serious and reasonable discussion.

Instead of trying to use the adversary as leverage for one's own effort to realize an ideal, nonviolence seeks only to enter into a dialogue with him in order to attain, together with him, the common good of *man*. Nonviolence must be realistic and concrete. Like ordinary political action, it is no more than the "art of the possible." But precisely the advantage of nonviolence is that it has a *more Christian and more humane notion of what is possible*. Where the powerful believe that only power is efficacious, the nonviolent resister is persuaded of the superior efficacy of love, openness, peaceful negotiation and above all of truth. For power can guarantee the interests of *some men* but it can never foster the good of *man*. Power always protects the good of some at the expense of all the others. Only love can attain and preserve the good of all. Any claim to build the security of *all* on force is a manifest imposture.

It is here that genuine humility is of the greatest importance. Such humility, united with true Christian courage (because it is based on trust in God and not in one's own ingenuity and tenacity), is itself a way of communicating the message that one is interested only in truth and in the genuine rights of others. Conversely, our authentic interest in the common good above all will help us to be humble, and to distrust our own hidden drive to self-assertion.

5. Christian nonviolence, therefore, is convinced that the manner in which the conflict for truth is waged will itself manifest or obscure the truth. To fight for truth by dishonest, violent, inhuman, or unreasonable means would simply betray the truth one is trying to vindicate. The absolute refusal of evil or suspect means is a necessary element in the witness of nonviolence.

As Pope Paul said before the United Nations Assembly in 1965, "Men cannot be brothers if they are not humble. No matter how justified it may appear, pride provokes tensions and struggles for prestige, domination, colonialism and egoism. In a word *pride shatters brotherhood*." He went on to say that the attempts to establish peace on the basis of violence were in fact a manifestation of human pride. "If you wish to be brothers, let the weapons fall from your hands. You cannot love with offensive weapons in your hands."

6. A test of our sincerity in the practice of nonviolence is this: are we willing to *learn something from the adversary*? If a *new truth* is made known

to us by him or through him, will we accept it? Are we willing to admit that he is not totally inhumane, wrong, unreasonable, cruel, etc.? This is important. If he sees that we are completely incapable of listening to him with an open mind, our nonviolence will have nothing to say to him except that we distrust him and seek to outwit him. Our readiness to see some good in him and to agree with some of his ideas (though tactically this might look like a weakness on our part), actually gives us power: the power of sincerity and of truth. On the other hand, if we are obviously unwilling to accept any truth that we have not first discovered and declared ourselves, we show by that very fact that we are interested not in the truth so much as in "being right." Since the adversary is presumably interested in being right also, and in proving himself right by what he considers the superior argument of force, we end up where we started. Nonviolence has great power, provided that it really witnesses to truth and not just to self-righteousness.

The dread of being open to the ideas of others generally comes from our hidden insecurity about our own convictions. We fear that we may be "converted"—or perverted—by a pernicious doctrine. On the other hand, if we are mature and objective in our open-mindedness, we may find that viewing things from a basically different perspective—that of our adversary—we discover our own truth in a new light and are able to understand our own ideal more realistically.

Our willingness to take *an alternative approach* to a problem will perhaps relax the obsessive fixation of the adversary on his view, which he believes is the only reasonable possibility and which he is determined to impose on everyone else by coercion.

It is the refusal of alternatives—a compulsive state of mind which one might call the "ultimatum complex"—which makes wars in order to force the unconditional acceptance of one oversimplified interpretation of reality. The mission of Christian humility in social life is not merely to edify, but to *keep minds open to many alternatives*. The rigidity of a certain type of Christian thought has seriously impaired this capacity, which nonviolence must recover.

Needless to say, Christian humility must not be

confused with a mere desire to win approval and to find reassurance by conciliating others superficially.

7. Christian hope and Christian humility are inseparable. The quality of nonviolence is decided largely by the purity of the Christian hope behind it. In its insistence on certain human values, the Second Vatican Council, following *Pacem in Terris*, displayed a basically optimistic trust *in man himself*. Not that there is not wickedness in the world, but today trust in God cannot be completely divorced from a certain trust in man. The Christian knows that there are radically sound possibilities in every man, and he believes that love and grace always have the power to bring out those possibilities at the most unexpected moments. Therefore if he has hopes that God will grant peace to the world it is because he also trusts that man, God's creature, is not basically evil: that there is in man a potentiality for peace and order which can be realized provided the right conditions are there. The Christian will do his part in creating these conditions by preferring love and trust to hate and suspiciousness. Obviously, once again, this "hope in man" must not be naïve. But experience itself has shown, in the last few years, how much an attitude of simplicity and openness can do to break down barriers of suspicion that had divided men for centuries.

In resume, the meekness and humility which Christ extolled in the Sermon on the Mount and which are the basis of true Christian nonviolence, are inseparable from an eschatological Christian hope which is completely open to the presence of God in the world and therefore to the presence of our brother who is always seen, no matter who he may be, in the perspectives of the Kingdom. Despair is not permitted to the meek, the humble, the afflicted, the ones famished for justice, the merciful, the clean of heart and the peacemakers. All the beatitudes "hope against hope," "bear everything, believe everything, hope for everything, endure everything" (I Corinthians 13:7). The beatitudes are simply aspects of love. They refuse to despair of the world and abandon it to a supposedly evil fate which it has brought upon itself. Instead, like Christ himself, the Christian takes upon his own shoulders the yoke of the Savior, meek and humble of heart. This yoke is the burden of the world's sin with all its confusions and all its problems. These sins, confusions and problems are our very own. We do not disown them.

83. Vincent Harding

The Religion of Black Power

Vincent Harding (b. 1931), Professor Emeritus of Religion and Social Transformation at the Iliff School of Theology in Denver, is a historian and civil rights activist who drafted Martin Luther King, Jr.'s famous Riverside Church speech against the Vietnam War ("Beyond Vietnam"). Harding, who is a Mennonite, was the first director of the King Center in Atlanta and is co-founder and chairperson of the Veterans of Hope Project: A Center for the Study of Religion and Democratic Renewal—an organization committed to social transformation through nonviolent, grassroots, and democratic action. Harding is the author of many books, including Martin Luther King: The Inconvenient Hero. *Below is an excerpt from his 1968 essay on Black Power, and its embrace of violence as a means of social transformation.*

Black Resurrection:
The Power and the Glory

What are the means to be used in building new black men, new black communities and a renewed, black-oriented world? Already certain pathways have been suggested. The new men must come partly from a new vision of themselves. Indeed the image that has been constantly used in this century involves more than new self-image, it presumes resurrection. Ever since Marcus Garvey preached an Easter sermon on "The Resurrection of the Negro" in 1922, the theme has been constantly renewed.... [There follows an analysis of Black Power's call for a temporary separation of blacks and whites.]

A question no less difficult arises in another step that Black Power takes towards the building of black men and the black community—the emphasis on self-defense. Speaking for his organization in 1966, Carmichael set the most obvious theme: "SNCC reaffirms the right of black men everywhere to defend themselves when threatened or attacked." Moving the idea from a right to an authentication of black freedom, Killens wrote, "Men are not free unless they affirm the right to defend themselves." But for those who would intelligently explore Black Power, even these explanations are insufficient. It was Killens who set out—largely by implication—the fuller and more profound psychological significance of self-defense for black men. He wrote in the same revealing article,

We black folk have a deep need to defend ourselves. Indeed we have an obligation. We must teach the brutalizers how it feels to be brutalized. We must teach them that it hurts. They'll never know unless we teach them.

The issues raised by this series of statements are worthy of thoughtful consideration, for they eventually move to a level of profound moment. On the surface they seem to be nothing more than an affirmation of the somewhat disreputable "American right" to self-defense. (A right, incidentally, which most Americans have no sound moral grounds for questioning when it suddenly appears among angry black men.)

In some ways this affirmation of self-defense is an obvious response to a situation in which black people find that neither separation, respect, nor love is forthcoming from the dominant portion of the society. On another, related level, it is a repetition of the earlier theme of judgment at the hands of the injured. As we have mentioned, in a world in which God is at least obscure, and where no one else seems a dependable agent of justice for black people, black men should stand firmly on their responsibility to do the necessary work. There is, however, an even more profound issue involved in what Killens describes so sensitively as "a deep need" for black men to defend themselves. What he seems to be implying is this: when men have long been forced to accept the wanton attacks of their oppressors, when they have had to stand by, and watch their women prostituted, it is crucial to their own sense of self-esteem that they affirm and be able to implement their affirmation of a right to strike back.

The basic human search for a definition of manhood is here set out in significant black lineaments. Does manhood indeed depend upon the capacity to defend one's life? Is this American shibboleth really the source of freedom for men? Is it possible that a man simply becomes a slave to another man's initiative when he feels obliged to answer his opponent on the opponent's terms? Is there perhaps a certain kind of bondage involved when men are so anxious about keeping themselves alive that they are ready to take the lives of others to prevent that occurrence? The question is really one of the image man was meant to reflect; what is it? Certain ways of looking at the world would suggest that such questions are pointless before they come from the lips. Other religious perspectives might suggest that manhood can be discussed, but only in terms of the capacity to create new grounds for response to danger, and in the act of bringing new life into being, rather than in the animal capacity to strike back.

In his characteristically vivid way, Karenga allows no circumventing of the issue. He writes, "If we fight we might be killed. But it is better to die as a man than to live like a slave." In the midst of a hostile, threatening environment the Zealot pathway is often chosen by those who are in honest search of their manhood, by those who seek to protect and avenge their oppressed community. Most persons who claim to be followers of the Man who introduced Zealots to a new way of response have chosen not to follow him at this point. And here is one of the most telling witnesses to the possibility that Black Power may be more fully bound to the traditions of the western Christian world than its proponents would ever dare believe.

Now, if it is possible that the fullest stature of man was found in one who honestly and sharply opposed his enemies but finally faced them with his cross, then Black Power may have chosen far less than the best available way. If it has chosen a bondage of death, the mistake is completely understandable. It is understandable not only because retaliatory violence is deeply etched into the American grain, but also because men who have been forced up against crosses all their lives find it difficult to take one up when the choice is fully theirs. It is understandable, too, because western society now seems unable to offer any normative response to the question, "What is man?" Moreover it appears totally without courage to experiment with possibilities beyond the old, "heroic," destructive replies.

Perhaps one possibility yet stands in the future, and Black Power's immediate choice must not be counted as its last. For who knows where the inner quest will lead black men if they are honestly in search of true manhood, true community, and true humanity? Are there not grounds for hope wherever men are soberly and devotedly engaged in the quest for new light?

Old White Models and New Black Hopes

If the relationship of self-defense to the building of black manhood is crucial on the personal level, then it is likely that the kinds of power [employed] by the black community is the focal question on the broader scale. Not only is it crucial, but it faces us with another set of religious issues of considerable force. Initially one must ask: what is the power necessary to build the new black community? Perhaps Stokely Carmichael best summarized the normative Black Power response when he wrote:

Almost from its beginning, SNCC sought to [build] a program aimed at winning political power for impoverished Southern blacks. We had to begin with politics because black Americans are a propertyless people in a country where property is valued above all. We had to work for power, because this country does not function by morality, love, and nonviolence, but by power.

Political, economic and social power with a final recourse to armed self-defense are at the heart of the black search, even though Carmichael has since gone on to espouse aggressive guerilla warfare. Ron Karenga, who feels the movement is not yet ready for such warfare, put the issues of power for the black community more colorfully, but no less directly when he said,

Like it or not, we don't live in a spiritual or moral world and the white boys got enough H-bombs, missiles, TVs, firehoses and dogs to prove it.

Therefore, he concluded, "we must move not spiritually but politically, i.e., with power."

In some ways it is understandable to hear the avowed revolutionaries among Black Power refer to political, economic, and military realities as the ultimate forces in life. It is even more interesting to note that same direction in the forceful statement of an impressive group of black churchmen who wrote on the subject of black and white power in 1966. In the midst of the national furor over the newly discovered term, the churchmen published a full-page advertisement in the *New York Times* which said, in part, "The fundamental distortion facing us in the controversy about 'black power' is rooted in a gross imbalance of power and conscience between Negroes and white Americans." After setting out this basic introduction to their thesis, the statement continued,

It is this distortion, mainly, which is responsible for the widespread though often inarticulate assumption that white people are justified in getting what they want through the use of power, but that Negro Americans must, either by nature or circumstances, make their appeal only through conscience. As a result, the power of white men and the conscience of black men have both been corrupted. The power of white men is corrupted because it meets little meaningful resistance from Negroes to temper it and keep white men from aping God.

Tracing the corruption of the black conscience, the churchmen attributed it to a condition in which,

having no power to implement the demands of conscience, the concern for justice is transmuted into a distorted form of love, which, in the absence of justice, becomes chaotic self-surrender. Powerlessness breeds a race of beggars. We are faced now with a situation where conscienceless power meets powerlessness conscience, threatening the very foundations of our nation.

It was evident that the churchmen were convinced that "conscience," or "love" as they later referred to it, was "powerless" without the coercive forces of the society. They appeared no less disturbed than John Killens about "unrequited love," and in a sophisticated adumbration, the group simply gave religious expression to the political views of Carmichael, Karenga and a host of other black spokesmen. Though it is not fully stated they seem to be saying that the ultimate weapons necessary for the building of the new black community are those now monopolized by white power leaders. Blacks have to get their hands on some of these weapons and perhaps depend upon their own consciences to "temper" black uses of the same instruments whites had used for destructive purposes. But when blacks begin getting their proper share of the power, it would appear that they might be less dependent upon the development of "conscience"—unless it was theirs in large supplies "by nature" rather than "by circumstance." How then would Black Power be tempered?

A question at least as compelling is this: Does the theological position implicit in the churchmen's statement carry a doctrine of two kingdoms with it? Do these leaders seek the Kingdom of the weaponless, defenseless, homeless King at certain times, and the Kingdom of the armed, propertied, politically powerful, American, white (soon to be technicolored) King at another time? Where do the kingdoms meet? Are the guidelines to the nature of human community as blurred as those for the nature of man? On issues of ultimate power, are the insights of Christian ministers only accidentally the same as Stokely Carmichael's and Ron Karenga's?

The implications of the churchmen's statement are numerous and provocative but it is important to supplement that statement with an even more theologically astute brief for Black Power by one of the individual senators, Nathan Wright. Dr. Wright, who is also chairman of the National Conference on Black Power, recently wrote of the image of God and its relationship to power among black men. He said,

In religious terms, a God of power, of majesty and of might, who has made men to be in His image and likeness, must will that His creation reflect in the immediacies of life His power, His majesty and His might. Black Power raises … the far too long overlooked need for power, if life is to become what in the mind of its Creator it is destined to be.

In a fascinating way Karenga, one of the best trained and most thoughtful of the Black Power leaders, picks up the precise theme set down by Wright. In all likeliness he does it independently, so it is even more significant and illuminating that his definition of Black Power should also find its basis in a powerful deity. He writes, "God is God who moves in power; God is God who moves in change and creates something out of nothing. If you want to be God just think about that." (Karenga's last sentence is not random rhetoric. Evidently he has so imbibed the homocentric orientation of the American society that he upstages the Mormons by telling men that they become Gods now by entering into Godlike action. Indeed, the emphasis on autonomous black action is another of the hallmarks of Black Power ideology, a hallmark that leaves little room for any dependence on what might be called grace—a hallmark that would stamp it as far more Protestant than one might desire.)

The difficulty with the analogy evoked by Wright and Karenga is its failure to recognize another aspect of the power of God within the biblical tradition. If Wright and the other black churchmen put any serious stock in the life and teachings of Jesus of Nazareth as the clearest possible window to the face of God, then one must at least examine another way of power. That is, one must see the power of God demonstrated in weakness and in humiliation. Is it not possible that the God who dies for his enemies, who rejects their terms and their weapons—and their kind of power—is also worthy of consideration as a model for the empowerment of the black community?

Though it is difficult to propound, it would appear that such a question may have some possible validity when one remembers some of the goals of Black Power. May not one properly ask if a new black community will be created by the appropriation of the old American weapons of power? More specifically, what of Karenga's insight into the nature of racism?

Racist minds create racist institutions. Therefore you must move against racism, not institutions. For even if you tear down the institutions that same mind will build them up again.

How does one "move against racism"? Surely, not with "H-bombs, missiles, TVs, firehoses ... dogs" and all the other institutions of political power now possessed by "the white boy." And what of Stokely Carmichael's strangely religious metaphor: "For racism to die, a totally different America must be born"? Will a black community in search of a new society really participate in the process of new birth by a reactionary fixation on all the kinds of power which have helped to corrupt the nation? How does new birth come?

Talk of weakness and death, quests for new birth, all tend to be at once sources of fascination and anathema for the current black breed. It is likely that the apparently contradictory references to such matters in their writings are largely unconscious, and that the conscious stance is one of opposition to Gods who die on crosses. As we have seen, black men have been chained to weakness for so long that any talk of voluntarily choosing a way that the society counts as weak is considered sheer madness....

84. James Douglass

The Nonviolent Cross

James Douglass (b. 1937) is a longtime Catholic peacemaker who, with his wife, Shelley, helped to found the Ground Zero Center for Nonviolent Action in 1975. This group led public protests of the construction of a Trident missile nuclear submarine base in Washington, as well as other anti-nuclear weapons protests. Before founding Ground Zero, Douglass was a leader in the campaign against the Vietnam War, and below is a selection from his popular book The Nonviolent Cross, *published in the middle of the war. Douglass later joined with Shelley in founding Mary's House, a hospitality house that cares for the poor and ill in Birmingham, Alabama. In 2008 he published* JFK and the Unspeakable: Why He Died and Why It Matters.

The way of truth in a world of injustice is revolution. There is a sense in which every Christian must follow Ivan Karamazov in his revolt against a world in which children suffer. As Jean Daniélou has observed, "Because of the scandal of the suffering of the innocent the world stands convicted, and revolt is justified." Such a world cries out for transformation, and any man of faith who keeps his gaze heavenward while his suffering neighbors appeal for a new earth will, we are told (Matthew 25), depart ultimately with the curse of the Son into the eternal fire. In the contemporary world of affluence and poverty, where man's major crime is murder by privilege, revolution against the established order is the criterion of a living faith. Pope Paul has put it in the form of a program: "The new name of peace is development" (*Populorum Progressio)*. Jesus stated its alternative: "Truly, I say to you, as you did not to one of the least of these, you did it not to me" (Matthew 25:45). The murder of Christ continues. Great societies build on dying men.

But Ivan's revolt against injustice needs Alyosha's love and acceptance of responsibility in order to become the grain of wheat which—as Dostoevsky quotes from John's Gospel in his epigraph—by dying will bear much fruit. Ivan's revolt turns against the Creator, blaming Him for the sins of men, and becomes a sterile gesture toward his own autonomy. The revolt against injustice becomes a revolt against dependence. Alyosha, on the other hand, hears the counsel of Father Zossima, who by an acceptance of man's responsibility for man points toward the Revolution of Peace:

There is only one means of salvation, then take yourself and make yourself responsible for all men's sins, that is the truth, you know, friends, for as soon as you sincerely make yourself responsible for everything and for all men, you will see at once that it is really so, and that you are to blame for every one and for all things.

The innocents of the world suffer, just as the Son suffered, because every living man makes them suffer. It is man's responsibility, in and through the cross of the Son, to see that the innocents stop suffering. Man either gives life by himself taking on their suffering in that community of Christ working toward a new earth or he murders by turning from the God in man to the idolatry of a distant deity. There is only one God, and he has become man. Man can possess no life in God apart from God's life in the Suffering Servant.

The Servant's suffering love is the power to redeem evil. Evil is not absolute. Its existence in the world is profound, yet dependent on the prior existence of Good. Evil is relative to the Good and can be redeemed by the Love on which even it is dependent. When evil is thought to be absolute, as in the thought of Jean-Paul Sartre, the only way remaining for the man who in conscience knows the world's suffering is to respond to the executioners with absolute violence. Thus the anguished cry for a return violence by Frantz Fanon. But violence cannot liberate the wretched of the earth. To press this way upon them, as Che Guevara and other men hungering for justice have sought to do, is to confuse revolution with the evil it must overcome. History knows no liberation through the sword. Arnold Toynbee has made the point well:

An instrument that has once been used to destroy life cannot then be used to preserve life at the user's convenience. The function of weapons is to kill; and a ruler who has not scrupled to "wade through slaughter to a throne" will find—if he tries to maintain his power thereafter without further recourse to the grim arts which have gained it—that sooner or later he will be confronted with a choice between letting the power slip through his fingers or else renewing his lease of it by means of another bout of bloodshed. The man of violence cannot both genuinely repent of his violence and permanently profit by it.

To use a term of Martin Buber, whose thought offers a supreme affirmation of the possibilities of redemption, the way of redeeming evil lies along a "narrow ridge" between the false positions of reducing evil to illusion or objective error on the one hand and of absolutizing its existence on the other. Such a dialectical attitude toward evil, acknowledging evil's profound presence at the same time as its possibilities of redemption, draws one into the cross at the world's center, as Buber shows in *I and Thou*:

Love is responsibility of an *I* for a *Thou*. In this lies the likeness—impossible in any feeling whatsoever—of all who love, from the smallest to the greatest and from the blessedly protected man, whose life is rounded in that of a loved being, to him who is all his life nailed to the cross of the world, and who ventures to bring himself to the dreadful point—to love *all men....*

It is Christians' living denial of Jesus' humanity which is the incarnational heresy characteristic of the modern Church. Only through an existential reaffirmation, in the lives of Christians, of Jesus' suffering, living humanity can his messianic character begin to become generally manifest again. St. Paul told the Colossians that he had to suffer in order to complete Christ's sufferings in the Church (Col. 1:24). Even though mankind is already justified by Christ's suffering, this redemptive act has to be made present in the world through its embodiment in the life of the Church.

In his book *The Grave of God,* Father Robert Adolfs calls for the re-creation of such a "kenotic Church," a Church which will empty herself of wealth and power and become poor again in the deepest evangelical sense so as to rule only by love; a servant Church reflecting the Son who emptied himself of all claims to wealth and power for the sake of man. A group of Protestant Christians in East Germany which has sought out of necessity to live such a vision put it more sharply: "It is not the church we try to preserve now, but the Gospel." Perhaps it was Peter Maurin, though, who possessed the deepest sense of the revolution rising in the Church for the sake of the world:

It is about time
to blow the lid off
so the Catholic Church
may again become
the dominant social dynamic force.

But even as the Church still hesitates before blowing the lid off her crucified Power, Christ's presence in the world today is manifest in scattered communities of men of all faiths whose lives are centered on the redemptive reality of suffering love, as it works to transform them and their societies. Danilo Dolci and his development teams in Sic-

ily, Caesar Chavez and the Mexican farm workers, Vinoba Bhave and his walking revolution, U Thant and his co-workers for global peace—in such communities circling the earth and in their common commitment to the redemptive reality the face of Christ appears, just as it appeared in the lives of Gandhi, King, Hammarskjöld, and Pope John. "Our ultimate end," said Martin King, "must be the creation of the beloved community." Christ becomes present now as he became present in such men, in the constant crucifixion of self and resurrection of man which is the liberating basis for the Revolution of Peace. The humanity of God is men suffering and loving. His divinity becomes manifest in the community of grace their suffering love reveals.

The baptism into Christ which men are undergoing today, both within and without the Church, is not of water but of blood—their suffering for the community of man, a suffering accepted out of love and the hope for a new earth. This baptism of suffering draws men into the heart of the redemptive event, crucifixion, and through their response of faith and hope in mankind raises them in Christ to the community of love which is God's life in man. Christ's love and power, given through the sacrament of suffering, is the Holy Spirit. The power of the Holy Spirit is remaking the earth. Beside it nuclear weapons are impotent.

But we remain distant from an understanding of the reality of power. Those men who have understood the power of the Spirit, and in whom we sense its radiating life, remain enigmas in their efforts to tell us what it is. For an age in which a breakaway technology has determined the meaning of "power," the power of the Spirit is always a sign of contradiction. Never has man's self-defined power been so enormous and so impotent.

A remarkable statement by Gandhi, the most powerful man of our time, indicates the amount of reconstruction necessary if we are ever to understand the meaning of true power. On one occasion during a period of evening prayer a member of Gandhi's Ashram asked him: "Bapuji, what would be your first act if at this moment you would have the power to shape the destinies of mankind?" After the suspense of silence, with all eyes pinned on Gandhi, he replied: "I would pray for the courage instantly to renounce that power."

Paul defined his power with a similar paradox in his second letter to the Corinthians: "I will all the more gladly boast of my weaknesses, that the power of Christ may rest upon me. For the sake of Christ, then, I am content with weaknesses, insults, hardships, persecutions, and calamities; for when I am weak, then I am strong" (12:9-10).

When man knows his weakness and accepts full responsibility for the evil in himself and in the world, he becomes strong in love and in the Spirit. By taking on the cross man is raised. By embracing the search in love and responsibility as Alyosha did, man is prepared by God to build the City of Man into the City of God.

With enormous power and authority man's evil stands resistant to him at the center of history. In apparent surrender man in God lies on the cross and accepts the full impact of evil's hammerblows, and evil falls back finally in exhaustion as the cross is raised against the sky. With its destructive energy spent, the evil in man waits expectantly as the Son cries out in agony to the Father. But the cry only affirms that God is truly man, that heaven and earth have met in the cross, and that man's evil is therefore overcome. For as the suffering and the cry affirm God's humanity, the death and the open tomb initiate man's divinity. As the man of the cross dies, the centurion who nailed him there is raised to life: "Truly this was the Son of God." Evil's violence accepted in love is evil overcome, for evil is man's effort to create himself, and cannot withstand his power in God to be re-created in love. Within history, which is from one standpoint the history of his sin, evil is one side of man. When man accepts that side of himself on the cross, he is reconciled to himself through suffering love. Evil demands suf-fering love as its cost of reconciliation. It is only when man reverses the cross and seeks to destroy his evil with a sword that he becomes impotent and self-destructive in facing his darker self. The Revolution of Peace is man taking responsibility for his evil in the cross and thereby becoming himself in God.

The world's beauty and mystery is the cross at its center extending outward through history and divinizing man through the power of Love. The nonviolent cross is not unique to the prophets of peace mentioned here. The cross of suffering love is God's continuing presence in each man on this earth. The Son lives today as the redeemed, in the community of peace being constantly created through the sacrifice of love. A man cannot live without loving someone, however much his life as a whole may be consumed by hatred or deadened by indifference. For that someone he will suffer gladly and thus realize his humanity. To love is to suffer in joy, for the perfect union sought by love can be approached only through sacrifice. Love's price of suffering extended across the world is the price of redeeming man's violence. The violence within man is what prevents him from realizing a perfect union of love, and can be overcome progressively only through the fire of voluntary suffering. Suffering itself is evil, the result of sin. Love seeks union and community, not suffering. But in a world in which man has first crucified his brother, love's only way to union is through the reversal of violence in suffering. And the way has been divinized. By becoming man God has sacramentalized man's suffering so that man might become God through the cost of love. Love is the Power, but Power incarnate on the cross....

85. DANIEL BERRIGAN

Our Apologies, Good Friends

Daniel Berrigan (b. 1921) is a Jesuit priest who has devoted his life to writing, teaching, and acting for Christian peace and nonviolence. He came to prominence especially in 1968 when he, his brother Philip, and several other activists (eventually known as the Catonsville Nine) protested the Vietnam War by using homemade napalm to destroy hundreds of draft files in the parking lot next to the draft board based in Catonsville, Maryland—an event he reflects on here in "Our Apologies, Good Friends." Berrigan was sentenced to three years imprisonment for this act of civil disobedience. Rather than surrender to imprisonment, he went underground and earned a place on the FBI's most wanted list before he was captured at the home of a fellow radical Christian—William Stringfellow—and imprisoned shortly thereafter.

Next week nine of us will, if all goes well (ill?) take our religious bodies during this week to a draft center near Baltimore. There we shall, of purpose and forethought, remove the A-1 files, sprinkle them in the public street with homemade napalm and set them afire. For which act we shall, beyond doubt, be placed behind bars for some portion of our natural lives, in consequence of our inability to live and die content in the plagued city, to say peace peace when there is no peace, to keep the poor poor, the homeless homeless, the thirsty and hungry thirsty and hungry.

Our apologies, good friends, for the fracture of good order, the burning of paper instead of children, the angering of the orderlies in the front parlor of the charnel house. We could not, so help us God, do otherwise.

For we are sick at heart, our hearts give us no rest for thinking of the Land of Burning Children. And for thinking of that other Child, of whom the poet Luke speaks. The infant was taken up in the arms of an old man, whose tongue grew resonant and vatic at the touch of that beauty. And the old man spoke: this child is set for the fall and rise of many in Israel, a sign that is spoken against.

Small consolation; a child born to make trouble, and to die for it, the first Jew (not the last) to be subject of a "definitive solution." He sets up the cross and dies on it; in the Rose Garden of the executive mansion, on the D.C. Mall, in the courtyard of the Pentagon. We see the sign, we read the direction; you must bear with us, for His sake. Or if you will not, the consequences are our own.

For it will be easy, after all, to discredit us. Our record is bad: troublemakers in church and state, a priest married despite his vows, two convicted felons. We have jail records, we have been turbulent, uncharitable, we have failed in love for the brethren, have yielded to fear and despair and pride, often in our lives. Forgive us.

We are no more, when the truth is told, than ignorant beset men, jockeying against all chance, at the hour of death, for a place at the right hand of the dying One.

We act against the law at a time of the Poor People's March; at a time, moreover, when the government is announcing even more massive paramilitary means to confront disorder in the cities. The implications of all this must strike horror in the mind of the thinking person. The war in Vietnam is more and more literally being brought home to us. Its inmost meaning strikes the American ghettoes: one war, one crime against the poor, waged (largely) by the poor, in servitude to the affluent. We resist and protest this crime.

Finally, we stretch out our hands to our brothers and sisters throughout the world. We who are priests, to our fellow priests. All of us who act against the law, turn to the poor of the world, to the Vietnamese, to the victims, to the soldiers who kill and die; for the wrong reasons, for no reason at all, because they were so ordered—by the authorities of that public order which is in effect a massive institutionalized disorder.

We say killing is disorder. Life and gentleness and community and unselfishness is the only order we recognize. For the sake of that order, we risk our liberty, our good name. The time is past when good people can remain silent, when obedience can segregate people from public risk, when the poor can die without defense.

We ask our fellow Christians to consider in their hearts a question that has tortured us, night and day, since the war began:

How many must die before our voices are heard, how many must be tortured, dislocated, starved, maddened? How long must the world's resources be raped in the service of legalized murder? When, at what point, will you say no to this war?

We wish also to place in question by this act all suppositions about normal times, longings for an untroubled life in a somnolent church, that neat timetable of ecclesiastical renewal, which in respect to the needs of people, amounts to another form of time serving.

Redeem the times! The times are inexpressibly evil. Christians pay conscious—indeed religious—tribute to Caesar and Mars; by approval of overkill tactics, by brinkmanship, by nuclear liturgies, by racism, by support of genocide. They embrace their society with all their heart, and abandon the cross. They pay lip service to Christ and military service to the powers of death.

And yet, and yet, the times are inexhaustibly good, solaced by the courage and hope of many.

The truth rules, Christ is not forsaken. In a time of death, some men and women—the resisters, those who work hardily for social change, those who preach and embrace the unpalatable truth—such men and women overcome death, their loves are bathed in the light of the resurrection, the truth has set them free. In the jaws of death, of contumely, of good and ill report, they proclaim their love of the people.

We think of such men and women in the world, in our nation, in the churches, and the stone in our breast is dissolved. We take heart once more.

86. CÉSAR CHÁVEZ

Letter from Delano

César Chávez (1927-1993) was a Mexican-American labor leader who focused his life efforts on securing rights for farm workers, especially migrant workers in California. In 1962, Chávez resigned from an activist position with the Community Service Organization, a Latino civil rights group, to help found the National Farm Workers Association (which later became the United Farm Workers of America). As head of this labor group, Chávez organized numerous nonviolent protests—fasts, boycotts, marches, and strikes—to advance workers' rights. A devout Catholic, Chávez often incorporated religious symbols, such as Our Lady of Guadalupe, into his public protests. One of his most famous campaigns resulted in a first-ever contract between vineyard owners and farm workers in California. In the campaign, Chávez used a 300-mile march from Delano to Sacramento that attracted ten thousand marchers; a national boycott of table grapes; personal fasts; and numerous public statements, including the following 1969 letter he wrote to E. L. Barr, the president of the California Grape and Tree Fruit League.

Dear Mr. Barr:

I am sad to hear about your accusations in the press that our union movement and table grape boycott have been successful because we have used violence and terror tactics. If what you say is true, I have been a failure and should withdraw from the struggle; but you are left with the awesome moral responsibility, before God and Man, to come forward with whatever information you have so that corrective action can begin at once. If for any reason you fail to come forth to substantiate your charges, then you must be held responsible for committing violence against us, albeit of the tongue. I am convinced that you as a human being did not mean what you said but rather acted hastily under pressure from the public relations firm that has been hired to try to counteract the tremendous moral force of our movement. How many times we ourselves have felt the need to lash out in anger and bitterness.

Today on Good Friday, 1969, we remember the life and the sacrifice of Martin Luther King, Jr., who gave himself totally to the nonviolent struggle for peace and justice. In his *Letter from a Birming-*

ham Jail Dr. King describes better than I could our hopes for the strike and boycott: "Injustice must be exposed, with all the tensions its exposure creates, to the light of human conscience and the air of national opinion before it can be cured." For our part I admit that we have seized upon every tactic and strategy consistent with the morality of our cause to expose that injustice and thus to heighten the sensitivity of the American conscience so that farmworkers will have, without bloodshed, their own union and the dignity of bargaining with their agribusiness employers. By lying about the nature of our movement, Mr. Barr, you are working against nonviolent social change. Unwittingly perhaps, you may unleash that other force which our union by discipline and deed, censure and education has sought to avoid, that panacean shortcut: that senseless violence which honors no color, class or neighborhood.

You must understand—I must make you understand—that our membership and the hopes and aspirations of the hundreds of thousands of the poor and dispossessed that have been raised on our account are, above all, human beings, no better and no worse than any other cross-section of human society; we are not saints because we are poor, but by the same measure neither are we immoral. We are men and women who have suffered and endured much, and not only because of our abject poverty but because we have been kept poor. The colors of our skins, the languages of our cultural and native origins, the lack of formal education, the exclusion from the democratic process, the numbers of our men slain in recent wars—all these burdens generation after generation have sought to demoralize us, to break our human spirit. But God knows that we are not beasts of burden, agricultural implements or rented slaves; we are men. And mark this well, Mr. Barr, we are men locked in a death struggle against man's inhumanity to man in the industry that you represent. And this struggle itself gives meaning to our life and ennobles our dying.

As your industry has experienced, our strikers here in Delano and those who represent us throughout the world are well trained for this struggle. They have been under the gun, they have been kicked and beaten and herded by dogs, they have been cursed and ridiculed, they have been stripped and chained and jailed, they have been sprayed with poisons used in the vineyards; but they have been taught not to lie down and die nor to flee in shame, but to resist with every ounce of human endurance and spirit. To resist not with retaliation in kind but to overcome with love and compassion, with ingenuity and creativity, with hard work and longer hours, with stamina and patient tenacity, with truth and public appeal, with friends and allies, with mobility and discipline, with politics and law, and with prayer and fasting. They were not trained in a month or even a year; after all, this new harvest season will mark our fourth full year of strike and even now we continue to plan and prepare for the years to come. Time accomplishes for the poor what money does for the rich.

This is not to pretend that we have everywhere been successful enough or that we have not made mistakes. And while we do not belittle or underestimate our adversaries—for they are the rich and the powerful and they possess the land—we are not afraid nor do we cringe from the confrontation. We welcome it! We have planned for it. We know that our cause is just, that history is a story of social revolution, and that the poor shall inherit the land.

Once again, I appeal to you as the representative of your industry and as a man. I ask you to recognize and bargain with our union before the economic pressure of the boycott and strike takes an irrevocable toll; but if not, I ask you to at least sit down with us to discuss the safeguards necessary to keep our historical struggle free of violence. I make this appeal because as one of the leaders of our nonviolent movement, I know and accept my responsibility for preventing, if possible, the destruction of human life and property. For these reasons, and knowing of Gandhi's admonition that fasting is the last resort in place of the sword, during a most critical time in our movement last February 1968 I undertook a 25-day fast. I repeat to you the principle enunciated to the membership at the start of the fast: if to build our union required the deliberate taking of life, either the life of a grower or his child, or the life of a farmworker or his child, then I choose not to see the union built.

Mr. Barr, let me be painfully honest with you. You must understand these things. We advocate militant nonviolence as our means for social revolution and to achieve justice for our people, but we are not blind or deaf to the desperate and moody winds of human frustration, impatience and rage that blow among us. Gandhi himself admitted that if his only choice were cowardice or violence, he would choose violence. Men are not angels, and time and tide wait for no man. Precisely because of these powerful human emotions, we have tried to involve masses of people in their own struggle. Participation and self-determination remain the best experience of freedom, and free men instinctively prefer democratic change and even protect the rights guaranteed to seek it. Only the enslaved

in despair have need of violent overthrow.

This letter does not express all that is in my heart, Mr. Barr. But if it says nothing else it says that we do not hate you or rejoice to see your industry destroyed; we hate the agribusiness system that seeks to keep us enslaved and we shall overcome and change it not by retaliation or bloodshed but by a determined nonviolent struggle carried on by those masses of farm workers who intend to be free and human.

Sincerely yours,
César E. Chávez

87. JACQUES ELLUL

Violence: Reflections from a Christian Perspective

Jacques Ellul (1912-1994) was a French sociologist and theologian based for many years at the University of Bordeaux. He first achieved fame with the 1954 publication of The Technological Society, *a penetrating critique of modern society's preference for the mechanics of technological efficiency over ethical thinking. Ellul also became a favorite among Christian anarchists when he argued that the goals of Christianity were closely connected with those of anarchy. As a leading Christian intellectual, Ellul subjected violence to a devastating critique, and his most famous work on this was* Violence: Reflections from a Christian Perspective *(1969), excerpted below.*

Necessity and Legitimacy

… Christian realism leads to the conclusion that violence is natural and normal to man and society, that violence is a kind of necessity imposed on governors and governed, on rich and poor. If this realism scandalizes Christians, it is because they make the great mistake of thinking that what is *natural* is *good* and what is *necessary* is *legitimate*. I am aware that the reader will answer at once: "You have shown that violence is inevitable and necessary in undertakings of any kind; *therefore* violence is legitimate, it *must* be used." This is anti-Christian reasoning par excellence. What Christ does for us above all is to make us free. Man becomes free through the Spirit of God, through conversion to and communion with the Lord. This is the one

way to true freedom. But to have true freedom is to escape necessity or, rather, to be free to struggle against necessity. Therefore I say that only one line of action is open to the Christian who is free in Christ. He must struggle against violence precisely *because,* apart from Christ, violence is the form that human relations normally and necessarily take. In other words, the more completely violence seems to be of the order of necessity, the greater is the obligation of believers in Christ's Lordship to overcome it by challenging necessity.

This is the fixed, the immutable, and the radical basis of the Christian option in relation to violence. For the order of necessity is the order of separation from God. Adam, created by God and in communion with God, is free; he is not subject to any kind of destiny. God lays on him only one commandment, a commandment that is a word of God and therefore also both a gospel and an element in dialogue between persons. This commandment is not a law limiting his freedom from without. Adam knows nothing of necessity, obligation, inevitability. If he obeys the word, he does so freely. It is not at all necessary for him to labor, to *produce,* to defend the Garden against anyone. Necessity appears when Adam breaks his relation with God. Then he becomes subject to an order of obligation, the order of toil, hunger, passions, struggle against nature, etc., from which there is no appeal. At that moment necessity becomes part of the order of nature—not of nature as God wished it to be, but of nature henceforth made for death. And death is then the most total of all necessities. Necessity is definable as what man does because he cannot do otherwise. But when God reveals himself, necessity ceases to be destiny or even inevitability. In the Old Testament, man shatters the necessity of eating by fasting, the necessity of toil by keeping the Sabbath; and when he fasts or keeps the Sabbath he recovers his real freedom, because he has been found again by the God who has reestablished communion with him. The institution of the order of Levites likewise shatters the normal institutional order of ownership, duty, provision for the future, etc. And this freedom is fully accomplished by and through Jesus Christ. For Christ, even death ceases to be a necessity: "I give my life for my sheep; it is not taken from me, I give it." And the constant stress on the importance of giving signifies a breaking away from the necessity of money.

Here then—all too briefly described—are the considerations basic to understanding the problem of violence. The temptation is always to yield to fatality, as Father Maillard does when he takes the extreme positions referred to above. "All life is a struggle," he says. "Life itself is violent. And it is in struggling that we realize ourselves. Every action is necessarily imperfect and impure.... We are caught in a terrible machine which can thrust us into situations of violence in spite of ourselves. Let us distrust the temptation to purity." But Father Maillard confuses the situation he perceives so realistically with the will of God.

Violence is inevitable, but so far as concerns society it has the same character as the univer-

sally prevailing law of gravitation, which is not in any way an expression of God's love in Christ or of Christian vocation. Whenever I stumble over an obstacle and fall, I am obeying the law of gravitation, which has nothing to do with Christian faith or the Christian life. We must realize that violence belongs to the same order of things. And so far as we understand that the *whole* of Christ's work is a work of liberation—of our liberation from sin, death, concupiscence, fatality (and from ourselves)—we shall see that violence is not simply an ethical option for us to take or leave. Either we accept the order of necessity, acquiesce in and obey it—and this has nothing at all to do with the work of God or obedience to God, however serious and compelling the reasons that move us—or else we accept the order of Christ; but then we must reject violence root and branch.

For the role of the Christian in society, in the midst of men, is to shatter fatalities and necessities. And he cannot fulfill this role by using violent means, simply because violence is of the order of necessity. To use violence is to be of the world. Every time the disciples wanted to use any kind of violence they came up against Christ's veto (the episode of the fire pouring from heaven on the cities that rejected Christ, the parable of the tares and the wheat, Peter's sword, etc.). This way of posing the problem is more radical than that implicit in the usual juxtaposition of violence and love. For as we shall see, there is a "violence of love," and there is necessarily a quarrel between "handless" love and effectual love. Naturally, there are those who protest: "But can anyone say that he loves the exploited poor of South America when he does nothing for them; and can anything be done without violence?" On the contrary, there is no escaping the absolute opposition between the order of necessity and the order of Christ.

... The better we understand that violence is necessary, indispensable, inevitable, the better shall we be able to reject and oppose it. If we are free in Jesus Christ, we shall reject violence *precisely because* violence is necessary! ... And, mind, this means *all* kinds and ways of violence: psychological manipulation, doctrinal terrorism, economic imperialism, the venomous warfare of free competition, as well as torture, guerilla movements, police action. The capitalist who, operating from his headquarters, exploits the mass of workers or colonial peoples is just as violent as the guerilla; he must absolutely not assume the mantle of Christianity. What he does is of the order of necessity, of estrangement from God; and even if he is a faithful churchgoer and a highly educated man, there is no freedom in him.

But if this is true, the opposite is also true. Christians must freely admit and accept the fact that non-Christians use violence.... We must accept and try to understand this man who does not know Christ's freedom. But let us distinguish clearly between him and the man who has known Christ and calls himself a Christian. The latter cannot be excused if he uses violence for his own ends. So, too, the capitalist or the colonialist who exploits and oppresses his fellow men, and the government leader who uses police or military violence, are to be radically condemned. Toward them, the church can only take the attitude that St. Ambrose took toward Theodore. On the other hand, the non-Christian—the one who, living under a tyrannous regime or in a society where, it seems, social justice will never end, wants to kill the tyrant or destroy the society; the one who, exploited or degraded by a colonialist regime, wants to kill the oppressor; the man who, victimized by a racist society, wants to avenge by violence the indignities heaped upon him—all these, along with their violence, their hatred, their folly, must be accepted by those of us who are Christians. We know that they will only unleash violence, that they will solve no problems and will not bring in a better world; that such elements will appear, again and again, in a world of slavery and fear. But we cannot condemn these people. We must understand that when a man considers violence the only resort left him, when he sees it, not as a remedy and the harbinger of a new day, but as at least an indictment of the old, unjust order, when he thinks of violence as a way of affirming his outraged human dignity (his pride!)—in all these cases he is yielding to a normal urge, he is being natural, he is, though he is outside the law, at least being truthful.

For after all, there is no need to deny that violence has its virtues. It can bring about the disorder that is necessary when the established order is only a sanctimonious injustice, therefore condemnable and condemned. Within the system of necessities, violence may be a valid means.... Violence is undoubtedly the only means for exploding facades, for exposing hypocrisy and hidden oppression for what they are; only violence reveals reality....

... Thus—speaking as a Christian—I say that while I cannot call violence good, legitimate, and just, I find its use condonable (1) when a man is in despair and sees no other way out, or (2) when a hypocritically just and peaceful situation must be exposed for what it is in order to end it. But I must emphasize that in these cases, too, violence is "of the order of necessity," therefore contradictory to the Christian life, whose root is freedom. Moreover, I must emphasize that this understandable, acceptable, condonable violence may change quickly. Opposing an unjust order, creating a state of disorder out of which (depending on how fluid the situation is) renewal may issue—this is acceptable, provided that the users of violence do not pretend that they are creating order; what they are creating is one more injustice. The Christian simply cannot believe that *this* violence will bring in a new order, a free society....

Moreover, violence cannot be accepted when it is made a factor in strategy. We must sympathize with the man whose suffering explodes in violence, but we must refuse to countenance the one who considers violence a tool, a strategic tactic he is free to use at will. My objection to Che Guevara or Stokely Carmichael is that incitement to violence is (or was) a factor in their strategy—which is to say that they betray the people whose suffering drives them into anger and brutality. Thus human suffering and anger are turned into strings to operate marionettes, and these leaders reveal a hatred of humanity as deep as that of the leaders they oppose. It seems to me that a Christian cannot but sympathize with spontaneous violence. But calculated violence, violence incited as part of a strategy, is in no respect different from the violence of the general who orders his soldiers to their death and in the same breath praises them for their patriotism, etc. This is the lesson that Lenin taught us.

Now a problem arises as regards the violence the Christian finds understandable and acceptable:

what should his relation to it be? … It is true that where man is exploited, crushed, degraded by man, the Christian can neither avoid involvement by escape into the realm of spiritual values, nor side by default with the dominating party (as he has done so often in the course of history). Necessarily in virtue of the calling to which Christ has called him, in virtue of the Lord's example, in virtue of the order of love, he is on the side of the little people, the poor. His place in the world is there—the only place the way of love leads to.…

If the Christian, because of his solidarity with the poor and the oppressed, joins their movement of distress, stands with them in their revolt, he may never use violence himself, nor even unreservedly condone their violence. The Christian may not commit murder or arson even to defend the poor. Moreover, he must be on guard against creating the impression that his presence in the movement gives it a kind of moral guarantee. "The Christians are on or side" is interpreted as "God is on our side." It seems to me that, though there is some confusion about it, the case of Camilo Torres is in point here. Torres, readers will remember, was the Columbian priest who, seeing the terrible misery of his country's peasants and workers, became convinced that there was only one remedy for it, namely, the guerilla movement. So he joined the guerillas. But he could not participate in their violence; he could only meet death at their side. Giving his life was his way of witnessing to Christ's presence among the poor and the afflicted. But I cannot say that it exemplifies Christian truth, for violence was directly involved here. Moreover, in such a case the Christian becomes a propaganda factor and the "good conscience" of men who have no hope in Jesus Christ. The only lesson to be drawn here is that Christians who share the suffering of men must bear witness to our Lord and Savior Jesus Christ in the worst and most dangerous situations. It is good and necessary that testimony to Jesus Christ be given among the guerillas; but this is the only justification for a Christian's presence in such company, even if his presence is an act of heroism.

It may, however, happen that the Christian himself uses violence. He has indeed often done so in the course of history.…

Be that as it may, his being a revolutionary

(and, as I have said, I believe that Christianity is profoundly revolutionary), his participation in the suffering of men, may lead a Christian to use violence.… The important thing is that, when he uses violence, the Christian knows very well that he is doing wrong, sinning against the God of Love, and (even if only in appearance) is increasing the world's disorder. He cannot conscientiously use violence in defense of the revolution of the poor, cannot believe that the violence he commits is in conformity with the divine will and the divine order. The only thing he can do is to admit that he is acting so out of his own fears and emotions (not to defend oneself in battle is difficult, more difficult than to accept a death sentence calmly); or else he can say that he is fighting *for* others, not to save his own life. To say that, however, is to recognize that violence is a necessity. In a revolution or a resistance movement, for instance, there are things that cannot be evaded, that have to be done; violence must be used—it is a necessity. But in such a situation the Christian must realize that he has fallen back into the realm of necessity; that is, he is no longer the free man God wills and redeemed at great cost. He is no longer a man conformed to God, no longer a witness to truth. Of course, he can say that he is only a man among men—but that is not at all the calling to which God has called him. He is once more traveling the rutted roads of this godless world. To be sure, the Bible tells of a great many men who "made history," but these were not the men God wished them to be. To fight even the worst of men is still to fight a man, a potential image of God.

Thus violence can never be justified or acceptable before God. The Christian can only admit humbly that he could not do otherwise, that he took the easy way and yielded to necessity and the pressures of the world. That is why the Christian, even when he permits himself to use violence in what he considers the best of causes, cannot either feel or say that he is justified; he can only confess that he is a sinner, submit to God's judgment, and hope for God's grace and forgiveness.…

So, if a Christian feels that he must participate in a violent movement (or in a war!), let him do so discerningly. He ought to be the one who, even as he acts with the others, proclaims the injustice and the unacceptability of what he and they are doing. He ought to be the mirror of truth in which his comrades perceive the horror of their action. He ought to be the conscience of the movement; the one who, in behalf of his unbelieving comrades, repents, bears humiliation, and prays to the Lord; the one who restrains man from glorifying himself for the evil he does....

88. WILLIAM STRINGFELLOW

Authority over Death

William Stringfellow (1928-1985) was a prolific Episcopal lay theologian with a law degree from Harvard and a passion for social justice and peace. As a committed Christian pacifist, Stringfellow and poet Anthony Towne gave sanctuary to Daniel Berrigan when he was a fugitive following his conviction for civil disobedience during the Vietnam War, and below is a sermon that Stringfellow preached in 1970, shortly after Berrigan's capture by federal authorities.

As I regard myself, I have never been especially religious, and, having been reared as an Episcopalian, the pietism of which I may be guilty has been ambiguous—a casual matter and an inconvenience more than a matter of consistency or fixed conviction. Still, as a younger person, particularly while an undergraduate, I had been precocious theologically, and instead of being attentive to whatever it was that students, in those days, may have been interested in, I concentrated much, in the privacy of my mind, on theology and upon what might be called theologizing.

I do not mean that I often studied or even read the works of theologians, because I did not do that, but I did begin then to read the Bible, in an unordered and spontaneous way, and I did begin, thus, to be caught up in a dialectic between an experience with the biblical witness and my everyday existence as a human being. I recall, in this, that there seemed to me to be a strong opposition between both the biblical story and my own life, on one side, and religion and religious moralism, on the other. After a while that opposition took on greater clarity, and I could discern that the former has to do with living humanly, while the latter has to do with dying in a moral sense and, indeed, with dying in *every* sense.

To anyone who knows this about me, it will come as no surprise to learn that in the immediate aftermath of the seizure by the federal authorities of Daniel Berrigan, at Eschaton, the home that Anthony Towne and I share on Block Island, I spent what time our suddenly hectic circumstances would afford with the New Testament. This was no exercise in solace; neither Anthony nor I had any regret or grief to be consoled, and we had each beheld the serenity of Dan as he was taken into the anxious custody of the FBI. The coolness of Berrigan had been a startling contrast to the evident shame and agitation of the agents, and we both understood that, whatever Dan was suffering in his transition from fugitive to captive, he had no need for pity or remorse, least of all from us.

To open, then, the Bible was an obvious, straightforward, natural thing to do. Berrigan had done something similar, publicly, when he preached to the Germantown congregation, relying upon texts from the Letter to the Hebrews. It is a wholly characteristic recourse for Christians, since, in the Bible, they find a holy history which is human history transfigured and since, in turn, they realize that human history is holy history and since, thus, they dwell in the continuity of the biblical word and the present moment.

Through the late spring and the summer, I had been engaged with the Babylon passages in the Book of Revelation, and that effort had influenced my participation in the conversations which were taking place with Daniel and Anthony. With the abrupt interruption of our talk on August 11th, I put aside—though not out of ready reach—the Babylon texts to return to the Acts of the Apostles and to some of the Letters that are thought to be chronologically proximate to Acts, specifically James and First Peter.

These testimonies, of course, deal with the issues of the Apostolic Church struggling to distinguish itself from the sects of Judaism, while at the same time confronting the political claims and challenges of the zealots, on one hand, and the manifest blasphemy and idolatry of the civic religion of Rome, on the other. All these subjects are so familiar in contemporary American reference that it is a temptation to treat them fatalistically … .

The immediate trauma of the aggression against our household, in which Dan had been taken, spared me from speculations of that sort, however, and I realized while reading Acts that more rudimentary and more fundamental problems had to be faced. I remembered vividly, moreover, how the same matters had plagued and confounded me, years earlier, for all my precocity, and how, in a sense, the situation of August 11th, 1970, had been long since foreshadowed. The episode of the arrest of Peter and John, as told in Acts, following upon the healing of the lame beggar at the temple gate, sums up the issues:

> And as they were speaking to the people, the priests and the captain of the temple and the Sadducees came upon them, annoyed because they were teaching the people and proclaiming in Jesus the resurrection from the dead. And they arrested them and put them in custody….(Acts 4:1-3a)

I read this and read it and read it; the most difficult questions of my initiation in Bible study returned: *What does "the resurrection from the dead" mean if proclaiming it is cause for arrest? Why is healing a cripple so threatening and provocative to the public authorities? Why should this apparent good work count as a crime?*

This arrest of Peter and John, associated publicly with the healing of the lame man and the open preaching of the resurrection, portended a wider persecution of Christians and an official repres-

sion of the Gospel, but it also relates back to the reasons for the condemnation and execution of Jesus, in which, it must not be overlooked, Jesus' own ministry of healing was interpreted by the incumbent authorities as if it were political agitation and was deemed by them to be a threat to their political authority. Where healing or, more broadly, where the witness to the resurrection is involved, the comprehension and response of Caesar and his surrogates to Christ as well as to the Apostles is, significantly, consistent. Such a witness is judged as a crime against the State.

There is a sentimentalistic (and unbiblical) tradition of "bible stories" in American Christendom which, when coupled with the thriving naïveté of Americans toward their own nation, renders it difficult for many citizens, particularly church-folk, to assimilate the fact that the Christian witness is treated as a criminal offense, even though this is so bluntly and repeatedly reported in New Testament texts. Within the American churchly ethos, biblical references to healing, however they may be interpreted medically, as metaphors or magic or miracles, are generally supposed to be highly private, individual, and personal happenings, having nothing categorically to do with politics. Meanwhile, when it comes to the resurrection as an event and the meaning of the resurrection as the gist of the Gospel, the sentimentalization of Scripture has reached a quintessence of distortion, so that to regard the resurrection in a political context, as the New Testament does, seems a most radical incongruity: an unthinkable thought.

At the same time, the simplistic Constantinianism which informs American attitudes toward Christianity and the nation allows Americans to view Rome and the ancillary ecclesiastical-political establishment allowed in the Empire at the time of the Crucifixion and during the Apostolic era as an aberrant version of the State rather than as an archetypical symbol of all political institutions and authorities in any time or place. There are no doubt some serious distinctions to be kept between Rome and America or between the Nazi State and the United States or between Sweden and the U.S.A. or, for that matter, between Revolutionary America and contemporary America, but such issues must not obscure the truth that every nation, every political regime, every civil power shares a singular characteristic which outweighs whatever may be said to distinguish one from another. And it is *that* common attribute of the State as such to which the New Testament points where the texts deal with the witness in Christ being condemned as criminal.

The sanction—though it takes different forms, it is, in principle, the *only* sanction—upon which the State relies is death. In the healing episodes, as in other works within the ministry in Christ, as in the proclamation of the resurrection from the dead, the authority of Christ over the moral power of death is verified as well as asserted. It is this claim of the Gospel which the State beholds as threatening; it is the audacity to verify this claim in living—in thought and word and action—that the State condemns as crime. The preaching of the resurrection, far from being politically innocuous, and the healing incidents, instead of being merely private, are profound, even cosmic, political acts.

This is how, on August 11th, in the hours soon after Father Berrigan's capture and incarceration, I thought of Dan's ministry and the various ways in which he has exercised his vocation through the years that Anthony and I have known him: as prisoner, as guest, as fugitive, as convicted felon, as Catonsville defendant, as exile, as citizen in protest, as poet, as priest—as a man. Confronted with what I was reading in Acts, I marveled at the patience of Berrigan's witness; I sensed the humor of what he has said and done being construed, especially in the churches, as so radical. It seemed utterly obvious that Berrigan had taken his stand in the mainstream of the Apostolic tradition and that his course had been not at all unusual but simply normative.

I do not imply that Berrigan is engaged in some self-conscious imitation of Peter or John or any other of the earlier Christians; I simply mean that to proclaim the resurrection in word and act is an affront which the State cannot tolerate because the resurrection exposes the subservience of the State to death as the moral purpose of the society which the State purports to rule. As has been intimated, the clarity or literalness with which the moral dependence upon death of the State can be discerned may vary much, from time to time and from place to place, but, nonetheless, the American circumstances today represent an instance in which death is pervasive, aggressive, and undisguised in its moral domination of the nation's existence. Theologically speaking, the war in Vietnam is not just an improvident, wicked, or stupid venture, but it epitomizes the militancy and insatiability of death as a moral power reigning in the nation—as that morality in relation to which everything and everyone is supposedly judged and justified. Thus to oppose the war becomes much more than a difference over policy. From the viewpoint of the State, protest against the war undermines the *only* moral purpose which the State has—the work of death—and risks the only punishment of which the State is capable: consignment to death or to some status which embodies the same meaning as death—though it be short of execution—like imprisonment, prosecution, persecution, loss of reputation or property or employment, intimidation to beget silence and conformity....

In the days that followed upon Dan's capture, many Block Island neighbors, many other friends, and many strangers have told Anthony and myself of their outrage and their apprehension—whatever they might think of what the Catonsville Nine did or of Father Berrigan's fugitive interlude—that the State seemed so anxious and overreactive and was in such hot pursuit of, as one person put it, "a harmless man." In this tentative, uneasy perception, I believe, a host of citizens, otherwise passive, grasp the desperate issue in what is taking place in America now: the power of death incarnate in the State violating, enslaving, perverting, imprisoning, destroying human life in society. To fail or refuse to act against this amounts to an abdication of one's humanness, a renunciation of the gift of one's own life, as well as a rejection of the lives of other human beings, a very ignominious idolatry of death. In the face of that the only way—no matter how the State judges or what the State does—is to live in the authority over death which the resurrection is. A person cannot be human and be silent about that, as *Acts* attests:

So they called them and charged them not to speak or teach at all in the name of Jesus. But Peter and John answered them, "Whether it is right in the sight of God to listen to you rather that to God, you must judge; for we cannot but speak of what we have seen and heard." (Acts 4:18-20)

229

89. PHILIP BERRIGAN

An Open Letter to a Bishop

Philip Berrigan (1923-2002), like his brother Dan, was a socially active priest who attracted national and international attention by carrying out public acts of civil disobedience to protest the Vietnam War. A year before joining his brother in the Catonsville Nine action, Philip had joined three others who were part of a group, eventually called the Baltimore Four, who poured blood on draft records in Baltimore and then handed out New Testament literature as they waited to be arrested. Later, after his release from prison for these actions, he would leave the Catholic priesthood and marry Elizabeth McAlister, a former nun. Together they founded Jonah House, a resistance community in Baltimore, and devoted their lives to the struggle against nuclear war. Below is a 1971 letter that Berrigan sent to Catholic Bishop William Baum, who had invited Berrigan to share his thoughts on justice and peace.

Here are the few ideas I promised you. They are qualified, of course, by my status and by the two years I have already served. But I possessed them before imprisonment, my books are full of them, and, it goes without saying, I believe them profoundly enough to stake my life on them. I have not found many men who can say that about their ideas.

So if you find the following negative, caustic, angry—remember that they come from one who has questioned domestic racism and modern war for ten years; who has lived in the slums and seen the anguish of the poor; who has resisted militarism and war-making repeatedly; who has experienced not only prison but solitary confinement and long fasts; who has endured the charade of three political trials and who faces a fourth; and who probably will be in and out of prison for the remainder of his life. In sum, my experience has been out of the ordinary, and it comes purely from attempts to answer the question, "What does Christ ask of me?"

Despite the fact that we come from different frames of reference, and that the Berrigan view of the Gospel (Dan's and mine) is radically different from the hierarchy's, we will not admit that our own responsibilities differ from yours. In fact, we might imply that the Bishops have a deeper obligation to costly witness than we do because of the magisterium, their pastorship and charism. I tend to state the matter bluntly. On the issue of modern war, the hierarchy's default is very nearly total; it is so bad, in effect, that nuclear exchange would find Bishops unprepared to discuss anything but the morality of defending a shelter with a shotgun.

Apart from these observations, which I offer only in introduction, please convey our love and fraternity (Dan's and mine) to the Pope. It strikes me that we speak for those unable to do so, those sisters and brothers imprisoned around the world—priests, religious, laity—in Latin America, Africa, Europe, Indochina, the Marxist world. We constitute the Church in chains—advocates of resistance to naked power, disproportionate wealth, racism, war-making. We want to express our fidelity to the Church and to the Chair of Peter, even as we sorrow over Christian myopia, hardness of heart and even cowardice.

With these preliminaries, let me offer a few general observations as well. It impresses me that thinking in the Church today, now that we are over the Vatican II euphoria, is stereotyped, cautious, quasi-despairing. Bishops, theologians, and clergy are obviously operating under the housekeeping assumption: from top to bottom, from Rome to parish, more synods, councils, democracy, and guitars will see us through present world crises. We operate as though, under a divine and magical star, we will muckle through with minimal losses while grace and providence work for us—providing, however, we pretend hard enough that nuclear overkill does not exist, that genocide in Indochina has not been carried out, that the North Atlantic community does not control 50 percent of the world's wealth, that wealth and power are not identified with the white world, and poverty and desperation are not identified with the so-called colored world.

Those Catholics—clergy and laity—who have not expressed disillusionment with such realities by leaving the Church altogether are leisurely marking time, maintaining low profile, avoiding controversy, shoring up obsolescent structures, talking a species of ecclesiastical doublespeak, and rejecting any involvement in the social horrors of the day. Apparently they take lightly the admonition of a witness like Paul: "Bear the burdens of one another, and you will have fulfilled the law (of Christ)."

Implicit in attitudes like these, shockingly pervasive as they are, is a dreadful and ill-defined fear—fear that we're not going to make it; fear that the Church will go down with the Powers of this world; fear of questioning, initiative, creativity, courage; fear of sacrifice, loneliness, criticism; fear finally of self, of neighbor, of Gospel, of Christ. (I remember President Johnson saying, with an off-the-cuff honesty quite foreign to him: "Peace is going to demand more than we counted on!") In the same manner, Catholics are discovering that Christ will demand more than we counted on. And generally, the thought fills them with dread.

The Church in America—in fact, in the West as a whole—has accepted as religion a kind of cultural syncretism, culminating in near-perfect allegiance to the State. Not a few of its more prominent Bishops have even waited upon the Presidency like court jesters. And now the culture is being violently challenged, and the State doesn't so much govern as rule by force. To whom do we turn?

A case in point is the Catholic response to the Indochinese war. It is a classic case of burning incense to Caesar. After twenty-two years' involvement in Indochina (President Truman committed American support to the French in 1949); after millions of Indochinese deaths (6 to 8 might be a conservative estimate); after as many as 100,000 American dead (Pentagon figures are probably half the total); after war expenditures of 300 bil-

lion; after documented ecocide and genocide; after all this, thirty-two American Bishops have finally condemned the immorality of the war. In a tragedy of this magnitude, worldwide in its ramifications, the American Church, supposedly the most vital expression of universal Catholicism, has mustered 32 tepid, episcopal voices, most of them recent. This, despite crushing evidence of the war's illegality—United Nations Charter, Geneva Accords, the SEATO agreement, the U.S. Constitution. Why so long for episcopal word, why so late and feeble? So late, in fact, that few listen and few care.

We have obviously surpassed the German Church in negligence both moral and criminal. (Resistance to Hitler, for example, meant totalitarian reprisal, which is not the case here.) Despite the clarity of Paul VI's stand, despite Constitutional protections, no Bishop has challenged the illegality of the war in serious fashion; no Bishop has broken patently immoral laws (the Apostles were martyred for refusing to obey the law); no Bishop (except Parrilla of Puerto Rico) has advocated nonviolent resistance to the war (Mayor Lindsay of New York City, a nebulous liberal at best, advocated such a course two years ago). And only two or three Bishops have visited Catholic resisters in jail, at least two of them virtually apologizing for their action: "This visit is a spiritual work of mercy, which I would perform for any of my flock." More to the point would be an explanation of why they themselves were not in jail.

Furthermore, no Bishop has questioned the marriage of Big Business and Big Military in Big Government, and how the marriage results in government by and for the wealthy and powerful. No Bishop has condemned the American rape of the developing world, nor the arms race in horror weapons, nor American arms salesmanship, nor the division of the world by superpowers.

On the contrary, the American episcopacy has docilely and silently stood by while their countrymen and spiritual sons established the American empire and ruled it with ruthless might. They stood by as spectator, or advocate, while their country plunged into perpetual hot and cold warring, spent 1 ¼ trillion dollars on war and weapons since 1946, and filled up Arlington Cemetery with the dead of Korea, the Dominican Republic, and Indochina.

And yet, the Church they lead, like the Savior, is come "to give life, and to give it more abundantly." What a gross irony!

Do I exaggerate? Perhaps. Some Catholics, who have suffered for dedication to Gospel and Church, would go much further, however. One layman I know, a superb student of Gospel politics and Gandhian nonviolence, currently in jail, would say this with a snort: "Shepherds? There is not one in the American Church! They are upper-management people for the most part. And they are the State's sheep!" Of him, I must say that he is capable of transcending mediocrity. He remains loyal in a sense that most Catholics and most Bishops cannot understand.

Perhaps in the above you might perceive my difficulty in speculating about the priesthood, and how it might serve man as physician and prophet. For who will finally legislate as to training, experience, freedom? And who will provide what is most crucial of all—example? The men and women who can address the subject realistically are concerned mainly with witnessing against institutionalized terror and death—and they are in severe jeopardy or in jail.

Moreover, there is this factor to consider. If Dan and I can serve as examples of repression by the Church—for nearly ten years now we have engaged in a constant, painful, running skirmish with Church authority, encountering ridicule, outrage, exile, reassignment, mistrust—the scales have, nevertheless, slowly balanced out. Today the episcopacy tolerates us, under the jurisdiction of the State. But episcopal hypocrisy has cut very deeply. Catholics who are today developing for themselves and their brothers "the freedom with which Christ has made us free," are extremely skeptical of Papal or episcopal pronouncements. They even tend to ignore them as shallow and devious. They want the pronouncement of action, feeling that it is very late for words.

In effect, thinking Catholics make little distinction between treatment by Church and State. They know that both desire malleability and conformity, that both fear conscience, that both are self-righteous and dogmatic, that both are ruthless in handling deviants. To be fair, the Church is quicker to forgive and to forget. On the other hand, the State may be quicker to learn. But the point is that Catholics increasingly tend to ignore the official Church since it says so little real about the questions of life and death, and lives less than it says. How could it be otherwise? they ask. The official Church is not about the Gospel, or the plight of what Pope John called "the majority of men." Therefore, how can it speak to either issue?

The understanding from this quarter is simply this: both Church and State are vast, sprawling bureaucracies which share an insufferably arrogant assumption that *they* offer the fundamental answers to the human condition. The understanding, further, is that, despite claims to the contrary, Church and State have brought Western civilization to its nadir, and have destroyed other civilizations in the process.

Critics have learned, or are learning in swelling numbers from history as well as from the Gospels, that nothing much makes sense except death to self and conversion to Christ and neighbor. All the virtues exemplified by the Lord—poverty, freedom in responsibility, the politics of community, willingness to risk jail and death for the exploited person—all these attack head-on the conceptions and realities of bureaucracies whether in Church or State. The goals of bureaucracies are simply not the goals of Christ.

To apply all this seriously to contemporary problems of priesthood—especially as an American—is enormously difficult, simply because we are so cut off from the mind and life of Christ. About all one can do is fumble with a few critical questions, and then labor with the complications of response.

The Catholic priest in America—and in the West generally—is more of a cultural phenomenon than he is a Gospel man. He is a nationalistic, white supremacist, and uncritical toward affluence and its source. His training reflects nuances of these cultural fixations, but, beyond that, it schools him merely in neutrality toward life. By that I mean, he tends to take a purely institutional view of threats to life, whether they be its abuse or destruction. Indeed, if he is sensitive, he will go through immense convolutions to escape such brutalities. Or if he is hardened, he will advocate them, or remain casual in face of them.

Therefore the problem becomes—how to instill

convictions strong enough to resist dehumanization, in oneself, in others, in structures. How to instruct him in nonviolence as a way of life, as mark of the new man, as instrument of human revolution and social regeneration? How to teach him the realities of power in all its nuances, from the will to dominate others to the will to exploit whole nations and peoples? How to toughen him so that one will understand and accept persecution, contempt, ostracism, jail or death on account of conscience and (above all) on account of the suffering brother? How to infuse him with such sensitivity to human rights and dignity that one will confront violence in every turn of his life—in himself, in the culture, in the State? How to convince him that Christ's man must integrate word and act, in full recognition that this might lead him to death, even as it did his Lord?

I don't know, because one can neither teach the above nor administer it. But the Church can beg the grace of God, the Church can provide the setting; even though it be modern catacombs, the Church can begin, realizing that her life must always constitute beginnings, and never endings. And if such fidelity means a vocation of opposition to Powers and Principalities as they operate in government and in the circle of prestige for which the government exists, so be it. If it means the outlawry of the Church, persecution … the Lord spoke of that too: "The time will come when those who kill you will think they are doing a service to God." But in the process, the Church would serve humanity, would even help to give humanity a future on this planet which it could not otherwise have.

As for the impending deliberations on world justice and peace, I have anguished questions about them. Do the American Bishops accept the implications of their country's control over one-half the world's productive capacity and finance? Do they realize that, despite our affluence, we have insti-

tutionalized poverty for perhaps one-quarter of our own people, plus millions in the developing world? Will they admit that these appalling realities are not an accident, but a cold calculation, that they follow the logic of profit and policy? Can they comprehend that war, particularly modern war, decides what nation or "security bloc" will control the profits, and that on the success or failure of the Indochinese war hinges the American Open Door policy to the developing world? (Policymakers fear that if the Indochinese force us out, certainty will spread among the world's poor that wars of liberation can succeed.) Do they understand that a few hundred American corporations, with hundreds of billions in assets and international holdings, are empires in their own right, exerting political and economic dominion wherever they are? To deliberate justice and peace while overlooking such realities is both ignorant and dishonest. Just as it is dishonest to deny that while most men starve, most Bishops live in comfort and affluence, welcome the dividends of offending corporations, and remain discreetly silent before the excesses of capitalism.

In closing, I hope and pray this letter is a source of help to you, and not a cause for pain and shock. You are an unusual man and Christian—intelligent, open, compassionate. Obviously you love the Church as I do. But before the tragedy and ruin of the times we must love the Church even more—enough to criticize honestly and charitably, enough to pick up heavier burdens, enough to lose everything in order that others might discover life. In essence, what would the wretched of the earth have us do to offer them hope, to lift from them the horror of war and starvation, to extend a sense of dignity and destiny in God and human community?

Our prayers go with you. And our wishes for the light, the strength, the peace of Christ.

Fraternally,
Philip Berrigan, S.S.J.

90. Dom Helder Camara

Dom Helder Camara (1909-1999) was the Roman Catholic Archbishop of Olinda and Recife, an outspoken advocate for the poor, and a sharp critic of the military dictatorship in Brazil, even in the face of numerous threats to his life. While conservative interests in the church and the state opposed him in public and private, Pope Paul VI offered Camara his personal support. Camara earned an international following among those attracted to his writings on peace and justice, and below is his landmark analysis of violence from a book titled Spiral of Violence *(1970)—an analysis that has since been used countless times by Christian theologians and ethicists. Following Camara's reflections on the spiral of violence is a section on the limitations of violence.*

Spiral of Violence

1. Looking at the Earth

How easy it is to find injustices everywhere; injustices of varying nature and varying degree, but injustices for all that.

In the underdeveloped countries these injustices—which are perhaps unknown elsewhere—affect millions of human beings, children of God, reducing them to a subhuman condition.

But what exactly do we mean by a "subhuman condition"? Isn't it perhaps too strong a term, too tinged with demagogy? Not at all. There exists very often what could be called a heritage of poverty. It is common knowledge that poverty kills just as surely as the most bloody war. But poverty does more than kill, it leads to physical deformity (just think of Biafra), to psychological deformity (there are many cases of mental subnormality for which hunger is responsible), and to moral deformity (those who, through a situation of slavery, hidden but nonetheless real, are living without prospects and without hope, foundering in fatalism and reduced to a begging mentality).

But we must be careful! Injustices are not the monopoly of the underdeveloped countries. They exist in the developed countries too, just as much on the capitalist side as on the socialist....

At the moment the developed world is proud and self-confident, with its nuclear bombs, and thinks it can afford to laugh at that giant with feet of clay, the underdeveloped world. But do the masters of the H-bomb really grasp the scope and consequences of the poverty bomb?

This is the situation of humanity at the beginning of the second development decade. If true development implies the development of *the whole man and of all men,* then there is not in fact a single truly developed country in the world.

But there is another unavoidable conclusion which is still more serious, a conclusion we must draw attention to because of its tragic consequences, and it is this. Look closely at the injustices in the underdeveloped countries, in the relations between the developed world and the underdeveloped world. You will find that everywhere the injustices are a form of violence. One can and must say that they are everywhere the basic violence, violence no. 1.

2. Violence Attracts Violence

No one is born to be a slave. No one seeks to suffer injustices, humiliations and restrictions. A human being condemned to a subhuman condition is like an animal—an ox or a donkey—wallowing in the mud.

Now the egoism of some privileged groups drives countless human beings into this subhuman condition, where they suffer restrictions, humiliations, injustices; without prospects, without hope, their condition is that of slaves.

This established violence, this violence No. 1, attracts violence No. 2, revolt, either of the oppressed themselves or of youth, firmly resolved to battle for a more just and human world.

Certainly there are, from continent to continent, from country to country, from city to city, variations, differences, degrees, nuances, in violence No. 2, but generally in the world today the oppressed are opening their eyes.

The authorities and the privileged are alarmed by the presence of agents coming from outside whom they call "subversive elements," "agitators," "communists."

Sometimes they are indeed people committed to an ideology of the extreme left who are fighting for the liberation of the oppressed and have opted for armed violence. At other times they are people moved by religious feeling, who can no longer tolerate religion interpreted and lived as an opium for the masses, as an alien and alienating force, but want to see it at the service of the human development of those who are imprisoned in a subhuman condition....

In those places where the oppressed masses have an opportunity for direct action they engage in more or less thoroughgoing, bitter and prolonged agitation. When the masses have fallen into a kind of fatalism for lack of hope, or when a too violent reaction cows them for an instant, then it is the young who rise.

The young no longer have the patience to wait for the privileged to discard their privileges. The young very often see governments too tied to the privileged classes. The young are losing confidence in the churches, which affirm beautiful principles—great texts, remarkable conclusions—but without ever deciding, at least so far, to translate them into real life.

The young then are turning more and more to radical action and violence.

In some places the young are the force of idealism, fire, hunger for justice, thirst for authenticity. In others, with the same enthusiasm, they adopt extremist ideologies and prepare for "guerilla warfare" in town or country.

If there is some corner of the world which has remained peaceful, but with a peace based on injustices—the peace of a swamp with rotten matter fermenting in its depths—we may be sure that that peace is false. Violence attracts violence. Let us repeat fearlessly and ceaselessly: injustices bring revolt, either from the oppressed or from the young, determined to fight for a more just and more human world.

3. And Then Comes Repression

When conflict comes out into the streets, when violence No. 2 tries to resist violence No. 1, the authorities consider themselves obliged to preserve or reestablish public order, even if this means using force; this is violence No. 3. Sometimes they go even further, and this is becoming increasingly common: in order to obtain information, which may indeed be important to public security, the logic of violence leads them to use moral and physical torture—as though any information extracted through torture deserved the slightest attention! ...

Let us have the honesty to admit, in the light of the past and, perhaps, here and there, in the light of some typical reactions, that violence No. 3—governmental repression, under the pretext of safeguarding public order, national security, the free world—is not a monopoly of the underdeveloped countries.

There is not a country in the world which is in no danger of falling into the throes of violence....

****

The Limitations of Violence

Allow me the humble courage of taking a stand: I respect those who have felt obliged in conscience to opt for violence, not the facile violence of armchair-guerillas, but that of the men who have proved their sincerity by the sacrifice of their lives. It seems to me the memory of Camilo Torres and Che Guevara deserves as much respect as that of Dr. Martin Luther King. I accuse the real abettors of violence, all those on the right or on the left who wrong justice and prevent peace.

My personal vocation is to be a pilgrim of peace, following the example of Paul VI. Personally I would prefer a thousand times more to be killed than to kill anyone.

This personal position is founded on the Gospel.... We need only to turn to the Beatitudes—the quintessence of the Gospel message—to see that the option for Christians is clear. We, as Christians, are on the side of nonviolence, and this is in no way an option for weakness and passivity. Opting for nonviolence means to believe more strongly in the power of truth, justice, and love than in the power of wars, weapons, and hatred.

Let me tell you why I have no faith in violence. I have two reasons. As I constantly repeat, I am quite aware that already, in Latin America, violence is established. Because, if a quite small minority exists whose wealth is based on the misery of a great number, that is already violence. But if we caused a war of liberation to explode, it would immediately be crushed by the imperialistic powers. Powers, in the plural. The United States cannot accept a second Cuba in Latin America, its sphere of influence. And Soviet Russia would obviously come immediately. And Red China and Cuba.

Ever since the small attempts at revolution in Bolivia and Colombia, there are military bases everywhere in Latin America, capable of crushing every sort of guerilla warfare. The strength of the guerilla fighters was in training their men in regions where modern armaments are completely meaningless. But today, at the anti-guerilla bases, soldiers are being trained precisely for those infernos, those inaccessible regions. I was in Colombia and I saw, in regions that were formerly the domain of the guerilleros, an anti-guerilla base where, for example, the soldiers let themselves be bitten by snakes in order to be vaccinated and prepared for no matter what test.

That is my first reason. I have no interest at all in causing a war to break out, even a war of liberation, if I am convinced that it would be immediately crushed.

And I have another reason. The revolution will not be fought either by the students or the priests or the artists or the intellectuals; it will be fought by the masses, the oppressed, and they will be the victims of that repressive action of the powers.

I am in direct contact with the masses, and I know that underdevelopment, both physical and material, unfortunately carries with it a spiritual underdevelopment. There is a discouragement, a lack of reasons for living, a fatalism. Why die? Very often in Latin America the masses have risen in revolt only to die and cause others to die. But they know all too well that the great of the world may change among themselves, but as for the oppressed, they always remain sunk in misery. They have no real reasons to live.

It seems to me that in the next ten or fifteen years there will really be no possibility of mobilizing the masses for a war of liberation.

I respect and shall always respect those who, with a clear conscience, have chosen or choose or will choose violence. I do not respect the drawing room guerrilleros, but the real ones. Yes, I respect them. But since they recognize that there are no real chances for violence in the next ten or fifteen years, I tell them, "Then give me that time. I am going to do an experiment."

I think Camilo Torres was one of many young priests and laymen who lost faith, not in Christ, but in the institutional church, when they saw all the fine resolutions of the Vatican Council trapped by human weakness and ecclesiastical prudence. Like others, Camilo Torres believed that the only way he could really help to liberate his people was through guerilla warfare, and he chose to join a Communist underground group. I also think that the Colombian Communists took advantage of Torres's reputation and deliberately sent him on a mission where he was likely to be killed. For them the end justified the means. The end was to make known and to popularize the existence of the guerilla movement. The means was to have a celebrated martyr.

Camilo Torres died, and neither the young people nor the workers of Colombia came forward to help the guerillas. Our Colombian brethren were very frustrated.

But you see it was like Che Guevara's failure in Bolivia. Che Guevara had a natural genius for guerilla warfare, and he had seen its effects in Cuba. But his mistake was to forget that a mass of people is not the same as a united people. A mass only becomes a united people after a long and difficult campaign during which the people are gradually and quietly made more aware. The majority of Bolivians, like nearly all Latin Americans, were living in subhuman conditions; but since they had no reason for living they also had no reason for dying. The Bolivian peasants welcomed Che Guevara and his men because they were armed. But afterward, when the government soldiers came, they welcomed them as well and told them everything they knew about the guerillas and their hiding places.

All of this only made me more and more certain that liberation could never be achieved through armed struggle.

PART VIII
Late Twentieth Century
(1975-2000)

91. SHELLEY DOUGLASS

Nonviolence and Feminism

Like her husband, Jim, Shelley Douglass (b. 1944) is a longtime Catholic peacemaker who helped to found the Ground Zero Center for Nonviolent Action in 1975. This group led public protests against the construction of a Trident missile nuclear submarine base in Washington, as well as other anti-nuclear weapons protests. Douglass later joined Jim in founding Mary's House, a Catholic Worker hospitality house that cares for the poor and ill in Birmingham, Alabama. She is a former chair of the national council of the Fellowship of Reconciliation and has been arrested numerous times for protesting violence. Below is her 1975 article titled "Nonviolence and Feminism."

There was a great controversy among antislavery radicals in the 1850s over the "woman question." Women formed a large part of the strength of abolitionist sentiment, supplied many of the most vocal leaders. But women themselves were nonpersons oppressed and subject to ridicule when, infrequently, they took a public stand. Many women saw their cause as bound up with the abolitionist cause: equality for all people, men and women. The reaction of the movement of that time was to tell the women to wait. It was not yet their turn to be heard; by pushing their untimely issue they would likely deprive the black man of his base of support.

Women were not important. For women who have come through the civil rights and peace movements over the last fifteen years, there is a kind of ironic familiarity in reading the history of the abolitionist/feminist debate. We've heard the same arguments in our own time!

My experience as a woman in the movement is fairly typical, I think. Since my early college years in 1962, I've been progressively more involved with the movement, living and working as part of it. Our experience as women has been one of awakening to a reality that was often harsh: we were welcomed into the movement in lower-echelon positions, as somebody's woman, girl, old lady, wife, as sex objects, as workhorses. Women were expected to make coffee and provide refreshments while men planned strategy and did resistance actions. Women kept the home-fires burning while men organized, acted, and went to jail. Women bore and raised children and created the homes to which the men returned. Women did leaflets in the thousands, typed letters, licked stamps, marched in demonstrations. We rarely spoke at demonstrations; our actions did not make us celebrities like the men. When women went to jail, they lacked strong community support. They had no knowledge, by and large, of their historic role in the peace movement. With a few exceptions (Dorothy Day, for example), women lost contact with the contributions of others like ourselves.

The reasons for this were many. At the time, most of us believed in women's place, too. We thought we were appointed to certain functions, and that if we were worthy we would eventually become equal. Those times took a heavy toll. In most cities there are women who have been in the peace movement for years. They have been the backbone of the movement, keeping things going when everyone else was too busy or too discouraged. Because they were women, they had the time for peace work; but because they were women, they were never taken seriously. Miraculously, some of these women were strong enough, well-balanced enough, to cope with the pressures and go on. Others, who should not be forgotten, women with good minds and great concern, cracked or warped under the pressure. They are now the proverbial "little old ladies in tennis shoes"; they could have been matriarchs of the movement. Yet this tragic waste of potential and unconscious dehumanization took place in a movement that only wanted the common good.

During the late 1960s women began to share some of their private problems and their maladjustments to the system in which they lived. We realized that our feelings were not just personal problems; they were political, the results of a system that exploited us all. We were not unique; this oppressive mentality pervaded even the movement itself. Insofar as it was patriarchal, the movement was simply part of the system. When this realization hit home, it was an extremely difficult time for many people in the movement. Attempts to share insights with male companions were met (understandably) with fierce resistance. There was a slow groping toward trust among sisters and disillusion with a movement that fought for other people's freedom while standing upon our backs. There was the shuddering realization of our victimization, our status as sex objects. Even worse was the knowledge that we had believed the lie and the rage we felt at again being pushed aside for another, "more important" issue. There was the growing problem of how to deal with oppression within the movement for liberation. How do we resist the resister? For many of us, the answer was simply to break contact, to work only with women on peace or women's issues. For others (less angry? less independent? more hopeful?) there seemed a chance that the peace movement could become a real movement for peace in all its meanings. We have stayed on.

As women concerned with feminism, we still find hostility, lack of comprehension, even ridicule, within the ranks. We also find more understanding, more honesty, more willingness to face the issue. In ourselves, we find the experience of being women a good one, joyful and strong. We are reclaiming our history—remembering all those founding mothers, all those women who kept the movement going without credit for so long, all the contributions we women have made and undervalued. The experience of being a woman is still one of isolation, frustration, anger. It is also one of confidence, strength, support, and pride. We are; we are becoming. I think we often feel impatient with those who lag behind, who don't see the problems or the possibilities. Not rage, just impatience. Women are strong; women will move forward; women have a crucial insight and a life-giving contribution to make.

Having sounded an optimistic note on women's position and contribution to the movement, I would qualify it. With the end of the Vietnam War and the widespread acceptance of the principle of equality for women, both the peace movement and the women's movement face crucial decisions. The peace movement cannot survive or hope for revolution without joining the women's movement—partly because there is no peace and justice to be built upon the backs of any people, partly because the insights of the feminist movement are necessary to the formation of a new, organic worldview, a basis for thought and action which will be more complete and profound, because more inclusive, than any we've had before. Feminist insights into the nature of God, of humankind, of violence and nonviolence, oppression and resistance, and into a whole life are the life-giving gift of women.

However, there are crucial questions also to be raised from the other side. For years we've asked the Catholic church: "How come you're so upset about abortion but say nothing about Vietnam?" As Dan Berrigan has pointed out, that question can legitimately be turned back upon us. We have been concerned about Vietnam, but what about abortion? Simplistic answers—abortion is anti-life, therefore it's wrong; or, women must control their own bodies, therefore it's necessary—are not enough. There must be a way to take seriously the societal changes, and all the female agony, the male refusal of responsibility, the pain of poverty or of being stretched too thin. No position on abortion is realistic if it does not take these into consideration. The basic question for both movements now is this: Do we want to keep trying to improve a system by disregarding human rights and the sacredness of life, or do we want to struggle to bring to birth a truly new world community in which both war and abortion are unnecessary and unthinkable? Insofar as the peace movement remains patriarchal, it is part of the system of oppression. Insofar as the women's movement accepts the brutal methods and rewards the current patriarchal society, it joins the oppressors of all peoples. I believe that the insights of feminism and of the nonviolent resistance movement can come together, painfully and honestly, to create a new, organic, human vision. Neither is complete without the other. With both together, we may be able to survive as a world.

92. RICHARD MCSORLEY

It's a Sin to Build a Nuclear Weapon

Richard McSorley (1914-2002) experienced torture at the hands of Japanese soldiers in World War II, an event that no doubt crystallized his life work for peace and justice. After the war, McSorley became a Jesuit priest, marched for civil rights with Martin Luther King, Jr., and eventually landed a teaching spot at Georgetown University, where he founded the school's peace center. McSorley also helped to establish Pax Christi USA, the national Catholic peace movement, in the early 1970s. He was a veteran opponent of the Vietnam War by the time Pax Christi USA came into existence, and he later helped guide the peace movement into campaigns against nuclear weapons. The force of his activism was matched only by the power of his numerous writings on peace and war, and below is his most famous work—a 1976 reflection titled "It's a Sin to Build a Nuclear Weapon."

Does God approve of our intent to use nuclear weapons?

No, I don't believe so. Moreover, I do not believe God approves of even the possession of nuclear weapons.

The danger of world suicide through nuclear war "compels us to undertake an evaluation of war with an entirely new attitude," Vatican II said. Einstein put it this way: "When we released the energy from the atom, everything changed except our way of thinking. Because of that we drift towards unparalleled disaster." Something of what Einstein meant is this: We still look upon war as a conflict between two armies. The armies try to break through each other's front line to reach the civilian population. When they do, the suffering is so great that the war is ended. However, war with nuclear weapons will reach the civilian immediately. Nuclear missiles take only twenty-four minutes to travel between Moscow and Washington. Both the speed and total penetrability are so different from war in the past that the word "war" should not be used. Something like "mutual suicide," "Doomsday," or "Apocalypse" would be more accurate.

What can a nuclear weapon do? In his book, *Nuclear Disaster*, Dr. Tom Stonier of Manhattan College describes what would happen if a 20-megaton nuclear weapon was detonated in the center of New York City.

The first result would be death: Ten times as many deaths as all the battle deaths that occurred in all the wars of US history—from the Revolution up to and including the 55,000 battle deaths in the Vietnam War. Seven million people would die from blast, firestorm, and radiation. The blast would cover a radius of ten miles. It would dig a crater 650 feet deep and a mile and a half across, even if it was dropped in solid rock. All living things, even in the subways, would die. Trucks and automobiles would be hurled about like giant Molotov cocktails spewing gasoline and fire. Most of the victims would be killed by falling buildings.

As the shock front moved out to its ten-mile radius, the huge vacuum at its center would begin to draw the winds back at speeds up to 125 miles per hour. A house or tree caught in this double pressure would be blasted from both sides.

Above the blast a ball of fire would form. This fireball, four miles wide, would swiftly rise to a height of about 20,000 feet. At its center the heat would be eight times hotter than the sun, its heat so intense that the unexposed human body forty miles away would receive second-degree burns; 250 miles away, as far as Washington, D.C., many people would suffer severe eye damage.

Within a thirty-nine mile radius a sea of fire would roll and boil fanned by the winds of the shock wave. Asphalt, which we do not generally consider combustible, would pass its combustion point of 800 degrees and burn.

From the huge cavern dug by the blast, vaporized material pulled up into the air by the fireball would form a radioactive cloud of death. This cloud would blow with the wind over Connecticut towards Hyannisport and out to the ocean. The cigar-shaped cloud would grow until it covered an area of 4800 square miles. At the center the radiation intensity would be measured at about 2300 roentgen units. One roentgen unit is severe enough to damage a primate cell. Four hundred roentgen units are fifty percent lethal. The lethal capacity of this radiation would decrease as it got farther from New York. What would a person need for protection from radiation? A shelter enclosed on all sides by two feet of concrete or three feet of earth with its own oxygen, food, and water supply for at least ninety-six hours, perhaps twelve days. At the end of ten months there would be still a dosage of 100 roentgen units over most of the area.

This is not imaginary. It is carefully deduced from scales made through US testing and through measurements from the Hiroshima and Nagasaki bombings.

How many bombs do we really need? If it were not sinful to make a nuclear weapon, how many could we get by with? Between 200 and 400 megatons delivered on an enemy would be enough to destroy the possible enemy as a viable society. Former Secretary of Defense Robert McNamara once argued this before Congress. No one has contested his figures. Delivery of twenty to 400 megatons would destroy seventy-five percent of the industrial capacity of the Soviet Union or any other collection of enemies.

The Soviet Union has roughly 200 cities with a population over 100,000. A bomb or two delivered on these cities would destroy them. McNamara's argument was that we won't need any more than 200 to 400 weapons delivered on target. He was trying to show the Congress and the country that beyond that amount we are not dealing with deterrence but overkill.

How many nuclear weapons do we have in our stockpile today? We have over 30,000 nuclear weapons—8,000 large (strategic) weapons and 22,000 smaller (tactical) weapons. We are making one new nuclear weapon every eight hours. We have enough weapons in our arsenal to deliver over 615,000 Hiroshima bombs. We can destroy every Soviet city of 100,000 or more forty-five times over. The Soviet Union can destroy every American city of 100,000 or more thirteen times over.

Can the use of these weapons be reconciled with the Gospel? Can even their existence be reconciled with the command "Love your enemies"? The United States policy is that we will retaliate with massive nuclear destruction if we are attacked. This is the very heart of our nuclear-deterrence policy. This is what we mean by deterrence. Is there any way that the Christian conscience can accept this policy of nuclear deterrence?

There are only two ways in which Christians have tried to reconcile war with the Gospel. One is the way practiced by the Christians in the first three centuries. During the first three centuries Christians considered joining the army incompatible with the following of Christ. The other is the just/unjust-war theory of St. Augustine of the fourth century. This theory holds among other conditions that in any war there be a proportionality between the evil done and the good to be hoped for, and that there be no direct killing of the innocent. Have we in the nuclear-war age reached the point where we finally must say that war is incompatible with the Christian conscience? Can we imagine Jesus pushing the button that would release nuclear weapons on millions of people? Vatican II says that military personnel who refuse orders of this kind are worthy of the highest commendation. Vatican II calls the arms race a trap in which humanity is caught. Vatican II points out that the massive outlay of money for the weapons of death ensures the hunger and deprivation of the masses of poor of the world. Vatican II condemns the use of weapons that destroy whole areas with all their people. Nuclear weapons will do all these things.

Can we go along with the intent to use nuclear weapons? What it is wrong to do, it is wrong to intend to do. If it is wrong for me to kill you, it is wrong for me to plan to do it. If I get my gun and go to your house to retaliate for a wrong done me, then find there are police guarding your house, I have already committed murder in my heart. I have intended it.

Likewise, if I intend to use nuclear weapons in massive retaliation, I have already committed massive murder in my heart.

The taproot of violence in our society today is our intent to use nuclear weapons. Once we have agreed to that, all other evil is minor by comparison. Until we have agreed to that, all other evil is minor by comparison. Until we squarely face the question of our consent to use nuclear weapons, any hope of large-scale improvement of public morality is doomed to failure. Even the possession of weapons which cannot be morally used is wrong. They are a threat to peace and might even be the cause of nuclear war. Human history shows that every weapon possessed is finally used. Since use of nuclear weapons is sinful, and possession leads to use, possession itself is sinful. Just as possession of alcohol is wrong for an alcoholic, and possession of drugs is wrong for a drug addict, so possession of morally unusable weapons is wrong for a government addicted to using weapons. The nuclear weapons of communists may destroy our bodies. But our intent to use nuclear weapons destroys our souls. Our possession of them is a proximate occasion for sin.

Technology in the nuclear age teaches us what we should have learned from our faith. As John Kennedy said at the United Nations in 1962: "Because of the nuclear sword of Damocles that hangs over us, we must cooperate together on this planet, or perish together in its flames through the weapons of our own hands."

93. OSCAR ROMERO

Last Sunday Sermon

Oscar Romero (1917-1980) served as a conservative priest and bishop in El Salvador before experiencing a conversion to the cause of the poor and the oppressed. His conversion took place soon after his appointment as Archbishop of San Salvador in 1977 and, more particularly, when his friend and fellow priest Rutilio Grande was assassinated as a result of his advocacy for the rights of peasant farmers. Deeply moved by Grande's martyrdom, Romero began to speak out against the injustices in El Salvador and the brutal violations of human rights perpetrated by the military government. In 1980 Romero called on the U.S. government to cut off support to the government. In his last Sunday sermon, reprinted below, he pleaded with members of the military to cease their repression. He was assassinated the next day, on March 24, 1980, while celebrating Mass.

Let no one be offended because we use the divine words read at our mass to shed light on the social, political and economic situation of our people. Not to do so would be unchristian. Christ desires to unite himself with humanity, so that the light he brings from God might become life for nations and individuals.

I know many are shocked by this preaching and want to accuse us of forsaking the gospel for politics. But I reject this accusation. I am trying to bring to life the message of the Second Vatican Council and the meetings at Medellin and Puebla. The documents from these meetings should not just be studied theoretically. They should be brought to life and translated into the real struggle to preach the gospel as it should be for our people. Each week I go about the country listening to the cries of the people, their pain from so much crime, and the ignominy of so much violence. Each week I ask the Lord to give me the right words to console, to denounce, to call for repentance. And even though I may be a voice crying in the desert, I know that the church is making the effort to fulfill its mission....

Every country lives its own "exodus"; today El Salvador is living its own exodus. Today we are passing to our liberation through a desert strewn with bodies and where anguish and pain are devastating us. Many suffer the temptation of those who walked with Moses and wanted to turn back and did not work together. It is the same old story. God, however, wants to save the people by making a new history ....

History will not fail; God sustains it. That is why I say that insofar as historical projects attempt to reflect the eternal plan of God, to that extent they reflect the kingdom of God. This attempt is the work of the church. Because of this, the church, the people of God in history, is not attached to any one social system, to any political organization,

to any party. The church does not identify herself with any of those forces because she is the eternal pilgrim of history and is indicating at every historical moment what reflects the kingdom of God and what does not reflect the kingdom of God. She is the servant of the kingdom of God.

The great task of Christians must be to absorb the spirit of God's kingdom and, with souls filled with the kingdom of God, to work on the projects of history. It's fine to be organized in popular groups; it's all right to form political parties; it's all right to take part in the government. It's fine as long as you are a Christian who carries the reflection of the kingdom of God and tries to establish it where you are working, and as long as you are not being used to further worldly ambitions. This is the great duty of the people of today. My dear Christians, I have always told you, and I will repeat, that the true liberators of our people must come from us Christians, from the people of God. Any historical plan that's not based on what we spoke of in the first point—the dignity of the human being, the love of God, the kingdom of Christ among people—will be a fleeting project. Your project, however, will grow in stability the more it reflects the eternal design of God. It will be a solution of the common good of the people every time, if it meets the needs of the people .... Now I invite you to look at things through the eyes of the church, which is trying to be the kingdom of God on earth and so often must illuminate the realities of our national situation.

We have lived through a tremendously tragic week. I could not give you the facts before, but a week ago last Saturday, on 15 March, one of the largest and most distressing military operations was carried out in the countryside. The villages affected were La Laguna, Plan de Ocotes and El Rosario. The operation brought tragedy: a lot of ranches were burned, there was looting, and—

inevitably—people were killed. In La Laguna, the attackers killed a married couple, Ernesto Navas and Audelia Mejia de Navas, their little children, Martin and Hilda, thirteen and seven years old, and eleven more peasants.

Other deaths have been reported, but we do not know the names of the dead. In Plan de Ocotes, two children and four peasants were killed, including two women. In El Rosario, three more peasants were killed. That was last Saturday.

Last Sunday, the following were assassinated in Arcatao by four members of ORDEN: peasants Marcelino Serrano, Vincente Ayala, twenty-four years old, and his son, Freddy. That same day, Fernando Hernandez Navarro, a peasant, was assassinated in Galera de Jutiapa, when he fled from the military.

Last Monday, 17 March, was a tremendously violent day. Bombs exploded in the capital as well as in the interior of the country. The damage was very substantial at the headquarters of the Ministry of Agriculture. The campus of the national university was under armed siege from dawn until 7 P.M. Throughout the day, constant bursts of machine-gun fire were heard in the university area. The archbishop's office intervened to protect people who found themselves caught inside.

On the Hacienda Colima, eighteen persons died, at least fifteen of whom were peasants. The administrator and the grocer of the ranch also died. The armed forces confirmed that there was a confrontation. A film of the events appeared on TV, and many analyzed interesting aspects of the situation.

At least fifty people died in serious incidents that day: in the capital, seven persons died in events at the Colonia Santa Lucia; on the outskirts of Tecnillantas, five people died; and in the area of the rubbish dump, after the evacuation of the site by the military, were found the bodies of four workers who had been captured in that action.

Sixteen peasants died in the village of Montepeque, thirty-eight kilometers along the road to Suchitoto. That same day, two students at the University of Central America were captured in Tecnillantas: Mario Nelson and Miguel Alberto Rodriguez Velado, who were brothers. The first one, after four days of illegal detention, was handed over to the courts. Not so his brother, who was wounded and is still held in illegal detention. Legal Aid is intervening on his behalf.

Amnesty International issued a press release in which it described the repression of the peasants, especially in the area of Chalatenango. The week's events confirm this report in spite of the fact the government denies it. As I entered the church, I was given a cable that says, "Amnesty International confirmed today [that was yesterday] that in El Salvador human rights are violated to extremes that have not been seen in other countries." That is what Patricio Fuentes (spokesman for the urgent action section for Central America in Swedish Amnesty International) said at a press conference in Managua, Nicaragua.

Fuentes confirmed that, during two weeks of investigations he carried out in El Salvador, he was able to establish that there had been eighty-three political assassinations between 10 and 14 March. He pointed out that Amnesty International recently condemned the government of El Salvador, alleging that it was responsible for six hundred political assassinations. The Salvadoran government defended itself against the charges, arguing that Amnesty International based its condemnation on unproved assumptions.

Fuentes said that Amnesty had established that in El Salvador human rights are violated to a worse degree than the repression in Chile after the coup d'état. The Salvadoran government also said that the six hundred dead were the result of armed confrontations between army troops and guerrillas. Fuentes said that during his stay in El Salvador, he could see that the victims had been tortured before their deaths and mutilated afterward.

The spokesman of Amnesty International said that the victims' bodies characteristically appeared with the thumbs tied behind their backs. Corrosive liquids had been applied to the corpses to prevent identification of the victims by their relatives and to prevent international condemnation, the spokesman added. Nevertheless, the bodies were exhumed and the dead have been identified. Fuentes said that the repression carried out by the Salvadoran army was aimed at breaking the popular organizations through the assassination of their leaders in both town and country.

According to the spokesman of Amnesty International, at least three thousand five hundred peasants have fled from their homes to the capital to escape persecution. "We have complete lists in London and Sweden of young children and women who have been assassinated for being organized," Fuentes stated ....

I would like to make a special appeal to the men of the army, and specifically to the ranks of the National Guard, the police and the military. Brothers, you come from our own people. You are killing your own brother peasants when any human order to kill must be subordinate to the law of God which says, "Thou shalt not kill." No soldier is obliged to obey an order contrary to the law of God. No one has to obey an immoral law. It is high time you recovered your consciences and obeyed your consciences rather than a sinful order. The church, the defender of the rights of God, of the law of God, of human dignity, of the person, cannot remain silent before such an abomination. We want the government to face the fact that reforms are valueless if they are to be carried out at the cost of so much blood. In the name of God, in the name of this suffering people whose cries rise to heaven more loudly each day, I implore you, I beg you, I order you in the name of God: stop the repression!

The church preaches your liberation just as we have studied it in the holy Bible today. It is a liberation that has, above all else, respect for the dignity of the person, hope for humanity's common good, and the transcendence that looks before all to God and only from God derives its hope and its strength.

94. DANIEL BERRIGAN

We Could Not Not Do This

On September 9, 1980, Daniel Berrigan (b. 1921), his brother Philip, and six others—the Plowshares Eight—trespassed on the property of the General Electric Nuclear Missile Reentry Division in King of Prussia, Pennsylvania, where they hammered on the nose cones of Mark 12A nuclear warheads, poured blood on related documents, and prayed aloud for peace. Their bold move sparked the Plowshares movement, with its focus on nuclear disarmament, around the world.

The question of why we did our action takes me back to those years when my conscience was being formed, back to a family that was poor, and to a father and mother who taught, quite simply, by living what they taught. And if I could put their message very shortly, it would go something like this: In a thousand ways they showed that you do what is right because it is right, that your conscience is a matter between you and God, that nobody owns you.

If I have a precious memory of my mother and father that lasts to this day, it is simply that they lived as though nobody owned them. They cheated no one. They worked hard for a living. They were poor, and perhaps most precious of all, they shared what they had. And that was enough, because in the life of a young child, the first steps of conscience are as important as the first steps of one's feet. They set the direction where life will go. And I feel that direction was set for my brothers and myself. There is a direct line between the way my parents turned our steps and this action. That is no crooked line.

That was the first influence. The second has to do with my religious order. When I was eighteen I left home for the Jesuit order. I reflect that I am sixty years old, and I have never been anything but a Jesuit, a Jesuit priest, in my whole life. We have Jesuits throughout Latin America today, my own brothers, who are in prison, who have been under torture; many of them have been murdered. On the walls of our religious communities both here and in Latin America are photos of murdered priests who stood somewhere because they believed in something. Those faces haunt my days. And I ask myself how I can be wishy-washy in the face of such example, example of my own lifetime, my own age.

This is a powerful thing, to be in a common bond of vows with people who have given their lives because they did not believe in mass murder, because such crimes could not go on in their name.

Dear friends of the jury, you have been called the conscience of the community. Each of us eight comes from a community. I don't mean just a biological family, I mean that every one of us has brothers and sisters with whom we live, with whom we pray, with whom we offer the Eucharist, with whom we share income, and, in some cases, the care of children. Our conscience, in other words, comes from somewhere. We have not come from outer space or from chaos or from madhouses to King of Prussia.

We have come from years of prayer, years of life together, years of testing—testing of who we are in the church and in the world. We would like to speak to you, each of us in a different way, about our communities; because, you see, it is our conviction that nobody in the world can form his or her conscience alone.

What are we to do in bad times? I am trying to say that we come as a community of conscience before your community of conscience to ask you: Are our consciences to act differently than yours in regard to the lives and deaths of children? A very simple question, but one that cuts to the bone. We would like you to see that we come from where you come. We come from churches. We come from neighborhoods. We come from years of work. We come from America. And we come to this, a trial of conscience and motive. And the statement of conscience we would like to present to you is this.

We could not *not* do this. We could not not do this! We were pushed to this by all our lives. Do you see what I mean? All our lives.

When I say I could not do this, I mean, among other things that with every cowardly bone in my body I wished I hadn't had to enter the GE plant. I wish I hadn't had to do it. And that has been true every time I have been arrested, all those years. My stomach turns over. I feel sick. I feel afraid. I don't want to go through this again.

I hate jail. I don't do well there physically. But I cannot not go on, because I have learned that we must not kill if we are Christians. I have learned that children, above all, are threatened by these weapons. I have read that Christ our Lord underwent death rather than inflict it. And I am supposed to be a disciple. All kinds of things like that. The push, the push of conscience is a terrible thing.

So at some point your cowardly bones get moving, and you say, "Here it goes again," and you do it. And you have a certain peace because you did it, as I do this morning in speaking with you.

One remains honest because one has a sense, "Well, if I cheat, I'm really giving over my humanity, my conscience." Then we think of these horrible Mark 12A missiles, and something in us says, "We cannot live with such crimes." Or our consciences turn in another direction. And by a thousand pressures, a thousand silences, people begin to say to themselves, "We can live with that. We know it's there. We know what it is for. We know that many thousands will die if only one of these exploded."

And yet we act like those employees, guards, experts we heard speak here; they close their eyes, close their hearts, close their briefcases, take their paychecks—and go home. It's called living with death. And it puts us to death before the missile falls.

We believe, according to the law, the law of the state of Pennsylvania, that we were justified in saying, "We cannot live with that," justified in saying it publicly, saying it dramatically, saying it with blood and hammers, as you have heard; because that weapon, the hundreds and hundreds more being produced in our country, are the greatest evil conceivable on this earth. There is no evil to compare with that. Multiply murder. Multiply desolation. The mind boggles.

So we went into that death factory, and in a modest, self-contained, careful way, we put a few dents in two missiles, awaited arrest, and came willingly into court to talk to you. We believe with all our hearts that our action was justified.

We have never taken actions such as these, perilous, crucial, difficult as they are, without the most careful preparation of our hearts, our motivation, our common sense, our sense of one another. This is simply a rule of our lives; we don't go from the street to do something like the King of Prussia action. We go from prayer. We go from reflection. We go from worship, always. And since we realized that this action was perhaps the most difficult of all our lives, we spent more time in prayer this time than before. We passed three days together in a country place. We prayed, and read the Bible, and shared our fears, shared our second and third thoughts. And in time we drew closer. We were able to say, "Yes, we can do this. We can take the consequences. We can undergo whatever is required." All of that.

During those days we sweated out the question of families and children—the question of a long separation if we were convicted and jailed. I talked openly with Jesuit friends and superiors. They respected my conscience and said, "Do what you are called to." That was the immediate preparation. And what it issued in was a sense that, with great peacefulness, with calm of spirit, even though with a butterfly in our being, we could go ahead and we did.

This enters into my understanding of conscience and justification, a towering question, which has faced so many good people in history, in difficult times, now in the time of the bomb. What helps people? What helps people understand, in difficult times, now, in the time of the bomb? What helps people understand who they are in the world, who they are in their families, who they are with their children, with their work? What helps?

That was a haunting question for me. Will this action be helpful? Legally, we could say that this was our effort to put the question of justification. Will our action help? Will people understand that this "lesser evil," done to this so-called "property," was helping turn things around in the church, in the nation? Will the action help us be more reflective about life and death and children and all life?

We have spent years and years of our adult lives keeping the law. We have tried everything, every access, every means to get to public authorities within the law. We come from within the law, from within.

We are deeply respectful of a law that is in favor of human life. And as we know, at least some of our laws are. We are very respectful of those laws. We

want you to know that. Years and years we spent writing letters, trying to talk to authorities, vigiling in public places, holding candles at night, holding placards by day, trying, trying, fasting, trying to clarify things to ourselves as we were trying to speak to others; all of that within the law, years of it.

And then I had to say, I could not not break the law and remain human. That was what was in jeopardy: what I call my conscience, my humanity, that which is recognizable to children, to friends, to good people, when we say, "There is someone I can trust and love, someone who will not betray."

We spent years within the law, trying to be that kind of person, a non-betrayer. Then we found we couldn't. And if we kept forever on this side of the line, we would die within ourselves. We couldn't look in the mirror, couldn't face those we love, had no Christian message in the world, nothing to say if we went on that way. I might just as well wander off and go the way of a low-grade American case of despair: getting used to the way things are. That is what I mean by dying. That is what we have to oppose. I speak for myself.

The Jesuit order accepted me as a member. The Catholic Church ordained me as a priest. I took all that with great seriousness. I still do, with all my heart. And then Vietnam came along, and then the nukes came along. And I had to continue to ask myself at prayer, with my friends, with my family, with all kinds of people, with my own soul, "Do you have anything to say today?" I mean, beyond a lot of prattling religious talk.

Do you have anything to say about life today, about the lives of people today? Do you have a word, a word of hope to offer, a Christian word? That's a very important question for anyone who takes being a priest, being a Christian, being a human being seriously: "Do you have anything to offer human life today?"

It is a terribly difficult question for me. And I am not at all sure that I do have something to offer. But I did want to say this. I am quite certain that I had September 9, 1980, to say. And I will never deny, whether here or in jail, to my family, or friends, or to the Russians, or the Chinese, or anyone in the world, I will never deny what I did.

More than that. Our act is all I have to say. The only message I have to the world is: We are not allowed to kill innocent people. We are not allowed to be complicit in murder. We are not allowed to be silent while preparations for mass murder proceed in our name, with our money, secretly.

I have nothing else to say to the world. At other times one could talk about family life and divorce and birth control and abortion and many other questions. But this Mark 12A is here. And it renders all other questions null and void. Nothing, nothing can be settled until this is settled. Or this will settle us, once and for all.

It's terrible for me to live in a time where I have nothing to say to human beings except, "Stop killing." There are other beautiful things that I would love to be saying to people. There are other projects I could be very helpful at. And I can't do them. I cannot. Because everything is endangered. Everything is up for grabs. Ours is a kind of primitive situation, even though we would call ourselves sophisticated. Our plight is very primitive from a Christian point of view. We are back where we started. Thou shalt not kill. We are not allowed to kill.

95. ELISE BOULDING

The Re-creation of Relationship, Interpersonal and Global

Elise Boulding (1920-2010) was a professor of sociology at Dartmouth College, where she played a leading role in developing one of the first peace and conflict studies programs in the United States. She also served as secretary general of the International Peace Research Association and as international chairperson of the Women's International League for Peace and Freedom. Boulding combined her Quaker principles with her work as a sociologist and built a reputation for analyzing cultures of peace and the family as a foundational unit for peacemaking. The selection below is taken from a 1981 pamphlet published by the Wider Quaker Fellowship.

... In some ways it is harder to think of world community and world family today than it was fifty years or one hundred years ago because we are much more aware now of the complexity of the international system. That system has many components which interconnect in many ways. Because it is intellectually paralyzing to try to think about what this means, it is helpful to begin by grounding ourselves in familiar metaphors. The metaphor is a wonderful tool we have for understanding intuitively very complex things. Having created the big picture, we can stand back and learn from the metaphor itself. It can teach us. We can pray about it, we can meditate about it, and we can study it.

The world as a family is a very familiar metaphor indeed .... Another metaphor very important to us is that of the world as the Peaceable Garden, or Peaceable Commonwealth. Every great religious and cultural tradition has had a vision of a Peaceable Garden; this is not something that arises uniquely in Isaiah. In the Homeric epics you find the vision of the Peaceable Garden in the Elysian fields, those green and verdant expanses where people laid aside their swords and shields and discoursed upon poetry and philosophy. The Koran has images of a green and lovely garden in the desert, where people live in peace. Concepts of humans laying down weapons and delighting in one another, delighting in poetry, delighting in the Creator and in the oneness of everything are not rare. There is always sharing in these visions. There is no injustice in the Peaceable Garden.

It is enormously comforting that every civilization has had this kind of a vision. There is something about the way we think and dream as human beings that keeps generating it. And it is good to know we are like that. As Christians, the Peaceable Garden is something we share with the other peoples of the Book, the Old Testament. We share it with Jews and with the community of Islam.

249

When we add that in the Garden we are God's family, we have said something profoundly important. The image of the family is not complete, however, unless we know in the deepest sense of knowing that God is our mother as well as our father. We use the metaphor of God's family wrongly if we only think of it as a patriarchal family. Let us use the metaphor for all that it can mean and acknowledge God our mother, and God our father. Let us also realize that such metaphors can become meaningless clichés. They can be used in crude and obnoxious ways that deaden the spirit, or they can be the gateway through which our prayer life can be entered. They can be the means for gaining a deeper understanding of our call than intellectual analysis can provide.

Metaphor is the beginning of vision, and a doorway into the future. We must consider the task of visioning as an integral part of our peace work, taking the courage to link poetic and prophetic visioning with images of the social and political and economic conditions that might obtain if we lived in a world without weapons. In working for disarmament, the one major stumbling block we face is that no one really believes we could have a weaponless world. Such a world is just not credible. In fact, we more and more use hedging terms like "a less armed world" and "arms control." General and complete disarmament, which one could talk about uninhibitedly in the early 1940s, is a term we are really embarrassed to use now because it seems so unreal. It seems to suggest we are hiding our heads in the sand. There is a somber aspect to this dilemma. If we cannot delineate in our mind a world without weapons—what relationships would be like, how economic activities would be carried on, how family life would go on, how community life would go on—then we are not serious about disarmament. There is no possibility of moving toward a goal that we cannot even see with our mind's eye.

A basic aspect of working for social change of any kind is the visualization of that which we are working for. We do it all the time for specific community projects; we dream up buildings and we dream up new organizations and we dream up new services. We develop very specific images of them. But few of us have seriously tried the task of delin-eating in our minds the contours of a weaponless world.

Since the early 1980s, some of us have brought together military personnel, diplomats, United Nations staff, scholars, church people, and community leaders for experiments in visualizing a world without weapons. The concept is to place before people an imaginary *de facto* situation: the weapons are gone. "Now describe the world," we say to the participants ....

Once having seen the contours of this future world, we work ourselves back year by year to the present. This way a sense of process and strategy emerges that is quite different from anything you might dream up if you start in the present and ask what we should do now to bring about disarmament. It involves linkage of the tasks of visioning and imagining with the skills of articulating what we know about how society works. This linkage enables us to break through some of the deadlocks and impasses and the sense of helplessness we now experience.

Another task we should try in addition to visioning the social, economic, and political dimensions of the future is the visioning of the religious dimension of a world without arms. What will be the spiritual state of this weaponless world? What will be its religious habits and ways of thinking and being? There are some interesting possibilities in trying to bring our Christian vision into world perspective by putting it alongside the visions for a weaponless world that come out of the communities of Judaism, Islam, Buddhism, and Hinduism. Each of these communities has well-tested methods for conflict resolution, for sharing, and for social justice. We have already taken the Jewish vision of the holy mountain where none shall hurt or destroy, "for the earth shall be full of the knowledge of the Lord" (Isaiah 11:9), as a central vision within Christendom. The kibbutz movement in present day Israel must be appreciated as a serious attempt to re-create the old vision, however one evaluates the political context of that attempt. The Taoists have taught nonviolence for centuries, and the contemporary Buddhist *shramadana* movement, which links spiritual awakening to community action, gives us new insights into peacemaking. The Hindu tradition of *sarvodaya*, seeking the welfare of all through *satya-*

graha (nonviolent doing and becoming), and the Islamic concept of the *tauhid,* the loving community of believers that holds the earth's resources in trust for the Creator, can all add to our understanding of the Christian call to peacemaking. The fact that many of the countries where these religious traditions are found are experiencing a great deal of violence tells us that the human race still has a great deal of maturing to do before spiritually based nonviolence can be effectively practiced.

Obedience, responsibility, and compassion are religious universals. We can draw on these principles with our brothers and sisters of every tradition in building a more peaceful world. And what do we, the Christians, bring? We bring the love of God, made manifest in the life of Jesus. We bring something that is very special to us that we feel makes us different. God has taught the peoples of each religious tradition in the way that they could hear. Each people has its *charismata,* its special manifestations of the Holy Spirit. We are by no means alike. Whatever spiritual unity we at our best can experience comes out of profound diversity. We each bring our particular gifts to the creation of world community, both to imagining a peaceful world and to the making of tools to practice peace.

We already have an important tool for practicing peace across nation-state boundaries: the networks of international nongovernmental organizations (NGOs). More than eighteen thousand groups are organized around religious, cultural, economic, political, and educational purposes, and operate across national boundaries. Each one of these organizations represents a special set of human intentions that reaches across borders to realize a global identity; that is why they are often termed "transnationals." Their purposes transcend the nation-state, and peace is always one of their purposes. Along with peace, they seek understanding, the improvement of the human condition and the furtherance of certain specific human skills ....

Everyone is connected with transnational communities, usually in several different ways. For peacemakers, churches and peace organizations are important transnational links. There are hundreds of religious nongovernmental organizations

and they are very important to the international peace movement ....

Religious NGOs are unique because they are the only ones that potentially reach into every home on the planet. Most organizations have a very selective membership .... But if you are talking about the World Council of Churches and its constituent denominational members, you are talking about families in local congregations in the towns and villages of every country of the world.

... As we become aware of the capacity to communicate within and between these transnational religious organizations, we are potentially reaching into individual homes. We are reaching out to men, women, and children where they live. That is not true of any other type of NGO. We have a very unique set of pathways across the planet in our religious transnational organizations. Most people don't think of communication that way. They think of getting important issues before their own parliament. They think of sending resolutions to the United Nations, to heads of other governments, but not to their sister communities around the world.

When we really look at NGOs as our world communication network, we can see how rapidly the net is growing.... With more organizations come new kinds of sharing, new kinds of information. NGOs are growing in their capacity to carry human caring. They are beginning to carry grassroots concerns.

What do NGOs actually make possible? What goes on in the networks? During the International Year of the Child, some of these NGOs actually trained children between the ages of nine and twelve to go into their own neighborhoods and monitor the illnesses of their own and other households. The children were trained to test water supplies and perform small services which would improve the health of the community. Nine-to twelve-year-olds carry a lot of responsibility in most parts of the world, but their work is not acknowledged. Now NGOs are finally acknowledging the importance of the work of children, and are using their networks to spread skill and training from one country to another. The networks are not only for service, but for learning, for celebration, for human playfulness. They give countless new dimensions to the human identity.

We need to know ourselves in these expanding network identities, for that is how we reach each other from home to home, village to village, town to town. This kind of family-based outreach is the core of our task as peacemakers. Our task isn't just to speak to governments. Our task is to speak to families, to the wise elders, to the children, to the middle-year folks, and use every means at hand to share our vision with others.

The task of peacemaking, however, goes beyond sharing a vision of peace to living a life of peace. That requires practical action skills. If we are to live in "that life and power that takes away the occasion of all wars," as Friends put it, we must figure out how to live our own lives in such a way that the seeds of war are not found there. We take responsibility for an active withdrawal of support from military institutions. This can happen in different ways for different individuals. Generally it takes the form of nonsupport of draft and registration for the draft, and can extend to nonpayment of some or all taxes. In some way, each person who responds to the call takes responsibility for countermanding the military enterprise.

Taking responsibility for removing the seeds of war means going further than nonsupport of the military, however. We are taken right to the Judaic call to the Jubilee Year in the Old Testament:

And ye shall hallow the fiftieth year, and proclaim liberty throughout all the land unto the inhabitants thereof: it shall be a jubilee year unto you; and ye shall return every man unto his possession and ye shall return every man unto his family…. And if thou sell ought unto thy neighbor, or buyest ought of thy neighbor's hand, ye shall not oppress one another. (Leviticus 25:10, 14)

This marvelous call to redistribution and social justice was never carried out in practice in Israel as far as we know, but the instructions are there. Suddenly the concept becomes fresh for us in these decades as we struggle under renewed pressure from the Third World to figure out what a new international economic order would really look like. It certainly means dealing with the inequities that have developed through two centuries of industrial revolution.

Nurturing the processes of peace takes more than an intention to distribute, however. It takes the skills of arbitration, mediation, and conflict resolution in the context of the practice of community, of neighboring. We must develop these skills. Another very important skill which we in the Christian community haven't given enough attention to is what I call "prophetic listening." We all know about prophetic speaking, but prophetic listening means listening to others in such a way that we draw out of them the seeds of their own highest understanding, their own obedience, their own vision—seeds that they themselves may not have known were there. Listening can draw out of people things that speaking to them cannot. If everybody listened and no one spoke, it would be a strange world. But prophetic listening is something we might all want to practice.

… If we're going to explore prophetic listening, there is a word we will have to eliminate from our vocabulary, especially from our religious vocabulary. That word is "enemy." … We have an enormous amount of trouble from this word. An enemy has to be either killed or converted. There really aren't any other things to do with enemies ….

I would like to suggest a new word to replace enemy. The word is "stranger." It's a very old word, and a good one. We have no more enemies but we have strangers. Sometimes we are estranged from ourselves and from God. When we meet a person we call a stranger, that person has to be listened to. We have to find out who he is and what basis for discourse exists. There is no tribal group to my knowledge that does not have a tradition for dealing with the stranger. That is, when a person you have no way of labeling or categorizing appears on the horizon, that person is defined as a stranger. An emissary is sent out to question the stranger until some basis for relationship has been found. When, through lengthy discussion, that basis has been found, the stranger is brought to the community and introduced: "Here is so-and-so, and this is how we are connected to her." Now the former stranger has an identity. This process of dialoguing with a person to find a basis for relationship, not agreement or consensus but simply a basis for relationship, is a widely practiced ritual in many parts of the world. Oddly enough, we have lost it in industrial society. Therefore we have enemies. We don't have rituals for deciding the basis of relationships. The stranger has to be killed or converted.

I suggest that we try to think of those we used to call enemies as strangers and see what it does for our capacity to establish relationship. Jesus taught us how to do this. In all of his dialogues, he never talked with an enemy—never. But he certainly dialogued with strange people. We can learn how to dialogue from the Gospels. If we abolish enemies and dialogue with strangers, then we may be in a position to speak a new word to old quarrels. One of the most troubling things that lies ahead for the world community has to do with quarrels within Islam, much exacerbated by superpower arming of folk societies that until very recently fought face to face with swords. With western technology, they are now destroying each other's resources and peoples at a rate that they do not themselves comprehend .... One of the most important calls for peacemaking now is for Christian groups to begin dialoguing with the thoughtful and caring leaders of Islamic thought. We need to know, we need to see what the hopes and fears are as they emerge within these internally conflicted societies. Much of their suffering we have helped inflict, through colonialism. It will not be an easy dialogue ....

We need to learn these skills of dialogue. We cannot go on invading the Holy Lands, as we began doing in the Middle Ages in what we called the Crusades. Neither can we make scapegoats of, or denigrate, the communities of faith that live there. We have ancient, unfinished business with these communities going back a thousand years and more. We share a world, and we must listen to one another ....

We are the ultimate interface between the personal and the global. Each of us is the interface. If we understand and pay attention to the connections at whatever point we touch one another, we will be world builders. We don't have to do it all the time, but it is good sometimes to place our daily actions within the context of the planetary networks to which we actually belong through our own individual membership commitments. We can in imagination trace out all the local branches of an organization, and start visualizing the households in a community at whose doors we could knock because they too are members. Because the imagination is a wonderful thing, we can actually knock at those doors. There is a welcome and a pot of tea for each of us in so many thousands of places, when we travel the NGO pathways the human family now has under construction. And we in turn must have our own pot of tea ready for those who knock at our door. If our bodies cannot travel, our voices and our letters can. Each of us is a link between the international and the personal.

The future we envision requires that we travel those pathways with our minds and hearts. Besides visioning, we have much to do. We must work to develop far better peacemaking skills than we now have, including the skills of sharing, of prophetic listening, and of building the institutions we need, such as an effective U.S. Institute of Peace. We must learn the dialogue that turns stranger into friend and makes the word enemy obsolete. All this is hard, for the times are dangerous and frightening, and we are not very wise or clever. But we do nothing alone. Wherever we put our hand or foot, wherever we cast our eyes, God is there and moves with us so that we cannot get lost.

96. DOROTHY FRIESEN

Social Action and the Need for Prayer

Dorothy Friesen (b. 1949) and her husband, Gene Stolzfus (1940-2010), carried out peacemaking work in the Philippines for many years as representatives of the Mennonite Central Committee. Dorothy and Gene also founded Synapses, a grassroots organization centered on domestic and international peace, before becoming part of Christian Peacemaker Teams. As the article below suggests, Friesen has given sustained attention to nurturing the inner life for peacemaking in the wider world.

People who are deeply involved in social justice work—even those who are religious—have often been suspicious of prayer as belonging to the realm of those pious ones who hide behind words to avoid involvement. But the split between people of prayer and people of action is a false and harmful one, especially for those of us in peace and justice work.

My husband and I were forced to our knees a few years ago when we lived and worked in the Philippines. Each day we had to deal with problems stemming from economics and our class background on a personal and emotional level. Each day we had to face our neighbors: squatters with no secure home who had been pushed off their farmland by the onslaught of multinational agribusiness. They came to the cities to find work, but most were underemployed and unable to afford both food and housing. Needing food, they had to live as squatters where they could. From begged and borrowed material they constructed makeshift houses on marginal, often swampy land, which they filled in themselves with hand-carried garbage and stones. Each day we had to face the violence of people we knew being arrested or "salvaged," a euphemistic term which means that the Philippine military killed them after they were tortured to extort any information they might have. We had to face homeless people sitting beside their bulldozed crops after business, the military, and the government joined forces to evict small rice-and-corn tenants and make way for export crops like bananas and pineapples.

How could we cope with it? How could we respond? We felt powerless in the face of this violence, fueled by the military, with economic and political support from our American government. The objective situation and our own internal longing brought us to this question:

How can we stand before God while walking with the people? We were forced to place ourselves—together with our contradictions, our guilt, and the objective wounds of Philippine society—in the presence of God. Broken, angry, and confused, we held these problems up to the light. But we had hesitations about prayer. We did not want to slip into magic or mail-order prayers, which would simply send up and order to have the goods delivered.

Partly, we did not even know what to ask for. We did not know how to pray. We could only offer up our confusion. As we did that, we began to realize that it was not our definition or assessment of the problem which was determinative. When we place ourselves in the presence of God, a transformation takes place. *Who God is* becomes important. Emptying ourselves so that we may take in the person of God becomes the essential thing. It shapes our view of the situation; it shapes the nature of our involvement.

In our groping, painful search we found the writings of Catherine de Hueck Doherty, founder of Madonna House, a lay apostolate for prayer and hospitality. Her book *Poustinia* helped us to understand the need for a desert: a holy quiet place where we could hear God. *Poustinia* is the Russian word for desert, but with many more rich meanings than our English understanding. To "make a *poustinia*" is to go to a quiet, enclosed place with simple food, a Bible, pen, and notebook for at least twenty-four hours of total silence. That experience can cleanse us so that we are prepared to start anew. But it is a special discipline, perhaps better done after building up with short periods of silence daily. Silence can be terrifying.

We were helped along the way, as well, by the example of Taize Brothers. Founded in Taize, France, during the Second World War by Brother Roger Schutz, these lay ecumenical brothers live simply among the poor, work for their living, and pray together three times a day. Some brothers lived in a little squatter house in the poorest area of the Philippine city where we were. They knew the country and the culture because of their ability to listen. At any time, they were spiritually prepared to go as deep with another person as that person was willing to go. Because they were centered within, they could act as a wedge into the world, pointing to another reality, an alternative.

In our busy, noisy lives, we can hardly imagine the time and space that would allow us the inner centeredness to stand before God. We know that in our modern, alienated society there are many internal and external obstacles to overcome before we can make contact and touch our innermost selves. Often we can't pray because we feel we aren't good enough; or we think we won't have enough discipline to continue; or we have had a fight with our husband or wife, and we know we can't pray before we are reconciled. But this concern carries in it some false understandings of the work and person of God. Doherty writes that Westerners often believe they are not worthy that God should speak to them. "Of course we are not worthy . . . but God still speaks," she writes. Pierre Yves Emery, a member of the Taize Community, offers us a new way of seeing these blockages. "The days during which we experience only a bitter powerlessness to hold ourselves in dignity before God can often be the days when prayer is most authentic, if we offer that powerlessness as an appeal and as confidence."

Another obstacle is the suspicion that prayer is an excuse to do nothing. People who are passionately concerned about what is happening to God's creatures and creation are right to be suspicious of cheap and easy answers. Jesus' prayerful life was neither cheap nor easy.

Throughout church history, saints and mystics have drawn the connection between material wealth and spiritual poverty. St. Ambrose of Milan minced no words: "It was in common and for all alike that the earth was created. Why then, O rich, do you take to yourselves the monopoly of owning land? It is not with your wealth that you give alms to the poor, but with a fraction of their own which you give back, for you are usurping for yourself something meant for the common good of all." St. John Chrysostom connects possessions with war when he writes, "It is because some try to take possession of what belongs to everyone that quarrels and wars break out. It is the poor's wealth of which you are trustees even in cases where you possess it through honest labor or inheritance …. And is not the earth the Lord's with all that therein is? Everything which belongs to God is for the use of all."

Economics and a healthy prayer life are deeply interrelated. Praying means readiness to let go of our certainty and to move ahead from where we are now. It demands that we take to the road again and again, leaving our houses and looking forward to a new land. Praying demands the readiness to live a life in which we have nothing to lose, so that we can always begin afresh. Whenever we willingly choose this poverty, we make ourselves vulnerable, but we also become free to see the world as it really is.

Contemplation (as part of prayer) helps us to overcome our great temptation to try to "control" God by making demands and hoping that God will do what we ask. Emery describes contemplation as "digging deep within the self to rediscover human life as it first burst forth, created by God and grafted onto Christ. God in the most inward part of ourselves, his love at the root of our being. It is there that he awaits us."

Although contemplation implies a certain withdrawal and the firm desire to quiet the inner noises, it is not an escape from life. The renunciation of control becomes the sign of God's presence. But going deep within is never disconnected from concern for peacemaking. Brother Roger writes, "One thing is certain. All contact with God leads to one's neighbor."

In our busy world, how do we prepare ourselves for this experience before God? It is important that each of us finds what is appropriate to us, without trying to squeeze ourselves into a prescribed mold. We are freed when we realize that God infinitely respects our sensibilities, our rhythms, and our inner life. After all, God created us in all our variety. Most of us will have to make changes that are essential to our becoming quiet and which are in tension with the way our society functions. We will probably have to trim our schedules in order to make room for quietness. It is possible to have brief relays of prayer in the gaps within our schedules, but sooner or later we will need a longer time to disengage ourselves and leave time for God to fill us.

Each person needs to find his or her own way, but sometimes suggestions of what other people have done can be helpful. A "baby step" is to set aside twenty minutes a day for silence or meditation. It is often helpful if one sits quietly at the same time each day and in the same place. A candle, incense, or a picture can help to focus and bring thoughts together. Sometimes beginning with a biblical passage, an event, or a question can also direct the twenty-minute reflection.

Keeping a journal can help to focus the mind over a period of time. This means not only keeping a record of events but also your reflections on events and dreams, on biblical passages, or on your twenty-minute daily meditation. While we must come to this centeredness ourselves—no one can do it for us—a partner can be helpful, either to sit with us during our meditation time or to check with periodically on the progress of our discipline.

We must always remember that centering and emptying is not done for oneself, for purity, or even to be one with God. Catherine Doherty warns that we must go beyond such motivation and "take upon ourselves the pain of humanity." The uniqueness of this kind of deep prayer for peacemaking is that it is brought into the marketplace. A *poustinia* in the marketplace, says Doherty, is carried within persons who go about their work. She makes the comparison to a pregnant woman who engages in day-to-day life like everyone else, but everyone knows she carries a special life within her. In her being, she is a witness to life.

Once we have let go, we are ready to intercede for others without getting caught in the mail-order syndrome. Overwhelming events or concern for justice action can bring us to prayer, but the movement between contemplation and action goes both ways. Justice action can rise out of the prayer meeting in the local congregation. In fact, that is a better place to root action than in the church bureaucracy or central office. If we pray together with a group, interceding on behalf of some concern, there will surely be some meaningful action that we are called to take. Real prayer is risky in that it demands commitment and responsibility when we speak our concern out loud.

Praying is the most critical activity we are capable of. For a person who prays is never satisfied with the world of here and now. We know it is possible to enter into dialogue with God and so work at renewing the earth. Prayer can move us to take local action together, but what about larger issues, where we cannot take direct, personal action so immediately? Pierre Yves Emery offers a helpful response:

If we dare to entrust to the love of God those problems which are vastly beyond our capacities to solve, such as peace or justice, we can do so honestly only in the knowledge that at least on our own level we must be workers for peace and justice. Our prayers must bring us back to the specific, in order to take a large view without being abstract. Our prayers must bring us back to our immediate and concrete responsibilities, as well as to that larger and more indirect relationship which is political and economic. Everything is interrelated, in a tenuous and usually hidden way. Intercessory prayer cannot get along without information on the life of the world.

But Emery adds that it is possible to pray for causes or individuals whom we cannot help personally in any way. How do we pray honestly? He says this: "Relying on the limited but serious involvement that is properly mine, my prayer can legitimately reach out to needs in areas where other men and women are seeking to bring answers." Intercession for events far away emphasizes our unity with others who also work and pray for peace and justice.

When we pray, we open ourselves to the influence of the power which has revealed itself as love. Once touched by this power, we have found a center for ourselves that gives creative distance, so that everything we see and hear and feel can be tested against this source. Prayer means breaking through the veil of existence and allowing ourselves to be led by God's vision. It is this rootedness and being in touch with the source of life that can give hope and energy to our peace-and-justice efforts. Prayer can save us from cynicism in the face of overwhelming odds.

As we receive God in our depths, we come to know that amid all the greed and selfish misuse of people and resources of the good earth, amid frantic effort and failure, there is still another stream of events that goes on. God is letting seeds grow, secretly and mysteriously, to the end that God plans. Through prayer, our inner eye is sharpened so that we can see the future sprouting, growing, and blooming from the seeds that we sow now.

97. Ronald J. Sider

God's People Reconciling

Ronald Sider (b. 1939) is an evangelical theologian and activist known especially for his groundbreaking work in encouraging evangelicals to become socially engaged for peace and justice in biblically responsible ways. As a founding member and president of Evangelicals for Social Action, Sider has advocated for evangelicals to fight poverty, racial discrimination, ecological injustice, and violence. Below is an excerpt of a landmark speech he delivered at the Mennonite World Conference in Strasbourg, France, in the summer of 1984. The speech eventually resulted in the founding of Christian Peacemaker Teams, an organization devoted to grassroots peacemaking in violent contexts, and it remains the most important contemporary statement of the Anabaptist commitment to peacemaking.

Over our past 450 years of martyrdom, migration and missionary proclamation, the God of shalom has been preparing us Anabaptists for a late twentieth-century rendezvous with history. The next twenty years will be the most dangerous—and probably the most vicious and violent—in human history. If we are ready to embrace the cross, God's reconciling people might save millions of lives and profoundly impact the course of history.

Violent economic structures annually maim and murder the poor by the millions. Idolatrous nationalism, religious bigotry, racial prejudice, and economic selfishness turn people against people in terrifying orgies of violence in Northern Ireland, the Middle East, Southern Africa, and Latin America. The competing self-righteous ideologies of the United States and the Soviet Union trample arrogantly on the people's dreams for justice and freedom in Central America and Afghanistan, the Philippines and Poland. Always, behind every regional conflict which kills thousands or millions, lurks the growing possibility of a nuclear exchange between the superpowers which would kill hundreds of millions. We teeter on the brink of nuclear disaster.

Our 450 years of commitment to Jesus' love for enemies finds its kairos, its special hour of decision and fulfillment, in these two terrifying decades. This could be our finest hour. Never has the world needed our message more. Never has it been more

open. Now is the time to risk everything for our belief that Jesus is the only way to peace. If we still believe it, now is the time to live it.

To rise to this challenge of our Lord and of history, we need to do three things: we need, first, to reject the ways we have misunderstood or weakened Jesus' call to be peacemakers; second, we need to embrace the full biblical understanding of shalom; and third, we need to prepare to die, by the thousands.

Jesus' Call to Be Peacemakers

First, the misunderstandings. Too often we fall into an isolationist nonresistance which silently ignores or gladly profits from injustice and war as long as our boys don't have to fight. As long as conscientious objector status protects our purity and safety, our neighbors need not fear that we will raise troubling questions about the injustice their armies reinforce or the civilians they maim and kill. The most famous advocate of our time, Mahatma Gandhi, once said that if the only two choices are to kill or to stand quietly by doing nothing while the weak are oppressed and killed, then, of course, we must kill. I agree.

But there is always a third option. We can always prayerfully and nonviolently place ourselves between the weak and the violent, between the oppressed and the oppressor. Do we have the courage to move from the back lines of isolationist nonresistance to the front lines of nonviolent peacemaking?

Sometimes we justify our silence with the notion that pacifism is a special vocation for us peculiar Anabaptists. It is not for other Christians. But this approach will not work. In fact, it is probably the last stop before total abandonment of our historic peace witness. If pacifism is not God's will for all Christians, then it is not His will for any. On the other hand, if the one who taught us to love our enemies is the eternal Son who became flesh in the carpenter who died and rose and now reigns as Lord of the universe, then the peaceful way of nonviolence is for all who believe and obey him. Do we have the courage to summon the entire church to forsake the way of violence?

Sometimes we weaken and confuse our peace witness with an Anabaptist version of Martin Luther's two-kingdom doctrine. Luther said that in the spiritual kingdom, God rules by love. Therefore in our private lives as Christians, we dare never act violently. But in the secular kingdom, God rules by the sword. Therefore, the same person in the role of executioner or soldier rightly kills. I was talking recently with one of our Anabaptist church leaders for whom I have the deepest respect. He said that he was a pacifist and believed it would be wrong for him to go to war. But he quickly added that the government is supposed to have armies. The United States, he said, had unfortunately fallen behind the Soviet Union and therefore President Reagan's nuclear build-up was necessary and correct. I fear that he and many other Western Mennonites and Brethren in Christ have endorsed the current arms race at the ballot box ....

If we want wars to be fought, then we ought to have the moral integrity to fight them ourselves. To vote for other people's sons and daughters to march off to death while ours safely register as conscientious objectors is a tragic form of confused hypocrisy. If, on the other hand, we believe that Jesus' nonviolent cross is the way to peace, then we need to implore everyone to stop seeking security in ever more lethal weapons. Jesus wept over Jerusalem's coming destruction because it did not recognize his way of peace. Do we have the courage with love and tears to warn the governments of the world

that the upward, ever upward, spiral of violence will lead, finally, to annihilation?

Finally, the affluent are regularly tempted to separate peace from justice. Affluent Anabaptists, in North America and Western Europe, can do that by focusing all of our energies on saving our own skins from nuclear holocaust and neglecting the fact that injustice now kills millions every year. We can also do it by denouncing revolutionary violence without also condemning and correcting the injustice that causes that violence. In Central America today, fifty percent of the children die before the age of five because of starvation and malnutrition. At the same time, vast acres of the best land in Central America grow export crops for North Americans and Western Europeans. Unjust economic structures today murder millions of poor folk. Our call to reject violence, whether it comes from affluent churches in industrialized countries or middle-class congregations in Third World nations, will have integrity only if we are willing to engage in costly action to correct injustice. Thank God for the courageous youth that our Mission Boards and Mennonite Central Committee have sent to stand with the poor. Thank God for the costly courage of poor Mennonite congregations in Central America and persecuted Mennonite churches in Ethiopia and elsewhere. But that is only a fraction of what we could have done. The majority of our people continue to slip slowly into numbing, unconcerned affluence. Do we have the courage as a united people in our congregations to show the poor of the earth that our peace witness is not a subtle support for an unjust status quo, but rather a commitment to risk danger and death so that justice and peace may embrace?

Embrace the Biblical Vision of Shalom

Acknowledging past temptations and misunderstandings is essential. But we need not—indeed we dare not remain mired in our failures. Instead we can allow the fullness of the biblical vision of peace, of shalom, to transform us into a reconciling people ready to challenge the madness of the late twentieth century.

The richness of the biblical vision of peace is conveyed in the Hebrew word for peace, "shalom." Shalom means right relationships in every direction—with God, with neighbor, and with the earth ....

Leviticus 26:3-6 describes the comprehensive shalom which God will give to those who walk in obedient relationship to God. The earth will yield rich harvests, wild animals will not ravage the countryside, and the sword will rest. Shalom means not only the absence of war but also a land flowing with milk and honey. It also includes just economic relationships with the neighbor. It means the fair division of land so that all families can earn their own way. It means the Jubilee and sabbatical release of debts so that great extremes of wealth and poverty do not develop among God's people. The result of such justice, Isaiah says, is peace (32:16-17). And the psalmist reminds us that God desires that "justice and peace will kiss each other" (Psalm 85:10). If we try to separate justice and peace, we tear asunder what God has joined together.

Tragically, the people of Israel refused to walk in right relationship with God and neighbor. They ran after false gods, and they oppressed the poor. So God [punished] them. But the prophets looked beyond the tragedy of national destruction to a time when God's Messiah, the Prince of Peace, would come to restore right relationships with God and neighbor (e.g., Isaiah 9:2ff.; 11:1ff.). "And they shall beat their swords into plowshares and their spears into pruning hooks; nation shall not lift up sword against nation, neither shall they learn war anymore" (Isaiah 2:4).

Jesus Christ was the long-expected Messiah. And just as the prophets had promised, shalom was at the heart of his messianic work and message. But Jesus' approach to peacemaking was not to lapse into passive nonresistance; it was not to withdraw to isolated solitude; it was not to teach one ethic for the private sphere and another for public life. Jesus modeled an activist challenge to the status quo, summoning the entire Jewish people to accept his nonviolent messianic strategy instead of the Zealot's militaristic methods.

Jesus' approach was not one of passive nonresistance. If Jesus' call not to resist one who is evil in Matthew 5:39 was a summons to pure nonresistance and the rejection of all forms of pressure and coercion, then Jesus regularly contradicted his own teaching. Jesus unleashed a blistering attack on the Pharisees, denouncing them as blind guides, fools, hypocrites, and snakes—surely psychological coercion of a vigorous type as is even the most loving church discipline which Jesus prescribed (Matthew 18:15ff.).

Nor was Jesus nonresistant when he cleansed the temple! He engaged in aggressive resistance against evil when he marched into the temple, drove the animals out with a whip, dumped the money tables upside down, and denounced the moneychangers as robbers. If Matthew 5:39 means that all forms of resistance to evil are forbidden, then Jesus sinfully disobeyed his own command. Jesus certainly did not kill the moneychangers. I doubt that he even used his whip on them. But he certainly resisted their evil.

Or consider Jesus' response when a soldier unjustly struck him on the cheek at his trial (John 18:19-24). Instead of turning the other cheek and meekly submitting to this injustice, he protested! "If I have spoken wrongly, bear witness to the wrong; but if I have spoken rightly, why do you strike me?" Apparently Jesus thought that protesting police brutality or engaging in civil disobedience in a nonviolent fashion was entirely consistent with his command not to resist the one who is evil.

Jesus would never have ended up on the cross if he had exemplified the isolationist pacifism of withdrawal that has so often tempted us Mennonites. Nor would he have offended anyone if he had simply conformed to current values as we are often tempted to do when we abandon the pattern of isolation. Rejecting both isolation and accommodation, Jesus lived at the heart of his society challenging the status quo at every point where it was wrong ....

Repeatedly in our history, the terror of persecution and the temptation of security have lured us to retreat to the safety of isolated rural solitude where our radical ideas threaten no one. But that was not Jesus' way. He challenged his society so vigorously and so forcefully that the authorities had only two choices. They had to accept his call to repentance and change or they had to get rid of him. Do we have the courage to follow in his steps? ...

It is hardly surprising that Christians have been tempted to weaken Jesus' call to costly self-sacrifice—whether by postponing its application to the millennium, labeling it an impossible ideal, or restricting its relevance to some personal private sphere. The last is perhaps the most widespread and the most tempting. Did Jesus merely mean that although the individual Christian in his personal role should respond nonviolently to enemies, that same person as public official should kill?

In his historical context, Jesus came as the Messiah of Israel with a plan and an ethic for the entire Jewish people. He advocated love toward political enemies as his specific political response to centuries of violence. His radical nonviolence was a conscious alternative to the contemporary Zealots' call for violent revolution to usher in the messianic kingdom. There is no hint that Jesus' reason for objecting to the Zealots was that they were unauthorized individuals whose violent sword would have been legitimate if the Sanhedrin had only given the order. On the contrary, his point was that the Zealots' whole approach to enemies, even unjust oppressive imperialists, was fundamentally wrong. The Zealots offered one political approach; Jesus offered another. But both appealed to the entire Jewish people.

The many premonitions of national disaster in the Gospels indicate that Jesus realized that the only way to avoid destruction and attain messianic shalom was through a forthright rejection of the Zealots' call to arms. In fact, Luke places the moving passage about Jesus' weeping over Jerusalem immediately after the triumphal entry—just after Jesus had disappointed popular hopes with his insistence on a peaceful messianic strategy. "And when he drew near and saw the city he wept over it, saying, 'Would that even today you knew the things that make for peace!'" (Luke 19:4ff.).

Zealot violence, Jesus knew, would lead to national destruction. It was an illusion to look for peace through violence. The way of the Suffering Servant was the only way to messianic shalom. Jesus' invitation to the entire Jewish people was to believe that the messianic kingdom was already breaking into the present. Therefore, if they would accept God's forgiveness and follow his Messiah, they could begin now to live according to the peaceful values of the messianic age. Understood in this historical setting, Jesus' call to love enemies can hardly be limited to the personal sphere of private life.

Furthermore, the personal-public distinction also seems to go against the most natural, literal meaning of the text. There is no hint whatsoever in the text of such a distinction. In fact, Jesus' words are full of references to public life. "Resist not evil" applies, Jesus says, when people take you to court (Matthew 5:40) and when foreign rulers legally demand forced labor (v. 41). Indeed, the basic norm Jesus transcends (an eye for an eye) was a fundamental principle of the Mosaic legal system. We can safely assume that members of the Sanhedrin and other officials heard Jesus' words. The most natural conclusion is that Jesus intended his words to be normative not just in private but also in public life.

We have examined the horizontal shalom with the neighbor which Jesus brought. But Jesus also announced and accomplished a new peace with God. Constantly he proclaimed God's astonishing forgiveness to all who repent. And then he obeyed the Father's command to die as the atonement for God's sinful enemies.

God's attitude toward sinful enemies revealed at the cross is the foundation of biblical nonviolence. Let us never ground our pacifism in sentimental imitation of the gentle Nazarene or in romantic notions of heroic martyrdom. Our commitment to nonviolence is rooted in the heart of historic Christian orthodoxy. It is grounded in the incarnation of the eternal Son of God and in his substitutionary atonement at the cross.

Jesus said that God's way of dealing with enemies was to take their evil upon Himself. "Love your enemies and pray for those who persecute you." Why? "So that you may be sons and daughters of your Creator in heaven." In fact, Jesus went even further. The crucified criminal hanging limp on the middle cross is the eternal Word who in the beginning was with God and indeed was God, but for our sake became flesh and dwelt among us. Only when we grasp that that is who the crucified one was, do we begin to fathom the depth of Jesus' teaching that God's way of dealing with enemies is the way of suffering love. By powerful parable and dramatic demonstration, Jesus had taught that God forgives sinners. Then he died on the cross to accomplish that reconciliation. The cross is the most powerful statement about God's way of dealing with enemies. Jesus made it very clear that he intended to die and that he understood that death as a ransom for others.

Romans 5 says: "God shows His love for us in that while we were yet sinners, Christ died for us. . . . While we were enemies we were reconciled to God by the death of His Son." Jesus' vicarious death for sinners is the foundation, and the deepest expression, of Jesus' command to love our enemies. We are enemies of God in a double sense. For one thing, because sinful persons are hostile to God, and for another, because the just, holy Creator cannot tolerate sin. For those who know the law, failure to obey it results in a divine curse. But Christ redeemed us from that curse by becoming a curse for us. Jesus' blood on the cross was an expiation for us sinful enemies of God. He who knew no sin was made sin for you and me.

Jesus' vicarious death for sinful enemies of God is the foundation of our Anabaptist commitment to nonviolence. The incarnate one knew that God was loving and merciful even toward sinful enemies. That's why he associated with sinners, forgave their sins, and completed his mission by dying for them on the cross. And it was precisely the same understanding of God that prompted him to command his followers to love their enemies. We as God's children are to imitate the loving characteristics of our heavenly God who rains mercifully on the just and the unjust. That's why we should love our enemies. The vicarious cross of Christ is the fullest expression of the character of God. At the cross God suffered for sinners. We'll never understand all of the mystery there. But it's precisely because the one hanging limp on the middle cross was the word who became flesh that we know two interrelated things. First, that a just, holy God mercifully accepts us sinful enemies just as we are. And second, that He wants us to go and treat our enemies exactly the same way. What a fantastic fulfillment of the messianic promise of shalom. Jesus did bring right relationships, with God and neighbor. In fact, he created a new community of shalom, a reconciled and reconciling people. As Ephesians 2 shows, peace with God through the cross demolishes hostile divisions among all those who stand together

under God's unmerited forgiveness. Women and slaves became persons. Jews accepted Gentiles. Rich and poor shared their economic abundance. So visibly different was this new community of shalom that onlookers could only exclaim: "Wow—behold how they love one another." Their common life validated their gospel of peace.

And so it must always be. Only if persons see a reconciled people in our homes and our congregations will they be able to hear our invitation to forsake the way of retaliation and violence. If I am not allowing the Holy Spirit to heal any brokenness in my relationship with my wife, I have little right to speak to my president about international reconciliation. If our Mennonite and Brethren in Christ congregations are not becoming truly reconciled communities, it is a tragic hypocrisy for us to try to tell secular governments how to overcome international hostility. It is a farce for the church to try to legislate what our congregations will not begin to live.

On the other hand, living models impact history. Even small groups of people practicing what they preach, laying down their lives for what they believe, influence society all out of proportion to their numbers. I believe the Lord of history wants to use our small family of Anabaptists scattered across the globe to help save life and promote justice. In short, to help shape modern history at the end of this dangerous twentieth century.

Die by the Thousands

But to do that, we must not only abandon mistaken ideas and, second, embrace the full biblical concept of shalom. One more thing is needed. We must take up our cross and follow Him to Golgotha. We must be ready to die by the thousands.

Those who have believed in peace through the sword have not hesitated to die. Proudly, courageously, they have marched off to death. Again and again, they sacrificed bright futures to the tragic illusion that one more righteous crusade would bring peace in their time. For their loved ones, for justice, and for peace, they have laid down their lives by the millions.

Why do we pacifists think that our way—Jesus' way—to peace will involve so little cost? On our way to Strasbourg, my family visited a spot in Switzerland called the Anabaptist bridge. High up in the Swiss mountains, our Mennonite ancestors met in secret under this bridge in order to avoid detection and death. As our family prayed together, I felt pride and joy at their courageous faith—this courageous faith of our mothers and fathers. But I asked myself: do I have the courage to follow in their steps today? Unless we Mennonites and Brethren in Christ are ready to start to die by the thousands in dramatic vigorous new exploits for peace and justice, we should sadly confess that we really never meant what we said. We did, of course, in earlier times. In previous centuries, we died for our convictions. Today we have grown soft and comfortable.

Unless comfortable North American and European Mennonites and Brethren in Christ are prepared to risk injury and death in nonviolent opposition to the injustice our societies foster and assist in Central America, the Philippines, and South Africa, we dare never whisper another word about pacifism to our sisters and brothers in those desperate lands. Unless the Mennonites of Latin America are willing to risk the torture of dictators and the sneer of guerillas in an aggressive, active, yet nonviolent, reconciling search for justice, we should confess that we fear to obey the one we worship. Unless we are ready to die developing new nonviolent attempts to reduce international conflict, we should confess that we never really meant the cross was an alternative to the sword. Unless the majority of our people in nuclear nations are ready as Anabaptist congregations to risk social disapproval and government harassment in a clear ringing call to live without nuclear weapons, we should sadly acknowledge that we have betrayed our peacemaking heritage. Making peace is as costly as waging war. Unless we are prepared to pay the cost of peacemaking, we have no right to claim the label or preach the message.

Our world is at an impasse. The way of violence has led us to the brink of global annihilation. Desperately, our contemporaries look for an alternative. They will never find Jesus' way to peace credible unless those of us who have proudly preached it are willing to die for it.

Last spring I attended a conference on the nuclear arms race, I met a former chief of the U.S. Air Force. I talked about a new, nonviolent action in Nicaragua, the Witness for Peace. He said he would be ready to do that because he was desperately searching for new ways to resolve international conflict.

A number of us Mennonites and Brethren in Christ are involved in that. A few dozen Christians are on that border all the time, witnessing silently for peace. A few dozen, of course, cannot stop that war. But think of what a few thousand could do! What would happen if the Christian church stationed as many praying Christians as the U.S. government has sent armed guerrillas across that troubled border?

What would happen if we in the Christian church today developed a new nonviolent peacekeeping force of 100,000 persons ready to move into violent conflicts and stand peacefully between warring parties in Central America, Northern Ireland, Poland, Southern Africa, the Middle East, and Afghanistan? Frequently we would get killed by the thousands. But everyone assumes that for the sake of peace it is moral and just for soldiers to get killed by the hundreds of thousands, even millions. Do we not have as much courage and faith as soldiers?

Again and again, I believe, praying, Spirit-filled, nonviolent peacekeeping forces would by God's special grace, be able to end the violence and nurture justice. Again and again, we would discover that love for enemies is not utopian madness or destructive masochism but rather God's alternative to the centuries of escalating violence that now threatens the entire planet. But we must face the cross—the cross, death by the thousands by those who believe Jesus, is the only way to convince our violent world of the truth of Christ's alternative.

I want to plead with the Mennonites, Brethren in Christ, and others in the Historic Peace Churches to take the lead in the search for new nonviolent approaches to conflict resolution. We could decide to spend 25 million dollars in the next three years developing a sophisticated, highly trained nonviolent peacekeeping force. The most sophisticated expertise in diplomacy, history, international politics, and logistics would be essential. So would a radical dependence on the Holy Spirit. Such a peacekeeping task force of committed Christians would immerse all of its activity in intercessory prayer. Perhaps in your small groups this morning, you can discuss this idea. There would be prayer chains in all our congregations as a few thousand of our best youth walked into the face of death, inviting all parties to end the violence and work together for justice.

If as a body we began to do this, we would, of course, invite the rest of the Christian church to join us. Maybe we could have 100,000 Christians in a new, nonviolent peacekeeping force. In fact, as the Witness for Peace shows, others have already begun. If we are not careful, God will raise up others to live out the heritage we have feared to apply to the problems of our day. Together the Christian church could afford to train and deploy 100,000 persons in a new nonviolent peacekeeping force. The result would not be utopia, or even the abolition of war. But it might tug our trembling planet back from the abyss.

I have one final plea. I know we live in a vicious, violent world. I know it takes more than winning smiles and moral advice to enable sinners to love their enemies. Sinners will never be able to fully follow Jesus' ethic. But they ought to. That they do not is the measure of their sinful rebellion. But regenerated Spirit-filled Christians can follow Jesus. Our only hope is a mighty peace revival that converts sinners and revives the church.

In the next decades, I believe we will see disaster and devastation on a scale never before realized in human history, unless God surprises our unbelieving world with a mighty worldwide peace revival. Therefore, my final plea is that we fall on our knees in intercessory prayer pleading with God for a global peace revival. At the worst of times in the past, God has broken into human history in mighty revivals that led to social movements that changed history. The Wesleyan revival in the eighteenth century resulted in Wilberforce's great crusade against slavery that changed the British Empire. The same could happen in the next few decades. Pray that God revives millions of lukewarm Christians. Pray that God draws millions of non-Christians into a personal living relationship with the risen Lord. Pray that millions and millions of people in all the continents of our small planet come to see that Jesus is the way to peace and peace is the way of Jesus. Pray that with our eyes fixed on the crucified one, the church will dare to pay the cost of being God's reconciling people in a broken world.

My brothers and sisters, today is the hour of decision. The long upward spiral of violence and counter violence today approaches its catastrophic culmination. Either the world repents and changes or it self-destructs. For centuries we Anabaptists have believed there is a different way, a better way. Our world needs that alternative. Now. But the world will be able to listen to our words only if large numbers of us live out the words we say. Our best sons and daughters, our leaders, and all of our people must be ready to risk death. The cross comes before the resurrection. There is finally only one question: Do we believe Jesus enough to pay the cost of following him? Do you? Do I?

98. STANLEY HAUERWAS

Peacemaking: The Virtue of the Church

Stanley Hauerwas (b. 1940) is the Gilbert T. Rowe Professor of Theological Ethics at Duke University. He and John Howard Yoder were the most influential Protestant peace intellectuals of the latter half of twentieth-century America. Just one of Hauerwas's primary contributions to the Christian peace movement is his theological argument, detailed in the 1985 essay below, that "peacekeeping is that virtue of the Christian community that is required if the church is to be a community of people at peace with one another in truth."

If your brother sins against you, go and tell him his fault, between you and him alone. If he listens to you, you have gained a brother. But if he does not listen, take one or two others along with you, that every word may be confirmed by the evidence of two or three witnesses. If he refuses to listen to them, tell it to the church; and if he refuses to listen even to the church, let him be to you as a Gentile and a tax collector. Truly, I say to you whatever you bind on earth shall be bound in heaven, and whatever you loose on earth shall be loosed in heaven. Again I say to you, if two of you agree on earth about anything they ask, it will be done for them by my Father in heaven. For where two or three are gathered in my name, there am I in the midst of them. Then Peter came up and said to him, "Lord, how often shall my brother sin against me, and I forgive him? As many as seven times?" Jesus said to him, "I do not say to you seven times, but seventy times seven." (Matthew 18:15-22)

This is surely a strange text to begin an article on peacemaking as a virtue. The text does not seem about peacemaking, but about conflict making. For it does not say if you have a grievance you might think about confronting the one you believe has wronged you. The text is much stronger than that. It says if you have a grievance you must, you are obligated to, confront the one you believe has sinned against you. You cannot overlook a fault on the presumption that it is better not to disturb the peace. Rather you must risk stirring the waters, causing disorder, rather than overlook the sin.

But on what possible grounds could Christians, people supposedly of peace, be urged actively to confront one another? It seems out of character for Jesus to urge us to do so and out of character for the Christian community to follow such an admonition. Yet I want to suggest that we will only understand peacemaking as a virtue when we see that such confrontation is at the heart of what it means to be a peacemaker. Even more important, however, I think that by attending to this passage we will be able to see how peacemaking, as well as any virtue, is correlative to a community's practices.

This is a crucial issue if we are to appreciate peacemaking as a virtue. For it is interesting to note how seldom peacemaking is treated as a virtue. Courage, temperance, and even humility are usually acknowledged as virtues much more readily than is peacemaking. For many peacemaking may sound like a "good thing," but they would be hesitant to call it a virtue. Peacemaking is usually seen more as a matter of political strategy than a disposition forming the self. Some people may even be peaceful, but that hardly seems a virtue.

Why do we seem reticent to think of peacemaking as a virtue? I suspect it is because we think of virtues as personal characteristics that everyone should possess irrespective of their membership in any specific community. But as I hope to show, such an understanding of virtue is far too limited if not an outright mistake. For as Aristotle argues, some virtues, such as justice and friendship, are correlative to certain kinds of relations and cannot exist without those relations being valued by a community. Peacemaking is that sort of virtue insofar as the church believes that peace (and a very particular kind of peace at that) is an essential characteristic of its nature.

But as important as understanding why we rightly consider peacemaking a virtue is how we understand what kind of activity it is. It is in this context that the passage from Matthew is so important for helping us understand peacemaking as a virtue. For normally we tend to think of peacemaking as the resolution of conflict rather than the encouragement of conflict. That such is the case I suspect is also one of the reasons that peacekeeping, even if it is understood as a virtue, is not really all that appealing. For have you ever known anyone, yourself included, who would rush out to see a movie or a play about peace?

We say we want peace but in fact we know we love conflict and even war. Indeed I suspect one of the deepest challenges for those of us who call ourselves pacifists is that on the whole peace just does not seem very interesting to most people. We may all say that we want peace, but I suspect most of us would be deeply upset if we got it. We want to work for peace, we like the struggle for peace, but the idea that peace might actually be achieved would actually scare us to death. For we associate peace with rest. But we fear that rest without conflict is but another name for death. We thus pray like Augustine to give us peace—but not yet.

We simply have to admit that for most of us peace is boring. Of course in the midst of terrible turmoil we may well think we could stand a bit of boredom, but it is interesting how often people look back on past "troubles" nostalgically. Life needs movement which rightly or wrongly most of us believe entails conflict. Therefore peacemaking for most of us appears a bit like Bernard Shaw's views of heaven—on reflection he thought he preferred hell since at least hell promised to contain some interesting people.

But this text from Matthew puts the issue of peacemaking in quite a different light. For as I noted above, Jesus does not suggest that, if you have a grievance against someone in the community it might be a good idea for you to "try to work it out." Rather he says that you must go and speak to the one whom you believe has sinned against you. Such a speaking, of course, may well involve nothing less than confrontation. You must do it first alone, but if reconciliation does not take place then you must "go public," taking witnesses with you. If that still is not sufficient you must take the matter before the whole church.

Our first reaction to this text is that surely this procedure is far too extreme for most of our petty conflicts. I may get mad at someone but if I wait I discover I get over it. Moreover who wants to appear like someone who is too easily offended? No one likes people who tend to make mountains out of molehills, especially when they claim to be doing so only because of the "principle involved." Even more important, most of us learn that time heals all wounds and thus we are better off waiting for some conflicts to die through the passage of time.

Yet Jesus seems to have been working with a completely different set of presuppositions about what is necessary to be a community of peace and peacemaking. For it seems that peace is not the name of the absence of conflict, but rather peacemaking is that quality of life and practices engendered by a community that knows it lives as a forgiven people. Such a community cannot afford to "overlook" one another's sins because they have learned that such sins are a threat to being a community of peace.

For the essential presupposition of peacemaking as an activity among Christians is our common belief that we have been made part of a community in which people no longer regard their lives as their own. We are not permitted to harbor our grievances as "ours." When we think our brother or sister has sinned against us such an affront is not just against us but against the whole community. A community established as peaceful cannot afford to let us relish our sense of being wronged without exposing that wrong in the hopes of reconciliation. We must learn to see wrongs as "personal," because we are part of a community where the "personal" is crucial to the common good.

It is an unpleasant fact, however, that most of our lives are governed more by our hates and dislikes than by our loves. I seldom know what I really want, but I know what or whom I deeply dislike and even hate. It may be painful to be wronged, but at least such wrongs give me a history of resentments that in fact constitute who I am. How would I know who I am if I did not have my enemies?

Yet it seems it is exactly our enemies whom Jesus is forcing us to confront. For he tells us that we cannot cherish our wrongs. Rather we are commanded to engage in the difficult task of confronting those whom we believe have sinned against us. Such confrontation is indeed hard because it makes us as vulnerable as the one we confront. For the process of confrontation means we may well discover that we have been mistaken about our being wronged. Still more troubling it means that even if we have been wronged, by confronting our brother or sister we will have to envision the possibility, like Jonah, that he or she may repent and we will therefore have to be reconciled. I will be forced to lose the subject of my hatred.

From this perspective peacemaking is anything but boring. Rather it is the most demanding of tasks. For one of the interesting aspects of this passage in Matthew is that it assumes that the Christian community will involve conflict and wrongs. The question is not whether such conflict can be eliminated but rather how we are to deal with the conflict. Conflict is not to be ignored or denied, but rather conflict, which may involve sins, is to be forced into the open. That we are to do so must surely be because the peace that Jesus brings is not a peace of rest but rather a peace of truth. Just as love without truth cannot help but be accursed, so peace without truthfulness cannot help but be deadly. In short, peacekeeping is that virtue of the Christian community that is required if the church is to be a community of people at peace with one another in truth.

The truth seems to be about the last thing we want to know about ourselves. We may say that the truth saves, but in fact we know that any truth worth knowing is as disturbing as it is fulfilling. Surely that is why Jesus is so insistent that those who would follow him cannot simply let sins go unchallenged. For when we fail to challenge sinners, we in fact abandon them to their sin. We show we care little for them by our unwillingness to engage in the hard work of establishing a truthful peace.

That the church is such a community of truthful peace depends on its being a community of the forgiven. As the text from Matthew notes, Peter realized that Jesus' command that we confront the sinner is not an easy one. For such confrontation is based on the presupposition that forgiveness is also to be offered. But how often, Peter asks, can forgiveness be offered—seven times? We cannot help but be sympathetic with Peter's question for it just seems to be against good sense to be ready to offer forgiveness. What kind of community would ever be sustained on the presupposition that forgiveness is always available?

Yet there seems to be no limit to forgiveness, as Jesus elaborates his response to Peter by telling the story of the servant who, having been forgiven his debt, refuses to forgive a fellow servant his debt. The lord of the unforgiving servant on being told of his servant's behavior, threw him in jail until he paid his debt. And so we are told our "heavenly Father will do to every one of you, if you do not forgive your brother from your heart" (Matthew 18:35). What it seems we must remember, if we are to be peacemakers capable of confronting one another with our sins, is that we are the forgiven and we are part of a community of the forgiven. Our ability to be truthful peacemakers depends on our learning that we owe our lives to God's unrelenting forgiveness.

The forgiveness that makes peacemaking possible, moreover, does not mean judgment as withheld. The question is not whether we should hold one another accountable but the basis for doing so and how it is done. To be sinned against or to know we have sinned requires that we have a language and correlative habit that makes it possible to know what it is to be a sinner. Only on such a basis do we have the capacity to avoid arbitrariness of judgment as we learn to see our relations with one another as part of a continuing tradition of discourse that helps us serve a common good. That good, at least among Christians, is to be a community of the forgiven empowered to witness to God's kingdom of peace wrought through Jesus of Nazareth.

We, therefore, do not confront one another from a position of self-righteousness; we must come to the other as one who has been forgiven. Such a perspective, I think, throws quite a different light on this passage than is often given it. Too often it is assumed that this text legitimates our confrontation with the brother or sister on the assumption that we have power over the brother because we have been wronged and thus can decide to forgive. Forgiveness from such a position is but another form of power since I assume I am in a superior position. But the whole point of this text is we confront one another not as forgivers, not as those who use forgiveness as power, but first and foremost as people who have learned the truth about ourselves—namely that we are all people who need to be and have been forgiven.

That is why we must and can confront one another as sinners, because we understand ourselves to share with the other our having been forgiven. We thus share a common history of forgiveness and repentance that makes our willingness to confront one another a process of peace rather than simply another way to continue our war with one another. That is why those who refuse to listen must be treated as a Gentile or tax collector, for they are acting as those who have not learned that they have been forgiven. To act as one not needing forgiveness is to act against the very basis of this community as a community of peacemaking. That is why they must be excluded, since they must learn they are not living like those who have found they are peacemakers exactly because they have been forgiven. From such a perspective there is no more violent act than the unwillingness to accept reconciliation freely and honestly offered. But the truth is that few of us are willing to be so reconciled.

From this perspective we should not be surprised if peacemakers and peacemaking appear anything but peaceful. Moreover, if the church is to be a community of peace in a world at war it cannot help but be a community that confronts the world in uncompromising manner. For the task of peacemaking cannot ignore real wrongs past or present. The peace that the world knows too often is but order built on forgetfulness, but that is not the peace of the church that is built on forgiveness. No genuine peace can come from simply forgetting past wrongs, but rather must come by encompassing those wrongs in a history of forgiveness. Those peacemakers, however, who insist on reminding us of our past sins, cannot help but appear often as troublemakers.

This is particularly true when so often the wrongs that we must remember are those that no amount of effort or goodwill can make right. No matter how hard Christians work against anti-Semitism, there is finally nothing that can be done to make "right" the terror of the Holocaust. If there is to be a reconciliation between Christians and Jews, it cannot come through forgetting such a terrible wrong, but by learning to face that history as a forgiven people.

That is but to remind us that peacemaking as a virtue has a peculiar state in the temporal. Peace, as well as forgiveness, must take place in time. Disembodied beings cannot know peace; only beings who know themselves as timeful are capable of being at peace. As we are told in Ephesians, the relation between Israel and the Gentiles has not been resolved by some atemporal decree. But rather

> now in Christ Jesus you who once were far off have been brought near in the blood of Christ. For he is our peace, who has made us both one, and has broken down the dividing wall of hostility, by abolishing in his flesh the law of commandments and ordinances, that he might create in himself one new man in the place of the two, so making peace, and might reconcile us both to God in one body

through the cross, thereby bringing the hostility to an end. And he came and preached peace to you who were far off and peace to those who were near; for through him we both have access in one spirit to the Father. (Ephesians 2:13-18)

Peacemaking among Christians, therefore, is not simply one activity among others, but rather the very form of the church insofar as the church is the form of the one who "is our peace." Peacemaking is the form of our relations in the church as we seek to be in unity with one another which at least means we begin to share a common history. Such unity is not that built on shallow optimism that we can get along together as long as we respect one another's differences. Rather it is a unity that profoundly acknowledges our differences because we have learned those differences are not accidental to our being a truthful people—even when they require us to confront one another as those who have wronged us.

But if peacemaking as a virtue is intrinsic to the nature of the church, what are we to say about those without the church? First, I think we must say that it is the task of the church to confront and challenge the false peace of the world that is too often built on power rather than truth. To challenge the world's sense of peace may well be dangerous, because often when sham peace is exposed it threatens to become violent. The church, however, cannot be less truthful with the world than it is expected to be with itself. If we are such we have no peace to offer to the world.

Secondly, Christians are prohibited from ever despairing of the peace possible in the world. For we know that as God's creatures we are not naturally violent nor are our institutions unavoidably violent. As God's people we have been created for peace. Rather what we must do is help the world find the habits of peace whose absence so often makes violence seem like the only alternative. For peacemaking as a virtue is an act of imagination built on long habits of the resolution of differences. The great problem in the world is that our imagination has been stilled since it has not made a practice of confronting wrongs so that violence might be avoided. In truth we must say that the church has too often failed the world by our failure to witness in our own life the kind of conflict necessary to be a community of peace. Without an example of a peacemaking community, the world has no alternative but to use violence as the means to settle disputes.

I have tried to show how peacekeeping as a virtue is community specific—that is, how it is an activity intrinsic to the nature of the church. Yet the fact that peacekeeping is community specific does not mean it ought to be community restrictive. The "brother" referred to in Matthew is no doubt a member of the Christian community, but the Matthean community is also one that understood it was to go among the nations as witness to God's peace. Therefore the habits of peacekeeping acquired in the church are no less relevant when the church confronts those not part of our community and who may even threaten or wrong our community. For it is our belief that God is no less present in our enemy calling us to find the means of reconciliation.

If the line I have taken is close to being right, then I think it puts pacifism into a different perspective than is normal. For pacifism is often associated with being passive in the face of wrong. As a result some even suggest that pacifism is immoral insofar as the pacifist suffers wrong and as a result fails to fulfill the obligation to the brother by resisting his injustice. But peacemaking is not a passive response; rather it is an active way to resist injustice by confronting the wrongdoer with the offer of reconciliation. Such reconciliation is not cheap, however, since no reconciliation is possible unless the wrong is confronted and acknowledged.

Contrary to usual stereotypes, this means that peacekeepers, rather than withdraw from politics, must be the most political of animals. For peacekeeping requires the development of the processes and institutions that make possible confrontation and resolution of differences so that violence can be avoided. The problem with politics, at least as politics is currently understood, is not that it involves compromises, but that it so little believes in truth. As a result, it becomes but a form of coercion without due acknowledgement that it is so. In such a situation the church can be a peacemaker by being the most political of institutions.

No doubt peacemaking, as I have tried to depict it, is a demanding business. I think it is impossible to sustain if it is thought to be a virtue of heroic individuals. Rather peacemaking must be a virtue of a whole community, so that the kind of support and care necessary to sustain peacemaking as an ongoing task will be forthcoming. As Christians, however, we cannot help but rejoice that God has called us to be peacemakers for what could possibly be a more joyful and exciting task than to be a part of God's peace?

99. John Howard Yoder

A Theological Critique of Violence

John Howard Yoder (1927-1997) was for many years a professor of Christian ethics at the University of Notre Dame and the Associated Mennonite Biblical Seminary in Goshen, Indiana. In the latter half of the twentieth century, he led the way in revitalizing the intellectual credibility of Christian nonviolence and in encouraging Christians to understand the church as its own polis. Yoder's most famous work was The Politics of Jesus, *which has since become a classic in Christian political thought. Below is an excerpt of his trenchant critique of violence, published posthumously in* The War of the Lamb: The Ethics of Nonviolence and Peacemaking *(2009).*

… First I propose to begin where the Bible does, by telling and interpreting a very ancient story. I shall not lay a prior theoretical groundwork by explaining why telling stories is a respectable theological thing to do, though that discussion is much in vogue in the guild. I shall not justify the authority of the book where we find these stories, although in some circles that would need to be done. I shall not throw any etymological light on the word *violence* or its Hebrew counterparts, as if definitions could settle moral matters.

As soon as the human story is situated outside the original innocence of the garden of Eden, one man kills his brother (Gen. 4). The first epistle of John tells us one reason for the murder, but Genesis does not. Cain represents the culture of the farmer, tied to the land from which he drew the vegetables that he offered in sacrifice but that Yahweh did not accept. Abel represents the flock-herding nomad. Genesis does not tell us why either of them brought sacrifices. There had been no account thus far of the origins of sacrifice. Nor are we told why the shepherd's sacrifice was more acceptable to Yahweh, although an anthropologist could offer some hunches.

It is not for us to make Genesis consistent by explaining what Abel was doing with flocks when Genesis 2 had foreseen a vegetarian culture. Ritually sacrificing and eating animals does not come until chapter 9. What we can say *is* in the intention of the text is that this first homicide drags Yahweh back into the fallen history which he had thought he had banished from his presence. We might think that divine intervention becomes necessary to protect the rest of humanity against the danger of this murderer in their midst. But the opposite is the case. Yahweh acts to protect Cain against the primeval vengeance he had every reason to fear. But why does Cain have reason to fear it?

A century ago, amid the debates around Darwinism, the mocking question was "where did Cain get his wife?" In Genesis, the rest of humanity is first alluded to not as a resource for affection or procreation or community, but as a threat. The very first reference to the rest of humanity is "whoever finds me will slay me."

That is the primeval definition of *violence* for our present purposes: that there are people out there whose response to Cain's deed is *mimetic*. They will quasi-automatically, as by reflex, want to do to him what he had done to Abel. It will not occur to them not to do so. It will seem self-evident to them that that is what he has asked for by what he did.

… Yahweh himself has no interest in vengeance. He does warn Cain that the earth that he has soiled with his brother's blood will no longer nourish him. That is more a statement of fact than a judicial pronouncement. In anthropological terms, Cain will move from agriculture to the cultural stage of crafts and city-building. But the divine initiative that matters is that *Yahweh intervenes to protect Cain's life from the universally threatening vengeance.* The sign of the protection is a mark placed on Cain; its verbal formula is a threat of vengeance: "If any one slays Cain, vengeance shall be taken on him sevenfold." The threat is so massive that it will not need to be carried out. No one will attack Cain, even though he has it coming, for fear of the sevenfold backlash. This was an extreme measure, but it worked. Cain did survive, to become the ancestor of urban culture, of metalworking, and of music.

The strand of the story soon reaches its dead end, however, with the boast of Cain's distant descendant Lamech. Whereas in Cain's case Yahweh's threat of sevenfold retaliation does not need to be carried out, Lamech boasts that he himself retaliates seventy-sevenfold (Gen. 4:23-24). That suffices to characterize the way in which the retaliatory reflex, by its very nature, runs amok. It breaks loose from the preventive, protective function that it was supposed to discharge and becomes itself the engine of destruction.

René Girard, literary critic turned anthropologist, has been attracting increasing attention to his general theory of the origins of primitive culture in a foundational transaction prior to history but reflected in myth and legend. By that foundational covenant, the escalating spiral of retaliation is broken off before it explodes. At that point a transaction, redirecting the communal vengeance against an innocent victim, replaces the spiral as the guarantee of society's peace.

Girard's theory is too complex for the ordinary nonspecialist like me to know whereby it might be validated or falsified, but in any case the threads he pulls together impress one with a kind of genial verisimilitude. His reconstruction seems to fit with stories like that of Lamech. The only way to keep Lamech's pride in his incommensurate retaliation from putting an end to history was to find some way to soak it up, to buffer it, to keep it from running free, yet without ignoring its provocation. The civil order arises to replace private violent vengeance: regulating it, mitigating it, yet also thereby legitimizing it.

… But my concern here cannot be to pose as an amateur anthropologist. Whether or not the Girardian etiology represents ancient prehistory with total accuracy, the metaphor is very helpful. I propose to make do with the kind of argument that Girard represents: namely, that the bloodiness of ancient human culture is not best understood as compatible with later rationalizations, either functionally as part of maintaining social order, or theologically as maintaining a cosmic balance. Those interpretations are modern. They are rationalizations in the technical sense: i.e., they are efforts to impose by a mental exercise a sense-giving framework upon realities that do not have that kind of meaning. That is why our struggles in the name of enlightenment against xenophobia, militarism, patriarchy, or the death penalty are so far from the mark.

But then if the phenomenon of violence is not rational in its causes, its functions, and its objectives, neither will its cure be rational. The cure will have to be something as primitive, as elemental, as the evil. It will have to act upon the deep levels of meaning and motivation, deeper than mental self-definition and self-control. It will have to be *sacrifice*. There will have to be innocent suffering.

… More than ethics is involved, then, in our coming to grips with what violence means. Whether that *more* needs to be sought deeper in the order of the impersonal cosmos that surrounds us, or deeper in the psyche inside us, or deeper in the decree of a person-like God, who responds to misbehavior in ways that can be compared to an angry person, is a choice we need not resolve. Why could it not be all of the above? For our purposes it suffices to recognize that *there is a destructive reflex at work, which will not go away and whereby violence propagates itself.*

One thing that can be done with this reflex is to channel it by the application of a justification that is at the same time a restraint; we call that the *state*, or *law and order*. Or we can attempt to manage it by appealing to the world of magic and metaphor; we call that *sacrament*. We can attempt to come to grips with it in the framework of a set of mental constructs; we may label it *mimesis* as does René Girard or compare it to the eye-for-eye balancing of the ancient Hebrews. We may call it *retribution* or *compensation*, as does legal theory. We may call it *expiation*, or the restoring the balance of a tilted cosmos. In another context, another discipline, the word will be *deterrence* or *self-affirmation*. C. S. Lewis argues that the imperative of equivalent retribution is part of the human dignity of the offender.

To Overcome the Retributive Impulse, We Need the Sacrifice of the Cross

Not long ago the television news hounds, with their usual nose for blood, were interviewing the father of one of the victims of the first man in years whom California was going to execute for murder. The father was rejoicing in the prospect of attending the execution, but said he would like even more to be able to replicate formally, as a means of execution, the chase and the stabbing as they took place in the original murder. His reason? "An eye for an eye, ya' know."

It is a fascinating fluke of culture transmission that this phrase, "an eye for an eye," whose primary place in the Christian canon is that Jesus set it aside, should lead its own life down through Western history as validation for the reflex of mimetic destruction. That phrase appears only three times in the Mosaic corpus, never in a literarily important place. In none of the three places does the text call for the death penalty for murder. The phrase is used once when death is prescribed for accidentally killing a woman in the course of fighting a man, once for blasphemy, and once for perjury in a capital case. In short: the notion of cosmic symmetry is there in the ancient rhymed phrases but not in the actual Hebrew jurisprudence, and not in the nature of God.

Nevertheless, that ancient rhyme rolls on down

through Western civilization as if it were the law of gravity. René Girard would say that it *is* the law of gravity.

By putting the facts about the violence reflex in an explanatory and (some hope) regulatory framework, these efforts to channel it or manage it have several things in common:

1. They are undertaken after the fact. None of them can or does claim to describe the *origin* of the phenomenon of reflexive vengeance.
2. They grant, concede, or posit that the reality of the destructive reflex cannot be managed or removed by describing, defining, or explaining it.

The response that is needed then is not a new way to *think* about it—what we might properly call a *theological critique*—but something to be *done* about it. The response is divine judgment; not an explanation, not an evaluation, but an intervention.

The name of that intervention is "Jesus." How best to interpret the meaning of Jesus, and especially of his becoming victim, will depend on which of the descriptions of the problem we choose to draw on. I mention only a few of these descriptions. If you can make sense of a sacrificial worldview, Jesus is the last high priest and the last victim. If your worldview is juridical, then Jesus is the last vicarious offender who bears the penalty humanity had earned. If your worldview is political realism, Jesus is the advocate of the people whose leadership called down on him the death penalty of the Romans. Psychodynamic analysis, or Girard's deep anthropological vision, or feminism can say it yet other ways. Tolstoy, the doctrinaire poetic oversimplifier, could speak of "breaking the chain" of evil. Gandhi, and Gandhi's pupil Martin Luther King Jr., replicated it as a model for social change in our time.

What all of these (in detail deeply different) modes of connection have in common is that the thing to do with violence is not to understand it *but to undergo it*. In no case is the solution that we should escalate our power to coerce. We cannot beat the destructive reflex at its own game. Whichever idiom we use to articulate its claim on us, for our own setting and for the mental agenda of our particular interlocutors, the answer is the cross.

Sometime in August of 1525, in the pastor's residence of the parish of St. Martin's in Basel, Johannes Hausschyn, who as a humanist preferred to use the Hellenized name Oecolampadius, was confronted by some men called Anabaptists. They were responding to his having attacked them from the pulpit. While they were talking, a man from Zurich joined the group. He exclaimed that, "what is needed is divine wisdom, in order to discern honor in the cross, and life in death. We must deny ourselves and become fools."

I have been working away at the problem of violence, beginning with the bad news rather than the good, because that was our assigned theme. The good news, however, is that out of death life has come and does come. The salvation of the world comes not from shrewder management or better luck but from the divine condescension of the cross.

This is not a rare insight, present only at one place, one high point, within the apostolic writings. Every major strand of the New Testament, each in its own way, interprets the acceptance by Jesus of the violence of the cross as the means, necessary and sufficient, of God's victory over the rebellious powers. Violence is not merely a problem to solve, a temptation to resist, a mystery to penetrate, or a challenge to resolve with a theodicy. It is all of that, but that is not yet the good news. The good news is that the violence with which we heirs of Cain respond to our brothers' differentness is the occasion of our salvation. *Were it not for that primeval destructive reflex, there would have been no suffering servant, and no wisdom and power of God in the cross.*

That this is the case does not make it any less necessary to review and update the arguments about the legitimacy of violence in the defense of victims or against oppression. That is the theme of the rest of this essay. Yet this observation may encourage us to direct our energies less toward explaining and evaluating, and more toward participation in the reconciliation story.

Paul wrote to the church at Corinth: "The weapons of our combat are not fleshly." We would expect the sentence to go on to say something like, "not fleshly *but spiritual.*" That would fit with Paul's acceptance of his weakness, expressed elsewhere in the same letter, as his own privileged mode of ministry. But that is not what he says. He says, "The weapons of our combat are not fleshly but mighty." They can "destroy strongholds." The opposite of "flesh" is *strength*. If we can face the great tacit assumption of Genesis 4—that the destructive reflex characterizes the fallen world—we may be empowered to see clearly that the cross of Jesus Christ is not only cultic but also *cosmic*. Innocent suffering is the victory over the vengeful urge, and over the institutions that exploit it, on an anthropologically far more fundamental level than our usual theories of the state or of social hygiene.

To illustrate: In our society, unlike in the rest of the industrialized world, the forces of enlightenment have been losing ground for twenty years in the effort to abolish the death penalty. Some of the reasons for the setbacks were tactical. It may have been a mistake in the long run to trust the courts to set aside as "cruel and unusual," or otherwise as unconstitutional, penalties that legislatures could reinstate. It may have been a tactical mistake to base so much of the case against judicial killing upon the racial and economic inequities of its application in some states. But I have come to the impression that there was a deeper mistake.

We have projected the tacit claim that there is something uncouth about the destructive reflex itself, rather than granting it a deep anthropological legitimacy. Instead of posing the foundations for a nonretributive society upon ways of processing the deep demand of blood for blood, such as Jewish reverence for the sacredness of life, or the Christian interpretation of the cross of Christ in word and sacrament (and in discipleship), or on Enlightenment visions of restraining governmental absolutism, or even on psychodynamic therapeutic analogues of all the above, we have tried to make our culture ashamed of its vengefulness. That shame has backfired in a new wave of executions.

We have not been able to transfer to capital punishment the insight that Gandhi and King taught us about racial oppression, namely that *the victim of violence most to be pitied is its perpetrator*. The perpetrator is not as free, or as in control, or as effective, or as satisfied with himself or herself as he or she thinks. This was the case for the imperial bureaucrats Gandhi faced, as well as for the white police officers King faced. This is hardly less true when the power being abused is that of office, or that of gender. Only when we retrieve an awareness of the foundational place of retribution in our social psyche can we hope to discover the role of redemption in a newly pertinent form....

Celebrating the Faith in the Face of Violence

"I believe," the creed says, "in one God, the Father Almighty, Maker of heaven and earth, and of all things visible and invisible." That God is almighty will have something to do with why we assume we need to impose our choice of the lesser evil on world history. But for now I note that if "all things visible and invisible" are of God's making, if (as Locke said much later about human creativity) God has "mixed his labor" with things, then they are God's. That is why we should not violate them. What is wrong with violence is that what is violated is a creature of the sovereign God. Of human life in particular, Genesis further says (although the creed does not) that the creature is characterized by the "image and likeness" of God. I do not propose to review the various meanings given to that Hebrew phrase; *any* possible meaning must be part of what makes it wrong to violate the life or dignity of a human being.

The theological critique of violence begins, then, by recognizing that *the majesty of the creator God is what is under attack*. To reduce a life-threatening situation to a clash of quantifiable group interests without recognizing the uniqueness of the human life one proposes to destroy is not merely misdirected politics or cost-benefit pragmatism with the coefficients wrong; it is first of all *blasphemy*.

There are many ways to sin against God and neighbor, but it is a mistake to level them all out as if the values at stake were all of the same size or shape. Some argue that in order to be consistent we must treat all sins the same and not make one sin worse than another. Yet to shed human blood is, according to Genesis 9, an offense against the divine image; that is not said of lying or stealing, coveting, bearing false witness, or disrespect to parents. *Violence* is qualitatively on a different level from other offenses. Many other offenses would be less drastic if not escalated by the admixture of coercion. After other offenses one can make amends to the victim; not after killing. Fratricide, as demonstrated in Genesis 4 and 1 John 3, is the chief of sins, because God's making my fellow human to be my partner in the care of the cosmos is the crown of creation.

The creed goes on: "I believe in one Lord Jesus Christ" and then uses seven words to describe the action of Christ: begotten, crucified, buried, risen, ascended, seated, coming. For our purposes we can concentrate on the verbs. First there is the triptych-like, threefold downward movement: three passive verbs, *kenosis*, and all past tense. Then the threefold victory: three active verbs, also past. Then comes the dangling seventh verb, in timeless present: "coming."

The theological critique of violence implicit in the first triptych addresses the pride and self-justification presupposed by the just war argument. The just war argument presupposes the possession of power. That is why Christians did not think that way during the first three centuries. The early Christians were not pacifist in the sense that, when called by the draft, they did not serve. There was no draft. They were not pacifist in the sense of asking Nero to call off the superpower struggle against the Parthians. Neither they nor Nero, not having read Locke or Rousseau, thought of Nero as being accountable to "the people" in general or to Christians in particular. But they *were* nonviolent. They saw in the passion and death of their Lord the model of divine-human virtue to place over against other visions of human prospering. Doing without dominion was not for them a second-best alternative to glory; *it was the way to participate in the victory of redemption.*

The theological critique of violence implicit in the active panel of the triptych addresses the element of despair in the just war argument. Violence is the only way, the last resort, the just war common sense says, *because there is no other actor for good on the scene.* We must tough-mindedly take on the dirty work and the moral ambivalence of dealing death to our fellow creatures, because otherwise history would get out of hand. But confessing Jesus Christ risen, ascended, and seated at the right hand of the Father meant, in the first century, that his-

tory *cannot* get out of hand. The medieval and high Protestant word for "seated at the right hand" was *providence.* There is a potential for saving outcomes in the human drama, and there is a potential for redemptive outcomes out of suffering, if Jesus Christ is viceroy over the cosmos. We short-circuit that providential potential when we decide to be providence ourselves, at the expense of the fellow humans on whom we inflict the violence that we claim is lesser.

The critique of violence implied in the final verb, "coming [to judge]," re-states as vindication what the three active participles [risen, ascended, seated at the right hand of God] described as authority. The redemption that is now going on in history under providence will be ratified as the last word. The evil that is now being condoned by the patience of God will come to an end. That the way of the suffering servant is after all the way of the Lord of hosts, which today we have to believe against appearances, will then be manifest so that every knee will bow.

That should be enough, but the creed goes on: "I believe in the Holy Spirit, the Church Universal, Forgiveness, Resurrection, and Eternal Life, Amen." That the human communion in which our trust centers is not a nation-state or a regime, that sins are forgiven, that the sanction of death is revoked: these are not major new theological affirmations, yet they round out the holism of our vision of the world where violence is out of order. This third article is not just an addendum. All of this concrete reconciliation and community is the work of the Spirit, who is no less Godself than are the Father and the Son.

My point in putting doxology before ethics was that too often our cultural ethics, especially social ethics, is reduced to a form of engineering: how to do what you have to with the least pain. We calculate costs and benefits on the basis of a deterministic understanding of how history goes. Then the place of piety is to help us live with the inevitable pain. If you are more Wesleyan, your warmed heart will make you try harder. If you are more Calvinist, your confidence in predestination will make you try harder. If you are Lutheran, your trust in God's forgiving you will make you stop trying so hard, but by the paradox of grace that will make you do just as well. For all of the above, dogma and spirituality contribute to the setting or the mood of ethics, but not to its substance.

For our apostolic predecessors, the form of the life of faith in society was not in that sense derivative. They did not have in one corner of their casuistry a place to discuss the pros and cons of killing in extreme circumstances. They were living in and into a new world, one in which that corner had no place.

Jesus and the Politics of Violence

One more exposition: I said nothing until now about the human career of the Jesus of the Gospels, because the creed does not. The creed skips from Bethlehem to Golgotha, from Mary to Pilate. But of course the Gospels do not make that leap, nor did the real story. If there had not been the story in between, there would have been no creed. Because of the metaphysical invasion of our world bespoken by the verb "begotten," there had to be the story in between, for which my name is *The Politics of Jesus*. Named by angelic imperative for the liberator Joshua, greeted by the magi as liberator-designate, and targeted for massacre by Herod for the same reason, Jesus faced the temptation of violence as no other. Our sources give no information concerning his inclinations to covet, steal, bear false witness, or commit adultery. But from the first testing in the desert to the last one in the garden, his unceasing temptation was the plea of the crowds and even of some of his disciples that he should strike out on the path of righteous kingship.

The Gospel Is Not about Delegitimizing Violence So Much as about Overcoming It

Violence, we saw already at the other end of the story, is not a sin like any other. For Jesus it was not a temptation like any other. Jesus did not refrain from violence because he was scrupulous about bloodguilt. He did not, like a cartoon figure incarnating unconditional love so absolutely as to be historically impossible, step off the scale of political pertinence in order to be true to the hyperbolic logic of the Sermon on the Mount (as Reinhold Niebuhr would interpret it in the 1930s). Jesus chose the cross as an alternative social strategy of strength, not weakness. As Paul would write a generation later, it was God's wisdom and power, what God ultimately does about violence.

In thus repeating the classical critical agenda evoked by the case for violence, I do not want to be thought unaware of the misuse that can be made of the gospel themes I have touched upon. What I referred to above as "doing without dominion" can, in the wrong hands, be twisted into an acceptance of evil systems on the grounds of the claim that God is in control. Suffering servanthood can, when involuntary, become pathological. Trusting providence can be twisted into passivity. Discerning in violence a destructive quality *sui generis* can keep us from discerning all of the latent ways we hurt each other without drawing blood. All of these distortions of the cross are connected to the effort to do ethics without piety, social ethics without ecclesiology, law without gospel.

The review of the justification for violence ends where the interpretation of its anthropological origins ended. Violence has been made a problem and has called forth our critique because some advocate its use on various kinds of grounds. But the gospel is not about delegitimizing violence so much as about overcoming it. We overcome it partly by demythologizing its moral pretensions, partly by refusing to meet it on its own terms, partly by replacing it with other more humane strategies and tactics of moral struggle, partly by innocent suffering, and partly by virtue of the special restorative resources of forgiveness and community. Yet all of those coping resources are derivative. At bottom violence is judged—*critiqued* in the deep sense of the verb—because of the passion events.

We participate in that judgment by participating in the cross, the resurrection, the ascension, and the pouring out of the Spirit. That we thus participate in the gathered life of believers goes without saying. What matters for our present study is to appropriate it as grace so that we can participate in the same process no less within the struggles of our wounded world.

100. On the Care of Creation: An Evangelical Declaration on the Care of Creation

In 1994 the Evangelical Environmental Network released the following Christian declaration on care for the creation. The declaration attracted the signatures of more than a hundred leading evangelical scholars and activists, and resulted in other evangelical declarations on the environment, including one on climate change at the beginning of the new century. Most striking about the document for the purposes of this book is the connections it draws between peace and care for creation.

The Earth is the Lord's, and the fullness thereof
—Psalm 24:1

As followers of Jesus Christ, committed to the full authority of the Scriptures, and aware of the ways we have degraded creation, we believe that biblical faith is essential to the solution of our ecological problems.

Because we worship and honor the Creator, we seek to cherish and care for the creation.

Because we have sinned, we have failed in our stewardship of creation. Therefore we repent of the way we have polluted, distorted, or destroyed so much of the Creator's work.

Because in Christ God has healed our alienation from God and extended to us the first fruits of the reconciliation of all things, we commit ourselves to working in the power of the Holy Spirit to share the Good News of Christ in word and deed, to work for the reconciliation of all people in Christ, and to extend Christ's healing to suffering creation.

Because we await the time when even the groaning creation will be restored to wholeness, we commit ourselves to work vigorously to protect and heal that creation for the honor and glory of the Creator—whom we know dimly through creation, but meet fully through Scripture and in Christ. We and our children face a growing crisis in the health of the creation in which we are embedded, and through which, by God's grace, we are sustained. Yet we continue to degrade that creation.

These degradations of creation can be summed up as 1) land degradation; 2) deforestation; 3) species extinction; 4) water degradation; 5) global toxification; 6) the alteration of atmosphere; 7) human and cultural degradation.

Many of these degradations are signs that we are pressing against the finite limits God has set for creation. With continued population growth, these degradations will become more severe. Our responsibility is not only to bear and nurture children, but to nurture their home on earth. We respect the institution of marriage as the way God has given to insure thoughtful procreation of children and their nurture to the glory of God.

We recognize that human poverty is both a cause and a consequence of environmental degradation.

Many concerned people, convinced that environmental problems are more spiritual than technological, are exploring the world's ideologies and religions in search of non-Christian spiritual resources for the healing of the earth. As followers of Jesus Christ, we believe that the Bible calls us to respond in four ways:

First, God calls us to confess and repent of attitudes which devalue creation, and which twist or ignore biblical revelation to support our misuse of it. Forgetting that "the earth is the Lord's," we have often simply used creation and forgotten our responsibility to care for it.

Second, our actions and attitudes toward the earth need to proceed from the center of our faith, and be rooted in the fullness of God's revelation in Christ and the Scriptures. We resist both ideologies which would presume the Gospel has nothing to do with the care of non-human creation and also ideologies which would reduce the Gospel to nothing more than the care of that creation.

Third, we seek carefully to learn all that the Bible tells us about the Creator, creation, and the human task. In our life and words we declare that full good news for all creation which is still waiting "with eager longing for the revealing of the children of God" (Rom. 8:19).

Fourth, we seek to understand what creation reveals about God's divinity, sustaining presence, and everlasting power, and what creation teaches us of its God-given order and the principles by which it works.

Thus we call on all those who are committed to the truth of the Gospel of Jesus Christ to affirm the following principles of biblical faith, and to seek ways of living out these principles in our personal lives, our churches, and society.

The cosmos, in all its beauty, wildness, and life-giving bounty, is the work of our personal and loving Creator.

Our creating God is prior to and other than creation, yet intimately involved with it, upholding each thing in its freedom, and all things in relationships of intricate complexity. God is transcendent, while lovingly sustaining each creature; and immanent, while wholly other than creation and not to be confused with it.

God the Creator is relational in very nature, revealed as three persons in One. Likewise, the creation which God intended is a symphony of individual creatures in harmonious relationship.

The Creator's concern is for all creatures. God declares all creation "good" (Gen. 1:31); promises care in a covenant with all creatures (Gen. 9:9-17); delights in creatures which have no human apparent usefulness (Job 39-41); and wills, in Christ, "to reconcile all things to himself" (Col.1:20).

Men, women, and children have a unique responsibility to the Creator; at the same time we are creatures, shaped by the same processes and embedded in the same systems of physical, chemical, and biological interconnections which sustain other creatures.

Men, women, and children, created in God's image, also have a unique responsibility for creation. Our actions should both sustain creation's fruitfulness and preserve creation's powerful testimony to its Creator.

Our God-given, stewardly talents have often been warped from their intended purpose: that we know, name, keep and delight in God's creatures; that we nourish civilization in love, creativity and obedience to God; and that we offer creation and civilization back in praise to the Creator. We have ignored our creaturely limits and have used the earth with greed, rather than care.

The earthly result of human sin has been a perverted stewardship, a patchwork of garden and wasteland in which the waste is increasing. "There is no faithfulness, no love, no acknowledgment of God in the land ... Because of this the land mourns, and all who live in it waste away" (Hosea 4:1, 3). Thus, one consequence of our misuse of the earth is an unjust denial of God's created bounty to other human beings, both now and in the future.

God's purpose in Christ is to heal and bring to wholeness not only persons but the entire created order. "For God was pleased to have all his fullness dwell in him, and through him to reconcile to himself all things, whether things on earth or things in heaven, by making peace through his blood shed on the cross" (Col. 1:19-20).

In Jesus Christ, believers are forgiven, transformed and brought into God's kingdom. "If anyone is in Christ, there is a new creation" (II Cor. 5:17). The presence of the kingdom of God is marked not only by renewed fellowship with God, but also by renewed harmony and justice between people, and by renewed harmony and justice between people and the rest of the created world. "You will go out in joy and be led forth in peace; the mountains and the hills will burst into song before you, and all the trees of the field will clap their hands" (Isa. 55:12).

We believe that in Christ there is hope, not only for men, women and children, but also for the rest of creation which is suffering from the consequences of human sin.

Therefore we call upon all Christians to reaffirm that all creation is God's; that God created it good; and that God is renewing it in Christ.

We encourage deeper reflection on the substantial biblical and theological teaching which speaks of God's work of redemption in terms of the renewal and completion of God's purpose in creation.

We seek a deeper reflection on the wonders of God's creation and the principles by which creation works. We also urge a careful consideration of how our corporate and individual actions respect and comply with God's ordinances for creation.

We encourage Christians to incorporate the extravagant creativity of God into their lives by increasing the nurturing role of beauty and the arts in their personal, ecclesiastical, and social patterns.

We urge individual Christians and churches to be centers of creation's care and renewal, both delighting in creation as God's gift, and enjoying it as God's provision, in ways which sustain and heal the damaged fabric of the creation which God has entrusted to us.

We recall Jesus' words that our lives do not consist in the abundance of our possessions, and therefore we urge followers of Jesus to resist the allure of wastefulness and overconsumption by making personal lifestyle choices that express humility, forbearance, self restraint and frugality.

We call on all Christians to work for godly, just, and sustainable economies which reflect God's sovereign economy and enable men, women and children to flourish along with all the diversity of creation. We recognize that poverty forces people to degrade creation in order to survive; therefore we support the development of just, free economies which empower the poor and create abundance without diminishing creation's bounty.

We commit ourselves to work for responsible public policies which embody the principles of biblical stewardship of creation.

We invite Christians—individuals, congregations and organizations—to join with us in this evangelical declaration on the environment, becoming a covenant people in an ever-widening circle of biblical care for creation.

We call upon Christians to listen to and work with all those who are concerned about the healing of creation, with an eagerness both to learn from them and also to share with them our conviction that the God whom all people sense in creation (Acts 17:27) is known fully only in the Word made flesh in Christ the living God who made and sustains all things.

We make this declaration knowing that until Christ returns to reconcile all things, we are called to be faithful stewards of God's good garden, our earthly home.

101. DUANE FRIESEN AND GLEN STASSEN

Just Peacemaking

Duane Friesen (b. 1940) and Glen Stassen (b. 1936) are two of the leading theorists of a movement they refer to as just peacemaking. Friesen is the Edmund G. Kaufman Professor Emeritus of Bible and Religion at Bethel College, and a longtime peace advocate with the Mennonite Central Committee. Stassen, a Baptist, is the Lewis B. Smedes Professor of Christian Ethics at Fuller Theological Seminary, and an active board member of Peace Action, a group that calls for a new U.S. foreign policy focused on resolving conflicts peacefully.

The Historical Kairos

Several historical forces have come together in our time to produce the Just Peacemaking Theory. Over fifty years ago the world was stunned by the horror of the devastation of World War II and the threat of atomic and nuclear weapons. The reality of that threat persuaded people and institutions to develop new networks and practices they hoped would prevent another world war and use of nuclear weapons. Now over fifty years have passed, and so far we have avoided those two specters. New practices are actually getting results in ways many have not noticed. We believe we live in a moment of *kairos* when it is useful to name these practices, call attention to them, and support them ethically.

In this new era, after the Cold War and at the turn of the millennium, people lack a clear vision of what sort of peacemaking is effective and is in fact happening. Hence, they do not know how they can contribute. The result is confusion, cognitive dissonance, apathy, and inward-turning—ironically just when the opportunity and need for spreading zones of peace is most at hand.

Just Peacemaking Theory is intended to give a road map to individual people, grassroots groups, voluntary associations, and groups in churches, synagogues, mosques, or meetings. The theory shows what people can do to fan the flames of peace.

… [T]here is in our time a growing sense of the inadequacy of the debate between just war theory and pacifism. This has been the major division among Christians on the question of war. Debates dominated by these two paradigms inevitably focus on whether or not to make war.

That crucial question will not go away if the just peacemaking paradigm succeeds. However, in that two-sided debate another question regularly gets slighted: What essential steps should be taken to make peace? Have they been taken? Or should they yet be taken?

The just peacemaking question fills out the original intention of the other two paradigms. It encourages pacifists to be what their name, derived from the Latin, *pacem-facere,* means: peace-*makers*. And it calls just war theorists to fill in the contents of their underdeveloped principles of last resort and just intention. It invites them to spell out what resorts must be tried before moving to the last resort, what intention there is to restore a just and endurable peace—and then to act on the peace-promoting suggestions emerging from such discernment.

Ten Practices of Just Peacemaking

The ten practices of just peacemaking presented here are based on and grounded in the Christian faith. But we also offer them to others who can adapt them to their own faith perspectives. We divide the practices into three groups: *cooperative forces, justice,* and *peacemaking initiatives.* The first group, *cooperative forces,* may be seen as a dimension of love, realistically rather than sentimentally understood. A key dimension of love in scriptural teaching is breaking down barriers to community and participation in cooperative community.

Justice, the second grouping, is a central biblical theme. Third, growing numbers of us interpret grace-based peacemaking in terms of specific *peacemaking initiatives, or transforming initiatives.* The theological comments which follow our list of the ten just peacemaking practices show how these are grounded in Christian faith.

Strengthen Cooperative Forces

1. *Recognize emerging cooperative forces in the international system and work with them.* Historically, cooperative institutions like the League of Nations have broken down. But there are trends in today's world that make it much more possible to sustain voluntary associations for peace and other purposes.

The utility of war has declined, with trade and the economy taking priority over war. International exchanges, communications, transactions, and networks are growing stronger. There is a gradual ascendancy of liberal representative democracy and a mixture of welfare-state and *laissez-faire* market economy. We should act so as to strengthen these trends and the international associations they make possible, insofar as they genuinely advance the common good and do not further hurt the poor and powerless.

When churches teach the wrongness and futility of war, send and receive missionaries, and welcome refugees, they are encouraging cooperative forces. Churches strengthen ties in this emerging international system by themselves becoming internationalized in their membership and leadership. They can work at this by sending members to international conferences, service projects, and work camps as well as learning from fellow Christians across international and especially North/South divisions. Churches were pioneering these practices long before international relations scholars were writing about them, and we need more of such activity.

2. *Strengthen the United Nations and interna-*

tional efforts for cooperation and human rights. International relations increasingly involve not only the traditional military-diplomatic arena but also the modern arena of economic interdependence. Here governments are exposed to the forces of a global market they do not control. At the same time, the information revolution makes it harder for governments to control people's minds, and popular pressures can now set much of the agenda of foreign policies. States float in a sea of forces from outside their borders or from among their people. Acting alone, states cannot solve problems of trade, debt, interest rates; of pollution, ozone depletion, acid rain, global warming; of migrations and refugees seeking asylum; of military security when weapons rapidly penetrate borders.

As we approach the turning of the century, collective action is increasingly necessary. Citizens can encourage their governments to act in small and large crises in ways that strengthen the effectiveness of the United Nations and of regional organizations. We can include support for the United Nations as part of our church teaching and action or as an aspect of the strategy of peacemaking organizations in which we participate.

Many multilateral practices are building effectiveness to resolve conflicts; to monitor, nurture, and even enforce truces; and to replace violent conflict with the beginnings of cooperation. International cooperation is meeting human needs for food, hygiene, medicine, education, and economic interaction. Collective action sometimes includes UN-approved humanitarian intervention in cases like the former Yugoslavia, Haiti, Somalia, and Rwanda "when a state's condition or behavior results in … grave and massive violations of human rights."

Advance Justice for All

3. *Promote democracy, human rights, and religious liberty. Spreading democracy and respect for human rights, including religious liberty, is widening the zones of peace.* Democracies tend not to make war on each other. Established democracies fought *no wars* against one another during the entire twentieth century. And they generally devote lower shares of their gross national products (GNP) to military expenditures, which decreases threats to other countries. Influences that played significant parts in producing the recent extensive wave of transitions to democracy include church institutions that oppose governmental authoritarianism; citizens' groups and nongovernmental organizations dedicated to defending human rights; and states and international organizations more actively promoting human rights and democracy.

Powerful threats to democracy's spread exist. Among them are grim economic conditions in numerous struggling democracies; ethnic, racial, nationalistic, and religious conflict; instabilities during the transition to democracy; and external threats from nondemocratic neighbors.

The possibility of a widespread and growing zone of peace requires a network of persons who work together to gain public attention for those they are trying to protect from human rights violations.

4. *Foster just and sustainable economic development.* Supporting human rights and democracy also requires sustainable development. The needs of today must be met without threatening the needs of tomorrow. Those who lack adequate material and economic resources need to gain access, and those who have such resources must learn to control their use and prevent future exhaustion. Organizations like the Mennonite Central Committee and others have pioneered in fostering the development of appropriate technology. Sustainable development will require work on various levels. Access to resources such as water and land is a peace question in the Middle East, Latin America, and Asia.

Take Peacemaking Initiatives

5. *Reduce offensive weapons and weapons trade.* A key factor in the decrease of war between nations is that weapons have become so destructive that war is not worth the price. Offensive forces cannot destroy the enemy's defense before it does huge retaliatory damage. Further reduction of offensive weapons makes war even less likely. For example, President Gorbachev removed half the Soviet Union's tanks from Central Europe and all its river-crossing equipment. This freed NATO to agree to get rid of all medium-range and shorter-range nuclear weapons on both sides from Eastern and

Western Europe—the first dramatic step in ending the Cold War peacefully.

As nations turn toward democracy and human rights, their governments no longer need large militaries to keep them in power. As the ten practices of peacemaking reduce the threat of war, nations feel less need for weapons. As they struggle with their deep indebtedness, they have less ability to buy weapons. The International Monetary Fund now requires big reductions in weapons expenditures before granting loans. Arms imports by developing nations in 1995 dropped to one-quarter of their 1988 peak.

6. *Support nonviolent direct action.* Nonviolent direct action, used effectively by Gandhi in India and the civil rights movement in the United States, is spreading widely. In recent decades it has ended dictatorship in the Philippines, terminated rule by the Shah in Iran, and brought about nonviolent revolutions in Poland, East Germany, and Central Europe. Nonviolent action has transformed injustice into democratic change in human rights movements in Guatemala, Argentina, and elsewhere in Latin America; in the nonviolent parts of the Intifada campaign in Palestine; in the freedom campaign in South Africa; and in many other countries. In contrast we can point to the failures of violent campaigners in Bosnia, Somalia, and Northern Ireland. Christian peacemakers are teaching the methods of nonviolence worldwide.

7. *Take independent initiatives to reduce hostility.* The recently developed strategy of independent initiatives successfully freed Austria from Soviet domination in the 1950s in exchange for Austrian neutrality and nonoffensive military. The Atmospheric Test Ban Treaty of 1963 was made possible after U.S. Presidents Eisenhower and Kennedy halted atmospheric nuclear testing unilaterally. Independent initiatives led to dramatic reductions in nuclear weapons via the series of initiatives by President Gorbachev plus the U.S. Congress and President Bush. Peacemaking breakthroughs have occurred through small initiatives taken by Israel and its Arab neighbors and by adversaries in Northern Ireland.

Independent initiatives have a number of characteristics. They are independent of the slow process of negotiation and designed to decrease distrust by the other side—but not leave the initiator weak. Such initiatives are visible and verifiable actions, have a timing announced in advance and carried out regardless of the other side's bluster, and include a clearly announced purpose—to shift toward de-escalation and to invite reciprocation. These initiatives need to come in a series. If the other side does not reciprocate, small initiatives should continue to keep inviting reciprocation.

The strategy of independent initiatives was advocated in various church peace statements in the 1980s. However, it needs to be understood more widely so it can be noticed when it causes breakthroughs and so citizens can press governments to take such initiatives.

8. *Use partnership conflict resolution.* Conflict resolution is becoming a well-known practice at international as well as local levels. A key test of seriousness of governments' claims to be seeking peace is whether they develop imaginative solutions that show they understand their adversary's perspectives and needs.

We prefer the term *partnership* conflict resolution. By this we mean active partnership in developing solutions, not merely passive cooperation. Adversaries need help to listen to each other and experience each other's perspectives. This multicultural literacy must go beyond the surface positions and interests of the adversaries to include aspects of their culture, spirituality, story, history, and emotion. We seek long-term solutions which help prevent future conflict, even as we work to heal and resolve immediate conflict. Justice is a core component for sustainable peace.

Martin Luther King, Jr. said, "Peace is not the absence of tension, but the presence of justice." John Howard Yoder describes the New Testament practice of fraternal admonition, long practiced (but not frequently and consistently enough) by churches, as a predecessor of conflict resolution.

9. *Acknowledge responsibility for conflict and injustice; seek repentance and forgiveness.* The single most important initiative in German Chancellor Willy Brandt's *Ostpolitik* was the quest for reconciliation with then-Communist Poland. Poland, after all, was the first country to be blitzkrieged by the Nazi war machine and the country with the largest number of Holocaust victims (perhaps 3,000,000).

In December 1970, Brandt courageously (with no sure guarantee of parliamentary approval) signed a treaty accepting the Oder-Neisse frontier and therewith the cession of 40,000 square miles of German territory (Silesia and parts of Pomerania and East Prussia). This decision he personally dramatized by kneeling silently at the Warsaw war memorial as an act of atonement for German offenses against the Polish people. That Brandt, of all people, should assume such a posture of repentance was especially remarkable in view of his own anti-Nazi credentials and his exile in Norway throughout the war. It was an extraordinarily winsome, powerful, long-lasting act of personal leadership. It made peace a human possibility.

Conflict is not really resolved nor the resolution really internalized until confession and forgiveness occur. This dimension of gospel grace also is deeply needed worldwide.

10. *Encourage grassroots peacemaking groups and voluntary associations.* Just peacemaking requires associations of citizens organized independently of governments, and linked together across boundaries of nation, class, and race, to learn peacemaking practices and press governments to employ these practices. Governments should protect such associations in law and give them accurate information.

The existence of a growing worldwide people's movement constitutes one more historical force that makes just peacemaking possible. A transnational network of groups, including faith groups, can partly transcend captivity by narrow national or ideological perspectives. Citizens' groups are not so committed to status-quo institutional maintenance as bureaucracies often are, nor are they so isolated and only temporarily engaged as individuals often are. Thus they can provide long-term perseverance in peacemaking. They can serve as voices for the voiceless, as they did in churches in East Germany and in women's groups in Guatemala. They can help to initiate, foster, or support transforming initiatives where existing parties need support and courage to risk breaking out of cycles that perpetuate violence and injustice.

A citizens' network of NGOs (nongovernmental organizations) and INGOs (international nongovernmental organizations) can be a source of information which persons in positions of governmental authority may lack or resist acknowledging. NGOs can criticize injustice and initiate repentance and forgiveness. They can nurture a spirituality that sustains courage when peacemaking is unpopular, hope when despair or cynicism is tempting, and grace and forgiveness when peacemaking fails.

****

The practices of just peacemaking make pragmatic sense. We see historical evidence that these practices can accomplish the goals of peace and justice. However, we arrive at these normative practices of just peacemaking not only on pragmatic grounds but also from deeply held faith perspectives. With the eyes of faith we attribute the evidence that just peacemaking works to the "breaking in of God's reign" in history ....

102. CARTER HEYWARD

Compassion and Nonviolence: A Spiritual Path

Carter Heyward (b. 1945) was for many years the Howard Chandler Robbins Professor of Theology at the Episcopal Divinity School in Massachusetts. She was one of the first women ordained in the Episcopal Church, and she has played an influential role in the flourishing of feminist and queer theologies in the United States. Heyward's work on compassion and nonviolence, while underappreciated, is as important as her work in feminism and sexuality. The following is drawn from her 1999 book, Saving Jesus from Those Who Are Right: Rethinking What It Means to Be Christian.

None of us, including JESUS, needs to be destroyed so that the rest of us can live holy lives. We are envisioning in this chapter a spiritual path that leads us *away* from blood sacrifice as in any sense acceptable to the God whom JESUS loved.

We have reflected on several problems with the mainstream Christian atonement tradition:

1. It is steeped in the trivialization and deprecation of human experience as ungodly.
2. For this reason, it represents a more radically dualistic apprehension of the divine-human relation than most mainline theologians will admit.
3. It is built around an image of a deity whose "inexorable love" is experienced by human beings as punitive, shaming, cruel, and even sadistic in relation to people whose psychospiritualities have been shaped, to various degrees, by images of a god whose love is violent—toward others, toward His Son, and toward Himself.
4. It promotes blood sacrifice—that is to say, the sacralizing of violence against others and oneself—as a (or even the) way of spiritual liberation.
5. Finally, it reflects a deity made in the image of human impatience with one another, ourselves, and our Sacred Source. In the best, most mutual relationships that have been broken—relationships not only between individuals but also supported by strong, respectful friends and community—those who have been violated and those who have done wrong often can find ways to restore what has been lost or at least some significant part of it. In relationships more like the one that most of us actually experience between ourselves and God—in which time and again we turn away from the vocation to love justice and show mercy in our relations—it is hard to imagine how we might restore a right relation with the Spirit of justice-love and compassion. Furthermore, it is not hard to understand why so many Christians, like Anselm, Baillie, and countless others, have imagined that surely God had to exact a harsh penalty for the terrible sins of the world.

What these Christian believers have lacked is faith in God's inexorable patience as a significant dimension of God's love.

To be sure, the evil among us is rampant, exacting tolls too high for many of us to pay or even imagine. And we humans must do everything in our power to protect one another, ourselves, and other creatures from the violence that invariably results from the fear-based betrayals of our Sacred Power in mutual relation. This means that, in this real world of ours, we will always be looking for better ways of protecting ourselves and one another from violent people and from others whose fear, greed, dishonesty, or rage threatens to harm us or disrupt the relative stabilities we are able sometimes to create as communities and cultures.

But we must not confuse protecting ourselves and those we love with inflicting upon our enemies the same torture and brutality that they may have inflicted (or wished) upon us. Contrary to the prevailing religious, moral, and political sentiments on the Right today, might does *not* make right. Justice makes right relation. Justice-love *is* right relation. We do not need an "almighty" god, except insofar as God's love—Her justice-love, Her compassion—is Her strength and Her power.

Putting our faith in God's patience with us in this imperfect, morally cluttered, and often evil world generates greater social and spiritual space for us to be honest, gentle people with ourselves and one another—space in which we are able to cultivate humility rather than fear as the basis of our life together and thereby become more deeply moral people. We need more images of a patient God who loves the world so much that She gives her people time and resources like history and culture, human friends and animal companions, work and play, mountains and water, food and music, memory and reason, imagination and talents, and prayer and worship, and as many chances as we in our fear may need to come to our senses.

We need not sacrifice one more child to the bloody god who needs innocent victims, one more person or creature to a deity who must punish either us or himself in order to love the world.

There is another way to God, in which compassion replaces honor and even self-respect as the highest good and in which nonviolence becomes a way of life, a liberating response to the ongoing savaging of ourselves and one another.

It is my thesis in this book that these twin commitments—compassion and nonviolence—are *living sacraments*, outward and visible signs among us of an authentically liberative atonement tradition.

Compassion, Nonviolence and Loneliness

Let me say it again: *compassion* too often sounds to us like a soft feeling. It rings of pity and often patronizes those who are, or seem, "poorer" in some ways than we ourselves. In the prevailing reactionary political climate, for example, compassion is often used by liberals as a synonym for our own politics. In the realm of public policy, we "liberals" have compassion and "conservatives" don't. Not surprisingly, conservatives, in trying to present their own politics as compassionate, are likely to define their brand of compassion as "more realistic" than that of liberals. I dare say that no one who supported the "welfare reform" bill of 1996—not a single senator, congressperson, or President Clinton himself—thinks of him or herself as short on compassion; whereas those of us who were appalled by this "reform" believed that it lacked compassion. In short, we liberals are seen by conservatives as too soft, not realistic enough in our commitments to the common good, whereas we on the left view more conservative folk as very hard on the poor and not idealistic enough to even envision a *common* good.

Compassion challenges this prevailing liberal-conservative split. This does not mean that compassion is a non-political "spiritual" quality, as some folks might suggest. It means that compassion is not simply, as many liberals assume, an individual's free-floating emotional and mental inclination to "be for" any people and creatures who might need some help. Nor is compassion a harder-edged belief that those who think they know what's best for others can forge into public policies to benefit the common good regardless of what most common-folk might want, need, or think about this.

Compassion is not primarily a feeling or spiritualized state of being. It is not a package of patronization for the poor. Genuine compassion is a shared—communal—commitment to do everything in our power to struggle toward the well-being of all people and creatures, including our adversaries, and especially those whose ways of being in the world we do not like or understand. In a potentially conflictual, perhaps even violent, situation, compassion is a commitment to do no harm to our enemies if we can possibly help it.

We learn compassion through community and friendship, usually to the extent that we ourselves have benefited from it. Insofar as we have known compassion, as its beneficiaries, we can more likely embody it as a trustworthy personal commitment. Otherwise, "compassion" will usually float freely "in" us as a feeling (as in much liberal spirituality), or it will stick in our gut as an obligation to the "less fortunate" people (as in some conservative politics).

Nonviolence is a first fruit of compassion. It is also a collective, public force, seldom an option for individuals who are in harm's way. Nonviolence is the practical effect of the commitment not to harm our enemies if at all possible. The qualification—"if at all possible"—is intended to allow for *spontaneous* and *last-resort* defense of one another and ourselves that can find no other solution. Even in such situations, violence should be as minimal and nondestructive as possible. Here I am referring both to large-scale defense, like armed struggle against oppression, and to smaller encounters, such as a woman's defense against an abusive spouse.

It is important to keep nonviolence, as a movement, in historical perspective. I cannot overemphasize the fact that nonviolence is a collective public force, seldom a practical or very real option for individuals. It is true that we often associate the names of individuals with it—for example, pacifist Congresswoman Alice Paul, who cast the lone vote against U.S. entry into World War I; Mahatma Gandhi of the Indian struggle against British colonialism; Martin Luther King Jr. of the Civil Rights Movement in the United States; Mohammad Ali, Muslim pacifist who refused to fight in the Vietnam War; and the Vietnamese Buddhist monk and activist for global peace, Thich Nhat Hahn. But these persons have not been merely iconoclastic, boundary-breaking individuals. They have represented—and, in that sense, embodied—movements, communities of activists, public forces larger than any single person's commitments. This relational basis has been the source of their strength.

Nonviolence is not merely a political strategy, although it is certainly often that. It is never only a private opinion, although we may be strengthened and shaped individually in significant ways by our shared commitment. Nonviolence is a shared way of life that invites "a dialogue." By "dialogue," I do not mean simply "talking." I mean acting together in mutually empowering ways. "Dialogue" in this sense refers to a way of proceeding in life—dialogically, mutually, in such a way that all parties can be beneficiaries.

Nonviolence is dialogical. It is an effort not to act unilaterally. It is steeped in the presupposition that all others, even our enemies, are worthy of dignity and respect. It is a yearning for peace that will not settle for peace without justice because such "peace" is not peace at all. It is a way of life with roots in solidarity (really a public manifestation of compassion), in community and friendship; in *phantasy*; in prayer and meditation; and in humility. Like forgiveness, nonviolence is imaginable *only* through our power in mutual relation.

In our world today, a nonviolent way of life with its communal basis is also, paradoxically, a lonely life.

Looping back to our resources for forgiveness, let's look into this paradox to notice both the loneliness and the serenity, the sorrow and the joy, at the heart of the matter. Earlier I suggested that solidarity through community and friendship, together with humility, are cornerstones of our capacities to forgive and to accept the forgiveness of others in such a way that it makes a difference in our lives. I noted also the roles of the struggle for justice-love, emotional honesty, imagination and *phantasy*, and prayer and meditation in the spiritual and political work of forgiveness. What is it, in this way of being, that promises us lives filled with a "peace which passeth understanding" and yet moves us also into what John of the Cross called "the dark night of the soul"?

Community and friendship provide the joy and peace of knowing that we are not alone in life but rather are participants who share a common way. Ideally, this is a role of family, as our most intimate companions, not "family" as defined narrowly in the limited, modern, capitalist, and non-biblical sense that the Christian Right embraces with such enthusiasm. Family is, in reality, wherever we find ourselves at home in a womb of compassion.

> Meanwhile, standing near the cross of JESUS were his mother, and his mother's sister, Mary the wife of Clopas, and, Mary Magdalene. When Jesus saw his mother and the disciple whom he loved standing beside her, he said to his mother, "Woman, here is your son!" Then he said to the disciple, "Here is your mother!" and from that hour the disciple took her into his own home. (John 19:25b-27)

family is
wherever
we find our
selves at home
in a womb
of compassion.

> Let us behold one another as sisters
> and mothers, fathers and brothers,
> grannies and grampas, lovers and spouses,
> animal companions, friends and beloved
> children: family. Amen.

Through this sense of "beholding" one another, whoever and wherever we are, we cannot escape sorrow. Drawn by love and held intimately in connection with those whom we love, we experience death and loss and grief, and also the often less ultimate but no less dreadful experiences of betrayal, disappointment, and relational wounds of a thousand kinds. Our family is vast and global and at the same time, for most of us, a much smaller experience of simply being at home with those whom we love. In both larger and smaller arenas, compassion and humility are lenses through which we who are family learn to view one another. In these contexts of joy and the sorrows that come with it, nonviolence becomes a way of experiencing ourselves and one another.

We may experience nonviolence as an aspiration even if, in our particular contexts, we do not and cannot practice it with much consistency. Our inability even to imagine being a radically nonviolent people has much to do with the sad reality that our communities are so broken and so weak.

Even with nonviolence as only a desire and a prayer, however, we can become a more serene people, able to be more honest with ourselves and others and more fully at peace among and within ourselves. Conflict and pain do not disappear, but we more easily can take them in stride, not becoming undone by them. And as we become less afraid of anger and conflict, more grounded in compassion and nonviolence, our staying power gets rooted. We become better able to participate for the long haul in the ongoing struggles for justice, those closest at hand and sometimes those more national or global movements for liberation and freedom. We are likely to discover here, in the midst of social struggle, a stronger sense of personal peace and well-being.

This paradox is strengthened through the practices of prayer and meditation and the gifts of imagination and phantasy. Bearing witness to the power of Martin Luther King Jr.'s "dream," we are surrounded by clouds of witnesses, upheld by the communion of saints, empowered by the ancestors. Along this path, we come to know the world and one another, ourselves and the Spirit, more fully and honestly as family.

By no means is it ever a solitary struggle. We are never alone in it.

And yet, it is a lonely place for each and every one in it. It is lonely because it is so *radically* at odds with what it means to be either human or divine in the dominant patriarchal culture that is shaping the world around and (always to some degree) within us.

It is a lonely place because twenty-four hours a day the dominant world/church is pressing upon us definitions of "community" and "friendship," "compassion" and "humility," "justice" and "love," "God" and "world," "self" and "other," "struggle" and "serenity" that—if we accept such definitions—will exhaust us because they tend to be so individualistic, adversarial, and impossible to embody in healthy or holy ways. In this context of constant social and psycho-spiritual disappointment, loneliness is a protective wrapping for our souls, the place in us in which we meet and most fully love one another, ourselves, and the Spirit that is our power to love.

Though our lives may be filled with friends and intimacy, love and struggle, public participation and personal relationship, there is *always* a place in us that no one can reach or know. If people know us well, they know this place is there in us—and that they cannot reach it, not because we do not trust them, but because none of us (not our friends, and not us) can escape the yearning and the loneliness that comes with living passionately in God. Our best friends know this, usually from their own experiences as well, and they accept the lonely place for what it is: a spot that keeps us well on *our* terms, not the world's, rooted and grounded in a Spirit that "the world does not know."

The loneliness paradoxically is indispensable to our loving one another, ourselves, and God without needing to know everything about anyone or anything, including God. It is the taproot of our capacity to accept the mystery and unknowable dimensions of all that is, especially God.

What Keeps Forgiveness from Being Idealistic?

Speaking as one who knows deeply the fatigue of wrongdoing as both subject and object of betrayals that tear at the fabric of our human and creaturely well-being, I am all the more persuaded that learning forgiveness, however long it may take us and our people—learning to be its givers and recipients—is more than anything what we need in order to make right relation with one another throughout the world and to live more fully in the Spirit that empowers us.

Our very life as a planet and as communities of people and creatures depends upon it. A willingness to learn forgiveness is not an option for people who are serious about survival and quality of life. Forgiveness makes quality of life possible for its givers and recipients. Without it there will always be, as LeGuin recounts, some child kept in its own filth at the edge of town, someone hanging on a cross, some innocent offered up yet again as a living sacrifice for the rest of us.

When we are in conflictual situations, in which we and others honestly see things differently, and especially when some have been badly wounded by others, we are very near the heart of God—because this tends to be a real and honest, deeply human situation in which we and others are yearning for some healing and liberation.

This critical moment is often when some one(s) will get hung on a cross. It is also the moment, the "Eternal Now," in Tillich's language, in which the Spirit urges us to walk away from the violence in search of a better way.

We can find our way beyond violence only with those who are unwilling to offer us, themselves, or others as a living sacrifice for anything or anybody and certainly not for a God who surely recoils at the very notion of such sacrifice.

Along this spiritual path we may be destroyed, but it will not be because we have sacrificed ourselves or others. Whatever suffering comes our way will be because we have lived as fully as possible into our power to God, and because God has lived as possible through us.

It was now about noon, and darkness came over the whole land until three in the afternoon, while the sun's light failed; and the curtain of the temple was torn in two. Then JESUS, crying with a loud voice, said, "Father into your hands I commend my spirit." (Luke 23:44-46a)

aware that he was slipping
away JESUS entrusted

himself to the spirit
of an open future.

there was I guess no shutting
down of pain no casting out
of doubts no
rejection of those who had
hurt and betrayed denied
and crucified him.

there was simply I
guess a turning
of himself over
into the life love
and ongoingness
of the One whom he
trusted.

in turning ourselves
over we make
a relational trust
from which we and
others too can draw
courage and wisdom
serenity and hope
a day at a time.

103. EILEEN EGAN

Peace Be with You: Justified Warfare or the Way of Nonviolence

Eileen Egan (1911-2000) was a staff member of the American Catholic Relief Services, a founding member of Pax Christi USA, and a pioneering thinker of the ways in which peace work flows from the Catholic celebration of the Eucharist. Here is a selection from Peace Be with You: Justified Warfare or the Way of Nonviolence *(1999).*

If Jesus had simply left his teaching in words, and in the example of his willingly accepted suffering and death, where could his disciples, then and later, find the strength and the nourishment to meet the demands of living according to his way?

The way of nonretaliation, of no revenge-taking, of forgiveness, and of a love that would enfold the enemy and persecutor, called for a discipleship that would transcend human nature in all its "fallenness." How would it be possible for this fallen human nature to imitate the limitless largess of the Creator? The Trinitarian God did not leave us orphans; God left the Spirit to aid us in confronting the world's violence, the effect of the "fallenness," with total nonviolence grounded in love. God did not abandon us, but left as nourishment for the journey his resurrected body in the form of bread and wine.

The Lord's Supper is the very heart of a theology of nonviolence. As the memorial of the act of sacrificial, redemptive love on the cross, it is the central act which convenes the community of those who have been baptized in Christ. Those who approach the Table of the Lord know that they are coming to the heart of peace, the great peace between God and man. "God wanted all perfection to be found in him and all things to be reconciled through him and for him, everything in heaven and everything on earth, when he made peace by his death on the cross" (Col. 1:20; Jerusalem Bible).

According to Donald Senior, "Reconciliation is the byword of the kingdom." The followers of Jesus came to the Lord's Supper from many national groups, as Gentiles of many roots joined with the original Jewish community; the differences of class, of old antagonisms, were submerged in one spirit. "For just as the body is one and has many members, and all the members of the body, though many, are one body, so it is with Christ. For in the Spirit we are all baptized into one body whether Jews or Greeks, slaves or free persons, and we were all given to drink of one spirit" (I Cor. 12:12-13). By the shedding of his blood, Jesus healed the division between the people of Israel and the Gentiles. "But now in Christ Jesus, you who were once far off have become near by the blood of Christ. For he is our peace, he who made both [Jews and Gentiles] one and broke down the dividing wall of enmity" (Eph. 2:13-14). No wall divided those who met at the Lord's Table.

The message of Jesus was addressed to each person, but as each person received it and was transformed by it, he or she joined fellow believers at the Table of the Lord. Personal transformation led to the transformed community, the beloved community. The great mystery of the changing of the bread and wine into the body and blood of the Messiah occurred whenever a gathering took place under an ordained presider. The hands of a mortal man, perhaps stubby, work-worn hands, could draw down the Godhead so that the other mortals could partake of it.

Saints of the past describe how the Eucharist strengthens those who partake of Jesus in the lowly elements of bread and wine. "By communicating himself, therefore, as heavenly food," said St. Procopius of Gaza, "God nourishes souls in virtue, and inebriates and delights them with knowledge, spreading virtue and knowledge before them like the food of a spiritual banquet to which all are invited."

Saints also help us recapture, if we tend to lose it, the awe of partaking of the Godhead in the form of bread and wine. "For neither was it enough for him to be made man," said St. John Chrysostom, "to be smitten and slaughtered, but he also commingles himself with us, and not by faith only, but also in the very deed, makes us his body .... That which when angels behold, [they] tremble, and dare not so much look at it without awe on account of the brightness that comes thence, with this we are fed and with this we are commingled, and we are made one body and flesh with Christ."

The expression "commingled" is used also by St. Cyril of Alexandria:

All who eat Christ's holy flesh enter into bodily union with him, and not only with him who is in us through the flesh, but with each other. We are, then, clearly one with each other in Christ. He is the bond which unites, he who is both God and Man.

In a similar way, we may say that all of us who have one and the same Holy Spirit are, as it were, commingled with each other and with God. For though we are many separate individuals and Christ makes his and Father's Spirit dwell in each separate one, yet that Spirit is himself one and indivisible. He therefore makes those separately subsisting individuals a unity through his presence; he makes them all be, in a way, a single entity through union with himself. Just as the power of Christ's holy flesh makes those in whom he dwells to be co-corporeal with each other, so the indwelling Spirit of God, indivisibly, one and the same in all, forges all into spiritual unity.

Cyril concludes that under the influence of the Spirit, human beings are no longer simply human beings but sons and daughters of God and beings of a heavenly mold.

The church, whose saints couch the mystery of the Eucharist in terms for the lettered, also had the task over the centuries of presenting the mysteries to the unlettered and barely lettered. The attempt to transmit this overwhelming reality to the generations has been the church's never-ending challenge. For every generation, for the lettered and unlettered, the teaching has been carried unbroken in two words, the "Real Presence," the "Real Presence" of Jesus in the new covenant.

In the Upper Room on the night before he was betrayed and raised on the cross, Jesus gave the new covenant to the apostles: "Take and eat; this is my body .... Drink from it, all of you, for this is my blood of the covenant, which will be shed on behalf of many for the forgiveness of sins" (Matt. 26:26-28). The same covenant is repeated across the world by priests in parish churches on the mean streets of the crowded cities, in the tiny chapels of lonely missions, and in great cathedrals.

"Since we are united with Christ, who is our Peace," says St. Gregory of Nyssa, "let us put all enmity to death and thus prove by our lives that we believe in him. Let us reconcile not only those who oppose us from without but also those which cause inner disturbances within us; flesh and spirit."

To be the mature Christian described by St. Gregory, one able to put all enmity to death, is the goal of the ordinary Christian, a goal won by constant prayer as well as surrender of the will to God. During many periods of history, the goal seemed far distant, when causing the death of the enemy was chosen over causing death to enmity. But in all periods, the teaching of the Eucharist, of the holy flesh and blood of Christ, has been maintained. The Eucharist, with its concept of the human person as vaulting to the heavens, is a secure ground for Christian peace and peacemaking.

Can we, believing that the Eucharist is the body and blood of Christ, the Messiah, ever destroy the bodies and shed the blood of human beings for whom he gave his life on the cross?

104. JOHN PAUL LEDERACH

The Journey toward Reconciliation

John Paul Lederach (b. 1955) is Professor of International Peacebuilding at the Kroc Institute for International Peace Studies at the University of Notre Dame. As a committed Mennonite pacifist, Lederach has carried out pioneering work in the theory and practice of conflict transformation. His international reputation has emerged not only from his many writings but also from his peace work in Colombia, the Philippines, Nepal, Tajikistan, and Africa, among other places. The following selection is drawn from his 1999 book titled The Journey toward Reconciliation.

... [T]he story of Esau and Jacob has especially shaped the way I understand and look at reconciliation. It has provided me with a guiding framework for the other stories and ideas that I will explore. Let me start with the narrative in Genesis, chapters 25-33.

Esau and Jacob are brothers, sons of Isaac and Rebecca. Esau is the firstborn, the hunter, and the

pride of his father's eyes. Jacob stays near home and close to his mother. When Isaac is old and nearly blind, he calls Esau to bless him as the firstborn son.

Esau sets out to hunt for game to roast as the meal preceding that generational blessing. While he is gone, Rebecca shows Jacob how to trick the old man into believing that *he* is Esau. Not knowing and not seeing, Isaac bestows the revered blessing on his younger son, Jacob.

When Esau returns and brings the meal to his father, they both discover that they have been tricked. Esau moans with an "exceedingly great and bitter cry." He implores his father three times, "Bless me, me also, father. Have you not reserved a blessing for me? Have you only one blessing, father? Bless me, me also, father!" (from 27:34-38). But there is nothing further that Isaac can give. He has already released the blessing for the firstborn; like an arrow in flight, it cannot be recalled. Jacob has stolen Esau's birthright and his blessing.

Esau then shouts with a voice that carries out across the tent village, "I hate Jacob! I will kill my brother!" These are the last words we hear from Esau until the brothers meet years later. On hearing this threat, Jacob flees in fear. The brothers are bitter enemies.

For many years they live separately. They have families and become wealthy. When Jacob faces difficulties with his wives' brothers, he hears the Lord say, "Return to the land of your ancestors and to your kindred, and I will be with you" (31:3). He is to return to the land where Esau lives.

Jacob *turns his face* toward Esau and the land of Seir. And he is afraid.

As he progresses on his journey, he sends messengers with gifts to appease his brother. They return saying that Esau, hearing that Jacob is coming, has set out to meet him with four hundred men.

Jacob becomes greatly distressed. He cries out to God: "Deliver me from the hand of my brother, from the hand of Esau, for I am *afraid* of him. He may come and *kill us all*, the mothers with the children" (32:11, adapted). But Jacob continues the journey toward Esau, sending gifts ahead each day as he travels.

The night before Jacob meets Esau, he comes to a ford in the stream Jabbok. He sends his wives, children, and everything he has across the stream and stays behind, alone. During the night a man comes and wrestles with him until daybreak. When the man sees that he cannot overcome Jacob, he strikes Jacob's hip out of joint and demands to be let go. But Jacob will not let him go until he gives Jacob a blessing. The man then blesses him and gives him

a new name, Israel. Jacob says, "I have seen the *face of God*, and yet my life is preserved." He names the place Peniel, "The face of God," so it will be remembered (32:22-30).

The next morning Jacob rises to meet Esau. After he crosses the stream, he sees Esau coming with four hundred men. He arranges his family behind him. Turning toward his brother, Jacob bows to the ground seven times as he approaches Esau. But Esau runs to meet him, embraces him, falls on his neck, and kisses him. And they weep (33:1-4).

"What do you mean by sending me all these things?" Esau asks.

"I wanted to find your favor," Jacob replies.

"I have enough," Esau declares.

"No, please; … accept my present from my hand," Jacob says, "for truly to see *your face* is like seeing *the face of God*—since you have received me with such favor" (33:10).

Then after several days together, the brothers separate again. Each chooses a different valley, and they move apart.

This certainly is an amazing story of conflict and reconciliation. It leads through a metaphorical moment, "I have seen the face of God." It moves on to a powerful similitude, or point of comparison: "to see your face is like seeing the face of God."

When we read such narratives in the Bible, we too often lose track of the genuine human qualities. We tend to see the stories as sacred and removed from our own reality. But look closely. We can see and feel the real human nature woven into the telling. What I find most intriguing are the parts left untold in the story. We must explore them in our search for understanding the process of reconciliation.

We find two brothers, one who tricks the other. We feel the depth of Esau's pain in the deception. He cries time and again for his father to bless him. His cry turns to bitter hatred. We see Jacob flee in fear. His deceptive actions will haunt him. The brothers move apart both physically and emotionally.

Here we ponder profound questions about conflict and resolution. How and when do we surface and address the injustice that was committed? How and in what ways is putting distance between persons, moving apart, a necessary part of the journey toward reconciliation? How do we respond to people who are at this point in their journey? The pain is so deep, the injustice so clear and immediately present, and the emotions so high! Is it legitimate to separate?

Such a view of reconciliation means we must be cautious about quick formulas of "forgiveness" and being "nice" to each other. Well-intentioned people may advise estranged parties to quickly forgive and forget. Yet those parties may need a long time and geographical separation for healing to occur. As in the case of these two brothers, the separation might last for decades.

One of the least-understood aspects of reconciliation is how to think about and allow for spaces of separation as an acceptable stage in the spiritual journey toward reconciliation. At these times, we *wonder* and *wander*. We are perplexed, awestruck by events, and groping for direction. Where is justice? Why me? Where is God?

Years later, the Lord asks Jacob to return, to take the journey back to Esau. We hear Jacob's cry: "I am afraid. My brother, my sworn enemy, may kill me and my entire family."

Behind Jacob's cry is the voice we have all felt and the question we all have asked: *How can I journey toward that which threatens my life and creates in me the greatest fear?* The biblical account does not give us a detailed explanation. We are missing information at perhaps the most crucial point.

Jacob's earlier journey took him away from Esau, and now he turns his face back toward the thing that scares him the most. What makes this *turn* possible? Is it his life experiences and maturity? Has he suffered injustice? Is it uniquely divine intervention? If that is the case, how do we hear God when all of our human senses are telling us the opposite?

How can people who work for reconciliation help create conditions where this sort of turning is possible? How can we accompany those who are in a long process of turning?

I have learned that there is no magical formula or technique we can apply to create the turn. The mystery of reconciliation is the most significant aspect of the journey. *The turn* is not something we can humanly produce or control.

We follow Jacob's journey of fear and struggle back to Esau. He moves toward that fear in a journey that will ultimately involve a struggle with himself and with God. He walks to meet his enemy. We are given no explanation for Esau's journey or window into it. We follow Jacob, who is guilty of manipulation, lying, and wrongdoing.

A few clues along the way tell us how Jacob's journey proceeds. Nothing tells us how Esau moves through his bitter anger, how he turns toward his offender and oppressor, and then embraces him as a long-missed brother. What makes such grace possible? Is it Jacob's visible repentance? How can Esau be sure that Jacob's repentance is not another manipulation? How would Esau have responded if Jacob had not repented?

What if Esau had not fared well over the years and the outcome of the injustice was a life of misery for him? How do we accompany the many Esaus in their journeys toward and through bitter anger and injustice and ultimately toward their oppressors? How do we accompany Jacob on his journey toward self-understanding, facing his fear, and returning to his enemy?

We feel the intense emotion when the brothers meet. In great fear, Jacob finds a brother who embraces him. Esau finds a lost brother. They weep with each other. Several important signposts in this story provide me with a way to understand the complex scenery that marks the landscape of reconciliation. I will return to these signposts frequently.

Reconciliation as a Journey

The primary metaphor in the story of Esau and Jacob is setting out on a *journey*. In the first journey, the brothers separate, moving away from each other. For Jacob, the journey of separation is driven by fear and perhaps a deep inner sense of guilt that cannot be faced. For Esau, it seems driven by bitterness and hatred, rooted in a profound experience of injustice.

We are not told in detail how each overcomes what has driven them, nor how much time it takes to change. We are told something that is consistent with nearly every other story of reconciliation in the Bible. The Lord says, "Turn. Go back. Take the journey toward your enemy. I will be with you." As a journey, reconciliation is understood as both the *flight away* and the daring *trip back*.

Ultimately, reconciliation is a journey *toward* and *through* conflict. In this instance, God does not promise to do the work for Jacob. God does not promise that he will take care of everything and level the road for Jacob. God promises to accompany him, to be present.

Reconciliation as Encounters

One cannot lightly set out on the journey through conflict nor conduct it without a high cost. We see the pain and anguish in the encounters. In general, we think about reconciliation as a single encounter bound to the time and place where enemies meet face to face. Yet in the story of Esau and Jacob, there are at least three encounters during the journey. What happens is not neatly bound up in a single encounter.

Along the way, encounters happen episodically, as metaphorical moments when we notice God's truth breaking into our lives. I believe there are encounters in every journey of reconciliation. They are different, yet at points interwoven and almost indistinguishable. They are the encounters with *self*, with *God*, and with *other(s)*.

The journey through conflict toward reconciliation always involves turning to face oneself. Jacob has to face his fear. To turn toward his brother, his enemy, he first has to deal with himself, his own fears, and his past actions. In this sense, at least, we can understand the long night of fighting alone with the stranger. During that night he fights with his own past and his fears about the future, then sees the face of God.

The journey toward reconciliation is not a path for the weak and feeble. Facing oneself and one's own fears and anxieties demands an outward *and* an inward journey. Along the journey of conflict, we always encounter ourselves, and in doing so, we come face to face with God, our Maker, whose image we bear, and who calls on us to "return."

Fear and bitterness are rooted in the experiences we have had with others. The journey toward reconciliation always involves turning toward the people who have contributed to our pain. As in the case of Jacob, it means turning toward the enemy.

There are two important changes during Jacob's journey: First, he *turns toward* Esau. Second, he *seeks the face* of his brother. It is impossible for us to make significant process on the journey of reconciliation without these two elements.

We turn and begin to walk in the direction of the person we fear. When we turn, we face a new destiny. We are not moving away from a person and a place. Instead, we are moving toward a place of reconciliation. That place is the face of the enemy that we seek. The story tells of Jacob "seeing" the face of Esau. He looks for and into that which he has feared the most.

In both actions—to turn and to seek—I find profound challenges. The journey of reconciliation requires us to expose our faces in a way that seems enormously risky. We feel vulnerable. Yet we must turn toward what most frightens us in the depths of our souls: the face of our enemy. To seek that face is to see in our enemy a person.

As we set out on this messy and quite-human journey, we find that we encounter God. This is the paradox. When we fight all night in the darkness of our soul and fear, we struggle with God. When we turn to seek the face of our enemy, we look into the face of God.

This is Jacob's journey. He fights all night with the stranger; a long night of fighting himself and his fears, and he sees God face-to-face. The next day he is bowing himself to the ground seven times as he approaches his brother. Esau embraces him. Jacob exclaims, "To see your face is like seeing the face of God."

We will find God present throughout the journey toward reconciliation, in the depths of fear, in the hopelessness of dark nights, in the tears of reconnection. We experience dazzling insight, defining moments that show where we are going and who we are becoming in our relationships. The pathway through conflict toward reconciliation is filled with God-encounters, if we have the eyes to see, the ears to hear, and the heart to feel.

Reconciliation as a Place

This journey leads to a place. In the story of Esau and Jacob, that place involves heartfelt reunion. We sometimes think of this as the ultimate resolution, the ending place. But we need to understand that the journey has many places along the way. Each of the major encounters—with the self, with the enemy, and with God—is marked by a place. A *place* is a specific time and space where certain things *come together* in the journey.

In the story of Esau and Jacob, these places are marked, named, and memorialized. In these places people have met their enemies, God has met people, and individuals have encountered themselves and gained new awareness. Here again it is the extraordinary dual nature of reconciliation: It is both a place we are trying to reach and a journey we take to get there.

Usually we, as individuals and societies, mark our encounters by remembering those aspects of conflict that have produced pain, loss, and sacrifice. For example, most of our official remembrance markers refer to war, places of great loss, or important military victories. But in the story of Esau and Jacob, the altars are built and the places are named to help people remember where God has encountered a person on the journey toward the enemy and reconciliation.

Once Jacob and Esau reach the place of reconciliation where they meet face-to-face, it is still not the end. The journey goes on, but the two brothers do not stay together. This story does not have a fairy-tale ending with everyone living together happily ever after. The journey leads to an encounter and a place; that encounter and place lead to new journeys. Such is the lifelong walk with self, the other, and God.

The story of Esau and Jacob leaves us with this landscape of memorialized places that celebrate metaphorical moments. Reconciliation is a journey, an encounter, and a place. God calls us to set out on this journey. It is a journey through conflict, marked by places where we see the face of God, the face of the enemy, and the face of our own self.

PART IX
Twenty-first Century

105. Dorothee Soelle

Violence and Nonviolence

Dorothee Soelle (1929-2003) was a German Protestant theologian who taught at Union Theological Seminary in New York City from 1975 to 1987. Although she never held a full professorship at a German university, Soelle attracted a worldwide following by closely identifying, in both her writings and activism, Christian mysticism and radical politics. In 1968 she and her husband, Fulbert Steffensky, founded Politisches Nachtgebet—late-evening prayers that focused on politics—in Cologne, Germany. An ardent opponent of violence, she played a leading role in Christian opposition to wars and nuclear weapons. Below is an excerpt from her 2001 book on Christian resistance and mysticism.

It is beyond dispute that a child, even before it begins to write the alphabet and gathers worldly knowledge, should know what the soul is, what truth is, what love is and what forces are hidden in the soul. It should be the essence of true education that every child learns this and in the struggle of life be able more readily to overcome hatred by love, falsehood by truth and violence by taking suffering on oneself.
—Gandhi, *The Unity of All Living Beings*

Mysticism creates a new relation to the three powers that, each in its own totalitarian way, hold us in prison: the ego, possession, and violence.

Mysticism relativizes them, frees us from their spell, and prepares us for freedom. Those powers project themselves in very diverse ways. The ego that keeps on getting bigger presents itself most often as well-mannered and civilized, even when it seeks to get rid of every form of ego-lessness. Possession, which according to Francis of Assisi makes for a condition that forces us to arm ourselves, appears in a neutralized, unobtrusive form. The fact that the very entities with which we destroy creation—namely possession, consumption and violence—have fashioned themselves into a unity in our world makes no impact, whether by design or through ignorance.

When women, like Dorothy Day, are not fixated

on their own egos, or when fools without possessions, like some of Saint Francis's sons and daughters, live different, liberated lives, they are met with smiles of derision. But when they dare to take real steps out of the violence-shaped actuality of our condition, they come into conflict with the judiciary or wind up in jail. More than anything else, violence must hide itself and always put on new garments, disguising itself in the form of imperatives, such as security, protection, technological necessity, public order, or defensive measures.

Here is an inconspicuous example. In June 1997, a member of the White Fathers, a religious community that is part of the "Order for Peace," was fined for having demonstrated outside the Chancellor's Office in Bonn with a picket-sign saying "Cancel Third World Debts." The office had refused to accept a petition, signed by 12,000 people, sponsored by the campaign "Development Needs Forgiveness of Debts." The harmless name of the violence behind which the Chancellor's Office was hiding is the law of inviolable precincts; under present circumstances it is one of the many, actually quite sensible garments of state power. But the law is abused when the office of state protects itself against democratic interventions and expects submission to or passivity in face of economic violence rather than a decisive No! of noncooperation.

This rather insignificant example of civil disobedience illustrates how people make use of violence. For many it is no longer good enough to behave nonviolently in their personal lives and to submit to administrative regulations. For in such nonviolence and submission, as the powerful of this world define them, the real violence that renders the countries of the Third World destitute is left untouched. To exist free of violence means much more than that: it means to think and act with other living beings in a common life. These forms of the freedom of opposition and resistance have multiplied in the last centuries also in Europe in the face of the militaristic and technocratic coercion. An essential and new role is played here by the basic insights of mysticism, such as those of the tradition of Gandhi as well as the Quakers.

In the eighties I was occasionally asked, especially within the contexts of civil disobedience against nuclear arms, whether I did not sense something in myself of the power and spirit of the other, the enemy: "Where is the Ronald Reagan in you?" I was in no mood to respond with a speculation about my shadow side. I do not think that a pacifist has to be complemented by a bellicist. Perhaps I did not understand correctly the seriousness of the question that seeks to grasp the unity of all human beings; to me the question seemed intent on neutralizing or mollifying what we were about. When I ask myself seriously what the principalities and powers that rule over me as structural powers claim from me, the answer is that it is my own cowardice that they seek to make use of. Those who submit to those powers also are part of the violence under whose velvet terror we live and destroy others.

Before he found his way to nonviolent resistance, Gandhi used to describe that time by saying that it was as a coward that he accommodated himself to violence. I understand this in a twofold sense. First, I submitted to external violence, which is to say I knuckled under, paid my taxes with which more weapons were produced, I followed the advice of my bank, and I consumed as much as the advertisers commanded. Worse still, I hankered after violence, wanted to be like "them" in the advertisements, as successful, attractive, aesthetic, and intelligent as they were. The existential step that the word nonviolence signals leads out of the forced marriage between violence and cowardice. And that means in practice that one becomes unafraid of the police and the power of the state.

The forms of resistance that revoke the common consensus about how we destroy creation have deep roots in a mysticism that we often do not recognize as such. It is the mysticism of being at one with all that lives. One of the basic mystical insights in the diverse religions envisions the unity of all human beings, indeed, of all living beings. It is part of the oldest wisdom of religion that life is no individual and autonomous achievement. Life cannot be made, produced, or purchased, and is not the property of private owners. Instead, life is a mystery of being bound up with and belonging one to another. Gandhi believed that he could live a spiritual life only when he began to identify himself with the whole of humankind, and he could do that only by entering into politics. For him the entire range of all human activities is an indivisible whole. Social, economic, political, and religious concerns cannot be cultivated in sterile plots that are hermetically sealed off from one another. To bring those sterile, sealed-off plots together in a related whole is one of the aims of the mysticism whose name is resistance.

In a long poem, Thich Nhat Hanh … names the identification with all that lives in all its contradictoriness:

> I am the mayfly that flits on the river's watery surface.
> And I am also the bird that dashes down to catch it.
>
> I am the frog that happily swims in the pond's clear water.
> And I am the grass snake that devours the frog in the stillness.
>
> I am the child from Uganda, just skin and bones with
> legs thin as bamboo sticks;
> And I am the arms-trader selling the weapons that rain
> death on Uganda.
>
> I am the twelve-year old girl,
> refugee in a small boat,
> that was raped by pirates
> and now only seeks death in the Ocean;
> and I am also the pirate—
> my heart is not yet able to understand and to love.

The poem is entitled "Name Me by My True Name" and the writer gives himself the most diverse names. He is the "caterpillar in the heart of a flower," a "jewel hidden in stone," but also a "member of the Politburo" and, at the same time, its victim who, slowly dying, pays "its bloodguilt in a forced labor camp." Animals and plants become the "name" of the immersing and expanding I. In his poems, the Zen teacher and poet who developed the concept of the "engaged Buddhist" sends his learners on their own search for names, a search which, without them knowing, can never end. Friends and foes

are distinguished; perpetrators such as the rapist are judged to be blind but not excluded—on them too does God's sun shine, as Jesus put it. That life has horrible, violent enemies is not denied. But this realism of naming is overcome into the mystical sense of being one. Difference is acknowledged but not absolutized in the destruction of community and the postmodern denial of every kind of universality.

> Call me by the my true name, please,
> so that I may hear all at once
> all my crying and laughing,
> so that I may see that my joy
> and my pain are now one,
> so that from now on the door of
> my heart may stand open—
> the door of sympathy.

According to Buddhist teaching, dissociating the self is one of the four causes of suffering next to greed, hate, and infatuation. The division of I and non-I, in other words, the delimitation of the self from others, is the onset of violence. If I "am" not the fly—in the changed mystical sense that the word "to be" gains here—then I can also kill it. If I "am" not the trader of arms to Uganda, then I cannot enter into a dialogue about economic alternatives or a blockade. The trader remains for me an accomplice in murder and I remain a spectator. The everyday question, "What business is that of yours?" lives by the dissociation of the self and allows violence to spread. What does not concern the I does not exist, and in our culture the non-identity of the I and the non-I is virtually built-up and transfigured. The dissociation of the I is a self-expression of actualized, legitimated, or suffered violence.

This violence is overcome when the belief in the I is expanded and transposed until, as the poem declares, one finally lives "recognizing oneself in everything." Buddhist wisdom teaches, "what I am, they are also; when one makes oneself thus equal with the other, one does not wish to kill or permit killing."

The mystical foundation of the life that, according to Albert Schweitzer, "desires life in the midst of other life" is the foundation of the ever-to-besearched-for freedom from the practice of violence and of the at least equally dangerous habituation to violence that rules among us. When one renounces one's attachment to the self, the consequences are truly great: no killing or acquiescence in it.

It is high time to stop playing the part of the "willing executioners" or of the allegedly uninvolved onlookers. The toil for possible alternatives to violence, which takes place, for example, in prison-work, in youth groups, and in the resistance against the violence of the nuclear industry, always recalls the spiritual basis of community. Devotions and meditative elements of very different kinds are today part of blockades or protest actions. The inner peace, as freedom from greed and the limitation of the self, translates itself into the practice of peace. The mystical peaceableness of the many "true names" leads to new forms of creating peace....

"Our Weapon Is to Have None": Martin Luther King Jr.

At Union Theological Seminary, during one of my seminars on mysticism and resistance, a student came to me wanting to talk about Martin Luther King Jr. (1929-1968). Somewhat confused I asked, "King, terrific but—a mystic?" He asked me whether I knew about the kitchen table experience. I had no idea, but this is how I came to know something about the "dark night of the soul" in King's life.

It all began on a bus in December 1955 as a forty-two-year-old black seamstress was traveling home from work. Even though 40 percent of the inhabitants of Montgomery were black, seats on the buses were reserved primarily for whites. Rosa Parks was seated in the section segregated for blacks; as more people got on the bus the driver told her to give her seat to a white passenger. She was tired and remained seated. The driver called the police; she was arrested, and, as was the custom, put in jail. "I was not tired physically, or no more tired than I usually was at the end of a working day," she writes in her memoirs. "No, the only tired I was, was tired of giving in." At the time, she was the honorary secretary of an antiracist organization that had been founded in 1909, in honor of Abraham Lincoln, to provide legal assistance and voter registration.

The evening following the arrest of this highly respected woman, young Reverend King invited well-known and influential black citizens to his church. The atmosphere was explosive. A boycott of the bus line was decided upon, and most black citizens honored the call not to ride the buses. For a year the buses drove their routes empty; taxi drivers took the strikers to their destinations for the price of bus fare. In the course of time, Baptist preacher King became the spokesperson for the local civil rights movement. At the same time he had to cope with threats and fears that the well-educated son of a Baptist minister had never encountered before. His father had taught him that "no one can make a slave of you as long as you do not think like a slave."

In January 1956, Martin Luther King Jr. was jailed for the first time under the pretext that he had exceeded the legal speed limit of 25 miles per hour by 5 miles. On the way to prison he became scared: the car he was being taken in was being driven out of town. Was he going to be lynched? A few months before, a black fourteen-year-old had been abducted and sadistically murdered; the three white perpetrators were never punished. With good reason to be scared, King also had reason enough for relief when he was taken "only" to the run-down jail, a place reeking of urine and overflowing with homeless people, vagrants, drunks, and thieves. "Don't forget us," they shouted as he was released on bail.

It was not much better at home: the family received between thirty and forty telephone calls and hate letters per day. "Get out of town or else. KKK." "You niggers are getting yourself in a bad place. We need and will have a Hitler to get our country straightened out." King and Coretta, his wife, could not disconnect the telephone because they depended on calls from their friends. They jumped every time it rang and had to listen to threats, unspeakable obscenities, and hatred.

A white friend informed King of a serious plot to kill him. King did not know which way to turn. He came home from a meeting exhausted, wrung out from a long day, and he went to sleep. Again the phone rang, he picked up the receiver and heard an ugly voice telling him: "Listen, nigger, we've taken from you all we want. Before next week you'll be sorry you ever came to Montgomery." King could bear it no longer; he got up and walked the floor. For the first time he feared for his life. He went to the kitchen table and put on a pot of coffee. Then he sat down at the table and wondered how he could leave Montgomery without appearing to be a coward. There was no alternative; he had to get away. He thought about his father. At this point, King Jr. was just twenty-seven years old. Something inside him said, "You can't call Daddy now. He's up in Atlanta, a hundred and seventy-five miles away. You have to call on that something, that being, that your Daddy told you about, this power that finds a way where there is none." Later King said that he discovered then that religion was for real, and that "I had to get to know God for myself." Sitting at the kitchen table and bowed over it, he began to pray aloud: "O, Lord. I'm down here trying to do what is right.… The people are looking to me for leadership, and if I stand before them without strength or courage, they too will falter. I am at the end of my powers. I have nothing left. I can't face it alone." Subsequently, King himself told what happened to him then at the kitchen table in Montgomery. "It seemed that an inner voice was speaking to him with quiet assurance: 'Martin Luther, stand up for righteousness. Stand up for justice. Stand up for truth. And lo, I will be with you even unto the end of the world.'" King heard the voice of Jesus telling him to keep up the struggle. He then heard or sang a hymn rooted in black piety: "He promised never to leave me, never to leave me alone." In that moment, King was to say later, he felt God's presence like never before. His fears left him all of a sudden, his uncertainty vanished, and he was ready to face anything. He made his decision, he did not quit, and he did not take the easier route of going along. He realized that suffering taken up voluntarily has a transforming power.

Years later King explained what this meant. He assumed that society was diseased with racism and hatred, and bent on keeping its privileges and advantages. These diseases are not healed if all that we do is try to make misery known, for example, by taking photos of starving children in Africa. Such diseases become treatable when minorities actually stand up for justice in economic relations, and when they do not let themselves be defeated by failures and ridicule, by being told that they are inferior, or by being rendered invisible.

When white racists threw a bomb on the porch of the King house, enraged blacks gathered in a crowd, armed with pistols, knives, sticks and stones. Arriving at the house, King implored the crowd not to answer violence with violence. Those who answer violence with violence, bombs with bombs, and killing with killing solve no problems but descend to the level of the enemy. He told the outraged people to take their guns home or to throw them into the sea. "Our weapon is to have none," he said. "When I decided that, as a teacher of the philosophy of nonviolence, I couldn't keep a gun, I came face to face with the question of death and I dealt with it. And from that point on, I no longer needed a gun nor have I been afraid. Ultimately, one's sense of manhood must come from within him." King had read Gandhi in his student days and for him also pacifism was not a "method for cowards." He called hooligans reactionaries because they resemble too much their enemies; he himself was a moderate radical, proud of being "badly adjusted." He favored methods of direct action but only after precise analysis of the situation. Action is to be taken only after negotiating with the other side has been tried as long as possible. Nonviolence means to forgo the desire to win and to avoid the defeat of enemies, which always includes their humiliation. The issues of peace, justice, and—as must be added today—creation are always the enemies' issues as well; they, too, need air to breathe. Their issue is also ours. Every form of the spirit of hostility has to be rejected. King called white racists "our sick white brothers," which angered some of his comrades in the struggle.

An important component of nonviolence for King was the unearned suffering that resulted from the conflicts. He said that there would be rivers of blood, but we are determined to make sure that it is not the blood of the enemy. And so the method or the different style of living out nonviolence gives precisely to the disenfranchised and powerless a different sense of their own dignity. This was rooted deeply in the piety of blacks, more deeply than King had initially assumed. Simplicity, clarity, depth—learned during centuries of suffering—is how King understood the Sermon on the Mount.

He had learned much from the Black theologian and philosopher Howard Thurman (1899-1981), who, as a teacher of the way of mysticism, spoke on behalf of the disenfranchised and underprivileged. In his lectures on "Mysticism and Social Change," Thurman wrote in reference to the well-known words of the socialist Eugene Debs: "It is not only the socialist but also the confirmed mystic or the man seeking the fullness of the vision of God who must say truly, 'while there is a lower class, I am in it. While there is a criminal element, I am of it. While there is a man in jail, I am not free.' The distinction between personal selfishness and social selfishness, between personal religion and social religion which we are wont to make, must forever remain artificial and unrealistic." The inheritance of this humane mystical tradition of unity is what King took up and, in his admirable rhetorical talent, declared it to be valid for his own people as well as for this century. "We shall match your capacity to inflict suffering by our capacity to endure suffering. We will meet your physical force with soul force. Do to us what you will and we will still love you. We cannot in all conscience obey your unjust laws and bide by the unjust system, because non-cooperation with evil is as much a moral obligation as is cooperation with good, and so throw us in jail and we will still love you. Bomb our homes and threaten our children, and, as difficult as it is, we will still love you. Send your hooded perpetrators of violence into our communities at the midnight hour and drag us out on some wayside road and leave us half-dead as you beat us up, and we will still love you."

Between Hopes and Defeats

... This fluctuation between defeats and hopes must be something a religious culture of resistance cannot avoid. Religiosity borne by "positive thinking" always strikes me as being embarrassingly void of spirit and opiate-like. This "dark night of the soul" cannot be voted out of existence, nor will buttons calling us to "Take Jesus!" help us to get over it, much less over the dark night of creation. That we are and shall always be in God's hand, according to the woman cited earlier, becomes credible when with Teresa of Avila we also know, mystically, that God has no other hands but ours. To be aware of the "silent cry" in our world means to become one with it.

106. Miroslav Volf

Forgiveness, Reconciliation, and Justice: A Christian Contribution to a More Peaceful Environment

Miroslav Volf (b. 1956) is the Henry B. Wright Professor of Systematic Theology at Yale Divinity School, a leader in international interfaith and ecumenical dialogues, and the author of numerous books on Christian theology and ethics. Below is an excerpt of a lecture he delivered at the John F. Kennedy School of Government at Harvard University in February 2001.

In this essay I want to contest the claim that the Christian faith, as one of the major world religions, predominantly fosters violence, and to argue, instead, that it should be seen as a contributor to more peaceful social environments. I will not argue that the Christian faith was not and is not often employed to foster violence. Obviously, such an argument cannot be plausibly made; not only have Christians committed atrocities and other lesser forms of violence but they have also drawn on religious beliefs to justify them. Neither will I argue that the Christian faith has been historically less associated with violence than other major religions; I am not at all sure that this is the case.

Rather, I will argue that at least when it comes to Christianity, the cure against religiously induced or legitimized violence is not less religion, but, in a carefully qualified sense, more religion. Put differently, the more we reduce Christian faith to vague religiosity or conceive of it as exclusively a private affair of individuals, the worse off we will be; and inversely, the more we nurture it as an ongoing tradition that by its intrinsic content shapes behavior and by the domain of its regulative reach touches the public sphere, the better off we will be. "Thick" practice of the Christian faith will help reduce violence and shape a culture of peace....

Will to Embrace, Actual Embrace

So what is the relationship between reconciliation and justice that is inscribed in the very heart of the Christian faith? Partly to keep things rhetorically simpler, I will substitute the more poetic "embrace" for "peace" as the terminal point of the reconciliation process as I explore this issue in the remainder of my text. The Christian tradition can be plausibly construed to make four central claims about the relation between justice and embrace.

The Primacy of the Will to Embrace

The starting point is the primacy of the will to embrace the other, even the offender. Since the God Christians worship is the God of unconditional and indiscriminate love the will to embrace the other is the most fundamental obligation of Christians. The claim is radical, and precisely in its radicality, so socially significant. The will to give ourselves to others and to welcome them, to readjust our identities to make space for them, is prior to any judgment about others, except that of identifying them in their humanity. The will to embrace precedes any "truth" about others and any reading of their action with respect to justice. This will is absolutely indiscriminate and strictly immutable; it transcends the moral mapping of the social world into "good" and "evil."

The primacy of the will to embrace is sustained negatively by some important insights into the nature of the human predicament. Since the Christian tradition sees all people as marred by evil and since it conceives of evil not just as act but as a

power that transcends individual actors, it rejects the construction of the world around exclusive moral polarities—here, on our side, "the just, the pure, the innocent," and there, on the other side, "the unjust, the defiled, the guilty." Such a world does not exist. If our search for peace is predicated on its existence, in its factual absence we will be prone to make the mistake of refusing to read conflicts in moral terms and thus lazily fall back on either establishing symmetries in guilt or proclaiming all actors as irrational. Instead of conceiving of our search for peace as a struggle on behalf of "the just, the pure, the innocent," we should understand it as an endeavor to transform the world in which justice and injustice, innocence and guilt, crisscross and intersect, and we should do so guided by the recognition that the economy of undeserved grace has primacy over the economy of moral desert.

Attending to Justice as a Precondition of Actual Embrace

Notice that I have described the will to embrace as unconditional and indiscriminate, but not the embrace itself. A genuine embrace, an embrace that neither play-acts acceptance nor crushes the other, cannot take place until justice is attended to. Hence the will to embrace includes in itself the will to determine what is just and to name wrong as wrong. The will to embrace includes the will to rectify the wrongs that have been done, and it includes the will to reshape the relationships to correspond to justice. And yet, though an actual embrace requires attending to justice, it does not require establishment of strict justice. Indeed, the pursuit of embrace is precisely an alternative to constructing social relations around strict justice. It is a way of creating a genuine and deeply human community of harmonious peace in an imperfect world of inescapable injustice. Without the grace of embrace, humane life in our world in which evil is inescapably committed but our deeds are irreversible would be impossible.

Will to Embrace as Framework for the Search for Justice

To emphasize the will to embrace means more than to advocate learning how to live with inescapable injustice while not giving up on the pursuit of justice. For the will to embrace is also a precondition of (even tenuous) convergences and agreements on what is just in a world of strife. Without the will to embrace, each party will insist on the justness of their own cause, and strife will continue. For, given the nature of human beings and their interaction, there is too much injustice in an uncompromising struggle for justice.

The will to embrace—love—sheds the light of knowledge by the fire it carries with it. Our eyes need the light of this fire to perceive any justice in the causes and actions of our enemies. Granted, our enemies may prove to be as unjust as they seem, and what they insist is just may in fact be a perversion of justice. But if there is any justice in their causes and actions, only the will to embrace will make us capable of perceiving it, because it will let us see both them and ourselves with their eyes. Similarly, the will to exclude—hatred—blinds by the fire it carries with it. The fire of exclusion directs its light only on the injustice of others; any justness they may have is enveloped in darkness or branded as covert injustice—a merely contrived goodness that makes their evil all the more deadly. Both the "clenched fist" and the "open arms" are epistemic stances; they are moral conditions of adequate moral perception. The clenched fist hinders the perception of the possible justness of our opponents and thereby reinforces injustice; the open arms help detect any justness that may hide behind what seems to be the manifest unjustness of our opponents and thereby reinforces justice. To agree on justice in situations of conflict you must want more than justice; you must want embrace.

Embrace as the Horizon
of the Struggle for Justice

As in many of our activities, in the struggle for justice much depends on the *telos* of the struggle. Toward what is the struggle oriented? Is it oriented simply toward ensuring that everyone gets what they deserve? Or is it oriented toward the larger goal of healing relationships? I think the latter is the case. Hence the embrace should be the *telos* of the struggle for justice. If not, reconciliation will not even be attempted until the "right" side has won. And unless reconciliation is the horizon of the struggle for justice from the outset, it is not clear why reconciliation should even be attempted after the victory of the "right" side has been achieved.

Pulling all four features of the relation between reconciliation and justice together we can say that reconciliation describes primarily a process whose goal is the creation of a community in which each recognizes and is recognized by all and in which all mutually give themselves to each other in love. As such, the concept of reconciliation stands in opposition to any notion of self-enclosed totality predicated on various forms of exclusion. And far from standing in contrast to justice, for such a notion of reconciliation justice is an integral element. Though reconciliation may be seen from one angle to issue *ultimately* in a state "beyond justice," it does so precisely by attending to justice rather than by circumventing it.

Forgiveness and the Primacy of Embrace

Forgiveness can be properly understood and practiced only in the context of the stance which gives primacy to reconciliation but does not give up the pursuit of justice. So what is the relation between forgiveness and justice?

First, forgiveness does not stand outside of justice. To the contrary, forgiveness is possible only against the backdrop of a tacit affirmation of justice. Forgiveness always entails blame. Anyone who has been forgiven for what she has *not* done will attest to that. Forgiveness should therefore not be confused with acceptance of the other. Acceptance is a purely positive concept; any notion of negation is foreign to it, except, obviously, that it implies negation of non-acceptance. But negation is constitutive of forgiveness. To offer forgiveness is at the same time to condemn the deed and accuse the doer; to receive forgiveness is at the same time to admit to the deed and accept the blame.

Second, forgiveness presupposes that justice—full justice in the strict sense of the term—has not been done. If justice were fully done, forgiveness would not be necessary, except in the limited and inadequate sense of not being vindictive; justice itself would have fully repaid for the wrongdoing. Forgiveness is necessary because strict justice is not done and strictly speaking cannot be done.

Third, forgiveness entails not only the affirmation of the claims of justice but also their transcendence. More precisely, by forgiving we affirm the claims of justice in the very act of not letting them count against the one whom we forgive. By stating that the claims of justice need not be (fully) satisfied, the person who forgives indirectly underscores the fact that what the sense of justice claims to be a wrongdoing is indeed a wrongdoing.

Fourth, since it consists in forgoing the affirmed claims of justice, forgiveness, like any instantiation of grace, involves self-denial and risk. One has let go of something one had a right to, and one is not fully certain whether one's magnanimity will bear fruit either in one's inner peace or in a restored relationship. Yet forgiveness is also laden with promise. Forgiveness is the context in which wrongdoers can come to the recognition of their own injustice. To accuse wrongdoers by simply insisting on strict justice is to drive them down the path of self-justification and denial before others and before themselves. To accuse wrongdoers by offering forgiveness is to invite them to self-knowledge and release. Such an invitation has a potential of leading the wrongdoer to admit guilt and to repent, and thereby healing not only wrongdoers but also those who have been wronged by them.

Fifth, the *first step* in the process of forgiveness is unconditional. It is not predicated on repentance on the part of the wrongdoer or on her willingness to redress the wrong committed. Yet, full-fledged and completed forgiveness is not unconditional. It is true that repentance—the recognition that the deed committed was evil coupled with the willingness to mend one's ways—is not so much a prerequisite of forgiveness as, more profoundly, its possible result. Yet repentance is the kind of result of forgiveness whose absence would amount to a refusal to see oneself as guilty and therefore a refusal to receive forgiveness as forgiveness. Hence an unrepentant wrongdoer must in the end remain an unforgiven wrongdoer—the unconditionality of the first step in the process of forgiveness notwithstanding.

Finally, forgiveness is best received if in addition to repentance there takes place some form of restitution. Indeed, one may ask whether the repentance is genuine if the wrongdoer refuses to restore something of what she has taken away by the wrongdoing—provided that she is capable of doing so.

In sum, forgiveness is an element in the process of reconciliation, a process in which the search for justice is an integral and yet subordinate element.

Conclusion

In the later part of this essay I sought to explicate the social significance of the foundational act of the Christian faith—the death of Christ. This step from the narrative of what God has done for humanity on the cross of Christ to the account of what human beings ought to do in relation to one another was often left unmade in the history of Christianity. The logic of God's action, it was sometimes argued, was applicable to the inner world of human souls plagued by guilt and shame; the outer relationships in family, economy, and state ought to be governed by another logic, more worldly logic. At least in Protestantism, this disjunction between the inner and the outer was one important reason why the Christian faith could be misused to legitimize violence. Emptied of their social import, religious symbols nonetheless floated loosely in the social world and could be harnessed to purposes that are at odds with their proper content. Significantly, this disjunction is never to be found in the New Testament; instead, the central religious narratives and rituals are intended to shape all domains of early Christians' lives. Arguably, the central Christian rituals, Baptism and Eucharist, enact the narrative of divine action precisely as the pattern for lives of believers.

It may well be the case, someone may respond, that the Christian faith at its heart fosters peace rather than violence. But in what ways can it do so in concrete social and political settings? First, the narrative of divine action can motivate and shape behavior of individual actors in conflict situations. Depending on their position, such individual actors can be significant and even decisive for the future of conflicts. Second, this narrative can shape broader cultural habits and expectations that make peaceful solutions possible. It takes a particular cultural soil for the seed of peace to bear fruit. Of course, the narratival portrayal of divine redemptive action cannot be simply mirrored in human interaction, be that on individual, communal, or political planes. Instead, one has to aim at culturally and situationally appropriate practical analogies as near or distant echoes of the divine redemptive action that lies at the heart of the Christian faith.

Finally, the narrative of divine action as it applies to human interaction can help shape social institutions. One way to think about how this may be the case is to recall the concluding words of Anthony Giddens's book *Modernity and Self-Identity*. After noting the emergence in the high modernity of what he calls "life politics" (as distinct from "emancipatory politics"), which demands a remoralization of social life, he writes:

> How can we remoralize social life without falling prey to prejudices? The more we

return to existential issues, the more we find moral disagreements; how can these be reconciled? If there are no transhistorical moral principles, how can humanity cope with clashes of "true believers" without violence? Responding to such problems will surely require a major reconstruction of emancipatory politics as well as the pursuit of the life-political endeavors.

The narrative of the God of unconditional love who reconciles humanity without condoning injustice along with its intended patterning in the lives of human beings and communities, contains, I suggest, at least some resources for such a reconstruction of politics.

107. John Dear

Compassion and Nonviolence from New York to Afghanistan: Reflections after September 11th

John Dear (b. 1959) is a Jesuit priest who represents the new generation of Catholic activists in the tradition of Daniel and Philip Berrigan. As a member of the Plowshares movement, Dear has been arrested numerous times for his protests against war, nuclear weapons, and, more recently, the use of drone attacks in the so-called war on terror. He is the author of more than twenty books, including his autobiography, A Persistent Peace, *and is a former executive director of the Fellowship of Reconciliation. Dear's peacebuilding efforts landed him in New York City after the 9/11 attack on the World Trade Center, and they have taken him across the globe, especially to war-torn regions in developing countries.*

Like thousands of other New Yorkers, I started volunteering immediately after the World Trade Center disaster. Within a few days, the Red Cross asked me to help coordinate the chaplain program at the Family Assistance Center, the site run by the government and the Red Cross for families.

I've been working there ever since. These past few weeks, I have met some 1,500 grieving family members, police officers and firefighters.

All we can do is stand with them in their grief, share their pain, listen, hold them, pray with them, encourage and bless them.

I remember the Long Island Catholic man who came to turn in DNA evidence only to discover his

missing brother-in-law's name on the short list of recovered bodies; the retired New Jersey couple looking for their son, sitting with them as they swabbed their mouths for DNA; the young man who flew alone from Italy looking for his missing mother, crying and shaking; a young man looking for his missing father; holding several mothers weeping for their lost sons.

I recall the young wife desperate to find her husband, asking me through her tears and anger, about God; the many firefighters who stopped me and asked for a blessing; the young woman looking for her husband, wanting to pray and become a Christian; the businessman who lost over fifty colleagues on one of the top floors; and the many low-income security guards, window washers and restaurant workers who narrowly escaped with their lives, who now mourn the loss of their friends and seek financial assistance.

There are so many people that I no longer remember them all, but I lift them up in prayer.

After a week, I stood at Ground Zero amidst the twisted steel and debris, and spoke and prayed with hundreds of workers. Then, I began escorting fifty family members at a time by ferry to Ground Zero, only to hold them as they wept before the horrific devastation. I felt like John standing with Mary and the women on Calvary, at the foot of the cross.

The grief has been overwhelming. But though September 11th remains horrific and still impossible to take in, unfortunately, it is understandable. We mourn nearly 5,400 people who died at the Trade towers in New York City, but in Iraq, they mourn over one million children and women dead from the US sanctions imposed since 1990. In the West Bank and Gaza Strip, parents mourn the hundreds of young people shot by Israeli soldiers. Tens of thousands die daily from starvation around the world, a result of Western economic and military hegemony.

As we begin to realize the massive grief around the world, we begin to understand why after years of bombs, sanctions and killings, powerless people are enraged with anger, and why several pursued the insanity of suicidal terrorism.

These days, I find myself walking from grieving families to Ground Zero to peace vigils, comforting the sorrowful, and speaking out against retaliation and war.

The U.S. bombing of Afghanistan began as 10,000 of us marched through Times Square with the message that inflicting further grief on the Muslim, Arabic world would only insure further terrorist attacks upon us. At another rally, I told how one crying mother, who lost her thirty-year-old son on the 105th floor of the First Tower, said that the deaths of innocent Afghanistan women and children would not bring her son back or make her feel safe, only increase her sorrow.

As we live through these sorrowful times, our task is to proclaim the simple Gospel truth that war is not the answer, that war doesn't work, that war is not the will of God, that war is never justified, and that war is never blessed by God.

We need to pray for peace, forgive and ask for forgiveness, pursue social justice and teach the lessons of peace: that there is no security in war, nuclear weapons, bombing raids, missile shields or greed, only in nonviolence, love, justice, compassion and the God of peace.

As war fever spreads, we can quietly quote Gandhi's insight: "An eye for an eye only makes the whole world blind." Violence in response to violence only leads to further violence. State-sanctioned terrorism will not stop terrorism, but only lead to further terrorism. Missile shields will not protect us from hijacked airplanes. Peaceful means are the only way to a peaceful future and to the God of peace. These are hard lessons, but they are the teachings of Jesus.

Jesus lived, taught and practiced the third way of active nonviolence. If we dare be his friends and followers, we too must live, teach and practice loving nonviolence.

The Gospel is crystal clear: love your enemies, forgive those who hurt you, bless those who persecute you, seek justice for the poor, and be compassionate like God. In other words, practice active, creative nonviolence. It's the only way out. We are not allowed to kill.

Standing at Ground Zero, I think of Jesus as he approached Jerusalem, weeping, saying, "If only you had understood the way to peace!" When his disciples wanted to call down "fire from heaven" upon their enemies, he rebuked them. When they took out the sword to defend him, he cried out, "Put away the sword."

In his name, we call for an immediate end to the war, the bombing raids, the sanctions on Iraq, the oppression of the Palestinian people and the international debt. We insist that our government throw away the Star Wars proposal, dismantle every nuclear weapon and every weapon of mass destruction, undertake international treaties for nuclear disarmament, and redirect those billions of dollars toward the hard work for a lasting peace through international cooperation for nonviolent alternatives, interfaith dialogue, feeding every child on the planet, joining the world court and international law, protecting the earth and showing compassion toward every human being on the planet.

"The moral to be drawn from the tragedy of destruction is that it cannot be resolved by counter-bombs," Gandhi said after World War II, "even as violence cannot be ended by counter-violence. Humanity has to get out of violence only through nonviolence. Hatred can be overcome only by love. Violence can only be overcome by nonviolence."

We can find hope in these dark days by remaining faithful to the nonviolent Jesus. He is the light in our darkness. By staying close to him and his story, we can find the courage and the love to gather for prayer and scripture study in our communities, to hold candlelight peace vigils in our towns, to organize teach-ins on nonviolence, to befriend our Muslim sisters and brothers and to act publicly for an end to war, nuclear weapons and injustice.

The grieving families of New York City have taught me once again that life is precious, that violence breeds violence, and that our only hope is in the wisdom of God's nonviolence.

But they give me hope. If we can walk with the grieving and suffering at home and abroad; love one another and love our enemies; and offer the truth of disarmament and nonviolence, I believe we will sow seeds of peace that will help bring a harvest of peace.

All we have to do is turn back to the God of peace with all our hearts.

108. MEL WHITE

Letter to Jerry Falwell

Mel White (b. 1940), an evangelical Christian, is the founder and president of Soulforce, an organization that uses the nonviolent principles of Martin Luther King, Jr., and Mohandas Gandhi in educational and direct-action campaigns "to end religious and political oppression of lesbian, gay, bisexual, transgender, queer, and questioning people." White is a former ghostwriter for Billy Graham, Pat Robertson, Jim Bakker, and Jerry Falwell, and in 2002 he and his partner, Gary Nixon, moved across the street from Falwell's church in Lynchburg, Virginia, to bear nonviolent witness to their belief that the love of God extends—unconditionally—to the gay community.

Below is a 2002 letter in which White extends an invitation to Falwell and informs him of a pending nonviolent campaign. Falwell did not accept the invitation, and on October 25, a day before hundreds celebrated the first gay-pride festival in Lynchburg, 150 nonviolent activists held a prayer vigil outside of Falwell's church. White stated that the purpose of the weekend of nonviolent protest was "to stand up and speak out against the toxic rhetoric spoken by Christian fundamentalists like Rev. Jerry Falwell. The pride event celebrated who we are and who God created us to be. The vigils called attention to the fact that fundamentalist rhetoric leads to violence and suffering for God's GLBT children."

Dear Jerry,

By now you know that Gary, my partner for more than twenty years, and I have moved to Lynchburg. We've signed a year's lease on a little cottage across the street from your Church on Thomas Road. Now we are your neighbors not just in spirit but in fact. We will be attending your services, study-ing the Bible and worshipping with you and your people. Our goal is simple: We have come to bear witness to the truth that gay people love God, this nation, and their partners with as much integrity and commitment as you and your people do.

Two by two, Gary and I will be inviting members of your congregation as well as staff and students from Liberty University to share a meal, meet for coffee, or just sit around our little living room not to debate or even discuss the topic that divides us, but to just get acquainted.

During the next six weeks, Sunday after Sunday, we will be joined by more and more friends (gay and straight alike) who will unite with us in this witness. On October 25, hundreds of our allies will gather to present our printed and video response to the charges you've made against us. We'll go door-to-door to the entire community.

We believe that your congregation, your students and staff, and the people of Lynchburg are interested in hearing both sides of this controversial question and that they can and will make their own decisions based on the data they find most convincing. You've never explained to them that there is another side, that most scholars, researchers, mental health professionals, Bible scholars, and thousands of clergy and lay leaders believe that homosexuality is another mystery of creation, that homosexuals should accept their sexual orientation as another of God's gifts, that homosexuals should not be asked to change, that when they are loved, accepted, and given support, most live healthy, happy, even holy lives.

On Sunday, October 27, after we have presented our case, hundreds of us will attend your services and sit beside your people to sing, pray, and hear the Word read and proclaimed. We are planning a picnic that same afternoon and hope you and Macel, members of your congregation and students from Liberty University will join us in Riverside Park on Rivermont for that occasion.

We know that your views are sincere, though we find them sincerely wrong about sexual and gender minorities. Consider our presence a kind of gift to you. We know that you have often been the first to change, to take a stand, to lead the way. We want to be your allies in that process. We know that you probably won't be convinced by the growing mountain of scientific, historic, or even biblical evidence that disproves your anti-homosexual beliefs.

But one day you will be changed because of one special homosexual person you know and love whose spiritual commitment and responsible, productive life cannot be denied. We're going to surround you with such people and at the same time pray daily that God will bless you with a gay grandson or lesbian granddaughter. When that day comes, truth will triumph over untruth. And you will realize at last the terrible mistake you've made all these decades in caricaturing and condemning God's beloved gay, lesbian, bisexual, and transgender children.

In the meantime, will you and Macel come to dinner any night next week, September 16? 20? I promise you, we will limit our conversation to the happy memories we share from working together on your autobiography. We'll call to confirm. Greetings to Ron. We hope he'll join us on a separate (or the same) evening. Gary is a great cook and we promise you an evening to remember.

Sincerely,
Mel White and Gary Nixon

109. DONALD KRAYBILL

Death in Disguise

Donald B. Kraybill, Distinguished College Professor and Senior Fellow in the Young Center for Anabaptist and Pietist Studies at Elizabethtown College, is not only the world's leading authority on the Amish—he is also a committed Christian pacifist. Kraybill is the author or editor of more than twenty-five books, and his book on the ethics of Jesus, The Upside-Down Kingdom, *excerpted below, has become a classic both within and beyond Anabaptist communities.*

Detours around Agape

Many scholars agree that nonviolence is central to Jesus' teachings and to the message of the New Testament. The early church practiced nonviolence for nearly three centuries after Jesus' death. Nevertheless, the call to love enemies has baffled human logic over the centuries. Even the church has condoned the use of violent means in various ways.

Christians have evaded the message of the Prince of Peace through several detours. One tempting excuse arises from warfare in the Old Testament. Didn't God send Israel into battle? At first glance this looks like a license to fight. Modern warfare, however, doesn't follow Old Testament strategies. When Yahweh commanded Israel to engage in military action, it was clear that Yahweh was the head warrior who would triumph. Thus military force was deliberately scaled *down* so any victory would be a miraculous one that would applaud Yahweh's divine intervention. If we took the ancient biblical model of warfare seriously, our modern armies would dramatically *reduce* their size and firepower and rely on God's miraculous intervention for victory!

Beyond this key difference, and more importantly, Jesus introduced a new norm, the Torah of love. As God's full and definitive revelation, Jesus is the key for interpreting all of Scripture. He is the supreme authority. As the final word in God's progressive revelation, Jesus offers a new way that transforms, and goes beyond, the old tit-for-tat patterns.

A second detour emerged in the eleventh to thirteenth centuries when Christian crusades, supposedly under the banner of God's blessing, slaughtered Muslims who had conquered Christian holy areas in the Middle East. In this sad and tragic moment, Christians deceived themselves into believing that God was on their side, blessing their use of violence. The temptation to think that God blesses and fights for particular nations, as Yahweh did in ancient Israel, continues even today.

The seductive power of nationalism seeks to wrap God's blessing around national destinies that have nothing to do with Christian faith. Some Christians still prostitute the gospel by justifying military crusades under the flag of God's blessing.

For example, singing "God Bless America," while marching off to war, turns God into a tribal deity that favors pet nations. This distortion of the gospel imagines that God smiles warmly on the military endeavors of some countries, but not on others. The use of God-talk to justify militarism spans many centuries—from holy crusades to modern versions—with claims that God "blesses" military action. Coins inscribed with "In God We Trust" are a mockery when a nation spends billions of dollars for defense. Americans obviously trust weapons, not God.

A third detour, the idea of a "just war," emerged in Christian thinking in the third century, as the church melted more into Roman society and sought ways to justify its defense. Although based on the premise that war should only be a last resort, the just war doctrine put a divine blessing on the use of violence for self-defense and the protection of innocent victims. Just war guidelines specified *when* a war was justifiable and proper rules for *how* it could be fought.

Over the centuries the just war approach enabled political leaders to receive a blessing from the church when using violence. This also made it acceptable for Christians to participate in various roles in military operations. Ironically, however, enemies in the same conflict often called their cause "just," leading both sides to claim God's blessing. One Christian scholar has argued that instead of trying to justify war, we should develop specific policies and steps for just peacemaking.

A fourth detour suggests that Jesus only calls us to love personal enemies. Jesus' words, in this view, apply only to interpersonal relationships. Because God institutes governments, we're obligated to obey the call of conscription and defend the country. We should love our personal enemies, yes, but not national ones. Making this distinction strikes a line between personal morality and one's obligation to the state. This view elevates national allegiance *above* kingdom loyalty.

The classic Christian text that calls for submission to government (Rom. 13:1-7) is sandwiched between two ardent pleas by the apostle Paul for suffering love. In addition there is a big difference between obeying government and submitting to its authority without resorting to violence when we disagree. Furthermore, this passage will sound very different in the context of a democratic government versus a tyrannical one. Often interpreting out of context, we use this passage to place national loyalties above kingdom values, thus negating allegiance to Jesus and bowing down to tribal deities.

We take a fifth detour when churches affirm the way of peace in public statements but view it as an appendage to the gospel. Instead of seeing forgiveness and its social implications as the core of salvation, we see it as marginal. Nonviolence is merely seen as an accessory that's nice when it works. Furthermore, we deem peacemaking a question of "individual conscience," not a gospel mandate. We can take it or leave it. Likewise military service is a matter of individual conscience, we conclude. What is at stake here is our ultimate allegiance. National loyalty often rises above our allegiance to Jesus.

Nagging Questions

Despite Jesus' clear call to peacemaking, many thorny questions lurk in our minds. May violence be used for self-protection? Is it ever God's will for Christians to use violence to further justice? For example, may violence be used to protect innocent victims? Jesus does not speak directly to the issue, but based on his teaching and ministry, his likely response is neither flight nor fight, but nonviolent resistance. His own actions suggest this. He was not a passive bystander in the face of Roman oppression, but neither did he lead an armed revolt. In fact, it may take more courage to engage in nonviolent resistance than to pull a trigger or press a button to launch a missile.

The issues of peacemaking and violence in our world stir many difficult ethical questions. I am fully persuaded that Jesus rejected the use of violence to confront evil, but I realize there are many nagging questions. In a short survey I cannot explore these issues in depth but do want to note some of the questions with which Christians of good faith struggle as they seek to practice the nonviolent way of Jesus amid a world of evil.

Is there a difference between using force and lethal violence? Governments use force to restrain violent criminals. Is the use of non-lethal force acceptable to restrain evil? Is it morally okay to shoot to cripple belligerent bullies as long as we don't kill them?

Are police-keeping actions to maintain order within a society different than using military means for national self-defense? May Christians participate in police actions to keep civic order?

Can a moral line be drawn between private acts of aggression and the use of lethal force by military units of legitimate governments? Is there a difference between murder and state-sanctioned killing? Or is all killing murder?

Is there an ethical difference between using violence for self-aggression, for self-defense, or for protecting innocent victims? Can Christians in good faith use violent force to defend innocent people against tyrants who might kill them? Is it acceptable to shoot a bully wounding or threatening smaller kids in a schoolyard? A bully in an international conflict?

Do Jesus' instructions on peacemaking apply only to his followers or to others as well? Should Christians expect and urge governments to practice nonviolence? In other words, are the ethics of nonviolence applicable to international relations?

Even though we know violence is not the way of Jesus, is it ever necessary to knowingly sin (engage in violence) to protect others and restrain evil?

These are difficult questions without easy or simple answers. Despite their moral complexity, Jesus' call to love the enemy slices through the issues with simplicity and clarity. We are easily trapped into thinking that violence is the most effective way to solve problems. Jesus calls us to faithfulness; to faithfully embody God's loving forgiveness. Many times, such love may, in the long run, be more effective than resorting to violence. Nevertheless, it's hard to discard our belief that violence is the ultimate answer to many problems.

The Myth of Redemptive Violence

… The myth of redemptive violence thrives whenever we assume violence is the most effective way to solve a problem. Terrible as it is, we are tempted to believe violence can bring good things out of a bad scene. Indeed, violence assumes a virtuous character whenever we expect it to save us from evil. The myth of redemptive violence fills video games, movies, and typical interpretations of national and global history.

If we believe that violence works, that it redeems bad things, then we readily turn to it when we face a fight. When we want to fix things that have gone awry, we reach for guns, bombs, and missiles. But sadly, when we try to redeem things through violent means, we may actually become the very evil we hate.

Talk of lovable enemies is hard to hear in a world loaded with weapons of mass destruction. Superpower nations have the capacity to pulverize each other many times over. A single submarine *alone* has the capacity to destroy some 400 separate cities each with a blast five times stronger than the bomb used on Hiroshima. Weapon after weapon, system after system—the overkill capacity is mind-boggling. Preparations for war rob the world's poor of basic necessities, such as food, shelter, and healthcare. Building stockpiles of weapons of mass destruction is an immoral waste of resources when one fourth of the world community lives in squalor.

When we believe violence redeems, the upward spiral of violence never ends. Threats beget more threats. Acts of violence trigger more violence. Wars against terrorism breed more terror and birth more terrorists. Amid wars and acts of terror, the Carpenter's appeal to love our enemies suddenly sounds like good advice. Isn't it more reasonable to learn to live with our enemies and to seek diplomatic solutions than to use weapons that not only destroy but also fuel the fires of hatred? Christians in every land must insist that war in the name of peace is really death in disguise. Imagine the global impact if Christians in every country were willing to pledge that they will never kill another human being.

110. Richard B. Hays, George Hunsinger, Richard Pierard, Glen Stassen, and Jim Wallis

Confessing Christ in a World of Violence

In October 2004, five leading evangelicals in the United States—Richard B. Hays, George Washington Ivey Professor of New Testament at Duke Divinity School; George Hunsinger, Hazel Thomas McCord Professor of Systematic Theology at Princeton Theological Seminary; Richard V. Pierard, Stephen Phillips Professor of History at Gordon College; Glen Stassen, Lewis Smedes Professor of Christian Ethics at Fuller Theological Seminary; and Jim Wallis, editor of Sojourners—*reacted to a brewing messianic theology of war by drafting, disseminating, and publicizing the following confession of Christ. Not more than two years earlier, President George W. Bush had described Iran, Iraq, and North Korea as part of an "axis of evil" that harbored terrorists and sought weapons of mass destruction.*

Our world is wracked with violence and war. But Jesus said: "Blessed are the peacemakers, for they shall be called the children of God" (Matt. 5:9). Innocent people, at home and abroad, are increasingly threatened by terrorist attacks. But Jesus said: "Love your enemies, pray for those who persecute you" (Matt. 5:44). These words, which have never been easy, seem all the more difficult today.

Nevertheless, a time comes when silence is betrayal. How many churches have heard sermons on these texts since the terrorist atrocities of September 11? Where is the serious debate about what it means to confess Christ in a world of violence? Does Christian "realism" mean resigning ourselves to an endless future of "pre-emptive wars"? Does it mean turning a blind eye to torture and massive civilian casualties? Does it mean acting out of fear and resentment rather than intelligence and restraint?

Faithfully confessing Christ is the church's task,

and never more so than when its confession is co-opted by militarism and nationalism.

A "theology of war," emanating from the highest circles of American government, is seeping into our churches as well.

The language of "righteous empire" is employed with growing frequency.

The roles of God, church, and nation are confused by talk of an American "mission" and "divine appointment" to "rid the world of evil."

The security issues before our nation allow no easy solutions. No one has a monopoly on the truth. But a policy that rejects the wisdom of international consultation should not be baptized by religiosity. The danger today is political idolatry exacerbated by the politics of fear.

In this time of crisis, we need a new confession of Christ.

1. Jesus Christ, as attested in Holy Scripture, knows no national boundaries. Those who confess his name are found throughout the earth. Our allegiance to Christ takes priority over national identity. Whenever Christianity compromises with empire, the gospel of Christ is discredited.

We reject the false teaching that any nation-state can ever be described with the words, "the light shines in the darkness and the darkness has not overcome it." These words, used in scripture, apply only to Christ. No political or religious leader has the right to twist them in the service of war.

2. Christ commits Christians to a strong presumption against war. The wanton destructiveness of modern warfare strengthens this obligation. Standing in the shadow of the Cross, Christians have a responsibility to count the cost, speak out for the victims, and explore every alternative before a nation goes to war. We are committed to international cooperation rather than unilateral policies.

We reject the false teaching that a war on terrorism takes precedence over ethical and legal norms. Some things ought never be done—torture, the deliberate bombing of civilians, the use of indiscriminate weapons of mass destruction—regardless of the consequences.

3. Christ commands us to see not only the splinter in our adversary's eye, but also the beam in our own. The distinction between good and evil does not run between one nation and another, or one group and another. It runs straight through every human heart.

We reject the false teaching that America is a "Christian nation," representing only virtue, while its adversaries are nothing but vicious. We reject the belief that America has nothing to repent of, even as we reject that it represents most of the world's evil. "All have sinned and fallen short of the glory of God" (Rom. 3:23).

4. Christ shows us that enemy-love is the heart of the gospel. "While we were yet enemies, Christ died for us" (Rom. 5:8, 10). We are to show love to our enemies even as we believe God in Christ has shown love to us and the whole world. Enemy-love does not mean capitulating to hostile agendas or domination. It does mean refusing to demonize any human being created in God's image.

We reject the false teaching that any human being can be defined as outside the law's protection. We reject the demonization of perceived enemies, which only paves the way to abuse; and we reject the mistreatment of prisoners, regardless of supposed benefits to their captors.

5. Christ teaches us that humility is the virtue befitting forgiven sinners. It tempers all political disagreements, and it allows that our own political perceptions, in a complex world, may be wrong.

We reject the false teaching that those who are not for the United States politically are against it or that those who fundamentally question American policies must be with the "evil-doers." Such crude distinctions, especially when used by Christians, are expressions of the Manichaean heresy, in which the world is divided into forces of absolute good and absolute evil.

The Lord Jesus Christ is either authoritative for Christians, or he is not. His Lordship cannot be set aside by any earthly power. His words may not be distorted for propagandistic purposes. No nation-state may usurp the place of God.

We believe that acknowledging these truths is indispensable for followers of Christ. We urge them to remember these principles in making their decisions as citizens. Peacemaking is central to our vocation in a troubled world where Christ is Lord.

111. JIM FOREST

Salt of the Earth: An Orthodox Christian Approach to Peacemaking

Jim Forest (b. 1941) and his wife, Nancy Forest, are co-secretaries of the Orthodox Peace Fellowship. After leaving the U.S. Navy as a conscientious objector, Jim devoted his life to peacemaking. He has edited both The Catholic Worker *and* Fellowship *(the magazine of the Fellowship of Reconciliation), served as co-founder of the Catholic Peace Fellowship and as general secretary of the International Fellowship of Reconciliation, and authored many books, including* The Road to Emmaus: Pilgrimage as a Way of Life. *The selection below is an excerpt from a lecture that Forest delivered at St. Vladimir's Seminary in Yonkers, New York, in November 2004.*

Consider three key words: Orthodox, Christian and peace.

Often the word "orthodox" is used as a synonym for rigidity. Not often is it understood in its real sense: the true way to give praise, and also true belief. Attach it to the word "Christian" and it becomes a term describing a person who is trying to live according to the Gospel. He may have far to go, but this is the direction he is trying to take. "To be an Orthodox Christian," said Metropolitan Anthony Bloom, "is to attempt to live a Christ-centered life. We should try to live in such a way that if the Gospels were lost, they could be rewritten by looking at us."

To be an Orthodox Christian means belonging to the Orthodox Church. It is not possible to follow Christ and remain alone. I am part of a vast, time-spanning community of people with a collective memory that goes back as far as Adam and Eve. It is a community that includes the Church Fathers, whose words we are encouraged to read.

It is also a Church of Councils. We hold ourselves accountable to the results of those councils even though they met many centuries ago. This means not letting my own opinions or those of my peers take charge of my faith. This requires guarding myself from the various ideologies that dominate the world I live in.

We are also a Church of saints. Day by day we remember them. We bear their names. We call on them for help. We remember what they did and

sometimes what they said. We have icons of some of them in our churches and homes.

Attention to the Church Fathers and the saints can be a bewildering experience. For example we discover one Church Father showers the highest praise on marriage while another regards marriage as a barely tolerable compromise for those unable to embrace the real Christian calling: celibate monastic life. It can be disconcerting to discover that on various questions different Church Fathers may have different ideas or different emphases or just plain disagree.

Or we look at the saints and find one who was martyred for refusing to be a soldier, then the next day discover a saint who was a hero on the battlefield. Or we read about a saint who wore the rich clothing of a prince and then find another saint whose only clothing was his uncut beard. Here is a saint who was a great scholar while there is a saint who was a holy fool. Here is a saint who raced to the desert, while over there is a saint who refused to leave the city and was critical of those who did. Each saint poses a challenge and each saint raises certain questions and even certain problems. The puzzle pieces don't always fit. We discover that neither the Church Fathers nor the saints on the calendar are a marching band, all in step and playing in perfect harmony.

Devotion to the saints solves some problems and raises others. In the details of their lives, they march in a thousand different directions. They also made mistakes. They were not saints every minute of every day. Like us, they had sins to confess. But their virtues overwhelm their faults. In different ways, each saint gives us a window for seeing Christ and his Gospel more clearly.

To be an Orthodox Christian means, as St. Paul says, that we are no longer Greek or Jew. Nationality is secondary. It is not the national flag that is placed on the altar but the Gospel. For us, even though we find ourselves in an Orthodox Church divided on national or jurisdictional lines, it means we are no longer American or Russian or Egyptian or Serbian. Rather we are one people united in baptism and faith whose identity and responsibility includes but goes beyond the land where we were born or the culture and mother tongue that shaped us.

On to the next word: peace. This is a damaged word. It's like an icon so blackened by candle smoke that the image is completely hidden. "Peace" is a word that has been covered with a lot of smoke from the fires of propaganda, politics, ideologies, war and nationalism. In Soviet Russia there were those omnipresent slogans proclaiming peace while the Church was often obliged to take part in state-organized and state-scripted "peace" events. As a boy growing up in New Jersey, it was almost the same situation. "Peace is our profession" was the slogan of the Strategic Air Command, whose apocalyptic task—fighting nuclear war—was on stage center in the film "Doctor Strangelove." In more recent years, there was a nuclear missile christened "The Peacemaker."

Not only governments but peace groups have damaged the word "peace." Anti-war groups often reveal less about peace than about anger, alienation and even hatred. It's always a surprise to find a peace group that regards unborn children as being among those whose lives need to be protected.

In wartime talk of peace can put you on thin ice. I recently heard a story that dates back to the first Gulf War. Three clergymen were being interviewed on television. Two of them insisted that the war was a good and just war and had God's blessing. The third opened his Bible and read aloud the words of Jesus: "Blessed are the peacemakers … Love your enemies …" But he was cut short by a shout from the angry pastor next to him: "That's not relevant now! We're at war!"

War does this to us. Parts of the Gospel are simply abandoned. They are seen as temporarily irrelevant, an embarrassment to the patriotic Christian. "Peace" is put in the deep freeze, a word to be thawed out after the war is over. Thus the salt loses it savor and sugar takes its place.

Part of our job is to clean words like "peace." It's a work similar to icon restoration. Otherwise it will be hard to understand the Gospel or the Liturgy and impossible to translate the Gospel and the Liturgy into daily life.

Peace is one of the characteristics of the Kingdom of God compressed into a single word. Consider how often and in what significant ways Christ uses the word "peace" in the Gospel: "And if the house is worthy, let your peace come upon it." "And he awoke and rebuked the wind, and said to the sea, 'Peace! Be still!'" "And he said to her, 'Daughter, your faith has made you well; go in peace, and be healed of your disease.'" "And he said to the woman, 'Your faith has saved you; go in peace.'" "Whatever house you enter, first say, 'Peace be to this house!'" "Would that even today you knew the things that make for peace!" "Peace I leave with you; my peace I give to you; not as the world gives do I give to you. Let not your hearts be troubled, neither let them be afraid." His greeting after the resurrection is, "Peace be with you." In Mark's Gospel, once again we come upon the metaphor of salt: "Have salt in yourselves, and be at peace with one another."

In the Slavic liturgical tradition, the custom is to sing the Beatitudes while the Gospel Book is carried in procession through the church. Why? Because the Beatitudes are a short summary of the Gospel. These few verses describe a kind of ladder to heaven, starting with poverty of spirit and ascending to readiness to suffer for Christ and at last to participate in the Paschal joy of Christ. Near the top we come to the words, "Blessed are the peacemakers."

Christ's peace is not passive nor has it anything to do with the behavior of a coward or of the person who is polite rather than truthful. Christ says, in Matthew's Gospel: "Do not think that I have come to bring peace on earth; I have not come to bring peace, but a sword." He means the sword metaphorically, as Luke makes clear in his version of the same passage: "Do you think that I have come to give peace on earth? No, I tell you, but rather division." To live truthfully rather than float with the tide means most of the time to swim against the tide, risking penalties if not punishment for doing so. Christ had, and still has, opponents. Christ's words and actions often brought his opponents' blood to a boil. Think of his words of protest about the teachings of the Pharisees who laid burdens on others they would not carry themselves. Think of him chasing the moneychangers from the Temple. No one was injured, but God's lightning flashed in the Temple courtyard.

Jesus speaks the truth, no matter how dangerous a task that may be. He gives us an example of spiritual and verbal combat. But his hands are not bloodstained. Think about the fact that Christ killed no one. Neither did he bless any of his followers to kill anyone. There are many ways in which Christ is unique. This is one of them. His final miracle before his crucifixion is to heal the injury of a temple guard whom Peter had wounded. He who preached the love of enemies took a moment to heal an enemy while on his way to the Cross.

In the early centuries, Christians got into a lot of trouble for their attitude toward the state. You get a sense of what that was like in this passage from second-century hieromartyr, St. Justin: "From Jerusalem there went out into the world, men, twelve in number, and these illiterate, of no ability in speaking: but by the power of God they proclaimed to every race of men that they were sent by Christ to teach to all the word of God; and we who formerly used to murder one another do not only now refrain from making war upon our enemies, but also, that we may not lie nor deceive our examiners, willingly die confessing Christ."

The big problem for early Christians, a problem that so often got them into trouble, was their refusal to regard any ruler as a god. This doesn't mean simply a ruler who claims to be a god, but the persistent tendency of so many rulers down to the present day to behave as gods and expect to be treated that way. Christians were obedient members of society in every way they could be without disobeying God, but were prepared to suffer even the most cruel death rather than place obedience to Caesar before obedience to God.

While eventually the baptismal requirements of the Church were relaxed, it was once the case that those who did not renounce killing, whether as a soldier or judge, could not be baptized. It is still the case that those who have killed another human being, even in self-defense or by accident, are excluded from serving at the altar. Presumably this would also bar anyone whose words incite others to kill.

What's the problem? Killing in war is often awarded with medals. Aren't soldiers only doing their duty, however horrible it may be? Is there not virtue in their deeds, however bloody? I am reminded of an interview with an American soldier in Iraq that I heard on television recently: "A part of your soul is destroyed in killing someone else." He might have said, but didn't, that a part of your soul is wounded when you kill another. The Church looks for ways to heal such wounds.

Christ is not simply an advocate of peace or an example of peace. He is peace. To want to live a Christ-like life means to want to participate in the peace of Christ. Yes, we may fail, as we fail in so many things, but we must not give up trying....

Occasionally the question is raised: "Why are we judged together and not one by one as we die?" It is because our life is far from over when we die. Our acts of love, and failures to love, continue to have consequences until the end of history. What Adam and Eve did, what Moses did, what Plato did, what Pilate did, what the Apostles did, what Caesar did, what Hitler did, what Martin Luther King did, what Mother Maria Skobtsova did, what you and I have done—all these lives, with their life-saving or murderous content, continue to have consequences for the rest of history. What you and I do, and what we fail to do, will matter forever.

It weighs heavily on many people that Jesus preached not only heaven but hell. There are many references to hell in the Gospels, including in the Sermon on the Mount. How can a loving God allow a place devoid of love?

A response to this question that makes sense to me is one I first heard in a church in Prague in the Communist period. God allows us to go wherever we are going. We are not forced to love. Communion is not forced on us. We are not forced to recognize God's presence. It is all an invitation. We can choose. We can choose life or death. Perhaps we can even make the choice of heaven while in hell. In *The Great Divorce*, C. S. Lewis has a tour bus leaving daily from hell to heaven. But the bus is never full and tends to return with as many passengers as it took on the trip out of hell. Heaven is too painful, its light too intense, its edges too sharp, for those who are used to the dullness of hell. In fact the older we are, the more we live by old choices, and defend those choices, and make ideologies, even theologies, out of our choices, and finally become slaves to them.

We can say, not just once but forever, as Peter once said of Jesus, "I do not know the man." There are so many people about whom we can say, to our eternal peril, "I do not know the man," to which we can add that he is worthless and has no one to blame for his troubles but himself, that his problems aren't our business, that he is an enemy, that he deserves to die—whether of frostbite or violence matters little.

As St. John Chrysostom said, "If you cannot find Christ in the beggar at the church door, you will not find Him in the chalice." If I cannot find the face of Jesus in the face of those who are my enemies, if I cannot find him in the unbeautiful, if I cannot find him in those who have the wrong ideas, if I cannot find him in the poor and the defeated, how will I find him in bread and wine, or in the life after death? If I do not reach out in this world to those with whom he has identified himself, why do I imagine that I will want to be with him, and them, in heaven? Why would I want to be for all eternity in the company of those whom I despised and avoided every day of my life?

Christ's Kingdom would be hell for those who avoided peace and devoted their lives to division. But heaven is right in front of us. At the heart of what Jesus says in every act and parable is this: Now, this minute, we can enter the Kingdom of God. This very day we can sing the Paschal hymn: "Christ is risen from the dead, trampling down death by death, and to those in the tomb he has given life!"

112. VALERIE WEAVER-ZERCHER

One Mean Mennonite Mama: A Pacifist Parent Faces Her Anger

Valerie Weaver-Zercher (b. 1973) is an essayist, editor, poet, and parent. Her writing has won several national awards, and has appeared in Sojourners, Christian Century, The Mennonite, *and several leading secular publications. The 2006 essay below represents the relatively rare genre of parenting and peacemaking.*

I did something not long ago that I've always claimed I'd never do: I spanked my child. Not only did I spank him, but I did it in a moment of complete, unfettered rage. Even if you think spanking is effective discipline, everyone knows you're not supposed to do it out of anger.

My 5-year-old was disappointed that he couldn't go to a picnic and was slamming doors, kicking and yelling, "Bad Mama!" (Considering what happened next, this was probably a fitting moniker.) The 3-year-old and 1-year-old were also throwing minor fits, and I was facing several more hours with these tykes. I was depleted, and after almost six years of parenting, I should have been able to read the handwriting on the wall: You are tired. You are angry. You will hurt your child if you do not shut yourself in the bathroom and repeat the Christ Prayer 20 times while breathing deeply.

But I couldn't read the warning signs because my vision was blurred with fury—

Or maybe I chose not to read the signs, because rage has such a strangely delicious taste. So instead of walking away or praying or calling a friend, I grabbed my eldest with my left hand and delivered several robust whacks to his bottom with my right.

Fortunately my arms are puny, and fortunately I woke up from my fuming stupor after about five whacks. I held him close and apologized profusely,

313

and somehow we both straightened up enough to make it through the evening with a semblance of normalcy.

Let me be clear: I know better. I've taken conflict transformation classes, and I've led trainings on anger management. Yet I have talked to enough other parents to know that I'm not the only one who should know better and doesn't. Several friends admit to grabbing their children's arms, hard, and one friend slapped her son for repeatedly dropping a book out of a wagon.

So what can we do once we've faced the truth that we're not the peaceable parents we'd like to be? I want to explore how we can forgive ourselves, how we can listen to our anger, how we can counteract our own fury with loving household rituals and how we can even transform our rage into a deeper, holier outrage at things that deserve our anger more than our children.

1. **Find forgiveness.** Receiving forgiveness from a 5-year-old is the easy part; forgiving myself is more difficult. Realizing that I can become furious enough to want to hurt a child is humiliating and terrifying. Before having children I didn't understand, at least in any visceral way, the importance of confession. Now I find it a formative act, and one I need to perform every day.

I must also learn to distinguish between anger and action. In those fragile, shame-filled moments after wanting to hurt a child, I am tempted to consider my rage a sin. Later, however, as I unfurl the strands of emotion and incident that led to my outburst, I remember that conceptualizing anger as a sin is riskier than seeing it as a signal that something needs to be changed. "I wonder if controlling my anger also makes me angry," writes Garret Keizer in *The Enigma of Anger: Essays on a Sometimes Deadly Sin*. "Trying to see everyone's point of view, trying to be patient beyond reason, trying to remember that the other person is also a child of God … how far do you go with all this before you explode from accumulated grievance?"

So while I seek forgiveness for my violence, I do not seek it for my anger. Instead I want to see my fury as a signal, a flare on the horizon that I'd do best not to ignore.

2. **Learn to decipher my own code of anger.** Losing my temper takes me completely off-guard.

But as Anne Lamott writes in her essay "Mother Anger: Theory and Practice": "When we blow up at our kids, we only think we're going from zero to 60 in one second. Our surface and persona are so calm that when the problem first begins, we sound in control when we say, 'Now, honey, stop that,' or 'that's enough.' But it's only an illusion," she writes. "Because actually we've been storing up grievances all day—against husbands and bosses and mothers and neighbors—and not been aware of them. So when the problem with your kid starts up, you're actually starting at 59, only you're not moving. You're in high idle already, but you are not even aware of how vulnerable and disrespected you already feel."

Reading my own anger also means developing rituals of release that allow me to vent in a way that doesn't hurt myself or my children. Maybe I should take my own advice to my kids and go punch a pillow. I've been known to yell at the couch, and my sister-in-law admits to emitting a foghorn-like cry before yelling, "Uh, oh, Mama's gonna blow!" It's amazing how thin the line is between rage and humor and how healing the crossing of it can be.

3. **Sanctify my house as often as I rage within it.** When my family sits down for dinner, we light four candles before we pray: one for God the Creator, one for God who came in Jesus, one for God who comforts us through the Holy Spirit and one for someone we want to pray for that evening. At bedtime we read, pray and sing hymns. These small acts work as flags of sorts, ways to stake my family's loyalty to God's reign of peace and love rather than to the government of our fickle emotions.

While wallowing in parental shame, I underestimate the power of rituals like these. Such traditions function as antidotes to the angry episodes that all households experience. "The sanctification of our household through prayer, custom and ceremonies of tenderness works to curb anger," writes Keizer. At the most basic level, sacramental acts give our children memories of us when we're not seething ogres. They remind us of our own commitments to peaceful living, which run stronger and deeper than a day of shouting and spanking here and there. Such traditions also help us reground ourselves in our love for our children: it's harder to scream at someone when you remember you have to sing and pray with them in a couple hours.

4. **Follow the path of my household frustrations toward holier anger.** The irony of parental anger is that in a world where there is much to be angry about—injustice, war, racism, sexism—I express my anger most strongly at those who deserve it least: children. How is it that I rage more often at three little preschoolers than at the sin and inequity that deprive millions of food and water and education? How can I fume more often at the insolence of a 5-year-old than I do at the disrespect humans show to God through our disregard for creation?

Perhaps I can learn to shift the target of my anger from my children to these larger issues of injustice and inequity. Sue Monk Kidd speaks of transfiguring anger from rage to outrage. "Rage, or what might be called untransfigured anger, can become a calcified bitterness," Monk Kidd writes in *The Dance of the Dissident Daughter*. "What rage wants and needs is to move outward toward positive social purpose.... Outrage is love's wild and unacknowledged sister."

Holy outrage is what motivated Christ to overturn the moneychangers' tables in the temple. Perhaps my anger at the small particulars of household life with children—tantrums, clutter and whining—can be transfigured into holy outrage at the things that enrage God.

It is important to discern when one's anger can be dealt with through a few commitments like these and when one's rage is truly injuring others or ourselves. We may need the help of pastors or friends to determine this.

Most parents I know, however, are too hard on themselves. For them, Keizer provides a reassuring image. "A house where no one ever gets mad might not be any more healthy to live in than a house where no one ever opens a window," he writes.

"Aside from the obvious pathological exceptions, I do not think it is the big blows that cause the greatest harm anyway, but rather the constant and petty outbreaks of simmering ill temper—what the poet [Robert] Hayden so aptly calls 'the chronic angers of that house.'"

It's disconcerting to realize that anger is a force that I and my household will always need to harness. Yet it's also strangely comforting to think that I will have many opportunities to practice these commitments. Carla Barnhill, in her book *The Myth of the Perfect Mother*, writes that motherhood—and, I would add, fatherhood—is best conceived not as a job or an identity but as a practice through which we are formed. Drawing from Alasdair MacIntyre's idea that an ethical life includes a cycle of practices that, upon perseverance, turn into virtues, Barnhill conceives of parenthood as not unlike Scripture reading, fasting and worship. Only through practice are such spiritual disciplines able to form us into the likeness of Christ. "What matters in the practice of mothering is our willingness to be open to God's work in our lives, our ability to grow and change with our children, our vulnerability and honesty in the face of the challenges that every brand of spiritual development presents," Barnhill writes.

When we view parenting as a spiritual discipline, Jesus' answer to his disciples' question about how often they should forgive suddenly doesn't sound so exaggerated. "Seventy times seven" sounds low, actually, when one considers the unrelenting practice of parenting.

In fact, in light of my commitment to peacemaking and my consistent inability to live it out, "seventy times seven" doesn't sound anything like drudgery or obligation. It sounds a lot more like a second and third—and 490th—chance for one fuming, tired parent to find God's grace.

113. ROBERT JOHANSEN

The Politics of Love and War: What Is Our Responsibility?

Robert Johansen (b. 1940) is a Senior Fellow at the Kroc Institute for International Peace Studies at the University of Notre Dame. His areas of specialty include issues of international ethics and global governance, the United Nations and the maintenance of peace and security, and peace and world order studies. He is the author of numerous books, including Toward an Alternative Security System: Moving Beyond the Balance of Power in the Search for World Security *(1983).*

Throughout their history Christians have faced this question: Can I refuse to kill others and still be morally responsible when violent, aggressive groups threaten other people? Can Christian love respond effectively to political violence? Can we love our enemies and still exercise moral responsibility toward others in an age of terrorism, preemptive and preventive wars, ruthless dictators, weapons of mass destruction, and a too often divided United Nations? Another question also interests us: How can we translate our charitable motives into the prevention of hostile violence and the avoidance of war altogether? I address these questions here speaking as a political scientist for whom ethics matter, not as a theologian.

To address the preceding questions, I will describe, first, the main criticism of Christian pacifism, particularly the claim that the Christian pacifist is not politically responsible. This criticism has dominated most political thought since the origins of our present international system, which grew out of the 1648 Peace of Westphalia, a response to the European religious wars that preceded it.

Second, I will examine the claim that nonpacifists are politically responsible because they are willing to fight wars. I will argue that new conditions in world affairs increasingly call that claim into question. To be sure, political violence and war do threaten us in new ways. But it does not necessarily follow that focusing on preparation for war is the best way to address current and future threats of armed conflict.

Third, I will argue that a comprehensive expression of Christian pacifism, if understood in its full potentiality, can be a responsible way to live.

Finally, I will sketch a future world on which many pacifists and nonpacifists could agree if they would take Christian values more seriously or, for those throughout the world who are not Christian, if they would take seriously what we might call the values of human dignity. These are values of respect for human life rooted in the world's major living religious traditions, even though they are expressed internationally not in religious language but in the lingua franca of international law found in seminal documents like the Universal Declaration of Human Rights, the human rights provisions of the United Nations Charter, and major human rights treaties.

Evaluating the Claim That Pacifists Are Not Politically Responsible

The influential Protestant theologian Reinhold Niebuhr and political theorists such as Max Weber authored some of the most telling, classic criticisms of pacifism. These and more recent similar criticisms continue to express the dominant school of thought in international relations. Policymakers in Washington, as well as political leaders in most capitals throughout the world, reject pacifism as politically irresponsible and ineffective in opposing military threats. Widespread acceptance of political killing in war occurred much earlier in history, of course, going back to ancient times. In the 1500s, Niccolo Machiavelli developed arguments legitimizing military killing that are still widely accepted. In *The Prince*, he advocated the use of military force whenever a ruler calculated that it would bring substantial political or economic gain to do so. Although this perspective, which views war as a morally acceptable instrument of normal statecraft, is called "realism," it is not necessarily more realistic in the sense of having an accurate grasp of reality than some other ways of thinking that are less ideological and more sensitive to empirical observation of the causes of war and the conditions for establishing peace.

Niebuhr considered himself to be a political realist, even a Christian realist. There are many varieties of realists; Machiavelli and Niebuhr typify realism as I use the term in this essay. They advised political leaders not to be constrained by moral reservations about killing when war seemed necessary for security. Political realists include people such as Otto von Bismarck (known for practicing realpolitik, the German term for political realism), and more contemporary political scientists such as Hans Morgenthau, Henry Kissinger, Kenneth Waltz, and John Mearsheimer. And although she often seems driven by ideological preferences, former Secretary of State Condoleezza Rice calls herself a realist. Most policymakers and scholars of international relations do also.

Political realists believe that officials should focus on maximizing the power of the state, measured primarily in terms of military power and secondarily economic strength. Moral principles and humanitarian values should not stop political leaders from using violence when they deem it necessary. The Christian realist—a term I use here interchangeably with "nonpacifist"—says that war in general is acceptable, but that a particular war can be considered legitimate only when it meets the standards for a just war. Political realism has dominated U.S. foreign policy regardless of which political party has been in power. It has shaped high school civics classes, television programs, talk radio, and movies. It has influenced most people's minds and limited our imaginations in ways that discourage us, even without being conscious of it, from thinking about genuine possibilities for non-military strategies to build peace. Religious pacifists have not always been immune to these influences. Indeed, the influence of some military thinking in our culture could be seen as a modern analogue to the influence of idol worship that led the ancient Hebrews astray.

Niebuhr acknowledged that pacifists, in refusing to fight wars, might be more faithful in following Jesus' example and teaching of nonviolent love than are soldiers. But he also said that they are not politically responsible. He was particularly concerned that pacifist thinking might discourage the United States from fighting Hitler in World War II. Later, he worried that pacifism could weaken public support for a U.S. military buildup against the Soviet Union during the Cold War. According to Niebuhr, to keep a clean conscience by not killing, pacifists refused to support high levels of military preparedness and to fight wars even though these were necessary to protect the United States from hostile violence. Centuries earlier Augustine had said that, although it was wrong for Christians to kill others in order to defend themselves, because that would be too selfish and self-interested, they did have a duty to fight and kill, when necessary, in order to protect other innocent people against attacks by ruthless, aggressive armies. However, despite the selfless origin for this thinking, it has led in practice to using violence for self-defense or self-aggrandizement more than for defense of the most innocent. Niebuhr said that willingness to kill in order to protect one's society was a duty. In short, Christian realists may acknowledge that pacifists are faithful to Jesus' teachings of nonviolent love for all, even enemies, but they also usually condemn pacifists for not being responsible in defending the political order. Realists say that pacifists have too much faith in God, even a naïve faith that political conflicts will turn out in acceptable ways if people live as nonviolently as Jesus did.

How do pacifists respond to this criticism? Although there are many kinds of pacifists, most Christian pacifists historically have not claimed to be politically responsible. We can find exceptions, but in general religious pacifists claimed to be ethically responsible in following Jesus. They chose not to worry about political effectiveness. They believed that a Christian should place more emphasis on being faithful in following Jesus than on estimating the possible political consequences of being faithful and then watering down faithfulness in order to become more "effective" politically. Being effective in such instances usually has meant protecting one's own state through killing other people.

Those Christian pacifists who are also political activists point out that realists are in error if they say that pacifists do nothing to resist military aggression. Many pacifists oppose military aggression in every way they can while still keeping their actions consistent with agape. They refuse to kill others in their opposition to aggression, but they, like Brethren pacifist Ted Studebaker who died in Vietnam in 1971, are willing to put their lives on the line in the struggle to prevent hostile violence from engulfing the world.

If pacifists are not focused on the political effectiveness of their actions, are they guilty as charged, then, of not being responsible? "Responsibility" means having a duty to another, or being legally or ethically responsible for the welfare of another. To assess responsibility we need to ask, Responsible to whom? And for what? A person may be responsible to God, to family and friends, to fellow citizens in one's society, to all people, or particularly for the Christian, to "the least of these" described in Matthew 25. There Jesus explained, "I was hungry and you gave me food, … I was thirsty and you gave me drink, … I was a stranger and you welcomed me, I was naked and you clothed me, I was sick and you took care of me, I was in prison and you visited me" (Matt. 25:35-36). Jesus seems to be saying that these downtrodden ones are the people to whom his followers should express responsibility in this world because that is a practical way of being faithful to God. This is an important passage because it is the basis for God's judgment about who has lived rightly, and, as Jesus says in verse 34, this standard of compassion has been in place since "the foundation of the world." It expresses both God's will for our lives and our most authentic or true selves as God created us. Any other conduct expresses a false self and contradicts God's will.

We also need to ask, Responsible for what? The pacifist says that we are responsible for showing compassion for the "least of these," and for loving all people, as Jesus loved. In contrast, Christian realists emphasize that we are responsible for protecting our country and its way of life and for protecting the political order based on independent states in the inter-state system. In my view, God is the one to whom Christians should express first responsibility. In honoring this responsibility to love God, we discover our second responsibility: to love our neighbor and especially to express compassion for the poor and downtrodden. If we do this for the least of these, says Jesus, we have loved God and been faithful, or we might say "responsible."

Let us use the label "type 1 responsibility" to refer to being responsible to God by being faithful to the ethic that Jesus taught. Let us call "type 2 responsibility" being responsible to those people who are most in need of help because of their possible victimization by hostile violence and poverty—the people Jesus referred to as "the least of these." Let us label "type 3 responsibility" the idea of political realists that we should shoulder responsibility for protecting the political order and the people who benefit from living in the political order. There is less Biblical authority for type 3 responsibility. Indeed, some pacifists might deny that we have a type 3 responsibility. But because political institutions provide benefits of law and order and economic organization, let us keep this third type of responsibility in view.

Type 1 and type 2 responsibility both emphasize being faithful to the Biblical injunction to be loving rather than to be calculating how to be politically effective. This emphasis is the reason that the Church of the Brethren, for example, since its origins in 1708, has opposed war in all its forms and has affirmed repeatedly at its annual meetings over the years that "all war is sin." In opposing all war, Brethren do not ask, as nonpacifist Protestants, Roman Catholics, and Orthodox should, whether a particular war meets the standards for a just war. For Brethren, there can be no ethically acceptable war, no justifiable cause for killing, even if a war satisfies just war criteria. Type 1 responsibility emphasizes principles to follow and only secondarily pays attention to the consequences of following them. This approach is sometimes called a deontological or rule-based ethic.

Let me sum up the argument so far. To the claim by nonpacifists that pacifists are not responsible, pacifists respond: Pacifists are responsible in fulfilling type 1 responsibility to God, and in fulfilling type 2 responsibility to neighbors, at least in part by not killing anyone in war and by helping the "least of these." Whether or not pacifists fulfill type 3 responsibility depends upon whether one considers nonviolent instruments of defense to be a satisfactory defense of the existing political order. Pacifists probably would; nonpacifists would not. However, we still need to discuss whether it is ethically desirable to fulfill type 3 responsibility when defined as defending the existing international political order. Before we do that, let us examine the seldom-examined assumption that those who are willing to fight are responsible.

Evaluating the Claim That Nonpacifists Are Responsible

To be responsible, according to Christian realists, Christians should honor their duty to defend through military means the existing political order when it is threatened by hostile violence, and particularly to defend democratic nation-states and the balance-of-power system in which nation-states enjoy political independence. Refusal to defend the political order with violence would result, they claim, in capitulation to the most ruthless and aggressive political leaders. Christian just war thinkers have said since the time of Augustine that Christians are justified in using violence to protect other innocent people who might be attacked. Nonpacifists argue that without U.S. military force poised against Kaiser Wilhelm in World War I, against Hitler and Tojo in World War II, against Stalin in the Cold War, against North Korea in the Korean War, and against Iraq and Iran and North Korea today, evil forces would take over. At first glance, it appears that realists should receive high marks for type 3 responsibility. They sacrifice and struggle to uphold the political order and protect their society against intruders. But upon further examination, it turns out that, in practice, realists or nonpacifists have serious problems in meeting all three forms of responsibility.

As for type 1 responsibility to God and Jesus' teachings, even Niebuhr admits that nonpacifist realists do not do as well as pacifists in imitating Jesus' love for neighbor and enemy. In type 2 responsibility to other people, nonpacifists have found it difficult to support justifiable wars without unintentionally also encouraging unjustifiable

reliance on high levels of military preparedness and other militaristic policies for security. Realists' endorsement of high military preparedness and overseas deployments may have inadvertently encouraged subsequent reactive cycles of competitive armament, counter threats, and terrorism. The emphasis on a Christian duty to use military force has often moved people away from strict adherence to just war doctrine and to encouragement of unjustifiable threats and uses of military force. Many Christians have supported the George W. Bush administration's attack on Iraq, for example, even though it did not meet generally accepted just war standards. It began as a preventive war that the United States chose to start, not as a war of last resort or of defense against an imminent attack. If a U.S. adversary had waged such a war, many in the United States would probably have called it a war of aggression. Yet it was possible for the United States to wage this particular war with impunity because of Christian realist acceptance of war in general.

Another negative consequence of endorsing political violence is that this endorsement, over time, changes our values, our ways of thinking, and ourselves. As the psychiatrist Robert Jay Lifton, who has studied moral degeneration produced by relying on military power, has concluded, the way we survive determines the future we create. If we survive by the sword, we will create a world with many swords pointed at us. Or as Seneca said more than 2000 years ago, "Power over life and death—don't be proud of it. Whatever [others] … fear from you, you'll be threatened with." To illustrate, every offensive weapon we have procured in the past to protect ourselves has eventually come back to haunt us when others have obtained it. Throughout the Cold War we were, in our nuclear deterrence policies, fully prepared to kill millions of innocent Russians for the misdeeds of their government over which they had no control. Christian realists became numb to threatening this sort of mass murder. In nuclear deterrence policies the United States threatened to kill more innocent civilians than were killed by the ruthless aggressive states in World War II. We also built a military-industrial complex so large that now it has begun to control the government rather than the other way around. We still have not been willing to say that we would never use nuclear weapons first in battle, even though willingness to use nuclear weapons first, let alone use them at all, cannot be squared with Christian ethics or even with the United Nations Charter, which prohibits both the threat and the use of force except in self-defense.

The failure to meet type 2 responsibility to love other people is further indicated by a look at contemporary violent conflicts. Seventy to 90 percent of the people killed in modern intrastate wars are civilians. In interstate wars also, often more civilians than soldiers are killed. It is difficult to show that these wars are primarily wars about protecting the innocent from harm, the only possible way Christians could justify them.

Another negative consequence of endorsing war as a legitimate instrument is that wars and preparation for wars encourage deceit. Wars are almost always justified in highly moralistic terms, but often they serve much narrower, selfish purposes, so governments mislead people in order to elicit their support. Prolonged deceit, which accompanies both cold and hot wars, conditions a society to accept military solutions to problems where military means are not necessary or the most effective means. High levels of military preparedness also interfere with devoting money and energy to helping the poor and alleviating conditions that give rise to violence. General acceptance of war and of nuclear deterrence as legitimate instruments of foreign policy brings so many negative consequences that this acceptance hardly fulfills type 2 responsibility to other people.

What about type 3 responsibility—to defend the existing political order and one's own society within it? Nonpacifists' endorsement of high levels of military preparedness, over time, perpetuates the present balance of power system, which is ultimately a military balance of power and a war-based system of international relations. This system encourages national governments to rely on military means for their security, encourages arms competition, discourages policies aimed at replacing the rule of military force with the rule of international law, and disadvantages the poor and the weak, who are most in need of being protected. Although the international system has positive features, such as the diversity among different societies that it facili-

tates, the negative consequences of this system lead us to ask the question, Is upholding the present international political order a Christian responsibility? Does this order need reform at least as badly as it needs to be maintained? The continuation, year after year, of extreme poverty, lawlessness, and gross violations of human rights in the current international system suggests that prevailing institutions and priorities do not meet our responsibilities to love God and our neighbor. They need deep change. The failure of existing national and global institutions calls into question whether the third responsibility, defined by nonpacifists as the need to uphold the political order, is really an ethically desirable responsibility.

Indeed, to perpetuate the present international system may not be consistent with Christian ethics, *if* a better system can be created. The present system provides many material incentives for national selfishness, military rivalries, gross violations of human rights, and related unchristian conduct. The possibility that what we have defined as type 3 responsibility (to protect the existing political order) is not a Christian duty is much more likely today than when Niebuhr wrote. Although the mixed results of the present international system are debatable, the poorest half of the world's population does not find this systemic structure congenial to human life.

It is possible today to take steps toward more effective and more democratic global governance in which the rule of law would, gradually over many years, replace the rule of force in international affairs. Yet even modest steps in this direction, such as ratifying treaties to limit nuclear weapons testing and production, or to prevent deploying weapons in space, are not being taken. Indeed such steps have been opposed by the United States. Washington has refused to ratify the Comprehensive Test Ban Treaty, which would have prohibited all nuclear weapons testing by signatories. At the same time, the United States strongly opposes efforts by some other states to move closer to testing nuclear weapons. Washington withdrew from the anti-ballistic missile treaty because U.S. officials did not want to be legally bound to stop testing space weapons, even though they do not want other states to test them. This treaty had already been ratified, had become international law, and was working to discourage deployment of weapons in space. The United States leads in military technology for space by a huge margin. But rather than seek a total ban of all weapons in space, the United States seems eager to put its own weapons in orbit. If it does, they will be followed by weapons from others that will eventually make us all less secure than we are now.

Because the United States and some other great powers actively oppose creating a more stable and peaceful international system in which international mechanisms for war prevention could be enhanced gradually until eventually they would become quite reliable, those governments can hardly claim that war for them is a last resort. They have refused to take reasonable peacetime steps to build institutions to constrain war. As a result, even from a Christian realist standpoint, one cannot be politically responsible in endorsing wars by these governments because their wars cannot satisfy a fundamental just war standard, namely, that war is justified only after all other avenues have been tried in good faith and failed.

Ironically, the most worrisome violent threats that U.S. citizens face today cannot be effectively addressed through primarily military means. Yet it is in military means that a majority of people continue to place their ultimate faith. We cannot eliminate terrorism with war or military threats. Such threats, together with the maintenance of an inequitable global system, are likely to generate terrorism. Even U.S. national intelligence reports conclude that terrorism has been made worse by the war in Iraq, a war that the U.S. elected to start. To address terrorism, we need good civilian police, international sharing of intelligence, effective internal and equitable international legal processes, cooperation from nearly every country on earth, and genuine efforts to address the conditions that give rise to terrorism.

Similarly, the proliferation of weapons of mass destruction cannot be effectively addressed through primarily military means. In fact, it is in part because North Korea and Iran have felt threatened militarily by the United States that they want nuclear technology. Their fears grew, following the U.S. attack on Iraq, that the United States might

attack governments that it does not like unless they have some means of striking back at the United States to deter it.

To justify his willingness to attack Iraq without UN authorization, President George W. Bush famously said in a nationally televised address before both houses of Congress that the United States would never seek a permission slip to use military force. As he spoke, nearly every member of Congress in our revered Capitol building rose in a standing ovation and cheered upon hearing no "permission slip." This is an understandable reaction to an understandable statement when one places faith in military power. Subsequently, President Bush and the same members of Congress now wish that North Korea and Iran would seek a permission slip before they obtain the weapons that the United States already has set an example for obtaining.

In the long run, security threats, including the impending deployment of weapons in space, can be dealt with most successfully and sustainably through equitable arms control agreements that are solidly verified and enforced. Yet Christian realist support for war and for the present international system in practice impedes efforts to meet security threats through nonmilitary means and to transform our system of world order. The present international system has been around so long that we think of it as natural or necessary, even though it is neither. It is analogous to other institutional structures that have existed for centuries but then were dramatically changed. Slavery is an example of a time-honored institution that was so undesirable that people dismantled it. The present international system, like feudalism, slavery, and the institutions of the Roman Empire, is an institution created by humans and able to be transformed by humans. The meaning of political responsibility today should include a willingness to establish a different political order if it would do better in fulfilling type 3 responsibility for preventing war, building peace, and implementing justice.

To sum up this look at the claim that nonpacifists are politically responsible, we have discovered that many people who acquiesce in current policies—the policies that may have brought some semblance of security in an earlier age—are not very effectively exercising responsibility in today's international context. Those policies and institutions are no longer producing security nor are they dedicated to helping the "least of these." They appear to be incapable of producing security in the future because technologies of death and destruction are too readily available to those governments and nongovernmental actors willing to kill. The United States has led the way in producing many of these technologies with the support of Christian realists. If nonpacifists continue on the present path, they may not fulfill type 1, type 2, or, surprisingly, even type 3 responsibilities.

Possibilities for Becoming More Responsible

We have been looking at two different ethical approaches to fulfilling responsibility: Christian pacifists emphasize following moral principles, such as loving neighbors and enemies; Christian realists emphasize the consequences of how one's conduct helps to defend the political order. Although both groups may give some attention to both the moral principles that they should follow and the consequences, the Christian pacifist emphasizes the first more than the second, and the Christian realist emphasizes the second more than the first. Perhaps both can benefit from further reflection. Pacifists could look more fully at the meaning and consequences of their pacifism, not to weaken their commitment to a nonviolent ethic, which can be morally responsible, but to see how to apply their ethical principles more effectively and comprehensively to round out their love of others and to move far beyond simply not killing them or simply acquiescing in the existing, unsatisfactory political order. It is time to develop a new theology of peace that explores how to create a more compassionate political, economic, and environmental world order that would do better at war prevention.

At the same time, Christian nonpacifists need to pay more attention to ensuring that the consequences that they want to achieve, such as peace and stability, are in fact attained through the means they choose rather than undermined by them, as now often seems to be the case. If one consequence of chronic high levels of military preparedness is to encourage unjustifiable wars and killings and to reinforce an unrepresentative, violence-prone international system that appears to be a form of global apartheid for the poor, then new policies are required. If both pacifists and nonpacifists reflect, they may both find some common ground in building a more effective, more democratic, and more peaceful form of global governance with enhanced capabilities to discourage war.

Pacifists can work at their responsibility in several ways. First, to fulfill their responsibility to the "least of these," pacifists can do more than refuse to kill others in war. The same love for neighbor that leads pacifists to non-killing should also motivate them to intense efforts to end poverty, ensure access to public education, and promote justice throughout the world. Their desire not to kill should lead them also to do their utmost to see that other people are not killed, harmed, or their lives shortened substantially by the economic and political structures within which they live (sometimes called "structural violence"). In doing this, pacifists can in part address the Niebuhrian and Augustinian criticism of pacifists that they do not do enough to protect the victims of aggression and injustice.

Thoughtful pacifists may also witness to the need for fundamental changes in the international system because the poverty perpetuated by the present international system kills more people, day after deadly day, than are being killed in war. "About 50,000 human deaths per day are due to poverty-related causes and therefore avoidable insofar as poverty itself is avoidable." Today 800 million people are malnourished; a billion lack access to safe drinking water, adequate shelter, and basic health services. More than two billion lack basic sanitation. The ratio of income between the richest fifth of the world's population to poorest fifth was three to one in the early 1800s. It was seven to one in 1870, eleven to one in 1913, thirty to one in 1960, sixty to one in 1990, and seventy-four to one in 1997. Can a global system that has done this over the past 200 years possibly be consistent with Jesus' teachings about concern for the poor? The members of the historic peace churches in the past have favored dismantling military conscription because it forced young people into a killing organization. It might follow logically that they should also favor reforming the international system because it is forcing people to kill indirectly. We do not choose this form of killing, but we are trapped by the present balance-of-power system into going along with it and being part of it.

The same compassion for others that leads pacifists not to kill can also be an act of political responsibility if they communicate a simple vote of "no confidence" to elected officials who support present priorities. Pacifists can educate their families and churches and work with fellow citizens, including nonpacifists, to nudge the U.S. government and other governments to change. Pacifists can make it clear that they do not intend to endorse war and inequitable global economic structures, because more effective and equitable global governance could be established to increase human security while gradually reducing reliance on military instruments.

Pacifists need to be clear not only where they stand on U.S. political issues, but also on acts of violence by others everywhere in the world. Loving enemies means genuine concern for their wellbeing and a principled evaluation of their conduct, especially if it is violent conduct. Evaluations of international conduct can be globally more legitimate when they are done cooperatively with people of other faiths and by applying international law equally on all governments and people. Over the long course of history, the politically most responsible path toward peace and justice and the most loving path toward enemies are likely to be same path, especially when diverse nationalities are seen as part of one global human community.

In considering and possibly implementing the measures suggested here, Christian pacifists can be responsible in a new way: by building global peace and justice, not simply refraining from killing. If pacifists exercise all three types of responsibility even while prioritizing type 1 and type 2 responsibilities, they can help usher in new national and international initiatives to advance peace and justice. The refusal to fight, if the reasons for the refusal are carefully communicated and combined with new work for economic justice and system change, can be more responsible than an easy readiness to send troops into crises as they arise. Easy endorsement of military combat today

reveals an unwarranted faith in the utility of military power and, perhaps, an ideological mindset. In our era and in the foreseeable future, military power is useful mainly for destruction but not for social integration and peacebuilding. Yet the power to promote healthy social integration is the form of power most needed today, even by the greatest military the world has known. The United States military can easily destroy any other army on earth, but it has not provided minimal security or kept the lights on in a small country that it occupied in the Middle East, even after several years of trying and the expenditure of nearly a trillion dollars.

As a result of these changes, Christian pacifists today can exercise a more influential political role, if they choose to do so, in a context where the utility of military power has declined drastically and the many-faceted costs of relying on military preparedness and war have risen enormously. Moreover, humans' ability to achieve global security through nonmilitary means has increased sufficiently to make war obsolescent, given the will to do so.

Christian pacifism, of course, does not solve all problems. For example, Christian pacifists understandably struggle with the agony of Christian-Muslim violence wherever it occurs, and especially among friends in Kenya, Nigeria, Sudan, and elsewhere. When religious bigots or militia bent on ethnic cleansing knock on the door, when an airplane is deliberately crashed into the World Trade Center, when families are sent to the gas chambers or die in bombing raids, there are no simple answers. Of course Christian realists have not solved all problems either, as much of history shows, so the inability of the Christian pacifist to solve every problem is in itself not a reason to take a more violent position.

A Future on Which Many Pacifists and Nonpacifists Might Agree?

To continue relying on military policies that have not worked in the past is not likely to make sense to someone who is a careful consequentialist or a thoughtful realist (as compared to someone following ideology or political dogma). Some who call themselves realists, however, appear not to look carefully at the consequences, in terms of all the losses, that flow from their endorsement of war. Governments often try to hide the consequences of war and do not want pictures on television to show the consequences of war policies, such as soldiers' flag-draped coffins. When blindfolded by political leaders, the public more readily follows. Ideological proclivity to accept killing appears, in this era of global interdependence and weapons of mass destruction, to be more at odds with rule-based pacifism in the quest for moral responsibility than is a morally cautious consequentialism. This proclivity seems widespread in U.S. culture today, even among some Christians.

Why do many in the peace churches fail to appreciate how relevant and responsible pacifists can be? Why do they not feel confident that their best beliefs offer supremely valuable guidelines for how the world can successfully address its major problems? Is it because the great Christian pacifist traditions have inadvertently internalized too much of the larger culture's ideological skepticism of those who refuse to kill? Have people in these traditions believed too much of the political realists' criticism that pacifists are unrealistic and are not politically responsible? Perhaps members of the peace churches need to live their own faith more deeply, more creatively. They can confidently interact with Christian nonpacifists and people of other faiths who share their aversion to war even though they are not pacifists. Although Christian pacifists ought not replace their traditional emphasis on faithfulness with an over-emphasis on political responsibility, they may be strengthened in their faith by the knowledge that being faithful, in the fullest sense, brings with it highly responsible consequences as well.

It is good to follow the ethic of agape for its own sake and also to consider more carefully the consequences of where following this ethic leads. Christian responsibility calls us to make the right choices, not to achieve great political outcomes. Our choices we can determine; political outcomes are usually beyond our control. Type 1 responsibility to God and type 2 responsibility to love "the least of these" should shape our choices about how we carry out type 3 responsibility to the political order. Pacifists' refusal to endorse war should highlight their commitment to building more just, peaceful, democratic, and compassionate international and national political orders. Pacifists can work with all people of goodwill in making peace through peaceful means and by trying harder to replace the rule of force with the rule of law in world affairs.

When facing hostile violence over the long run, it is not necessary to limit ourselves to a two-fold choice between surrender and sending in the troops. The possibility of establishing a third alternative, a rule-of-law society on the global level, makes it likely that refusing to endorse war is a politically responsible way to live in today's violent world, especially if one does this with humility about what this position does not solve, because it points the way toward the third alternative.

For both pacifists and nonpacifists, the political ends they seek are never assured, no matter what they do. For both, the means they have chosen are imperfect, in that they do not solve all problems. But in examining the two sets of imperfect means, the least imperfect appears to be that of the politically responsible Christian who chooses not to kill and to move toward a more peaceful global system. Taking the non-killing path expresses a humble responsibility to God (type 1) and to the "least of these" (type 2), while also opening a door toward enhanced responsibility for building a peaceful, just, democratic world society (type 3).

114. Gene Stolzfus

Interrogation and Martyrdom

Gene Stolzfus (1940-2010) was a founding member and director of the Christian Peacemaker Teams (CPT). With its focus on fieldwork, CPT trains and places Christian peacemakers in conflict-ridden areas like Iraq, the West Bank, Colombia, and native communities in the United States and Canada. Stolzfus spent considerable time in Iraq in 1991 and again in 2003, doing peacebuilding with the various sides of the conflict. His life of peacemaking was rooted partly in his experience as a conscientious objector during the Vietnam War and his work with International Voluntary Service.

I have talked to survivors of military interrogation around the world who at some point thought they would not live for another day. I never write about it in the U.S. and Canada because it seems so unbelievable and out of place in a world of sanitized shopping malls and super highways. When I retell their stories I notice that people here fidget. But interrogation processes are one way in which martyrs are created. Martyrs in the original sense are "witnesses to the truth," with a deep commitment of conscience that sustains them through moments of cruelty and abuse.

Some people are killed during interrogation. They never get to tell the story themselves. So I have learned to listen to those who narrowly avoid interrogation's brush with death. This might be the time that you will prefer not to read on. But if you stop here you will skip over an important part of living and dying that stretches around the world and touches the entire human family.

I spent two hours in Iraq talking to a 22-year-old student who was arrested in a house raid along with two of his brothers. Until the time of his capture he was relatively uninvolved with anything political, not an unusual story in the Iraq of 2003. After his capture by American military personnel he was not allowed to sleep for two days. After 48 hours the American GIs told him that he would be killed unless he told them where Saddam Hussein was hiding. He was continuously blindfolded. He was told that his brother, taken into custody at the same time, was just now being shot. In the distance he could hear a gun being fired. If he didn't want to die, he must tell all. Then nearby he heard a gun being cocked and felt a revolver touching his head. He expected to die. There was more shouting from the soldiers and then silence.

"I believed I would die," he told me. "And then after a long wait I felt my hand to be sure I was still alive." His blindfold was temporarily removed and then he was marched off to one of Iraq's prison camps where he met others who experienced similar beatings and moments of terror. He was released three months later because of persistent outside intervention—an advantage that many disappeared people do not have.

My time with him left me exhausted and jolted me to wonder how I would respond to interrogation. Would I make up a story? Would I lie? Would something I say implicate others? Would I respond with anger or physical struggle? Would I go quietly to my death as some martyrs are reported to have done? Would anyone know how I died?

After my talk with the unlikely martyr, the connection of this Muslim student to my own ancestors in 16th-century Europe fluttered in my mind. Did the stories I read in my youth about the Anabaptist martyrs prepare me for this? Death by burning or drowning is now little practiced, but current authorities still believe that truth can be accessed by means of brutality. The pattern of torture used for their interrogation blended now with the people I was meeting. The Anabaptist stories recorded in the *Martyrs Mirror* (subtitled "The Bloody Theatre of the Anabaptists or Defenseless Christians Who Suffered and Were Slain from the Time of Christ until the Year AD 1660) are part of the continuous tapestry of state-sponsored cruelty reaching to our very own day.

In the late 1970s I worked in the Philippines. One day I was invited to meet a pastor and former political prisoner. The Marcos dictatorship had sent its military and paramilitary to his community and their tactics were designed to control popular discontent through cruelty, terror, domination, killing and confiscation of property. The pastor felt bound by his convictions to do what was possible to protect the people of his church. He was arrested and interrogated for weeks. His body was spent. Finally he was encased in a blindfold and told he would be killed. He felt the barrel of a revolver that touched the temple of his head and rested there for a time while his interrogator demanded that he give names of the people with whom he worked. "I was silent because I couldn't think any more," he told me.

"Were you afraid you would endanger others?" I asked. "Of course I was worried that what I said would implicate others but when the gun was put to my head I just expected to die. I couldn't think of anything to say. I even thought about being a pastor but that didn't seem very important in the moment. I was ready to die. I just told them to get it over with. During those days I thought about the martyrs. The interrogator didn't pull the trigger. I don't know why."

I felt my gut twitch after the pastor described the near-death moment. Was there anything I could say or do? Anything healing? Anything personal? The pastor, like the Iraqi student 25 years later, only requested that I tell the world what happened to him. That was enough.

Accounts like these stories of people living on borrowed time reach back centuries to pre-Roman times and show me that the impulse to domination is still alive in our as-yet-uncivilized reptilian brain stem. In our time the word "martyr" has morphed from its root meaning of "witness to the truth" to a description of someone who dies for his or her beliefs. The Greeks and early Christians who used the term understood death to be a possible outcome of the path towards truth and light. Eventually "martyr" referred exclusively to those who died for their belief. Those who began as witnesses to truth became martyrs at the time of death. For the Muslim, *shahada* (martyrdom) also springs from the internal struggle that results in the witness to truth. Both religious traditions have departed from the core understanding of martyrdom in times of political conflict and triumphalism. From where did my childhood curiosity arise to steal into my father's study to read about the martyrs? Those drawings of torture and burning bodies awakened wonder within me. In one of my early return journeys to North America from the lands of torture—before I understood that torture techniques had their home here—I was introduced to a new psychological disease called the martyr complex—seeking persecution to fulfill an inward need. Had I been the unwitting recipient of this disease? Or was the use of the term "martyr complex" the work of a psychologist who had never met a torture victim or known the honored path to witness practiced by martyrs?

Church buildings pay tribute to martyrs, including long-forgotten soldiers who died in distant lands to protect the nation or empire. Their deeds are celebrated and interwoven with patriotism. I have visited churches in the Netherlands, the birthplace of Anabaptist martyrs, where they place the *Martyrs Mirror* on their altars before the service of worship and return it to a locked closet after the service. I once inquired about the influence of the book of martyrs in the life of worshipers and was told that, "Most of us have no idea about the stories in that book. It's from another time."

Why are soldiers and interrogators still trained in the craft of torture? Can moral outrage and attempts to protect the prisoner change things? Why do Christian crusaders or Muslim suicide bombers slip into patterns of domination that kill and destroy in a manner that cannot possibly reveal truth? Can respect for and veneration of martyrs draw us closer to the truth when the patterns of our lives are so remote from the authentic truth-seeking represented in martyrs?

Genuine martyrs appear when people believe that their witness on earth is connected to the whole of the universe. Martyrs are not inclined to draw attention to themselves, but their path can draw people to the glory and faith of a vision. Martyrs have all the foibles of the rest of us. Some may not deserve the label. In our human family great movements that push us to transcend boundaries with visions of hope produce martyrs. But organizations and movements become emasculated and ineffectual when they protect themselves too much from the risk of bold witness. On the other hand, they also undercut themselves when they slide into violence against others in order to try to control the outcome of their vision. We have the challenge of incarnating a blend of vulnerability and boldness.

The test of martyrdom is whether that particular witness to the truth helps to support and sustain the community's commitment to a full-bodied vision of peace and justice. The martyrs are present with us and may be more powerful for their witness in death than they ever could have been in life.

115. Andy Alexis-Baker

Policing and Christian Forgiveness

Andy Alexis-Baker (b. 1975) is a new—and important—voice in the field of Christian peace studies. He is a doctoral candidate at Marquette University, has taught peace studies at Goshen College, and has authored several significant articles on peacemaking. Below is his article on the Christian ethics of policing—a topic that has recently attracted sustained attention as leading peace advocates have called for just policing as a viable way of solving conflict on the domestic and international levels.

After the attacks on the World Trade Center and the Pentagon on September 11, 2001, several Christian ethicists urged the U.S. government to respond within a framework of criminal law rather than war. Most notably, Jim Wallis suggested that the international community create a global police force that could safeguard innocent lives as they pursued the perpetrators and help prevent future attacks in a way military action could not. Similarly, Mennonite ethicist John Paul Lederach called for a multi-faceted approach to address the attack's root causes, which included a proposal for "domestic and international policing." Since that time, pacifist-minded Christians have increased calls for policing as an alternative to war. Central to their proposals is the belief that police are less violent than soldiers because law restricts police actions.

Despite the widespread belief in this theory among Christian ethicists and other thinkers, they have not adequately established or tested the claim's validity. This ahistorical argument does not account for real police practices or current police theory. Consequently it does not acknowledge the possibility that adopting a policing model for international conflicts might sustain or even worsen violence, not lessen it. Furthermore, looking to secular policing instead of distinct Christian practices of forgiveness prohibits us from exploring more faithful ways of peacemaking.

Police Historiography and the Common Good

Christian ethicists who claim police represent the common good and protect the weak incorrectly treat the police as an ancient institution. Yet police are a recent invention. The typical Greek and Roman *polis* had neither a police nor a military force available to apprehend common criminals; citizens themselves performed these tasks. In Acts 21, for instance, Paul's presence in the temple caused some people to shout, "Men of Israel, help . . ." Customarily, when someone called for help like this, everyone nearby gathered to aid the person. Thus a crowd dragged Paul from the temple. Seeing an apparent riot, the Roman military intervened, exhibiting their duty to suppress riots and rebellions, not routine law enforcement. Classicist Wilfried Nippel argues further that "We do not even know to what degree (if at all) the Roman authorities undertook prosecution of murder." Yet this informal "hue and cry" system prevailed through the Middle Ages into the early American colonies.

In the United States, professionalized preventative policing developed from emerging racial and class conflicts. Southern police forces evolved from slave patrols designed to catch runaway slaves, monitor their social behavior, restrict their movement, and thwart revolt. Armed patrols guarded countryside roads to verify that traveling slaves had a valid pass. In the process patrolmen generally harassed and abused black people. After the Civil War, the patrols morphed into the first American police forces. The leading causes of arrest—disorderly conduct, public intoxication, loitering, arrest "on suspicion," "on warrant," larceny and prostitution—allowed police to target and control the black population, provoking statements from blacks like this: "We have lived in Atlanta twenty-seven years, and we have heard the lash sounding from the cabins of slaves, poured on by their masters, but we have never seen a meaner set of low-down cut throats, scrapes, and murderers than the city of Atlanta has to protect the peace."

In the North, police departments emerged in the nineteenth century to suppress the "dangerous class." In city after city, fledgling police forces combated vices of the poor such as drinking and vagrancy, instead of violent crime. For example, arrest records from St. Louis in 1874—then a city of 300,000—show that police arrested over 2,500 for vagrancy, 8,000 for drunkenness, 1,600 for profane language and 3,300 for disturbing the peace. Yet they arrested only 42 people for felonious violence (murder, robbery and rape) and 16 for burglary.

Besides maintaining class order, northern police also helped consolidate political power. In most cities, police backed current politicians because new regimes customarily replaced existing police with loyalists. This happened following elections in Los Angeles (1889), Kansas City (1895), Chicago (1897) and Baltimore (1897). Consequently, the police promoted voter turnout, monitored voting stations, ignored ballot stuffing, and beat citizens who voted against the current administration.

Thus instead of promoting the common good or protecting the weak, police have historically promoted particular interests, siding with their employers and with dominant racial and economic groups. The police did not result from inevitable historical forces but from calculated moves to maintain social stratification that continue into the present.

Rule of Law and Discretion

Aside from overlooking police history, ethicists who advocate policing as a solution to international violence also overlook the ways police operate as a sovereign power that stands above the law. Although in theory the police are supposed to be restricted by law, in practice the central police power of discretion—the ability to decide whether to uphold or circumvent particular rules or laws within a specific situation—enables police to trump the law. Instead of mechanically enforcing the law in every situation, the police determine when, where and upon whom they will implement

it. Because police operate in "low visibility" conditions, the only people likely to know that the police officer decided not to invoke the law are the police officer and the suspect. Thus these discretionary decisions are unreviewable and risk becoming arbitrary and prejudiced, particularly in cases of racial profiling, police brutality and class bias. Practices of discretion and legal interpretation are routine, daily occurrences that are executed and encouraged within the policing function. Yet at the same time, this discretion transforms the police into a sovereign power, which opposes an essential democratic ideal—the rule of law.

Community Policing and Violence

In exercising discretion, police primarily maintain order rather than enforce law. Community policing theorists have long recognized this distinction and therefore advocate for broader discretionary police power, not less. Communitarians argue that the rule of law unduly constrains the police to respect the individual's legal rights over the broader community's welfare. Under the liberal idea that law should rule above all else, procedural rules and laws have prevented police from ridding the community of disorderly people who undermine residents' sense of safety and order. Under community policing theory, police should have discretionary powers, including racial profiling, even if these actions are not "easily reconciled with any conception of due process or fair treatment" and would probably "not withstand a legal challenge."

The underlying premise of community policing, however, makes violence much more likely because of its tendency to scapegoat people and bifurcate community into "good" and "bad" people. In the community policing paradigm, allowing even law-abiding homeless people or panhandlers to go unchecked creates an atmosphere of negligence that invites unscrupulous outsiders with a penchant for criminal activity to invade the neighborhood. In order to prevent a later influx of dangerous low-level nuisances even those who are only engaged in seemingly harmless behavior like loitering become scapegoats and are criminalized as a result. Consequently, this shift from a policing model governed by liberal rights and rule of law, which is already undermined by the sovereign use of discretion, to the model of community policing opens the door to more police violence. Such is the case in New York City and other cities that have switched to community policing.

Criminals and Enemies

This scapegoating tendency reveals a more trenchant problem that the hope to lessen the violence of war through policing does not acknowledge. One of the differences between war and policing is the way in which each model conceives of "the other" to whom it is opposed. In war, the other is an enemy who has a political identity to whom there are certain duties and obligations. Therefore, in a just war the aim is not to eradicate moral evil or punish criminals, but rather to resolve conflict between two equal bodies. Furthermore, in war it is possible to negotiate an end to hostilities that does not essentialize the enemy as immoral. However, when a conflict becomes a police action that defines the enemy as criminal, negotiating an end to hostility becomes nearly impossible because one does not bargain with criminals. Triumph over the criminal demands the absolute victory of those engaged in police action over those who broke the law, or in community policing, threatening the good of the neighborhood. Therefore, categorizing enemies as criminals and redefining war as police action turns conflict into international civil war under the guise of criminal justice. Violence becomes more, not less, intractable with the shift in political identity from enemy to criminal. How then do we address violence and evil?

Christian Forgiveness

In determining how to bring God's justice and peace into difficult and disillusioning situations, we must first confess our inability to completely end violence and that some conflicts may be beyond our capacity to resolve. Second, we need to explore Christian practices of forgiveness. Instead of advocating for aggressive and potentially deadly police measures, Christians can encourage truth and reconciliation processes with the goal of forgiveness. Evidence abundantly suggests the possibility

and workability of forgiveness in politics. Archbishop Desmond Tutu claims there could not have been a peaceful solution to a multiracial democracy if black South Africans had insisted on punishing whites who had abused them. The victory would have sown the seeds for future conflict. Instead, black South Africans turned to forgiveness and set up the Truth and Reconciliation Commission. Although truth commissions have limitations, they have effectively promoted a reconciling and forgiving culture and have helped reduce violence.

In situations like 9/11, Christians should call for both sides to halt their hostilities, engage in a mutual truth-telling and implore leaders and representatives to confess their role in violence. Without diminishing the horrors experienced on September 11, 2001, Christians like Wallis missed the opportunity to confess that neither Al Qaeda nor the U.S. has been innocent. The attacks were not unprovoked and solely bent on killing: they, like the U.S. response, had reasons and rationales for their violence. These reasons *do not excuse* the brutality, but they do refute the idea of the enemy's "radical evil" beyond redemption and the truth of the cross. Christians therefore can and should invite American and British governments to begin a process of truth-telling and mutual forgiveness, which at minimum means forgoing vengeance. This process precludes cheap grace if both sides commit not only to truth-telling, but also to restoring what has been taken and compensating for what cannot be restored.

Although research shows that forgiveness is psychologically and physically healthy, most studies focus on individual victims choosing to overcome anger and to forgive. Yet Amish practices show the communality of forgiveness. Following the 2006 Nickel Mines shooting in which five Amish school girls were killed and five wounded, the Amish forgave the perpetrator's family. But this forgiveness was not primarily charged to the victims or their families. Instead, the Amish *community* forgave the man and his family. Here forgiveness exemplifies Amish mutual aid in which people unite to complete a task that individuals would be unable to finish. In numerous tragedies, Amish have forsworn revenge and forgave the perpetrators. Through prayer, communion and fasting, the Amish have cultivated a habitually forgiving culture. While neither simple nor easy, the demands of Anabaptist discipleship have shaped them into a people for whom holding grudges and hunting down and killing perpetrators is unthinkable. Forgiveness in this sense can be a pure gift, unattached to whether the other party feels remorse.

The Amish, however, would distinguish between forgiveness and pardon. When members persistently break community rules, they are subject to shunning or excommunication. To be restored to the community, the offender would have to show contriteness and repentance. Thus in Amish discipline, it is possible to forgive somebody for a wrong, while maintaining community discipline.

The Amish example is instructive because they re-narrate wrongs received within the gospel story. Thus all "trespasses" become occasions for obeying and imitating God's redemptive love. Through confession, the stories we tell about conflict in which righteous revenge plays a prominent role must be transformed through forgiveness into mutually binding stories that tie together people on both sides of a conflict in new patterns of tolerance. A primary task of Christian theologians, therefore, is to debunk the self-righteous histories which dominant powers construct so as to justify violence and to criminalize the other. The task of the theologian is not chaplaincy and underwriting the violence of empire or terror, but to speak of God's love in Jesus.

When Christians accept forgiveness, we also accept duties and obligations to set ourselves on a new path through restoring and repairing harms we have done. We neither ignore our past sins and their consequences nor reduce justice to vengeance. Christians do not use forgiveness to excuse atrocity and grant ourselves amnesty for what we have done, but as an opportunity to obey and imitate Jesus. When people who call themselves Christian export exploitative economics, deal in weapons, and treat some people as less than God's created beings, we sow the seeds for conflict. If those Christians then call for police or military action against those who have reacted to our violence, we have betrayed the forgiveness we accepted.

Conclusion

Contrasting the Amish willingness to forgive with America's response to 9/11, Diane Butler Bass asked,

> What if the Amish were in charge of the war on terror? What if, on the evening of Sept. 12, 2001, we had gone to Osama bin Laden's house (metaphorically, of course, since we didn't know where he lived!) and offered him forgiveness? What if we had invited the families of the hijackers to the funerals of the victims of 9/11? What if a portion of The September 11th Fund had been dedicated to relieving poverty in a Muslim country? What if we dignified the burial of their dead by our respectful grief? What if, instead of seeking vengeance, we had stood together in human pain, looking honestly at the shared sin and sadness we suffered? What if we had tried to *make* peace?

But this did not happen. Christian pacifists called not for truth and reconciliation, but for police action to hunt down those who had planned the atrocity. Yet the experiences of the Amish communities and those of many other larger societies who have forgone retribution teach us that Christian pacifists have not only theological resources, but practical experience to draw upon that allows us to witness far beyond police violence.

116. Tracy Wenger Sadd

A Prayer for Peace

Tracy Wenger Sadd (b. 1964) serves as Chaplain and Director of Religious Life, as well as Lecturer in Religion, at Elizabethtown College. She is the author of several books and is co-editor of God and Country? Diverse Perspectives on Christianity and Patriotism. *Sadd is one of the best contemporary writers of Christian prayers, and an example of her powerful writing appears in* Resist! Christian Dissent for the Twenty-first Century. *The following is a new prayer, written expressly to conclude this volume.*

God,
Whose holy mountain is a house for all peoples
Whose Spirit told the Hebrew prophet
    Of a day
        when the lion and the lamb
            will lie down together
        when humankind will study war no more,

This is a day
    when we join
        with voices echoing through the ages
            to say: *Dona nobis pacem.*
                Grant us peace.

Yet, Lord, we must confess our complicity
    in the ceaseless and senseless violence
        of this world.
We have believed tempting lies
    which are the enemies of peace:
        that good fences make good neighbors,
        that our unexamined sectarianism
            is the only truth,
        that our passivity is a noble pacifism,
        that our tolerance could never be a mask
            for indifference or quiet condescension,
        that we are not controlled
            by a paralyzing social fear,
        that a low-risk short-term strategy
            can take the place
                of long-term commitment,
        that our actions toward one generation
            will be forgotten by the next,
        that peace is a political cause,
            rather than an orientation
                toward all of life.

God of all who have ever been despised,
        oppressed, or repressed
Whose dream for the universe
        and its galaxies unknown
    is greater even than we can imagine,
Forgive us,
    and renew in us a holy reverence
        for the world and all its creatures—
            each one a part of Your divine symphony—
            from the tranquility of the birdsong
                to the laughter of the child
                to the roiling and rolling
                    of the thunderstorm.
Help us to find—
    in the midst of the anxieties, threats,
        and fears of living—
    glimpses of the ineffable oneness of all things
        experienced by mystics of all times and places
            who have sought You unrelentingly.

God whom some have called
    An infinite sphere
        Whose center is everywhere
        Whose circumference—nowhere.
Make us mindful of the boundless opportunities
        to build bridges across borders
        to collaborate on common ground.
Give us courage to take risks
        in both creative thought
            and innovative action.
Empower us with the knowledge
        that we walk in the footsteps
                of the multitude of generations
        who understood the cost
            of confronting injustice

of including the outsider
of serving the enemy
of resisting the sword.

Lord, who can accomplish more
than we can ever ask,
Consecrate us to be the living incarnation
of Your *shalom*,
the blessed peacemakers of the third way
following Jesus, the prince of peace,
who is our peace.

Sustain us with a blissful confidence
in Your illimitable love
for us and for all creation.
Grant us hearts and souls
that remain unconquered.
Make us tireless ambassadors of reconciliation
who will not be satisfied
until righteousness and peace
are realized on this earth
as they are in heaven.
Amen.

Sources and Permissions

The editor is grateful for permission to publish the documents listed below. All efforts have been made to clear permissions for copyrighted material. We will gladly rectify any omissions in a future printing.

Part I
Scriptures of Peace

1. Hebrew Scriptures
Isaiah 11:6-9; Jeremiah 6:13-14; Micah 4:1-4. The New Revised Standard Version Bible (New York: Oxford University Press, 1989). The Scripture quotations contained herein are from the New Revised Standard Version Bible, copyright © 1989 by the Division of Christian Education of the National Council of the Churches of Christ in the U.S.A., and are used by permission. All rights reserved.

2. Walter Brueggemann
Living toward a Vision. From Walter Brueggemann, *Peace* (St. Louis: Chalice Press, 2001), 13-23. Used by permission.

3. Sermon on the Mount
Matthew 5:1-12, 38-48. The New Revised Standard Version Bible (New York: Oxford University Press, 1989). See source no. 1.

4. Walter Wink
Jesus and Nonviolence: A Third Way. From *Jesus and Nonviolence: A Third Way* by Walter Wink © 2003 Fortress Press, admin. Augsburg Fortress Publishers. Reproduced by permission.

5. New Testament Texts
Romans 5:8-10; 12:14, 16a, 17-21; Hebrews 10:32-34; I Peter 2:21, 23. The New Revised Standard Version Bible (New York: Oxford University Press, 1989). See source no. 1.

6. Richard B. Hays
Violence in Defense of Justice. "Violence in Defense of Justice" (pp. 317-46) from *The Moral Vision of the New Testament* by Richard B. Hays. Copyright © 1996 by Richard B. Hays. Reprinted by permission of HarperCollins Publishers.

Part II
Early Christian Voices

I am especially indebted to Professor Louis J. Swift for helping me to negotiate my way through the voluminous writings of the early Christian fathers. His book *The Early Fathers on War and Military Service* (Wilmington, DE: Michael Glazier, Inc., 1983), proved to be an excellent source for this section.

7. Justin Martyr
First Apology. Early Christian Fathers, vol. 1, trans. and ed. Cyril C. Richardson (Philadelphia: Westminster Press, 1953), 243-67. Reproduced from *Early Christian Fathers* (Library of Christian Classics Series), edited by Cyril C. Richardson. Used by permission of Westminster John Knox Press. www.wjkbooks.com.
Dialogue with Trypho. The Ante-Nicene Fathers, vol. 1, ed. Alexander Roberts and James Donaldson (Buffalo: Christian Literature Publishing Company, 1885), 253-54.

8. Athenagorus
A Plea Regarding Christians. Early Christian Fathers, vol. 1, trans. and ed. Cyril C. Richardson (Philadelphia: Westminster Press, 1953), 300-311, 339. Reproduced from *Early Christian Fathers* (Library of Christian Classics Series), edited by Cyril C. Richardson. Used by permission of Westminster John Knox Press. www.wjkbooks.com.

9. *Letter to Diognetus*
Early Christian Fathers, vol. 1, trans. and ed. Cyril C. Richardson (Philadelphia: Westminster Press, 1953), 213-24. Reproduced from *Early Christian Fathers* (Library of Christian Classics Series), edited by Cyril C. Richardson. Used by permission of Westminster John Knox Press. www.wjkbooks.com.

10. Tertullian
Apology. In *The Ante-Nicene Fathers,* vol. 3, ed. Alexander Roberts and James Donaldson (Buffalo: Christian Leadership Publishing Company, 1870), 45.
On Idolatry. In *The Ante-Nicene Fathers,* vol. 3, ed. Alexander Roberts and James Donaldson (Buffalo: Christian Leadership Publishing Company, 1870), 73.
The Shows. In *The Ante-Nicene Fathers,* vol. 3, ed. Alexander Roberts and James Donaldson (Buffalo: Christian Leadership Publishing Company, 1870), 79-80.
On the Crown. Excerpted in Swift, *Early Fathers,* 43-46. Used by permission.
On Marcion. In *The Ante-Nicene Fathers,* vol. 3, ed. Alexander Roberts and James Donaldson (Buffalo: Christian Leadership Publishing Company, 1870), 332-333.
On Patience. In *The Ante-Nicene Fathers,* vol. 3, ed. Alexander Roberts and James Donaldson (Buffalo: Christian Leadership Publishing Company, 1870), 708.

11. Origen
Against Celsus. In *The Ante-Nicene Fathers,* vol. 4, ed. Alexander Roberts and James Donaldson (Buffalo: Christian Leadership Publishing Company, 1885), 620-21.
Homilies on Joshua. Excerpted in Swift, *Early Fathers,* 59. Used by permission.

12. Cyprian
To Donatus. In *The Ante-Nicene Fathers,* vol. 5, ed. Alexander Roberts and James Donaldson (Buffalo: Christian Leadership Publishing Company, 1885), 276-79.
On the Advantage of Patience. In *The Ante-Nicene Fathers,* vol. 5, ed. Alexander Roberts and James Donaldson (Buffalo: Christian Leadership Publishing Company, 1885), 485-88.

13. Apostolic Tradition
Hippolytus, *On the Apostolic Tradition,* intro. and commentary by Alistair Stewart-Sykes (Crestwood, NY: St. Vladimir's Seminary Press, 2001), 99-100. Used by permission.

14. Early Christian Martyrs
The Acts of Maximilian. Excerpted in Swift, *Early Fathers,* 72-73. Used by permission.
The Acts of Marcellus. Acts of the Christian Martyrs, ed. Herbert Musurillo (Oxford: Clarendon Press, 1972), 250.

15. Arnobius
Against the Heathen. In *The Ante-Nicene Fathers,* vol. 6, ed. Alexander Roberts and James Donaldson (Buffalo: Christian Leadership Publishing Company, 1885), 415, 433-434.

16. Lactantius
The Divine Institutes. In *The Ante-Nicene Fathers,* vol. 7, ed. Alexander Roberts and James Donaldson (Buffalo: Christian Leadership Publishing Company, 1885), 143-46, 155-58, 172-75, 185-88. See Swift, *Early Fathers,* 61-68.

Part III
Medieval Voices

I am especially indebted to Professor Ronald Musto for helping me to identify the Catholic peacemakers selected in Parts III and IV. Professor Musto's outstanding work can be found in his three-volume series titled *Catholic Peacemakers: A Documentary History* and at his Web site titled PeaceDocs.

17. Basil of Caesaria
Canon 13 and John Anthony McGuckin, *Nonviolence and Peace in Early and Eastern Christianity.* John Anthony McGuckin, "Nonviolence and Peace in Early and Eastern Christianity," in *Religion, Terrorism and Globalization—Nonviolence: A New Agenda,* ed. K. K. Kuriakose (New York: Nova Science Publishers, Inc., 2006), 189-201. Used by permission.

18. Pelagius
On Riches. B. R. Rees, *Pelagius: Life and Letters* (Rochester, NY: Boydell Press, 1998); excerpted in *Radical Christian Writings: A Reader,* ed. Andrew Bradstock and Christopher Rowland (Oxford: Blackwell), 15-16. Used by permission.

19. Paulinus of Nola
Poem 17. In *The Poems of St. Paulinus of Nola,* trans. P. G. Walsh (New York: Newman Press, 1975), 107-13; excerpted in Musto, *Catholic Peacemakers,* vol. 1, 265-66. Reprinted by permission of Paulist Press, Inc. www.paulistpress.com.
Letter 18. In *Letters of St. Paulinus of Nola,* trans. P. G. Walsh (New York: Newman Press, 1966). 175-77. Reprinted by permission of Paulist Press, Inc. www.paulistpress.com.
Letter 25. Excerpted in Swift, *Early Fathers,* 152-53. Used by permission.

20. Sulpicius Severus
Life of St. Martin. Reprinted in *Nicene and Post-Nicene Fathers,* second series, vol. 11, ed. Philip Schaff and Henry Wace (Grand Rapids: Eerdmans, 1955), 4-6.

21. Benedict of Nursia
The Rule of St. Benedict. From *St. Benedict's Rule,* trans. Patrick Barry (Mahwah, NJ: HiddenSpring, 2004), 66-73. Excerpts from *St. Benedict's Rule* by Patrick Barry, OSB, copyright © 2004 by Ampleforth Abbey Trustees. Paulist Press, Inc., New York/Mahwah, NY. Reprinted by permission of Paulist Press, Inc. www.paulistpress.com.

22. Penitentials
Penitential of Finnian. From *Medieval Handbooks of Penance,* trans. John T. McNeil and Helena M. Gamer. Copyright © 1990 Columbia University Press. Reprinted with permission of the publisher. Excerpted from pp. 86-89.
Penitential of Theodore. From *Medieval Handbooks of Penance,* trans. John T. McNeil and Helena M. Gamer. Copyright © 1990 Columbia University Press. Reprinted with permission of the publisher. Excerpted from p. 187.
Penitential Ascribed to Bede. From *Medieval Handbooks of Penance,* trans. John T. McNeil and Helena M. Gamer. Copyright © 1990 Columbia University Press. Reprinted with permission of the publisher. Excerpted from p. 225.

23. Smaragdus
Commentary on the Rule of Saint Benedict. From Smaragdus of Saint-Mihiel, *Commentary on the Rule of Saint Benedict,* trans. David Barry (Kalamazoo, MI: Cistercian Publications, 2007), 57-62. Copyright 2007 by Cistercian Publications. Published by Liturgical Press, Collegeville, MN. Reprinted with permission.

24. Peace of God
Select Doctrines of European History, 800-1492 (New York: Henry Holt, 1929), 19. Excerpted in *The Ethics of War: Classic and Contemporary Readings,* ed. Gregory M. Reichberg, Henrik Syse, and Endre Begby (Oxford: Blackwell, 2006), 94-95. *The Ethics of War: Classic and Contemporary Readings,* ed. Gregory M. Reichberg, Henrik Syse, and Endre Begby. Copyright © 2006. Reproduced with permission of Blackwell Publishing, Ltd.

25. The Martyrdom of Boris and Gleb
From *Medieval Russia's Epics, Chronicles, and Tales,* trans. and ed. Serge A. Zenkovsky (New York: Meridian, 1963), 100-105.

26. Truce of God
The Earliest Truce of God, Proclaimed in the Diocese of

Elne, 1027. From *Select Doctrines of European History, 800-1492* (New York: Henry Holt, 1929), 19-20. The editor has followed, with gratitude, the excerpts reprinted in *The Ethics of War: Classic and Contemporary Readings* (Oxford: Blackwell, 2006), 95.

Truce of God, Proclaimed at the Council of Norbonne, August 25, 1054. From *Select Doctrines of European History, 800-1492* (New York: Henry Holt, 1929), 20-21. The editor has followed, with gratitude, the excerpts reprinted in Reichberg et al., *The Ethics of War,* 95-96.

Canons of the Second Lateral Council, 1123. From *Disciplinary Decrees of the General Councils: Text, Translation and Commentary* (St. Louis: B. Herder, 1937), 195-213. The editor has followed, with gratitude, the excerpts reprinted in Reichberg et al., *The Ethics of War,* 96-97.

27. Peter Damian
Letter to Bishop Olderic. Excerpted from Ronald G. Musto, *Catholic Peacemakers: A Documentary History.* Vol. 1. *From the Bible to the Era of the Crusades,* 482-86. Translated by Ronald G. Musto. Used by permission of Ronald G. Musto.

28. Francis of Assisi
The Earlier Rule 1209/10-1221. From *Francis of Assisi: Early Documents,* vol. 1, ed. Regis J. Armstrong, J. A. Wayne Hellmann and William J. Short (New York: New City Press, 1999), 72-74, 79, 113-14. Used by permission.

29. Humbert of Romans
Short Work in Three Parts. Excerpted from Ronald G. Musto, *Catholic Peacemakers.* Vol. 1. *From the Bible to the Era of the Crusades,* pp., 658-661. Translated by Ronald G. Musto. Used by permission of Ronald G. Musto.

30. The Twelve Conclusions of the Lollards
Creeds and Confessions of Faith in the Christian Tradition, ed. Jaroslav Pelikan and Valerie Hotchkiss (New Haven, CT: Yale University Press, 2003), 786, 789-90. Reprinted with permission of Cambridge University Press.

31. Peter Chelcicky
On the Triple Division of Society. From Peter Chelcicky, "On the Triple Division of Society," trans. Howard Kaminsky, *Studies in Medieval and Renaissance History,* vol. 1, ed. William M. Bowsky (Lincoln, NE: University of Nebraska Press, 1964), 137-67. Used by permission.

Part IV
Late Scholastic and Reformation

32. Desiderius Erasmus
The Education of a Christian Prince. From *The Education of a Christian Prince,* trans. Neil M. Cheshire and Michael J. Heath, *Erasmus: The Education of a Christian Prince,* ed. Lisa Jardine. Copyright © 1977 by Cambridge University Press. Reprinted with permission. Excerpted from 102-10.

33. Conrad Grebel
Letter to Thomas Muntzer. From *The Sources of Swiss Anabaptism: The Grebel Letters and Related Documents.* Copyright © 1985 by Herald Press, Scottdale, PA 15683. Used by permission. Excerpted from pp. 284-94.

34. Juan Luis Vives
Introduction to Wisdom. Reprinted by permission of the publisher. From Marian Leona Tobriner (ed), *Vives' Introduction to Wisdom.* New York: Teachers College Press. Copyright © 1968 by Teachers College Press. All rights reserved. Excerpted in Musto, *Catholic Peacemakers,* vol. 2 (New York: Garland Publishing, 1996), 81-82.

35. *Brotherly Union of a Number of Children of God Concerning Seven Articles (The Schleitheim Confession).* From *The Legacy of Michael Sattler,* trans. and ed. by John H. Yoder. Copyright © 1973 by Herald Press, Scottdale, PA 15683. Used by permission. Excerpted from pp. 34-43.

36. Jakob Hutter
Letter to Johann Kuna von Kunstadt. From *Brotherly Faithfulness: Epistles from a Time of Persecution,* trans. The Hutterian Society of Brothers (Rifton, NY: Plough Publishing House, 1979), 65-74. Used with permission of publisher.

37. Peter Riedemann
Account of Our Religion, Doctrine and Faith. From *Account of Our Religion, Doctrine and Faith: Given by Peter Rideman of the Brothers Whom the Men Call Hutterians,* trans. The Hutterian Society of Brothers (Plough Publishing House, 1970), 102-12. Used with permission of publisher.

38. Menno Simons
Reply to False Accusations. From *The Complete Writings of Menno Simons,* trans. by Leonard Verduin and ed. by John Christian Wenger. Copyright © 1956 by Herald Press, Scottdale, PA 15683. Used by permission. Excerpted from pp. 543-77.

39. Bartolomé de Las Casas
The Only Way. Excerpted in Musto, *Catholic Peacemakers,* vol. 2 (New York: Garland, 1996), 112-21. From Bartolomé de Las Casas, *The Only Way,* ed. Helen Rand Parish, trans. Francis Patrick Sullivan (New York: Paulist Press, 1992). Reprinted by permission of Paulist Press, Inc. www.paulistpress.com.

Part V
Modern (1600-1900)

40. Gerrard Winstanley
The True Levellers Standard. Excerpted in *Radical Christian Writings: A Reader,* ed. Andrew Bradstock and Christopher Rowland (Oxford: Blackwell, 2002), 128-31; full text at luminarium.org. *Radical Christian Writings: A Reader,* ed. Andrew Bradstock and Christopher Rowland. Copyright © 2002. Reproduced with permission of Blackwell Publishing Ltd.

41. George Fox
Paper to Friends to Keep Out of Wars and Fights. From *Early Quaker Writings,* ed. Hugh Barbour and Arthur O. Roberts (Grand Rapids: Eerdmans, 1973), 406-7. Reproduced with permission.

42. Robert Barclay
Epistle of Love and Friendly Advice. From Robert Barclay,

An Epistle of Love and Friendly Advice to the Ambassadors of the Several Princes of Europe, Met at Nimeguen to Consult the Peace of Christendom, So Far As They Are Concerned, Wherein the True Cause of the Present War Is Discovered, and the Right Remedy and Means for a Firm and Settle Peace Is Proposed (Glenside, PA: Quaker Heritage Press, 2003; repr., 1692), 3-12.

43. William Penn

An Essay towards the Present and Future Peace of Europe. From *William Penn's Plan for a League of Nations*, ed. William I. Hull (Philadelphia: American Friends' Service Committee, 1919), 5-14.

44. John Woolman

Journal of John Woolman. From John Woolman, *Journal of John Woolman*, etext.lib.virginia.edu.

45. Pennsylvania Mennonites and German Baptists

A Short and Sincere Declaration. High Library, Elizabethtown College, Peace Pamphlets Collection.

46. David Dodge

War Inconsistent with the Religion of Jesus Christ. From David Low Dodge, *War Inconsistent with the Religion of Jesus Christ* (Boston: Ginn, 1905).

47. Priscilla Cadwallader

Sermon against War. Priscilla Cadwallader, *Memoir of Priscilla Cadwallader* (Philadelphia: T. Ellwood Zell, 1864), 73-79.

48. William Lloyd Garrison

Nonresistance Society: Declaration of Principles. From William Lloyd Garrison, "Declaration of Sentiments Adopted by the Peace Convention, Held in Boston, September 18, 19 and 20, 1838," *Selections from the Writings and Speeches of William Lloyd Garrison* (Boston: R. F. Walcutt, 1852), 72-77.

49. Frederick Douglass

My Opposition to War. Frederick Douglass, "My Opposition to War: An Address Delivered in London, England, on May 19, 1846," *Liberator* (July 3, 1846).

50. Adin Ballou

Christian Nonresistance. From Adin Ballou, *Christian Non-Resistance, in All Its Important Bearings, Illustrated and Defended* (Philadelphia: J. Miller M'Kim, 1846).

51. Alexander Campbell

An Address on War. Alexander Campbell, "An Address on War," *Millennial Harbinger*, 3rd ser., 5 (July 1848): 361-86. I am grateful to Professor Lee Campbell for providing this edited version.

52. Sojourner Truth

Narrative of Sojourner Truth. From Sojourner Truth, *Narrative of Sojourner Truth, a Northern Slave, Emancipated from Bodily Servitude by the State of New York, in 1828*, ed. Olive Gilbert (Boston: Printed for the Author, 1850); accessed at digital.library.upenn.edu.

53. William C. Thurman

Nonresistance, or the Spirit of Christianity Restored. William C. Thurman, *Nonresistance, or the Spirit of Christianity Restored* (Charlottesville, VA: Published by Author, 1862), 70, High Library, Elizabethtown College, Peace Pamphlets Collection.

54. Joshua Blanchard

Hostile Brotherhood. Joshua Blanchard, "Hostile Brotherhood," *Bond of Brotherhood* (March 1865), Joshua Pollard Blanchard Collected Papers, 1819-1868, CDG-A, Joshua Pollard Blanchard Scrapbook, Swarthmore College Peace Collection, Swarthmore College, Pennsylvania.

55. Lucretia Mott

The Subject of Peace Is Taking Hold. From Lucretia Mott, "The Subject of Peace Is Taking a Deep Hold," *Lucretia Mott: Her Complete Speeches and Sermons*, ed. Dana Greene (New York: Edwin Mellen, 1980), 343-48. Used with permission of The Edwin Mellen Press.

56. Charles Spurgeon

Periodical War Madness. C. H. Spurgeon, "Periodical War Madness," *The Sword and the Trowel* (April 1878).

57. Dwight L. Moody

Good News. From D. L. Moody, *Twelve Select Sermons* (Chicago: F. H. Revell, 1881), 32-44.

58. Jane Addams

The Subjective Necessity for Social Settlement. Jane Addams, "The Subjective Necessity for Social Settlements," in *Philanthropy and Social Progress, Seven Essays by Miss Jane Adams, Robert A. Woods, Father J. O. S. Huntington, Professor Franklin H. Giddings and Bernard Bosanquet. Delivered before the School of Applied Ethics at Plymouth, Mass., during the Session of 1892*, ed. Henry C. Adams (New York: Thomas Y. Crowell, 1893). Also from *Jane Addams*: Copyright © 2001 Jean Bethke Elshtain. Reprinted by permission of Basic Books, a member of the Perseus Books Group.

59. Leo Tolstoy

Letter to Ernest Howard Crosby. Leo Tolstoy, *Writings on Civil Disobedience and Nonviolence* (Philadelphia: New Society Publishers, 1987), 244-53.

Part VI
Early Twentieth Century (1900-1949)

60. Clarence Darrow

Resist Not Evil. Clarence S. Darrow, *Resist Not Evil* (Chicago, Charles H. Kerr, 1902), 11-32. Used by permission.

61. A. J. Tomlinson

The Awful War Seems Near. A. J. Tomlinson, "The Awful War Seems Near," *Church of God Evangel* (March 31, 1917): 1.

62. John Haynes Holmes

A Statement to My People on the Eve of War. From John Haynes Holmes, *The Messiah Pulpit: A Statement to My People on the Eve of War* (New York: Church of the Messiah), May 1917.

63. General Council of the Assemblies of God

Resolution Concerning the Attitude of the General Council of the Assemblies of God toward Any Military Service Which Involves the Actual Participation in the Destruction of Human Life. From "The Pentecostal Movement and the Conscription Law," *The Weekly Evangel* (August 4, 1917): 6.

64. Ammon Hennacy

Love Your Enemies? From Ammon Hennacy, *Book of Ammon*, ed. Jim Missey and Joan Thomas, 2nd ed. (Baltimore: Fortkamp Pub. Co., 1994). Used by permission of Wipf & Stock Publishers. www.wipfandstock.com.

65. Howard Thurman

Peace Tactics and a Racial Minority. Howard Thurman, "Peace Tactics and a Racial Minority," *The World Tomorrow* (December 1928): 505-7.

66. Harry Emerson Fosdick

The Unknown Soldier. "The Unknown Soldier" (pp. 88-98) from *The Secret of Victorious Living* by Harry Emerson Fosdick. Copyright 1934 by Harper & Brothers. Copyright renewed © 1962 by Harry Emerson Fosdick. Reprinted by permission of HarperCollins Publishers.

67. Evelyn Underhill

The Church and War. From Evelyn Underhill, *The Church and War* (disseminary.org: Hoopoe Publications, 2003).

68. Muriel Lester

Training. From Muriel Lester, *Training* (Nashville: Cokesbury Press, 1940); excerpted in *Ambassador of Reconciliation: A Muriel Lester Reader*, ed. Richard Deats (Philadelphia: New Society, 1991), 92-100. Used by permission.

69. Georgia Harkness

The Christian's Dilemma. Copyright © 1941 by the *Christian Century.* "The Christian's Dilemma" by Georgia Harkness is reprinted by permission from the August 6, 1941 issue of the *Christian Century.* The excerpt is from pp. 977-79.

70. Ernest Fremont Tittle

If America Is Drawn into the War, Can You, as a Christian, Participate in It, or Support It? Copyright © 1941 by the *Christian Century.* "If America Enters the War—What Shall I Do?" by Ernest Fremont Tittle is reprinted by permission from the February 5, 1941 issue of the *Christian Century.* The excerpt is drawn from pp. 178-80.

71. Dorothy Day

Our Country Passes from Undeclared War to Declared War; We Continue Our Christian Pacifist Stand. Dorothy Day, "Our Country Passes from Undeclared War to Declared War; We Continue Our Christian Pacifist Stand," *The Catholic Worker* (January 1942), 1, 4.

72. Bayard Rustin

Letter to Local Draft Board No. 63. Bayard Rustin to Local Draft Board No. 63, November 16, 1943, Bayard Rustin Papers, Library of Congress, Washington, DC. Used with permission by the Estate of Bayard Rustin.

73. André Trocmé

Message to the Church of Le Chambon-sur-Lignon. From André Trocmé, "Message to the Church of Le Chambon-sur-Lignon," André Trocmé and Magda Trocmé Papers, 1919-Date, DG 107, Series B. Box 10, Swarthmore College Peace Collection, Swarthmore College, Pennsylvania. Used by permission.

74. Takashi Nagai

The Bells of Nagasaki. From Takashi Nagai, *The Bells of Nagasaki,* trans. William Johnston (Tokyo: Kodansha International, 1984; repr., 1949), Used by permission.

75. Toyohiko Kagawa

We Have Abandoned War. From Toyohiko Kagawa, "We Have Abandoned War," *The Christian Century* 64 (December 3, 1947): 1483; repr., Kagawa Calendar for 1948.

76. A. J. Muste

Theology of Despair: An Open Letter to Reinhold Niebuhr. A. J. Muste, "Theology of Despair: An Open Letter to Reinhold Niebuhr," *Liberation* (April 21, 1948). Selected from *The Essays of A. J. Muste,* ed. Nat Hentoff (New York: Bobbs-Merrill, 1967), 302-7. Used by permission.

Part VII
Mid-Twentieth Century (1950-1974)

77. Kirby Page

The Faith of a Christian Pacifist. Kirby Page, "The Faith of a Christian Pacifist," *Christianity and Crisis* 10, no. 19 (November 13, 1950): 146-47.

78. Historic Peace Churches and the International Fellowship of Reconciliation Committee

Peace Is the Will of God. From "Peace Is the Will of God" by Historic Peace Churches and the International Fellowship of Reconciliation Committee in *A Declaration on Peace: In God's People the World's Renewal Has Begun* by Douglas Gwynn, George Hunsinger, Eugene F. Roop, and John Howard Yoder. Copyright © 1991 by Herald Press, Scottdale, PA 15683. Used by permission. Excerpted from pp. 53-77.

79. Martin Luther King, Jr.

Nonviolence and Racial Justice. Martin Luther King, Jr., "Nonviolence and Racial Justice," *Christian Century* (February 6, 1957): 165-67. Used by permission of the Estate of Martin Luther King, Jr.

80. Marjorie Swann

Statement by Marjorie Swann, Participant in Omaha Action. From Marjorie Swann, "Statement by Marjorie Swann, Participant in Omaha Action," July 21, 1959, Horace Champney Papers. Box 4, Swarthmore College Peace Collection, Swarthmore College, Pennsylvania. Used by permission.

81. Pope John XXIII

Pacem in Terris. From Pope John XXIII, *Pacem in Terris,* in *Proclaiming Justice & Peace: Documents from John XXIII-John Paul II,* ed. Michael Walsh and Brian Davies (Mystic, CT: Twenty-third Publications, 1984), 45-76. Copyright © Libreria Editrice Vaticana 1984. Used by permission.

82. Thomas Merton

Blessed Are the Meek: The Roots of Christian Nonviolence. From Thomas Merton, "Blessed Are the Meek: The Roots of Christian Nonviolence," *Fellowship* 33 (May 1967): 18-22. Used with expressed permission of the Fellowship of Reconciliation (www.forusa.org).

83. Vincent Harding

The Religion of Black Power. Vincent Harding, "The Religion of Black Power," in *The Religious Situation: 1968*, ed. Donald R. Cutler (Boston: Beacon), 3-38. Used by permission.

84. James Douglass

The Nonviolent Cross. James W. Douglass, *The Nonviolent Cross: A Theology of Revolution and Peace* (Eugene, OR: Wipf & Stock, 2006, repr., 1966), 284-92. Used by permission.

85. Daniel Berrigan

Our Apologies, Good Friends. Daniel Berrigan, *Night Flight to Hanoi* (New York: Macmillan, 1968), xiii-xix. Used by permission.

86. César Chávez

Letter from Delano. César Chávez, "Letter from Delano," farmmovement.org.

87. Jacques Ellul

Violence: Reflections from a Christian Perspective. From Jacques Ellul, *Violence: Reflections from a Christian Perspective*, trans. Cecelia Gaul Kings (New York: Seabury, 1969), 127-75.

88. William Stringfellow

Authority over Death. "Authority Over Death," from the book *Suspect Tenderness* by William Stringfellow and Anthony Towne. Copyright © 1971 by Holt, Rinehart and Winston. Reprinted by permission of Henry Holt and Company, LLC. Excerpted from pp. 69-76.

89. Philip Berrigan

An Open Letter to a Bishop. Philip Berrigan, "Open Letter to a Bishop," in *Peace and Nonviolence: Basic Writings*, ed. Edward Guinan (New York: Paulist Press, 1973), 17-24. Reprinted by permission of Paulist Press, Inc. www.paulistpress.com.

90. Dom Helder Camara

Spiral of Violence. Dom Helder Camara, *Spiral of Violence* (London: Sheed and Ward, 1971), 25-40.
The Limitations of Violence. Dom Helder Camara, *The Conversions of a Bishop: An Interview with Jose de Broucker* (London: Collins, 1979), 176-77; excerpted in *Dom Helder Camara: Essential Writings* (Modern Spiritual Masters Series), selected with an introduction by Francis McDonagh (Maryknoll, NY: Orbis Books, 2009). Used by permission.

Part VIII
Late Twentieth Century (1975-2000)

91. Shelley Douglass

Nonviolence and Feminism. Shelley Douglass, "Nonviolence and Feminism," *Fellowship* (July-August 1975); excerpted in *Peace Is the Way: Writings on Nonviolence from the Fellowship of Reconciliation*, ed. Walter Wink (Maryknoll, NY: Orbis Books, 2000), 46-48. Used with expressed permission of the Fellowship of Reconciliation (www.forusa.org).

92. Richard McSorley

It's a Sin to Build a Nuclear Weapon. Richard McSorley, *It's a Sin to Build a Nuclear Weapon*, ed. John Dear (Baltimore: Fortkamp, 1991), 93-97. Used by permission of Wipf & Stock. www.wipfandstock.com.

93. Oscar Romero

Last Sunday Sermon. Oscar Romero, "Last Sunday Sermon," *The Church and Human Liberation* (March 14, 1980); accessed at www.haverford.edu.

94. Daniel Berrigan

We Could Not Not Do This. Daniel Berrigan, *Cloud of Witnesses* (Maryknoll, NY: Orbis Books, 1991), 221-27. Used by permission of Sojouners (www.sojo.net).

95. Elise Boulding

The Re-creation of Relationship, Interpersonal and Global. Elise Boulding, *The Re-creation of Relationship, Interpersonal and Global* (Philadelphia: Wider Quaker Fellowship, 1981). Used by permission.

96. Dorothy Friesen

Social Action and the Need for Prayer. Dorothy Friesen, "Social Action and the Need for Prayer," *Fellowship* (July-August 1981); excerpted in *Peace Is the Way: Writings on Nonviolence from the Fellowship of Reconciliation*, ed. Walter Wink (Maryknoll, NY: Orbis Books, 2000), 124-28. Used with expressed permission of the Fellowship of Reconciliation (www.forusa.org).

97. Ronald J. Sider

God's People Reconciling. Ronald J. Sider, "God's People Reconciling," cpt.org/resources/writings/sider. Used by permission.

98. Stanley Hauerwas

Peacemaking: The Virtue of the Church. Stanley Hauerwas, "Peacemaking," *The Furrow* 36, no. 10 (October 1985): 605-12. Reproduced by permission.

99. John Howard Yoder

A Theological Critique of Violence. John Howard Yoder, "A Theological Critique of Violence," *New Conversations* 16, no. 3 (1995): 2-15.

100. On the Care of Creation: An Evangelical Declaration on the Care of Creation

Evangelical Environmental Network, *On the Care of Creation: An Evangelical Declaration on the Care of Creation*, creationcare.org.

101. Duane Friesen and Glen Stassen

Just Peacemaking. From "Just Peacemaking" by Duane K. Friesen and Glen H. Stassen in *Transforming Violence: Linking Local and Global Peacemaking*, ed. by Judy Zimmerman Herr and Robert Herr. Copyright © 1998 by Herald Press, Scottdale, PA 15683. Used by permission. Excerpted from pp. 54-67.

102. Carter Heyward

Compassion and Nonviolence: A Spiritual Path. From *Saving Jesus from Those Who Are Right: Rethinking What It Means to Be Christian,* by Carter Heyward © 1999 Fortress Press, admin. Augsburg Fortress Publishers. Reproduced by permission. (Minneapolis: Fortress Press, 1999).

103. Eileen Egan

Peace Be with You: Justified Warfare or the Way of Nonviolence. From Eileen Egan, *Peace Be with You: Justified Warfare or the Way of Nonviolence* (Maryknoll, NY: Orbis Books, 1999), 162-65. Used by permission.

104. John Paul Lederach

The Journey toward Reconciliation. The Journey toward Reconciliation by John Paul Lederach. Copyright © 1999 by Herald Press, Scottdale, PA 15683. Used by permission. Excerpted from pp. 17-26.

Part IX
Twenty-first Century

105. Dorothee Soelle

Violence and Nonviolence. From *The Silent Cry: Mysticism and Resistance* by Dorothee Soelle copyright © 2001 Fortress Press. Reproduced by permission. Excerpt from pp. 259-77.

106. Miroslav Volf

Forgiveness, Reconciliation, and Justice: A Christian Contribution to a More Peaceful Environment. Miroslav Volf, "Forgiveness, Reconciliation, and Justice: A Christian Contribution to a More Peaceful Environment," livedtheology. org. Used by permission.

107. John Dear

Compassion and Nonviolence from New York to Afghanistan: Reflections after September 11th. John Dear, "Compassion and Nonviolence from New York to Afghanistan: Reflections after September 11th," johndear.org. Used by permission.

108. Mel White

Letter to Jerry Falwell. Mel White to Jerry Falwell, September 12, 2002, soulforce.org. Used by permission.

109. Donald Kraybill

Death in Disguise. From *The Upside-Down Kingdom* by Donald B. Kraybill. Copyright © 1978 by Herald Press, Scottdale, PA 15683. Used by permission. Excerpted from pp. 186-91 of the third edition (2003).

110. Richard B. Hays, George Hunsinger, Richard Pierard, Glen Stassen, and Jim Wallis,

Confessing Christ in a World of Violence. Confessing Christ in a World of Violence: This article originally appeared on Sojourners' God's Politics blog. Visit the blog at http://blog. sojo.net.

111. Jim Forest

Salt of the Earth: An Orthodox Christian Approach to Peacemaking. Jim Forest, "Salt of the Earth: An Orthodox Christian Approach to Peacemaking," incommunion.org. Used by permission.

112. Valerie Weaver-Zercher

One Mean Mennonite Mama: A Pacifist Parent Faces Her Anger. Valerie Weaver-Zercher, "One Mean Mennonite Mama: A Pacifist Parent Faces Her Anger," *The Mennonite* (October 3, 2006), mennonite.org. Used by permission.

113. Robert Johansen

The Politics of Love and War: What Is Our Responsibility? Robert C. Johansen, "The Politics of Love and War: What Is Our Responsibility?" *Journal of Religion, Conflict and Peace* (Fall 2008), plowsharesproject.org. This online version is a reprint from *Lines, Places and Heritage: Essays Commemorating the 300th Anniversary of the Church of the Brethren,* ed. Stephen L. Longenecker and Jeff Bach (Rockland, ME: Penobscot Press, 2008). Used by permission of Bridgewater College.

114. Gene Stolzfus

Interrogation and Martyrdom. Gene Stolzfus, "Worth Living for—Worth Dying for," March 10, 2010, peaceprobe. word press.com. Used by permission.

115. Andy Alexis-Baker

Policing and Christian Forgiveness. This is an original contribution to the volume.

116. Tracy Wenger Sadd

A Prayer for Peace. This is an original contribution to the volume.

Acknowledgments

Perhaps the most basic form of peacemaking is simply recognizing that we do not exist alone and then giving thanks to those who help us grow and flourish in our interdependent role as peacemakers. With this in mind and heart, I send my thanks to the community of peacemakers who have played such important roles behind *Christian Peace and Nonviolence*.

Robert Ellsberg of Orbis Books expressed enthusiasm for this project shortly after I contacted him, and I cannot thank him enough for his commitment to publish this volume. Robert's brilliant career at Orbis demonstrates a fierce commitment to publishing works of peace, justice, and spirituality, and all of us who are concerned about these issues—this way of life—are indebted to him for enriching our lives so deeply through the written word.

Stanley Hauerwas has offered nothing less than breathtaking contributions to contemporary expressions of Christian nonviolence, and I could not be more pleased than I am that he has written the foreword for this book.

Mr. and Mrs. Harold Isbell made it possible for us to secure copyright permissions, and I remain deeply grateful for their generous support of this project.

Sari Mauro, my diligent research assistant, tracked down one article after another, typed more words than I could use, proofread texts until her eyes went bleary, and secured permissions—all the while maintaining a professional and even cheery disposition. I am indebted not only to Sari but also to other students and friends who helped with typing and proofreading, especially Sharon Herr, Alyson Shade, John Mackey, and Sara Neumann. Thanks to these good folks, I was able to complete the manuscript ahead of schedule.

My beautiful friends Alyson Shade and Sharon Herr offered precious support along the way.

Numerous individuals gave of their time and expertise in answering my countless questions about individuals, movements, and texts. These generous folks include Louis Swift, Euon Cameron, Ronald Musto, Patricia Applebaum, Ron Sider, Jim Forest, Irven Resnick, Kip Kosek, Rose Berger, Murray Wagner, Bill Wylie-Kellermann, Tobias Winwright, Michael Cartwright, Dana Greene, Christopher Densmore, Wendy Chmielewski, Mark Yurs, Richard Taylor, Jeff Bach, Colman McCarthy, Ridgeway Addison, David King, Warren Goldstein, Byron Borger, William Lindsay, John Dear, Paul Alexander, Wally Landes, Richard Deats, Thomas Curran, Dorothy Friesen, Andy Alexis-Baker, Scott Gustafson, Larry Rasmussen, Larry Ingle, Richard Hughes, Theron Schlabach, Willard Swartley, J. Denny Weaver, Ellen Ross, Richard Mahoney, Anthony Dancer, and Marilee Melvin.

I consulted numerous readers in peace, war, justice, and Christianity along the way, and my gratitude extends to those who have edited these excellent collections, especially Ronald Musto, Howard

340

Zinn, Christopher Rowland, Andrew Bradstock, E. Morris Sider, Luke Keefer, Jr., Joseph J. Fahey, Richard Armstrong, Staughton Lynd, Alice Lynd, Edward Guinan, Charles Chatfield, Ruzanna Ilukhina, Arthur Weinberg, Lila Weinberg, Gregory Reichberg, Henry Syse, Endre Begby, Walter Wink, Bruce B. Lawrence, Asiha Karim, Louis Swift, Mulford Sibley, Jean Bethke Elshtain, Cornel West, Eddie Glaude, Jr., F. L. Cross, E. A. Livingstone, James Duke, Carter Lindberg, Christopher Ocker, and Rebecca Weaver. These scholars provided me with wonderful models, and I am grateful for their works.

Jefferey Long, a renowned scholar of Hinduism and a wonderful man of peace, chairs the Department of Religious Studies at Elizabethtown College, my home institution, and I am always grateful for his words of support and encouragement. My thanks also goes out to the staff at High Library—especially Sylvia Morra, Pete Depuydt, Louise Hyder-Darlington, and Anna Pilston—for offering me help beyond help. Carol Ouimet also provided invaluable administrative support.

Finally, I thank Karin for parenting our sons with love and justice, care and concern, tenderness and toughness. And I thank Jackson and Nate for the sheer joy they bring to my life, even when they wield light sabers against me as I write about the way—the more excellent way—of resisting the sword.

INDEX